2.95

P9-CRB-668

INTRODUCTION TO
ST. THOMAS AQUINAS

Introduction to
SAINT
THOMAS AQUINAS

Edited with an Introduction by
ANTON C. PEGIS
Pontifical Institute of
Mediaeval Studies, Toronto

THE MODERN LIBRARY · *New York*

THE MODERN LIBRARY
is published by RANDOM HOUSE, INC.

Manufactured in the United States of America

To Mary, Paul
and Lucille

PREFACE

THE present volume represents selections of materials, drawn entirely from *Basic Writings of St. Thomas Aquinas,* which Random House published in 1945. Its intention is to serve the purpose of an introduction to St. Thomas. Since it is only an introduction, it cannot pretend to achieve the objective that *Basic Writings* had in view. Nevertheless, in spite of the special difficulties surrounding the selection of these introductory texts, I hope that the work is sufficiently representative in its choices, compact in its argumentation and broad in its interests to meet the needs of a first approach to St. Thomas.

The selection of the citations which go to make up the Modern Library edition has been an extremely difficult undertaking. The *Summa Theologica,* from which this volume, like *Basic Writings,* is drawn, is a work that is continuous in its analysis and its matter. Hence, having risked displeasing a good many readers of St. Thomas by being forced to exclude some of their favorite texts from *Basic Writings,* I must now risk displeasing even more readers by the great compactness of this *Introduction.* But I have not made my selections with an eye to the opinions of specialists; I have aimed at meeting what seemed to me the needs of the college student who is a beginner in St. Thomas. Such a student will find in this book St. Thomas' mature views of the most crucial questions of natural theology, psychology, theory of knowledge and ethics.

It is to be hoped that the reader of this *Introduction* will follow St. Thomas' own indications and look elsewhere in his writings for the background or possible developments of the various pieces in the present volume. An introduction is of itself an incomplete sort of thing; or rather, its completion comes from reaching the reality to which it has been its purpose to lead. To seek completeness in an introduction is an

illusion, not to say a contradiction. My aim has rather been
to achieve, not at all a total picture of St. Thomas, but reasonably continuous doctrinal threads, which might serve as
an invitation to the student to undertake his own adventures
within the philosophical thought of St. Thomas.

Anton C. Pegis

CONTENTS

	PAGE
Preface	vii
Introduction	xi

1. GOD:
Summa Theologica, I, qq. 1, 2, 3 (aa. 3, 4, 7), 5, 6, 7, 11-17, 19 (aa. 1-10), 22, 25 (aa. 1-3). ... 3

2. CREATION:
Summa Theologica, I, qq. 44, 45 (a. 5), 46, 47, 48 (aa. 3-4), 49. ... 233

3. MAN; HIS POWERS; HIS KNOWLEDGE:
Summa Theologica, I, qq. 75 (aa. 1, 2, 4, 6), 76 (aa. 1-4), 77 (aa. 1-3, 5), 78, 79 (aa. 1-5, 11), 80-81, 82 (aa. 1, 2, 4), 83, 84, 85, 86 (a. 1), 87 (a. 1). ... 280

4. THE END OF MAN:
Summa Contra Gentiles, Book III, Chapters 2, 3, 16-20, 25-26, 37-40, 47-48, 51-54, 61. ... 429

5. HUMAN ACTS:
Summa Theologica, I-II, qq. 6, 8 (a. 2), 9, 12 (aa. 1-2), 13 (aa. 1, 3-5), 18, 20 (a. 4). ... 478

6. HABITS AND VIRTUES:
Summa Theologica, I-II, qq. 49 (a. 4), 51, 54 (aa. 2-3), 55 (aa. 1, 4), 56 (a. 1), 57 (aa. 2-5), 58 (aa. 1-2), 60 (a. 1), 61 (aa. 1-2), 62, 63, 64 (aa. 1-2). ... 544

PAGE

7. LAW:
Summa Theologica, I-II, qq. 90, 91, 93 (aa.
1-3), 94, 95 (aa. 1-2).   609

8. GRACE:
Summa Theologica, I-II, qq. 109, 112.   651

Bibliography   682

INTRODUCTION

THE comparatively short life of St. Thomas Aquinas covers the second and third quarters of the thirteenth century. At the beginning of his life, Greek and Arabian philosophy was just entering the Latin world; three years after his death, the large-scale condemnation of Aristotelianism in Paris by Bishop Stephen Tempier signalized what turned out to be a defeat for Christian thinkers in the presence of Greek and Arabian philosophers, Platonists and Aristotelians alike. Between these termini, the thought of St. Thomas unfolded with an interior calmness of order and an assurance of judgment that the historian of the thirteenth century must record with increasing perplexity. His age influenced him much more than it listened to him. It gave him the problems with which he was to be concerned; in many cases it even set for him directions that he was to follow, explore and complete. It is impossible to understand the works of St. Thomas without seeing them in the context of his world; yet it is astonishing to observe how little that world understood and followed his reflections on its fundamental issues during that critical third quarter of the thirteenth century which marked the first decisive philosophical encounter between Hellenism and Christianity.

St. Thomas Aquinas was born in the Castle of Roccasecca, near Aquino, Italy, early in 1225. From 1231 to 1239 he remained in the Benedictine Monastery of Monte Cassino where his parents had entered him as an oblate. In 1239 he went to study the liberal arts at the newly established University of Naples. Having decided, in 1244, to become a Dominican, he set out for Paris and arrived there in the summer of 1245. Whether he remained there or went for his studies to Cologne is a disputed point. In any case, when St. Albert the Great was sent to Cologne in 1248 to found a house of studies, St. Thomas became his pupil and remained with him in Cologne until 1252. In that year he returned to the Dominican convent of St. James in Paris, where he commented on the Gospels (1252-1254) and on the *Sentences* of Peter Lombard (1254-1256), receiving his license to teach from the University of Paris in 1256. During the next three years he inaugurated his career as a professor of theology in Paris, fulfilling in this way the desire, which he was to express at the beginning of the *Contra Gentiles,* of being a teacher of divine wisdom. In 1259 St. Thomas returned to Italy where he taught at the Papal Curia: at Anagni (1259-1261), Orvieto (1261-1265), Rome (1265-1267), Viterbo (1267-1268). St. Thomas' meeting with his fellow Dominican William of Moerbeke at Orvieto led to William's translation of the writings of Aristotle from Greek originals as well as St. Thomas' commentaries on the Philosopher. Returning to Paris in 1268, by way of Bologna and Milan, he entered into the struggles against the Latin Averroists in the Faculty of Arts and against the new attacks by the seculars on the religious orders. Finding himself under attack by the Augustinians, he was finally relieved of his teaching duties in 1272 and commissioned by his Order to establish a new house of studies in Naples. On his way to the Council of Lyons in 1274, to which he had been summoned by Pope Gregory X, he died at the Cistercian monastery of Fossanuova, March 7, 1274. He was canonized by Pope John XXII on July 18, 1323. In 1567 Pope Pius V pronounced him the *Angelic Doctor.* Since 1880, when he was named Patron of Catholic Schools by Pope Leo XIII, St. Thomas has received many official honors from the Church.

St. Thomas' writings belong to many fields of activity and are a faithful mirror of his participation in the religious and intellectual life of his age. His theological writings are a landmark in the history of theology. The Commentary on *The Four Books of Sentences* of Peter Lombard (*Scriptum in IV Libros Sententiarum*) was written in 1254-1256(?). The famous *Summa Contra Gentiles* dates from about 1260. The *Summa Theologica,* left unfinished, is a classic synthesis of Christian thought and represents St. Thomas at his distinctive best. The work belongs to the years 1256-1272. I may add in passing that, though tradition has honored the use of the name *Summa Theologica,* the correct title of the work is either *Summa* or *Summa Theologiae.* In this same group of writings we must also locate the *Compendium of Theology* (*Compendium Theologiae,* 1273).

Of St. Thomas' commentaries, mention must be made of those on Boethius (*De Trinitate, De Hebdomadibus,* 1257-1258), on Dionysius the pseudo-Areopagite (*De Divinis Nominibus,* about 1261), as well as on the anonymous and extremely influential *Book of Causes* (*Liber de Causis,* 1268). St. Thomas' commentaries on Aristotle (1261-1272) are a decisive moment in his career. There are commentaries on almost the whole Aristotelian corpus: *Physics, Metaphysics, Nicomachean Ethics, Politics, On the Soul, Posterior Analytics, On Interpretation, On the Heavens, On Generation and Corruption. The Disputed Questions* deals with many topics: *On Truth* (*De Veritate,* 1256-1259), *On the Power of God* (*De Potentia Dei,* 1259-1263), *On Evil* (*De Malo,* 1263-1268), *On Spiritual Creatures* (*De Spiritualibus Creaturis, 1269*), *On the Soul* (*De Anima,* 1269-1270). St. Thomas has also written short treatises or *Opuscula,* of which mention must be made at least of the following: *On Being and Essence* (*De Ente et Essentia,* 1256), *On the Eternity of the World* (*De Aeternitate Mundi,* 1270), *On the Unity of the Intellect* (*De Unitate Intellectus,* 1270), *On Separate Substances* (*De Substantiis Separatis,* 1272).

II

An age which had as many philosophical masters (Greek, Arabian and Jewish) as did the thirteenth century, and in which these masters had very brilliant disciples, cannot be represented by any neat historical formula. On the other hand, those who yield to the impulse to treat the history of mediaeval philosophy with impeccable scholarship joined to philosophical neutrality are being learned spectators whereas the reality which they are investigating, namely, philosophy as it has existed in history, requires that their learning be an instrument of their philosophical understanding of that which in history is itself philosophical. Certainly, a patient reading of the theologians and the philosophers of the thirteenth century suggests that, though they are the heirs and the disciples of many and conflicting philosophical traditions, which crossed and re-crossed one another in the course of a long history, yet they had many problems in common; and

behind the more particular problems, a good many of the
thinkers of the thirteenth century saw the emergence, on the
boundary between Greek and Christian thought, of issues
which were more basic not only because they contained the
distinctively Greek contribution to philosophy, but also because they revealed what was permanently philosophical and
permanently true in the Greeks. That is why St. Thomas
Aquinas, for example, studied the history of philosophy not
merely as though it were the record of human opinions, but
also and even more as though within this record there was
to be found the unfolding of philosophy itself. That is why
his diagnosis of the history of philosophy meant to him a
philosophical inquiry depending on the intelligibility and
truth of philosophical doctrines. The Plato who was a philosopher in the fifth and fourth centuries B.C. was a philosopher none the less; and while the historical Plato is inseparably wedded in his individuality to the calamitous age of
Athens between the Peloponnesian War and the rise of Philip
of Macedon, Platonism remains in any age an understandable philosophical phenomenon, however much it may be
true that it belongs to the half century following the death
of Socrates. And to St. Thomas, at least, Platonism in the
course of history has meant primarily a reasonably coherent
philosophical doctrine and method which could grow in the
hands of Platonic disciples from Proclus to Avicenna but
which retained in its very growth the original inspiration of
the doctrine and the method to which Plato gave existence.
In any case, we must recognize that a Greek Plato, a Persian
Avicenna and a Jewish Maimonides were to St. Thomas
Aquinas, as to many others of his age, philosophical contemporaries. We must recognize further that in following the
practice of calling Aristotle *The Philosopher,* St. Thomas
had no intention of burying philosophy in the fourth century
B.C.; on the contrary, what he intended to do was to insist
on the fact that, though philosophy can exist at any time
only on the condition of being original, yet some philosophical doctrines began by being original with Aristotle.

The most important result of St. Thomas' attitude toward
philosophy and its history is what may be called the historically social character of his own philosophical work. He lives
and thinks in the company of others. When he reaches a
certain philosophical conclusion, he will very often go out

of his way to say that such a conclusion had been reached by one or more of his predecessors; or he might say that he disagreed with Avicenna or Averroes in reaching it; or even that Plato and Aristotle may have formulated the principle that he used, even though they may not have followed through their principle to the end. In short, St. Thomas' use of the history of philosophy, far from being accessory ornamentation, was a necessary part of his own philosophical argument and a sign of his allegiance and discipleship to those who had made that argument possible for him. When he said, therefore, that we study what men have thought in order to discover the truth, he was giving expression, in a remarkably accurate way, to the conviction that philosophy has a history not in the sense that it is ever old but in the sense that those who explore its perpetual newness become an increasing company from generation to generation.

We must be prepared to go very far indeed in the direction of respecting with St. Thomas Aquinas the living character of philosophy before we understand fully the genuinely philosophical character of his conversations with the Greek and Arabian philosophers. Platonism, to repeat, is not for him a convenient abstraction designating a group of thinkers with vague family likenesses; before it is the name of a group, it is the name of a doctrine and of a method. But we must go further than this; for St. Thomas' historical relations to Platonism are very special. There are not many philosophical aberrations that were either inherited or developed by the thinkers of the thirteenth century that St. Thomas does not trace to the Platonic metaphysics, psychology and epistemology. Whether the problem be the nature of God and the divine goodness, the procession of creatures from God, their constitution and unity, their causality and autonomy under the creative causality of God, the unity and economy of man's composite being—the ultimate issue for St. Thomas is Platonism because it is for him the ultimate source to which the many and seemingly varied positions of later thinkers were reducible. Nor are the Platonic errors in these different domains fundamentally many. They are basically one error, running like a guiding thread in all the directions of the Platonic philosophical fabric. They are, in St. Thomas' estimation, errors of *existence*. If St. Thomas disagrees with Plato on the nature of God, creation, the divine transcend-

ence and the divine causality, the constitution of creatures
as beings, the economy of their natures, and particularly the
economy of man's nature, the reason is one and the only one,
even though it has many consequences. Plato, so the reason
runs, did not know the nature of being; and in the Platonic
unawareness of being *from the point of view of existence* we
are invited by St. Thomas Aquinas to locate the many tan-
gled threads of the most serious philosophical issues in the
thirteenth century.

It is worthwhile following St. Thomas' conversation with
Plato. It will introduce us to the crucial issues of St. Thomas'
age. It will enable us to understand that in turning to Aristotle St. Thomas was doing so for motives that were ulti-
mately not to be found in Aristotle himself. Finally, it will
enable us to appreciate, however briefly, the distinctive trait
of what it is now fashionable to call the existentialism of
St. Thomas Aquinas.

III

Of the many issues in the thirteenth century in which St.
Thomas was involved and which were eminently issues of
existence three are particularly significant, namely, the nature of *being,* the nature of *man* and the nature of *knowledge.*
It seemed to St. Thomas Aquinas that on these three issues
his ultimate opponent was Plato himself. And though history
could offer to him Platonists of many sorts, and even of many
degrees, nevertheless, what especially interested him was the
fundamental attitude and method of the Platonic philosophy.
If Platonism is the name of a school, that is true because it
is first and foremost the name of a philosophical doctrine and
method. That doctrine concerns the parallelism and simi-
larity of treatment which St. Thomas has observed in the
Platonic answer to three specific problems.

There is (A) the Platonic separation of being from becoming, of the intelligible and stable Ideas or Forms from
changing and unstable sensible things. There is (B) the
problem of the relations between intellectual knowledge and
sensation. Intellectual knowledge neither comes from sensible things, nor is it about them; and to say that reminiscence
is a necessary moment in the origin of intellectual knowledge
is to admit this precise fact, namely, that such knowledge is
neither *from* nor *of* sensible things. There is (C) the separa-

tion of soul from body, according to which Platonism has the tendency to say that man is a *soul* using a body rather than a *composite* of soul and body. The implication of this tendency is that the whole nature of man is to be found in the soul, and that the body is a sort of residence for man—a residence which is sometimes a workshop, sometimes a prison, sometimes a grave.

The common enemy in the Platonic effort to separate being from becoming, mind from sense and soul from body is matter. Plato has tried to protect the purity of intelligible essences, the universality and immateriality of intellectual knowledge, as well as the rational dignity of the soul, from the stain of matter. True being is the world of intelligible essences, true knowing is intellectual, the true man is the rational soul alone. These are surely cherished Platonic dreams, and St. Thomas Aquinas was both respectful and careful in their presence; and if he finally parted company with Plato, it was precisely at that moment when he was called upon to account for the role and the reality of matter in the universe.

Here, be it observed, St. Thomas differs from Plato by a principle. For since matter is a creature in a world of creatures, it has an intelligible role to play in the structure and organization of the world. Matter is not a barbarian, for in a world of creatures which depend for their whole being upon a creating God, there are no natural barbarians. In any case, Plato's effort to save essences, mind and knowledge from the barbarism of matter was to St. Thomas Aquinas a sign that Plato had not succeeded in looking upon all of reality from a truly unified point of view.

For, why should a philosopher cut off some parts and aspects of reality in order to save them from the rest? Why honor the Ideas with the name being at the price of keeping becoming in the outer darkness of the imitation of being? To this there can be but one answer. Only the philosopher who has not seen being as a whole, who has not seen the order and the unity of being from the point of view of being itself —only such a philosopher can reserve the name *being* for some realities and deny it to others. But what does this mean? It means, among other things, that when Plato separated being from becoming as that which truly *is* from that which *is imitationally*, he was basing his notion of being, not on existence, but on the private characteristics of a certain sort of being.

It is here that the Platonic *method*, which is for St. Thomas Aquinas the cornerstone of Platonism, makes itself apparent. And it is this method, so widely practiced by his contemporaries, that St. Thomas has singled out with a steady insistence throughout his writings and with remarkable elaborateness in his commentary on the *Liber de Causis*. What is this method? It is the method of modeling the properties of existing beings on the abstractions of the human intellect. In other words, it is the method of thinking that being takes its characteristics *as being* from what it reveals of itself *in the state of being thought*. One need not argue that Plato modeled being on thought, as though he examined thought in order to discover the attributes of being. Nor did St. Thomas Aquinas ever so argue. But one can and must argue that Plato set out to investigate being by using reason and thought alone. Assuredly, Plato did not measure being by thought; but he did, as it is clear from the *Phaedo*, deliberately make the effort to become a pure and solitary reason, free from the body and from sensation, in order to investigate being adequately. Now, in St. Thomas' view, this Platonic method fails by as much as the human reason or human abstract thought is powerless, *by itself*, to apprehend and to know the conditions of actually existing things. For, according to St. Thomas, there are many and profoundly important aspects of existence that thought alone or the reason alone cannot know about things; and the most important of these important aspects and conditions is *existence*.

The Ideas are, as St. Thomas repeatedly contends, the center of the Platonic metaphysics. They are true being, they exclude the imperfect conditions of sensible matter, and man must become a pure mind in order to know them. Now it is St. Thomas' conviction that the method which led Plato to posit the Ideas was intended by Plato himself to transcend the imperfections of sensible things; but, according to St. Thomas, that method succeeded in forcing Plato to have a dis-existentialized view of being, of man and of knowledge. Why so? Because the more Plato sought to discover the ultimate conditions of reality by means of a reason which had methodically cut itself off from the body and from all sensible experience, the more he was investing with the name of being the abstract essences which were the only objects that such a methodically isolated reason could reach; and the more abstract essences became the center of Plato's world, the more Plato found himself incapable of explaining those conditions of actual beings which he could not derive from, or envisage within the economy of, the abstract essences which were the exemplars of his world.

Whether we examine the Platonic conception of the nature and the origin of being or the interior economy of such a being as man, the Platonic commitment to abstract essences as the ultimate models and, in some sense, the sources of the sensible beings around us, can lead to only one result. To be adequately the models and exemplars of reality, the Platonic Ideas would have to be creative divine ideas; and they would have to transcend the world of sensible things as the Creator transcends His creatures. But, in fact, the Ideas, being in St. Thomas' estimation of no more power and transcendence than are human abstractions, are powerless to cause within sensible things the very conditions of matter which they yet represent abstractly. This is the most ultimate conflict in Platonism, the conflict between being and essence. Consider the case of man as an example. How does it happen that man is entirely intelligible as an essence but not entirely intelligible as a being? For the Platonic man is entirely intelligible as a rational animal, but he is not quite so intelligible as soul and body. Why are being and essence thus at odds with one another? Because being and essence are related to matter in radically different ways within Platonism. Corporeal matter disturbs the economy of man's being, but not the economy of his essence. And this must mean that according to Platonism the whole being of man is not included within the ordering of the world by the Platonic Ideas. In other words, it means that matter escapes the causality of the Ideas, and to this extent sensible beings are not entirely intelligible in their origin. Matter enters the economy of the sensible world, not within the providence of God, nor as a co-principle within the economy of composite essences, but radically outside the whole domain and source of intelligibility. Matter is there as an unreduced stranger within reality, an unintelligible and barbaric alien. It is there to be ordered, but it does not serve essentially the intelligible structure of reality. For Plato, the Ideas are not divine ideas of individual being whose composite being is entirely intelligible to God. Conceivably, the Ideas might serve as the definitions of the essences of composite beings; but they cannot be the productive causes of the being of composite things.

By as much, therefore, as the Ideas are models of material things whose materiality they are yet powerless to cause, by so much Plato excludes from his explanation of reality the existential conditions of sensible beings. This does not mean merely that Plato was unable to account for the existence of matter, or to include matter within the causality of the intelligible source of all being. The malady is much deeper than this. Plato's flight from matter is bound to be a flight from existence; for a metaphysics which does not deal with being as a whole does not deal with being at all. Plato could not successfully exclude matter and becoming from the domain of being, however much he may have tried; rather, by trying to exclude them, he excluded himself. And this is another way of saying that the Platonic metaphysics of the Ideas is a metaphysics of flight from existence.

But the dilemmas of a metaphysics which turns its back on existence in order to avoid matter can prove embarrassing not only in the problem of the origin of things but also in the problem of their interior constitution and economy. If in the problem of the origin of the world St. Thomas opposed Platonic participation, he also found it necessary to carry this opposition through to its logical results in the further contention that, on Platonic grounds, we are unable to explain the unity of any being as a being and the unity of its nature. Once more, let us take man as an example. It is known how indefatigably St. Thomas Aquinas defended the unity of man's being as well as the unity of the composite economy of his nature. What it is necessary to see in this defense is that the issue between St. Thomas and Plato (an issue deliberately raised by St. Thomas himself) is, once more, a question of existence.

Composite in nature, man yet is for St. Thomas one being. *There* is a mystery to consider. And the mystery is manifold. For if man, though composed of soul *and* body, is one being, then he has one nature, that is to say, an internal organization and order serving *as a whole* one specific and final purpose. To say, however, that man has a unity of nature is to say that he has an ordered relationship among his various powers, so that they work and function together for an end which is expressive of the very nature of man. Yet we are not to suppose that this ordered relationship among man's many powers (intellect, will, imagination, memory, sight, hearing, etc.) exists as a meaningless reflection of the unity of man's nature. On the contrary, if man is a composite being, if he is soul *and* body, if, therefore, he has many and varied powers within the unity of his nature, to St. Thomas that means that man is the sort of being that requires the *simultaneous* and *inter-ordinated* activity of his several powers to achieve the unitary purpose of his nature. St. Thomas does not think of man as a unity as though his various functions do not interfere with one another; man is rather a unity in the sense that he has to act through several powers *at the same time*, contributing to one another, so that by their togetherness one work, distinctively human, may be the result.

Is man one being? And if so, to what purpose?

To the first of these questions St. Thomas' answer proved very disconcerting to his contemporaries. They all agreed, certainly, that man was *one* being; but sometimes some of them did not mind saying that man was one being because he was the union of two beings. This position, which is not exactly unknown in modern philosophy, struck St. Thomas Aquinas as bad arithmetic and worse philosophy. If man is the *sum* of two actually constituted beings, then he is two beings; in which case there would arise all sorts of embarrassing questions. Why this two-in-one? And how could something that was two beings act as one being—*be* one agent? You could try to relieve the difficulty by saying that man is not a soul and a body, but a soul *with* a body. This would make man a unity by the expedient of saying that man was a soul using and ruling a body. This is the position which St. Thomas attributes to Plato and to St. Augustine.

But it will not work. For man is not a soul, if that means that his whole nature as man is verified in the soul alone, since precisely the notion of a rational animal is not verified in the soul alone. To put man's whole nature in the soul might evade the difficulty of making man two beings; but it poses the other difficulty that the soul alone, though a spiritual substance, is not a complete being. St. Thomas, therefore, offers to his Platonic contemporaries two dilemmas. If, as everybody admitted, the knowledge of truth was the end and purpose of the soul as a spiritual substance, how could the soul accomplish this purpose by itself? Assuming that this question receives some sort of answer, how did they account for the fact that man, who is for them very little less than the angels, is yet an incarcerated angel? What, after all, is an angel doing with a body?

St. Thomas' conviction is that there are no adequate Platonic answers to these questions. As he sees the problem, any explanation, to be acceptable, must satisfy at least two conditions, both posed by the fact to be explained—man himself. The human soul is in itself a spiritual substance; it does not need the body in order to exist, since precisely it can and does exist through itself. And yet this spiritual substance, which exists *through* itself, does not exist *by* itself; it does not exist as a soul alone. Now how can man be one being? And what is the *why* of such a being?

To the first of these questions St. Thomas answers that man can be one being if the whole composite receives actual existence through one cause or principle. For St. Thomas, at least, being *one* being follows from *being* one being. Such a principle is the soul. Subsistent in itself, it is nevertheless also the principle through which the whole composite exists. The famous Thomistic doctrine of the unicity of the substantial form in man, so resisted by the thinkers of the late thirteenth century, has for its purpose to explain how man is one being in his very existence. To say that man is a composite being can be ambiguous. It should not mean that man is made up of two beings; it must rather mean that, though man is composed of soul and body, the body exists in and through the existence of the soul. That is why we may say that, existentially considered, it is the body that is in the soul, not the soul in the body.

That this is a paradoxical thesis needs scarcely to be denied. But we must add immediately that it is no more paradoxical than the paradox it is trying to explain. What a creature is man! He is spirit and matter together. He is not an imprisoned angel; he is by nature an incarnate spirit. This is the fact to explain—without changing it and without explaining it away. But the more we are true to the fact of man as an incarnate spirit, to the fact of a subsistent and spiritual soul which is yet by nature a part of man, the more we are driven to ask the why of such a being. And we are equally driven to exclude as impossible all explanations of man which render the facts impossible. What is, is possible; and man is. And because man is an observable reality, he poses the problem of the unity of his being and of his nature.

The Thomistic explanation of the unity of man is historically decisive far beyond the confines of the thirteenth century. There are, according to St. Thomas, two things that cannot be said on this point. In the first place, we cannot say that an intellectual substance is joined to a body as a consequence of being an intellectual substance. For the good of such a substance is a spiritual good, the knowledge of truth. It is not, therefore, in the line of the essential purpose of the soul as an intellectual substance that it should be joined to a body. On the other hand, we cannot say that the soul is joined to a body for the good of the body itself, since matter serves form rather than making it its servant. What, then? There is, in St. Thomas' view, only one answer which remains true to the fact without violating any principles. If an intellectual substance is joined to a body neither precisely because it is intellectual nor for the sake of a body, then it must be so joined because it is unequal *by itself* to the task of accomplishing the work proper to an intellectual substance. That is to say, a spiritual substance such as the human soul, which is intellectual in its nature and purpose, and which yet is part of the human composite, must require to be such a part in order to become completely an intellectual substance. We are invited by St. Thomas Aquinas, therefore, to look upon the human composite of soul and body as being the complement of the intellectual nature of the soul. If the knowledge of truth is the aim of a spiritual substance, and if the soul, which is such a substance, is an incarnate spirit, then it is incarnate in order to do the work of a spirit; and, what is no less decisive, it must do a spiritual work as an incarnate spirit.

We are now standing in the presence of a philosophical decision which is unique in history. To say that man must do a spiritual work as an incarnate spirit is to say that *as a knower* man is a composite being. Where the Platonic knower is a pure reason, and the Cartesian knower a pure mind, the Thomistic knower is, *as knower*, the composite of soul and body. Let us say this in another way. Man as a knower must be partly material in order to be adequately a knower. Of course, such a notion is bound to sound scandalous to modern ears. For we are the heirs of generations of philosophic speculations according to which man is a *thinker* and a *mind*. Now it is a fact that the Thomistic man is a knower rather than a thinker, and he is a composite being rather than a mind. In fact, St. Thomas does not even have in his vocabulary a term corresponding to 'the term thinker: you cannot translate such a term into Thomistic Latin. If we are to judge matters as St. Thomas has done, we are bound to say that the European man became a thinker after he ruined himself as a knower; and we can now even trace the steps of that ruination—from Augustinian Platonism to the nominalistic isolationism of Ockham to the despairing and desperate methodism of Descartes. For what we call the decline of mediaeval philosophy was really a transition from man as a knower to man as a thinker—from man knowing the world of sensible things to man thinking abstract thoughts in separation from existence. What is thinking but dis-existentialized knowing?

There is no need to dwell on man as a thinker except perhaps to say that the recent revolts by existential theologians and existential philosophers, not to mention existential historians, is a critical lesson for all to consider. Philosophers have tried to be thinkers; they have tried to give a conceptual and totally abstract reproduction of reality; some of them have even played at being God in order to give, from the point of view of mind, a total and totally abstract presentation of reality. Now, what the contemporary revolt by existentialists will lead to no one will predict. But what it means is clear enough; it means the emptiness of abstract thought closed on abstractions. It is equally clear that, in the violence of their revolt, some existentialists should circle round man's existence very closely, very anxiously and very desperately. And well they should. For an existential revolt against abstractions is historically understandable and philosophically salutary. But a revolt of existence, which turns out to be a revolt against intelligibility in the world, merely ruins the world in order to save existence. The remedy for meaning without a world is not a world without meaning. For, granted that thinking without existence is empty, existence without intelligibility is just as empty.

The Thomistic doctrine of man, in which the knowing subject is a composite being, an incarnate spirit, yields neither to the impulse to conceptualize existence nor to the impulse to stop conceptualization in the presence of existence. Rather, St. Thomas sets himself the problem to explain how it is that we know concrete sensible being. It is not abstractions that we know, though we use abstractions; it is things. What is more, we know things as being, not as essences; we say that things have essences, not that they are essences. How is this knowing of *beings* to be explained? And how is it that we are able to pronounce the very *to be*? Being is not the name of any essence, and in the sense in which we are said to conceive essences we cannot say that we conceive being. We have, to be sure, a concept of being, but it is not the concept of an essence, nor is it abstracted as essential concepts are; for, far from excluding the individuals from which it is abstracted, it includes them, since that to which it refers is individual in every individual being—namely, its act of to be.

The notion of act is fundamental in the metaphysics and epistemology of St. Thomas. For him, the name being takes its origin from the act of to be; it is therefore a name of things from the standpoint of act, not from the standpoint of essence. Essence itself, as St. Thomas understands it, is not a thing or a reality in itself. If you ask: *what* is a thing? to St. Thomas the question means: what sort of being does a thing have? But because a thing is called a being from its act of to be, to ask what is is to be concerned with the sortness of its act of to be. To be a man is to be humanly.

How then can *being*—that being which has been such a stranger from the philosophical horizons of Plato and of most modern philosophers—how can being be known? For it cannot be conceived as an essence, since it is not an essence. But, be it observed, the being that is in question here is not some abstraction. It is the being of sensible things; it *is* sensible things. The being that we are called upon to know, and the knowledge of which we are called upon to explain, is concrete sensible being—manifold and multiple, changing and indefinitely varied. Now, how can such being—such beings— be known, given that, because they are beings and not essences, they cannot be completely conceptualized?

To this question, too, St. Thomas thinks that there is but

one answer. The first requisite of knowledge is that the thing known be in the knower. The second requisite is that the thing known, since it is a being and not an essence, be in the knower as a being and not as an essence. The third requisite is that, since the thing to be known is a concrete sensible being, it must be in the knower as a concrete sensible being. Without these requisites, there would not be knowledge as St. Thomas understands it; there would not be a human knowing which is the knowing of sensible beings.

The Thomistic doctrine that man as a knower is a composite being, that *he* knows through the use of his several powers together and inter-ordinated, is the exact complement of knowing understood in the light of the above requisites. Man must as a knower *be* sensible things in order to know them. Man as a knower must be such that he can give existence, within his knowledge, not to abstract essences, but to sensible beings. That is why man as a knower needs a body; for, through the senses of his body he can give sensible existence in the order of knowing to that which is sensible in the order of being. The body as part of the knowing man answers for St. Thomas Aquinas the two questions which knowledge poses for him. In knowing sensible being, how do we know it as sensible, which it is, and as being, which it likewise is? St. Thomas' answer is that sensible being exists in our knowledge as sensible being; its actuality exists in our sensible knowledge as sensible actuality, and not as an abstraction. And it is because we can give sensible actuality, within our knowledge, to what is a sensible actuality in the order of existence that we can say we know sensible beings.

It is important to stress this approach to human knowledge from the point of view of the act of being in sensible things. To know is to be; to know sensible things is, by means of knowing, to be sensible things. To St. Thomas, knowing first presents itself in the mode of act; for it is the mode of act which is the mode of being. If we think of knowledge as intellectual abstraction, we shall never explain why we know being from the point of view of its actuality. If St. Thomas believes that abstraction is not working in a void, and that conceptualization is rooted in the actuality of things, it is because before the work of abstraction and conceptualization by the intellect (or, rather, by man through the intellect) there is the work of giving sensible existence, within man's knowledge, to the sensible being of things. In other words, being (the being of and in sensible things) first comes to us in the way that it is, as sensible actuality, and human knowing begins by being the exercise by man of the sensible act of being in things.

That is why abstraction as St. Thomas understands it is not a separation from existence; it is the consideration by the intellect of the essential elements within the actuality of things. In other words, given St. Thomas' view of sensible knowledge, we are bound to say that for him abstraction always takes place within the apprehended actuality of things. That is why we can use concepts and form judgments. For a judgment is not built on abstractions; it is in the line of the act of being, not in the line of essence. In going from concepts to judgments we do not miraculously get something from nothing—as though we begin knowledge with conceptualized essences and then by the employment of judgment we begin to speak the language of being. Conceptualized essences, unless they be conceptualized within our apprehension of being, will never enable us to form judgments. For judgments, including attributive judgments, depend for their possibility on our apprehension of being as act, and of essence itself from the viewpoint of act; for it is act which unifies being, and it is within the unity of being that we must seek the unity of essence and therefore the ground of judgment.

IV

There would be many more names and many more struggles within the thirteenth century that we would have to consider in order to give a complete picture of St. Thomas and his age. But perhaps, in a general appreciation of the philosophical spirit of St. Thomas, it is not unjust to concentrate our attention on his relations to Plato. The Thomistic critique of Plato is a permanent and decisive aspect of Thomism, just as it is a permanent and decisive issue in the thirteenth century. Nor is it difficult to see the role assigned to Aristotle by St. Thomas Aquinas. Where the Platonic method in philosophy threatens to leave man in a void of abstractions, the Aristotelian critique of Plato has the basic merit of saving the reality of the world from Platonic abstractionism. But in following the direction of the Aristotelian critique of Plato,

St. Thomas breathed into Aristotle's conception of the world a vision that the Stagirite himself had never known. The world which St. Thomas analyzes by means of the principles of the Aristotelian *Physics* is a world of creatures, something that Aristotle had never known; and while it is true that Averroes and the Averroists used the Aristotelian doctrine of motion against the Christian doctrine of creation, St. Thomas Aquinas preferred to interpret it as failing to reach the idea of creation, rather than as denying it.

It has always been a problem for students of St. Thomas to explain his comparatively milder treatment of Aristotle than of Plato. No doubt, he agreed with Aristotle much more than he ever did with Plato; although it is a fact that he has had occasion to side with Plato against Aristotle. Now one has only to think of all the principles and doctrines which St. Thomas received from Aristotle in order to recognize that the most obvious reason for his mildness toward Aristotle is that, after all, no other attitude is possible in the circumstances. It is quite probable, too, that the intellectual situation in the world around him suggested to St. Thomas the attitude he adopted. For that situation, so rampant with Platonism, some of which even masqueraded under the name of Aristotle, required precisely the sort of use of Aristotle which St. Thomas actually made. An Aristotle, in fact, whose *De Anima, Physics* and *Metaphysics* are made to be stout weapons in defense of truth against Plato's isolation of soul from body, his sacrifice of being in the name of its intelligibility, his disparaging attitude toward the world of sense and toward sense knowledge—such an Aristotle was a veritable ally of every Catholic theologian in the thirteenth century.

What is, however, perplexing about such an Aristotle is not the timeliness of his arrival in the Paris of St. Thomas during the middle of the thirteenth century, nor the extent of his services to the cause of philosophy and theology. What is perplexing is, rather, that such an Aristotle existed, to a great extent, only in the mind of St. Thomas Aquinas; and what is no less perplexing is that St. Thomas has criticized Aristotle often enough to leave no doubt on this point. What many still like to call the Aristotelian-Thomistic synthesis is the result of more than one benign Thomistic interpretation of the Philosopher. To identify St. Thomas with an Aristotle who is, in many important respects, his own creation, is a compliment to St. Thomas himself. To do so without realizing that St. Thomas' Aristotle is a Thomist who, on some basic fundamentals, was never an Aristotelian is a historical illusion that is both dangerous and without justification in our own day. For whereas St. Thomas could and did transform Aristotle according to the needs and purposes of the thirteenth century, and thus served the cause of truth in his world, to identify Aristotle and St. Thomas today, or to speak without grave qualification of "the Aristotelianism of St. Thomas," is to risk the danger of ignoring and even losing those very doctrines which are the work of the personal genius of St. Thomas himself. And the point of this loss is not merely that it would be an injustice to an eminent Catholic theologian; the point is that we would be the losers.

Admittedly, the historian of St. Thomas does not have the right to alter his mildness toward Aristotle. Yet he has also the duty to point out, no matter how briefly, that the Aristotle of history bequeathed to the thirteenth century many doctrines and dilemmas which increased the philosophical turmoil of that age. If Plato had transformed man into a reason and freed him from matter by turning him from existence toward abstractions, Aristotle freed man from the reign of matter and motion by likewise transforming him into a reason and by likewise turning him from existence toward thought. To confine man within reason in order to escape matter is, in its own way, a form of dis-existentialization. Nor is the Aristotelian theology any less a dis-existentialized one, however much St. Thomas may have used the *Metaphysics* of Aristotle for a genuinely existential appreciation of being. The end of man is surely an embarrassingly obscure point in the Aristotelian ethics, and the problem of the relations between soul and body in man is equally so. All this is not to say that we must disparage Aristotle in order to magnify St. Thomas. Quite the contrary, the only point in calling attention to these and similar Aristotelian embarrassments is to free ourselves of the illusion that we can be Thomists (supposing, for the moment, that at least some of us do) by means of the Aristotelianism which led to these embarrassments.

It will be abundantly clear to those who read the following pages that St. Thomas Aquinas was the disciple of his predecessors, and even their spokesman, at the very moment of

being their critic. For by his own practice we are warranted
in saying that St. Thomas' predecessors helped him to reach
the truths that he did. Sometimes they helped him by reaching them before him; sometimes they helped by struggling
toward them and, by their very failures, revealing to all who
could read what would have to be done in order to succeed
where they failed. If he was a critic of his predecessors, it was
in their name that St. Thomas was their critic. If his doctrines were new, he yet managed to find many beginnings of
these doctrines in the past. Nothing is newer in the history
of Christian thought than St. Thomas' notion of existence;
and, speaking from the historical vantage point of the twen-
tieth century, let us add that nothing has been rarer in the
history of philosophy since the thirteenth century than that
notion of existence. And yet the same St. Thomas Aquinas,
who loved truth much more than he was aware of his own
novelty, presents many of his most distinctive notions as
having a long birth in the history of Christian thought before
him. "According to reason and Aristotle," he has often said.
He stood on a giant past; and though he himself was a giant,
he always looked upon his intellectual stature with the genu-
ine humility of one who, even in his highest speculative
reaches, accepted the fruits of philosophical victory as much
in the name of those who went before him as in his own.

Anton C. Pegis

INTRODUCTION TO
ST. THOMAS AQUINAS

GOD

THE SUMMA THEOLOGICA

Part One

Question I

THE NATURE AND DOMAIN OF SACRED DOCTRINE

(*In Ten Articles*)

To PLACE our purpose within definite limits, we must first investigate the nature and domain of sacred doctrine. Concerning this there are ten points of inquiry:—

(1) Whether sacred doctrine is necessary? (2) Whether it is a science? (3) Whether it is one or many? (4) Whether it is speculative or practical? (5) How it is compared with other sciences? (6) Whether it is a wisdom? (7) Whether God is its subject-matter? (8) Whether it is argumentative? (9) Whether it rightly employs metaphors and similes? (10) Whether the Sacred Scripture of this doctrine may be expounded in different senses?

First Article

WHETHER, BESIDES THE PHILOSOPHICAL SCIENCES, ANY FURTHER DOCTRINE IS REQUIRED?

We proceed thus to the First Article:—

Objection 1. It seems that, besides the philosophical sciences, we have no need of any further knowledge. For man should not seek to know what is above reason: *Seek not the things that are too high for thee* (*Ecclus*. iii. 22). But whatever is not above reason is sufficiently considered in the phil-

3

osophical sciences. Therefore any other knowledge besides
the philosophical sciences is superfluous.

Obj. 2. Further, knowledge can be concerned only with being, for nothing can be known, save the true, which is convertible with being. But everything that is, is considered in
the philosophical sciences—even God Himself; so that there
is a part of philosophy called theology, or the divine science,
as is clear from Aristotle.[1] Therefore, besides the philosophical sciences, there is no need of any further knowledge.

On the contrary, It is written (*2 Tim.* iii. 16): *All Scripture inspired of God is profitable to teach, to reprove, to correct, to instruct in justice.* Now Scripture, inspired of God, is
not a part of the philosophical sciences discovered by human
reason. Therefore it is useful that besides the philosophical
sciences there should be another science—*i.e.,* inspired of
God.

I answer that, It was necessary for man's salvation that
there should be a knowledge revealed by God, besides the
philosophical sciences investigated by human reason. First,
because man is directed to God as to an end that surpasses
the grasp of his reason: *The eye hath not seen, O God, besides Thee, what things Thou hast prepared for them that
wait for Thee* (*Isa.* lxiv. 4). But the end must first be known
by men who are to direct their thoughts and actions to the
end. Hence it was necessary for the salvation of man that
certain truths which exceed human reason should be made
known to him by divine revelation. Even as regards those
truths about God which human reason can investigate, it was
necessary that man be taught by a divine revelation. For the
truth about God, such as reason can know it, would only be
known by a few, and that after a long time, and with the
admixture of many errors; whereas man's whole salvation,
which is in God, depends upon the knowledge of this truth.
Therefore, in order that the salvation of men might be
brought about more fitly and more surely, it was necessary
that they be taught divine truths by divine revelation. It was
therefore necessary that, besides the philosophical sciences
investigated by reason, there should be a sacred science by
way of revelation.

Reply Obj. 1. Although those things which are beyond
man's knowledge may not be sought for by man through his

[1] *Metaph.,* V, 1 (1026a 19).

reason, nevertheless, what is revealed by God must be accepted through faith. Hence the sacred text continues, *For many things are shown to thee above the understanding of man* (*Ecclus.* iii. 25). And in such things sacred science consists.

Reply Obj. 2. Sciences are diversified according to the diverse nature of their knowable objects. For the astronomer and the physicist both prove the same conclusion—that the earth, for instance, is round: the astronomer by means of mathematics (*i.e.*, abstracting from matter), but the physicist by means of matter itself. Hence there is no reason why those things which are treated by the philosophical sciences, so far as they can be known by the light of natural reason, may not also be treated by another science so far as they are known by the light of the divine revelation. Hence the theology included in sacred doctrine differs in genus from that theology which is part of philosophy.

Second Article

WHETHER SACRED DOCTRINE IS A SCIENCE?

We proceed thus to the Second Article:—

Objection 1. It seems that sacred doctrine is not a science. For every science proceeds from self-evident principles. But sacred doctrine proceeds from articles of faith which are not self-evident, since their truth is not admitted by all: *For all men have not faith* (2 *Thess.* iii. 2). Therefore sacred doctrine is not a science.

Obj. 2. Further, science is not of individuals. But sacred doctrine treats of individual facts, such as the deeds of Abraham, Isaac and Jacob, and the like. Therefore sacred doctrine is not a science.

On the contrary, Augustine says that *to this science alone belongs that whereby saving faith is begotten, nourished, protected and strengthened.*[2] But this can be said of no science except sacred doctrine. Therefore sacred doctrine is a science.

I answer that, Sacred doctrine is a science. We must bear in mind that there are two kinds of sciences. There are some which proceed from principles known by the natural light of

---

[2] *De Trin.,* XIV, 1 (PL 42, 1037).

the intellect, such as arithmetic and geometry and the like. There are also some which proceed from principles known by the light of a higher science: thus the science of optics proceeds from principles established by geometry, and music from principles established by arithmetic. So it is that sacred doctrine is a science because it proceeds from principles made known by the light of a higher science, namely, the science of God and the blessed. Hence, just as music accepts on authority the principles taught by the arithmetician, so sacred science accepts the principles revealed by God.

Reply Obj. 1. The principles of any science are either in themselves self-evident, or reducible to the knowledge of a higher science; and such, as we have said, are the principles of sacred doctrine.

Reply Obj. 2. Individual facts are not treated in sacred doctrine because it is concerned with them principally; they are rather introduced as examples to be followed in our lives (as in the moral sciences), as well as to establish the authority of those men through whom the divine revelation, on which this sacred scripture or doctrine is based, has come down to us.

Third Article

WHETHER SACRED DOCTRINE IS ONE SCIENCE?

We proceed thus to the Third Article:—

Objection 1. It seems that sacred doctrine is not one science, for according to the Philosopher *that science is one which treats only of one class of subjects.*[3] But the creator and the creature, both of whom are treated in sacred doctrine, cannot be grouped together under one class of subjects. Therefore sacred doctrine is not one science.

Obj. 2. Further, in sacred doctrine we treat of angels, corporeal creatures and human morality. But these belong to separate philosophical sciences. Therefore sacred doctrine cannot be one science.

On the contrary, Holy Scripture speaks of it as one science: *Wisdom gave him the knowledge [scientiam] of holy things (Wis.* x. 10).

I answer that, Sacred doctrine is one science. The unity of

[3] *Post. Anal.,* I, 28 (87a 38).

a power or habit is to be gauged by its object, not indeed, in its material aspect, but as regards the formality under which it is an object. For example, man, ass, stone, agree in the one formality of being colored; and color is the formal object of sight. Therefore, because Sacred Scripture (as we have said) considers some things under the formality of being divinely revealed, all things which have been divinely revealed have in common the formality of the object of this science. Hence, they are included under sacred doctrine as under one science.

Reply Obj. 1. Sacred doctrine does not treat of God and creatures equally, but of God primarily, and of creatures only so far as they are referable to God as their beginning or end. Hence the unity of this science is not impaired.

Reply Obj. 2. Nothing prevents inferior powers or habits from being diversified by objects which yet agree with one another in coming together under a higher power or habit; because the higher power or habit regards its own object under a more universal formality. Thus, the object of the *common sense* is the sensible, including, therefore, whatever is visible or audible. Hence the *common sense*, although one power, extends to all the objects of the five senses. Similarly, objects which are the subject-matter of different philosophical sciences can yet be treated by this one single sacred science under one aspect, namely, in so far as they can be included in revelation. So that in this way sacred doctrine bears, as it were, the stamp of the divine science, which is one and simple, yet extends to everything.

Fourth Article

WHETHER SACRED DOCTRINE IS A PRACTICAL SCIENCE?

We proceed thus to the Fourth Article:—

Objection 1. It seems that sacred doctrine is a practical science, for a practical science is that which ends in action, according to the Philosopher.[4] But sacred doctrine is ordained to action: *Be ye doers of the word, and not hearers only* (*Jas.* i. 22). Therefore sacred doctrine is a practical science.

Obj. 2. Further, sacred doctrine is divided into the Old and the New Law. But law belongs to moral science, which

[4] *Metaph.*, Ia, 1 (993b 21).

is a practical science. Therefore sacred doctrine is a practical science.

On the contrary, Every practical science is concerned with the things man can do; as moral science is concerned with human acts, and architecture with buildings. But sacred doctrine is chiefly concerned with God, Who is rather the Maker of man. Therefore it is not a practical but a speculative science.

I answer that, Sacred doctrine, being one, extends to things which belong to the different philosophical sciences, because it considers in each the same formal aspect, namely, so far as they can be known through the divine light. Hence, although among the philosophical sciences some are speculative and others practical, nevertheless, sacred doctrine includes both; as God, by one and the same science, knows both Himself and His works.

Still, it is more speculative than practical, because it is more concerned with divine things than with human acts; though even of these acts it treats inasmuch as man is ordained by them to the perfect knowledge of God, in which consists eternal beatitude.

This is a sufficient answer to the Objections.

Fifth Article

WHETHER SACRED DOCTRINE IS NOBLER THAN OTHER SCIENCES?

We proceed thus to the Fifth Article:—

Objection 1. It seems that sacred doctrine is not nobler than other sciences, for the nobility of a science depends on its certitude. But other sciences, the principles of which cannot be doubted, seem to be more certain than sacred doctrine; for its principles—namely, articles of faith—can be doubted. Therefore other sciences seem to be nobler.

Obj. 2. Further, it is the part of a lower science to draw upon a higher; as music draws upon arithmetic. But sacred doctrine does draw upon the philosophical sciences; for Jerome observes, in his Epistle to Magnus, that *the ancient doctors so enriched their books with the doctrines and thoughts of the philosophers, that thou knowest not what more to admire in them, their profane erudition or their scriptural learning.*[5] Therefore sacred doctrine is inferior to other sciences.

On the contrary, Other sciences are called the handmaidens of this one: *Wisdom sent her maids to invite to the tower* (*Prov.* ix. 3).

I answer that, Since this science is partly speculative and partly practical, it transcends all other sciences, speculative and practical. Now one speculative science is said to be nobler than another either by reason of its greater certitude, or by reason of the higher dignity of its subject-matter. In both these respects this science surpasses other speculative sciences: in point of greater certitude, because other sciences derive their certitude from the natural light of human reason, which can err, whereas this derives its certitude from the light of the divine knowledge, which cannot err; in point of the higher dignity of its subject-matter, because this science treats chiefly of those things which by their sublimity transcend human reason, while other sciences consider only those things which are within reason's grasp. Of the practical sciences, that one is nobler which is ordained to a more final end, as political science is nobler than military science; for the good of the army is directed to the good of the state. But the purpose of this science, in so far as it is practical, is eternal beatitude, to which as to an ultimate end the ends of all the practical sciences are directed. Hence it is clear that from every standpoint it is nobler than other sciences.

Reply Obj. 1. It may well happen that what is in itself the more certain may seem to us the less certain because of the weakness of our intellect, *which is dazzled by the clearest objects of nature; as the owl is dazzled by the light of the sun.*[6] Hence the fact that some happen to doubt about the articles of faith is not due to the uncertain nature of the truths, but to the weakness of the human intellect; yet the slenderest knowledge that may be obtained of the highest things is more desirable than the most certain knowledge obtained of the lowest things, as is said in *De Animalibus* xi.[7]

Reply Obj. 2. This science can draw upon the philosophical sciences, not as though it stood in need of them, but only

[5] *Epist.* LXX (PL 22, 668).   [6] Aristotle, *Metaph.,* Ia, 1 (993b 9).
[7] Aristotle, *De Part. Anim.,* I, 5 (644b 31).

in order to make its teaching clearer. For it accepts its principles, not from the other sciences, but immediately from
God, by revelation. Therefore it does not draw upon the
other sciences as upon its superiors, but uses them as its
inferiors and handmaidens: even so the master sciences make
use of subordinate sciences, as political science of military
science. That it thus uses them is not due to its own defect or
insufficiency, but to the defect of our intellect, which is more
easily led by what is known through natural reason (from
which proceed the other sciences), to that which is above
reason, such as are the teachings of this science.

Sixth Article

WHETHER THIS DOCTRINE IS A WISDOM?

We proceed thus to the Sixth Article:—

Objection 1. It seems that this doctrine is not a wisdom.
For no doctrine which borrows its principles is worthy of the
name of wisdom, seeing that the wise man directs, and is not
directed.[8] But this doctrine borrows its principles. Therefore
it is not a wisdom.

Obj. 2. Further, it is a part of wisdom to prove the principles of other sciences. Hence it is called the chief of sciences,
as is clear in *Ethics* vi.[9] But this doctrine does not prove
the principles of other sciences. Therefore it is not a wisdom.

Obj. 3. Further, this doctrine is acquired by study, whereas
wisdom is acquired by God's inspiration, and is accordingly
numbered among the gifts of the Holy Spirit (*Isa.* xi. 2).
Therefore this doctrine is not a wisdom.

On the contrary, It is written (*Deut.* iv. 6): *This is your
wisdom and understanding in the sight of nations.*

I answer that, This doctrine is wisdom above all human
wisdoms not merely in any one order, but absolutely. For
since it is the part of a wise man to order and to judge, and
since lesser matters can be judged in the light of some higher
cause, he is said to be wise in any genus who considers the
highest cause in that genus. Thus in the realm of building,
he who plans the form of the house is called wise and architect, in relation to the subordinate laborers who trim the

[8] Aristotle, *Metaph.*, I, 2 (982a 18).   [9] Aristotle, *Eth.*, VI, 7 (1141a
20).

wood and make ready the stones: thus it is said, *As a wise architect I have laid the foundation* (*1 Cor.* iii. 10). Again, in the order of all human life, the prudent man is called wise, inasmuch as he directs his acts to a fitting end: thus it is said, *Wisdom is prudence to a man* (*Prov.* x. 23). Therefore, he who considers absolutely the highest cause of the whole universe, namely God, is most of all called wise. Hence wisdom is said to be the knowledge of divine things, as Augustine says.[10] But sacred doctrine essentially treats of God viewed as the highest cause, for it treats of Him not only so far as He can be known through creatures just as philosophers knew Him—*That which is known of God is manifest in them* (*Rom.* i. 19)—but also so far as He is known to Himself alone and revealed to others. Hence sacred doctrine is especially called a wisdom.

Reply Obj. 1. Sacred doctrine derives its principles, not from any human knowledge, but from the divine knowledge, by which, as by the highest wisdom, all our knowledge is ordered.

Reply Obj. 2. The principles of the other sciences either are evident and cannot be proved, or they are proved by natural reason in some other science. But the knowledge proper to this science comes through revelation, and not through natural reason. Therefore it is not its business to prove the principles of the other sciences, but only to judge them. For whatsoever is found in the other sciences contrary to the truth of this science must be condemned as false. Hence, it is said: *Destroying counsels and every height that exalteth itself against the knowledge of God* (*2 Cor.* x. 4, 5).

Reply Obj. 3. Since judgment pertains to wisdom, in accord with a twofold manner of judging there is a twofold wisdom. A man may judge in one way by inclination, as whoever has the habit of a virtue judges rightly of what is virtuous by his very inclination towards it. Hence it is the virtuous man, as we read,[11] who is the measure and rule of human acts. In another way, a man may judge by knowledge, just as man learned in moral science might be able to judge rightly about virtuous acts, though he had not virtue. The first manner of judging divine things belongs to that wisdom

[10] *De Trin.*, XII, 14 (PL 42, 1009).—Cf. Cicero, *De Officiis*, II, 2 (p. 80).   [11] Aristotle, *Eth.*, X, 5 (1176a 17).

which is numbered as a gift of the Holy Ghost: *The spiritual man judgeth all things* (*1 Cor.* ii. 15). And Dionysius says: *Hierotheus is taught not only as one learning, but also as experiencing divine things.*[12] The second manner of judging belongs to this doctrine, inasmuch as it is acquired by study, though its principles are obtained by revelation.

Seventh Article

WHETHER GOD IS THE SUBJECT-MATTER OF THIS SCIENCE?

We proceed thus to the Seventh Article:—

Objection 1. It seems that God is not the subject-matter of this science. For, according to the Philosopher,[13] in every science the essence of its subject is presupposed. But this science cannot presuppose the essence of God, for Damascene says: *It is impossible to express the essence of God.*[14] Therefore God is not the subject-matter of this science.

Obj. 2. Further, whatever conclusions are reached in any science must be comprehended under the subject-matter of that science. But in Holy Scripture we reach conclusions not only concerning God, but concerning many other things, such as creatures and human morality. Therefore God is not the subject-matter of this science.

On the contrary, The subject-matter of a science is that of which it principally treats. But in this science the treatment is mainly about God; for it is called theology, as treating of God. Therefore God is the subject-matter of this science.

I answer that, God is the subject-matter of this science. The relation between a science and its subject-matter is the same as that between a habit or a power and its object. Now properly speaking the object of a power or habit is that under whose formality all things are referred to that power or habit, as man and stone are referred to sight in that they are colored. Hence colored things are the proper object of sight. But in sacred doctrine all things are treated under the aspect of God, either because they are God Himself, or because

---

[12] *De Div. Nom.,* II, 9 (PG 3. 648).   [13] *Post. Anal.,* I, 1 (71a 13).
[14] *De Fide Orth.,* I, 4 (PG 94, 797).

they refer to God as to their beginning and end. Hence it follows that God is in very truth the subject-matter of this science. This is made clear also from the principles of this science, namely, the articles of faith, for faith is about God. The subject-matter of the principles and of the whole science must be the same, since the whole science is contained virtually in its principles.

Some, however, looking to what is treated in this science, and not to the aspect under which it is treated, have asserted the subject-matter of this science to be something other than God—that is, either things and signs,[15] or the works of salvation,[16] or the whole Christ, that is, the head and members.[17] Of all these things, in truth, we treat in this science, but so far as they are ordered to God.

Reply Obj. 1. Although we cannot know in what consists the essence of God, nevertheless in this doctrine we make use of His effects, either of nature or of grace, in the place of a definition, in regard to whatever is treated in this doctrine concerning God; even as in some philosophical sciences we demonstrate something about a cause from its effect, by taking the effect in the place of a definition of the cause.

Reply Obj. 2. Whatever other conclusions are reached in this sacred science are comprehended under God, not as parts or species or accidents, but as in some way ordained to Him.

Eighth Article

WHETHER SACRED DOCTRINE IS ARGUMENTATIVE?

We proceed thus to the Eighth Article:—

Objection 1. It seems this doctrine is not argumentative. For Ambrose says: *Put arguments aside where faith is sought.*[18] But in this doctrine faith especially is sought: *But these things are written that you may believe* (*Jo.* xx. 31). Therefore sacred doctrine is not argumentative.

Obj. 2. Further, if it is argumentative, the argument is either from authority or from reason. If it is from authority, it seems unbefitting its dignity, for the proof from authority

[15] Peter Lombard, *Sent.*, I, i, 1 (I, 14); cf. St. Augustine, *De Doc. Christ.*, I, 2 (PL 34, 19).   [16] Hugh of St. Victor, *De Sacram.*, Prol., 2 (PL 176, 183).   [17] Robert Grosseteste, *Hexaëm.* (p. 176); Robert Kilwardby, *De Nat. Theol.* (p. 17).   [18] *De Fide*, I, 13 (PL 16, 570).

is the weakest form of proof according to Boethius.[19] But if
from reason, this is unbefitting its end, because, according
to Gregory, *faith has no merit in those things of which human reason brings its own experience.*[20] Therefore sacred
doctrine is not argumentative.

On the contrary, The Scripture says that a bishop should
*embrace that faithful word which is according to doctrine,
that he may be able to exhort in sound doctrine and to con-
vince the gainsayers* (*Tit.* i. 9).

I answer that, As the other sciences do not argue in proof
of their principles, but argue from their principles to demonstrate other truths in these sciences, so this doctrine does not
argue in proof of its principles, which are the articles of faith,
but from them it goes on to prove something else; as the
Apostle argues from the resurrection of Christ in proof of the
general resurrection (*1 Cor.* xv, 12). However, it is to be
borne in mind, in regard to the philosophical sciences, that
the inferior sciences neither prove their principles nor dispute with those who deny them, but leave this to a higher
science; whereas the highest of them, viz., metaphysics, can
dispute with one who denies its principles, if only the opponent will make some concession; but if he concedes nothing, it can have no dispute with him, though it can answer
his arguments. Hence Sacred Scripture, since it has no science above itself, disputes argumentatively with one who
denies its principles only if the opponent admits some at least
of the truths obtained through divine revelation. Thus, we
can argue with heretics from texts in Holy Scripture, and
against those who deny one article of faith we can argue from
another. If our opponent believes nothing of divine revelation, there is no longer any means of proving the articles of
faith by argument, but only of answering his objections—if
he has any—against faith. Since faith rests upon infallible
truth, and since the contrary of a truth can never be demonstrated, it is clear that the proofs brought against faith are
not demonstrations, but arguments that can be answered.

Reply Obj. 1. Although arguments from human reason
cannot avail to prove what belongs to faith, nevertheless,
this doctrine argues from articles of faith to other truths.

Reply Obj. 2. It is especially proper to this doctrine to

[19] *In Top. Cicer.,* I (PL 64, 1166); *De Differ. Top.,* III (PL 64,
1199).   [20] *In Evang.,* II, hom. 26 (PL 76, 1197).

argue from authority, inasmuch as its principles are obtained by revelation; and hence we must believe the authority of those to whom the revelation has been made. Nor does this take away from the dignity of this doctrine, for although the argument from authority based on human reason is the weakest, yet the argument from authority based on divine revelation is the strongest. But sacred doctrine also makes use of human reason, not, indeed, to prove faith (for thereby the merit of faith would come to an end), but to make clear other things that are set forth in this doctrine. Since therefore grace does not destroy nature, but perfects it, natural reason should minister to faith as the natural inclination of the will ministers to charity. Hence the Apostle says: *Bringing into captivity every understanding unto the obedience of Christ* (*2 Cor.* x. 5). Hence it is that sacred doctrine makes use also of the authority of philosophers in those questions in which they were able to know the truth by natural reason, as Paul quotes a saying of Aratus: *As some also of your own poets said: For we are also His offspring* (*Acts* xvii. 28). Nevertheless, sacred doctrine makes use of these authorities as extrinsic and probable arguments, but properly uses the authority of the canonical Scriptures as a necessary demonstration, and the authority of the doctors of the Church as one that may properly be used, yet merely as probable. For our faith rests upon the revelation made to the apostles and prophets, who wrote the canonical books, and not on the revelations (if any such there are) made to other doctors. Hence Augustine says: *Only those books of Scripture which are called canonical have I learned to hold in such honor as to believe their authors have not erred in any way in writing them. But other authors I so read as not to deem anything in their works to be true, merely because of their having so thought and written, whatever may have been their holiness and learning.*[21] •

Ninth Article

WHETHER HOLY SCRIPTURE SHOULD USE METAPHORS?

We proceed thus to the Ninth Article:—
Objection 1. It seems that Holy Scripture should not use

[21] *Epist.* LXXXII, 1 (PL 33, 277).

metaphors. For that which is proper to the lowest science
seems not to befit this science, which holds the highest place
of all. But to proceed by the aid of various similitudes and
figures is proper to poetic, the least of all the sciences. Therefore it is not fitting that this science should make use of such
similitudes.

Obj. 2. Further, this doctrine seems to be intended to make
truth clear. Hence a reward is held out to those who manifest it: *They that explain me shall have life everlasting* (*Ecclus.* xxiv. 31). But by such similitudes truth is obscured.
Therefore to put forward divine truths under the likeness of
corporeal things does not befit this doctrine.

Obj. 3. Further, the higher creatures are, the nearer they
approach to the divine likeness. If therefore any creature be
taken to represent God, this representation ought chiefly to
be taken from the higher creatures, and not from the lower;
yet this is often found in the Scriptures.

On the contrary, It is written (*Osee* xii. 10): *I have multiplied visions, and I have used similitudes by the ministry of
the prophets.* But to put forward anything by means of similitudes is to use metaphors. Therefore sacred doctrine may
use metaphors.

I answer that, It is befitting Holy Scripture to put forward
divine and spiritual truths by means of comparisons with
material things. For God provides for everything according
to the capacity of its nature. Now it is natural to man to
attain to intellectual truths through sensible things, because
all our knowledge originates from sense. Hence in Holy
Scripture spiritual truths are fittingly taught under the likeness of material things. This is what Dionysius says: *We
cannot be enlightened by the divine rays except they be hidden within the covering of many sacred veils.*[22] It is also befitting Holy Scripture, which is proposed to all without distinction of persons—*To the wise and to the unwise I am a
debtor* (*Rom.* i. 14)—that spiritual truths be expounded by
means of figures taken from corporeal things, in order that
thereby even the simple who are unable by themselves to
grasp intellectual things may be able to understand it.

Reply Obj. 1. Poetry makes use of metaphors to produce a
representation, for it is natural to man to be pleased with

representations. But sacred doctrine makes use of metaphors as both necessary and useful.

Reply Obj. 2. The ray of divine revelation is not extinguished by the sensible imagery wherewith it is veiled, as Dionysius says;[23] and its truth so far remains that it does not allow the minds of those to whom the revelation has been made, to rest in the likenesses, but raises them to the knowledge of intelligible truths; and through those to whom the revelation has been made others also may receive instruction in these matters. Hence those things that are taught metaphorically in one part of Scripture, in other parts are taught more openly. The very hiding of truth in figures is useful for the exercise of thoughtful minds, and as a defense against the ridicule of the unbelievers, according to the words, *Give not that which is holy to dogs* (*Matt.* vii. 6).

Reply Obj. 3. As Dionysius says,[24] it is more fitting that divine truths should be expounded under the figure of less noble than of nobler bodies; and this for three reasons. First, because thereby men's minds are the better freed from error. For then it is clear that these things are not literal descriptions of divine truths, which might have been open to doubt had they been expressed under the figure of nobler bodies, especially in the case of those who could think of nothing nobler than bodies. Second, because this is more befitting the knowledge of God that we have in this life. For what He is not is clearer to us than what He is. Therefore similitudes drawn from things farthest away from God form within us a truer estimate that God is above whatsoever we may say or think of Him. Third, because thereby divine truths are the better hidden from the unworthy.

Tenth Article

WHETHER IN HOLY SCRIPTURE A WORD MAY HAVE SEVERAL SENSES?

We proceed thus to the Tenth Article:—

Objection 1. It seems that in Holy Scripture a word cannot have several senses, historical or literal, allegorical, tropological or moral, and anagogical. For many different senses in one text produce confusion and deception and destroy all

[23] *Ibid.*   [24] *Op. cit.,* II, 2 (PG 3, 136).

force of argument. Hence no argument, but only fallacies, can be deduced from a multiplicity of propositions. But Holy Scripture ought to be able to state the truth without any fallacy. Therefore in it there cannot be several senses to a word.

Obj. 2. Further, Augustine says that *the Old Testament has a fourfold division: according to history, etiology, analogy, and allegory.*[25] Now these four seem altogether different from the four divisions mentioned in the first objection. Therefore it does not seem fitting to explain the same word of Holy Scripture according to the four different senses mentioned above.

Obj. 3. Further, besides these senses, there is the parabolical, which is not one of these four.

On the contrary, Gregory says: *Holy Scripture by the manner of its speech transcends every science, because in one and the same sentence, while it describes a fact, it reveals a mystery.*[26]

I answer that, The author of Holy Scripture is God, in Whose power it is to signify His meaning, not by words only (as man also can do), but also by things themselves. So, whereas in every other science things are signified by words, this science has the property that the things signified by the words have themselves also a signification. Therefore that first signification whereby words signify things belongs to the first sense, the historical or literal. That signification whereby things signified by words have themselves also a signification is called the spiritual sense, which is based on the literal, and presupposes it. Now this spiritual sense has a threefold division. For as the Apostle says (*Heb.* x. 1) the Old Law is a figure of the New Law, and Dionysius says *the New Law itself is a figure of future glory.*[27] Again, in the New Law, whatever our Head has done is a type of what we ought to do. Therefore, so far as the things of the Old Law signify the things of the New Law, there is the allegorical sense; so far as the things done in Christ, or so far as the things which signify Christ, are signs of what we ought to do, there is the moral sense. But so far as they signify what relates to eternal glory, there is the anagogical sense. Since

[25] *De Util. Cred.,* III (PL 42, 68).   [26] *Moral.,* XX, 1 (PL 76, 135).
[27] *De Eccles. Hier.,* V, 2 (PG 3, 501).

the literal sense is that which the author intends, and since
the author of Holy Scripture is God, Who by one act comprehends all things by His intellect, it is not unfitting, as
Augustine says,[28] if, even according to the literal sense, one
word in Holy Scripture should have several senses.

Reply Obj. 1. The multiplicity of these senses does not
produce equivocation or any other kind of multiplicity, seeing that these senses are not multiplied because one word
signifies several things, but because the things signified by
the words can be themselves signs of other things. Thus in
Holy Scripture no confusion results, for all the senses are
founded on one—the literal—from which alone can any argument be drawn, and not from those intended allegorically,
as Augustine says.[29] Nevertheless, nothing of Holy Scripture
perishes because of this, since nothing necessary to faith is
contained under the spiritual sense which is not elsewhere
put forward clearly by the Scripture in its literal sense.

Reply Obj. 2. These three—history, etiology, analogy—
are grouped under the literal sense. For it is called history,
as Augustine expounds,[30] whenever anything is simply related; it is called etiology when its cause is assigned, as when
Our Lord gave the reason why Moses allowed the putting
away of wives—namely, because of the hardness of men's
hearts (*Matt.* xix, 8); it is called analogy whenever the
truth of one text of Scripture is shown not to contradict the
truth of another. Of these four, allegory alone stands for
the three spiritual senses. Thus Hugh of St. Victor includes
the anagogical under the allegorical sense, laying down three
senses only—the historical, the allegorical and the tropological.[31]

Reply Obj. 3. The parabolical sense is contained in the
literal, for by words things are signified properly and figuratively. Nor is the figure itself, but that which is figured, the
literal sense. When Scripture speaks of God's arm, the literal
sense is not that God has such a member, but only what is
signified by this member, namely, operative power. Hence it
is plain that nothing false can ever underlie the literal sense
of Holy Scripture.

---

[28] *Confess.*, XII, 31 (PL 32, 844).   [29] *Epist.* XCIII, 8 (PL 33, 334).
[30] *De Util. Cred.*, 3 (PL 42, 68).   [31] Cf. *De Sacram.*, I, 4 (PL 176.
184).—Cf. also *De Scriptur. et Scriptor. Sacris,* 3 (PL 175, 11).

THE EXISTENCE OF GOD

(*In Three Articles*)

BECAUSE the chief aim of sacred doctrine is to teach the knowledge of God not only as He is in Himself, but also as He is the beginning of things and their last end, and especially of rational creatures, as is clear from what has been already said,[1] therefore, in our endeavor to expound this science, we shall treat: (1) of God; (2) of the rational creature's movement towards God;[2] (3) of Christ Who as man is our way to God.[3]

In treating of God there will be a threefold division:—

For we shall consider (1) whatever concerns the divine essence. (2) Whatever concerns the distinctions of Persons.[4] (3) Whatever concerns the procession of creatures from Him.[5]

Concerning the divine essence, we must consider:—

(1) Whether God exists? (2) The manner of His existence, or, rather, what is *not* the manner of His existence.[6] (3) Whatever concerns His operations—namely, His knowledge,[7] will,[8] power.[9]

Concerning the first, there are three points of inquiry:—

(1) Whether the proposition *God exists* is self-evident? (2) Whether it is demonstrable? (3) Whether God exists?

First Article

WHETHER THE EXISTENCE OF GOD IS SELF-EVIDENT?

We proceed thus to the First Article:—

Objection 1. It seems that the existence of God is self-evident. For those things are said to be self-evident to us the knowledge of which exists naturally in us, as we can see in regard to first principles. But as Damascene says, *the knowledge of God is naturally implanted in all.*[10] Therefore the existence of God is self-evident.

---

[1] Q. 1, a. 7.   [2] *S.T.*, II.   [3] *S.T.*, III.   [4] Q. 27.   [5] Q. 44.   [6] Q. 3.
[7] Q. 14.   [8] Q. 19.   [9] Q. 25.   [10] *De Fide Orth.*, I, 1; 3 (PG 94, 789; 793).

Obj. 2. Further, those things are said to be self-evident which are known as soon as the terms are known, which the Philosopher says is true of the first principles of demonstration.[11] Thus, when the nature of a whole and of a part is known, it is at once recognized that every whole is greater than its part. But as soon as the signification of the name *God* is understood, it is at once seen that God exists. For by this name is signified that thing than which nothing greater can be conceived. But that which exists actually and mentally is greater than that which exists only mentally. Therefore, since as soon as the name *God* is understood it exists mentally, it also follows that it exists actually. Therefore the proposition *God exists* is self-evident.

Obj. 3. Further, the existence of truth is self-evident. For whoever denies the existence of truth grants that truth does not exist: and, if truth does not exist, then the proposition *Truth does not exist* is true: and if there is anything true, there must be truth. But God is truth itself: *I am the way, the truth, and the life* (*Jo.* xiv. 6). Therefore *God exists* is self-evident.

On the contrary, No one can mentally admit the opposite of what is self-evident, as the Philosopher states concerning the first principles of demonstration.[12] But the opposite of the proposition *God is* can be mentally admitted: *The fool said in his heart, There is no God* (*Ps.* lii. 1). Therefore, that God exists is not self-evident.

I answer that, A thing can be self-evident in either of two ways: on the one hand, self-evident in itself, though not to us; on the other, self-evident in itself, and to us. A proposition is self-evident because the predicate is included in the essence of the subject: *e.g., Man is an animal,* for animal is contained in the essence of man. If, therefore, the essence of the predicate and subject be known to all, the proposition will be self-evident to all; as is clear with regard to the first principles of demonstration, the terms of which are certain common notions that no one is ignorant of, such as being and non-being, whole and part, and the like. If, however, there are some to whom the essence of the predicate and subject is unknown, the proposition will be self-evident in itself, but

---

[11] *Post. Anal.*, I, 3 (72b 18).   [12] *Metaph.*, III, 3 (1005b 11); *Post. Anal.*, I, 10 (76b 23).

not to those who do not know the meaning of the predicate and subject of the proposition. Therefore, it happens, as Boethius says, that there are some notions of the mind which are common and self-evident only to the learned, as that incorporeal substances are not in space.[13] Therefore I say that this proposition, *God exists*, of itself is self-evident, for the predicate is the same as the subject, because God is His own existence as will be hereafter shown.[14] Now because we do not know the essence of God, the proposition is not self-evident to us, but needs to be demonstrated by things that are more known to us, though less known in their nature— namely, by His effects.

Reply Obj. 1. To know that God exists in a general and confused way is implanted in us by nature, inasmuch as God is man's beatitude. For man naturally desires happiness, and what is naturally desired by man is naturally known by him. This, however, is not to know absolutely that God exists; just as to know that someone is approaching is not the same as to know that Peter is approaching, even though it is Peter who is approaching; for there are many who imagine that man's perfect good, which is happiness, consists in riches, and others in pleasures, and others in something else.

Reply Obj. 2. Perhaps not everyone who hears this name *God* understands it to signify something than which nothing greater can be thought, seeing that some have believed God to be a body.[15] Yet, granted that everyone understands that by this name *God* is signified something than which nothing greater can be thought, nevertheless, it does not therefore follow that he understands that what the name signifies exists actually, but only that it exists mentally. Nor can it be argued that it actually exists, unless it be admitted that there actually exists something than which nothing greater can be thought; and this precisely is not admitted by those who hold that God does not exist.

Reply Obj. 3. The existence of truth in general is self-

---

[13] *De Hebdom.* (PL 64, 1311).   [14] Q. 3, a. 4.   [15] Cf. *C. G.*, I, 20.—Cf. also Aristotle, *Phys.*, I, 4 (187a 12); St. Augustine, *De Civit. Dei*, VIII, 2; 5 (PL 41, 226; 239); *De Haeres*, 46, 50, 86 (PL 42, 35; 39; 46); *De Genesi ad Litt.*, X, 25 (PL 34, 427); Maimonides, *Guide*, I, 53 (p. 72).

evident, but the existence of a Primal Truth is not self-evident to us.

Second Article

WHETHER IT CAN BE DEMONSTRATED THAT GOD EXISTS?

We proceed thus to the Second Article:—

Objection 1. It seems that the existence of God cannnot be demonstrated. For it is an article of faith that God exists. But what is of faith cannot be demonstrated, because a demonstration produces scientific knowledge, whereas faith is of the unseen, as is clear from the Apostle (*Heb.* xi. 1). Therefore it cannot be demonstrated that God exists.

Obj. 2. Further, essence is the middle term of demonstration. But we cannot know in what God's essence consists, but solely in what it does not consist, as Damascene says.[16] Therefore we cannot demonstrate that God exists.

Obj. 3. Further, if the existence of God were demonstrated, this could only be from His effects. But His effects are not proportioned to Him, since He is infinite and His effects are finite, and between the finite and infinite there is no proportion. Therefore, since a cause cannot be demonstrated by an effect not proportioned to it, it seems that the existence of God cannot be demonstrated.

On the contrary, The Apostle says: *The invisible things of Him are clearly seen, being understood by the things that are made* (*Rom.* i. 20). But this would not be unless the existence of God could be demonstrated through the things that are made; for the first thing we must know of anything is, whether it exists.

I answer that, Demonstration can be made in two ways: One is through the cause, and is called *propter quid,* and this is to argue from what is prior absolutely. The other is through the effect, and is called a demonstration *quia;* this is to argue from what is prior relatively only to us. When an effect is better known to us than its cause, from the effect we proceed to the knowledge of the cause. And from every effect the existence of its proper cause can be demonstrated, so long as its effects are better known to us; because, since every effect depends upon its cause, if the effect exists, the

[16] *De Fide Orth.,* I, 4 (PG 94, 800).

cause must pre-exist. Hence the existence of God, in so far as it is not self-evident to us, can be demonstrated from those of His effects which are known to us.

Reply Obj. 1. The existence of God and other like truths about God, which can be known by natural reason, are not articles of faith, but are preambles to the articles; for faith presupposes natural knowledge, even as grace presupposes nature and perfection the perfectible. Nevertheless, there is nothing to prevent a man, who cannot grasp a proof, from accepting, as a matter of faith, something which in itself is capable of being scientifically known and demonstrated.

Reply Obj. 2. When the existence of a cause is demonstrated from an effect, this effect takes the place of the definition of the cause in proving the cause's existence. This is especially the case in regard to God, because, in order to prove the existence of anything, it is necessary to accept as a middle term the meaning of the name, and not its essence, for the question of its essence follows on the question of its existence. Now the names given to God are derived from His effects, as will be later shown.[17] Consequently, in demonstrating the existence of God from His effects, we may take for the middle term the meaning of the name *God*.

Reply Obj. 3. From effects not proportioned to the cause no perfect knowledge of that cause can be obtained. Yet from every effect the existence of the cause can be clearly demonstrated, and so we can demonstrate the existence of God from His effects; though from them we cannot know God perfectly as He is in His essence.

Third Article

WHETHER GOD EXISTS?

We proceed thus to the Third Article:—

Objection 1. It seems that God does not exist; because if one of two contraries be infinite, the other would be altogether destroyed. But the name *God* means that He is infinite goodness. If, therefore, God existed, there would be no evil discoverable; but there is evil in the world. Therefore God does not exist.

Obj. 2. Further, it is superfluous to suppose that what can

[17] Q. 13, a. 1.

be accounted for by a few principles has been produced by many. But it seems that everything we see in the world can be accounted for by other principles, supposing God did not exist. For all natural things can be reduced to one principle, which is nature; and all voluntary things can be reduced to one principle, which is human reason, or will. Therefore there is no need to suppose God's existence.

On the contrary, It is said in the person of God: *I am Who am* (*Exod.* iii. 14).

I answer that, The existence of God can be proved in five ways.

The first and more manifest way is the argument from motion. It is certain, and evident to our senses, that in the world some things are in motion. Now whatever is moved is moved by another, for nothing can be moved except it is in potentiality to that towards which it is moved; whereas a thing moves inasmuch as it is in act. For motion is nothing else than the reduction of something from potentiality to actuality. But nothing can be reduced from potentiality to actuality, except by something in a state of actuality. Thus that which is actually hot, as fire, makes wood, which is potentially hot, to be actually hot, and thereby moves and changes it. Now it is not possible that the same thing should be at once in actuality and potentiality in the same respect, but only in different respects. For what is actually hot cannot simultaneously be potentially hot; but it is simultaneously potentially cold. It is therefore impossible that in the same respect and in the same way a thing should be both mover and moved, *i.e.,* that it should move itself. Therefore, whatever is moved must be moved by another. If that by which it is moved be itself moved, then this also must needs be moved by another, and that by another again. But this cannot go on to infinity, because then there would be no first mover, and, consequently, no other mover, seeing that subsequent movers move only inasmuch as they are moved by the first mover; as the staff moves only because it is moved by the hand. Therefore it is necessary to arrive at a first mover, moved by no other; and this everyone understands to be God.

The second way is from the nature of efficient cause. In the world of sensible things we find there is an order of efficient causes. There is no case known (neither is it, indeed, possible) in which a thing is found to be the efficient cause of itself; for so it would be prior to itself, which is impossible. Now in efficient causes it is not possible to go on to infinity, because in all efficient causes following in order, the first is the cause of the intermediate cause, and the intermediate is the cause of the ultimate cause, whether the intermediate cause be several, or one only. Now to take away the cause is to take away the effect. Therefore, if there be no first cause among efficient causes, there will be no ultimate, nor any intermediate, cause. But if in efficient causes it is possible to go on to infinity, there will be no first efficient cause, neither will there be an ultimate effect, nor any intermediate efficient causes; all of which is plainly false. Therefore it is necessary to admit a first efficient cause, to which everyone gives the name of God.

The third way is taken from possibility and necessity, and runs thus. We find in nature things that are possible to be and not to be, since they are found to be generated, and to be corrupted, and consequently, it is possible for them to be and not to be. But it is impossible for these always to exist, for that which can not-be at some time is not. Therefore, if everything can not-be, then at one time there was nothing in existence. Now if this were true, even now there would be nothing in existence, because that which does not exist begins to exist only through something already existing. Therefore, if at one time nothing was in existence, it would have been impossible for anything to have begun to exist; and thus even now nothing would be in existence—which is absurd. Therefore, not all beings are merely possible, but there must exist something the existence of which is necessary. But every necessary thing either has its necessity caused by another, or not. Now it is impossible to go on to infinity in necessary things which have their necessity caused by another, as has been already proved in regard to efficient causes. Therefore we cannot but admit the existence of some being having of itself its own necessity, and not receiving it from another, but rather causing in others their necessity. This all men speak of as God.

The fourth way is taken from the gradation to be found in things. Among beings there are some more and some less good, true, noble, and the like. But *more* and *less* are predicted of different things according as they resemble in their different ways something which is the maximum, as a thing is said to be hotter according as it more nearly resembles that which is hottest; so that there is something which is truest, something best, something noblest, and, consequently, something which is most being, for those things that are greatest in truth are greatest in being, as it is written in *Metaph.* ii.[18] Now the maximum in any genus is the cause of all in that genus, as fire, which is the maximum of heat, is the cause of all hot things, as is said in the same book.[19] Therefore there must also be something which is to all beings the cause of their being, goodness, and every other perfection; and this we call God.

The fifth way is taken from the governance of the world. We see that things which lack knowledge, such as natural bodies, act for an end, and this is evident from their acting always, or nearly always, in the same way, so as to obtain the best result. Hence it is plain that they achieve their end, not fortuitously, but designedly. Now whatever lacks knowledge cannot move towards an end, unless it be directed by some being endowed with knowledge and intelligence; as the arrow is directed by the archer. Therefore some intelligent being exists by whom all natural things are directed to their end; and this being we call God.

Reply Obj. 1. As Augustine says: *Since God is the highest good, He would not allow any evil to exist in His works, unless His omnipotence and goodness were such as to bring good even out of evil.*[20] This is part of the infinite goodness of God, that He should allow evil to exist, and out of it produce good.

Reply Obj. 2. Since nature works for a determinate end under the direction of a higher agent, whatever is done by nature must be traced back to God as to its first cause. So likewise whatever is done voluntarily must be traced back to some higher cause other than human reason and will, since these can change and fail; for all things that are changeable and capable of defect must be traced back to an immovable and self-necessary first principle, as has been shown.

[18] *Metaph.* Ia, 1 (993b 30).   [19] *Ibid.* (993b 25).   [20] *Enchir.*, XI (PL 40, 236).

ON THE SIMPLICITY OF GOD

WHEN the existence of a thing has been ascertained, there remains the further question of the manner of its existence, in order that we may know its essence. Now because we cannot know what God is, but rather what He is not, we have no means for considering how God is, but rather how He is not.

Therefore, we must consider (1) how He is not; (2) how He is known by us;[1] (3) how He is named.[2]

Now it can be shown how God is not, by removing from Him whatever does not befit Him—viz., composition, motion, and the like. Therefore (1) we must discuss His simplicity, whereby we remove composition from Him. And because whatever is simple in material things is imperfect and a part of something else, we shall discuss (2) His perfection;[3] (3) His infinity;[4] (4) His immutability;[5] (5) His unity.[6]

Concerning His simplicity, there are eight points of inquiry: (1) Whether God is a body? (2) Whether He is composed of matter and form? (3) Whether in Him there is composition of quiddity or essence (or nature) and subject? (4) Whether there is in Him a composition of essence and being? (5) Whether He is composed of genus and difference? (6) Whether He is composed of subject and accident? (7) Whether He is in any way composite, or wholly simple? (8) Whether He enters into composition with other things?

Third Article

WHETHER GOD IS THE SAME AS HIS ESSENCE OR NATURE?

We proceed thus to the Third Article:—

Objection 1. It seems that God is not the same as His essence or nature. For nothing is in itself. But the essence or nature of God—*i.e.*, the Godhead—is said to be in God. Therefore it seems that God is not the same as His essence or nature.

Obj. 2. Further, the effect is assimilated to its cause; for

[1]Q. 12.　　[2]Q. 13.　　[3]Q. 4.　　[4]Q. 7.　　[5]Q. 9.　　[6]Q. 11.

every agent produces its like. But in created things the *suppositum* is not identical with its nature; for a man is not the same as his humanity. Therefore God is not the same as His Godhead.

On the contrary, It is said of God that He is life itself, and not only that He is a living thing: *I am the way, the truth, and the life (Jo.* xiv. 6). Now the relation between Godhead and God is the same as the relation between life and a living thing. Therefore God is His very Godhead.

I answer that, God is the same as His essence or nature. To understand this, it must be noted that in things composed of matter and form, the nature or essence must differ from the *suppositum,* for the essence or nature includes only what falls within the definition of the species; as humanity includes all that falls within the definition of man, for it is by this that man is man, and it is this that humanity signifies, that, namely, whereby man is man. Now individual matter, with all the individuating accidents, does not fall within the definition of the species. For this particular flesh, these bones, this blackness or whiteness, etc., do not fall within the definition of a man. Therefore this flesh, these bones, and the accidental qualities designating this particular matter, are not included in humanity; and yet they are included in the reality which is a man. Hence, the reality which is a man has something in it that humanity does not have. Consequently, humanity and a man are not wholly identical, but humanity is taken to mean the formal part of a man, because the principles whereby a thing is defined function as the formal constituent in relation to individuating matter. The situation is different in things not composed of matter and form, in which individuation is not due to individual matter—that is to say, to *this* matter—but the forms themselves are individuated of themselves. Here it is necessary that the forms themselves should be subsisting *supposita.* Therefore *suppositum* and nature in them are identified. Since, then, God is not composed of matter and form, He must be His own Godhead, His own Life, and whatever else is so predicated of Him.

Reply Obj. 1. We can speak of simple things only as though they were like the composite things from which we derive our knowledge. Therefore, in speaking of God, we use concrete nouns to signify His subsistence, because with us only those things subsist which are composite, and we use abstract nouns to signify His simplicity. In speaking therefore of Godhead, or life, or the like as being in God, we indicate the composite way in which our intellect understands, but not that there is any composition in God.

Reply Obj. 2. The effects of God do not imitate Him perfectly, but only as far as they are able. It pertains to defect in imitation that what is simple and one can be represented only by a multiplicity. This is the source of composition in God's effects, and therefore in them *suppositum* is not the same as nature.

Fourth Article

WHETHER ESSENCE AND BEING ARE THE SAME IN GOD?

We proceed thus to the Fourth Article:—

Objection 1. It seems that essence and being [*esse*] are not the same in God. For if it be so, then the divine being has nothing added to it. Now being to which no addition is made is the being-in-general which is predicated of all things. Therefore it follows that God is being-in-general which can be predicated of everything. But this is false: *For men gave the incommunicable name to stones and wood* (*Wis.* xiv. 21). Therefore God's being is not His essence.

Obj. 2. Further, we can know *whether* God exists, as was said above,[7] but we cannot know *what* He is. Therefore God's being is not the same as His essence—that is, as His quiddity or nature.

On the contrary, Hilary says: *In God being is not an accidental quality, but subsisting truth.*[8] Therefore what subsists in God is His being.

I answer that, God is not only His own essence, as has been shown, but also His own being. This may be shown in several ways. First, whatever a thing has besides its essence must be caused either by the constituent principles of that essence (like a proper accident that necessarily accompanies the species—as the faculty of laughing is proper to a man—and is caused by the constituent principles of the species), or by some exterior agent,—as heat is caused in water by

[7] Q. 2, a. 2.   [8] *De Trin.,* VII (PL 10, 208).

fire. Therefore, if the being of a thing differs from its essence, this being must be caused either by some exterior agent or by the essential principles of the thing itself. Now it is impossible for a thing's being to be caused only by its essential constituent principles, for nothing can be the sufficient cause of its own being, if its being is caused. Therefore that thing, whose being differs from its essence, must have its being caused by another. But this cannot be said of God, because we call God the first efficient cause. Therefore it is impossible that in God His being should differ from His essence.

Second, being is the actuality of every form or nature; for goodness and humanity are spoken of as actual, only because they are spoken of as being. Therefore, being must be compared to essence, if the latter is distinct from it, as actuality to potentiality. Therefore, since in God there is no potentiality, as shown above, it follows that in Him essence does not differ from being. Therefore His essence is His being. Third, just as that which has fire, but is not itself fire, is on fire by participation, so that which has being, but is not being, is a being by participation. But God is His own essence, as was shown above. If, therefore, He is not His own being, He will be not essential, but participated, being. He will not therefore be the first being—which is absurd. Therefore, God is His own being, and not merely His own essence.

Reply Obj. 1. A thing-that-has-nothing-added-to-it can be understood in two ways. Either its essence precludes any addition (thus, for example, it is of the essence of an irrational animal to be without reason), or we may understand a thing to have nothing added to it, inasmuch as its essence does not require that anything should be added to it (thus the genus animal is without reason, because it is not of the essence of animal in general to have reason; but neither is it of the essence of animal to lack reason). And so the divine being has nothing added to it in the first sense; whereas being-in-general has nothing added to it in the second sense.

Reply Obj. 2. *To be* can mean either of two things. It may mean the act of being, or it may mean the composition of a proposition effected by the mind in joining a predicate to a subject. Taking *to be* in the first sense, we cannot understand God's being (or His essence); but only in the second sense. We know that this proposition which we form about

God when we say *God is,* is true; and this we know from
His effects, as was said above.[9]

Seventh Article

WHETHER GOD IS ALTOGETHER SIMPLE?

We proceed thus to the Seventh Article:—

Objection 1. It seems that God is not altogether simple.
For whatever is from God imitates Him. Thus from the first
being are all beings, and from the first good are all goods.
But in the things which God has made, nothing is altogether
simple. Therefore neither is God altogether simple.

Obj. 2. Further, whatever is better must be attributed to
God. But with us that which is composite is better than that
which is simple: thus, chemical compounds are better than
elements, and elements than the parts that compose them.
Therefore it cannot be said that God is altogether simple.

On the contrary, Augustine says, *God is truly and absolutely simple.*[10]

I answer that, The absolute simplicity of God may be
shown in many ways. First, from the previous articles of this
question. For there is neither composition of quantitative
parts in God, since He is not a body; nor composition of
form and matter; nor does His nature differ from His *suppositum*; nor His essence from His being; neither is there in
Him composition of genus and difference, nor of subject and
accident. Therefore, it is clear that God is in no way composite, but is altogether simple. Secondly, because every composite is posterior to its component parts, and is dependent
on them; but God is the first being, as has been shown
above.[11] Thirdly, because every composite has a cause, for
things in themselves diverse cannot unite unless something
causes them to unite. But God is uncaused, as has been
shown above,[12] since He is the first efficient cause. Fourthly,
because in every composite there must be potentiality and
actuality (this does not apply to God) for either one of the
parts actualizes another, or at least all the parts are as it
were in potency with respect to the whole. Fifthly, because
nothing composite can be predicated of any one of its parts,

[9] Q. 2, a. 2.   [10] *De Trin.,* VI, 6 (PL 42, 928).   [11] Q. 2, a. 3.
[12] *Ibid.*

And this is evident in a whole made up of dissimilar parts; for no part of a man is a man, nor any of the parts of the foot, a foot. But in wholes made up of similar parts, although something which is predicated of the whole may be predicated of a part (as a part of the air is air, and a part of water, water), nevertheless certain things are predicable of the whole which cannot be predicated of any of the parts; for instance, if the whole volume of water is two cubits, no part of it can be two cubits. Thus in every composite there is something which is not it itself. But, even if this could be said of whatever has a form, viz., that it has something which is not it itself, as in a white object there is something which does not belong to the essence of white, nevertheless, in the form itself there is nothing besides itself. And so, since God is absolute form, or rather absolute being, He can in no way be composite. Hilary touches upon this argument when he says: *God, Who is strength, is not made up of things that are weak; nor is He, Who is light, composed of things that are dark.*[13]

Reply Obj. 1. Whatever is from God imitates Him, as caused things imitate the first cause. But it is of the essence of a thing caused to be in some way composite; because at least its being differs from its essence, as will be shown hereafter.[14]

Reply Obj. 2. With us composite things are better than simple things, because the perfection of created goodness is not found in one simple thing, but in many things. But the perfection of divine goodness is found in one simple thing, as will be shown hereafter.[15]

[13] *De Trin.*, VII (PL 10, 223).   [14] Q. 50, a. 2.   [15] Q. 4, a. 1; Q. 6, a. 3.

Question V

ON GOODNESS IN GENERAL

(*In Six Articles*)

WE NEXT consider goodness:—

First, goodness in general. Secondly, the goodness of God.[1]
Under the first head there are six points of inquiry:—

(1) Whether goodness and being are the same really? (2)
Granted that they differ only in idea, which is prior in
thought? (3) Granted that being is prior, whether every
being is good? (4) To what cause should goodness be reduced? (5) Whether goodness consists in limit, species and
order? (6) Whether goodness is divided into the befitting,
the useful, and the pleasant?

First Article

WHETHER GOODNESS DIFFERS REALLY FROM BEING?

We proceed thus to the First Article:—

Objection 1. It seems that goodness differs really from
being. For Boethius says: *I perceive that in nature the fact
that things are good is one thing, that they are is another.*[2]

Obj. 2. Further, nothing can be its own form. *But that is
called good which has the form of being,* according to the
commentary on the *Book of Causes.*[3] Therefore goodness
differs really from being.

Obj. 3. Further, goodness is receptive of more and less.
But being cannot receive more and less. Therefore goodness
differs really from being.

On the contrary, Augustine says that, *inasmuch as we are,
we are good.*[4]

I answer that, Goodness and being are really the same, and
differ only in idea; which is clear from the following argument. The essence of goodness consists in this, that it is in
some way desirable. Hence the Philosopher says: *Goodness is
what all desire.*[5] Now it is clear that a thing is desirable only
in so far as it is perfect, for all desire their own perfection.

[1] Q. 6.　[2] *De Hebdom.* (PL 64, 1312).　[3] *De Causis,* XX (p.
177).　[4] *De Doct. Christ.,* I, 32 (PL 34, 32).　[5] *Eth.,* I, 1 (1094a
3).

But everything is perfect so far as it is actual. Therefore it is clear that a thing is perfect so far as it is being; for being is the actuality of every thing, as is clear from the foregoing.[6] Hence it is clear that goodness and being are the same really. But goodness expresses the aspect of desirableness, which being does not express.

Reply Obj. 1. Although goodness and being are the same really, nevertheless, since they differ in thought, they are not predicated of a thing absolutely in the same way. For since being properly signifies that something actually is, and actuality properly correlates to potentiality, a thing is, in consequence, said absolutely to have being accordingly as it is primarily distinguished from that which is only in potentiality; and this is precisely each thing's substantial being. Hence it is by its substantial being that everything is said to have being absolutely; but by any further actuality it is said to have being relatively. Thus to be white signifies being relatively, for to be white does not take a thing out of absolutely potential being, since it is added to a thing that actually has being. But goodness expresses perfection, which is something desirable, and hence it expresses something final. Hence, that which has ultimate perfection is said to be absolutely good, but that which has not the ultimate perfection it ought to have (although, in so far as it is at all actual, it has some perfection) is not said to be perfect absolutely nor good absolutely, but only relatively. In this way, therefore, viewed in its first (*i.e.*, substantial) being, a thing is said to be absolutely, and to be good relatively *i.e.*, in so far as it has being); but viewed in its complete actuality a thing is said to be relatively, and so be good absolutely. Hence the saying of Boethius, *that in nature the fact that things are good is one thing, that they are is another*,[7] is to be referred to being good absolutely, and being absolutely. Because, regarded in its first actuality, a thing is a being absolutely; and regarded in its complete actuality, it is good absolutely, though even in its first actuality, it is in some way good, and even in its complete actuality, it is in some way being.

Reply Obj. 2. Goodness is a form so far as it is understood absolutely according to complete actuality.

---

[6] Q. 3, a. 4; q. 4, a. 1, ad 3.   [7] *De Hebdom.* (PL 64, 1312).

Reply Obj. 3. Again, goodness is spoken of as more or less according to a superadded actuality, for example, according to knowledge or virtue.

Second Article

WHETHER GOODNESS IS PRIOR IN IDEA TO BEING?

We proceed thus to the Second Article:—

Objection 1. It seems that goodness is prior in idea to being. For names are arranged according to the arrangement of the things signified by the names. But Dionysius assigned the first place, among other names of God, to His goodness rather than to His being.[8] Therefore in idea goodness is prior to being.

Obj. 2. Further, that which is the more extensive is prior in idea. But goodness is more extensive than being, because as Dionysius notes,[9] *goodness extends to things both existing and non-existing; whereas being extends to existing things alone.* Therefore goodness is in idea prior to being.

Obj. 3. Further, what is more universal is prior in idea. But goodness seems to be more universal than being, since goodness has the aspect of the desirable. Now to some non-existence is desirable, for it is said of Judas: *It were better for him, if that man had not been born (Matt.* xxvi. 24). Therefore in idea goodness is prior to being.

Obj. 4. Further, not only is being desirable, but life, knowledge, and many other things besides. Thus it seems that being is a particular appetible, and goodness a universal appetible. Therefore, absolutely, goodness is prior in idea to being.

On the contrary, It is said in the *Book of Causes* that *the first of created things is being.*[10]

I answer that, In idea being is prior to goodness. For the meaning signified by the name of a thing is that which the intellect conceives of the thing and intends by the word that stands for it. Therefore, that is prior in idea which is first conceived by the intellect. Now the first thing conceived by the intellect is being, because everything is knowable only inasmuch as it is actually.[11] Hence, being is the proper object

---

[8] *De Div. Nom.,* III, 1 (PG 3, 680).   [9] *Op. cit.,* V, 1 (PG 3, 816).
[10] *De Causis,* IV (p. 164).   [11] Aristotle, *Metaph.,* VIII, 9 (1051a 31).

of the intellect, and is thus the first intelligible, as sound is the first audible. Therefore in idea being is prior to goodness.

Reply Obj. 1. Dionysius defines the divine names according as they imply some causal relation in God; for we name God, as he says,[12] from creatures, as a cause from its effects. But goodness, since it has the aspect of the desirable, implies the idea of a final cause, the causality of which is first among causes, since an agent does not act except for some end; and by an agent matter is moved to its form. Hence the end is called the cause of causes. Thus goodness, as a cause, is prior to being, as is the end to the form. Therefore among the names signifying the divine causality, goodness precedes being. Again, according to the Platonists, who, through not distinguishing primary matter from privation,[13] said that matter was non-being,[14] goodness is more extensively participated than being; for primary matter participates in goodness as seeking it, for all seek their like, but it does not participate in being, since it is presumed to be non-being. Therefore Dionysius says that *goodness extends to the non-existent*.[15]

Reply Obj. 2. The same solution applies to this objection. Or it may be said that goodness extends to existing and non-existing things, not so far as it can be predicated of them, but so far as it can cause them—if, indeed, by the non-existent we understand not unqualifiedly those things which do not exist, but those which are potential, and not actual. For goodness has the aspect of the end in which not only actual things find their completion, but also towards which tend even those things which are not actual, but merely potential. But being implies the relation of a formal cause only, either inherent or exemplar; and its causality does not extend save to those things which are actual.

Reply Obj. 3. Non-being is desirable, not of itself, but only relatively—*i.e.*, inasmuch as the removal of an evil, which is removed by non-being, is desirable. Now the removal of an evil cannot be desirable, except so far as this evil deprives a thing of some being. Therefore it is being which is desirable of itself, while non-being is desirable only relatively, viz., inasmuch as one seeks some being of which

---

[12] *De Div. Nom.*, I, 7 (PG 3, 596).   [13] Cf. Aristotle, *Phys.*, I, 9 (192a 2).   [14] Cf. Aristotle, *ibid.* (192a 3).   [15] *De Div. Nom.*, V, 1 (PG 3, 816).

one cannot bear to be deprived; and thus it happens that even non-being can be spoken of as relatively good.

Reply Obj. 4. Life, wisdom, and the like, are desirable only so far as they are actual. Hence in each one of them some sort of being is desired. And thus nothing is desirable except being, and consequently nothing is good except being.

Third Article

WHETHER EVERY BEING IS GOOD?

We proceed thus to the Third Article:—

Objection 1. It seems that not every being is good. For goodness is something superadded to being, as is clear from what has been said. But whatever is added to being limits it; as substance, quantity, quality, etc. Therefore goodness limits being. Therefore not every being is good.

Obj. 2. Further, no evil is good: *Woe to you that call evil good, and good evil* (*Isa.* v. 20). But some things are called evil. Therefore not every being is good.

Obj. 3. Further, goodness implies desirability. Now primary matter does not imply desirability, but rather that which desires. Therefore primary matter does not contain the formality of goodness. Therefore not every being is good.

Obj. 4. Further, the Philosopher observes that in *mathematics goodness does not exist.*[16] But mathematicals are entities, or otherwise there would be no science of mathematics. Therefore not every being is good.

On the contrary, Every being that is not God, is God's creature. Now *every creature of God is good* (*1 Tim.* iv. 4): and God is the greatest good. Therefore every being is good.

I answer that, Every being, as being, is good. For all being, as being, has actuality and is in some way perfect, since every act is some sort of perfection, and perfection implies desirability and goodness, as is clear from what has been said. Hence it follows that every being as such is good.

Reply Obj. 1. Substance, quantity, quality, and everything included in them, limit being by applying it to some essence or nature. Now in this sense, goodness does not add

---

[16] *Metaph.,* II, 2 (996b 1).

anything to being beyond the aspect of desirability and perfection, which is also proper to being, whatever its nature. Hence goodness does not limit being.

Reply Obj. 2. No being is said to be evil, considered as being, but only so far as it lacks being. Thus a man is said to be evil, because he lacks the being of virtue; and an eye is said to be evil, because it lacks the power to see well.

Reply Obj. 3. As primary matter has only potential being, so it is only potentially good. Although, according to the Platonists,[17] primary matter may be said to be a non-being because of the privation added to it, nevertheless, it does participate to a certain extent in goodness, viz., by its ordination to, or aptitude for, goodness. Consequently, not to be desirable, but to desire, befits it.

Reply Obj. 4. Mathematicals do not subsist as separate beings, for if they subsisted there would be in them some good, viz., their very being; but they have a separate existence only in the reason, inasmuch as they are abstracted from motion and matter; and it is thus that they are abstracted from an end whose nature it is to act as a moving cause. Nor is it repugnant that in some logical entity we do not find the good, or the character of goodness; for the idea of being is prior to the idea of goodness, as was said in the preceding article.

Fourth Article

WHETHER GOODNESS HAS THE ASPECT OF A FINAL CAUSE?

We proceed thus to the Fourth Article:—

Objection 1. It seems that goodness has not the aspect of a final cause, but rather of the other causes. For, as Dionysius says, *Goodness is praised as beauty.*[18] But beauty has the aspect of a formal cause. Therefore goodness has the aspect of a formal cause.

Obj. 2. Further, goodness is self-diffusive; for Dionysius says that goodness is that whereby all things subsist, and are.[19] But to be self-giving implies the aspect of an efficient

---

[17] Cf. Aristotle, *Phys.*, I, 9 (192a 2).   [18] *De Div. Nom.*, IV, 7 (PG 3, 701).   [19] *Op. cit.*, IV, 4; 20 (PG 3, 700; 720); cf. also, *op. cit.*, IV, 1 and 4 (PG 3, 693; 697).

cause. Therefore goodness has the aspect of an efficient cause.

Obj. 3. Further, Augustine says that *we exist, because God is good.*[20] But we are from God as from an efficient cause. Therefore goodness implies the aspect of an efficient cause.

On the contrary, The Philosopher says that *that is to be considered as the end and the good of other things, for the sake of which something is.*[21] Therefore goodness has the aspect of a final cause.

I answer that, Since goodness is that which all things desire, and since this has the aspect of an end, it is clear that goodness implies the aspect of an end. Nevertheless, the idea of goodness presupposes the idea of an efficient cause, and also of a formal cause. For we see that what is first in causing is last in the thing caused. Fire, *e.g.,* heats first of all before it reproduces the form of fire, though the heat in the fire follows from its substantial form. Now in causing, first comes goodness and the end, moving the agent to act; secondly, the action of the agent moving to the form; thirdly, comes the form. Hence in that which is caused the converse ought to take place, so that there should be, first, the form whereby it is a being; secondly, we consider in it its effective power, whereby it is perfect in being, *for a thing is perfect when it can reproduce its like,* as the Philosopher says;[22] thirdly, there follows the formality of goodness which is the basic principle of perfection in a being.

Reply Obj. 1. Beauty and goodness in a thing are identical fundamentally, for they are based upon the same thing, namely, the form; and this is why goodness is praised as beauty. But they differ logically, for goodness properly relates to appetite (goodness being what all things desire), and therefore it has the aspect of an end (the appetite being a kind of movement towards a thing). On the other hand, beauty relates to a cognitive power, for those things are said to be beautiful which please when seen. Hence beauty consists in due proportion, for the senses delight in things duly proportioned, as in what is like them—because the sense too is a sort of reason, as is every cognitive power. Now, since knowledge is by assimilation, and likeness relates to form, beauty properly belongs to the nature of a formal cause.

[20] *De Doc. Christ.,* I, 32 (PL 34, 32).   [21] *Phys.,* II, 3 (195a 23).
[22] *Meteor.,* IV, 3 (380a 12).

Reply Obj. 2. Goodness is described as self-diffusive in the sense that an end is said to move.

Reply Obj. 3. He who has a will is said to be good, so far as he has a good will; because it is by our will that we employ whatever powers we may have. Hence a man is said to be good, not because he has a good intellect, but because he has a good will. Now the will relates to the end as to its proper object. Thus the saying, *we exist because God is good* [23] has reference to the final cause.

Fifth Article

WHETHER THE ESSENCE OF GOODNESS CONSISTS IN LIMIT, SPECIES AND ORDER?

We proceed thus to the Fifth Article:—

Objection 1. It seems that the essence of goodness does not consist in limit, species and order. For goodness and being differ logically. But limit, species and order seem to belong to the nature of being, for it is written: *Thou hast ordered all things in measure, and number and weight* (*Wis.* xi. 21). And to these three can be reduced species, limit and order, as Augustine says: *Measure fixes the limit of everything, number gives it its species, and weight gives it rest and stability.* [24] Therefore the essence of goodness does not consist in limit, species and order.

Obj. 2. Further, limit, form, and order are themselves good. Therefore if the essence of goodness consists in limit, species and order, then every limit must have its own limit, species and order. The same would be the case with species and order in endless succession.

Obj. 3. Further, evil is the privation of limit, species and order. But evil is not the total absence of goodness. Therefore the essence of goodness does not consist in limit, species and order.

Obj. 4. Further, that wherein consists the essence of goodness cannot be spoken of as evil. Yet we can speak of an evil limit, species and order. Therefore the essence of goodness does not consist in limit, species and order.

Obj. 5. Further, limit, species and order are caused by

[23] St. Augustine, *De Doc. Christ.*, I, 32 (PL 34, 32).   [24] *De Genesi ad Litt.*, IV, 3 (PL 34, 299).

weight, number and measure, as appears from the quotation from Augustine.[25] But not every good thing has weight, number and measure; for Ambrose says: *It is of the nature of light not to have been created in number, weight and measure.*[26] Therefore the essence of goodness does not consist in limit, species and order.

On the contrary, Augustine says: *These three—limit, species, order—as common good things, are in everything God has made; thus, where these three abound the things are very good; where they are less, the things are less good; where they do not exist at all, there can be nothing good.*[27] But this would not be unless the essence of goodness consisted in them. Therefore the essence of goodness consists in limit, species and order.

I answer that, Everything is said to be good so far as it is perfect; for in that way is it desirable (as has been shown above). Now a thing is said to be perfect if it lacks nothing according to the mode of its perfection. But since everything is what it is by its form (and since the form presupposes certain things, and from the form certain things necessarily follow), in order for a thing to be perfect and good it must have a form, together with all that precedes and follows upon that form. Now the form presupposes determination or commensuration of its principles, whether material or efficient, and this is signified by the limit: hence it is said that *measure fixes the limit.*[28] But the form itself is signified by the species, for everything is placed in its species by its form. Hence number is said to give the species, for *definitions signifying species are like numbers,* according to the Philosopher;[29] for as a unit added to, or taken from, a number, changes its species, so a difference added to, or taken from, a definition, changes its species. Further, upon the form follows an inclination to the end, or to an action, or something of the sort; for everything, in so far as it is in act, acts and tends towards that which befits it according to its form; and this belongs to weight and order. Hence the essence of goodness, so far as it consists in perfection, consists also in limit, species and order.

[25] *Ibid.*   [26] *Hexaëm.,* I, 9(PL 14, 154).   [27] *De Nat. Boni,* 3 (PL 42, 553).   [28] St. Augustine, *De Genesi ad Litt.,* IV, 3 (PL 34, 299).
[29] *Metaph.,* VIII, 3 (1043b 34).

Reply Obj. 1. These three follow upon being, only so far as it is perfect; and according to this perfection it is good.

Reply Obj. 2. Limit, species and order are said to be good, and to be beings, not as though they themselves were subsistents, but because through them other things are both beings and good. Hence they have no need of other things whereby to be good, for they are spoken of as good, not as though formally so constituted by something else, but as formally constituting others good: thus whiteness is not said to be a being because it exists in anything else, but because, by it, something else has accidental being, viz., a thing that is white.

Reply Obj. 3. All being is through some form. Hence, according to the particular being of a thing is its limit, species, order. Thus, a man has a limit, species and order, as a man; and another limit, species, and order, as he is white, virtuous, knowing, and so on, according to everything predicated of him. But evil deprives a thing of some sort of being, as blindness deprives us of that being which is sight; and so it does not destroy every limit, species and order, but only such as follow upon the being of sight.

Reply Obj. 4. As Augustine says, *Every limit, as limit, is good* (and the same can be said of species and order). *But an evil limit, species and order are so called as being less than they ought to be, or as not belonging to that to which they ought to belong; or they are called evil, because they are out of place and incongruous.*[30]

Reply Obj. 5. The nature of light is spoken of as being without number, weight and measure, not absolutely, but in comparison with corporeal things, because the power of light extends to all corporeal things inasmuch as it is an active quality of the first body that causes change, *i.e.,* the heavens.

Sixth Article

WHETHER GOODNESS IS RIGHTLY DIVIDED INTO THE BEFITTING, THE USEFUL AND THE PLEASANT?

We proceed thus to the Sixth Article:—
Objection 1. It seems that goodness is not rightly divided

---

[30] *De Nat. Boni,* 22 (PL 42, 558).

into the befitting, the useful and the pleasant. For goodness is divided by the ten predicaments, as the Philosopher says.[31] But the befitting, the useful and the pleasant can be found under one predicament. Therefore goodness is not rightly divided by them.

Obj. 2. Further, every division is made by opposites. But these three do not seem to be opposites, for the befitting is pleasing, and nothing unbefitting is useful; whereas this ought to be the case if the division were made by opposites, for then the befitting and the useful would be opposed, as also Tully observes.[32] Therefore the division is improper.

Obj. 3. Further, where one thing is because of another, there is only one thing. But the useful is not good, except so far as it is pleasing and befitting. Therefore the useful ought not to be divided from the pleasant and the befitting.

On the contrary, Ambrose makes use of this division of goodness in his *De Officiis.*[33]

I answer that, This division properly concerns human goodness. But if we consider the nature of goodness from a higher and more universal point of view, we shall find that this division properly concerns goodness as such. For a thing is good so far as it is desirable, and is a term of the movement of appetite. The term of this movement can be seen from a consideration of the movement of a natural body. The movement of a natural body terminates absolutely in the end, and relatively in the means through which it comes to the end, where the movement ceases; so that a term of movement is so called in so far as it terminates any part of that movement. Now the ultimate term of movement can be taken in two ways: either as the thing itself towards which it tends, *e.g.,* a place or form; or as a state of rest in that thing. Thus, in the movement of appetite, the thing desired that terminates the movement of appetite relatively, as a means of tending towards something else, is called the *useful*; that sought after as the last thing absolutely terminating the movement of the appetite, as a thing towards which for its own sake the appetite tends, is called the *befitting,* for the *befitting* is that which is desired for its own sake; but that which terminates the movement of appetite in the form of rest in the thing desired, is called the *pleasant.*

[31] *Eth.,* I, 6 (1096a 19). [32] *De Off.,* II, 3 (pp. 81-82). [33] *De Off.,* I, 9 (PL 16, 35).

Reply Obj. 1. Goodness, so far as it is really identical with being, is divided by the ten predicaments. But this division belongs to it according to its proper formality.

Reply Obj. 2. This division is not by opposite things, but by opposite aspects. Now those things are properly called pleasing which have no other formality under which they are desirable except the pleasant, although at times they are harmful and unbefitting. Whereas the useful applies to such as are undesirable in themselves, but are desired only as helpful to something further: *e.g.,* the taking of bitter medicine; while the befitting are said to be such as are desirable in themselves.

Reply Obj. 3. Goodness is not divided into these three as something univocal which is predicated equally of them all, but as something analogical which is predicated of them according to priority and posteriority. For it is predicated by priority of the befitting, then of the pleasant, and lastly of the useful.

THE GOODNESS OF GOD

(*In Four Articles*)

WE NEXT consider the goodness of God, under which head there are four points of inquiry: (1) Whether to be good belongs to God? (2) Whether God is the highest good? (3) Whether He alone is essentially good? (4) Whether all things are good by the divine goodness?

First Article

WHETHER TO BE GOOD BELONGS TO GOD?

We proceed thus to the First Article:—

Objection 1. It seems that to be good does not belong to God. For goodness consists in limit, species and order. But these do not seem to belong to God, since God is immense, and is not ordered to anything. Therefore to be good does not belong to God.

Obj. 2. Further, the good is what all things desire. But all things do not desire God, because all things do not know Him; and nothing is desired unless it is known. Therefore to be good does not belong to God.

On the contrary, It is written (*Lam.* iii. 25): *The Lord is good to them that hope in Him, to the soul that seeketh Him.*

I answer that, To be good belongs pre-eminently to God. For a thing is good according to its desirableness. Now everything seeks after its own perfection, and the perfection and form of an effect consist in a certain likeness to the agent, since every agent makes its like; and hence the agent itself is desirable and has the nature of good. For the very thing which is desirable in it is the participation of its likeness. Therefore, since God is the first producing cause of all things, it is manifest that the aspect of good and of desirableness belong to Him; and hence Dionysius attributes good to God as to the first efficient cause, saying that *God is called good as by Whom all things subsist.*[1]

---

[1] *De Div. Nom.,* 4 (PG 3, 700).

Reply Obj. 1. To have limit, species and order belongs to the essence of caused good; but good is in God as in its cause, and hence it belongs to Him to impose limit, species and order on others; wherefore these three things are in God as in their cause.

Reply Obj. 2. All things, by desiring their own perfection, desire God Himself, inasmuch as the perfections of all things are so many similitudes of the divine being, as appears from what is said above.[2] And so of those beings which desire God, some know Him as He is in Himself, and this is proper to a rational creature; others know some participation of His goodness, and this belongs also to sensible knowledge; and others have a natural desire without knowledge, as being directed to their ends by a higher knower.

Second Article

WHETHER GOD IS THE HIGHEST GOOD?

We proceed thus to the Second Article:—

Objection 1. It seems that God is not the *highest* good. For the *highest* good adds something to good, or otherwise it would belong to every good. But everything which is an addition to anything else is a composite thing: therefore the highest good is composite. But God is supremely simple, as was shown above.[3] Therefore God is not the highest good.

Obj. 2. Further, *Good is what all desire*, as the Philosopher says.[4] Now what all desire is nothing but God, Who is the end of all things: therefore there is no other good but God. This appears also from what is said (*Luke* xviii. 19): *None is good but God alone.* But we use the word highest in comparison with others, as, *e.g.,* the highest hot thing is used in comparison with all other hot things. Therefore God cannot be called the highest good.

Obj. 3. Further, highest implies comparison. But things not in the same genus are not comparable; as sweetness is not properly called greater or less than a line. Therefore, since God is not in the same genus as other good things, as appears above,[5] it seems that God cannot be called the highest good in relation to them.

[2] Q. 4, a. 3.   [3] Q. 3, a. 7.   [4] *Eth.,* I, 1 (1094a 3).   [5] Q. 3, a. 5; q. 4, a. 3.

On the contrary, Augustine says that the Trinity of the divine persons *is the highest good, discerned by purified minds.*[6]

I answer that, God is the highest good absolutely, and not only in any genus or order of things. For good is attributed to God, as was said, inasmuch as all desired perfections flow from Him as from the first cause. They do not, however, flow from Him as from a univocal agent, as was shown above,[7] but as from an agent that does not agree with its effects either in species or genus. Now the likeness of an effect in the univocal cause is found uniformly; but in the equivocal cause it is found more excellently, as heat is in the sun more excellently than it is in fire. Therefore as good is in God as in the first, 'but not the univocal, cause of all things, it must be in Him in a most excellent way; and therefore He is called the highest good.

Reply Obj. 1. The highest good does not add to good any absolute thing, but only a relation. Now a relation, by which something is said of God relatively to creatures, is not really in God, but in the creature, for it is in God in our idea only. In the same way, what is knowable is so called with relation to knowledge, not that it depends on knowledge, but because knowledge depends on it. Thus it is not necessary that there should be composition in the highest good, but only that other things be deficient in comparison with it.

Reply Obj. 2. When we say that *good is what all desire,* it is not to be understood that every kind of good thing is desired by all, but that whatever is desired has the nature of good. And when it is said, *None is good but God alone,* this is to be understood of the essentially good, as will be explained.[8]

Reply Obj. 3. Things not of the same genus are in no way comparable to each other if they are in diverse genera. Now we say that God is not in the same genus with other good things. This does not mean that He is in any other genus, but that He is outside genus, and is the principle of every genus. Thus He is compared to others by excess, and it is this kind of comparison that the highest good implies.

---

[6] *De Trin.,* I, 2 (PL 42, 822).   [7] Q. 4, a. 2 and 3.   [8] A. 3.

Third Article

WHETHER TO BE ESSENTIALLY GOOD BELONGS TO GOD ALONE?

We proceed thus to the Third Article:—

Objection 1. It seems that to be essentially good does not belong to God alone. For as *one* is convertible with *being,* so is *good,* as we said above.[9] But every being is one essentially, as appears from the Philosopher.[10] Therefore every being is good essentially.

Obj. 2. Further, if good is what all things desire, since being itself is desired by all, then the being of each thing is its good. But everything is a being essentially: therefore every being is good essentially.

Obj. 3. Further, everything is good by its own goodness. Therefore if there is anything which is not good essentially, it is necessary to say that its goodness is not its own essence. Therefore its goodness, since it is a being, must be good; and if it is good by some other goodness, the same question applies to that goodness also. Therefore we must either proceed to infinity, or come to some goodness which is not good by any other goodness. Therefore the first supposition holds good. Therefore everything is good essentially.

On the contrary, Boethius says that *all things but God are good by participation.*[11] Therefore they are not good essentially.

I answer that, God alone is good essentially. For everything is called good according to its perfection. Now perfection in a thing is threefold: first, according to the constitution of its own being; secondly, in respect of any accidents being added as necessary for its perfect operation; thirdly, perfection consists in the attaining to something else as the end. Thus, for instance, the first perfection of fire consists in its being, which it has through its own substantial form; its secondary perfection consists in heat, lightness and dryness, and the like; its third perfection is to rest in its own place. This triple perfection belongs to no creature by its own essence; it belongs to God only, Whose essence alone is His being, in Whom there are no accidents, since whatever be-

[9] Q. 5, a. 1.   [10] *Metaph.,* III, 2 (1003b 32).   [11] *De Hebdom.* (PL 64, 1313).

longs to others accidentally belongs to Him essentially: *e.g.*, to be powerful, wise, and the like, as appears from what is stated above.[12] Furthermore, He is not directed to anything else as to an end, but is Himself the last end of all things. Hence it is manifest that God alone has every kind of perfection by His own essence, and therefore He alone is good essentially.

Reply Obj. 1. *One* does not include the idea of perfection, but only of indivision, which belongs to everything according to its own essence. Now the essences of simple things are undivided both actually and potentially, but the essences of composite things are undivided only actually; and therefore everything must be one essentially, but not good essentially, as was shown above.

Reply Obj. 2. Although everything is good in that it has being, yet the essence of a creature is not being itself, and therefore it does not follow that a creature is good essentially.

Reply Obj. 3. The goodness of a creature is not its very essence, but something superadded; it is either its being, or some added perfection, or the order to its end. Still, the goodness itself thus added is called good, just as it is called being. But it is called being because by it something has being, not because it itself has being through something else. Hence it is called good because by it something is good, and not because it itself has some other goodness whereby it is good.

Fourth Article

WHETHER ALL THINGS ARE GOOD BY THE DIVINE GOODNESS?

We proceed thus to the Fourth Article:—

Objection 1. It seems that all things are good by the divine goodness. For Augustine says: *This and that are good. Take away this and that, and see good itself if thou canst; and so thou shalt see God, good not by any other good, but the good of every good.*[13] But everything is good by its own good: therefore everything is good by that very good which is God.

Obj. 2. Further, as Boethius says,[14] all things are called

---

[12] Q. 3, a. 6.   [13] *De Trin.*, VIII, 3 (PL 42, 949).   [14] *De Hebdom.* (PL 64, 1312).

good according as they are directed to God, and this is by reason of the divine goodness: therefore all things are good by the divine goodness.

On the contrary, All things are good inasmuch as they have being. But they are not called beings through the divine being, but through their own being: therefore all things are not good by the divine goodness, but by their own goodness.

I answer that, As regards relative things, we may admit extrinsic denomination. Thus, a thing is denominated *placed* from *place,* and *measured* from *measure.* But as regards what is said absolutely, opinions differ. Plato held the separate existence of the essences of all things, and that individuals were denominated by them as participating in the separate essences; for instance, that Socrates is called man according to the separate Form of man.[15] Now just as he laid down separate Forms of man and horse which he called absolute man and absolute horse,[16] so likewise he laid down separate Forms of *being* and of *one,* and these he called absolute being and absolute oneness,[17] and by participation in these everything was called *being* or *one.* What was thus absolute being and absolute one, he said was the highest good.[18] And because good is convertible with being, as is also one, he called the absolute good God,[19] from whom all things are called good by way of participation.[20]

Although this opinion appears to be unreasonable in affirming that there are separate forms of natural things subsisting of themselves—as Aristotle argues in many ways[21]—still, it is absolutely true that there is something first which is essentially being and essentially good, which we call God, as appears from what is shown above.[22] Aristotle agrees with this.[23] Hence from the first being, essentially being and good, everything can be called good and a being inasmuch as it participates in the first being by way of a certain assimilation,

[15] Cf. Aristotle, *Metaph.,* I, 6 (987b 7); St. Augustine, *Lib. 83 Quaest.,* q. 46 (PL 40, 30).   [16] Aristotle, *Metaph.,* II, 2 (997b 8). [17] *Op. cit.,* II, 4 (999b 26).   [18] Cf. Aristotle, *Eth.,* I, 6 (1096a 23); Macrobius, *In Somn. Scipion.,* I, 2 (p. 482).   [19] St. Augustine, *De Civit. Dei,* VIII, 8 (PL 41, 233); Plato, *Republic,* VI (p. 508c). [20] Cf. St. Augustine, *De Trin.,* VIII, 3 (PL 42, 949); St. Albert, *In Eth.,* I, tr. 5, ch. 13 (VII, 76).   [21] *Metaph.,* I, 9 (990a 33); VI, 7-8 (1031a 15); *Eth.,* I, 6 (1096a 11).   [22] O. 2, a. 3.   [23] *Metaph.,* Ia, 1 (993b 24); cf. above, q. 2, a. 3.

although distantly and defectively, as appears from the above.[24]

Everything is therefore called good from the divine goodness, as from the first exemplary, effective and final principle of all goodness. Nevertheless, everything is called good by reason of the likeness of the divine goodness belonging to it, which is formally its own goodness, whereby it is denominated good. And so of all things there is one goodness, and yet many goodnesses.

This is a sufficient Reply to the Objections.

[24] Q. 4, a. 3.

THE INFINITY OF GOD

(*In Four Articles*)

AFTER considering the divine perfection, we must consider God's infinity, and His existence in things;[1] for God is said to be everywhere, and in all things, inasmuch as He is boundless and infinite.

Concerning the first, there are four points of inquiry: (1) Whether God is infinite? (2) Whether anything besides Him is infinite in essence? (3) Whether anything can be infinite in magnitude? (4) Whether an infinite multitude can exist?

First Article

WHETHER GOD IS INFINITE?

We proceed thus to the First Article:—

Objection 1. It seems that God is not infinite. For everything infinite is imperfect, as the Philosopher says, because it has parts and matter, as is said in *Physics* iii.[2] But God is most perfect: therefore He is not infinite.

Obj. 2. Further, according to the Philosopher,[3] finite and infinite belong to quantity. But there is no quantity in God, for He is not a body, as was shown above.[4] Therefore it does not belong to Him to be infinite.

Obj. 3. Further, what is here in such a way as not to be elsewhere is finite according to place. Therefore, that which is this thing in such a way as not to be another thing is finite according to substance. But God is this, and not another; for He is not a stone or wood. Therefore God is not infinite in substance.

On the contrary, Damascene says that *God is infinite and eternal and boundless*.[5]

I answer that, All the ancient philosophers attribute infinitude to the first principle, as it is said,[6] and this *with rea-*

---

[1] Q. 8.   [2] Aristotle, *Phys.*, III, 6 (207a 27).   [3] *Op. cit.*, I, 2 (185b 2).   [4] Q. 3, a. 1.   [5] *De Fide Orth.*, I, 4 (PG 94, 800).   [6] Aristotle, *Phys.*, III, 4 (203a 1).

son;[7] for they considered that things flow forth infinitely from the first principle. But because some erred concerning the nature of the first principle, as a consequence they erred also concerning its infinity. For they asserted that matter was the first principle;[8] and consequently they attributed to the first principle a material infinity, asserting that some infinite body was the first principle of things.

We must consider therefore that a thing is called infinite because it is not finite. Now matter is in a way made finite by form, and the form by matter. Matter is made finite by form inasmuch as matter, before it receives its form, is in potentiality to many forms; but on receiving a form, it is terminated by that one. Again, form is made finite by matter inasmuch as form, considered in itself, is common to many; but when received in matter, the form is determined to this one particular thing. Now matter is perfected by the form by which it is made finite, and therefore infinity as attributed to matter has the nature of something imperfect, for it is as it were formless matter. On the other hand, form is not made perfect by matter, but rather is contracted by matter; and hence the infinite, regarded on the part of the form not determined by matter, has the nature of something perfect. Now being is the most formal of all things, as appears from the above.[9] Since therefore the divine being is not a being received in anything, but God is His own subsistent being (as was shown above[10]), it is clear that God Himself is infinite and perfect.

From this appears the Reply to the First Objection.

Reply Obj. 2. The term of quantity is, as it were, its form, and this can be seen in the fact that a figure which consists in the termination of quantity is a kind of quantitative form. Hence the infinite of quantity is in the order of matter, and such a kind of infinite cannot be attributed to God, as was said above.

Reply Obj. 3. The fact that the being of God is self-subsisting, not received in any other, and is thus called infinite, shows God to be distinguished from all other beings, and all others to be apart from Him; much as, were there such a thing as a self-subsisting whiteness, the very fact that it did

---

[7] *Ibid.* (203b 4).   [8] Aristotle, *Metaph.,* I, 3 (983b 6).   [9] Q. 4, a. 1.   [10] Q. 3, a. 4.

not exist in anything else would make it distinct from every other whiteness existing in a subject.

Second Article

WHETHER ANYTHING BUT GOD CAN BE ESSENTIALLY INFINITE?

We proceed thus to the Second Article:—

Objection 1. It seems that something else besides God can be essentially infinite. For the power of anything is proportioned to its essence. Now if the essence of God is infinite, His power must also be infinite. Therefore He can produce an infinite effect, since the extent of a power is known by its effect.

Obj. 2. Further, whatever has infinite power has an infinite essence. Now the created intellect has an infinite power, for it apprehends the universal, which can extend itself to an infinitude of singulars. Therefore every created intellectual substance is infinite.

Obj. 3. Further, primary matter is something other than God, as was shown above.[11] But primary matter is infinite. Therefore something besides God can be infinite.

On the contrary, The infinite cannot be from some principle, as is said in *Physics* iii.[12] But everything outside God is from God as from its first principle. Therefore nothing besides God can be infinite.

I answer that, Things other than God can be relatively infinite, but not absolutely infinite. For with regard to the infinite as applied to matter, it is manifest that everything actually existing possesses a form; and thus its matter is determined by form. But because matter, considered as existing under some substantial form, remains in potentiality to many accidental forms, what is absolutely finite can be relatively infinite. For example, wood is finite according to its own form, but still it is relatively infinite inasmuch as it is in potentiality to an infinite number of shapes. But if we speak of the infinite in reference to form, it is manifest that those things, the forms of which are in matter, are absolutely finite, and in no way infinite. If, however, any created forms are not received into matter, but are self-subsisting, as some think to

[11] Q. 3, a. 8.   [12] Aristotle, *Phys.* III, 4 (203b 7).

be the case with the angels,[13] these will be relatively infinite, inasmuch as such forms are not terminated, nor contracted, by any matter. But because a created form thus subsisting has being, and yet is not its own being, it follows that its being is received and contracted to a determinate nature. Hence it cannot be absolutely infinite.

Reply Obj. 1. It is against the nature of a produced thing for its essence to be its being, because subsisting being is not a created being; and hence it is against the nature of a produced thing to be absolutely infinite. Therefore, as God, although He has infinite power, cannot make a thing to be not made (for this would imply that two contradictories are true at the same time), so likewise He cannot make anything to be absolutely infinite.

Reply Obj. 2. The reason why the power of the intellect in a way extends itself to an infinity of things is that the intellect is a form not in matter; but it is either wholly separated from matter, as are angelic substances, or at least there is the separation of an intellectual power, which is not the act of any organ, in the intellectual soul joined to a body.

Reply Obj. 3. Primary matter does not exist by itself in nature, since it is not actual being, but only potential. Hence it is something concreated rather than created. Nevertheless, primary matter even as a potentiality is not absolutely infinite, but relatively, because its potentiality extends only to natural forms.

Third Article

WHETHER AN ACTUALLY INFINITE MAGNITUDE CAN EXIST?

We proceed thus to the Third Article:—

Objection 1. It seems that there can be something actually infinite in magnitude. For in mathematics there is no error, since *there is no lie in things abstract,* as the Philosopher says.[14] But mathematics uses the infinite in magnitude; and thus, the geometrician in his demonstrations says, *Let this line be infinite.* Therefore it is not impossible for a thing to be infinite in magnitude.

Obj. 2. Further, what is not against the nature of anything can agree with it. Now to be infinite is not against the nature

---

[13] Cf. below, q. 50, a. 2.   [14] Aristotle, *Phys.* II, 2 (193b 35).

of magnitude, but rather both the finite and the infinite seem to be attributes of quantity. Therefore it is not impossible for some magnitude to be infinite.

Obj. 3. Further, magnitude is infinitely divisible, for the continuous is defined as *that which is infinitely divisible,* as is clear from *Physics* iii.[15] But contraries are concerned about one and the same thing. Since, therefore, addition is opposed to division, and increase is opposed to diminution, it appears that magnitude can be increased to infinity. Therefore it is possible for magnitude to be infinite.

Obj. 4. Further, movement and time have quantity and continuity derived from the magnitude over which movement passes, as it is said in *Physics* iv.[16] But it is not against the nature of time and movement to be infinite, since every determinate indivisible in time and circular movement is both a beginning and an end. Therefore neither is it against the nature of magnitude to be infinite.

On the contrary, Every body has a surface. But every body which has a surface is finite, because surface is the term of a finite body. Therefore all bodies are finite. The same applies also to surface and to a line. Therefore nothing is infinite in magnitude.

I answer that, It is one thing to be infinite in essence, and another to be infinite in magnitude. For granted that there exists a body which is infinite in magnitude, as fire or air, yet this would not be infinite in essence, because its essence would be terminated in a species by its form, and confined to some individual by matter. And so, assuming from what has preceded that no creature is infinite in essence, it still remains to inquire whether any creature can be infinite in magnitude.

We must therefore observe that a body, which is a complete magnitude, can be considered in two ways: *mathematically,* in which case we consider its quantity only; and *naturally,* in which case we consider its matter and form.

Now it is manifest that a natural body cannot be actually infinite. For every natural body has some determined substantial form. Therefore, since accidents follow upon the substantial form, it is necessary that determinate accidents should follow upon a determinate form; and among these

[15] *Op. cit.,* III, 1 (200b 20).   [16] *Op. cit.,* IV, 11 (219a 12).

accidents is quantity. So every natural body has a greater or smaller determinate quantity. Hence it is impossible for a natural body to be infinite. The same appears from movement, because every natural body has some natural movement, whereas an infinite body could not have any natural movement. It cannot have one in a straight line, because nothing moves naturally by such a movement unless it is out of its place; and this could not happen to an infinite body, for it would occupy every place, and thus every place would be indifferently its own place. Neither could it move circularly, since circular motion requires that one part of the body be necessarily transferred to a place which had been occupied by another part, and this could not happen as regards an infinite circular body: for if two lines be drawn from the center, the farther they extend from the center, the farther they are from each other; and therefore, if a body were infinite, the lines would be infinitely distant from each other, and thus one could never occupy the place belonging to the other.

The same applies to a mathematical body. For if we imagine a mathematical body actually existing, we must imagine it under some form, because nothing is actual except by its form. Hence, since the form of quantity as such is figure, such a body must have some figure. It would therefore be finite, for figure is confined by a term or boundary.

Reply Obj. 1. A geometrician does not need to assume that a given line is actually infinite: he needs to take some actually finite line, from which he can subtract whatever he finds necessary; which line he calls infinite.

Reply Obj. 2. Although the infinite is not against the nature of magnitude in general, it is against the nature of any species of it. Thus, for instance, it is against the nature of a bicubical or tricubical magnitude, whether circular or triangular, and so on. Now what is not possible in any species cannot exist in the genus, and hence there cannot be any infinite magnitude, since no species of magnitude is infinite.

Reply Obj. 3. The infinite in quantity, as was shown above, belongs to matter. Now by division of the whole we approach to matter, since parts are as matter; but by addition we approach to the whole which is as a form. Therefore, the infinite is not found in the addition of magnitude, but only in division.

Reply Obj. 4. Movement and time are not actual as wholes, but successively, and hence they have potentiality mixed with actuality. But magnitude is an actual whole, and therefore the infinite in quantity refers to matter, and does not agree with the totality of magnitude; yet it agrees with the totality of time or movement: for to be in potentiality befits matter.

Fourth Article

WHETHER AN INFINITE MULTITUDE CAN EXIST?

We proceed thus to the Fourth Article:—

Objection 1. It seems that an actually infinite multitude is possible. For it is not impossible for a potentiality to be made actual. But number can be multiplied to infinity. Therefore it is possible for an infinite multitude actually to exist.

Obj. 2. Further, it is possible for any individual of any species to be actual. But the species of figures are infinite. Therefore an infinite number of actual figures is possible.

Obj. 3. Further, things not opposed to each other do not obstruct each other. But supposing a multitude of things to exist, there can still be many others not opposed to them. Therefore it is not impossible for others also to coexist with them, and so on to infinitude. Therefore an actual infinite number of things is possible.

On the contrary, It is written, *Thou hast ordered all things in measure, and number and weight* (*Wis.* xi. 21).

I answer that, A twofold opinion has obtained on this subject. Some, as Avicenna and Algazel,[17] said that *it was impossible for an absolutely infinite multitude to exist actually, but that an accidentally infinite multitude was not impossible. A multitude is said to be infinite absolutely, when an infinite multitude is necessary that something may exist.* Now this is impossible, because it would mean that something is dependent on an infinity for its existence; and hence its generation would never be accomplished, because it is impossible to traverse what is infinite.

A multitude is said to be accidentally infinite when its existence as such is not necessary, but accidental. This can be shown, for example, in the work of an artisan requiring a

---

[17] Cf. Averroes, *Destruct. Destruct.*, I (IX, 12vab).

certain absolute multitude, namely, art in the soul, the movement of the hand, and a hammer; and supposing that such
things were infinitely multiplied, the work would never be
finished, since it would depend on an infinite number of
causes. But the multitude of hammers, which results when
one hammer is broken and is replaced by another, is an accidental multitude; for it happens by accident that many hammers are used, and it matters little whether one or two, or
many are used, or an infinite number, if the work is carried
on for an infinite time. In this way they said that there can
be actually an accidentally infinite multitude.

This, however, is impossible, since every kind of multitude
must belong to a species of multitude. Now the species of
multitude are to be reckoned by the species of numbers. But
no species of number is infinite, for every number is multitude measured by one. Hence it is impossible that there be
an actually infinite multitude, either absolutely or accidentally. Furthermore, multitude in the world is created, and
everything created is comprehended under some definite intention of the Creator; for no agent acts aimlessly. Hence
everything created must be comprehended under a certain
number. Therefore it is impossible for an actually infinite
multitude to exist, even accidentally.

But a potentially infinite multitude is possible, because the
increase of multitude follows upon the division of a magnitude, since the more a thing is divided, the greater number
of things result. Hence, just as the infinite is to be found
potentially in the division of the continuous, because we thus
approach matter, as was shown above, in the same way the
infinite can also be found potentially in the addition of multitude.

Reply Obj. 1. Whatever exists potentially is made actual
according to its mode of being. For instance, a day is reduced
to act successively, and not all at once. Likewise the infinite
in multitude is reduced to act successively, and not all at
once, because every multitude can be succeeded by another
multitude to infinity.

Reply Obj. 2. Species of figures are infinite by the infinitude of number. Now there are various species of figures,
such as trilateral, quadrilateral and so on; and as an infinitely numerable multitude is not all at once reduced to act,
so neither is the multitude of figures.

Reply Obj. 3. Although the supposition of some things does not preclude the supposition of others, still the supposition of an infinite number is opposed to any single species of multitude. Hence it is not possible for any actually infinite multitude to exist.

Question XI

THE UNITY OF GOD

(In Four Articles)

AFTER the foregoing, we consider the divine unity, concerning which there are four points of inquiry: (1) Whether *one* adds anything to *being*? (2) Whether *one* and *many* are opposed to each other? (3) Whether God is one? (4) Whether He is in the highest degree one?

First Article

WHETHER *ONE* ADDS ANYTHING TO *BEING?*

We proceed thus to the First Article:—

Objection 1. It seems that *one* adds something to *being*. For everything is in a determinate genus by addition to being, which encompasses all genera. But *one* is in a determinate genus, for it is the principle of number, which is a species of quantity. Therefore *one* adds something to *being*.

Obj. 2. Further, that which divides something common is by addition to it. But *being* is divided by *one* and by *many*. Therefore *one* adds something to *being*.

Obj. 3. Further, if *one* does not add to *being, one* and *being* must have the same meaning. But it would be nugatory to call *being* by the name of *being*: therefore it would be equally so to call being *one*. Now this is false. Therefore *one* adds something to *being*.

On the contrary, Dionysius says: *Nothing which exists is not in some way one,*[1] which would be false if *one* were an addition to *being*, in the sense of limiting it. Therefore *one* is not an addition to *being*.

I answer that, One does not add any reality to *being*, but is only the negation of division; for *one* means undivided *being*. This is the very reason why *one* is convertible with *being*. For every being is either simple or composite. But what is simple is undivided, both actually and potentially; whereas what is composite has not being while its parts are divided, but after they make up and compose it. Hence it is

[1] *De Div. Nom.,* V, 2 (PG 3, 977).

manifest that the being of anything consists in indivision; and hence it is that everything guards its unity as it guards its being.

Reply Obj. 1. Some, thinking that the *one* convertible with *being* is the same as the *one* which is the principle of number, were divided into contrary opinions. Pythagoras and Plato, seeing that the *one* convertible with *being* did not add any reality to *being,* but signified the substance of *being* as undivided, thought that the same applied to the *one* which is the principle of number.[2] And because number is composed of unities, they thought that numbers were the substances of all things. Avicenna, however, on the contrary, considering that the *one* which is the principle of number added a reality to the substance of being (otherwise number made of unities would not be a species of quantity), thought that the *one* convertible with *being* added a reality to the substance of beings; as *white* adds to *man.*[3] This, however, is manifestly false, inasmuch as each thing is *one* by its substance. For if a thing were *one* by anything else but by its substance, since this again would be *one,* supposing it were again *one* by another thing, we should be driven on to infinity. Hence we must adhere to the former statement; therefore we must say that the *one* which is convertible with *being* does not add a reality to being; but that the *one* which is the principle of number does add a reality to *being,* belonging to the genus of quantity.

Reply Obj. 2. There is nothing to prevent a thing, which in one way is divided, from being in another way undivided, as what is divided in number may be undivided in species; thus it may be that a thing is in one way *one,* and in another way *many.* Still, if it is absolutely undivided, either because it is so according to what belongs to its essence (though it may be divided as regards what is outside its essence, as what is one in subject may have many accidents), or because it is undivided actually, and divided potentially (as what is *one* in the whole, and is *many* in its parts), in which case a thing will be *one* absolutely, and *many* accidentally. On the other hand, if it be undivided accidentally, and divided absolutely, as if it were divided in essence and undivided in idea or in

---

[2] Cf. Aristotle, *Metaph.,* I, 5 (987a 13; a 19); I, 6 (987b 23).—Cf. also St. Thomas, *In Metaph.,* I, lect. 7 and 8.   [3] *Metaph.,* III, 3 (79r).—Cf. also Averroes, *Destruct. Destruct.,* III (IX, 25ra).

principle or cause, it will be *many* absolutely, and *one* accidentally; as what are *many* in number, and *one* in species, or
one in principle. This is the way in which being is divided by
one and by *many*; as it were by *one* absolutely, and by *many*
accidentally. For multitude itself would not be contained under *being* unless it were in some way contained under *one*.
Thus Dionysius says that *there is no kind of multitude that
is not in a way one. But what are many in their parts are one
in their whole; and what are many in accidents are one in
subject; and what are many in number are one in species;
and what are many in species are one in genus; and what are
many in processions are one in principle.*[4]

Reply Obj. 3. It does not follow that it is nugatory to say
being is *one*; since *one* adds something to *being* logically.

Second Article

WHETHER ONE AND MANY ARE OPPOSED TO EACH OTHER?

We proceed thus to the Second Article:—

Objection 1. It seems that *one* and *many* are not mutually
opposed. For no opposite is predicated of its opposite. But
every *multitude* is in a certain way *one*, as appears from the
preceding article. Therefore *one* is not opposed to *multitude*.

Obj. 2. Further, no opposite is constituted by its opposite.
But *multitude* is constituted by *one*. Therefore it is not opposed to *multitude*.

Obj. 3. Further, each thing has one opposite. But the opposite of *many* is *few*. Therefore, the opposite is not *one*.

Obj. 4. Further, if *one* is opposed to *multitude*, it is opposed as the undivided is to the divided, and is thus opposed
to it as privation is to habit. But this appears to be incongruous, because it would follow that one comes after *multitude*, and is defined by it; whereas, on the contrary, *multitude* is defined by *one*. Hence there would be a vicious circle
in the definition; which is inadmissible. Therefore *one* and
many are not opposed.

On the contrary, Things which are opposed in idea are
themselves opposed to each other. But the idea of *one* consists in indivisibility; and the idea of *multitude* contains
division. Therefore *one* and *many* are opposed to each other.

[4] *De Div. Nom.,* XIII, 2 (PG 3, 980).

I answer that, One is opposed to *many,* but in various ways. The *one* which is the principle of number is opposed to *multitude* which is number as the measure is to the thing measured. For *one* implies the idea of a primary measure; and number is *multitude* measured by *one,* as is clear from *Metaph.* x.[5] But the *one* which is convertible with *being* is opposed to *multitude* by way of privation; as the undivided is to the divided.

Reply Obj. 1. No privation entirely takes away the being of a thing, inasmuch as privation means *negation in the subject,* according to the Philosopher.[6] Nevertheless, every privation takes away some being; and so in being, by reason of its community, the privation of being has its foundation in being; which is not the case in privations of special forms, as of sight, or of whiteness, and the like. And what applies to being applies also to one and to good, which are convertible with being, for the privation of good is founded in some good; likewise the removal of unity is founded in some one thing. Hence it happens that multitude is some one thing, and evil is some good thing, and non-being is some kind of being. Nevertheless, opposite is not predicated of opposite, since one is absolute, and the other is relative; for what is relatively being (*i.e.,* in potency) is non-being absolutely, *i.e.,* actually; or what is being absolutely in the genus of substance is non-being relatively as regards some accidental being. In the same way, what is relatively good is absolutely bad, or *vice versa;* likewise, what is absolutely *one* is relatively *many,* and *vice versa.*

Reply Obj. 2. A *whole* is twofold. In one sense it is homogeneous, composed of like parts; in another sense it is heterogeneous, composed of dissimilar parts. Now in every homogeneous whole, the whole is made up of parts having the form of the whole, as, for instance, every part of water is water; and such is the constitution of a continuous thing made up of its parts. In every heterogeneous whole, however, every part is wanting in the form belonging to the whole; as, for instance, no part of a house is a house, nor is any part of man a man. Now multitude is such a kind of whole. Therefore, inasmuch as its part has not the form of the multitude, the latter is composed of unities, as a house is composed of not

[5] Aristotle, *Metaph.,* IX, 1 (1052b 18); 6 (1057a 3).   [6] *Op. cit.,* III, 2 (1004a 15); cf. *Cat.,* X (12a 26).

houses; not, indeed, as if unities constituted multitude so far
as they are undivided, in which way they are opposed to
multitude, but so far as they have being; as also the parts
of a house make up the house by the fact that they are beings, not by the fact that they are not houses.

Reply Obj. 3. *Many* is taken in two ways: absolutely, and
in that sense it is opposed to *one*; in another way, as import-
ing some kind of excess, in which sense it is opposed to *few.*
Hence, in the first sense two are many; but not in the second
sense.

Reply Obj. 4. *One* is opposed to *many* privatively, inasmuch as the idea of *many* involves division. Hence division
must be prior to unity, not absolutely in itself, but according to our way of apprehension. For we apprehend simple
things by composite things; and hence we define a point to
be, *what has no part,* or *the beginning of a line. Multitude*
also, in idea, follows on *one*; because we do not understand
divided things to convey the idea of multitude except by the
fact that we attribute unity to every member. Hence *one* is
placed in the definition of *multitude*; but *multitude* is not
placed in the definition of *one.* But division comes to be understood from the very negation of being: so what first comes
to the intellect is being; secondly, that this being is not that
being, and thus we apprehend division as a consequence;
thirdly, comes the notion of one; fourthly, the notion of
multitude.

Third Article

WHETHER GOD IS ONE?

We proceed thus to the Third Article:—

Objection 1. It seems that God is not one. For it is written,
For there be many gods and many lords (*1 Cor.* viii. 5).

Obj. 2. Further, *one,* as the principle of number, cannot
be predicated of God, since quantity is not predicated of
God; likewise, neither can *one* which is convertible with *being* be predicated of God, because it imports privation, and
every privation is an imperfection, which cannot apply to
God. Therefore God is not one.

On the contrary, It is written, *Hear, O Israel, the Lord our
God is one Lord* (*Deut.* vi. 4).

I answer that, It can be shown from three sources that God

is one. First from His simplicity. For it is manifest that the
reason why any singular thing is *this particular thing* is
because it cannot be communicated to many, since that
whereby Socrates is a man can be communicated to many,
whereas what makes him this particular man is communicable only to one. Therefore, if Socrates were a man by what
makes him to be this particular man, as there cannot be
many Socrateses, so there could not in that way be many
men. Now this belongs to God alone; for God Himself is His
own nature, as was shown above.[7] Therefore, in the very
same way God is God and this God. It is impossible therefore
that there should be many gods.

Secondly, this is proved from the infinity of His protection.
For it was shown above that God comprehends in Himself
the whole perfection of being.[8] If, then, many gods existed,
they would necessarily differ from each other. Something,
therefore, would belong to one which did not belong to another. And if this were a privation, one of them would not be
absolutely perfect; but if a perfection, one of them would be
without it. So it is impossible for many gods to exist. Hence
also the ancient philosophers, constrained as it were by truth,
when they asserted an infinite principle, asserted likewise
that there was only one such principle.

Thirdly, this is shown from the unity of the world. For all
things that exist are seen to be ordered to each other since
some serve others. But things that are diverse do not come
together in the same order unless they are ordered thereto by
some one being. For many are reduced into one order by one
better than by many: because one is the *per se* cause of one,
and many are only the accidental cause of one, inasmuch as
they are in some way one. Since, therefore, what is first is
most perfect, and is so *per se* and not accidentally, it must be
that the first which reduces all into one order should be only
one. And this is God.

Reply Obj. 1. Gods are called many by the error of some
who worshipped many deities, thinking as they did that the
planets and other stars were gods, and also the particular
parts of the world. Hence the Apostle adds: *Our God is one,*
etc. (*1 Cor.* viii. 6).

Reply Obj. 2. *One* which is the principle of number is not predicated of God, but only of material things. For *one* which is the principle of number belongs to the *genus* of mathematicals, which are material in being, and abstracted from matter only in idea. But *one* which is convertible with being is something metaphysical and does not, in being, depend on matter. And although in God there is no privation, still, according to the mode of our apprehension, He is known to us by way only of privation and remotion. Thus there is no reason why certain privative terms should not be predicated of God, for instance, that He is *incorporeal,* and *infinite;* and in the same way it is said of God that He is *one.*

Fourth Article

WHETHER GOD IS SUPREMELY ONE?

We proceed thus to the Fourth Article:—

Objection 1. It seems that God is not supremely *one.* For *one* is so called from the privation of division. But privation cannot be greater or less. Therefore God is not more *one* than other things which are called *one.*

Obj. 2. Further, nothing seems to be more indivisible than what is actually and potentially indivisible; such as a point, and unity. But a thing is said to be more *one* according as it is indivisible. Therefore God is not more *one* than unity is *one* and a point is *one.*

Obj. 3. Further, what is essentially good is supremely good. Therefore, what is essentially *one* is supremely *one.* But every being is essentially *one,* as the Philosopher says.[9] Therefore, every being is supremely *one;* and therefore God is not *one* more than any other being is *one.*

On the contrary, Bernard says: *Among all things called one, the unity of the Divine Trinity holds the first place.*[10]

I answer that, Since *one* is an undivided being, if anything is supremely *one* it must be supremely being and supremely undivided. Now both of these belong to God. For He is supremely being inasmuch as His being is not determined by any nature to which it is adjoined; since He is being itself, subsistent, absolutely undetermined. And He is supremely undivided inasmuch as He is divided neither actually nor po-

[9] *Metaph.,* III, 2· (1003b 32).   [10] *De Consider.,* V, 8 (PL 182, 799).

tentially by any mode of division; since He is altogether simple, as was shown above.[11] Hence it is manifest that God is *one* in the supreme degree.

Reply Obj. 1. Although privation considered in itself is not susceptive of more or less, still according as its opposite is subject to more and less, privation also can be predicated according to more and less. Therefore, according as a thing is more or less or not at all divided or divisible, in that degree it is called more, or less, or supremely, *one*.

Reply Obj. 2. A point and unity, which is the principle of number, are not supremely being, inasmuch as they have being only in some subject. Hence neither of them can be supremely *one*. For as a subject cannot be supremely *one* because of the diversity of accident and subject, so neither can an accident.

Reply Obj. 3. Although every being is *one* by its substance, still every substance is not equally the cause of unity; for the substance of some things is composite, and of others not.

[11] Q. 3, a. 7.

Question XII

HOW GOD IS KNOWN BY US

(*In Thirteen Articles*)

As HITHERTO we have considered God as He is in Himself, we now go on to consider how He is in our knowledge, that is, how He is known by creatures. Concerning this there are thirteen points of inquiry. (1) Whether any created intellect can see the essence of God? (2) Whether the essence of God is seen by the intellect through any created species? (3) Whether the essence of God can be seen by the corporeal eye? (4) Whether any created intellectual substance is sufficient by its own natural powers to see the essence of God? (5) Whether the created intellect needs any created light in order to see the essence of God? (6) Whether, of those who see the essence of God, one sees it more perfectly than another? (7) Whether any created intellect can comprehend the essence of God? (8) Whether a created intellect, seeing the essence of God, knows all things in it? (9) Whether what is there known is known by any likenesses? (10) Whether the created intellect knows all at once what it sees in God? (11) Whether in the state of this life any man can see the essence of God? (12) Whether by natural reason we can know God in this life? (13) Whether there is in this life any knowledge of God through grace above the knowledge of natural reason?

First Article

WHETHER ANY CREATED INTELLECT CAN SEE THE ESSENCE OF GOD?

We proceed thus to the First Article:—

Objection 1. It seems that no created intellect can see the essence of God. For Chrysostom, commenting on *John* i. 18 (*No man hath seen God at any time*), says: *Not prophets only, but neither angels nor archangels have seen God. For how can a creature see what is uncreatable?*[1] Dionysius also,

---

[1] *In Ioann.*, hom. XV (PG 59, 98).

speaking of God, says: *Neither is there sense, nor image, nor opinion, nor reason, nor knowledge of Him.*[2]

Obj. 2. Further, everything infinite, as such, is unknown. But God is infinite, as was shown above.[3] Therefore in Himself He is unknown.

Obj. 3. Further, the created intellect knows only existing things. For what falls first under the apprehension of the intellect is being. Now God is not something existing; but He is rather super-existence, as Dionysius says.[4] Therefore God is not intelligible; but above all intellect.

Obj. 4. Further, there must be some proportion between the knower and the known, since the known is the perfection of the knower. But no proportion exists between the created intellect and God, for there is an infinite distance between them. Therefore a created intellect cannot see the essence of God.

On the contrary, It is written: *We shall see Him as He is* (*1 John* iii. 2).

I answer that, Since everything is knowable according as it is actual, God, Who is pure act without any admixture of potentiality, is in Himself supremely knowable. But what is supremely knowable in itself may not be knowable to a particular intellect, because of the excess of the intelligible object above the intellect; as, for example, the sun, which is supremely visible, cannot be seen by the bat by reason of its excess of light.

Therefore, some who considered this held that no created intellect can see the essence of God.[5] This opinion, however, is not tenable. For the ultimate beatitude of man consists in the use of his highest function, which is the operation of the intellect. Hence, if we suppose that a created intellect could never see God, it would either never attain to beatitude, or its beatitude would consist in something else beside God; which is opposed to faith. For the ultimate perfection of the rational creature is to be found in that which is the source of its being; since a thing is perfect so far as it attains to its source. Further, the same opinion is also against reason. For there resides in every man a natural desire to know the cause of any effect which he sees. Thence arises wonder in men. But

[2] *De Div. Nom.,* I, 5 (PG 3, 593).   [3] Q. 7, a. 1.   [4] *De Div. Nom.,* IV, 3 (PG 3, 697).   [5] Amaury of Bène (text in G. C. Capelle, *Amaury de Bène,* p. 105).

if the intellect of the rational creature could not attain to the first cause of things, the natural desire would remain vain.

Hence it must be granted absolutely that the blessed see the essence of God.

Reply Obj. 1. Both of these authorities speak of the vision of comprehension. Hence Dionysius premises immediately before the words cited, *He is universally to all incomprehensible*,[6] etc. Chrysostom, likewise, after the words quoted, says: *He says this of the most certain vision of the Father, which is such a perfect consideration and comprehension as the Father has of the Son.*[7]

Reply Obj. 2. The infinity of matter not made perfect by form, is unknown in itself, because all knowledge is through form; whereas the infinity of the form not limited by matter is in itself supremely known. God is infinite in this way, and not in the first way: as appears from what was said above.[8]

Reply Obj. 3. God is not said to be not existing as if He did not exist at all, but because He exists above all that exists, inasmuch as He is His own being. Hence it does not follow that He cannot be known at all, but that He transcends all knowledge; which means that He is not comprehended.

Reply Obj. 4. Proportion is twofold. In one sense it means a certain relation of one quantity to another, according to which double, treble and equal are species of proportion. In another sense, every relation of one thing to another is called proportion. And in this sense there can be a proportion of the creature to God, inasmuch as it is related to Him as the effect to its cause, and as potentiality to act; and in this way a created intellect can be proportioned to know God.

Second Article

WHETHER THE ESSENCE OF GOD IS SEEN BY A CREATED INTELLECT THROUGH A LIKENESS?

We proceed thus to the Second Article:—

Objection 1. It seems that the essence of God is seen by the created intellect through some likeness. For it is written: *We*

---

[6] *De Div. Nom.*, I, 5 (PG 3, 593).   [7] *In Ioann.*, hom. XV (PG 59, 99).   [8] Q. 7, a. 1.

know that when He shall appear, we shall be like to Him, and we shall see Him as He is (*1 John* iii. 2).

Obj. 2. Further, Augustine says: *When we know God, some likeness of God comes to be in us.*[9]

Obj. 3. Further, the intellect in act is the actual intelligible; as sense in act is the actual sensible. But this comes about inasmuch as the sense is informed with the likeness of the sensible thing, and the intellect with the likeness of the thing understood. Therefore, if God is seen actually by the created intellect, it must be that He is seen through some likeness.

On the contrary, Augustine says, that when the Apostle says, 'We see through a glass and in an enigma,' *by the terms 'glass' and 'enigma' certain likenesses are signified by him, which are accommodated to an understanding of God.*[10] But to see the essence of God is not an enigmatic or a reflected vision, but is, on the contrary, of an opposite kind. Therefore the divine essence is not seen through likenesses.

I answer that, Two things are required both for sensible and for intellectual vision—viz., power of sight, and union of the thing seen with the sight. For vision is made actual only when the thing seen is in a certain way in the seer. Now in corporeal things it is clear that the thing seen cannot be by its essence in the seer, but only by its likeness; as the likeness of a stone is in the eye, whereby the vision is made actual, whereas the substance of the stone is not there. But if the source of the visual power and the thing seen were one and the same thing, it would necessarily follow that the seer would possess both the visual power, and the form whereby it sees, from that one same thing.

Now it is manifest both that God is the author of the intellectual power and that He can be seen by the intellect. And since the intellectual power of the creature is not the essence of God, it follows that it is some kind of participated likeness of Him Who is the first intellect. Hence also the intellectual power of the creature is called an intelligible light, as it were, derived from the first light, whether this be understood of the natural power, or of some superadded perfection of grace or of glory. Therefore, in order to see God, there is

---

[9] *De Trin.,* IX, 11 (PL 42, 969).   [10] *Op. cit.,* XV, 9 (PL 42, 1069).

needed some likeness of God on the part of the visual power, whereby the intellect is made capable of seeing God. But on the part of the thing seen, which must in some way be united to the seer, the essence of God cannot be seen through any created likeness. First, because, as Dionysius says, *by the likenesses of the inferior order of things, the superior can in no way be known;*[11] as by the likeness of a body the essence of an incorporeal thing cannot be known. Much less therefore can the essence of God be seen through any created species whatever. Secondly, because the essence of God is His very being, as was shown above,[12] which cannot be said of any created form. Hence, no created form can be the likeness representing the essence of God to the seer. Thirdly, because the divine essence is uncircumscribed, and contains in itself supereminently whatever can be signified or understood by a created intellect. Now this cannot in any way be represented by any created species, for every created form is determined according to some aspect of wisdom, or of power, or of being itself, or of some like thing. Hence, to say that God is seen through some likeness is to say that the divine essence is not seen at all; which is false.

Therefore it must be said that to see the essence of God there is required some likeness in the visual power, namely, the light of glory strengthening the intellect to see God, which is spoken of in the *Psalm* (xxxv. 10): *In Thy light we shall see light.* The essence of God, however, cannot be seen by any created likeness representing the divine essence as it is in itself.

Reply Obj. 1. That authority speaks of the likeness which is caused by participation in the light of glory.

Reply Obj. 2. Augustine there speaks of the knowledge of God here on earth.[13]

Reply Obj. 3. The divine essence is being itself. Hence, as other intelligible forms which are not their own being are united to the intellect by means of some being whereby the intellect itself is informed and made in act, so the divine essence is united to the created intellect, as the object actually understood, making the intellect in act through itself.

[11] *De Div. Nom.*, I, 1 (PG 3, 588).   [12] Q. 3, a. 4.   [13] *De Trin.*, IX, 11 (PL 42, 969).

Third Article

WHETHER THE ESSENCE OF GOD CAN BE SEEN WITH THE BODILY EYE?

We proceed thus to the Third Article:—

Objection 1. It seems that the essence of God can be seen by the bodily eye. For it is written (*Job* xix. 26): *In my flesh I shall see . . . God,* and (*ibid.* xlii. 5), *With the hearing of the ear I have heard Thee, but now my eye seeth Thee.*

Obj. 2. Further, Augustine says: *Those eyes* (*namely, of the glorified*) *will therefore have a greater power of sight, not so much to see more keenly, as some report of the sight of serpents or of eagles* (*for whatever acuteness of vision is possessed by these creatures, they can see only corporeal things*), *but to see even incorporeal things.*[14] Now whoever can see incorporeal things, can be raised up to see God. Therefore the glorified eye can see God.

Obj. 3. Further, God can be seen by man through a vision of the imagination. For it is written: *I saw the Lord sitting upon a throne,* etc. (*Isa.* vi. 1). But an imaginary vision originates from sense; for imagination is a movement produced by the sense in act.[15] Therefore God can be seen by a vision of sense.

On the contrary, Augustine says: *No one has ever seen God as He is either in this life, or in the angelic life, in the manner that visible things are seen by corporeal vision.*[16]

I answer that, It is impossible for God to be seen by the sense of sight, or by any other sense or power of the sensitive part of the soul. For every such power is the act of a corporeal organ, as will be shown later.[17] Now act is proportioned to the being whose act it is. Hence no power of that kind can go beyond corporeal things. But God is incorporeal, as was shown above.[18] Hence, He cannot be seen by the sense or the imagination, but only by the intellect.

Reply Obj. 1. The words, *In my flesh I shall see God my Saviour,* do not mean that God will be seen with the eye of flesh, but that man existing in the flesh after the resurrection

---

[14] *De Civit. Dei,* XXII, 29 (PL 41, 799).   [15] Aristotle, *De An.,* III, 3 (429a 1).   [16] *Epist.* CXLVII, 11 (PL 33, 609).   [17] Q. 78, a. 1.   [18] Q. 3, a. 1.

will see God. Likewise the words, *Now my eye seeth Thee*,
are to be understood of the mind's eye, as the Apostle says:
*May He give unto you the spirit of wisdom . . . in the
knowledge of Him,* that *the eyes of your heart* may be *enlightened* (*Ephes.* i. 17, 18).

Reply Obj. 2. Augustine speaks[19] as one inquiring, and
conditionally. This appears from what preceded that remark:
Therefore they will have an altogether different power [viz.,
glorified eyes], *if through it they shall see that incorporeal
nature;* and afterwards he explains this, saying: *It is very
credible that we shall so see the mundane bodies of the new
heavens and the new earth, as to see most clearly God everywhere present and governing all corporeal things; not as we
now see the invisible things of God as understood by what
is made, but as when we see men among whom we live, living
and exercising the functions of human life, we do not believe
they live, but see it.* Hence it is evident that the glorified
eyes will see God in the way that now our eyes see the life
of another. But life is not seen with the bodily eye as a thing
in itself visible, but as the accidental object of the sense;
which indeed is not known by sense, but at once, together
with sense, by some other cognitive power. But that the
divine presence is known by the intellect immediately on
the sight of, and through corporeal things, happens from two
causes—viz., from the perspicacity of the intellect, and from
the refulgence of the divine glory infused into the body after
its renovation.

Reply Obj. 3. The essence of God is not seen in a vision
of the imagination, but the imagination receives some form
representing God according to some mode of likeness; as in
divine Scripture divine things are metaphorically described
by means of sensible things.

Fourth Article

WHETHER ANY CREATED INTELLECT BY ITS NATURAL
POWERS CAN SEE THE DIVINE ESSENCE?

We proceed thus to the Fourth Article:—
Objection 1. It seems that a created intellect can see the
divine essence by its own natural power. For Dionysius says:

[19] *De Civit. Dei,* XXII, 29 (PL 41, 780).

An angel is a pure mirror, most clear, receiving, if it is permissible to say so, the whole beauty of God.[20] But the original is seen when its reflection is seen. Therefore, since an angel understands himself by his natural power, it seems that by his own natural power he understands the divine essence.

Obj. 2. Further, what is supremely visible is made less visible to us by reason of our defective bodily or intellectual sight. But the angelic intellect has no defect. Therefore, since God is supremely intelligible in Himself, it seems that in like manner He is supremely so to an angel. Therefore, if the angel can understand other intelligible things by his own natural power, all the more can he understand God.

Obj. 3. Further, bodily sense cannot be raised up to understand incorporeal substance, since it is above its nature. Therefore, if to see the essence of God is above the nature of every created intellect, it follows that no created intellect can reach the vision of the essence of God at all. But this is false, as appears from what is said above. Therefore it seems that it is natural for a created intellect to see the divine essence.

On the contrary, It is written: *The grace of God is life everlasting* (*Rom.* vi. 23). But life everlasting consists in the vision of the divine essence, according to the words: *This is eternal life, that they may know Thee the only true God,* etc. (*Jo.* xvii. 3). Therefore, to see the essence of God is possible to the created intellect by grace, and not by nature.

I answer that, It is impossible for any created intellect to see the essence of God by its own natural power. For knowledge takes place according as the thing known is in the knower. But the thing known is in the knower according to the mode of the knower. Hence the knowledge of every knower is according to the mode of its own nature. If therefore the mode of being of a given thing exceeds the mode of the knower, it must result that the knowledge of that thing is above the nature of the knower. Now the mode of being of things is manifold. For some things have being only in this individual matter; such are all bodies. There are other beings whose natures are themselves subsisting, not residing in matter at all, which, however, are not their own being, but receive it: and these are the incorporeal substances called an-

---

[20] *De Div. Nom.*, IV, 22 (PG 3, 724).

gels. But to God alone does it belong to be His own subsistent being.

Therefore, what exists only in individual matter we know naturally, since our soul, through which we know, is the form of some particular matter. Now our soul possesses two cognitive powers. One is the act of a corporeal organ, which naturally knows things existing in individual matter; hence sense knows only the singular. But there is another kind of cognitive power in the soul, called the intellect; and this is not the act of any corporeal organ. Therefore the intellect naturally knows natures which exist only in individual matter; not indeed as they are in such individual matter, but according as they are abstracted therefrom by the consideration of the intellect. Hence it follows that through the intellect we can understand these things in a universal way; and this is beyond the power of sense. Now the angelic intellect naturally knows natures that are not in matter; but this is beyond the power of the intellect of the human soul in the state of its present life, united as it is to the body.

It follows, therefore, that to know self-subsistent being is natural to the divine intellect alone, and that it is beyond the natural power of any created intellect; for no creature is its own being, since its being is participated. Therefore, a created intellect cannot see the essence of God unless God by His grace unites Himself to the created intellect, as an object made intelligible to it.

Reply Obj. 1. This mode of knowing God is natural to an angel—namely, to know Him by His own likeness refulgent in the angel himself. But to know God by any created likeness is not to know the essence of God, as was shown above. Hence it does not follow that an angel can know the essence of God by his own power.

Reply Obj. 2. The angelic intellect is not defective, if defect be taken to mean privation, as if it were without anything which it ought to have. But if defect be taken negatively, in that sense every creature is defective, when compared with God, since it does not possess the excellence which is in God.

Reply Obj. 3. The sense of sight, as being altogether material, cannot be raised up to anything immaterial. But our intellect, or the angelic intellect, inasmuch as it is elevated above matter in its own nature, can be raised up above its own nature to a higher level by grace. An indication of this is that sight cannot in any way know in abstraction what it knows concretely; for in no way can it perceive a nature except as this one particular nature; whereas our intellect is able to consider in abstraction what it knows in concretion. For although it knows things which have a form residing in matter, still it resolves the composite into both elements, and considers the form separately by itself. Likewise, also, the intellect of an angel, although it naturally knows the being concreted in any nature, still it is able to separate that being by its intellect; since it knows that the thing itself is one thing, and its being is another. Since therefore a created intellect is naturally capable of apprehending the concreted form and the concreted being in abstraction, by way of a certain resolution, it can by grace be raised up to know separate subsisting substance and separate subsisting being.

Fifth Article

WHETHER THE CREATED INTELLECT NEEDS ANY CREATED LIGHT IN ORDER TO SEE THE ESSENCE OF GOD?

We proceed thus to the Fifth Article:—

Objection 1. It seems that the created intellect does not need any created light in order to see the essence of God. For what is of itself lucid in sensible things does not require any other light in order to be seen. Therefore the same applies to intelligible things. Now God is intelligible light [*lux*]. Therefore He is not seen by the means of any created light [*lumen*].

Obj. 2. Further, if God is seen through a medium, He is not seen in His essence. But if seen by any created light, He is seen through a medium. Therefore He is not seen in His essence.

Obj. 3. Further, what is created can be natural to some creature. Therefore, if the essence of God is seen through any created light, such a light could be made natural to some creature. And thus, that creature would not need any other light to see God; which is impossible. Therefore it is not necessary that every creature should require a superadded light in order to see the essence of God.

On the contrary, It is written: *In Thy light we shall see light* (*Ps.* xxxv. 10).

I answer that, Everything which is raised up to what exceeds its nature must be prepared by some disposition above its nature; as, for example, if air is to receive the form of fire, it must be prepared by some disposition for such a form. But when any created intellect sees the essence of God, the essence of God itself becomes the intelligible form of the intellect. Hence it is necessary that some supernatural disposition should be added to the intellect in order that it may be raised up to such a great height. Now since the natural power of the created intellect does not enable it to see the essence of God, as was shown above, it is necessary that its power of understanding should be increased by divine grace. Now this increase of the intellectual powers is called the illumination of the intellect, as we also call the intelligible itself by the name of light or illumination. And this is the light spoken of in the *Apocalypse* (xxi. 23): *The glory of God hath enlightened it*—viz., the society of the blessed who see God. By this light the blessed are made *deiform*—that is, like to God, according to the saying: *When He shall appear we shall be like to Him, and we shall see Him as He is* (*1 John* iii. 2).

Reply Obj. 1. A created light is necessary to see the essence of God, not in order to make the essence of God intelligible, which is of itself intelligible, but in order to enable the intellect to understand in the same way as a habit makes a power more able to act. In the same way, corporeal light is necessary as regards external sight, inasmuch as it makes the medium actually transparent, and susceptible of color.

Reply Obj. 2. This light is required to see the divine essence, not as a likeness in which God is seen, but as a perfection of the intellect, strengthening it to see God. Therefore it may be said that this light is not a medium *in which* God is seen, but one *by which* He is seen; and such a medium does not take away the immediate vision of God.

Reply Obj. 3. The disposition to the form of fire can be natural only to the subject of that form. Hence the light of glory cannot be natural to a creature unless the creature were to have a divine nature; which is impossible. For by this light the rational creature is made deiform, as was said above.

Sixth Article

WHETHER OF THOSE WHO SEE THE ESSENCE OF GOD, ONE SEES MORE PERFECTLY THAN ANOTHER?

We proceed thus to the Sixth Article:—

Objection 1. It seems that of those who see the essence of God, one does not see more perfectly than another. For it is written (*1 John* iii. 2): *We shall see Him as He is.* But He is only in one way. Therefore He will be seen by all in one way only; and therefore He will not be seen more perfectly by one and less perfectly by another.

Obj. 2. Further, Augustine says that one person cannot understand one and the same thing more perfectly than another.[21] But all who see God in His essence have an understanding of the divine essence; for God is seen by the intellect and not by sense, as was shown above. Therefore of those who see the divine essence, one does not see more clearly than another.

Obj. 3. Further, That anything be seen more perfectly than another can happen in two ways: either on the part of the visible object, or on the part of the visual power of the seer. On the part of the object, it may so happen because the object is received more perfectly in the seer, that is, according to a more perfect likeness; but this does not apply to the present question, for God is present to the intellect seeing His essence not through any likeness, but through His essence. It follows then that if one is to see Him more perfectly than another, this will happen according to a difference in intellectual power. Thus it follows too that the one whose intellectual power is the higher will see Him the more clearly; and this is incongruous, since equality with angels is promised to men as their beatitude.

On the contrary, Eternal life consists in the vision of God, according to *John* (xvii. 3): *This is eternal life, that they may know Thee the only true God,* etc. Therefore, if all see the essence of God equally in eternal life, all will be equal; the contrary to which is declared by the Apostle: *Star differs from star in glory* (*1 Cor.* xv. 41).

[21] *Lib. 83 Quaest.,* q. 32 (PL 40, 22).

I answer that, Of those who see the essence of God, one
sees Him more perfectly than another. This does not take
place as if one had a more perfect likeness of God than another, since that vision will not be through any likeness. But
it will take place because one intellect will have a greater
power or faculty to see God than another. The faculty of
seeing God, however, does not belong to the created intellect
naturally but through the light of glory, which establishes
the intellect in a kind of *deiformity*, as appears from what
is said above. Hence the intellect which has more of the light
of glory will see God the more perfectly. But he will have
a fuller participation of the light of glory who has more
charity, because where there is the greater charity, there is
the more desire, and desire in a certain manner makes the one
desiring apt and prepared to receive the object desired.
Hence he who possesses the more charity, will see God the
more perfectly, and will be the more beatified.

Reply Obj. 1. In the words, *We shall see Him as He is,* the
conjunction *as* determines the mode of vision on the part of
the object seen, so that the meaning is, we shall see Him to
be as He is, because we shall see His being, which is His
essence. But it does not determine the mode of vision on the
part of the one seeing; as if the meaning was that the mode
of seeing God will be as perfect as is the mode of God's being.

Thus appears the answer to the Second Objection. For
when it is said that one intellect does not understand one and
the same thing better than another, this would be true if
referred to the mode of the thing understood; for whoever
understands it otherwise than it really is does not understand
it truly. But if it is referred to the mode of understanding,
then the statement is not true, for the understanding of one
is more perfect than the understanding of another.

Reply Obj. 3. The diversity of seeing will not arise because
of the object seen, for the same object will be presented to
all—viz., the essence of God; nor will it arise from the diverse participation of the object through different likenesses;
but it will arise because of the diverse faculty of the intellect,
not, indeed, the natural faculty, but the glorified faculty, as
was said.

Seventh Article

WHETHER THOSE WHO SEE THE ESSENCE OF GOD COMPREHEND HIM?

We proceed thus to the Seventh Article:—

Objection 1. It seems that those who see the divine essence comprehend God. For the Apostle says (*Phil.* iii. 12): *But I follow after, if I may by any means comprehend.* But the Apostle did not follow in vain, for he himself said (*1 Cor.* ix. 26): *I . . . so run, not as at an uncertainty.* Therefore he comprehended; and in the same way others also, whom he invites to do the same, saying: *So run that you may comprehend.*

Obj. 2. Further, Augustine says: *That is comprehended which is so seen as a whole, that nothing of it is hidden from the seer.*[22] But if God is seen in His essence, He is seen whole, and nothing of Him is hidden from the seer, since God is simple. Therefore, whoever sees His essence, comprehends Him.

Obj. 3. Further, if it be said that He is seen as a *whole,* but *not wholly,* it may be contrarily urged that *wholly* refers either to the mode of the seer or to the mode of the thing seen. But he who sees the essence of God sees Him wholly, if the mode of the thing seen is considered, since he sees Him as He is; so, too, he sees Him wholly if the mode of the seer be meant, since the intellect will with its full power see the divine essence. Therefore all who see the essence of God see Him wholly; therefore they comprehend Him.

On the contrary, It is written: *O most mighty, great, and powerful, the Lord of hosts is Thy Name. Great in counsel, and incomprehensible in thought* (*Jer.* xxxii. 18, 19). Therefore, He cannot be comprehended.

I answer that, It is impossible for any created intellect to comprehend God; but *to attain to God with the mind in some degree is great beatitude,* as Augustine says.[23]

In proof of this we must consider that what is comprehended is perfectly known; and that is perfectly known which is known so far as it can be known. Thus, if anything which is capable of scientific demonstration is held only by

[22] *Epist.* CXLVIII, 9 (PL 33, 606).   [23] *Serm.* CXVII, 3 (PL 38, 663).

an opinion resting on a probable proof, it is not comprehended. For instance, if anyone knows by scientific demonstration that a triangle has three angles equal to two right
angles, he comprehends that truth; whereas if anyone accepts it as a probable opinion because wise men or most men
teach it, he does not comprehend the thing itself, because he
does not attain to that perfect mode of knowledge of which it
is intrinsically capable. But no created intellect can attain to
that perfect mode of the knowledge of the divine intellect
whereof it is intrinsically capable. Here is the proof. Everything is knowable according to its actuality. But God, Whose
being is infinite, as was shown above,[24] is infinitely knowable.
Now no created intellect can know God infinitely. For a
created intellect knows the divine essence more or less perfectly in proportion as it receives a greater or lesser light of
glory. Since therefore the created light of glory received into
any created intellect cannot be infinite, it is clearly impossible for any created intellect to know God in an infinite degree. Hence it is impossible that it should comprehend God.

   Reply Obj. 1. *Comprehension* is twofold: in one sense it
is taken strictly and properly, according as something is included in the one comprehending; and thus in no way is God
comprehended either by the intellect or by anything else;
for since He is infinite, He cannot be included in any finite
being, so that a finite being contain Him infinitely, as befits
Him. It is in this sense that we now take *comprehension.*
But in another sense *comprehension* is taken more largely as
opposed to *non-attainment*; for he who attains to anyone is
said to comprehend him when he attains to him. And in this
sense God is comprehended by the blessed, according to the
words, *I held him, and I will not let him go (Cant.* iii. 4);
in this sense also are to be understood the words quoted from
the Apostle concerning comprehension. According to this
meaning, *comprehension* is one of the three prerogatives of
the soul, answering to hope, as vision answers to faith, and
fruition answers to charity. For even among ourselves not
everything seen is held or possessed, since things sometimes
appear afar off, or they are not in our power of attainment.
Neither, again, do we always enjoy what we possess, either
because we find no pleasure in them, or because such things

²⁴ Q. 7, a. 1.

are not the ultimate end of our desire, so as to give it fulfillment and peace. But the blessed possess these three things in God, because they see Him, and in seeing Him, possess Him as present, having the power to see Him always; and possessing Him, they enjoy Him as the ultimate fulfillment of desire.

Reply Obj. 2. God is called incomprehensible not because anything of Him is not seen, but because He is not seen as perfectly as He is capable of being seen. Thus, when any demonstrable proposition is known by a probable reason only, it does not follow that any part of it is unknown, either the subject, or the predicate, or the composition; but as a whole it is not as perfectly known as it is capable of being known. Hence Augustine, in his definition of comprehension, says: *a whole is comprehended when it is seen in such a way that nothing of it is hidden from the seer, or when its boundaries can be completely viewed or traced;*[25] for the boundaries of a thing are said to be completely surveyed when the end of the knowledge of it is attained.

Reply Obj. 3. The word *wholly* denotes a mode of the object; not that the whole object does not come under knowledge, but that the mode of the object is not the mode of the one who knows. Therefore, he who sees God's essence sees in Him that He exists infinitely, and is infinitely knowable. Nevertheless, this infinite mode does not extend to enable the knower to know. infinitely; thus, for instance, a person can have a probable opinion that a proposition is demonstrable, although he himself does not know it as demonstrated.

Eighth Article

WHETHER THOSE WHO SEE THE ESSENCE OF GOD SEE ALL IN GOD?

We proceed thus to the Eighth Article:—

Objection 1. It seems that those who see the essence of God see all things in God. For Gregory says: *What do they not see, who see Him Who sees all things?* [26] But God sees all things. Therefore, those who see God see all things.

Obj. 2. Further, whoever sees a mirror, sees what is reflected in the mirror. But all actual or possible things shine

[25] *Epist.* CXLVII, 9 (PL 33, 606).   [26] *Dial.,* IV, 33 (PL 77, 376).

forth in God as in a mirror; for He knows all things in Himself. Therefore, whoever sees God, sees all actual things, and also all possible things.

Obj. 3. Further, whoever understands the greater, can understand the least, as is said in *De Anima* iii.[27] But all that God does, or can do, is less than His essence. Therefore, whoever understands God, can understand all that God does or can do.

Obj. 4. Further, the rational creature naturally desires to know all things. Therefore, if in seeing God it does not know all things, its natural desire will not rest satisfied. Hence, in seeing God it will not be fully happy; which is incongruous. Therefore, he who sees God knows all things.

On the contrary, The angels see the essence of God, and yet they do not know all things. For, as Dionysius says, *the inferior angels are cleansed from ignorance by the superior angels.*[28] Also they are ignorant of future contingent things, and of secret thoughts; for this knowledge belongs to God alone. Therefore, whosoever sees the essence of God does not know all things.

I answer that, A created intellect, in seeing the divine essence, does not see in it all that God does or can do. For it is manifest that things are seen in God according as they are in Him. But all things are in God as effects are in the power of their cause. Therefore all things are seen in God as an effect is seen in its cause. Now it is clear that the more perfectly a cause is seen, the more of its effects can be seen in it. For whoever has a lofty understanding, as soon as one demonstrative principle is put before him, can gather the knowledge of many conclusions; but this is beyond one of a weaker intellect, for he needs things to be explained to him separately. And so that intellect can know all the effects of a cause and the reasons for those effects in the cause itself which comprehends the cause wholly. Now no created intellect can comprehend God wholly, as was shown above. Therefore, no created intellect, in seeing God, can know all that God does or can do, for this would be to comprehend His power; but, among the things that God does or can do, any intellect can know the more, the more perfectly it sees God.

Reply Obj. 1. Gregory speaks concerning the sufficiency of

[27] Aristotle, *De An.*, III, 4 (429b 3).   [28] *De Cael. Hier.*, VII, 3 (PG 3, 208).

the object, namely, God, Who in Himself sufficiently contains and shows forth all things; but it does not follow that whoever sees God knows all things, for he does not perfectly comprehend Him.

Reply Obj. 2. It is not necessary that whoever sees a mirror should see all that is in the mirror, unless his glance comprehends the mirror itself.

Reply Obj. 3. Although it is greater to see God than to see all things else, still it is a greater thing to see Him so that all things are known in Him, than to see Him in such a way that not all things, but fewer or more, are known in Him. For it has already been shown that the number of things known in God varies according as He is seen more or less perfectly.

Reply Obj. 4. The natural desire of a rational creature is to know everything that belongs to the perfection of the intellect, namely, the species and genera of things and their essences, and these everyone who sees the divine essence will see in God. But to know other singulars, their thoughts and their deeds, does not belong to the perfection of a created intellect nor does its natural desire go out to these things; neither, again, does it desire to know things that as yet do not exist, but which God can call into being. But if God alone were seen, Who is the fount and source of all being and of all truth, He would so fill the natural desire for knowledge that nothing else would be desired, and the seer would be completely beatified. Hence Augustine says: *Unhappy the man who knoweth all these* [that is, all creatures] *and knoweth not Thee! but happy whoso knoweth Thee although he know not these. And whoso knoweth both Thee and them is not the happier for them, but for Thee alone.*[29]

Ninth Article

WHETHER WHAT IS SEEN IN GOD, BY THOSE WHO SEE THE DIVINE ESSENCE, IS SEEN THROUGH ANY LIKENESS?

We proceed thus to the Ninth Article:—

Objection 1. It seems that what is seen in God by those who see the divine essence is seen by means of some likeness. For every kind of knowledge comes about by the knower being assimilated to the object known. For thus the intellect

[29] *Confess.*, V, 4 (PL 32, 708).

in act becomes the actual intelligible, and the sense in act becomes the actual sensible, inasmuch as it is informed by a likeness of the object, as the eye by the likeness of color. Therefore, if the intellect of one who sees the divine essence understands any creatures in God, it must be informed by their likenesses.

Obj. 2. Further, what we have seen, we keep in memory. But Paul, seeing the essence of God while in rapture, when he had ceased to see the divine essence, as Augustine says,[30] remembered many of the things he had seen in that rapture; hence he said: I have *heard secret words which it is not granted to man to utter* (2 *Cor.* xii. 4). Therefore it must be said that certain likenesses of what he remembered remained in his mind; and in the same way, when he actually saw the essence of God, he had certain likenesses or species of what he actually saw in it.

On the contrary, A mirror and what is in it are seen by means of one species. But all things are seen in God as in an intelligible mirror. Therefore, if God Himself is not seen by any likeness but by His own essence, neither are the things seen in Him seen by any likenesses or species.

I answer that, Those who see the divine essence see what they see in God not by any likeness, but by the divine essence itself united to their intellect. For each thing is known in so far as its likeness is in the one who knows. Now this takes place in two ways. For as things which are like to one and the same thing are like to each other, a cognitive power can be assimilated to any knowable object in two ways. In one way, it is assimilated by the object itself, when it is directly informed by the likeness of the object; in which case the object is known in itself. In another way, when the cognitive power is informed by a species of something which resembles the object; and in this way the knowledge is not of the thing in itself, but of the thing in its likeness. For the knowledge of a man in himself differs from the knowledge of him in his image. Hence, to know things thus by their likeness in the one who knows, is to know them in themselves or in their own natures; whereas to know them by their likenesses pre-existing in God is to see them in God. Now there is a differ-

---

[30] *De Genesi ad Litt.,* XII, 28; 34 (PL 34, 478; 483); *Epist.* CXLVII, 13 (PL 33, 611).

ence between these two kinds of knowledge. Hence, according to the knowledge whereby things are known by those who see the essence of God, they are seen in God Himself not by any other likenesses but by the divine essence alone present to the intellect; by which also God Himself is seen.

Reply Obj. 1. The created intellect of one who sees God is assimilated to the things seen in God inasmuch as it is united to the divine essence, in which the likenesses of all things pre-exist.

Reply Obj. 2. There are some cognitive powers which can form other images from those first conceived: thus the imagination from the preconceived species of a mountain and of gold forms the likeness of a golden mountain; and the intellect, from the preconceived ideas of genus and difference, forms the idea of species. In like manner, from the likeness of an image we can form in our minds the likenesses of the original of the image. Thus Paul, or any other person who sees God, by the very vision of the divine essence, can form in himself the likenesses of the things seen in the divine essence; which remained in Paul even when he had ceased to see the essence of God. Still, this kind of vision, whereby things are seen by these species thus conceived, is not the same as that whereby things are seen in God.

Tenth Article

WHETHER THOSE WHO SEE THE ESSENCE OF GOD SEE ALL THEY SEE IN IT AT THE SAME TIME?

We proceed thus to the Tenth Article:—

Objection 1. It seems that those who see the essence of God do not see all they see in Him at one and the same time. For, according to the Philosopher: *It may happen that many things are known, but only one is understood.*[31] But what is seen in God, is understood; for God is seen by the intellect. Therefore, those who see God do not see many things in Him at the same time.

Obj. 2. Further, Augustine says, *God moves the spiritual creature according to time*[32]—that is, by intelligence and affection. But the spiritual creature is the angel, who sees

[31] *Top.*, II, 10 (114b 34).   [32] *De Genesi ad Litt.*, VIII, 20; 22 (PL 34, 388; 389).

God. Therefore those who see God understand and are affected successively; for time means succession.

On the contrary, Augustine says: *Our thoughts will not be unstable, going to and fro from one thing to another; but we shall see all we know at one glance.*[33]

I answer that, What is seen in the Word is seen not successively, but at the same time. In proof whereof, the reason why we ourselves cannot know many things all at once is because we understand many things by means of diverse species. But our intellect cannot be actually informed by diverse species at the same time, so as to understand by them; as one body cannot bear different shapes simultaneously. Hence, when many things can be understood by one species, they are understood at the same time; as the diverse parts of a whole are understood successively, and not all at the same time, if each one is understood by its own species, whereas if all are understood under the one species of the whole, they are understood simultaneously. Now it was shown above that things seen in God are not seen singly by their own similitude, but all are seen by the one essence of God. Hence they are seen simultaneously, and not successively.

Reply Obj. 1. We understand one thing only when we understand by one species; but many things understood by one species are understood simultaneously, as in the species of a *man* we understand *animal* and *rational,* and in the species of a *house* we understand the *wall* and the *roof.*

Reply Obj. 2. As regards their natural knowledge, whereby they know things by the diverse species with which they are endowed, the angels do not know all things simultaneously, and thus, in understanding, they are moved according to time; but as regards the things which they see in God, they see all at the same time.

Eleventh Article

WHETHER ANYONE IN THIS LIFE CAN SEE THE ESSENCE OF GOD?

We proceed thus to the Eleventh Article:—
Objection 1. It seems that in this life one can see the divine essence. For Jacob said: *I have seen God face to face (Gen.*

[33] *De Trin.,* XV, 16 (PL 42, 1079).

xxxii. 30). But to see Him face to face is to see His essence, as appears from the words: *We see now in a glass and in a dark manner, but then face to face* (*1 Cor.* xiii. 12). Therefore God can be seen in this life in His essence.

Obj. 2. Further, the Lord said of Moses: *I speak to him mouth to mouth, and plainly, and not by riddles and figures doth he see the Lord* (*Num.* xii. 8); but this is to see God in His essence. Therefore it is possible to see the essence of God in this life.

Obj. 3. Further, that wherein we know all other things, and whereby we judge of other things, is in itself known to us. But even now we know all things in God; for Augustine says: *If we both see that what you say is true, and we both see that what I say is true, where, I ask, do we see this? neither I in thee, nor thou in me; but both of us in that incommutable truth itself above our minds.*[34] He also says that, *We judge of all things according to the divine truth,*[35] and that, *it is the business of reason to judge of these corporeal things according to the incorporeal and eternal ideas; which, unless they were above the mind, could not be incommutable.*[36] Therefore even in this life we see God himself.

Obj. 4. Further, according to Augustine, those things that are in the soul by their essence are seen by intellectual vision.[37] But intellectual vision is of intelligible things, not by any likenesses, but by their very essences, as he also says there. Therefore, since God is in our soul by His essence, it follows that He is seen by us in His essence.

On the contrary, It is written, *Man shall not see Me, and live* (*Exod.* xxxiii. 20), and the *Gloss* upon this says: *In this mortal life God can be seen by certain images, but not by the likeness itself of His own nature.*[38]

I answer that, God cannot be seen in His essence by one who is merely man, except he be separated from this mortal life. The reason is, because, as was said above, the mode of knowledge follows the mode of the nature of the knower. But our soul, as long as we live in this life, has its being in corporeal matter; hence it knows naturally only what has a form in matter, or what can be known by such a form. Now

---

[34] *Confess.*, XII, 25 (PL 32, 840).   [35] *De Vera Relig.*, XXX; XXXI (PL 34, 146; 147).   [36] *De Trin.*, XII, 2 (PL 42, 999).   [37] *De Genesi ad Litt.*, XII, 24; 31 (PL 34, 474; 479).   [38] *Glossa ordin.* (I, 203B).

it is evident that the divine essence cannot be known through the nature of material things. For it was shown above that the knowledge of God by means of any created likeness is not the vision of His essence. Hence it is impossible for the soul of man in this life to see the essence of God. This can be seen in the fact that the more our soul is abstracted from corporeal things, the more it is capable of receiving abstract intelligible things. Hence in dreams and alienations of the bodily senses, divine revelations and foresight of future events are perceived the more clearly. It is not possible, therefore, that the soul in this mortal life should be raised up to the highest of intelligible objects, that is, to the divine essence.

Reply Obj. 1. According to Dionysius, *a man is said in the Scriptures to have seen God in the sense that certain figures were formed in the senses or imagination, according to some likeness representing something divine.*[39] So when Jacob says, *I have seen God face to face,* this does not mean the divine essence, but some figure representing God. And this is to be referred to some high mode of prophecy, so that God is seen to speak, though in an imaginary vision; as will later be explained in treating of the degrees of prophecy.[40] We may also say that Jacob spoke thus to designate some exalted intellectual contemplation, above the ordinary state.

Reply Obj. 2. As God works miracles in corporeal things, so also He does supernatural wonders above the common order, raising the minds of some living in the flesh, but who forego the use of the senses, even up to the vision of His own essence; as Augustine says of Moses, the teacher of the Jews, and of Paul, the teacher of the Gentiles.[41] This will be treated more fully in the question on rapture.[42]

Reply Obj. 3. All things are said to be seen in God, and all things are judged in Him, because by the participation of His light we know and judge all things; for the very light of natural reason is a participation of the divine light; as likewise we are said to see and judge of sensible things in the sun, that is, by the sun's light. Hence Augustine says, *The lessons of instruction can be seen only if they be il-*

[39] *De Cael. Hier.,* IV, 3 (PG 3, 180).   [40] *S.T.* II-II, q. 174, a. 3. [41] *De Genesi ad Litt.,* XII, 26; 27; 28; 34 (PL 34, 476; 477; 478; 482); *Epist.* CXLVII, 13 (PL 33, 610).   [42] *S.T.* II-II, q. 175, a. 3, 4, 5 and 6.

lumined by their own sun,[43] namely, God. Just as therefore, in order to see a sensible thing it is not necessary to see the substance of the sun, so in like manner to see something intelligible, it is not necessary to see the essence of God.

Reply Obj. 4. Intellectual vision is of the things which are in the soul by their essence, as intelligible things are in the intellect. And thus God is in the souls of the blessed; not thus is He in our soul, but by presence, essence, and power.

Twelfth Article

WHETHER GOD CAN BE KNOWN IN THIS LIFE BY NATURAL REASON?

We proceed thus to the Twelfth Article:—

Objection 1. It seems that by natural reason we cannot know God in this life. For Boethius says that *reason does not grasp a simple form.*[44] But God is a supremely simple form, as was shown above.[45] Therefore natural reason cannot attain to know Him.

Obj. 2. Further, the soul understands nothing by natural reason without an image.[46] But we cannot have an image of God, Who is incorporeal. Therefore we cannot know God by natural knowledge.

Obj. 3. Further, the knowledge of natural reason belongs to both good and evil, inasmuch as they have a common nature. But the knowledge of God belongs only to the good; for Augustine says: *The eye of the human mind is not fixed on that excellent light unless purified by the justice of faith.*[47] Therefore God cannot be known by natural reason.

On the contrary, It is written (*Rom.* i. 19), *That which is known of God,* namely, what can be known of God by natural reason, *is manifest in them.*

I answer that, Our natural knowledge begins from sense. Hence our natural knowledge can go as far as it can be led by sensible things. But our intellect cannot be led by sense so far as to see the essence of God; because sensible creatures are effects of God which do not equal the power of God, their cause. Hence from the knowledge of sensible things the whole

---

[43] *Solil.*, I, 8 (PL 32, 877).   [44] *De Consol.*, V, prose 4 (PL 63, 847).
[45] Q. 3, a. 7.   [46] Aristotle, *De An.*, III, 7 (431a 16).   [47] *De Trin.*, I, 2 (PL 42, 822).

power of God cannot be known; nor therefore can His essence be seen. But because they are His effects and depend on their cause, we can be led from them so far as to know of God *whether He exists*, and to know of Him what must necessarily belong to Him, as the first cause of all things, exceeding all things caused by Him.

Hence, we know His relationship with creatures, that is, that He is the cause of all things; also that creatures differ from Him, inasmuch as He is not in any way part of what is caused by Him; and that His effects are removed from Him, not by reason of any defect on His part, but because He superexceeds them all.

Reply Obj. 1. Reason cannot reach a simple form, so as to know *what it is*; but it can know *whether it is*.

Reply Obj. 2. God is known by natural knowledge through the images of His effects.

Reply Obj. 3. Since the knowledge of God's essence is by grace, it belongs only to the good, but the knowledge of Him by natural reason can belong to both good and bad; and hence Augustine says, retracting what he had said before: *I do not approve what I said in prayer, 'God who willest that only the pure should know truth.'* [48] *For it can be answered that many who are not pure know many truths,*[49] that is, by natural reason.

Thirteenth Article

WHETHER BY GRACE A HIGHER KNOWLEDGE OF GOD CAN BE OBTAINED THAN BY NATURAL REASON?

We proceed thus to the Thirteenth Article:—

Objection 1. It seems that by grace a higher knowledge of God is not obtained than by natural reason. For Dionysius says that whoever is the better united to God in this life, is united to Him as to one entirely unknown.[50] He says the same of Moses, who nevertheless obtained a certain excellence by the knowledge conferred by grace. But to be united to God, while not knowing of Him *what He is*, comes about also by natural reason. Therefore God is not more known to us by grace than by natural reason.

---

[48] *Solil.*, I, 1 (PL 32, 870).   [49] *Retract.*, I, 4 (PL 32, 589).   [50] *De Myst. Theol.*, I, 3 (PG 3, 1001).

Obj. 2. Further, we can acquire the knowledge of divine things by natural reason only through images; and the same applies to the knowledge given by grace. For Dionysius says that *it is impossible for the divine ray to shine upon us except as screened round about by the many colored sacred veils.*[51] Therefore we do know God more fully by grace than by natural reason.

Obj. 3. Further, our intellect adheres to God by the grace of faith. But faith does not seem to be knowledge; for Gregory says that *things not seen are the objects of faith, and not of knowledge.*[52] Therefore there is not given to us a more excellent knowledge of God by grace.

On the contrary, The Apostle says that *God hath revealed to us by His Spirit,* what *none of the princes of this world knew* (*1 Cor.* ii. 8, 10), namely, *the philosophers,* as the *Gloss* expounds.[53]

I answer that, We have a more perfect knowledge of God by grace than by natural reason. Which is proved thus. The knowledge which we have by natural reason requires two things: images derived from the sensible things, and a natural intelligible light enabling us to abstract intelligible conceptions from them.

Now in both of these, human knowledge is assisted by the revelation of grace. For the intellect's natural light is strengthened by the infusion of gratuitous light, and sometimes also the images in the imagination are divinely formed, so as to express divine things better than do those which we receive naturally from sensible things, as appears in prophetic visions; while sometimes sensible things, or even voices, are divinely formed to express some divine meaning; as in the Baptism, the Holy Ghost was seen in the shape of a dove, and the voice of the Father was heard, *This is My beloved Son* (*Matt.* iii. 17).

Reply Obj. 1. Although by the revelation of grace in this life we do not know of God *what He is,* and thus are united to Him as to one unknown, still we know Him more fully according as many and more excellent of His effects are demonstrated to us, and according as we attribute to Him some things known by divine revelation, to which natural

---

[51] *De Cael. Hier.,* I, 2 (PG 3, 121).   [52] *In Evang.,* II, hom. 26 (PL 76, 1202).   [53] *Glossa interl.,* super *1 Cor.* II, 10 (VI, 36r).

reason cannot reach, as, for instance, that God is Three and One.

Reply Obj. 2. From the images either naturally received from sense, or divinely formed in the imagination, we have so much the more excellent intellectual knowledge, the stronger the intelligible light is in man; and thus through the revelation given by the images a fuller knowledge is received by the infusion of the divine light.

Reply Obj. 3. Faith is a kind of knowledge, inasmuch as the intellect is determined by faith to some knowable object. But this determination to one object does not proceed from the vision of the believer, but from the vision of Him Who is believed. Thus, as far as faith falls short of vision, it falls short of the nature which knowledge has when it is science; for science determines the intellect to one object by the vision and understanding of first principles.

Question XIII

THE NAMES OF GOD

(*In Twelve Articles*)

AFTER the consideration of those things which belong to the divine knowledge, we now proceed to the consideration of the divine names. For everything is named by us according to our knowledge of it.

Under this head, there are twelve points for inquiry. (1) Whether God can be named by us? (2) Whether any names applied to God are predicated of Him substantially? (3) Whether any names applied to God are said of Him properly, or are all to be taken metaphorically? (4) Whether any names applied to God are synonymous? (5) Whether some names are applied to God and to creatures univocally or equivocally? (6) Whether, supposing they are applied analogically, they are applied first to God or to creatures? (7) Whether any names are applicable to God from time? (8) Whether this name *God* is a name of nature, or of operation? (9) Whether this name *God* is a communicable name? (10) Whether it is taken univocally or equivocally as signifying God, by nature, by participation, and by opinion? (11) Whether this name, *Who is,* is the supremely appropriate name of God? (12) Whether affirmative propositions can be formed about God?

First Article

WHETHER A NAME CAN BE GIVEN TO GOD?

We proceed thus to the First Article:—

Objection 1. It seems that no name can be given to God. For Dionysius says that, *Of Him there is neither name, nor can one be found of Him;*[1] and it is written: *What is His name, and what is the name of His Son, if thou knowest?* (*Prov.* xxx. 4).

Obj. 2. Further, every name is either abstract or concrete. But concrete names do not belong to God, since He is simple, nor do abstract names belong to Him, since they do not

[1] *De Div. Nom.,* I, 5 (PG 3, 593).

signify any perfect subsisting thing. Therefore no name can be said of God.

Obj. 3. Further, nouns signify substance with quality; verbs and participles signify substance with time; pronouns the same with demonstration or relation. But none of these can be applied to God, for He has no quality, or accident, or time; moreover, He cannot be felt, so as to be pointed out; nor can He be described by relation, inasmuch as relations serve to recall a thing mentioned before by nouns, participles, or demonstrative pronouns. Therefore God cannot in any way be named by us.

On the contrary, It is written (*Exod.* xv. 3): *The Lord is a man of war, Almighty is His name.*

I answer that, Since, according to the Philosopher,[2] words are signs of ideas, and ideas the similitudes of things, it is evident that words function in the signification of things through the conception of the intellect. It follows therefore that we can give a name to anything in so far as we can understand it. Now it was shown above that in this life we cannot see the essence of God;[3] but we know God from creatures as their cause, and also by way of excellence and remotion. In this way therefore He can be named by us from creatures, yet not so that the name which signifies Him expresses the divine essence in itself in the way that the name *man* expresses the essence of man in himself, since it signifies the definition which manifests his essence. For the idea expressed by the name is the definition.

Reply Obj. 1. The reason why God has no name, or is said to be above being named, is because His essence is above all that we understand about God and signify in words.

Reply Obj. 2. Because we come to know and name God from creatures, the names we attribute to God signify what belongs to material creatures, of which the knowledge is natural to us, as was shown above.[4] And because in creatures of this kind what is perfect and subsistent is composite, whereas their form is not a complete subsisting thing, but rather is that whereby a thing is, hence it follows that all names used by us to signify a complete subsisting thing must have a concrete meaning, as befits composite things. On the other hand, names given to signify simple forms signify a thing not

---

[2] *Perih.,* I (16a 3).   [3] Q. 12, a. 11 and 12.   [4] Q. 12, a. 4.

as subsisting, but as that whereby a thing is; as, for instance, whiteness signifies that whereby a thing is white. And since God is simple and subsisting, we attribute to Him simple and abstract names to signify His simplicity, and concrete names to signify His subsistence and perfection; although both these kinds of names fail to express His mode of being, because our intellect does not know Him in this life as He is.

Reply Obj. 3. To signify substance with quality is to signify the *suppositum* with a nature or determined form in which it subsists. Hence, as some things are said of God in a concrete sense, to signify His subsistence and perfection, so likewise nouns are applied to God signifying substance with quality. Further, verbs and participles, which signify time, are applied to Him because His eternity includes all time. For as we can apprehend and signify simple subsistents only by way of composite things, so we can understand and express simple eternity only by way of temporal things, because our intellect has a natural proportion to composite and temporal things. But demonstrative pronouns are applied to God as pointing to what is understood, not to what is sensed. For we can point to Him only as far as we understand Him. Thus, according as nouns, participles and demonstrative pronouns are applicable to God, so far can He be signified by relative pronouns.

Second Article

WHETHER ANY NAME CAN BE APPLIED TO GOD SUBSTANTIALLY?

We proceed thus to the Second Article:—

Objection 1. It seems that no name can be applied to God substantially. For Damascene says: *Everything said of God must not signify His substance, but rather show forth what He is not; or express some relation, or something following from His nature or operation.*[5]

Obj. 2. Further, Dionysius says: *You will find a chorus of holy doctors addressed to the end of distinguishing clearly and praiseworthily the divine processions in the denominations of God.*[6] This means that the names applied by the holy

[5] *De Fide Orth.*, I, 9 (PG 94, 833).   [6] *De Div. Nom.*, I, 4 (PG 3, 589).

doctors in praising God are distinguished according to the divine processions themselves. But what expresses the procession of anything does not signify anything pertaining to its essence. Therefore the names said of God are not said of Him substantially.

Obj. 3. Further, a thing is named by us according as we understand it. But in this life God is not understood by us in His substance. Therefore neither is any name we can use applied substantially to God.

On the contrary, Augustine says: *For God to be is to be strong or wise, or whatever else we may say of that simplicity whereby His substance is signified.*[7] Therefore all names of this kind signify the divine substance.

I answer that, Names which are said of God negatively or which signify His relation to creatures manifestly do not at all signify His substance, but rather express the distance of the creature from Him, or His relation to something else, or rather, the relation of creatures to Himself.

But as regards names of God said absolutely and affirmatively, as *good, wise,* and the like, various and many opinions have been held. For some have said that all such names, although they are applied to God affirmatively, nevertheless have been brought into use more to remove something from God than to posit something in Him. Hence they assert that when we say that God lives, we mean that God is not like an inanimate thing; and the same in like manner applies to other names. This was taught by Rabbi Moses.[8] Others[9] say that these names applied to God signify His relationship towards creatures: thus in the words, *God is good,* we mean, God is the cause of goodness in things; and the same interpretation applies to other names.

Both of these opinions, however, seem to be untrue for three reasons. First, because in neither of them could a reason be assigned why some names more than others should be applied to God. For He is assuredly the cause of bodies in the same way as He is the cause of good things; therefore if the words *God is good* signified no more than, *God is the cause of good things,* it might in like manner be said that God is a body, inasmuch as He is the cause of bodies. So also to say that He is a body implies that He is not a mere

[7] *De Trin.,* VI, 4 (PL 42, 927).   [8] *Guide,* I, 58 (p. 82).   [9] Alain of Lille, *Theol. Reg.* XXI; XXVI (PL 210, 631; 633).

potentiality, as is primary matter. Secondly, because it would follow that all names applied to God would be said of Him by way of being taken in a secondary sense, as healthy is secondarily said of medicine, because it signifies only the cause of health in the animal which primarily is called healthy. Thirdly, because this is against the intention of those who speak of God. For in saying that God lives, they assuredly mean more than to say that He is the cause of our life, or that He differs from inanimate bodies.

Therefore we must hold a different doctrine—viz., that these names signify the divine substance, and are predicated substantially of God, although they fall short of representing Him. Which is proved thus. For these names express God, so far as our intellects know Him. Now since our intellect knows God from creatures, it knows Him as far as creatures represent Him. But it was shown above that God prepossesses in Himself all the perfections of creatures, being Himself absolutely and universally perfect.[10] Hence every creature represents Him, and is like Him, so far as it possesses some perfection: yet not so far as to represent Him as something of the same species or genus, but as the excelling source of whose form the effects fall short, although they derive some kind of likeness thereto, even as the forms of inferior bodies represent the power of the sun. This was explained above in treating of the divine perfection.[11] Therefore, the aforesaid names signify the divine substance, but in an imperfect manner, even as creatures represent it imperfectly. So when we say, *God is good,* the meaning is not, *God is the cause of goodness,* or, *God is not evil;* but the meaning is, *Whatever good we attribute to creatures pre-exists in God,* and in a higher way. Hence it does not follow that God is good because He causes goodness; but rather, on the contrary, He causes goodness in things because He is good. As Augustine says, *Because He is good, we are.*[12]

Reply Obj. 1. Damascene says that these names do not signify what God is because by none of these names is what He is perfectly expressed; but each one signifies Him in an imperfect manner, even as creatures represent Him imperfectly.

Reply Obj. 2. In the signification of names, that from

[10] Q. 4, a. 2.   [11] Q. 4, a. 3.   [12] *De Doc. Christ.*, I, 32 (PL 34, 32).

which the name is derived is different sometimes from what it is intended to signify, as for instance this name *stone* [*lapis*] is imposed from the fact that it hurts the *foot* [*lædit pedem*]; yet it is not imposed to signify that which hurts the foot, but rather to signify a certain kind of body; otherwise everything that hurts the foot would be a stone. So we must say that such divine names are imposed from the divine processions; for as according to the diverse processions of their perfections, **creatures** are the representations of God, although in an imperfect manner, so likewise our intellect knows and names God according to each kind of procession. But nevertheless these names are not imposed to signify the processions themselves, as if when we say *God lives,* the sense were, *life proceeds from Him,* but to signify the principle itself of things, in so far as life pre-exists in Him, although it pre-exists in Him in a more eminent way than is understood or signified.

Reply Obj. 3. In this life, we cannot know the essence of God as it is in itself, but we know it according as it is represented in the perfections of creatures; and it is thus that the names imposed by us signify it.

Third Article

WHETHER ANY NAME CAN BE APPLIED TO GOD PROPERLY?

We proceed thus to the Third Article:—

Objection 1. It seems that no name is applied properly to God. For all names which we apply to God are taken from creatures, as was explained above. But the names of creatures are applied to God metaphorically, as when we say, God is a stone, or a lion, or the like. Therefore names are applied to God in a metaphorical sense.

Obj. 2. Further, no name can be applied properly to anything if it should be more truly denied of it than given to it. But all such names as *good, wise,* and the like, are more truly denied of God than given to Him; as appears from what Dionysius says.[13] Therefore none of these names is said of God properly.

Obj. 3. Further, corporeal names are applied to God in a

[13] *De Cael. Hier.,* II, 3 (PG 3, 141).

metaphorical sense only, since He is incorporeal. But all such names imply some kind of corporeal condition; for their meaning is bound up with time and composition and like corporeal conditions. Therefore all these names are applied to God in a metaphorical sense.

On the contrary, Ambrose says, *Some names there are which express evidently the property of the divinity, and some which express the clear truth of the divine majesty; but others there are which are said of God metaphorically by way of similitude.*[14] Therefore not all names are applied to God in a metaphorical sense, but there are some which are said of Him properly.

I answer that, According to the preceding article, our knowledge of God is derived from the perfections which flow from Him to creatures; which perfections are in God in a more eminent way than in creatures. Now our intellect apprehends them as they are in creatures, and as it apprehends them thus does it signify them by names. Therefore, as to the names applied to God, there are two things to be considered—viz., the perfections themselves which they signify, such as goodness, life, and the like, and their mode of signification. As regards what is signified by these names, they belong properly to God, and more properly than they belong to creatures, and are applied primarily to Him. But as regards their mode of signification, they do not properly and strictly apply to God; for their mode of signification befits creatures.

Reply Obj. 1. There are some names which signify these perfections flowing from God to creatures in such a way that the imperfect way in which creatures receive the divine perfection is part of the very signification of the name itself, as *stone* signifies a material being; and names of this kind can be applied to God only in a metaphorical sense. Other names, however, express the perfections themselves absolutely, without any such mode of participation being part of their signification, as the words *being, good, living,* and the like; and such names can be applied to God properly.

Reply Obj. 2. Such names as these, as Dionysius shows, are denied of God for the reason that what the name signifies does not belong to Him in the ordinary sense of its significa-

---

[14] *De Fide*, II, Prol. (PL 16, 583).

tion, but in a more eminent way. Hence Dionysius says also that God is above all substance and all life.[15]

Reply Obj. 3. These names which are applied to God properly imply corporeal conditions, not in the thing signified, but as regards their mode of signification; whereas those which are applied to God metaphorically imply and mean a corporeal condition in the thing signified.

Fourth Article

WHETHER NAMES APPLIED TO GOD ARE SYNONYMOUS?

We proceed thus to the Fourth Article:—

Objection 1. It seems that these names applied to God are synonymous names. For synonymous names are those which mean exactly the same. But these names applied to God mean entirely the same thing in God; for the goodness of God is His essence, and likewise it is His wisdom. Therefore these names are entirely synonymous.

Obj. 2. Further, if it be said that these names signify one and the same thing in reality, but differ in idea, it can be objected that an idea to which no reality corresponds is an empty notion. Therefore if these ideas are many, and the thing is one, it seems also that all these ideas are empty notions.

Obj. 3. Further, a thing which is one in reality and in idea is more one than what is one in reality and many in idea. But God is supremely one. Therefore it seems that He is not one in reality and many in idea; and thus the names applied to God do not have different meanings. Hence they are synonymous.

On the contrary, All synonyms united with each other are redundant, as when we say, *vesture clothing.* Therefore if all names applied to God are synonymous, we cannot properly say *good God,* or the like; and yet it is written, *O most mighty, great and powerful, the Lord of hosts is Thy name* (*Jer.* xxxii. 18).

I answer that, These names spoken of God are not synonymous. This would be easy to understand, if we said that these names are used to remove or to express the relation of cause to creatures; for thus it would follow that there are

---

[15] *De Cael. Hier.,* II, 3 (PG 3, 141).

different ideas as regards the diverse things denied of God, or as regards diverse effects connoted. But according to what was said above, namely, that these names signify the divine substance, although in an imperfect manner, it is also clear from what has been said that they have diverse meanings. For the idea signified by the name is the conception in the intellect of the thing signified by the name. But since our intellect knows God from creatures, in order to understand God it forms conceptions proportioned to the perfections flowing from God to creatures. These perfections pre-exist in God unitedly and simply, whereas in creatures they are received divided and multiplied. Just as, therefore, to the diverse perfections of creatures there corresponds one simple principle represented by the diverse perfections of creatures in a various and manifold manner, so also to the various and multiplied conceptions of our intellect there corresponds one altogether simple principle, imperfectly understood through these conceptions. Therefore, although the names applied to God signify one reality, still, because they signify that reality under many and diverse aspects, they are not synonymous.

Thus appears the solution of the First Objection, since synonymous names signify one thing under one aspect; for names which signify different aspects of one thing do not signify primarily and absolutely one thing, because a name signifies a thing only through the medium of the intellectual conception, as was said above.

Reply Obj. 2. The many aspects of these names are not useless and empty, for there corresponds to all of them one simple reality represented by them in a manifold and imperfect manner.

Reply Obj. 3. The perfect unity of God requires that what are manifold and divided in others should exist in Him simply and unitedly. Thus it comes about that He is one in reality, and yet multiple in idea, because our intellect apprehends Him in a manifold manner, as things represent Him.

Fifth Article

WHETHER WHAT IS SAID OF GOD AND OF CREATURES IS UNIVOCALLY PREDICATED OF THEM?

We proceed thus to the Fifth Article:—

Objection 1. It seems that the things attributed to God and creatures are univocal. For every equivocal term is reduced to the univocal, as many are reduced to one: for if the name *dog* be said equivocally of the barking dog and of the dogfish, it must be said of some univocally—viz., of all barking dogs; otherwise we proceed to infinitude. Now there are some univocal agents which agree with their effects in name and definition, as man generates man; and there are some agents which are equivocal, as the sun which causes heat, although the sun is hot only in an equivocal sense. Therefore it seems that the first agent, to which all other agents are reduced, is a univocal agent: and thus what is said of God and creatures is predicated univocally.

Obj. 2. Further, no likeness is understood through equivocal names. Therefore, as creatures have a certain likeness to God, according to the text of *Genesis* (i. 26), *Let us make man to our image and likeness,* it seems that something can be said of God and creatures univocally.

Obj. 3. Further, measure is homogeneous with the thing measured, as is said in *Metaph.* x.[16] But God is the first measure of all beings. Therefore God is homogeneous with creatures; and thus a name may be applied univocally to God and to creatures.

On the contrary, Whatever is predicated of various things under the same name but not in the same sense is predicated equivocally. But no name belongs to God in the same sense that it belongs to creatures; for instance, wisdom in creatures is a quality, but not in God. Now a change in genus changes an essence, since the genus is part of the definition; and the same applies to other things. Therefore whatever is said of God and of creatures is predicated equivocally.

Further, God is more distant from creatures than any creatures are from each other. But the distance of some creatures makes any univocal predication of them impossible, as

[16] Aristotle, *Metaph.,* IX, 1 (1053a 24).

in the case of those things which are not in the same genus. Therefore much less can anything be predicated univocally of God and creatures; and so only equivocal predication can be applied to them.

I answer that, Univocal predication is impossible between God and creatures. The reason of this is that every effect which is not a proportioned result of the power of the efficient cause receives the similitude of the agent not in its full degree, but in a measure that falls short; so that what is divided and multiplied in the effects resides in the agent simply, and in an unvaried manner. For example, the sun by the exercise of its one power produces manifold and various forms in these sublunary things. In the same way, as was said above, all perfections existing in creatures divided and multiplied pre-exist in God unitedly. Hence, when any name expressing perfection is applied to a creature, it signifies that perfection as distinct from the others according to the nature of its definition; as, for instance, by this term *wise* applied to a man, we signify some perfection distinct from a man's essence, and distinct from his power and his being, and from all similar things. But when we apply *wise* to God, we do not mean to signify anything distinct from His essence or power or being. And thus when this term *wise* is applied to man, in some degree it circumscribes and comprehends the thing signified; whereas this is not the case when it is applied to God, but it leaves the thing signified as uncomprehended and as exceeding the signification of the name. Hence it is evident that this term *wise* is not applied in the same way to God and to man. The same applies to other terms. Hence, no name is predicated univocally of God and of creatures.

Neither, on the other hand, are names applied to God and creatures in a purely equivocal sense, as some have said.[17] Because if that were so, it follows that from creatures nothing at all could be known or demonstrated about God; for the reasoning would always be exposed to the fallacy of equivocation. Such a view is against the Philosopher, who proves many things about God, and also against what the Apostle says: *The invisible things of* God *are clearly seen being understood by the things that are made* (*Rom.* i. 20). Therefore it must be said that these names are said of God and

[17] Maimonides, *Guide,* I, 59 (p. 84); Averroes, *In Metaph.,* XII, comm. 51 (VIII, 158r).

creatures in an *analogous* sense, that is, according to proportion.

This can happen in two ways: either according as many things are proportioned to one (thus, for example *healthy* is predicated of medicine and urine in relation and in proportion to health of body, of which the latter is the sign and the former the cause), or according as one thing is proportioned to another (thus, *healthy* is said of medicine and an animal, since medicine is the cause of health in the animal body). And in this way some things are said of God and creatures analogically, and not in a purely equivocal nor in a purely univocal sense. For we can name God only from creatures. Hence, whatever is said of God and creatures is said according as there is some relation of the creature to God as to its principle and cause, wherein all the perfections of things pre-exist excellently. Now this mode of community is a mean between pure equivocation and simple univocation. For in analogies the idea is not, as it is in univocals, one and the same; yet it is not totally diverse as in equivocals; but the name which is thus used in a multiple sense signifies various proportions to some one thing: *e.g., healthy,* applied to urine, signifies the sign of animal health; but applied to medicine, it signifies the cause of the same health.

Reply Obj. 1. Although in predications all equivocals must be reduced to univocals, still in actions the non-univocal agent must precede the univocal agent. For the non-univocal agent is the universal cause of the whole species, as the sun is the cause of the generation of all men. But the univocal agent is not the universal efficient cause of the whole species (otherwise it would be the cause of itself, since it is contained in the species), but is a particular cause of this individual which it places under the species by way of participation. Therefore the universal cause of the whole species is not a univocal agent: and the universal cause comes before the particular cause. But this universal agent, while not univocal, nevertheless is not altogether univocal (otherwise it could not produce its own likeness); but it can be called an analogical agent, just as in predications all univocal names are reduced to one first non-univocal analogical name, which is *being.*

Reply Obj. 2. The likeness of the creature to God is imperfect, for it does not represent the same thing even generically.[18]

Reply Obj. 3. God is not a measure proportioned to the things measured; hence it is not necessary that God and creatures should be in the same genus.

The arguments adduced in the contrary sense prove indeed that these names are not predicated univocally of God and creatures; yet they do not prove that they are predicated equivocally.

Sixth Article

WHETHER NAMES PREDICATED OF GOD ARE PREDICATED PRIMARILY OF CREATURES?

We proceed thus to the Sixth Article:—

Objection 1. It seems that names are predicated primarily of creatures rather than of God. For we name anything accordingly as we know it, since *names*, as the Philosopher says,[19] *are signs of ideas*. But we know creatures before we know God. Therefore the names imposed by us are predicated primarily of creatures rather than of God.

Obj. 2. Further, Dionysius says that we name God from creatures.[20] But names transferred from creatures to God are said primarily of creatures rather than of God; as *lion, stone*, and the like. Therefore all names applied to God and creatures are applied primarily to creatures rather than to God.

Obj. 3. Further, all names applied to God and creatures in common *are applied to God as the cause of all creatures*, as Dionysius says.[21] But what is applied to anything through its cause is applied to it secondarily; for *healthy* is primarily predicated of animal rather than of medicine, which is the cause of health. Therefore these names are said primarily of creatures rather than of God.

On the contrary, It is written, *I bow my knees to the Father of our Lord Jesus Christ, of Whom all paternity in heaven and earth is named (Ephes.* iii. 14, 15); and the same holds of the other names applied to God and creatures. Therefore these names are applied primarily to God rather than to creatures.

[18] Q. 4, a. 3.   [19] *Perih.,* I (16a 3).   [20] *De Div. Nom.,* I, 6 (PG 3, 596).   [21] *De Myst. Theol.,* I, 2 (PG 3, 1000).

I answer that, In names predicated of many in an analogical sense, all are predicated through a relation to some one thing; and this one thing must be placed in the definition of them all. And since *the essence expressed by the name is the definition,* as the Philosopher says,[22] such a name must be applied primarily to that which is put in the definition of the other things, and secondarily to these others according as they approach more or less to the first. Thus, for instance, *healthy* applied to animals comes into the definition of *healthy* applied to medicine, which is called healthy as being the cause of health in the animal; and also into the definition of *healthy* which is applied to urine, which is called healthy in so far as it is the sign of the animal's health.

So it is that all names applied metaphorically to God are applied to creatures primarily rather than to God, because when said of God they mean only similitudes to such creatures. For as *smiling* applied to a field means only that the field in the beauty of its flowering is like to the beauty of the human smile by proportionate likeness, so the name of *lion* applied to God means only that God manifests strength in His works, as a lion in his. Thus it is clear that applied to God the signification of these names can be defined only from what is said of creatures.

But to other names not applied to God in a metaphorical sense, the same rule would apply if they were spoken of God as the cause only, as some have supposed.[23] For when it is said, *God is good,* it would then only mean, *God is the cause of the creature's goodness*; and thus the name *good* applied to God would include in its meaning the creature's goodness. Hence *good* would apply primarily to creatures rather than God. But, as was shown above, these names are applied to God not as the cause only, but also essentially. For the words, *God is good,* or *wise,* signify not only that He is the cause of wisdom or goodness, but that these exist in Him in a more excellent way. Hence as regards what the name signifies, these names are applied primarily to God rather than to creatures, because these perfections flow from God to creatures; but as regards the imposition of the names, they are primarily applied by us to creatures, which we know first. Hence they

---

[22] Aristotle, *Metaph.,* III, 7 (1012a 23).   [23] Alain of Lille, *Theol. Reg.,* XXI; XXVI (PL 210, 631; 633).

have a mode of signification which belongs to creatures, as was said above.

Reply Obj. 1. This objection refers to the imposition of the name: to that extent it is true.

Reply Obj. 2. The same rule does not apply to metaphorical and to other names, as was said above.

Reply Obj. 3. This objection would be valid if these names were applied to God only as cause, and not also essentially, for instance, as *healthy* is applied to medicine.

Seventh Article

WHETHER NAMES WHICH IMPLY RELATION TO CREATURES ARE PREDICATED OF GOD TEMPORALLY?

We proceed thus to the Seventh Article:—

Objection 1. It seems that names which imply relation to creatures are not predicated of God temporally. For all such names signify the divine substance, as is universally held. Hence also Ambrose says that this name *Lord* is a name of power,[24] which is the divine substance; and *Creator* signifies the action of God, which is His essence. Now the divine substance is not temporal, but eternal. Therefore these names are not applied to God temporally, but eternally.

Obj. 2. Further, that to which something applies temporally can be described as made; for what is white temporally is made white. But to be made does not apply to God. Therefore nothing can be predicated of God temporally.

Obj. 3. Further, if any names are applied to God temporally because they imply relation to creatures, the same rule holds good of all things that imply relation to creatures. But some names implying relation to creatures are spoken of God from eternity; for from eternity He knew and loved the creature, according to the word: *I have loved thee with an everlasting love (Jer.* xxxi. 3). Therefore also other names implying relation to creatures, as *Lord* and *Creator,* are applied to God from eternity.

Obj. 4. Further, names of this kind signify relation. Therefore that relation must be something in God, or in the creature only. But it cannot be that it is something in the creature only, for in that case God would be called *Lord* from

[24] *De Fide,* I (PL 16, 553).

the opposite relation which is in creatures; and nothing is named from its opposite. Therefore the relation must be something in God. But nothing temporal can be in God, for He is above time. Therefore these names are not applied to God temporally.

Obj. 5. Further, a thing is called relative from relation; for instance, lord from lordship, and white from whiteness. Therefore if the relation of lordship is not really in God, but only in idea, it follows that God is not really Lord, which is plainly false.

Obj. 6. Further, in relative things which are not simultaneous in nature, one can exist without the other; as a knowable thing can exist without the knowledge of it, as the Philosopher says.[25] But relative things which are said of God and creatures are not simultaneous in nature. Therefore a relation can be predicated of God to the creature even without the existence of the creature; and thus these names, *Lord* and *Creator,* are predicated of God from eternity, and not temporally.

On the contrary, Augustine says that this relative appellation *Lord* is applied to God temporally.[26]

I answer that, Some names which import relation to creatures are applied to God temporally, and not from eternity.

To see this we must learn that some have said that relation is not a reality, but only an idea.[27] But this is plainly seen to be false from the very fact that things themselves have a mutual natural order and relation. Nevertheless it is necessary to know that, since a relation needs two extremes, there are three conditions that make a relation to be real or logical. Sometimes from both extremes it is an idea only, as when a mutual order or relation can be between things only in the apprehension of reason; as when we say that *the same is the same as itself.* For the reason, by apprehending one thing twice, regards it as two; and thus it apprehends a certain relation of a thing to itself. And the same applies to relations between *being* and *non-being* formed by reason, inasmuch as it apprehends *non-being* as an extreme. The same is true of those relations that follow upon an act of reason, as genus and species, and the like.

[25] Aristotle, *Cat.,* VII (7b 30).   [26] *De Trin.,* V, 16 (PL 42, 922). [27] Cf. Averroes, *In Metaph.,* XII, comm. 19 (VIII, 144r).—Cf. also St. Thomas, *De Pot.,* q. 8, a. 2.

Now there are other relations which are realities as regards both extremes, as when a relation exists between two things according to some reality that belongs to both. This is clear of all relations consequent upon quantity, as great and small, double and half, and the like; for there is quantity in both extremes. The same applies to relations consequent upon action and passion, as motive power and the movable thing, father and son, and the like.

Again, sometimes a relation in one extreme may be a reality, while in the other extreme it is only an idea. This happens whenever two extremes are not of one order, as sense and science refer, respectively, to sensible things and to knowable things; which, inasmuch as they are realities existing in nature, are outside the order of sensible and intelligible existence. Therefore, in science and in sense a real relation exists, because they are ordered either to the knowledge or to the sensible perception of things; whereas the things looked at in themselves are outside this order. Hence in them there is no real relation to science and sense, but only in idea, inasmuch as the intellect apprehends them as terms of the relations of science and sense. Hence, the Philosopher says that they are called relative, not because they are related to other things, but because others are related to them.[28] Likewise, *on the right* is not applied to a column, unless it stands on the right side of an animal; which relation is not really in the column, but in the animal.

Since, therefore, God is outside the whole order of creation, and all creatures are ordered to Him, and not conversely, it is manifest that creatures are really related to God Himself; whereas in God there is no real relation to creatures, but a relation only in idea, inasmuch as creatures are related to Him. Thus there is nothing to prevent such names, which import relation to the creature, from being predicated of God temporally, not by reason of any change in Him, but by reason of the change in the creature; as a column is on the right of an animal, without change in itself, but because the animal has moved.

Reply Obj. 1. Some relative names are imposed to signify the relational ordinations themselves, as *master* and *servant*, *father* and *son*, and the like; and these are called relatives *in being* [*secundum esse*]. But others are imposed to signify the

[28] *Metaph.*, IV, 15 (1021a 29).

things from which follow certain relations, as the *mover* and the *moved*, the *head* and the *being that has a head*, and the like; and these are called relatives *in name* [*secundum dici*]. Thus, there is the same twofold difference in divine names. For some signify the relation itself to the creature, as *Lord*, and these do not signify the divine substance directly, but indirectly, in so far as they presuppose the divine substance; as dominion presupposes power, which is the divine substance. Others signify the divine essence directly, and the corresponding relation consequently; as *Savior*, *Creator*, and the like, signify the action of God, which is His essence. Yet both kinds of names are said of God temporally so far as they imply a relation either principally or consequently, but not so far as they signify the essence, either directly or indirectly.

Reply Obj. 2. Just as relations applied to God temporally are in God only in our idea, so, *to become*, or *to be made* are applied to God only in idea, with no change in Him; as when we say, *Lord, Thou art become our refuge* (*Ps.* lxxxix. 1).

Reply Obj. 3. The operation of the intellect and will is in the operator, and therefore names signifying relations following upon the action of the intellect or will are applied to God from eternity; whereas those following upon the actions proceeding, according to our mode of thinking, to external effects are applied to God temporally, as *Savior*, *Creator*, and the like.

Reply Obj. 4. Relations signified by such names as are applied to God temporally are in God only in idea; but the opposite relations in creatures are real. Nor is it incongruous that God should be denominated from relations really existing in things, provided that the opposite relations be at the same time understood by us as existing in God, so that God is spoken of relatively to the creature inasmuch as the creature is related to Him; just as the Philosopher says that the object is said to be knowable relatively because knowledge relates to it.[29]

Reply Obj. 5. Since God is related to the creature for the reason that the creature is related to Him: and since the relation of subjection is real in the creature, it follows that God is Lord not in idea only, but in reality; for He is called Lord according to the manner in which the creature is subject to Him.

[29] *Ibid.* (1021a 30).

Reply Obj. 6. To know whether relations are simultaneous by nature or otherwise, it is not necessary to consider the order of things to which they belong but the meaning of the relations themselves. For if one includes another in its idea, and *vice versa*, then they are simultaneous by nature: as double and half, father and son, and the like. But if one includes another in its idea, and not *vice versa*, they are not simultaneous by nature. This is the way that science and its object are related, for the *knowable* expresses a possibility, and *science* expresses a possible habit, or an act. Hence the concept *knowable* according to its mode of signification is prior to *science*; but if the knowable object becomes actually known, then it is simultaneous with science in act; for the known object is nothing as such unless the knowledge of it exists. Hence, though God is prior to the creature, still, because the signification of Lord includes the idea of a servant and *vice versa*, these two relative terms, *Lord* and *servant*, are simultaneous by nature. Hence God was not *Lord* until He had a creature subject to Himself.

Eighth Article

WHETHER THIS NAME GOD NAMES A NATURE?

We proceed thus to the Eighth Article:—

Objection 1. It seems that this name, *God*, does not name a nature. For Damascene says that *God* (Θεός) *is so called from* θεεῖν *which means to take care of, and to cherish all things; or from* αἴθειν, *that is, to burn, for our God is a consuming fire; or from* θεᾶσθαι, *which means to consider all things*.[30] But all these names belong to operation. Therefore this name *God* signifies His operation and not His nature.

Obj. 2. Further, a thing is named by us as we know it. But the divine nature is unknown to us. Therefore this name *God* does not signify the divine nature.

On the contrary, Ambrose says that *God* names a nature.[31]

I answer that, Whence a name is imposed, and what the name signifies are not always the same thing. For just as we know substance from its properties and operations, so we sometimes name a substance from some operation or property: *e.g.*, we name the substance of a stone from a particular

---

[30] *De Fide Orth.*, I, 9 (PG 94, 835).   [31] *De Fide*, I, 1 (PL 16, 553).

action, namely, that it hurts the foot [*lædit pedem*]; but still this name is not meant to signify the particular action, but the stone's substance. On the other hand, when the things in question are known to us in themselves, such as heat, cold, whiteness, and the like, then they are not named from other things. Hence, as regards such things, the meaning of the name and its source are the same.

Because therefore God is not known to us in His nature, but is made known to us from His operations or His effects, it is from these that we can name Him, as was said above; hence this name *God* is a name of operation so far as relates to the source of its meaning. For this name is imposed from His universal providence over all things, since all who speak of God intend to name *God* that being which exercises providence over all. Hence Dionysius says: *The Deity watches over all with perfect providence and goodness.*[32] But though taken from this operation, this name *God* is imposed to signify the divine nature.

Reply Obj. 1. All that Damascene says refers to providence,[33] which is the source of the signification of the name *God*.

Reply Obj. 2. We can name a thing according to the knowledge we have of its nature from its properties and effects. Hence because we can know what stone is in itself from its property, this name *stone* signifies the nature of stone in itself; for it signifies the definition of stone, by which we know what it is, *for the essence which the name signifies is the definition*, as is said in *Metaph.* iv.[34] Now from the divine effects we cannot know the divine nature in itself, so as to know what it is; but only by way of eminence, causality, and negation, as was stated above.[35] So it remains that the name *God* signifies the divine nature. For this name was imposed to signify something existing above all things, the principle of all things, and removed from all things; for this is what those who name God intend to signify.

[32] *De Div. Nom.*, XII, 2 (PG 3, 969).   [33] *De Fide Orth.*, I, 9 (PG 94, 836).   [34] Aristotle, *Metaph.*, III, 7 (1012a 23).   [35] Q. 12, a. 12.

Ninth Article

WHETHER THIS NAME *GOD* IS COMMUNICABLE?

We proceed thus to the Ninth Article:—

Objection 1. It seems that this name *God* is communicable. For whosoever shares in the thing signified by a name shares in the name itself. But this name *God* signifies the divine nature, which is communicable to others, according to the words, *He hath given us great and precious promises, that by these we may be made partakers of the divine nature* (2 *Pet.* i. 4). Therefore this name *God* can be communicated to others.

Obj. 2. Further, only proper names are not communicable. Now this name *God* is not a proper, but an appellative noun; which appears from the fact that it has a plural, according to the text, *I have said, You are gods* (*Ps.* lxxxi. 6). Therefore the name *God* is communicable.

Obj. 3. Further, this name *God* comes from operation, as was explained. But other names given to God from His operations or effects are communicable; as *good, wise,* and the like. Therefore this name *God* is communicable.

On the contrary, It is written: *They gave the incommunicable name to wood and stones* (*Wis.* xiv. 21), in reference to the divine name. Therefore this name *God* is incommunicable.

I answer that, A name is communicable in two ways, properly, and through likeness. It is properly communicable if its whole signification can be given to many; through likeness it is communicable according to some part of the signification of the name. For instance, this name *lion* is properly communicated to all beings of the same nature as *lion*; through likeness it is communicable to those who share in something of the lion's nature, as for instance courage, or strength, and such are called lions metaphorically. To know, however, what names are properly communicable, we must consider that every form existing in a singular subject, by which it is individuated, is common to many either in reality or at least in idea; as human nature is common to many in reality and in idea, whereas the nature of the sun is not common to many in reality, but only in idea. For the nature of the sun can be understood as existing in many subjects; and the rea-

son is because the intellect understands the nature of every
species by abstraction from the singular. Hence, to be in
one singular subject or in many is outside the idea of the
nature of the species. So, given the idea of a species, it can be
understood as existing in many. But the singular, from the
fact that it is singular, is divided off from all others. Hence
every name imposed to signify any singular thing is incommunicable both in reality and idea: for the plurality of this
individual thing cannot be conceived. Hence no name signifying any individual thing is properly communicable to
many, but only by way of likeness; as a person can be called
Achilles metaphorically, because he may possess something
of the characteristics of Achilles, such as strength. On the
other hand, forms which are individualed not by any *suppositum,* but by and of themselves, as being subsisting forms,
if understood as they are in themselves, could not be communicable either in reality or in idea; but only perhaps by
way of likeness, as was said of individuals. But since we are
unable to understand simple self-subsisting forms as they
really are, and we understand them after the manner of composite things having forms in matter, therefore, as was said
in the first article, we give them concrete names signifying a
nature existing in some *suppositum.* Hence, so far as concerns
names, the same situation applies to names we impose to signify the nature of composite things as to names given by us
to signify simple subsisting natures.

Since, then, this name *God* is given to signify the divine
nature, as was stated above, and since the divine nature cannot be multiplied as was shown above,[36] it follows that this
name *God* is incommunicable in reality, but communicable in
human opinion; just as in the same way this name *sun* would
be communicable according to the opinion of those who say
there are many suns. Therefore, it is written: *You served
them who by nature are not gods* (*Gal.* iv. 8); and the *Gloss*
adds, *Gods not in nature, but in human opinion.*[37] Nevertheless, this name *God* is communicable, not in its whole signification, but in some part of it by way of some likeness; so that
they are called gods who share in divinity by likeness, according to the text, *I have said, You are gods* (*Ps.* lxxxi. 6).

[36] Q. 11, a. 3.   [37] Peter Lombard, *In Gal.,* super IV, 8 (PL 192,
139); cf. *Glossa interl.* (VI, 84v).

But if any name were given to signify God not as to His nature but as to His *suppositum*, according as He is considered as *this something*, that name would be absolutely incommunicable; as, for instance, perhaps the Tetragrammaton among the Hebrews; and this is like giving to the sun a name which signifies this individual one.

Reply Obj. 1. The divine nature is communicable only according to the participation of some likeness.

Reply Obj. 2. This name *God* is an appellative name, and not a proper name, for it signifies the divine nature as residing in some one possessing it; although God Himself in reality is neither universal nor particular. For names do not follow upon the mode of being in things, but upon the mode of being that things have in our knowledge. And yet *God* is incommunicable in reality, as was said above concerning the name *sun*.

Reply Obj. 3. These names *good, wise,* and the like, are imposed from the perfections proceeding from God to creatures; but they are not meant to signify the divine nature, but rather the perfections themselves absolutely; and therefore even in reality they are communicable to many. But this name *God* is given to God from His own proper operation, which we experience continually, to signify the divine nature.

Tenth Article

WHETHER THIS NAME *GOD* IS APPLIED TO GOD UNIVOCALLY, BY NATURE, BY PARTICIPATION, AND ACCORDING TO OPINION?

We proceed thus to the Tenth Article:—

Objection 1. It seems that this name *God* is applied to God univocally by nature, by participation, and according to opinion. For where a diverse signification exists, there is no contradiction of affirmation and negation; for equivocation prevents contradiction. But a Catholic who says: *An idol is not God*, contradicts a pagan who says: *An idol is God*. Therefore *God* in both instances is said univocally.

Obj. 2. Further, as an idol is God in opinion, and not in truth, so the enjoyment of carnal pleasures is called happiness in opinion, and not in truth. But this name *beatitude* is applied univocally to this opined happiness, and also to true happiness. Therefore this name *God* is also applied univocally to the true God and to God according to opinion.

Obj. 3. Further, those names are called univocal which are one in meaning. Now when a Catholic says: *There is one God*, he understands by the name *God* an omnipotent being, and one to be venerated above all things; while the pagan understands the same when he says: *An idol is God*. Therefore this name *God* is applied univocally to both.

On the contrary, That which is in the intellect is the likeness of what is in the thing, as is said in *Periherm.* i.[38] But the word *animal*, applied to a true animal and to a picture of one, is used equivocally. Therefore this name *God*, when applied to the true God and to God in opinion, is applied equivocally.

Further, No one can signify what he does not know. But the pagan does not know the divine nature. So when he says *an idol is God*, he does not signify the true Deity. On the other hand, a Catholic signifies the true Deity when he says there is one God. Therefore this name God is not applied univocally, but equivocally, to the true God and to God according to opinion.

I answer that, This name *God* in the three aforesaid significations is taken neither univocally nor equivocally, but analogically. This is apparent from this reason:—Univocal names have absolutely the same meaning, while equivocal names have absolutely diverse meanings; whereas in analogicals, a name taken in one signification must be placed in the definition of the same name taken in other significations; as, for instance, *being* which is applied to *substance* is placed in the definition of being as applied to *accident*; and *healthy* applied to animal is placed in the definition of healthy as applied to urine and medicine. For of health in the animal urine is the sign and medicine the cause.

The same applies to the question at issue. For this name *God*, as signifying the true God, includes the idea of God when it is used to signify God according to opinion or by participation. For when we name anyone god by participation, we understand by the name *god* some likeness of the true God. Likewise, when we call an idol *god*, by this name god we understand that something is signified which men

---

[38] Aristotle, *Perih.*, I (16a 5).

think to be God. It is thus manifest that *God* has different meanings, but that one of them is present in the others. Hence it is manifestly said analogically.

Reply Obj. 1. The multiplicity of names does not depend on the predication of a name, but on its signification: for this name *man*, of whomsoever it is predicated, whether truly or falsely, is predicated in one sense. But it would be multiplied if by the name *man* we meant to signify diverse things; for instance, if one meant to signify by this name *man* what man really is, and another meant to signify by the same name a stone, or something else. Hence it is evident that a Catholic saying that an idol is not God contradicts the pagan asserting that it is God; because each of them uses this name *God* to signify the true God. For when the pagan says an idol is God, he does not use this name as meaning God in opinion, for he would then speak the truth, as also Catholics sometimes use the name in that sense, as in the Psalm, *All the gods of the Gentiles are demons* (*Ps.* xcv. 5).

The same remark applies to the second and third Objections. For those arguments proceed according to a diversity in the predication of a name, and not according to a diverse signification.

Reply Obj. 4. *Animal* applied to a true and a pictured animal is not said in a purely equivocal way; for the Philosopher takes equivocal names in a large sense, according to which they include analogous names,[39] because *being* as well, which is predicated analogically, is something said to be predicated equivocally of diverse predicaments.

Reply Obj. 5. Neither a Catholic nor a pagan knows the very nature of God as it is in itself; but each one knows it according to some idea of causality, or excellence, or remotion as was said above.[40] So a pagan can take this name *God* in the same way when he says *an idol is God*, as the Catholic does in saying *an idol is not God*. But if there were someone entirely ignorant of God, he could not even name Him; unless, perhaps, as we utter names the meaning of which we do not know.

[39] *Cat.*, I (1a 1).   [40] Q. 12, a. 12.

Eleventh Article

WHETHER THIS NAME, *HE WHO IS*, IS THE MOST PROPER NAME OF GOD?

We proceed thus to the Eleventh Article:—

Objection 1. It seems that this name *HE WHO IS* is not the most proper name of God. For this name *God* is an incommunicable name. But this name, *HE WHO IS,* is not an incommunicable name. Therefore this name *HE WHO IS* is not the most proper name of God.

Obj. 2. Further, Dionysius says that *the name Good excellently manifests all the processions of God.*[41] But it especially belongs to God to be the universal source of all things. Therefore this name *GOOD* is supremely proper to God, and not this name *HE WHO IS.*

Obj. 3. Further, every divine name seems to imply relation to creatures, for God is known to us only through creatures. But this name *HE WHO IS* imports no relation to creatures. Therefore this name *HE WHO IS* is not the most proper name of God.

On the contrary, It is written that when Moses asked, *If they should say to me, What is His name? what shall I say to them?* the Lord answered him, *Thus shalt thou say to them, HE WHO IS hath sent me to you* (*Exod.* iii. 13, 14). Therefore this name, *HE WHO IS,* is the most proper name of God.

I answer that, This name, *HE WHO IS,* is the most proper name of God for three reasons:—

First, because of its signification. For it does not signify some form, but being itself. Hence, since the being of God is His very essence (which can be said of no other being),[42] it is clear that among other names this one most properly names God; for everything is named according to its essence.

Secondly, because of its universality. For all other names are either less universal, or, if convertible with it, add something above it at least in idea; hence in a certain way they inform and determine it. Now in this life our intellect cannot know the essence itself of God as it is in itself, but however it may determine what it understands about God, it falls

---

[41] *De Div. Nom.,* III, 1 (PG 3, 680).   [42] Q. 3, a. 4.

short of what God is in Himself. Therefore the less determinate the names are, and the more universal and absolute
they are, the more properly are they applied to God. Hence
Damascene says that, HE WHO IS *is the principal of all names
applied to God; for comprehending all in itself, it contains
being itself as an infinite and indeterminate sea of substance.*[43] Now by any other name some mode of substance is
expressed determinately, whereas this name HE WHO IS determines no mode of being, but is related indeterminately to
all; and that is why it names the *infinite ocean of substance.*

Thirdly, from its consignification, for it signifies being *in
the present*; and this above all properly applies to God,
whose being knows not past or future, as Augustine says.[44]

Reply Obj. 1. This name HE WHO IS is the name of God
more properly than this name *God,* both as regards its source,
namely, being, and as regards the mode of signification and
consignification, as was said above. But as regards the object
intended to be signified by the name, this name *God* is more
proper, as it is imposed to signify the divine nature; and still
more proper is the name Tetragrammaton, imposed to signify
the substance itself of God, incommunicable and, if one may
so speak, singular.

Reply Obj. 2. This name *Good* is the principal name of
God in so far as He is a cause, but not absolutely; for absolutely speaking, *being* is understood by us before *cause.*

Reply Obj. 3. It is not necessary that all the divine names
should import relation to creatures; it suffices that they be
imposed from some perfections flowing from God to creatures. Among these the first is being, from which comes this
name, HE WHO IS.

Twelfth Article

WHETHER AFFIRMATIVE PROPOSITIONS CAN BE FORMED ABOUT GOD?

We proceed thus to the Twelfth Article:—
Objection 1. It seems that affirmative propositions cannot

[43] *De Fide Orth.,* I, 9 (PG 94, 836).   [44] Cf. Peter Lombard, *Sent.,*
I, viii, 1 (I, 58); St. Isidore, *Etymol.,* VII, 1 (PL 82, 261); Rhabanus
Maurus, *In Exod.,* I, 6 (PL 108, 21).

be formed about God. For Dionysius says that *negations about God are true; but affirmations are vague.*[45]

Obj. 2. Further, Boethius says that *a simple form cannot be a subject.*[46] But God is most absolutely a simple form, as was shown.[47] Therefore He cannot be a subject. But everything about which an affirmative proposition is made is taken as a subject. Therefore an affirmative proposition cannot be formed about God.

Obj. 3. Further, every intellect is false which understands a thing otherwise than as it is. But God has being without any composition, as was shown above.[48] Therefore, since every intellect which makes an affirmation understands something as composite, it seems that a true affirmative proposition about God cannot be made.

On the contrary, What is of faith cannot be false. But some affirmative propositions are of faith; as that God is Three and One, and that He is omnipotent. Therefore true affirmative propositions can be formed about God.

I answer that, Affirmative propositions can be truly formed about God. To prove this we must observe that in every true affirmative proposition the predicate and the subject must signify in some way the same thing in reality, and diverse things in idea. And this appears to be the case both in propositions which have an accidental predicate and in those which have a substantial predicate. For it is manifest that *man* and *white* are the same in subject, and diverse in idea; for the idea of man is one thing, and that of whiteness is another. The same applies when I say, *man is an animal,* since the same thing which is man is truly animal; for in the same *suppositum* there is both a sensible nature by reason of which he is called animal, and the rational nature by reason of which he is called man; hence, here again, predicate and subject are the same as to *suppositum,* but diverse as to idea. But in propositions where the same thing is predicated of itself, the same rule in some way applies, inasmuch as the intellect considers as the *suppositum* what it places in the subject; and what it places in the predicate it considers as the nature of the form existing in the *suppositum,* according to the saying that *predicates are taken formally, and subjects materially.* To this diversity in idea corresponds the plurality of

[45] *De Cael. Hier.,* II, 3 (PG 3, 140).   [46] *De Trin.,* II (PL 64, 1250).
[47] Q. 3, a. 7.   [48] *Ibid.*

predicate and subject, while the intellect signifies the identity
of the thing by the composition itself.

God, however, as considered in Himself, is altogether one
and simple, yet our intellect knows Him according to diverse
conceptions because it cannot see Him as He is in Himself.
Nevertheless, although it understands Him under diverse
conceptions, it yet knows that absolutely one and the same
reality corresponds to its conceptions. Therefore the plurality
of predicate and subject represents the plurality of idea; and
the intellect represents the unity by composition.

Reply Obj. 1. Dionysius says that affirmations about God
are vague or, according to another translation, *incongruous*,
inasmuch as no name can be applied to God according to its
mode of signification,[49] as was said above.

Reply Obj. 2. Our intellect cannot apprehend simple subsisting forms as they really are in themselves; but it apprehends them after the manner of composite things in which
there is something taken as subject and something that is inherent. Therefore it apprehends the simple form as a subject
and attributes something else to it.

Reply Obj. 3. This proposition, *The intellect understanding anything otherwise than it is, is false,* can be taken in two
senses, according as this adverb *otherwise* modifies the verb
to understand from the standpoint of the thing understood,
or from the standpoint of the one who understands. Taken as
referring to the thing understood, the proposition is true, and
the meaning is: Any intellect which understands that a thing
is otherwise than it is, is false. But this does not hold in the
present case, because our intellect, in forming a proposition
about God, does not affirm that He is composite, but that He
is simple. But taken as referring to the one who understands,
the proposition is false. For our intellect understands in one
way, and things are in another. Thus it is clear that our intellect understands material things below itself in an immaterial
way; not that it understands them to be immaterial things:
but its way of understanding is immaterial. Likewise, when
it understands simple things above itself, it understands them
according to its own way, which is composite; yet not so as
to understand them to be composite things. And thus our intellect is not false in composing a judgment concerning God.

---

[49] *De Cael. Hier.*, II, 3 (PG 3, 140).

ON GOD'S KNOWLEDGE

(*In Sixteen Articles*)

HAVING considered what belongs to the divine substance, we have now to treat of what belongs to God's operation. And since one kind of operation is immanent, and another kind of operation proceeds to an exterior effect, we shall treat first of knowledge and of will[1] (for understanding abides in the intelligent agent, and will in the one who wills); and afterwards of the power of God, which is taken to be the principle of the divine operation as proceeding to an exterior effect.[2] Now because to understand is a kind of life, after treating of the divine knowledge, we must consider the divine life.[3] And as knowledge concerns truth, we shall have to consider truth[4] and falsehood.[5] Further, as everything known is in the knower, and the essences of things as existing in the knowledge of God are called *ideas,* to the consideration of knowledge there will have to be added a consideration of ideas.[6]

Concerning knowledge, there are sixteen points for inquiry: (1) Whether there is knowledge in God? (2) Whether God understands Himself? (3) Whether He comprehends Himself? (4) Whether His understanding is His substance? (5) Whether He understands other things besides Himself? (6) Whether He has a proper knowledge of them? (7) Whether the knowledge of God is discursive? (8) Whether the knowledge of God is the cause of things? (9) Whether God has knowledge of non-existing things? (10) Whether He has knowledge of evil? (11) Whether He has knowledge of individual things? (12) Whether He knows the infinite? (13) Whether He knows future contingent things? (14) Whether He knows whatever is enunciable? (15) Whether the knowledge of God is variable? (16) Whether God has speculative or practical knowledge of things?

[1] Q. 19. [2] Q. 25. [3] Q. 18. [4] Q. 16. [5] Q. 17. [6] Q. 15.

First Article

WHETHER THERE IS KNOWLEDGE IN GOD?

We proceed thus to the First Article:—

Objection 1. It seems that in God there is not knowledge [*scientia*]. For knowledge is a habit; and habit does not belong to God, since it is the mean between potentiality and act. Therefore knowledge is not in God.

Obj. 2. Further, since science is about conclusions, it is a kind of knowledge caused by something else, namely, the knowledge of principles. But nothing caused is in God; therefore science is not in God.

Obj. 3. Further, all knowledge is universal, or particular. But in God there is no universal or particular.[7] Therefore there is no knowledge in God.

On the contrary, The Apostle says, *O the depth of the riches of the wisdom and of the knowledge of God* (*Rom.* xi. 33).

I answer that, In God there exists the most perfect knowledge. To prove this, we must note that knowing beings are distinguished from non-knowing beings in that the latter possess only their own form; whereas the knowing being is naturally adapted to have also the form of some other thing, for the species of the thing known is in the knower. Hence it is manifest that the nature of a non-knowing being is more contracted and limited; whereas the nature of knowing beings has a greater amplitude and extension. That is why the Philosopher says that *the soul is in a sense all things.*[8] Now the contraction of a form comes through the matter. Hence, as we have said above, according as they are the more immaterial, forms approach more nearly to a kind of infinity.[9] Therefore it is clear that the immateriality of a thing is the reason why it is cognitive, and that according to the mode of immateriality is the mode of cognition. Hence, it is said in *De Anima* ii. that plants do not know, because of their materiality.[10] But sense is cognitive because it can receive species free from matter; and the intellect is still further cognitive, because it is more *separated from matter and unmixed,* as is

---

[7] Q. 13, a. 9, ad 2.   [8] *De An.,* III, 8 (431b 21).   [9] Q. 7, a. 2.
[10] Aristotle, *De An.,* II, 12 (424a 32).

said in *De Anima* iii.[11] Since therefore God is in the highest degree of immateriality, as was stated above,[12] it follows that He occupies the highest place in knowledge.

Reply Obj. 1. Because perfections flowing from God to creatures exist in a higher state in God Himself,[13] whenever a name taken from any created perfection is attributed to God, there must be separated from its signification anything that belongs to the imperfect mode proper to creatures. Hence knowledge is not a quality in God, nor a habit; but substance and pure act.

Reply Obj. 2. Whatever is divided and multiplied in creatures exists in God simply and unitedly as was said above.[14] Now man has different kinds of knowledge, according to the different objects of his knowledge. He has *understanding* as regards the knowledge of principles; he has *science* as regards knowledge of conclusions; he has *wisdom,* according as he knows the highest cause; he has *counsel* or *prudence,* according as he knows what is to be done. But God knows all these by one simple act of knowledge, as will be shown. Hence the simple knowledge of God can be named by all these names; in such a way, however, that there must be removed from each of them, so far as they are predicated of God, everything that savors of imperfection; and everything that expresses perfection is to be retained in them. Hence it is said, *With Him is wisdom and strength, He hath counsel and understanding.* (*Job* xii. 13).

Reply Obj. 3. Knowledge is according to the mode of the one who knows, for the thing known is in the knower according to the mode of the knower. Now since the mode of the divine essence is higher than that of creatures, divine knowledge does not exist in God after the mode of created knowledge, so as to be universal or particular, or habitual, or potential, or existing according to any such mode.

Second Article

WHETHER GOD UNDERSTANDS HIMSELF?

We proceed thus to the Second Article:—
Objection 1. It seems that God does not understand Him-

[11] *Op. cit.,* III, 4 (429a 18; b5).   [12] Q. 7, a. 1.   [13] Q. 4, a. 2.
[14] Q. 13, a. 4.

self. For it is said in the *Book of Causes, Every knower who knows his own essence returns completely to his own essence.*[15] But God does not go out from His own essence, nor is He moved at all; thus He cannot return to His own essence. Therefore He does not know His own essence.

Obj. 2. Further, *to understand is a kind of passion and becoming,* as the Philosopher says;[16] and knowledge also is a kind of assimilation to the object known, and the thing known is the perfection of the knower. But nothing becomes, or suffers, or is made perfect by itself; *nor,* as Hilary says, *is a thing its own likeness.*[17] Therefore God does not know Himself.

Obj. 3. Further, we are like to God chiefly in our intellect, because we are in the image of God in our mind, as Augustine says.[18] But our intellect understands itself only as it understands other things, as is said in *De Anima* iii.[19] Therefore God understands Himself only so far perchance as He understands other things.

On the contrary, It is written: *The things that are of God no man knoweth, but the Spirit of God* (*1 Cor.* ii. 11).

I answer that, God understands Himself through Himself. In proof whereof it must be known that, although in operations which pass to an external effect the object of the operation, which is taken as the term, exists outside the operator, nevertheless, in operations that remain in the operator, the object signified as the term of operation resides in the operator; and according as it is in the operator is the operation actual. Hence the Philosopher says that *the sensible in act is the sense in act, and the intelligible in act is the intellect in act.*[20] For the reason why we actually feel or know a thing is because our intellect or sense is actually informed by the sensible or intelligible species. And because of this only, it follows that sense or intellect is distinct from the sensible or intelligible object, since both are in potentiality.

Since therefore God has nothing in Him of potentiality, but is pure act, His intellect and its object must be altogether the same; so that He neither is without the intelligible spe-

---

[15] *De Causis,* XV (p. 173).   [16] *De An.,* III, 4 (429b 24) ; 7 (431a 6). [17] *De Trin.,* III, 23 (PL 10, 92).   [18] *De Genesi ad Litt.,* VII, 12 (PL. 34, 347) ; *De Trin.,* XV, 1 (PL 42, 1057).   [19] Aristotle, *De An.,* III, 4 (430a 2).   [20] *Op. cit.,* III, 2 (426a 16) ; 4 (430a 3).

cies, as is the case with our intellect when it understands
potentially, nor does the intelligible species differ from the
substance of the divine intellect, as it differs in our intellect
when it understands actually; but the intelligible species itself is the divine intellect itself, and thus God understands
Himself through Himself.

Reply Obj. 1. To return to its own essence means only that
a thing subsists in itself. Inasmuch as the form perfects the
matter by giving it being, it is in a certain way diffused in it;
and it returns to itself inasmuch as it has being in itself.
Therefore, those cognitive powers which are not subsisting,
but are the acts of organs, do not know themselves, as in
the case of each of the senses; whereas those cognitive powers which are subsisting know themselves, and this is why it
is said in the *Book of Causes* that *whoever knows his essence
returns to it.*[21] Now it supremely belongs to God to be self-
subsisting. Hence, according to this mode of speaking, He
supremely returns to His own essence and knows Himself.

Reply Obj. 2. Becoming and passion are taken equivocally
when *to understand is described as a kind of becoming or
passion,* as is stated in *De Anima* iii.[22] For to understand is
not the motion that is an act of something imperfect passing
from one state to another, but it is an act, existing in the
agent itself, of something perfect. Likewise, that the intellect
is perfected by the intelligible object, *i.e.*, is assimilated to
it, this belongs to an intellect which is sometimes in potentiality; because the fact of its being in a state of potentiality
makes it differ from the intelligible object and assimilates it
thereto through the intelligible species, which is the likeness
of the thing understood, and makes it to be perfected thereby,
as potentiality is perfected by act. On the other hand, the
divine intellect, which is in no way in potentiality, is not
perfected by the intelligible object, nor is it assimilated
thereto, but is its own perfection and its own intelligible object.

Reply Obj. 3. Its physical being does not belong to primary matter, which is a potentiality, unless it is reduced to
act by a form. Now our possible intellect has the same relation to intelligible objects as primary matter has to physical

[21] *De Causis*, XV (p. 173).   [22] Aristotle, *De An.*, III, 4 (429b 24);
7 (431a 6).

things; for it is in potentiality as regards intelligible objects, just as primary matter is to physical things. Hence our possible intellect can be exercised concerning intelligible objects only so far as it is perfected by the intelligible species of something; and thus it understands itself by an intelligible species, in the same way that it understands other things: for it is manifest that by knowing the intelligible object it understands also its own act of understanding, and by this act knows the intellectual power. But God is as pure act both in the order of being, as also in the order of intelligible objects; therefore He understands Himself through Himself.

Third Article

WHETHER GOD COMPREHENDS HIMSELF?

We proceed thus to the Third Article:—

Objection 1. It seems that God does not comprehend Himself. For Augustine says, that *whatever comprehends itself is finite to itself.*[23] But God is in all ways infinite. Therefore He does not comprehend Himself.

Obj. 2. If it be said that God is infinite to us, and finite to Himself, it can be urged to the contrary, that everything in God is truer than it is in us. If therefore God is finite to Himself, but infinite to us, then God is more truly finite than infinite; which is against what was laid down above.[24] Therefore God does not comprehend Himself.

On the contrary, Augustine says, *Everything that understands itself, comprehends itself.*[25] But God understands Himself. Therefore He comprehends Himself.

I answer that, God comprehends Himself perfectly, as can be thus proved. A thing is said to be comprehended when the end of the knowledge of it is attained, and this is accomplished when it is known as perfectly as it is knowable. Thus, a demonstrable proposition is comprehended when known by demonstration, not, however, when it is known by some probable argument. Now it is manifest that God knows Himself as perfectly as He is perfectly knowable. For everything is knowable according to the mode of its actuality, since a thing is not known according as it is in potentiality,

---

[23] *Lib. 83 Quaest.,* q. 15 (PL 40, 15).   [24] Q. 7, a. 1.   [25] *Lib. 83 Quaest.,* q. 15 (PL 40, 15).

but in so far as it is in actuality, as said in *Metaph.* ix.[26]
Now the power of God in knowing is as great as His actuality
in existing; because it is from the fact that He is in act and
free from all matter and potentiality, that God is cognitive,
as was shown above. Whence it is manifest that He knows
Himself as much as He is knowable; and for that reason He
perfectly comprehends Himself.

Reply Obj. 1. The strict meaning of *comprehension* signifies that one thing possesses and includes another; and in
this sense everything comprehended is finite, as also is everything included in another. But God is not said to be comprehended by Himself in this sense, as if His intellect were
another reality apart from Himself which contained and included Him; such ways of speaking are rather to be taken by
way of negation. For just as God is said to be in Himself inasmuch as He is not contained by anything outside of Himself; so He is said to be comprehended by Himself inasmuch
as nothing in Himself is hidden from Him. For Augustine
says that *The whole is comprehended when seen, if it is seen
in such a way that nothing of it is hidden from the seer.*[27]

Reply Obj. 2. When it is said, *God is finite to Himself,* this
is to be understood according to a certain proportional likeness, because He has the same relation in not exceeding His
intellect, as anything finite has in not exceeding a finite intellect. But God is not to be called finite to Himself in the
sense that He understands Himself to be something finite.

Fourth Article

WHETHER THE ACT OF GOD'S INTELLECT IS HIS
SUBSTANCE?

We proceed thus to the Fourth Article:—

Objection 1. It seems that the act of God's intellect is not
His substance. For to understand is an operation. But an
operation signifies something proceeding from the operator.
Therefore the act of God's intellect is not His substance.

Obj. 2. Further, to understand one's act of understanding
is to understand something that is neither great nor chiefly
understood, but secondary and accessory. If therefore God

[26] Aristotle, *Metaph.,* VIII, 9 (1051a 31).   [27] *Epist.* CXLVII, 9
(PL 33, 606).

be His own act of understanding, His act of understanding will be as when we understand our act of understanding: and thus God's act of understanding will not be something great.

Obj. 3. Further, every act of understanding involves understanding something. When therefore God understands Himself, if He Himself is not distinct from this act of understanding, He understands that He understands, and that He understands that He understands Himself; and so on to infinity. Therefore the act of God's intellect is not His substance.

On the contrary, Augustine says, *In God to be is the same as to be wise.*[28] But to be wise is the same thing as to understand. Therefore in God to be is the same thing as to understand. But God's being is His substance, as was shown above.[29] Therefore the act of God's intellect is His substance.

I answer that, It must be said that the act of God's intellect is His substance. For if His act of understanding were other than His substance, then something else, as the Philosopher says,[30] would be the act and perfection of the divine substance, to which the divine substance would be related as potentiality is to act; which is altogether impossible, because the act of understanding is the perfection and act of the one understanding. Let us now consider how this is. As was laid down above, to understand is not an act passing to anything extrinsic, but it remains in the operator as his own act and perfection; as being is the perfection of the one existing: for just as being follows on the form, so in like manner to understand follows on the intelligible species. Now in God there is no form which is something other than His being, as was shown above.[31] Hence, as His essence itself is also His intelligible species, it necessarily follows that His act of understanding must be His essence and His being.

Thus it follows from all the foregoing that in God intellect, the object understood, the intelligible species, and His act of understanding are entirely one and the same. Hence, when God is said to be understanding, no multiplicity is attached to His substance.

Reply Obj. 1. To understand is not an operation proceeding out of the operator, but remaining in him.

Reply Obj. 2. When that act of understanding which is

[28] *De Trin.,* VII, 2; VI, 4 (PL 42, 936; 927).   [29] Q. 3, a. 4.
[30] *Metaph.,* XI, 9 (1074b 18).   [31] Q. 3, a. 4.

not subsistent is understood, something great is not understood; as when we understand our act of understanding; and so this cannot be likened to the act of the divine understanding which is subsistent.

Thus appears the *Reply to Obj.* 3. For the act of divine understanding, which subsists in itself, belongs to its very self and is not another's; hence it need not proceed to infinity.

Fifth Article

WHETHER GOD KNOWS THINGS OTHER THAN HIMSELF?

We proceed thus to the Fifth Article:—

Objection 1. It seems that God does not know other things besides Himself. For all other things but God are outside of God. But Augustine says that *God does not behold anything out of Himself.*[32] Therefore He does not know things other than Himself.

Obj. 2. Further, the object understood is the perfection of the one who understands. If therefore God understands other things besides Himself, something else will be the perfection of God, and will be nobler than He; which is impossible.

Obj. 3. Further, the act of understanding is specified by the intelligible object, as is every other act from its own object. Hence the intellectual act is so much the nobler, the nobler the object understood. But God is His own intellectual act, as is clear from what has been said. If therefore God understands anything other than Himself, then God Himself is specified by something other than Himself; which cannot be. Therefore He does not understand things other than Himself.

On the contrary, It is written: *All things are naked and open to His eyes* (*Heb.* iv. 13).

I answer that, God necessarily knows things other than Himself. For it is manifest that He perfectly understands Himself; otherwise His being would not be perfect, since His being is His act of understanding. Now if anything is perfectly known, it follows of necessity that its power is perfectly known. But the power of anything can be perfectly known only by knowing to what that power extends. Since,

---

[32] *Lib. 83 Quaest.,* q. 46 (PL 40, 30).

therefore, the divine power extends to other things by the very fact that it is the first effective cause of all things, as is clear from the aforesaid,[33] God must necessarily know things other than Himself. And this appears still more plainly if we add that the very being of the first efficient cause—viz., God—is His own act of understanding. Hence whatever effects pre-exist in God, as in the first cause, must be in His act of understanding, and they must be there in an intelligible way: for everything which is in another is in it according to the mode of that in which it is.

Now in order to know how God knows things other than Himself, we must consider that a thing is known in two ways: in itself, and in another. A thing is known *in itself* when it is known by the proper species adequate to the knowable object itself; as when the eye sees a man through the species of a man. A thing is seen *in another* through the species of that which contains it; as when a part is seen in the whole through the species of the whole, or when a man is seen in a mirror through the species of the mirror, or by any other way by which one thing is seen in another.

So we say that God sees Himself in Himself, because He sees Himself through His essence; and He sees other things, not in themselves, but in Himself, inasmuch as His essence contains the likeness of things other than Himself.

Reply Obj. 1. The passage of Augustine in which it is said that God *sees nothing outside Himself* is not to be taken in such a way, as if God saw nothing that was outside Himself, but in the sense that what is outside Himself He does not see except in Himself, as was explained above.

Reply Obj. 2. The object understood is a perfection of the one understanding, not by its substance, but by its species, according to which it is in the intellect as its form and perfection. For, as is said in *De Anima* iii,[34] *a stone is not in the soul, but its species.* Now those things which are other than God are understood by God inasmuch as the essence of God contains their species, as was explained above; and hence it does not follow that anything is the perfection of the divine intellect other than the divine essence.

Reply Obj. 3. The intellectual act is not specified by what is understood in another, but by the principal object under-

[33] Q. 2, a. 3.   [34] Aristotle. *De An.*, III, 8 (431b 29).

stood in which other things are understood. For the intellectual act is specified by its object inasmuch as the intelligible form is the principle of the intellectual operation, since
every operation is specified by the form which is its principle
of operation, as heating by heat. Hence the intellectual operation is specified by that intelligible form which makes the
intellect to be in act. And this is the species of the principal
thing understood, which in God is nothing but His own essence in which all the species of things are comprehended.
Hence it does not follow that the divine intellectual act, or
rather God Himself, is specified by anything other than the
divine essence itself.

Sixth Article

WHETHER GOD KNOWS THINGS OTHER THAN HIMSELF BY PROPER KNOWLEDGE?

We proceed thus to the Sixth Article:—
Objection 1. It seems that God does not know things other
than Himself by proper knowledge. For, as was shown, God
knows things other than Himself according as they are in
Him. But other things are in Him as in their common and
universal first cause, and are therefore known by God as in
their first and universal cause. This is to know them by general, and not by proper, knowledge. Therefore God knows
things besides Himself by general, and not by proper knowledge.

Obj. 2. Further, the created essence is as distant from the
divine essence, as the divine essence is distant from the created essence. But the divine essence cannot be known through
the created essence, as was said above.[35] Therefore neither
can the created essence be known through the divine essence.
Thus, as God knows only by His essence, it follows that He
does not know what the creature is in its essence, so as to
know *what it is,* which is to have a proper knowledge of it.

Obj. 3. Further, proper knowledge of a thing can come
only through its proper likeness. But as God knows all things
by His essence, it seems that He does not know each thing
by its proper likeness; for one thing cannot be the proper
likeness of many and diverse things. Therefore God has not

[35] Q. 2, a. 2.

a proper knowledge of things, but a general knowledge; for to know things otherwise than by their proper likeness is to have only a common knowledge of them.

On the contrary, To have a proper knowledge of things is to know them not only in general, but as they are distinct from each other. Now God knows things in that manner. Hence it is written that He reaches *even to the division of the soul and the spirit, of the joints also and the marrow, and is a discerner of the thoughts and intents of the heart; neither is there any creature invisible in His sight* (*Heb.* iv. 12, 13).

I answer that, Some have erred on this point, saying that God knows things other than Himself only in general, that is, only as beings.[36] For as fire, if it knew itself as the principle of heat, would know the nature of heat, and all things else in so far as they are hot; so God, through knowing Himself as the source of being, knows the nature of being, and all other things in so far as they are beings.

But this cannot be. For to know a thing in general, and not in particular, is to have an imperfect knowledge of it. Hence our intellect, when it is reduced from potentiality to act, acquires first a universal and confused knowledge of things, before it knows them in particular; as proceeding from the imperfect to the perfect, as is clear from *Physics* i.[37] If therefore the knowledge of God regarding things other than Himself were only universal and not particular, it would follow that His understanding would not be absolutely perfect; therefore neither would His being. And this is against what was said above.[38] We must therefore say that God knows things other than Himself with a proper knowledge, not only in so far as being is common to them, but in so far as one is distinguished from the other.

In proof thereof we may observe that some, wishing to show that God knows many things by one means, bring forward some examples, as, for instance, that if the center knew itself, it would know all lines that proceed from the center;[39] or if light knew itself, it would know all colors.[40] Now although these examples are similar in part, namely, as regards

---

[36] Attributed to Averroes by St. Thomas, *In I Sent.*, d. xxxv, q. 1, a. 3.   [37] Aristotle, *Phys.*, I, 1 (184a 22).   [38] Q. 4, a. 1.   [39] Cf. Alex. of Hales, *Summa Theol.*, I, no. 166 (I, 249).   [40] Cf. Pseudo-Dionysius, *De Div. Nom.*, VII, 2 (PG 3, 870).

universal causality, nevertheless they fail in this respect, that multitude and diversity are caused by the one universal principle, not as regards that which is the principle of distinction, but only as regards that in which they communicate. For the diversity of colors is not caused by the light only, but by the diverse disposition of the diaphanous medium which receives it; and likewise, the diversity of the lines is caused by their diverse position. Hence it is that this kind of diversity and multitude cannot be known in its principle by a proper knowledge, but only in a general way. In God, however, it is otherwise. For it was shown above that whatever perfection exists in any creature wholly pre-exists and is contained in God in an excelling manner.[41] Now not only what is common to creatures—viz., being—belongs to their perfection, but also what makes them distinguished from each other; as living and understanding, and the like, whereby living beings are distinguished from the non-living, and the intelligent from the non-intelligent. Likewise, every form whereby each thing is constituted in its own species is a perfection. Hence it is that all things pre-exist in God, not only as regards what is common to all, but also as regards what distinguishes one thing from another. And therefore as God contains all perfections in Himself, the essence of God is compared to all other essences of things, not as the common to the proper, as unity is to numbers, or as the center [of a circle] to the radii, but as perfect act to imperfect acts; as if I were to compare man to animal, or six, a perfect number, to the imperfect numbers contained under it. Now it is manifest that by a perfect act imperfect acts can be known not only in general but also by proper knowledge; thus, for example, whoever knows a man, knows an animal by proper knowledge, and whoever knows the number six, knows the number three also by proper knowledge.

Since therefore the essence of God contains in itself all the perfection contained in the essence of any other being, and far more, God can know all things in Himself with a proper knowledge. For the nature proper to each thing consists in some particular participation of the divine perfection. Now God could not be said to know Himself perfectly unless He knew all the ways in which His own perfection can be

shared by others. Neither could He know the very nature
of being perfectly, unless He knew all the ways of being.
Hence it is manifest that God knows all things with a proper
knowledge, according as they are distinguished from each
other.

Reply Obj. 1. Thus to know a thing as it is in the knower
may be understood in two ways. In one way, according as
this adverb *thus* imports the mode of knowledge on the part
of the thing known; and in that sense it is false. For the
knower does not always know the object known according to
the being it has in the knower; since the eye does not know
a stone according to the being it has in the eye, but by the
species of the stone which is in it the eye knows the stone
according to its being outside the eye. And even if any
knower should know the object known according to the being
it has in the knower, the knower nevertheless knows it according to its being outside the knower; thus the intellect
knows a stone according to the intelligible being it has in
the intellect, inasmuch as it knows that it understands; and
yet it knows the being of a stone in its own nature. If however the adverb *thus* be understood to import the mode [of
knowledge] on the part of the knower, in that sense it is true
that only the knower has knowledge of the object known as
it is in the knower; for the more perfectly the thing known is
in the knower, the more perfect is the mode of knowledge.

We must say therefore that God knows not only that
things are in Him, but, by the fact that they are in Him, He
knows them in their own nature, and all the more perfectly,
the more perfectly each one is in Him.

Reply Obj. 2. The created essence is compared to the essence of God as the imperfect to the perfect act. Therefore
the created essence cannot sufficiently lead us to the knowledge of the divine essence, but rather the converse.

Reply Obj. 3. The same thing cannot be considered as the
proportioned likeness of diverse things. But the divine essence *excels* all creatures. Hence it can be taken as the proper
likeness of each thing according to the diverse ways in which
diverse creatures participate in it and imitate it.

Seventh Article

WHETHER THE KNOWLEDGE OF GOD IS DISCURSIVE?

We proceed thus to the Seventh Article:—

Objection 1. It seems that the knowledge of God is discursive. For the knowledge of God is not habitual knowledge, but actual knowledge. Now the Philosopher says: *The habitual knowledge may regard many things at once; but actual understanding regards only one thing at a time.*[42] Therefore as God knows many things, Himself and others, as was shown above, it seems that He does not understand all at once, but proceeds from one to another.

Obj. 2. Further, to know the effect through its cause belongs to discursive knowledge. But God knows other things through Himself, as effects through their cause. Therefore His knowledge is discursive.

Obj. 3. Further, God knows each creature more perfectly than we know it. But we know the effects in their created causes; and thus we go discursively from causes to things caused. Therefore it seems that the same applies to God.

On the contrary, Augustine says, *God does not see all things in their particularity or separately, as if He looked first here and then there; but He sees all things together at once.*[43]

I answer that, In the divine knowledge there is no discursiveness; the proof of which is as follows. In our knowledge there is a twofold discursion. One is according to succession only, as when we have actually understood anything, we turn ourselves to understand something else; while the other mode of discursion is according to causality, as when through principles we arrive at the knowledge of conclusions. The first kind of discursion cannot belong to God. For many things, which we understand in succession if each is considered in itself, we understand simultaneously if we see them in some one thing; if, for instance, we understand the parts in the whole, or see different things in a mirror. Now God sees all things in one thing alone, which is Himself. Therefore God sees all things together, and not successively. Likewise the second mode of discursion cannot be applied to God.

---

[42] *Top.,* II, 10 (114b 34).   [43] *De Trin.,* XV, 14 (PL 42, 1077).

First, because this second mode of discursion presupposes the first, for whosoever proceeds from principles to conclusions does not consider both at once; secondly, because to advance thus is to proceed from the known to the unknown. Hence it is manifest that when the first is known, the second is still unknown; and thus the second is known not in the first, but from the first. Now the term of discursive reasoning is attained when the second is seen in the first, by resolving the effects into their causes; and then the discursion ceases. Hence as God sees His effects in Himself as in their cause, His knowledge is not discursive.

Reply Obj. 1. Although the act of understanding is one in itself, nevertheless many things may be understood in something one, as was shown above.

Reply Obj. 2. God does not know first a cause and then, through it, its hitherto supposedly unknown effects; He knows the effects in the cause, and hence His knowledge is not discursive, as was shown above.

Reply Obj. 3. It is true that God sees the effects of created causes in the causes themselves, much better than we can; but still not in such a manner that the knowledge of the effects is caused in Him by the knowledge of the created causes, as is the case with us; and hence His knowledge is not discursive.

Eighth Article

WHETHER THE KNOWLEDGE OF GOD IS THE CAUSE OF THINGS?

We proceed thus to the Eighth Article:—

Objection 1. It seems that the knowledge of God is not the cause of things. For Origen says (on *Rom.* viii. 30): *A thing will not happen, because God knows it as future, but because it is future, it is on that account known by God before it exists.*[44]

Obj. 2. Further, given the cause, the effect follows. But the knowledge of God is eternal. Therefore if the knowledge of God is the cause of created things, it seems that creatures are eternal.

Obj. 3. Further, *The knowable thing is prior to knowledge,*

[44] *In Rom.*, VII, super VIII, 30 (PG 14, 1126).

and is its measure, as the Philosopher says.[45] But what is posterior and measured cannot be a cause. Therefore the knowledge of God is not the cause of things.

On the contrary, Augustine says, *Not because they are, does God know all creatures spiritual and temporal, but because He knows them, therefore they are.*[46]

I answer that, The knowledge of God is the cause of things. For the knowledge of God is to all creatures what the knowledge of the artificer is to things made by his art. Now the knowledge of the artificer is the cause of the things made by his art from the fact that the artificer works through his intellect. Hence the form in the intellect must be the principle of action; as heat is the principle of heating. Nevertheless, we must observe that a natural form, being a form that remains in that to which it gives being, denotes a principle of action according only as it has an inclination to an effect; and likewise, the intelligible form does not denote a principle of action in so far as it resides in the one who understands unless there is added to it the inclination to an effect, which inclination is through the will. For since the intelligible form has a relation to contraries (inasmuch as the same knowledge relates to contraries), it would not produce a determinate effect unless it were determined to one thing by the appetite, as the Philosopher says.[47] Now it is manifest that God causes things by His intellect, since His being is His act of understanding; and hence His knowledge must be the cause of things, in so far as His will is joined to it. Hence the knowledge of God as the cause of things is usually called the *knowledge of approbation.*

Reply Obj. 1. Origen[48] spoke in reference to that aspect of knowledge to which the idea of causality does not belong unless the will is joined to it, as is said above.

But when he says that the reason why God foreknows some things is because they are future, this must be understood according to the cause of consequence, and not according to the cause of being. For if things are in the future, it follows that God foreknows them; but the futurity of things is not the cause why God knows them.

Reply Obj. 2. The knowledge of God is the cause of things

[45] Aristotle, *Metaph.,* IX, 1 (1053a 33).   [46] *De Trin.,* XV, 13 (PL 42, 1076); VI, 10 (PL 42, 931).   [47] Aristotle, *Metaph.,* VIII, 5 (1048a 11).   [48] *In Rom.,* VII, super VIII, 30 (PG 14, 1126).

according as things are in His knowledge. But that things should be eternal was not in the knowledge of God; hence, although the knowledge of God is eternal, it does not follow that creatures are eternal.

Reply Obj. 3. Natural things are midway between the knowledge of God and our knowledge: for we receive knowledge from natural things, of which God is the cause by His knowledge. Hence, just as the natural things that can be known by us are prior to our knowledge, and are its measure, so the knowledge of God is prior to them, and is their measure; as, for instance, a house is midway between the knowledge of the builder who made it, and the knowledge of the one who gathers his knowledge of the house from the house already built.

Ninth Article

WHETHER GOD HAS KNOWLEDGE OF THINGS THAT ARE NOT?

We proceed thus to the Ninth Article:—

Objection 1. It seems that God has not knowledge of things that are not. For the knowledge of God is of true things. But *truth* and *being* are convertible terms. Therefore the knowledge of God is not of things that are not.

Obj. 2. Further, knowledge requires likeness between the knower and the thing known. But those things that are not cannot have any likeness to God, Who is very being. Therefore what is not, cannot be known by God.

Obj. 3. Further, the knowledge of God is the cause of what is known by Him. But it is not the cause of things that are not, because a thing that is not has no cause. Therefore God has no knowledge of things that are not.

On the contrary, The Apostle says: *Who . . . calleth those things that are not as those that are* (*Rom.* iv. 17).

I answer that, God knows all things whatsoever that in any way are. Now it is possible that things that are not absolutely should be in a certain sense. For, absolutely speaking, those things are which are actual; whereas things, which are not actual, are in the power either of God Himself or of a creature, whether in active power, or passive; whether in the power of thought or of imagination, or of any other kind whatsoever. Whatever therefore can be made, or thought, or said by the creature, as also whatever He Himself can do, all are known to God, although they are not actual. And to this extent it can be said that He has knowledge even of things that are not.

Now, among the things that are not actual, a certain difference is to be noted. For though some of them may not be in act now, still they have been, or they will be; and God is said to know all these with the *knowledge of vision*: for since God's act of understanding, which is His being, is measured by eternity, and since eternity is without succession, comprehending all time, the present glance of God extends over all time, and to all things which exist in any time, as to objects present to Him. But there are other things in God's power, or the creature's, which nevertheless are not, nor will be, nor have been; and as regards these He is said to have the knowledge, not of vision, but of *simple intelligence*. This is so called because the things we see around us have distinct being outside the seer.

Reply Obj. 1. Those things that are not actual are true in so far as they are in potentiality, for it is true that they are in potentiality; and as such they are known by God.

Reply Obj. 2. Since God is very being, everything is in so far as it participates in the likeness of God; as everything is hot in so far as it participates in heat. So, things in potentiality are known by God, even though they are not in act.

Reply Obj. 3. The knowledge of God is the cause of things when the will is joined to it. Hence it is not necessary that whatever God knows should be, or have been or is to be; but this is necessary only as regards what He wills to be, or permits to be. Further, it is not in the knowledge of God that these things be, but that they be possible.

Tenth Article

WHETHER GOD KNOWS EVIL THINGS?

We proceed thus to the Tenth Article:—

Objection 1. It seems that God does not know evil things. For the Philosopher says that the intellect which is not in potentiality does not know privation.[49] But *evil is the privation of good*, as Augustine says.[50] Therefore, as the intellect

---

[49] *De An.*, III, 6 (430b 23).   [50] *Confess.* III, 7 (PL 32, 688).

of God is never in potentiality, but always in act, as is clear
from the foregoing, it seems that God does not know evil
things.

Obj. 2. Further, all knowledge is either the cause of the
thing known, or is caused by it. But the knowledge of God
is not the cause of evil, nor is it caused by evil. Therefore
God does not know evil things.

Obj. 3. Further, everything known is known either by its
likeness, or by its opposite. But whatever God knows, He
knows through His essence, as is clear from the foregoing.
Now neither is the divine essence the likeness of evil, nor is
evil its contrary; for the divine essence has no contrary, as
Augustine says.[51] Therefore God does not know evil things.

Obj. 4. Further, what is known through another, and not
through itself, is imperfectly known. But evil is not known
by God through itself, otherwise evil would be in God; for
the thing known must be in the knower. Therefore if evil is
known through something else, namely, through good, it
will be known by Him imperfectly; which cannot be, for the
knowledge of God is not imperfect. Therefore God does not
know evil things.

On the contrary, It is written (*Prov.* xv. 11), *Hell and
destruction are before God.*

I answer that, Whoever knows a thing perfectly must
know all that can occur to it. Now there are some good things
to which corruption by evil may occur. Hence God would
not know good things perfectly, unless He also knew evil
things. Now a thing is knowable in the degree in which it is;
hence, since this is the essence of evil that it is the privation
of good, by the very fact that God knows good things, He
also knows evil things; as by light darkness is known. Hence
Dionysius says: *God through Himself receives the vision
of darkness, not otherwise seeing darkness except through
light.*[52]

Reply Obj. 1. The saying of the Philosopher must be understood as meaning that the intellect which is not in potentiality does not know privation by a privation existing in it;
and this agrees with what he had said previously, that a point
and every indivisible thing are known by privation of division. This is because simple and indivisible forms are in our

[51] *De Civit. Dei,* XII, 2 (PL 41, 350).   [52] *De Div. Nom.,* VII, 2
(PG 3, 869).

intellect, not actually, but only potentially; for were they in
our intellect actually, they would not be known by privation.
It is thus that simple things are known by separate substances. God therefore knows evil, not by a privation existing in Himself, but by its opposite, the good.

Reply Obj. 2. The knowledge of God is not the cause of
evil; it is the cause of the good whereby evil is known.

Reply Obj. 3. Although evil is not opposed to the divine
essence, which is not corruptible by evil, it is opposed to the
effects of God, which He knows by His essence; and knowing them, He knows the opposite evils.

Reply Obj. 4. To know a thing by something else only, belongs to imperfect knowledge, if that thing is knowable in
itself; but evil is not knowable in itself because the very nature of evil consists in the privation of good; therefore evil
can neither be defined nor known except by good.

Eleventh Article

WHETHER GOD KNOWS SINGULAR THINGS?

We proceed thus to the Eleventh Article:—

Objection 1. It seems that God does not know singular
things. For the divine intellect is more immaterial than the
human intellect. Now the human intellect, by reason of its
immateriality, does not know singular things; but as the
Philosopher says, *reason has to do with universals, sense
with singular things.*[53] Therefore God does not know singular
things.

Obj. 2. Further, in us those powers alone know the singular, which receive the species not abstracted from material
conditions. But in God things are in the highest degree abstracted from all materiality. Therefore God does not know
singular things.

Obj. 3. Further, all knowledge comes about through some
likeness. But the likeness of singular things, in so far as they
are singular, does not seem to be in God; for the principle of
singularity is matter, which, since it is in potentiality only,
is altogether unlike God, Who is pure act. Therefore God
cannot know singular things.

[53] *De An.,* II, 5 (417b 22).

On the contrary, It is written (*Prov.* xvi. 2), *All the ways of a man are open to His eyes.*

I answer that, God knows singular things. For all perfections found in creatures pre-exist in God in a higher way, as is clear from the foregoing.[54] Now to know singular things is part of our perfection. Hence God must know singular things. Even the Philosopher considers it incongruous that anything known by us should be unknown to God; and thus against Empedocles he argues that *God would be most ignorant if He did not know discord.*[55] Now the perfections which are found divided among inferior beings exist simply and unitedly in God; hence, although by one power we know the universal and immaterial, and by another we know singular and material things, nevertheless God knows both by His simple intellect.

Now some, wishing to show how this can be, said that God knows singular things through universal causes.[56] For nothing exists in any singular thing that does not arise from some universal cause. They give the example of an astronomer who knows all the universal movements of the heavens, and can thence foretell all eclipses that are to come. This, however, is not enough; for from universal causes singular things acquire certain forms and powers which, however they may be joined together, are not individuated except by individual matter. Hence he who knows Socrates because he is white, or because he is the son of Sophroniscus, or because of something of that kind, would not know him in so far as he is this particular man. Hence, following the above explanation, God would not know singular things in their singularity.

On the other hand, others have said that God knows singular things by the application of universal causes to particular effects.[57] But this will not hold; for no one can apply a thing to another unless he first knows that other thing. Hence the said application cannot be the reason of knowing the particular; it rather presupposes the knowledge of singular things.

Therefore we must propose another explanation. Since God is the cause of things by His knowledge, as was stated above, His knowledge extends as far as His causality extends. Hence, as the active power of God extends not only to forms,

[54] Q. 4, a. 2.   [55] *De An.,* I, 5 (410b 4); *Metaph.,* II, 4 (1000b 3).
[56] Cf. Avicenna, *Metaph.,* VIII, 6 (100rb).   [57] Cf. Averroes, *Destruct. Destruct.,* XI (IX, 47rb).

which are the source of universality, but also to matter, as we shall prove further on, the knowledge of God must extend to singular things, which are individuated by matter.[58] For since He knows things other than Himself by His essence, as being the likeness of things, or as their active principle, His essence must be the sufficing principle of knowing all things made by Him, not only in the universal, but also in the singular. The same would apply to the knowledge of the artificer, if it were productive of the whole thing, and not only of the form.

Reply Obj. 1. Our intellect abstracts the intelligible species from the individuating principles; hence the intelligible species in our intellect cannot be the likeness of the individual principles, and on that account our intellect does not know the singular. But the intelligible species in the divine intellect, which is the essence of God, is immaterial not by abstraction, but of itself, being the principle of all the principles which enter into the composition of the thing, whether these be principles of the species or principles of the individual; hence by it God knows not only universals, but also singular things.

Reply Obj. 2. Although the species in the divine intellect has no material conditions in its being like the species received in the imagination and sense, yet it extends to both immaterial and material things through its power.

Reply Obj. 3. Although matter, because of its potentiality, recedes from likeness to God, yet, even in so far as it has being in this wise, it retains a certain likeness to the divine being.

Twelfth Article

WHETHER GOD CAN KNOW INFINITE THINGS?

We proceed thus to the Twelfth Article:—

Objection 1. It seems that God cannot know infinite things. For the infinite, as such, is unknown, since the infinite is that which, *to those who measure it, leaves always something more to be measured,* as the Philosopher says.[59] Moreover, Augustine says that *whatever is comprehended by*

[58] Q. 44, a. 2.   [59] *Phys.,* III, 6 (207a 7).

knowledge is bounded by the comprehension of the knower.[60]
Now infinite things have no boundary. Therefore they cannot be comprehended by the knowledge of God.

Obj. 2. Further, if it be said that things infinite in themselves are finite in God's knowledge, against this it may be urged that the essence of the infinite is that it is untraversable, and of the finite that it is traversable, as is said in *Physics* iii.[61] But the infinite is not traversable either by the finite or by the infinite, as is proved in *Physics* vi.[62] Therefore the infinite cannot be bounded by the finite, nor even by the infinite; and so the infinite cannot be finite in God's knowledge, which is infinite.

Obj. 3. Further, the knowledge of God is the measure of what is known. But it is contrary to the essence of the infinite that it be measured. Therefore infinite things cannot be known by God.

On the contrary, Augustine says, *Although we cannot number the infinite, nevertheless it can be comprehended by Him whose knowledge has no number.*[63]

I answer that, Since God knows not only things actual but also things possible to Himself or to created things, as was shown above, and since these must be infinite, it must be held that He knows infinite things. Although the *knowledge of vision,* which has relation only to things that are, or will be, or have been, is not of infinite things, as some say,[64] for we do not hold that the world is eternal, nor that generation and movement will go on for ever, so that individuals be infinitely multiplied; yet, if we consider more attentively, we must hold that God knows infinite things even by the knowledge of vision. For God knows even the thoughts and affections of hearts, which will be multiplied to infinity since rational creatures will endure forever.

The reason of this is to be found in the fact that the knowledge of every knower is measured by the mode of the form which is the principle of knowledge. For the sensible species in the sense is the likeness of only one individual thing, and can give the knowledge of only one individual. But the intelligible species in our intellect is the likeness of the thing as regards its specific nature, which is participable

[60] *De Civit. Dei,* XII, 18 (PL 41, 368).   [61] Aristotle, *Phys.,* III, 4 (204a 3).   [62] *Op. cit.,* VI, 7 (238b 17).   [63] *De Civit. Dei,* XII, 18 (PL 41, 368).   [64] Cf. q. 7, a. 4; q. 46, a. 2, ad 8.

by infinite particulars. Hence our intellect by the intelligible species of man in a certain way knows infinite men, not however as distinguished from each other, but as communicating in the nature of the species; and the reason is because the intelligible species of our intellect is the likeness of man, not as to the individual principles, but as to the principles of the species. On the other hand, the divine essence, whereby the divine intellect understands, is a sufficing likeness of all things that are, or can be, not only as regards the universal principles, but also as regards the principles proper to each one, as was shown above. Hence it follows that the knowledge of God extends to infinite things, even according as they are distinct from each other.

Reply Obj. 1. The idea of the infinite pertains to quantity, as the Philosopher says.[65] But the idea of quantity implies an order of parts. Therefore to know the infinite according to the mode of the infinite is to know part after part; and in this way the infinite cannot be known, for whatever quantity of parts be taken, there will always remain something else outside. But God does not know the infinite, or infinite things, as if He enumerated part after part; since He knows all things simultaneously and not successively, as was said above. Hence there is nothing to prevent Him from knowing infinite things.

Reply Obj. 2. Transition imports a certain succession of parts; and hence it is that the infinite cannot be traversed by the finite, nor by the infinite. But equality suffices for comprehension, because that is said to be comprehended which has nothing outside the comprehender. Hence, it is not against the idea of the infinite to be comprehended by the infinite. And so, what is infinite in itself can be called finite to the knowledge of God as comprehended; but not as if it were traversable.

Reply Obj. 3. The knowledge of God is the measure of things, not quantitatively, for the infinite is not subject to this kind of measure, but because it measures the essence and truth of things. For everything has truth of nature according to the degree in which it imitates the knowledge of God, as the thing made by art agrees with the art. Granted, however, an actually infinite number of things (for instance,

---

[65] *Phys.,* I, 2 (185a 33).

an infinitude of men, or an infinitude in continuous quantity, as an infinite air, as some of the ancients held),[66] yet it is manifest that these would have a determinate and finite being, because their being would be limited to certain determinate natures. Hence they would be measurable as regards the knowledge of God.

Thirteenth Article

WHETHER THE KNOWLEDGE OF GOD IS OF FUTURE CONTINGENT THINGS?

We proceed thus to the Thirteenth Article:—

Objection 1. It seems that the knowledge of God is not of future contingent things. For from a necessary cause proceeds a necessary effect. But the knowledge of God is the cause of things known, as was said above. Since therefore that knowledge is necessary, what He knows must also be necessary. Therefore the knowledge of God is not of contingent things.

Obj. 2. Further, every conditional proposition, of which the antecedent is absolutely necessary, must have an absolutely necessary consequent. For the antecedent is to the consequent as principles are to the conclusion: and from necessary principles only a necessary conclusion can follow, as is proved in *Poster.* i.[67] But this is a true conditional proposition, *If God knew that this thing will be, it will be,*[68] for the knowledge of God is only of true things. Now, the antecedent of this conditioned proposition is absolutely necessary, because it is eternal, and because it is signified as past. Therefore the consequent is also absolutely necessary. Therefore whatever God knows is necessary; and so the knowledge of God is not of contingent things.

Obj. 3. Further, everything known by God must necessarily be, because even what we ourselves know must necessarily be; and, of course, the knowledge of God is much

[66] Attributed to Anaximenes and Diogenes by Aristotle, *Phys.*, III, 4 (203a 18); *Metaph.*, I, 3 (984a 5).   [67] Aristotle, *Post. Anal.*, I, 6 (75a 4).   [68] Cf. St. Anselm, *De Concord. Praesc. cum Lib. Arb.*, q. I, 1 (PL 158, 509); St. Augustine, *De Civit. Dei*, V, 9; XI, 21 (PL 41, 148; 334); *De Lib. Arb.*, III, 4 (PL 32, 1276); Boethius, *De Consol.*, V, prose 3; prose 6 (PL 63, 840; 860); Peter Lombard, *Sent.*, I, xxxviii, 2 (I, 244).

more certain than ours. But no future contingent thing must necessarily be. Therefore no contingent future thing is known by God.

On the contrary, It is written (*Ps.* xxxii. 15), *He Who hath made the hearts of every one of them, Who understandeth all their works,* that is, of men. Now the works of men are contingent, being subject to free choice. Therefore God knows future contingent things.

I answer that, Since, as was shown above, God knows all things, not only things actual but also things possible to Him and to the creature, and since some of these are future contingent to us, it follows that God knows future contingent things.

In evidence of this, we must observe that a contingent thing can be considered in two ways. First, in itself, in so far as it is already in act, and in this sense it is not considered as future, but as present; neither is it considered as contingent to one of two terms, but as determined to one; and because of this it can be infallibly the object of certain knowledge, for instance to the sense of sight, as when I see that Socrates is sitting down. In another way, a contingent thing can be considered as it is in its cause, and in this way it is considered as future, and as a contingent thing not yet determined to one; for a contingent cause has relation to opposite things: and in this sense a contingent thing is not subject to any certain knowledge. Hence, whoever knows a contingent effect in its cause only, has merely a conjectural knowledge of it. Now God knows all contingent things not only as they are in their causes, but also as each one of them is actually in itself. And although contingent things become actual successively, nevertheless God knows contingent things not successively, as they are in their own being, as we do, but simultaneously. The reason is because His knowledge is measured by eternity, as is also His being; and eternity, being simultaneously whole, comprises all time, as was said above.[69] Hence, all things that are in time are present to God from eternity, not only because He has the essences of things present within Him, as some say,[70] but because His glance is carried from eternity over all things as they are in their presentiality. Hence it is manifest that contingent things are

[69] Q. 10, a. 2, ad 4.   [70] Avicenna, *Metaph.*, VIII, 6 (100rb).

infallibly known by God, inasmuch as they are subject to the divine sight in their presentiality; and yet they are future contingent things in relation to their own causes.

Reply Obj. 1. Although the supreme cause is necessary, the effect may be contingent by reason of the proximate contingent cause; just as the germination of a plant is contingent by reason of the proximate contingent cause, although the movement of the sun, which is the first cause, is necessary. So, likewise, things known by God are contingent because of their proximate causes, while the knowledge of God, which is the first cause, is necessary.

Reply Obj. 2. Some say that this antecedent, *God knew this contingent to be future,* is not necessary, but contingent; because, although it is past, still it imports a relation to the future.[71] This, however, does not remove necessity from it, for whatever has had relation to the future, must have had it, even though the future sometimes is not realized. On the other hand, some say that this antecedent is contingent because it is a compound of the necessary and the contingent;[72] as this saying is contingent, *Socrates is a white man.* But this also is to no purpose; for when we say, *God knew this contingent to be future,* contingent is used here only as the matter of the proposition, and not as its principal part. Hence its contingency or necessity has no reference to the necessity or contingency of the proposition, or to its being true or false. For it may be just as true that I said a man is an ass, as that I said Socrates runs, or God is: and the same applies to necessary and contingent.

Hence it must be said that this antecedent is absolutely necessary. Nor does it follow, as some say, that the consequent is absolutely necessary because the antecedent is the remote cause of the consequent, which is contingent by reason of the proximate cause.[73] But this is to no purpose. For the conditional would be false were its antecedent the remote necessary cause, and the consequent a contingent effect; as, for example, if I said, *if the sun moves, the grass will grow.*

Therefore we must reply otherwise: when the antecedent

---

[71] St. Bonaventure, *In I Sent.,* d. xxxviii, a. 2, q. 2 (I, 678); St. Albert, *In I Sent.,* d. xxxviii, a. 4 (XXVI, 290).   [72] Robert Grosseteste, *De Lib. Arb.,* VI (p. 170).   [73] Alex. of Hales, *Summa Theol.,* I, no. 171 (I, 255); no. 184 (1, 270); Alain of Lille, *Theol. Reg.,* LXVI (PL 210, 653).

contains anything belonging to an act of the soul, the consequent must be taken, not as it is in itself, but as it is in the soul; for the being of a thing in itself is other than the being of a thing in the soul. For example, when I say, *What the soul understands is immaterial*, the meaning is that it is immaterial as it is in the intellect, not as it is in itself. Likewise if I say, *If God knew anything, it will be*, the consequent must be understood as it is subject to the divine knowledge, that is, as it is in its presentiality. And thus it is necessary, as is also the antecedent; *for everything that is, while it is, must necessarily be*, as the Philosopher says in *Periherm.* i.[74]

Reply Obj. 3. Things reduced to actuality in time are known by us successively in time, but by God they are known in eternity, which is above time. Whence to us they cannot be certain, since we know future contingent things only as contingent futures; but they are certain to God alone, Whose understanding is in eternity above time. Just as he who goes along the road does not see those who come after him; whereas he who sees the whole road from a height sees at once all those traveling on it. Hence, what is known by us must be necessary, even as it is in itself; for what is in itself a future contingent cannot be known by us. But what is known by God must be necessary according to the mode in which it is subject to the divine knowledge, as we have already stated, but not absolutely as considered in its proper causes. Hence also this proposition, *Everything known by God must necessarily be*, is usually distinguished,[75] for it may refer to the thing or to the saying. If it refers to the thing, it is divided and false; for the sense is, *Everything which God knows is necessary*. If understood of the saying, it is composite and true, for the sense is, *This proposition, 'that which is known by God is' is necessary*.

Now some urge an objection and say that this distinction holds good with regard to forms that are separable from a subject.[76] Thus if I said, *It is possible for a white thing to be black*, it is false as applied to the saying, and true as applied to the thing: for a thing which is white can become

[74] Aristotle, *Perih.*, I, 9 (19a 23).   [75] Cf. Wm. of Sherwood, *Introd. in Logicam* (p. 89); St. Albert, *In Prior. Anal.*, I, tr. 4, ch. 16 (I, 562). [76] Cf. St. Thomas, *In I Sent.*, d. xxxviii, q. 1, a. 5, ad 5-6; *De Ver.*, II, 12, ad 4.

black; whereas this saying, *a white thing is black,* can never be true. But in forms that are inseparable from a subject, this distinction does not hold: for instance, if I said, *A black crow can be white;* for in both senses it is false. Now to be known by God is inseparable from a thing; for what is known by God cannot be not known. This objection, however, would hold if these words *that which is known* implied any disposition inherent in the subject; but since they import an act of the knower, something can be attributed to the known thing in itself (even if it always be known) which is not attributed to it in so far as it falls under an act of knowledge. Thus, material being is attributed to a stone in itself, which is not attributed to it inasmuch as it is intelligible.

Fourteenth Article

WHETHER GOD KNOWS WHATEVER IS ENUNCIABLE?

We proceed thus to the Fourteenth Article:—

Objection 1. It seems that God does not know whatever is enunciable. For to know it belongs to our intellect as it composes and divides. But in the divine intellect there is no composition. Therefore God does not know whatever is enunciable.

Obj. 2. Further, every kind of knowledge takes place through some likeness. But in God there is no likeness of enunciables, since He is altogether simple. Therefore God does not know enunciables.

On the contrary, It is written: *The Lord knoweth the thoughts of men* (*Ps.* xciii. 11). But what can be enunciated is contained in the thoughts of men. Therefore God knows what can be enunciated.

I answer that, Since it is in the power of our intellect to form enunciations, and since God knows whatever is in His own power or in that of creatures, as was said above, it follows of necessity that God knows all enunciations that can be formed.

Now just as He knows material things immaterially, and composite things simply, so likewise He knows what can be enunciated, not after its own manner, as if in His intellect there were composition or division of enunciations, but He knows each thing by simple intelligence, by understanding the essence of each thing; as if we, by the very fact that we understand what man is, were to understand all that can be predicated of man. This, however, does not happen in the case of our intellect, which proceeds from one thing to another, since the intelligible species represents one thing in such a way as not to represent another. Hence, when we understand what man is, we do not forthwith understand other things which belong to him, but we understand them one by one, according to a certain succession. On this account, the things we understand as separated we must reduce to one by way of composition or division, by forming an enunciation. Now the species of the divine intellect, which is God's essence, suffices to manifest all things. Hence, by understanding His essence, God knows the essences of all things, and also whatever can be added to them.

Reply Obj. 1. This objection would be true if God knew enunciations according to their own limitations.

Reply Obj. 2. Composition in an enunciation signifies some sort of being in a thing; and so God, by His being, which is His essence, is the likeness of everything signified by enunciations.

Fifteenth Article

WHETHER THE KNOWLEDGE OF GOD IS VARIABLE?

We proceed thus to the Fifteenth Article:—

Objection 1. It seems that the knowledge of God is variable. For knowledge is related to what is knowable. But whatever imports relation to the creature is applied to God from time, and varies according to the variation of creatures. Therefore, the knowledge of God is variable according to the variation of creatures.

Obj. 2. Further, whatever God can make He can know. But God can make more things than He does. Therefore, He can know more than He knows. Thus, His knowledge can vary according to increase and diminution.

Obj. 3. Further, God knew that Christ would be born. But He does not know now that Christ will be born, because Christ is not to be born in the future. Therefore God does not know everything He once knew; and thus the knowledge of God is variable.

On the contrary, It is said, that in God *there is no change nor shadow of alteration* (*Jas.* i. 17).

I answer that, Since the knowledge of God is His substance, as is clear from the foregoing, just as His substance is altogether immutable, as was shown above,[77] so His knowledge likewise must be altogether invariable.

Reply Obj. 1. *Lord, Creator,* and the like, import relations to creatures in so far as they are in themselves. But the knowledge of God imports relation to creatures in so far as they are in God; because everything is actually understood according as it is in the one who understands. Now created things are in God in an invariable manner; while they exist variably in themselves.—Or we may say that *Lord, Creator,* and the like, import the relations consequent upon the acts which are understood as terminating in the creatures themselves as they are in themselves; and thus these relations are attributed to God variously, according to the variation of creatures. But *knowledge* and *love,* and the like, import relations consequent upon the acts which are understood to be in God; and therefore these are predicated of God in an invariable manner.

Reply Obj. 2. God knows also what He can make, and does not make. Hence from the fact that He can make more than He makes, it does not follow that He can know more than He knows, unless this be referred to the *knowledge of vision,* according to which He is said to know those things which actually exist in some period of time. But from the fact that He knows that some things can be which are not, or that some things can not-be which are, it does not follow that His knowledge is variable, but rather that He knows the variability of things. If, however, anything existed which God did not previously know, and afterwards knew, then His knowledge would be variable. But this is impossible, for whatever is, or can be in any period of time, is known by God in His eternity. Therefore, from the fact that a thing is said to exist in some period of time, we must say that it is known by God from all eternity. Therefore it cannot be granted that God can know more than He knows; because such a proposition implies that first of all He did not know, and then afterwards knew.

Reply Obj. 3. The ancient Nominalists said that it was the

[77] Q. 9, a. 1.

same thing to say *Christ is born* and *will be born*, and *was born*; because the same thing is signified by these three—viz., the nativity of Christ.[78] Therefore it follows, they said, that whatever God knew, He knows; because now He knows that Christ is born, which means the same thing as that Christ will be born. This opinion, however, is false, both because the diversity in the parts of a sentence causes a diversity in enunciations, and because it would follow that a proposition which is true once would always be true; which is contrary to what the Philosopher lays down when he says that this sentence, *Socrates sits,* is true when he is sitting, and false when he stands up.[79] Therefore, it must be conceded that this proposition, *Whatever God knew He knows,* is not true if referred to what is enunciated. But because of this, it does not follow that the knowledge of God is variable. For as it is without variation in the divine knowledge that God knows one and the same thing sometime to be, and sometime not, so it is without variation in the divine knowledge that God knows that an enunciation is sometime true, and sometime false. The knowledge of God, however, would be variable if He knew enunciations according to their own limitations, by composition and division, as occurs in our intellect. Hence our knowledge varies either as regards truth and falsity, for example, if when a thing is changed we retained the same opinion about it; or as regards diverse opinions, as if we first thought that someone was sitting, and afterwards thought that he was not sitting; neither of which can be in God.

Sixteenth Article

WHETHER GOD HAS A SPECULATIVE KNOWLEDGE OF THINGS?

We proceed thus to the Sixteenth Article:—

Objection 1. It seems that God has not a speculative knowledge of things. For the knowledge of God is the cause of things, as was shown above. But speculative knowledge is not the cause of the things known. Therefore the knowledge of God is not speculative.

---

[78] Cf. Abelard, *Introd. ad Theol.*, III, 5 (PL 178, 1102); Peter Lombard, *Sent.*, I, xli, 3 (I, 258).   [79] *Cat.*, V (4a 23).

Obj. 2. Further, speculative knowledge comes by abstraction from things; which does not belong to the divine knowledge. Therefore the knowledge of God is not speculative.

On the contrary, Whatever is the more excellent must be attributed to God. But *speculative knowledge is more excellent than practical knowledge,* as the Philosopher says in the beginning of the *Metaphysics*.[80] Therefore God has a speculative knowledge of things.

I answer that, Some knowledge is speculative only, some is practical only, and some is partly speculative and partly practical. In proof whereof it must be observed that knowledge can be called speculative in three ways: first, in relation to the things known, which are not operable by the knower; such is the knowledge of man about natural or divine things. Secondly, as regards the manner of knowing—as, for instance, if a builder were to consider a house by defining and dividing, and considering what belongs to it in general: for this is to consider operable things in a speculative manner, and not as they are operable; for *operable* means the application of form to matter, and not the resolution of the composite into its universal formal principles. Thirdly, as regards the end; *for the practical intellect differs from the speculative by its end,* as the Philosopher says.[81] For the practical intellect is ordered to the end of operation; whereas the end of the speculative intellect is the consideration of truth. Hence if a builder were to consider how a house can be made, but without ordering this to the end of operation, but only towards knowledge, this would be only a speculative consideration as regards the end, although it concerns an operable thing. Therefore, knowledge which is speculative by reason of the thing itself known is merely speculative. But that which is speculative either in its mode or as to its end is partly speculative and partly practical: and when it is ordained to an operative end it is strictly practical.

In accordance with this, therefore, it must be said that God has of Himself a speculative knowledge only; for He Himself is not operable.

But of all other things He has both speculative and practical knowledge. He has speculative knowledge as regards the mode; for whatever we know speculatively in things by

[80] *Metaph.,* I, 1 (982a 1).   [81] *De An.,* III, 10 (433a 14).

defining and dividing, God knows all this much more perfectly.

Now of things which He can make, but does not make at any time, He has not a practical knowledge, according as knowledge is called practical from the end. In this sense He has a practical knowledge of what He makes in some period of time. And, as regards evil things, although they are not operable by Him, yet they fall under His practical knowledge, as also do good things, inasmuch as He permits, or impedes, or directs them; just as sicknesses fall under the practical knowledge of the physician, inasmuch as he cures them by his art.

Reply Obj. 1. The knowledge of God is a cause, not indeed of Himself, but of other things. He is actually the cause of some, that is, of things that come to be in some period of time; He is virtually the cause of others, that is, of things which He can make, and which nevertheless are never made.

Reply Obj. 2. The fact that knowledge is derived from things known does not belong to speculative knowledge essentially, but only accidentally in so far as it is human.

In answer to what is objected to the contrary, we must say that perfect knowledge of operable things is obtainable only if they are known in so far as they are operable. Therefore, since the knowledge of God is in every way perfect, He must know what is operable by Him precisely in-so-far as it is operable, and not only in-so-far as it is speculative. Nevertheless this does not impair the nobility of His speculative knowledge, for He sees all things other than Himself in Himself, and He knows Himself speculatively; and so in the speculative knowledge of Himself, He possesses both speculative and practical knowledge of all other things.

Question XV

ON IDEAS

(*In Three Articles*)

AFTER considering the knowledge of God, it remains to consider ideas. And about this there are three points of inquiry: (1) Whether there are ideas? (2) Whether they are many, or one only? (3) Whether there are ideas of all things known by God?

First Article

WHETHER THERE ARE IDEAS?

We proceed thus to the First Article:—

Objection 1. It seems that there are no ideas. For Dionysius says that God does not know things by ideas.[1] But ideas are for nothing else except that things may be known through them. Therefore there are no ideas.

Obj. 2. Further, God knows all things in Himself, as has been already said.[2] But He does not know Himself through an idea; neither therefore other things.

Obj. 3. Further, an idea is considered to be the principle of knowledge and action. But the divine essence is a sufficent principle of knowing and effecting all things. It is not therefore necessary to posit ideas.

On the contrary, Augustine says, *Such is the power inherent in ideas, that no one can be wise unless they be understood.*[3]

I answer that, It is necessary to posit ideas in the divine mind. For the Greek word Ἰδέα is in Latin *Forma.* Hence by ideas are understood the forms of things, existing apart from the things themselves. Now the form of anything, existing apart from the thing itself, can be for one of two ends; either to be the exemplar of that of which it is called the form, or to be the principle of the knowledge of that thing, according as the forms of knowable things are said to be in him who

[1] *De Div. Nom.,* VII, 2 (PG 3, 868).   [2] Q. 14, a. 5.   [3] *Lib. 83 Quaest.,* q. 46 (PL 40, 29).

knows them. In either case we must posit ideas, as is clear
for the following reason:

In all things not generated by chance, the form must be
the end of any generation whatsoever. But an agent does not
act for the sake of the form, except in so far as the likeness
of the form is in the agent; which may happen in two ways.
For in some agents the form of the thing-to-be-made pre-
exists according to its natural being, as in those that act by
their nature; as a man generates a man, or fire generates
fire. Whereas in other agents the form of the thing-to-be-
made pre-exists according to intelligible being, as in those
that act by the intellect; and thus the likeness of a house
pre-exists in the mind of the builder. And this may be called
the idea of the house, since the builder intends to build his
house like the form conceived in his mind.

Since, then, the world was not made by chance, but by
God acting by His intellect, as will appear later,[4] there must
exist in the divine mind a form to the likeness of which the
world was made. And in this the notion of an idea consists.

Reply Obj. 1. God does not understand things according
to an idea existing outside Himself. Thus Aristotle likewise
rejects the opinion of Plato, who held that Ideas existed of
themselves, and not in the intellect.[5]

Reply Obj. 2. Although God knows Himself and all else by
His own essence, yet His essence is the operative principle
of all things, except of Himself. It has therefore the nature
of an idea with respect to other things; though not with respect to God Himself.

Reply Obj. 3. God is the likeness of all things according to
His essence; therefore an idea in God is nothing other than
His essence.

Second Article

WHETHER THERE ARE MANY IDEAS?

We proceed thus to the Second Article:—

Objection 1. It seems that there are not many ideas. For
an idea in God is His essence. But God's essence is one only.
Therefore there is only one idea.

Obj. 2. Further, as the idea is the principle of knowing

[4] Q. 47, a. 1.   [5] *Metaph.*, II, 2 (997b 6); VI, 6 (1031b 5).

and operating, so are art and wisdom. But in God there are not several arts or wisdoms. Therefore in Him there is no plurality of ideas.

Obj. 3. Further, if it be said that ideas are multiplied according to their relations to different creatures, it may be argued on the contrary that the plurality of ideas is eternal. If, then, ideas are many, but creatures temporal, then the temporal must be the cause of the eternal.

Obj. 4. Further, these relations are either real in creatures only, or in God also. If in creatures only, since creatures are not from eternity, the plurality of ideas cannot be from eternity, if ideas are multiplied only according to these relations. But if they are real in God, it follows that there is a real plurality in God other than the plurality of Persons: and this is against the teaching of Damascene, who says that in God all things are one, except *ingenerability, generation, and procession.*[6] Ideas therefore are not many.

On the contrary, Augustine says, *Ideas are certain original forms or permanent and immutable models of things which are contained by the divine intelligence. They are immutable because they themselves have not been formed; and that is why they are eternal and always the same. But though they themselves neither come to be nor perish, yet it is according to them that everything, which can come to be or pass away or which actually comes to be and passes away, is said to be formed.*[7]

I answer that, It must necessarily be held that ideas are many. In proof of which it is to be considered that in every effect the ultimate end is the proper intention of the principal agent, as the order of an army is the proper intention of the general. Now that which is best in things is the good of the order of the universe, as the Philosopher clearly teaches in *Metaph.* xii.[8] Therefore, the order of the universe is properly intended by God, and is not the accidental result of a succession of agents, as has been supposed by those who have taught that God created only the first creature, and that this creature created a second creature, and so on, until this great multitude of beings was produced.[9] According to this opinion, God would have an idea of the first created thing alone; whereas, if the very order of the universe was itself created

[6] *De Fide Orth.,* I, 10 (PG 94, 837).   [7] *Lib. 83 Quaest.,* q. 46 (PL 40, 30).   [8] *Metaph.,* XI, 10 (1075a 13).   [9] Cf. below, q. 45, a. 5.

by Him immediately, and intended by Him, He must have the idea of the order of the universe. Now there cannot be an idea of any whole, unless particular ideas are had of those parts of which the whole is made; just as a builder could not conceive the idea of a house unless he had the idea of each of its parts. So, then, it must needs be that in the divine mind there are the proper ideas of all things. Hence Augustine says *that each thing was created by God according to the idea proper to it;*[10] from which it follows that in the divine mind there are many ideas.

Now it can easily be seen how this is not repugnant to the simplicity of God, if we consider that the idea of the thing to be produced is in the mind of the producer as that which is understood, and not as the likeness whereby he understands, which is a form that makes the intellect in act. For the form of the house in the mind of the builder is something understood by him, to the likeness of which he forms the house in matter. Now, it is not repugnant to the simplicity of the divine mind that it understand many things; though it would be repugnant to its simplicity were God's understanding to be informed by a plurality of likenesses. Hence many ideas exist in the divine mind as that which is understood by it; as can be proved thus. Inasmuch as God knows His own essence perfectly, He knows it according to every mode in which it can be known. Now it can be known not only as it is in itself, but as it can be participated in by creatures according to some kind of likeness. But every creature has its own proper species, according to which it participates in some way in the likeness of the divine essence. Therefore, as God knows His essence as so imitable by such a creature, He knows it as the particular model and idea of that creature: and in like manner as regards other creatures. So it is clear that God understands many models proper to many things; and these are many ideas.

Reply Obj. 1. The divine essence is not called an idea in so far as it is that essence, but only in so far as it is the likeness or model of this or that thing. Hence ideas are said to be many, inasmuch as many models are understood through the self-same essence.

Reply Obj. 2. By wisdom and art we signify *that by which* God understands; but by an idea, *that which* God under-

[10] *Lib. 83 Quaest.*, q. 46 (PL 40, 30).

stands. For God by one principle understands many things, and that not only according as they are in themselves, but also according as they are understood; and this is to understand the several models of things. In the same way, an architect is said to understand a house, when he understands the form of the house in matter. But if he understands the form of a house, as devised by himself, from the fact that he understands that he understands it, he thereby understands the model or the idea of the house. Now not only does God understand many things by His essence, but He also understands that He understands many things by His essence. And this means that He understands the several models of things; or that many ideas are in His intellect as understood by Him.

Reply Obj. 3. Such relations, whereby ideas are multiplied, are caused not by the things themselves, but by the divine intellect comparing its own essence with these things.

Reply Obj. 4. Relations multiplying ideas do not exist in created things, but in God. Yet they are not real relations, such as those whereby the Persons are distinguished, but relations understood by God.

Third Article

WHETHER THERE ARE IDEAS OF ALL THINGS THAT GOD KNOWS?

We proceed thus to the Third Article:—

Objection 1. It seems that there are not ideas in God of all things that He knows. For the idea of evil is not in God; since it would follow that evil was in Him. But evil things are known by God. Therefore there are not ideas of all things that God knows.

Obj. 2. Further, God knows things that neither are, nor will be, nor have been, as has been said above.[11] But of such things there are no ideas, since, as Dionysius says: *Acts of the divine will are the determining and effective models of things.*[12] Therefore in God there are not ideas of all things known by Him.

Obj. 3. Further, God knows primary matter, of which there can be no idea, since it has no form. Hence the same conclusion.

[11] Q. 14, a. 9.   [12] *De Div. Nom.*, V, 8 (PG 3, 845).

Obj. 4. Further, it is certain that God knows not only species, but also genera, singulars, and accidents. But there are no ideas of these, according to Plato's teaching, who first taught ideas, as Augustine says.[13] Therefore there are not ideas in God of all things known by Him.

On the contrary, Ideas are exemplars existing in the divine mind, as is clear from Augustine.[14] But God has the proper exemplars of all the things that He knows; and therefore He has ideas of all things known by Him.

I answer that, As ideas, according to Plato,[15] were the principles of the knowledge of things and of their generation, an idea, as existing in the mind of God, has this twofold office. So far as the idea is the principle of the making of things, it may be called an *exemplar,* and belongs to practical knowledge. But so far as it is a principle of knowledge, it is properly called a *likeness,* and may belong to speculative knowledge also. As an exemplar, therefore, it is related to everything made by God in any period of time; whereas as a principle of knowledge it is related to all things known by God, even though they never come to be in time; and to all things that He knows according to their proper likeness, in so far as they are known by Him in a speculative manner.

Reply Obj. 1. Evil is known by God, not through its own likeness, but through the likeness of good. Evil, therefore, has no idea in God, neither in so far as an idea is an *exemplar,* nor so far as it is a *likeness.*

Reply Obj. 2. God has no practical knowledge, except virtually, of things which neither are, nor will be, nor have been. Hence, with respect to these there is no idea in God in so far as idea signifies an *exemplar,* but only in so far as it signifies a *likeness.*

Reply Obj. 3. Plato is said by some to have considered matter as not created;[16] and therefore he held, not that there was an idea of matter, but that an idea was a co-cause with matter. Since, however, we hold matter to be created by God, though not apart from form, matter has its idea in God, but not apart from the idea of the composite; for matter in itself can neither exist, nor be known.

[13] *Lib. 83 Quaest.,* q. 46 (PL 40, 29).   [14] *Ibid.* (PL 40, 30).
[15] Cf. below, q. 84, a. 4.—Cf. also Aristotle, *Metaph.,* I a, 9 (991b 3).
[16] Cf. Chalcidius, *In Timaeum,* CCXLVIII (p. 245).—Cf. also Peter Lombard, *Sent.* II, i, 1 (I, 306-307).

Reply Obj. 4. Genus can have no idea apart from the idea of species, in so far as idea denotes an *exemplar*; for genus cannot exist except in some species. The same is the case with those accidents that inseparably accompany their subject; for these come into being along with their subject. But accidents which are added to the subject have their special idea. For an architect produces through the form of the house all the accidents that originally accompany it; whereas those that are superadded to the house when completed, such as decorations, or any other such thing, are produced through some other form. Now individual things, according to Plato, have no other idea than that of the species,[17] both because singular things are individuated by matter, which, as some say, he held to be uncreated and a co-cause with the idea; and because the intention of nature aims at the species, and produces individuals only that in them the species may be preserved. However, divine providence extends not merely to species, but to individuals, as will be shown later.[18]

[17] Cf. Aristotle, *Metaph.*, I, 9 (990b 29).   [18] Q. 22, a. 2.

ON TRUTH

(*In Eight Articles*)

SINCE knowledge is of what is true, after the consideration of the knowledge of God, we must inquire concerning truth. About·this there are eight points of inquiry: (1) Whether truth resides in the thing, or only in the intellect? (2) Whether it resides only in the intellect composing and dividing? (3) On the comparison of the true with being. (4) On the comparison of the true with the good. (5) Whether God is truth? (6) Whether all things are true by one truth, or by many? (7) On the eternity of truth. (8) On the unchangeableness of truth.

First Article

WHETHER TRUTH RESIDES ONLY IN THE INTELLECT?

We proceed thus to the First Article:—

Objection 1. It seems that truth does not reside only in the intellect, but rather in things. For Augustine condemns this definition of truth, *That is true which is seen;*[1] since it would follow that stones hidden in the bosom of the earth would not be true stones, as they are not seen. He also condemns the following, *That is true which is as it appears to the knower, who is willing and able to know;* for hence it would follow that nothing would be true, unless someone could know it. Therefore he defines truth thus: *The true is which is.* It seems, then, that truth resides in things, and not in the intellect.

Obj. 2. Further, whatever is true, is true by reason of truth. If, then, truth is only in the intellect, nothing will be true except in so far as it is understood. But this is the error of the ancient philosophers, who said that whatever seems to be true is so.[2] Consequently contradictories can be true at

[1] *Solil.,* II, 5 (PL 32, 888).   [2] Attributed to Democritus and Protagoras by Aristotle, *De An.,* I, 2 (404a 28); *Metaph.,* III, 5 (1009a 8).

the same time, since contradictories seem to be true as seen by different persons at the same time.

Obj. 3. Further, *that because of which a thing is so, is itself more so,* as is evident from the Philosopher.[3] But *it is from the fact that a thing is or is not, that our thought or word is true or false,* as the Philosopher teaches.[4] Therefore truth resides rather in things than in the intellect.

On the contrary, The Philosopher says, *The true and the false reside not in things, but in the intellect.*[5]

I answer that, As *good* names that towards which the appetite tends, so *the true* names that towards which the intellect tends. Now there is this difference between the appetite and the intellect, or any knowledge whatsoever, that knowledge is according as the thing known is in the knower, while appetite is according as the desirer tends towards the thing desired. Thus the term of the appetite, namely good, is in the desirable thing, and the term of the intellect, namely the true, is in the intellect itself. Now as good exists in a thing so far as that thing is related to the appetite—and hence the aspect of goodness passes on from the desirable thing to the appetite, in so far as the appetite is called good if its object is good; so, since the true is in the intellect in so far as the intellect is conformed to the thing understood, the aspect of the true must needs pass from the intellect to the thing understood, so that also the thing understood is said to be true in so far as it has some relation to the intellect.

Now a thing understood may be in relation to an intellect either essentially or accidentally. It is related essentially to an intellect on which it depends as regards its being, but accidentally to an intellect by which it is knowable; even as we may say that a house is related essentially to the intellect of the architect, but accidentally to the intellect upon which it does not depend. Now we do not judge of a thing by what is in it accidentally, but by what is in it essentially. Hence, everything is said to be true absolutely, in so far as it is related to the intellect on which it depends; and thus it is that artificial things are said to be true as being related to our intellect. For a house is said to be true that fulfills the likeness of the form in the architect's mind; and words are said to be true so far as they are the signs of truth in the intellect.

[3] Aristotle, *Post. Anal.,* I, 2 (72a 29).   [4] *Cat.,* V (4b 8).   [5] *Metaph.,* V, 4 (1027b 25).

In the same way, natural things are said to be true in so far as they express the likeness of the species that are in the divine mind. For a stone is called true, which possesses the nature proper to a stone, according to the preconception in the divine intellect. Thus, then, truth resides primarily in the intellect, and secondarily in things according as they are related to the intellect as their source.

Consequently, there are various definitions of truth. Augustine says, *Truth is that whereby is made manifest that which is;*[6] and Hilary says that *Truth makes being clear and evident:*[7] and this pertains to truth according as it is in the intellect. As to the truth of things in so far as they are related to the intellect, we have Augustine's definition, *Truth is a supreme likeness, without any unlikeness, to its source;*[8] also Anselm's definition, *Truth is rightness, perceptible by the mind alone;*[9] for that is right which is in accordance with its source; also Avicenna's definition, *The truth of each thing is a property of the being which has been given to it.*[10] The definition that *Truth is the equation of thought and thing* is applicable to it under either aspect.

Reply Obj. 1. Augustine is speaking about the truth of things, and from the notion of this truth excludes relation to our intellect; for what is accidental is excluded from every definition.

Reply Obj. 2. The ancient philosophers held that the species of natural things did not proceed from any intellect, but came about by chance.[11] But as they saw that truth implies relation to intellect, they were compelled to base the truth of things on their relation to our intellect. From this fact there followed the various awkward consequences that the Philosopher attacks.[12] Such consequences, however, do not follow, if we say that the truth of things consists in their relation to the divine intellect.

Reply Obj. 3. Although the truth of our intellect is caused by the thing, yet it is not necessary that the essence of truth should be there primarily, any more than that of the essence of health should be primarily in medicine, rather than in·the

---

[6] *De Vera Relig.*, XXXVI (PL 34, 151).   [7] *De Trin.*, V (PL 10, 131).   [8] *De Vera Relig.*, XXXVI (PL 34, 152).   [9] *De Ver.*, XI (PL 158, 480).   [10] *Metaph.*, VIII, 6 (100r).   [11] Cf. below, q. 22, a. 2.   [12] *Metaph.*, III, 5 (1009a 6); 6 (1011a 3).

animal: for it is the power of medicine, and not its health, that is the cause of health, since the agent is not univocal. In the same way, the being of the thing, not its truth, is the cause of truth in the intellect. Hence the Philosopher says that an opinion or a statement is true *from the fact that a thing is, not from the fact that a thing is true.*[13]

Second Article

WHETHER TRUTH RESIDES ONLY IN THE INTELLECT COMPOSING AND DIVIDING?

We proceed thus to the Second Article:—

Objection 1. It seems that truth does not reside only in the intellect composing and dividing. For the Philosopher says that *as the senses are always true as regards their proper sensible objects, so is the intellect as regards what a thing is.*[14] Now composition and division are neither in the senses nor in the intellect knowing *what a thing is.* Therefore truth does not reside only in the intellect composing and dividing.

Obj. 2. Further, Isaac says in his book *On Definitions* that truth is the equation of thought and thing.[15] Now just as the intellect which forms judgments can be equated to things, so also can the intellect that simply apprehends essences; and this is true likewise of sense apprehending a thing as it is. Therefore truth does not reside only in the intellect composing and dividing.

On the contrary, the Philosopher says that *with regard to simple things and what a thing is, truth is not found either in the intellect or in things.*[16]

I answer that, As was stated before, truth resides, in its primary aspect, in the intellect. Now since everything is true according as it has the form proper to its nature, the intellect, in so far as it is knowing, must be true according as it has the likeness of the thing known, which is its form as a knowing power. For this reason truth is defined by the conformity of intellect and thing; and hence to know truth. But in no way does sense know this. For although sight has the

[13] *Cat.,* V (4b 8).   [14] *De An.,* III, 6 (430b 27).   [15] Cf. J. T. Muckle, "Isaac Israeli's Definition of Truth" (*Archives d'hist. doct. et litt. du moyen âge,* viii, 1933, pp. 5-8).   [16] *Metaph.,* V, 4 (1027b 27).

likeness of a visible thing, yet it does not know the comparison which exists between the thing seen and that which it itself is apprehending concerning it. But the intellect can know its own conformity with the intelligible thing; yet it does not apprehend it by knowing of a thing *what a thing is*. When, however, it judges that a thing corresponds to the form which it apprehends about that thing, then it first knows and expresses truth. This it does by composing and dividing: for in every proposition it either applies to, or removes from, the thing signified by the subject some form signified by the predicate. This clearly shows that the sense is true in regard to a given thing, as is also the intellect, in knowing *what a thing is*; but it does not thereby know or affirm truth. This is, in like manner, the case with propositions or terms. Truth, therefore, may be in the sense, or in the intellect knowing *what a thing is,* as in something that is as in something that is true; yet not as the thing known is in the knower, which is implied by the word *truth*; for the perfection of the intellect is truth *as known*. Therefore, properly speaking, truth resides in the intellect composing and dividing; and not in the sense, nor in the intellect knowing *what a thing is*.

And thus the Objections given are solved.

Third Article

WHETHER THE TRUE AND BEING ARE CONVERTIBLE TERMS?

We proceed thus to the Third Article:—

Objection 1. It seems that the true and being are not convertible terms. For the true resides properly in the intellect, as has been stated, while being is properly in things. Therefore they are not convertible.

Obj. 2. Further, that which extends to being and non-being is not convertible with being. But the true extends to being and non-being; for it is true that what is, is, and that what is not, is not. Therefore the true and being are not convertible.

Obj. 3. Further, things which stand to each other in order of priority and posteriority seem not to be convertible. But the true appears to be prior to being; for being is not understood except under the aspect of the true. Therefore it seems they are not convertible.

On the contrary, the Philosopher says that there is the same disposition of things in being and in truth.[17]

I answer that, As *good* has the nature of what is desirable, so *the true* is related to knowledge. Now everything is knowable in as far as it has being. Therefore it is said in *De Anima* iii. that *the soul is in some manner all things,*[18] through the senses and the intellect. And therefore, as good is convertible with being, so is the true. But as good adds to being the notion of the desirable, so the true adds a relation to the intellect.

Reply Obj. 1. The true resides in things and in the intellect, as was said before. But the true that is in things is substantially convertible with being, while the true that is in the intellect is convertible with being, as that which manifests is convertible with the manifested; for this belongs to the nature of truth, as has been said already. It may, however, be said, that being also is in things and in the intellect, as is the true; even though truth is primarily in the intellect, while being is primarily in things. This is so because truth and being differ in idea.

Reply Obj. 2. Non-being has nothing in itself whereby it can be known; but it is known in so far as the intellect renders it knowable. Hence the true is based on being, inasmuch as non-being is a certain logical being (apprehended, that is, by reason).

Reply Obj. 3. When it is said that being cannot be apprehended except under the notion of the true, this can be understood in two ways. In the one way, so as to mean that being is not apprehended without the idea of the true following upon the apprehension of being; and this is true. In the other way, so as to mean that being cannot be apprehended unless the notion of the true be also apprehended; and this is false. But the true cannot be apprehended unless the notion of being be also apprehended; since being is included in the notion of the true. The case is the same if we were to compare the intelligible object with being. For being cannot be under-

---

[17] *Op. cit.,* Ia, 1 (993b 30).   [18] *De An.,* III, 8 (431b 21).

stood except because being is intelligible. Yet being can be understood while its intelligibility is not understood. Similarly, being understood by the intellect is true; yet the true is not understood by understanding being.

Fourth Article

WHETHER GOOD IS LOGICALLY PRIOR TO THE TRUE?

We proceed thus to the Fourth Article:—

Objection 1. It seems that good is logically prior to the true. For what is more universal is logically prior, as is evident from *Physics* i.[19] But the good is more universal than the true, since the true is a kind of good, namely, of the intellect. Therefore the good is logically prior to the true.

Obj. 2. Further, good is in things, but the true in the intellect composing and dividing, as was said before. But that which is in things is prior to that which is in the intellect. Therefore good is logically prior to the true.

Obj. 2. Further, good is in things, but the true in the intellect composing and dividing, as was said before. But that which is in things is prior to that which is in the intellect. Therefore good is logically prior to the true.

Obj. 3. Further, truth is a species of virtue, as is clear from *Ethics* iv.[20] But virtue is included under good, since, as Augustine says, it is a good quality of the mind.[21] Therefore the good is prior to the true.

On the contrary, What is in more things is prior logically. But the true is in some things wherein good is not, as, for instance, in mathematics. Therefore the true is prior to good.

I answer that, Although the good and the true are convertible with being, as to suppositum, yet they differ logically. And in this manner the true, speaking absolutely, is prior to good, as appears from two reasons. First, because the true is more closely related to being which is itself prior to the good. For the true regards being itself absolutely and immediately, while the nature of good follows being in so far as being is in some way perfect; for thus it is desirable. Secondly, it is evident from the fact that knowledge naturally

---

[19] Aristotle, *Phys.*, I, 5 (189a 5).   [20] Aristotle, *Eth.*, IV, 7 (1127a 29).   [21] *De Lib. Arb.*, II, 19 (PL 32, 1267).

precedes appetite. Hence, since the true is related to knowledge, and the good to the appetite, the true must be prior in nature to the good.

Reply Obj. 1. The will and the intellect mutually include one another: for the intellect understands the will, and the will wills the intellect to understand. So then, among the things related to the object of the will, are comprised also those that belong to the intellect; and conversely. Whence, in the order of desirable things, good stands as the universal, and the true as the particular; whereas in the order of intelligible things the converse is the case. From the fact, then, that the true is a kind of good, it follows that the good is prior in the order of desirable things; but not that it is absolutely prior.

Reply Obj. 2. A thing is prior logically in so far as it is prior in the apprehension of the intellect. Now the intellect first apprehends being itself; secondly, it apprehends that it understands being; and thirdly, it apprehends that it desires being. Hence the notion of being is first, that of truth second, and the notion of good third, even though the good is in things.

Reply Obj. 3. The virtue which is called *truth* is not truth in general, but a certain kind of truth according to which man shows himself in deed and word as he really is. But truth as applied to *life* is used in a particular sense, inasmuch as a man fulfills in his life that to which he is ordained by the divine intellect; much as it has been said that truth exists in all other things. Furthermore, the truth of *justice* is found in man as he fulfills his duty to his neighbor, as ordained by law. Hence we cannot argue from these particular truths to truth in general.

Fifth Article

WHETHER GOD IS TRUTH?

We proceed thus to the Fifth Article:—

Objection 1. It seems that God is not truth. For truth consists in the intellect composing and dividing. But in God there is no composition and division. Therefore in God there is no truth.

Obj. 2. Further, truth, according to Augustine, is a *likeness to the source*.[22] But in God there is no likeness to a source. Therefore in God there is no truth.

Obj. 3. Further, whatever is said of God, is said of Him as of the first cause of all things. Thus the being of God is the cause of all being, and His goodness the cause of all good. If therefore there is truth in God, all truth will be from Him. But it is true that someone sins. Therefore this will be from God; which is evidently false.

On the contrary, Our Lord says, *I am the Way, the Truth and the Life (Jo.* xiv. 6).

I answer that, As was said above, truth is found in the intellect according as it apprehends a thing as it is; and in things according as they have being conformable to an intellect. This is to the greatest degree found in God. For His being is not only conformed to His intellect, but it is the very act of His intellect; and His act of understanding is the measure and cause of every other being and of every other intellect; and He Himself is His own being and act of understanding. Whence it follows not only that truth is in Him, but that He is the highest and first truth itself.

Reply Obj. 1. Although in the divine intellect there is neither composition nor division, yet in His simple act of intelligence He judges of all things and knows all propositions; and thus there is truth in His intellect.

Reply Obj. 2. The truth of our intellect is according to its conformity with its source, that is to say, the things from which it receives knowledge. The truth also of things is according to their conformity with their source, namely, the divine intellect. Now this cannot be said, properly speaking, of divine truth; unless perhaps in so far as truth is appropriated to the Son, Who has a source. But if we speak of divine truth in its essence, we cannot understand what Augustine has said unless the affirmative proposition be resolved into the negative one, as when one says: *the Father is of Himself, because He is not from another*. Similarly, the divine truth can be called *a likeness of its source*, inasmuch as His being is not unlike His intellect.

Reply Obj. 3. Non-being and privation have no truth of themselves, but only in the apprehension of the intellect.

[22] *De Vera Relig.*, XXXVI (PL 34, 152).

Now all apprehension of the intellect is from God. Hence all the truth that exists in the statement,—*that this person commits fornication is true,* is entirely from God. But to argue, *Therefore that this person fornicates is from God,* is a fallacy of accident.

Sixth Article

WHETHER THERE IS ONLY ONE TRUTH ACCORDING TO WHICH ALL THINGS ARE TRUE?

We proceed thus to the Sixth Article:—

Objection 1. It seems that there is only one truth according to which all things are true. For according to Augustine, *nothing is greater than the mind of man, except God.*[23] Now truth is greater than the mind of man; otherwise the mind would be the judge of truth: whereas in fact it judges all things according to truth, and not according to its own measure. Therefore God alone is truth. Therefore there is no other truth but God.

Obj. 2. Further, Anselm says that, *as is the relation of time to temporal things, so is that of truth to true things.*[24] But there is only one time for all temporal things. Therefore there is only one truth, by which all things are true.

On the contrary, it is written (*Ps.* xi. 2), *Truths are decayed from among the children of men.*

I answer that, In a sense there is one truth whereby all things are true, and in a sense not. In proof of which we must consider that when anything is predicated of many things univocally, it is found in each of them according to its proper nature; as animal is found in each species of animal. But when anything is predicated of many things analogically, it is found in only one of them according to its proper nature, and from this one the rest are denominated. So healthiness is predicated of animal, of urine, and of medicine; not that health is not only in the animal, but from the health of the animal, medicine is called healthy, in so far as it is the cause of health, and urine is called healthy, in so far as it indicates health. And although health is neither in medicine nor in urine, yet in either there is something whereby the one causes, and the other indicates health.

---

[23] *De Trin.*, XV, 1 (PL 42, 1057). [24] *De Ver.*, XIV (PL 158, 484).

Now we have said that truth resides primarily in the intellect, and secondarily in things, according as they are related to the divine intellect. If therefore we speak of truth as it exists in the intellect, according to its proper nature, then are there many truths in many created intellects; and even in one and the same intellect, according to the number of things known. Whence the *Gloss* on *Ps.* xi. 2 (*Truths are decayed from among the children of men*) says: *As from one man's face many likenesses are reflected in a mirror, so many truths are reflected from the one divine truth.*[25] But if we speak of truth as it is in things, then all things are true by one primary truth, to which each one is assimilated according to its own entity. And thus, although the essences or forms of things are many, yet the truth of the divine intellect is one, in conformity to which all things are said to be true.

Reply Obj. 1. The soul does not judge of all things according to any kind of truth, but according to the first truth, inasmuch as it is reflected in the soul, as in a mirror, by reason of the first principles of the understanding. It follows, therefore, that the first truth is greater than the soul. And yet, even created truth, which resides in our intellect, is greater than the soul, not absolutely, but to the extent that it is the perfection of the intellect; even as science may also be said to be greater than the soul. Yet it remains true that nothing subsisting is greater than the rational soul, except God.

Reply Obj. 2. The saying of Anselm is correct in so far as things are said to be true by their relation to the divine intellect.

Seventh Article

WHETHER CREATED TRUTH IS ETERNAL?

We proceed thus to the Seventh Article:—

Objection 1. It seems that created truth is eternal. For Augustine says, *Nothing is more eternal than the nature of a circle, and that two added to three make five.*[26] But the truth of these is a created truth. Therefore created truth is eternal.

---

[25] Peter Lombard, *In Psalm.*, super XI, 2 (PL 191, 155); cf. *Glossa interl.* (III, 102r).—Cf. also St. Augustine, *Enarr. in Psalm.*, super XI, 2 (PL 36, 158).   [26] *De Lib. Arb.*, II, 8 (PL 32, 1251); *Solil.*, II, 19 (PL 32, 901).

Obj. 2. Further, that which is always, is eternal. But universals are always and everywhere; therefore they are eternal. So therefore is truth, which is the most universal.

Obj. 3. Further, it was always true that what is true in the present was to be in the future. But as the truth of a proposition regarding the present is a created truth, so is that of a proposition regarding the future. Therefore some created truth is eternal.

Obj. 4. Further, all that is without beginning and end is eternal. But the truth of enunciations is without beginning and end. For if their truth had a beginning, then since it was not previously, it was true that truth was not, and true, of course, by reason of truth; so that truth was before it began to be. Similarly, if it be asserted that truth has an end, it follows that it is after it has ceased to be, for it will still be true that truth is not. Therefore truth is eternal.

On the contrary, God alone is eternal, as was laid down before.[27]

I answer that, The truth of enunciations is nothing other than the truth of the intellect. For an enunciation resides in the intellect, and in speech. Now according as it is in the intellect, it has truth of itself, but according as it is in speech, it is called enunciable truth, according as it signifies some truth of the intellect, and not because of any truth residing in the enunciation, as though in a subject. Thus urine is called healthy, not from any health within it but from the health of an animal which it indicates. In like manner, it has been already said that things are called true from the truth of the intellect. Hence, if no intellect were eternal, no truth would be eternal. Now because only the divine intellect is eternal, in it alone truth has eternity. Nor does it follow from this that anything else but God is eternal, since the truth of the divine intellect is God Himself, as has already been shown.

Reply Obj. 1. The nature of a circle, and the fact that two and three make five, have eternity in the mind of God.

Reply Obj. 2. That something is always and everywhere can be understood in two ways. In one way, as having in itself the power to extend to all time and to all places, as it belongs to God to be everywhere and always. In the other

[27] Q. 10, a. 3.

way, as not having in itself determination to any place or time; as primary matter is said to be one, not because it has one form, as man is one by the unity of one form, but by the absence of all distinguishing forms. In this manner, all universals are said to be everywhere and always, in so far as universals abstract from place and time. It does not, however, follow from this that they are eternal, except in an intellect, if one exists that is eternal.

Reply Obj. 3. What is now was to be, before it was, because its future lay in its cause. Hence, if the cause were removed, that thing's coming to be would not be future. But the first cause is alone eternal. Hence it does not follow that it was always true that what now is would be, except in so far as its future being was in the sempiternal cause; and God alone is such a cause.

Reply Obj. 4. Because our intellect is not eternal, neither is the truth of enunciable propositions, which are formed by us, eternal, but it had a beginning in time. Now before such truth existed, it was not true to say that such a truth did exist, except by reason of the divine intellect, wherein alone truth is eternal. But it is true now to say that that truth did not then exist: and this is true only by reason of the truth that is now in our intellect, and not by reason of any truth in the things. For this is truth concerning non-being, and non-being has no truth of itself, but only so far as our intellect apprehends it. Hence it is true to say that truth did not exist, in so far as we apprehend its non-being as preceding its being.

Eighth Article

WHETHER TRUTH IS IMMUTABLE?

We proceed thus to the Eighth Article:—
Objection 1. It seems that truth is immutable. For Augustine says that *Truth and mind do not rank as equals, otherwise truth would be mutable, as the mind is.*[28]

Obj. 2. Further, what survives all change is immutable; as primary matter is unbegotten and incorruptible, since it survives all generation and corruption. But truth survives all

---

[28] *De Lib. Arb.*, II, 12 (PL 32, 1259).

change; for after every change it is true to say that a thing is, or is not. Therefore, truth is immutable.

Obj. 3. Further, if the truth of an enunciation changes, it changes especially with the changing of the thing. But it does not thus change. For truth, according to Anselm, *is a certain rightness*, in so far as a thing answers to that which is in the divine mind concerning it.[29] But this proposition, *Socrates sits*, receiver from the divine mind the signification that Socrates does sit; and it has the same signification even though he does not sit. Therefore the truth of the proposition in no way changes.

Obj. 4. Further, where there is the same cause, there is the same effect. But the same thing is the cause of the truth of the three propositions, *Socrates sits, will sit, sat.* Therefore the truth of each is the same. But one or other of these must be the true one. Therefore the truth of these propositions remains immutable; and for the same reason that of any other proposition.

On the contrary, It is written (*Ps.* xi. 2), *Truths are decayed from among the children of men.*

I answer that, Truth, properly speaking, resides only in the intellect, as was said before; but things are called true in virtue of the truth residing in an intellect. Hence the mutability of truth must be regarded from the point of view of the intellect, the truth of which consists in its conformity to the things understood. Now this conformity may vary in two ways, even as any other likeness, through change in one of the two extremes. Hence, in one way, truth varies on the part of the intellect, from the fact that a change of opinion occurs about a thing which in itself has not changed, and, in another way, when the thing is changed, but not the opinion. In either way there can be a change from true to false. If, then, there is an intellect wherein there can be no alternation of opinions, and the knowledge of which nothing can escape, in this is immutable truth. Now such is the divine intellect, as is clear from what has been said before.[30] Hence the truth of the divine intellect is immutable. But the truth of our intellect is mutable, not because it is itself the subject of change, but in so far as our intellect changes from truth to falsity; for thus forms may be called mutable.

---

[29] *De Ver.*, VII; X (PL 158, 475; 478).   [30] Q. 14, a. 15.

But the truth of the divine intellect is that according to which natural things are said to be true, and this is altogether immutable.

Reply Obj. 1. Augustine is speaking of divine truth.

Reply Obj. 2. The true and being are convertible terms. Hence, just as being is not generated nor corrupted of itself, but accidentally, in so far as this being or that is corrupted or generated, as is said in *Physics* i.,[31] so does truth change, not so as that no truth remains, but because that particular truth does not remain which existed previously.

Reply Obj. 3. A proposition not only has truth, as other things are said to have it, namely, in so far as they correspond to that which is the design of the divine intellect concerning them, but it is said to have truth in a special way, in so far as it indicates the truth of the intellect, which consists in the conformity of the intellect with a thing. When this disappears, the truth of an opinion changes, and consequently the truth of the proposition. So therefore this proposition, *Socrates sits,* is true, as long as he is sitting, both with the truth of the thing, in so far as the expression is significative, and with the truth of signification, in so far as it signifies a true opinion. When Socrates rises, the first truth remains, but the second is changed.

Reply Obj. 4. The sitting of Socrates, which is the cause of the truth of the proposition, *Socrates sits,* has not the same status when Socrates sits, after he sits, and before he sits. Hence the truth which results varies, and is variously signified by these propositions concerning present, past, or future. Thus it does not follow, though one of the three propositions is true, that the same truth remains invariable.

[31] Aristotle, *Phys.,* I, 8 (191b 17).

CONCERNING FALSITY

(*In Four Articles*)

WE NEXT consider falsity. About this, four points of inquiry arise: (1) Whether falsity exists in things? (2) Whether it exists in the sense? (3) Whether it exists in the intellect? (4) Concerning the opposition of the true and the false.

First Article

WHETHER FALSITY EXISTS IN THINGS?

We proceed thus to the First Article:—

Objection 1. It appears that falsity does not exist in things. For Augustine says, *If the true is that which is, it will be concluded that the false exists nowhere; whatever reason may appear to the contrary.*[1]

Obj. 2. Further, false is derived from *fallere* [to deceive]. But things do not deceive; for, as Augustine says, they show nothing but their own species.[2] Therefore the false is not found in things.

Obj. 3. Further, the true is said to exist in things by conformity to the divine intellect, as was stated above.[3] But everything, in so far as it exists, imitates God. Therefore everything is true without admixture of falsity; and thus nothing is false.

On the contrary, Augustine says: *Every body is a true body and a false unity:* for it imitates unity without being unity.[4] But everything imitates the divine unity, yet falls short of it. Therefore in all things falsity exists.

I answer that, Since true and false are opposed, and since opposites stand in relation to the same thing, we must needs seek falsity where primarily we find truth, that is to say, in the intellect. Now, in things, neither truth nor falsity exists, except in relation to the intellect. And since every thing is denominated absolutely by what belongs to it essentially, but is denominated relatively by what belongs to it accidentally, a thing may be called false absolutely when compared with

---

[1] *Solil.*, II, 8 (PL 32, 892).   [2] *De Vera Relig.*, XXXVI (PL 34, 152).   [3] Q. 16, a. 1.   [4] *De Vera Relig.*, XXXIV (PL 34, 150).

the intellect on which it depends, and to which it is related essentially; but it may be called false relatively as ordered to another intellect, to which it is related accidentally.

Now natural things depend on the divine intellect, as artificial things on the human. Therefore, artificial things are said to be false absolutely and in themselves, in so far as they fall short of the form of the art; whence a craftsman is said to produce a false work, if it falls short of the proper operation of his art. In things that depend on God, falseness cannot be found, in so far as they are compared with the divine intellect; since whatever takes place in things proceeds from the ordinance of that intellect, unless perhaps in the case of voluntary agents only, who have it in their power to withdraw themselves from what is so ordained; wherein consists the evil of sin. Thus sins themselves are called untruths and lies in the Scriptures, according to the words of the text, *Why do you love vanity, and seek after lying?* (*Ps.* iv. 3); as on the other hand virtuous deeds are called the *truth of life* as being obedient to the order of the divine intellect. Thus it is said, *He that doth truth, cometh to the light* (*Jo.* iii. 21).

But in relation to our intellect, natural things, which are compared thereto accidentally, can be called false, not absolutely, but relatively; and that in two ways. In one way, according to the thing signified, and thus a thing is said to be false which is signified or represented by false speech or thought. In this manner, anything can be said to be false as regards any quality not possessed by it; as if we should say that a diameter is a false commensurable thing, as the Philosopher says.[5] So, too, Augustine says: *The tragedian is a false Hector*.[6] So, too, on the contrary, anything can be called true, in regard to that which belongs to it. In another way, a thing can be called false, by way of cause—and thus a thing is said to be false that naturally begets a false opinion. And because it is innate in us to judge of things by external appearances, since our knowledge takes its rise from sense, which principally and essentially deals with external accidents, therefore those external accidents which resemble things other than themselves are said to be false with respect to those things; thus gall is false honey, and tin, false

[5] *Metaph.*, IV, 29 (1024b 19).　　　[6] *Solil.*, II, 10 (PL 32, 893).

silver. Regarding this, Augustine says: *We call those things false that appear to our apprehension like the true;*[7] and the Philosopher says: *Things are called false that are naturally apt to appear such as they are not, or what they are not.*[8] In this sense a man is called false as delighting in false opinions or words, and not because he can invent them; for in that way many wise and learned persons might be called false, as is stated in *Metaph.* v.[9]

Reply Obj. 1. A thing compared with the intellect is said to be true in respect to what it is, and false in respect to what it is not. Hence, *The true tragedian is a false Hector*, as stated in *Soliloq.* ii.[10] As, therefore, in things that are there is found a certain non-being, so in things that are is found a certain character of falseness.

Reply Obj. 2. Things do not deceive by their own nature, but by accident. For they give occasion to falsity by the likeness they bear to things which they actually are not.

Reply Obj. 3. Things are said to be false, not as compared with the divine intellect, in which case they would be false absolutely, but as compared with our intellect; and thus they are false only relatively.

To the argument which is urged on the contrary: A defective likeness or representation does not involve the character of falsity except in so far as it gives occasion to false opinion. Hence a thing is not always said to be false because it resembles another thing, but only when the resemblance is such as naturally to produce a false opinion, not in some cases, but in general.

Second Article

WHETHER THERE IS FALSITY IN THE SENSES?

We proceed thus to the Second Article:—

Objection 1. It seems that falsity is not in the senses. For Augustine says: *If all the bodily senses report as they are affected, I do not know what more we can require from them.*[11] Thus it seems that we are not deceived by the senses. Therefore falsity is not in them.

---

[7] *Op. cit.*, II, 6 (PL 32, 889).   [8] *Metaph.*, IV, 29 (1024b 21).
[9] *Ibid.* (1025a 2).   [10] *Solil.*, II, 10 (PL 32, 893).   [11] *De Vera Relig.*, XXXIII (PL 34, 149).

Obj. 2. Further, the Philosopher says that falsity is not proper to the senses, but to the imagination.[12]

Obj. 3. Further, in concepts there is neither true nor false, but in judgments only. But affirmation and negation do not belong to the senses. Therefore in the senses there is no falsity.

On the contrary, Augustine says, *It appears that the senses entrap us into error by their deceptive similitudes.*[13]

I answer that, Falsity is not to be sought in the senses except as truth is in them. Now truth is not in them in such a way that the senses know truth, but in so far as they have a true apprehension of sensible things, as was said above.[14] This takes place through the senses apprehending things as they are; and hence it happens that falsity exists in the senses through their apprehending or judging things to be otherwise than they really are.

Now the knowledge of things by the senses is in proportion to the existence of their likeness in the senses; and the likeness of a thing can exist in the senses in three ways. In the first way, primarily and essentially, as in sight there is the likeness of colors and of other sensible objects proper to it. Secondly, essentially, though not primarily; as in sight there is the likeness of figure or bodily shape, and of other sensible objects common to more than one sense. Thirdly, neither primarily nor essentially, but accidentally; as in sight, there is the likeness of a man, not as man, but in so far as it happens to the colored object to be a man.

Sense, then, has no false knowledge about its proper objects, except accidentally and rarely, and then because of an indisposition in the organ it does not receive the sensible form rightly; just as other passive subjects because of their indisposition receive defectively the impressions of the agent. Hence, for instance, it happens that because of an unhealthy tongue sweet seems bitter to a sick person. But as to common objects of sense, and accidental objects, even a rightly disposed sense may have a false judgment, because the sense is referred to them not directly, but accidentally, or as a consequence of being related to other objects.

[12] *Metaph.*, III, 5 (1010b 2).   [13] *Solil.*, II, 6 (PL 32, 890).   [14] Q. 16, a. 2.

Reply Obj. 1. The affection of sense is its sensation itself. Hence, from the fact that sense reports as it is affected, it follows that we are not deceived in the judgment by which we judge that we are sensing something. Since, however, sense is sometimes affected otherwise than is the thing, it follows that it sometimes reports that thing otherwise than as it is; and thus we are deceived by sense about the thing, not about the fact of sensation.

Reply Obj. 2. Falsity is said not to be proper to sense, since sense is not deceived as to its proper object. Hence in another translation the text reads more plainly, *Sense, about its proper object, is never false.*[15] Falsity is attributed to the imagination, however, as it represents the likeness of something even in its absence. Hence, when anyone perceives the likeness of a thing as if it were the thing itself, falsity results from such an apprehension; and for this reason the Philosopher says that *shadows, pictures and dreams* are said to be false inasmuch as they convey the likeness of things without the substance.[16]

Reply Obj. 3. This argument proves that the false is not in the sense as in that which knows the true and the false.

Third Article

WHETHER FALSITY IS IN THE INTELLECT?

We proceed thus to the Third Article:—

Objection 1. It seems that falsity is not in the intellect. For Augustine says, *Everyone who is deceived understands not that in which he is deceived.*[17] But falsity is said to exist in any knowledge in so far as we are deceived therein. Therefore falsity does not exist in the intellect.

Obj. 2. Further, the Philosopher says that *the intellect is always right.*[18] Therefore there is no falsity in the intellect.

On the contrary, It is said in *De anima* iii. that *where there is composition of objects understood, there there is truth and falsehood.*[19] But such composition is in the intellect. Therefore truth and falsehood exist in the intellect.

I answer that, Just as a thing has being by its proper form,

[15] Cf. B. Geyer, in *Phil. Jahrbuch,* XXX (1917), p. 406.   [16] *Metaph.,* IV, 29 (1024b 23).   [17] *Lib. 83 Quaest.,* q. 32 (PL 40, 22).   [18] *De An.,* III, 10 (433a 26).   [19] *Op. cit.,* III, 6 (430a 27).

so the knowing power has knowledge by the likeness of the thing known. Hence, as natural things do not fall short of the being that belongs to them by their form, but may fall short of accidental or consequent qualities, even as a man may fail to possess two feet, but not fail to be a man; so the power of knowing cannot fail in the knowledge of the thing with the likeness of which it is informed, but may fail with regard to something consequent upon that form, or accidental thereto. For it has been said that sight is not deceived in its proper sensible, but about common sensibles that are consequent upon that proper object, or about accidental objects of sense. Now as the sense is directly informed by the likeness of its proper object, so is the intellect by the likeness of the essence of a thing. Hence the intellect is not deceived about the essence of a thing, as neither the sense about its proper object. But in affirming and denying, the intellect may be deceived by attributing to the thing, of which it understands the essence, something which is not consequent upon it, or is opposed to it. For the intellect is in the same position as regards judging of such things, as sense is as to judging of common, or accidental, sensible objects. There is, however, this difference, as was before mentioned regarding truth, that falsity can exist in the intellect not merely because the knowledge of the intellect is false, but because the intellect is conscious of that false knowledge, as it is conscious of truth;[20] whereas in the sense falsity does not exist as known, as was stated above.

But because falsity of the intellect is concerned essentially only with the composition of the intellect, falsity can occur accidentally also in that operation of the intellect whereby it knows the essence of a thing in so far as a composition of the intellect is involved in it. This can take place in two ways. In one way, by the intellect applying to one thing the definition proper to another; as that of a circle to a man. Therefore the definition of one thing is false of another. In another way, by composing a definition of parts which are mutually repugnant. For thus the definition is not only false of the thing, but false in itself. A definition such as 'a four-footed rational animal' would be of this kind, and the intellect false in making it; for such a statement as 'some rational animals are four-footed' is false in itself. For this reason the intellect cannot be false in its knowledge of simple essences; but it is either true, or it understands nothing at all.

Reply Obj. 1. Because the essence of a thing is the proper object of the intellect, we are properly said to understand a thing when we reduce it to its essence, and judge of it thereby; as takes place in demonstrations, in which there is no falsity. In this sense Augustine's words must be understood, *that he who is deceived understands not that wherein he is deceived;* and not in the sense that no one is ever deceived in any operation of the intellect.

Reply Obj. 2. The intellect is always right as regards first principles, since it is not deceived about them for the same reason that it is not deceived about *what a thing is.* For self-known principles are such as are known as soon as the terms are understood, from the fact that the predicate is contained in the definition of the subject.

Fourth Article

WHETHER TRUE AND FALSE ARE CONTRARIES?

We proceed thus to the Fourth Article:—

Objection 1. It seems that true and false are not contraries. For true and false are opposed as that which is to that which is not; for *the true,* as Augustine says, *is that which is.*[21] But that which is and that which is not are not opposed as contraries. Therefore true and false are not contraries.

Obj. 2. Further, one of two contraries is not in the other. But falsity is in truth, because, as Augustine says, *A tragedian would not be a false Hector, if he were not a true tragedian.*[22] Therefore true and false are not contraries.

Obj. 3. Further, in God there is no contrariety, *for nothing is contrary to the Divine Substance,* as Augustine says.[23] But falsity is opposed to God, for an idol is called a lie in Scripture. *They have laid hold on lying* (*Jer.* viii. 5), that is to say, *an idol,* as the *Gloss* says.[24] Therefore true and false are not contraries.

---

[21] *Solil.,* II, 5 (PL 32, 889).   [22] *Op. cit.,* II, 10 (PL 32, 893). [23] *De Civit. Dei,* XII, 2 (PL 41, 350).   [24] *Glossa interl.,* super *Jeremiah,* VIII, 5 (IV, 123v).—Cf. St. Jerome, *In Jerem.,* super VIII, 5 (PL 24, 765).

On the contrary, The Philosopher says that a false opinion is contrary to a true one.[25]

I answer that, True and false are opposed as contraries, and not, as some have said, as affirmation and negation.[26] In proof of which it must be considered that negation neither asserts anything nor determines for itself any subject. It can therefore be said of being as of non-being, for instance, not-seeing or not-sitting. But though privation asserts nothing, it determines a subject, for it is *negation in a subject,* as is stated in *Metaph.* iv.;[27] for blindness is not said except of one whose nature it is to see. Contraries, however, both assert something and determine a subject, for blackness is a species of color. Now falsity asserts something, for a thing is false, as the Philosopher says,[28] inasmuch as *something is said or seems to be something that it is not, or not to be what it really is.* For as truth implies an adequate apprehension of a thing, so falsity implies the contrary. Hence it is clear that true and false are contraries.

Reply Obj. 1. What is in things is the truth of the thing; but what is apprehended is the truth of the intellect, wherein truth primarily resides. Hence the false is that which is not as apprehended. But to apprehend being and non-being implies contrariety; for, as the Philosopher proves, the contrary of the statement *good is good* is, *good is not good.*[29]

Reply Obj. 2. Falsity is not founded in the truth which is contrary to it, just as evil is not founded in the good which is contrary to it, but in that which is its proper subject. This happens in both cases because *true* and *good* are universals and convertible with being. Hence, as every privation is founded in a subject that is a being, so every evil is founded in some good, and every falsity in some truth.

Reply Obj. 3. Because contraries, and opposites by way of privation, are by nature about one and the same thing, therefore there is nothing contrary to God, considered in Himself, either with respect to His goodness or His truth; for in His intellect there can be nothing false. But in our apprehen-

---

[25] *Perih.,* II, 14 (23b 35).   [26] Cf. Alex. of Hales, *Summa Theol.,* I, no. 101 (I, 159).   [27] Aristotle, *Metaph.,* III, 2 (1004a 15); IV, 22 (1022a 26).   [28] *Op. cit.,* III, 7 (1011b 26).   [29] *Perih.,* II, 14 (23b 35).

sion of Him, God has a contrary, for the false opinion concerning Him is contrary to the true. So idols are called lies which are opposed to the divine truth, inasmuch as the false opinion concerning them is contrary to the true opinion of the divine unity.

Question XIX

THE WILL OF GOD

(*In Twelve Articles*)

AFTER considering the things belonging to the divine knowledge, we consider what belongs to the divine will. The first consideration is about the divine will itself; the second, about what belongs to His will absolutely;[1] the third, about what belongs to the intellect in relation to His will.[2] About His will itself there are twelve points of inquiry: (1) Whether there is will in God? (2) Whether God wills things other than Himself? (3) Whether whatever God wills, He wills necessarily? (4) Whether the will of God is the cause of things? (5) Whether any cause can be assigned to the divine will? (6) Whether the divine will is always fulfilled? (7) Whether the will of God is mutable? (8) Whether the will of God imposes necessity on the things willed? (9) Whether God wills evil? (10) Whether God has free choice? (11) Whether the *will of sign* is distinguished in God? (12) Whether five signs of will are rightly held of the divine will?

First Article

WHETHER THERE IS WILL IN GOD?

We proceed thus to the First Article:—

Objection 1. It seems that there is no will in God. For the object of will is the end and the good. But we cannot assign any end to God. Therefore there is no will in God.

Obj. 2. Further, will is a kind of appetite. But appetite, since it is directed to things not possessed, implies imperfection, which cannot be imputed to God. Therefore there is no will in God.

Obj. 3. Further, according to the Philosopher, the will is a moved mover.[3] But God is the first mover, Himself unmoved, as is proved in *Physics* viii.[4] Therefore there is no will in God.

---

[1] Q. 20.　　[2] Q. 22.　　[3] *De An.*, III, 10 (433b 16).　　[4] Aristotle, *Phys.*, VIII, 6 (258b 10).

On the contrary, The Apostle says (*Rom.* xii. 2): *That you may prove what is the will of God.*

I answer that, There is will in God, just as there is intellect: since will follows upon intellect. For as natural things have actual being by their form, so the intellect is actually knowing by its intelligible form. Now everything has this disposition towards its natural form, that when it does not have it, it tends towards it; and when it has it, it is at rest therein. It is the same with every natural perfection, which is a natural good. This disposition to good in things without knowledge is called *natural appetite.* Whence also intellectual natures have a like disposition to good as apprehended through an intelligible form, so as to rest therein when possessed, and when not possessed to seek to possess it; both of which pertain to the will. Hence in every intellectual being there is *will,* just as in every sensible being there is *animal appetite.* And so there must be will in God, since there is intellect in Him. And as His knowing is His own being, so is His willing.

Reply Obj. 1. Although nothing apart from God is His end, yet He Himself is the end with respect to all things made by Him. And He is the end by His essence, for by His essence He is good, as was shown above:[5] for the end has the aspect of good.

Reply Obj. 2. Will in us belongs to the appetitive part, which, although named from appetite, has not for its only act to seek what it does not possess, but also to love and delight in what it does possess. In this respect will is said to be in God, as always possessing the good which is its object; since, as we have already said, it is not in essence distinct from this good.

Reply Obj. 3. A will, of which the principal object is a good outside itself, must be moved by another: but the object of the divine will is His goodness, which is His essence. Hence, since the will of God is His essence, it is not moved by another than itself, but by itself alone (in the same sense, of course, in which understanding and willing are said to be movements). This is what Plato meant when he said that the first mover moves himself.[6]

[5] Q. 6, a. 3.   [6] Cf. *S.T.*, q. 9, a. 1, ad. 1.

Second Article

WHETHER GOD WILLS THINGS OTHER THAN HIMSELF?

We proceed thus to the Second Article:—

Objection 1. It seems that God does not will things other than Himself. For the divine will is the divine being. But God is not other than Himself. Therefore He does not will things other than Himself.

Obj. 2. Further, the object willed moves the one who wills, as the appetible the appetite, as is stated in *De Anima* iii.[7] If, therefore, God wills anything apart from Himself, His will must be moved by another; which is impossible.

Obj. 3. Further, if what is willed suffices the one who wills, he seeks nothing beyond it. But His own goodness suffices God, and completely satisfies His will. Therefore God does not will anything other than Himself.

Obj. 4. Further, acts of the will are multiplied according to the number of their objects. If, therefore, God wills Himself and things other than Himself, it follows that the act of His will is manifold, and consequently His being, which is His will. But this is impossible. Therefore God does not will things other than Himself.

On the contrary, The Apostle says (*1 Thess.* iv. 3): *This is the will of God, your sanctification.*

I answer that, God wills not only Himself, but also things other than Himself. This is clear from the comparison made above. For natural things have a natural inclination not only towards their own proper good, to acquire it if not possessed, and, if possessed, to rest therein; but also to diffuse their own good among others so far as possible. Hence we see that every agent, in so far as it is perfect and in act, produces its like. It pertains, therefore, to the nature of the will to communicate as far as possible to others the good possessed; and especially does this pertain to the divine will, from which all perfection is derived in some kind of likeness. Hence, if natural things, in so far as they are perfect, communicate their good to others, much more does it pertain to the divine will to communicate by likeness its own good to others as much as is possible. Thus, then, He wills both Himself to be,

[7] Aristotle, *De An.,* III, 10 (433b 17).

and other things to be; but Himself as the end, and other things as ordained to that end, inasmuch as it befits the divine goodness that other things should be partakers therein.

Reply Obj. 1. Although in God to will is really the same as to be, yet they differ logically, according to the different ways of understanding them and signifying them, as is clear from what has been already said.[8] For when we say that God exists, no relation to any other thing is implied, as we do imply when we say that God wills. Therefore, although He is not anything other than Himself, yet He does will things other than Himself.

Reply Obj. 2. In things willed for the sake of the end, the whole reason for our being moved is the end; and this it is that moves the will, as most clearly appears in things willed only for the sake of the end. He who wills to take a bitter draught, in doing so wills nothing else than health; and this alone moves his will. It is different with one who takes a draught that is pleasant, which anyone may will to do, not only for the sake of health, but also for its own sake. Hence, although God wills things other than Himself only for the sake of the end, which is His own goodness, it does not follow that anything else moves His will, except His goodness. So, as He understands things other than Himself by understanding His own essence, so He wills things other than Himself by willing His own goodness.

Reply Obj. 3. From the fact that His own goodness suffices the divine will, it does not follow that it wills nothing other than itself, but rather that it wills nothing except by reason of its goodness. Thus, too, the divine intellect: although its perfection consists in its knowledge of the divine essence, yet in that essence it knows other things.

Reply Obj. 4. As the divine knowing is one, as seeing the many only in the one, in the same way the divine willing is one and simple, as willing the many only through the one, that is, through its own goodness.

[8] Q. 13, a. 4.

Third Article

WHETHER WHATEVER GOD WILLS HE WILLS NECESSARILY?

We proceed thus to the Third Article:—

Objection 1. It seems that whatever God wills He wills necessarily. For everything eternal is necessary. But whatever God wills, He wills from eternity, for otherwise His will would be mutable. Therefore whatever He wills, He wills necessarily.

Obj. 2. Further, God wills things other than Himself inasmuch as He wills His own goodness. Now God wills His own goodness necessarily. Therefore He wills things other than Himself necessarily.

Obj. 3. Further, whatever belongs to the nature of God is necessary, for God is of Himself necessary being, and the source of all necessity, as was above shown.[9] But it belongs to His nature to will whatever He wills; since in God there can be nothing over and above His nature, as is stated in *Metaph.* v.[10] Therefore whatever He wills, He wills necessarily.

Obj. 4. Further, being that is not necessary, and being that is possible not to be, are one and the same thing. If, therefore, God does not necessarily will a thing that He wills, it is also possible for Him not to will it, and therefore possible for Him to will what He does not will. And so the divine will is contingent, with respect to choosing determinately among these things; and also imperfect, since everything contingent is imperfect and mutable.

Obj. 5. Further, on the part of that which is indifferent to one or the other of two things, no action results unless it is inclined to one or the other by some other being, as the Commentator says on *Physics* ii.[11] If, then, the will of God is indifferent with regard to anything, it follows that His determination to a given effect comes from another; and thus He has some cause prior to Himself.

Obj. 6. Further, whatever God knows He knows necessarily. But as the divine knowledge is His essence, so is the

[9] Q. 2, a. 3.   [10] Aristotle, *Metaph.,* IV, 5 (1015b 15).   [11] *Phys.,* II, comm. 48 (IV, 31v).

divine will. Therefore whatever God wills He wills necessarily.

On the contrary, The Apostle says (*Ephes* i. 11): *Who worketh all things according to the counsel of His will.* Now, what we work according to the counsel of the will, we do not will necessarily. Therefore God does not will necessarily whatever He wills.

I answer that, There are two ways in which a thing is said to be necessary, namely, absolutely, and by supposition. We judge a thing to be absolutely necessary from the relation of the terms, as when the predicate forms part of the definition of the subject: thus it is necessary that man is an animal; or as when the subject forms part of the notion of the predicate: thus it is necessary that a number must be odd or even. In this way it is not necessary that Socrates sits: hence it is not necessary absolutely, but it may be so by supposition; for, granted that he is sitting, he must necessarily sit, as long as he is sitting.

Accordingly, as to things willed by God, we must observe that He wills something of absolute necessity; but this is not true of all that He wills. For the divine will has a necessary relation to the divine goodness, since that is its proper object. Hence God wills the being of His own goodness necessarily, even as we will our own happiness necessarily, and as any other power has a necessary relation to its proper and principal object, for instance the sight to color, since it is of its nature to tend to it. But God wills things other than Himself in so far as they are ordered to His own goodness as their end. Now in willing an end we do not necessarily will things that conduce to it, unless they are such that the end cannot be attained without them; as, we will to take food to preserve life, or to take a ship in order to cross the sea. But we do not will necessarily those things without which the end is attainable, such as a horse for a stroll, since we can take a stroll without a horse. The same applies to other means. Hence, since the goodness of God is perfect and can exist without other things, inasmuch as no perfection can accrue to Him from them, it follows that for Him to will things other than Himself is not absolutely necessary. Yet it can be necessary by supposition, for supposing that He wills a thing, then He is unable not to will it, as His will cannot change.

Reply Obj. 1. From the fact that God wills from eternity whatever He wills, it does not follow that He wills it necessarily, except by supposition.

Reply Obj. 2. Although God wills necessarily His own goodness, He does not necessarily will things willed because of His goodness; for it can exist without other things.

Reply Obj. 3. It is not natural to God to will any of those other things that He does not will necessarily; and yet it is not unnatural or contrary to His nature, but voluntary.

Reply Obj. 4. Sometimes a necessary cause has a non-necessary relation to an effect, owing to a deficiency in the effect, and not in the cause. Thus, the sun's power has a non-necessary relation to some contingent events on this earth owing to a defect, not in the solar power, but in the effect that proceeds not necessarily from the cause. In the same way, that God does not necessarily will some of the things that He wills, does not result from defect in the divine will, but from a defect belonging to the nature of the thing willed, namely, that the perfect goodness of God can be without it; and such defect accompanies every created good.

Reply Obj. 5. A naturally contingent cause must be determined to act by some external being. The divine will, however, which by its nature is necessary, determines itself to will things to which it has no necessary relation.

Reply Obj. 6. Just as the divine being is necessary of itself, so is the divine willing and the divine knowing; but the divine knowing has a necessary relation to the thing known; not the divine willing, however, to the thing willed. The reason for this is that knowledge is of things as they exist in the knower; but the will is related to things as they exist in themselves. Since, then, all other things have a necessary being inasmuch as they exist in God, but no absolute necessity to be necessary in themselves, in so far as they exist in themselves, it follows that God knows necessarily whatever He knows, but does not will necessarily whatever He wills.

Fourth Article

WHETHER THE WILL OF GOD IS THE CAUSE OF THINGS?

We proceed thus to the Fourth Article:—
Objection 1. It seems that the will of God is not the cause

of things. For Dionysius says: *As our sun, not by reasoning nor by choice, but by its very being, enlightens all things that can participate in its light, so the divine good by its very essence pours the rays of its goodness upon everything that exists.*[12] But every voluntary agent acts by reasoning and choice. Therefore God does not act by will; and so His will is not the cause of things.

Obj. 2. Further, the first in any order is that which is essentially so; thus in the order of burning things, that comes first which is fire by its essence. But God is the first agent. Therefore He acts by His essence; and that is His nature. He acts then by nature, and not by will. Therefore the divine will is not the cause of things.

Obj. 3. Further, whatever is the cause of anything, because it itself is such a thing, is a cause by nature, and not by will. For fire is the cause of heat, as being itself hot; whereas an architect is the cause of a house, because he wills to build it. Now Augustine says, *Because God is good, we exist.*[13] Therefore God is the cause of things by His nature, and not by His will.

Obj. 4. Further, of one thing there is one cause. But the cause of created things is the knowledge of God, as was said before.[14] Therefore the will of God cannot be considered the cause of things.

On the contrary, It is said (*Wis.* xi. 26), *How could anything endure, if Thou wouldst not?*

I answer that, We must hold that the will of God is the cause of things, and that He acts by the will, and not, as some have supposed, by a necessity of His nature.

This can be shown in three ways: First, from the order itself of agent causes. Since both *intellect and nature* act for an end, as is proved in *Physics* ii.,[15] the natural agent must have the end and the necessary means predetermined for it by some higher intellect; as, the end and definite movement is predetermined for the arrow by the archer. Hence the intellectual and voluntary agent must precede the agent that acts by nature. Hence, since God is first in the order of agents, He must act by intellect and will.

This is shown, secondly, from the character of a natural agent, to which it belongs to produce one and the same ef-

[12] *De Div. Nom.*, IV, 1 (PG 3, 693).   [13] *De Doct. Christ.*, I, 32 (PL 34, 32).   [14] Q. 14, a. 8.   [15] Aristotle, *Phys.*, II, 5 (196b 21).

fect; for nature operates in one and the same way, unless
it be prevented. This is because the nature of the act is according to the nature of the agent, and hence as long as it
has that nature, its acts will be in accordance with that nature; for every natural agent has a determinate being. Since,
then, the divine being is undetermined, and contains in Himself the full perfection of being, it cannot be that He acts
by a necessity of His nature, unless He were to cause something undetermined and indefinite in being; and that this is
impossible has been already shown.[16] He does not, therefore,
act by a necessity of His nature, but determined effects proceed from His own infinite perfection according to the determination of His will and intellect.

Thirdly, it is shown by the relation of effects to their
cause. For effects proceed from the agent that causes them
in so far as they pre-exist in the agent; since every agent
produces its like. Now effects pre-exist in their cause after
the mode of the cause. Therefore, since the divine being is
His own intellect, effects pre-exist in Him after the mode of
intellect, and therefore proceed from Him after the same
mode. Consequently, they proceed from Him after the mode
of will, for His inclination to put in act what His intellect
has conceived pertains to the will. Therefore the will of God
is the cause of things.

Reply Obj. 1. Dionysius in these words does not intend to
exclude election from God absolutely, but only in a certain
sense, in so far, that is, as He communicates His goodness
not merely to certain beings, but to all; whereas election implies a certain distinction.

Reply Obj. 2. Because the essence of God is His intellect
and will, from the fact of His acting by His essence it follows
that He acts after the mode of intellect and will.

Reply Obj. 3. Good is the object of the will. The words,
therefore, *Because God is good, we exist,* are true inasmuch
as His Goodness is the reason of His willing all other things,
as was said before.

Reply Obj. 4. Even in us the cause of one and the same
effect is knowledge as directing it, whereby the form of the
thing to be done is conceived, and will as commanding it,
since the form as it is only in the intellect is not determined

[16] Q. 7, a. 2.

to exist or not to exist actually, except by the will. Hence, the speculative intellect has nothing to say as to operation. But the power of the agent is cause, as executing the effect, since it denotes the immediate principle of operation. But in God all these things are one.

Fifth Article

WHETHER ANY CAUSE CAN BE ASSIGNED TO THE DIVINE WILL?

We proceed thus to the Fifth Article:—

Objection 1. It seems that some cause can be assigned to the divine will. For Augustine says: *Who would venture to say that God made all things irrationally?* [17] But to a voluntary agent, the reason for acting is also the cause of willing. Therefore the will of God has some cause.

Obj. 2. Further, in things made by one who wills to make them, and whose will is influenced by no cause, there can be no cause assigned except the will of him who wills. But the will of God is the cause of all things, as has been already shown. If, then, there is no cause of His will, in the whole realm of natural things we cannot seek any cause, except the divine will alone. Thus all the sciences would be in vain, since science seeks to assign causes to effects. This seems inadmissible, and therefore we must assign some cause to the divine will.

Obj. 3. Further, what is done by the one who wills, because of no cause, depends absolutely on his will. If, therefore, the will of God has no cause, it follows that all things made depend absolutely on His will, and have no other cause. But this also is not admissible.

On the contrary, Augustine says: *Every efficient cause is greater than the thing effected. But nothing is greater than the will of God. We must not then seek for a cause of it.* [18]

I answer that, In no wise has the will of God a cause. In proof of which we must consider that, since the will follows from the intellect, the cause explaining the willing of one who wills is the same as the cause explaining the knowing of one who knows. The case with the intellect is this: that if

[17] *Lib. 83 Quaest.*, q. 46 (PL 40, 30).   [18] *Op. cit.*, q. 28 (PL 40, 18).

the principle and its conclusion are understood separately
from each other, the understanding of the principle is the
cause that the conclusion is known. But if the intellect perceive the conclusion in the principle itself, apprehending
both the one and the other at the same glance, in this case
the knowledge of the conclusion would not be caused by understanding the principles, since a thing cannot be its own
cause; and yet, it would be true that the intellect would understand the principles to be the cause of the conclusion. It
is the same with the will, with respect to which the end
stands in the same relation to the means as principles to the
conclusions in the intellect.

Hence, if anyone in one act wills an end, and in another
act the means to that end, his willing the end will be the
cause of his willing the means. This cannot be the case if
in one act he wills both end and means; for a thing cannot
be its own cause. Yet it will be true to say that he wills to
order to the end the means to the end. Now as God by one
act understands all things in His essence, so by one act He
wills all things in His goodness. Hence, as in God to understand the cause is not the cause of His understanding the
effect (for He understands the effect in the cause), so, in
Him, to will an end is not the cause of His willing the means;
yet He wills the ordering of the means to the end. Therefore
He wills this to be as means to that; but He does not will
this because of that.

Reply Obj. 1. The will of God is reasonable, not because
anything is to God a cause of willing, but in so far as He
wills one thing to be because of another.

Reply Obj. 2. Since God wills effects to proceed from definite causes, for the preservation of order in the universe, it
is not unreasonable to seek for causes secondary to the divine will. It would, however, be unreasonable to do so, if
such were considered as primary, and not as dependent on
the will of God. In this sense Augustine says: *Philosophers
in their vanity have thought fit to attribute contingent effects to other causes, being utterly unable to perceive the
cause that is above all others, the will of God.*[19]

Reply Obj. 3. Since God wills that effects be because of
their causes, all effects that presuppose some other effect do
not depend solely on the will of God, but on something else

[19] *De Trin.,* III, 2 (PL 42, 871).

besides: but the first effect depends on the divine will alone. Thus, for example, we may say that God willed man to have hands to serve his intellect by their work, and an intellect, that he might be man; and willed him to be man that he might enjoy Him, or for the completion of the universe. But this cannot be reduced to further created secondary ends. Hence such things depend on the simple will of God; but the others on the order of other causes.

Sixth Article

WHETHER THE WILL OF GOD IS ALWAYS FULFILLED?

We proceed thus to the Sixth Article:—

Objection 1. It seems that the will of God is not always fulfilled. For the Apostle says (*1 Tim.* ii. 4): *God will have all men to be saved, and to come to the knowledge of the truth.* But this does not happen. Therefore the will of God is not always fulfilled.

Obj. 2. Further, as is the relation of knowledge to truth, so is that of the will to good. Now God knows all truth. Therefore He wills all good. But not all good actually exists; for much more good might exist. Therefore the will of God is not always fulfilled.

Obj. 3. Further, since the will of God is the first cause, it does not exclude intermediate causes. But the effect of a first cause may be hindered by a defect of a secondary cause; as the effect of the locomotive power of the body may be hindered by the incapacity of a leg. Therefore the effect of the divine will may be hindered by a defect of the secondary causes. The will of God, therefore, is not always fulfilled.

On the contrary, It is said (*Ps.* cxiii. 11): *God hath done all things, whatsoever He would.*

I answer that, The will of God must needs always be fulfilled. In proof of which we must consider that, since an effect is conformed to the agent according to its form, the rule is the same with agent causes as with formal causes. The rule in forms is this: that although a thing may fall short of any particular form, it cannot fall short of the universal form. For though a thing may fail to be a man or a living being, for example, yet it cannot fail to be a being. Hence the same must happen in agent causes. Something may escape the order of any particular agent cause, but not the order of the universal cause under which all particular causes are included; and if any particular cause fails of its effect, this is because of the hindrance of some other particular cause, which is included within the order of the universal cause. Therefore, an effect cannot possibly escape the order of the universal cause. This is clearly seen also in corporeal things. For it may happen that a star is hindered from producing its effects; yet whatever effect does result within the realm of corporeal things, as a consequence of this hindrance of a corporeal cause, must be referred through intermediate causes to the universal influence of the first heavens.

Since, then, the will of God is the universal cause of all things, it is impossible that the divine will should not produce its effect. Hence that which seems to depart from the divine will in one order, returns into it in another; as does the sinner, who by sin falls away from the divine will as much as lies in him, yet falls back into the order of that will, when by its justice he is punished.

Reply Obj. 1. The words of the Apostle, *God will have all men to be saved*, etc., can be understood in three ways. First, by a restricted application, in which case they would mean, as Augustine says, *God wills all men to be saved that are saved, not because there is no man whom He does not wish saved, but because there is no man saved whose salvation He does not will.*[20] Secondly, they can be understood as applying to every class of individuals, not to every individual of each class; in which case they mean that God wills some men of every class and condition to be saved, males and females, Jews and Gentiles, great and small, but not all of every condition. Thirdly, according to Damascene, they are understood of the antecedent will of God; not of the consequent will.[21] This distinction must not be taken as applying to the divine will itself, in which there is nothing antecedent or consequent, but to the things willed.

To understand this we must consider that everything, in so far as it is good, is willed by God. A thing taken in its primary sense, and absolutely considered, may be good or evil, and yet, when some additional circumstances are taken

[20] *Enchir.*, CIII (PL 40, 280).   [21] *De Fide Orth.*, II, 29 (PG 94, 968).

into account, by a consequent consideration may be changed into the contrary. Thus that a man should live is good; and that a man should be killed is evil, absolutely considered. But if in a particular case we add that a man is a murderer or dangerous to society, to kill him is a good; that he live is an evil. Hence it may be said of a just judge, that antecedently he wills all men to live; but consequently wills the murderer to be hanged. In the same way, God antecedently wills all men to be saved, but consequently wills some to be damned, as His justice exacts. Nor do we will absolutely what we will antecedently, but rather we will it in a qualified manner; for the will is directed to things as they are in themselves, and in themselves they exist under particular conditions. Hence we will a thing absolutely inasmuch as we will it when all particular circumstances are considered; and this is what is meant by willing consequently. Thus it may be said that a just judge wills absolutely the hanging of a murderer, but in a qualified manner he would will him to live, namely, inasmuch as he is a man. Such a qualified will may be called a velleity rather than an absolute will. Thus it is clear that whatever God wills absolutely takes place; although what He wills antecedently may not take place.

Reply Obj. 2. An act of the cognitive power takes place according as the thing known is in the knower; while an act of the appetitive power is directed to things as they exist in themselves. But all that can have the nature of being and truth is virtually in God, though it does not all exist in created things. Therefore God knows all truth, but does not will all good, except in so far as He wills Himself, in Whom all good exists virtually.

Reply Obj. 3. A first cause can be hindered in its effect by deficiency in the secondary cause, when it is not the universal first cause, including under itself all causes; for then the effect could in no way escape the order of this cause. And thus it is with the will of God, as was said above.

Seventh Article

WHETHER THE WILL OF GOD IS CHANGEABLE?

We proceed thus to the Seventh Article:—
Objection 1. It seems that the will of God is changeable.

For the Lord says (*Gen.* vi. 7): *It repenteth Me that I have made man.* But whoever repents of what he has done, has a changeable will. Therefore God has a changeable will.

Obj. 2. Further, it is said in the person of the Lord: *I will speak against a nation and against a kingdom, to root out, and to pull down, and to destroy it; but if that nation shall repent of its evil, I also will repent of the evil that I have thought to do to them* (*Jer.* xviii. 7, 8). Therefore God has a changeable will.

Obj. 3. Further, whatever God does, He does voluntarily. But God does not always do the same thing, for at one time He ordered the law to be observed, and at another time forbade it. Therefore He has a chanageable will.

Obj. 4. Further, God does not will of necessity what He wills, as was said before. Therefore He can both will and not will the same thing. But whatever can incline to either of two opposites is changeable; as that which can exist and not exist is changeable substantially, and that which can exist in a place or not in that place is changeable locally. Therefore God is changeable as regards His will.

On the contrary, It is said: *God is not as a man, that He should lie, nor as the son of man, that He should be changed* (*Num.* xxiii. 19).

I answer that, The will of God is entirely unchangeable. On this point we must consider that to change the will is one thing; to will that certain things should be changed is another. For it is possible to will a thing to be done now and its contrary afterwards, and yet for the will to remain permanently the same; whereas the will would be changed if one should begin to will what before he had not willed, or cease to will what he had willed before. This cannot happen, unless we presuppose change either in the knowledge or in the disposition of the substance of the one who wills. For since the will is concerned with the good, a man may in two ways begin to will a thing. In one way, when that thing begins to be good for him, and this does not take place without a change in him. Thus when the cold weather begins, it becomes good to sit by the fire; though it was not so before. In another way, when he knows for the first time that a thing is good for him, though he did not know it before. For, after all, we take counsel in order to know what is good for us. Now it has already been shown that both the substance of God and His knowledge are entirely unchangeable.[22] Therefore His will must be entirely unchangeable.

Reply Obj. 1. These words of the Lord are to be understood metaphorically, and according to the likeness of our nature. For when we repent, we destroy what we have made; although we may even do so without change of will, as, when a man wills to make a thing, at the same time intending to destroy it later. Therefore, God is said to have repented by way of comparison with our mode of acting, in so far as by the deluge He removed from the face of the earth man whom He had previously made.

Reply Obj. 2. The will of God, as it is the first and universal cause, does not exclude intermediate causes that have power to produce certain effects. Since, however, all intermediate causes are inferior in power to the first cause, there are many things in the divine power, knowledge and will that are not included in the order of inferior causes. Thus in the case of the raising of Lazarus, one who looked only at inferior causes could have said: *Lazarus will not rise again;* but looking at the divine first cause, he could have said: *Lazarus will rise again.* And God wills both: that is, that a thing shall happen in the order of the inferior cause, but that it shall not happen in the order of the higher cause; or He may will conversely. We may say, then, that God sometimes declares that a thing shall happen according as it falls under the order of inferior causes (for example, the dispositions of nature or the merits of men), which yet does not happen, as not being in the designs of the divine and higher cause. Thus He foretold to Ezechias: *Take order with thy house, for thou shalt die, and not live* (*Isa.* xxxviii. 1). Yet this did not take place, since from eternity it was otherwise disposed in the divine knowledge and will, which is unchangeable. Hence Gregory says: *The sentence of God changes, but not His counsel* [23]—that is to say, the counsel of His will. When therefore He says, *I also will repent,* His words must be understood metaphorically. For men seem to repent, when they do not fulfill what they have threatened.

Reply Obj. 3. It does not follow from this argument that God has a will that changes, but that He wills that things should change.

[22] Q. 9, a. 1; q. 14, a. 15.   [23] *Moral.,* XVI, 10 (PL 75, 1127).

Reply Obj. 4. Although God's willing a thing is not by absolute necessity, yet it is necessary by supposition, because of the unchangeableness of the divine will, as has been said above.

Eighth Article

WHETHER THE WILL OF GOD IMPOSES NECESSITY ON THE THINGS WILLED?

We proceed thus to the Eighth Article:—

Objection 1. It seems that the will of God imposes necessity on the things willed. For Augustine says: *No one is saved, except whom God has willed to be saved. He must therefore be asked to will it; for if He wills it, it must necessarily be.*[24]

Obj. 2. Further, every cause that cannot be hindered produces its effect necessarily, because, as the Philosopher says, *nature always works in the same way, if there is nothing to hinder it.*[25] But the will of God cannot be hindered. For the Apostle says (*Rom.* ix. 19): *Who resisteth His will?* Therefore the will of God imposes necessity on the things willed.

Obj. 3. Further, whatever is necessary by its antecedent cause is necessary absolutely; it is thus necessary that animals should die, being compounded of contrary elements. Now things created by God are related to the divine will as to an antecedent cause, whereby they have necessity. For this conditional proposition is true: *if God wills a thing, it comes to pass:* and every true conditional proposition is necessary. It follows therefore that all that God wills is necessary absolutely.

On the contrary, All good things that exist God wills to be. If therefore His will imposes necessity on the things willed, it follows that all good happens of necessity; and thus there is an end of free choice, counsel, and all other such things.

I answer that, The divine will imposes necessity on some things willed, but not on all. The reason of this some have chosen to assign to intermediate causes, holding that what God produces by necessary causes is necessary, and what He produces by contingent causes contingent.

---

[24] *Enchir.,* CIII (PL 40, 280).   [25] Aristotle, *Phys.,* II, 8 (199b 18).

This does not seem to be a sufficient explanation, for two reasons. First, because the effect of a first cause is contingent because of the secondary cause, from the fact that the effect of the first cause is hindered by deficiency in the second cause, as the sun's power is hindered by a defect in the plant. But no defect of a secondary cause can hinder God's will from producing its effect. Secondly, because if the distinction between the contingent and the necessary is to be referred only to secondary causes, this must mean that the distinction itself escapes the divine intention and will; which is inadmissible.

It is better therefore to say that this happens because of the efficacy of the divine will. For when a cause is efficacious to act, the effect follows upon the cause, not only as to the thing done, but also as to its manner of being done or of being. Thus from defect of active power in the seed it may happen that a child is born unlike its father in accidental points, which belong to its manner of being. Since then the divine will is perfectly efficacious, it follows not only that things are done which God wills to be done, but also that they are done in the way that He wills. Now God wills some things to be done necessarily, some contingently, so that there be a right order in things for the perfection of the universe. Therefore to some effects He has attached unfailing necessary causes, from which the effects follow necessarily; but to others defectible and contingent causes, from which effects arise contingently. Hence it is not because the proximate causes are contingent that the effects willed by God happen contingently; but God has prepared contingent causes for them because He has willed that they should happen contingently.

Reply Obj. 1. By the words of Augustine we must understand a necessity in things willed by God that is not absolute, but conditional. For the conditional proposition that *if God wills a thing, it must necessarily be,* is necessarily true.

Reply Obj. 2. From the very fact that nothing resists the divine will, it follows not only that those things happen that God wills to happen, but that they happen necessarily or contingently according to His will.

Reply Obj. 3. Consequents have necessity from their antecedents according to the mode of the antecedents. Hence things effected by the divine will have that kind of necessity that God wills them to have, either absolute or conditional. Not all things, therefore, are necessary absolutely.

Ninth Article

WHETHER GOD WILLS EVILS?

We proceed thus to the Ninth Article:—
Objection 1. It seems that God wills evils. For every good that exists, God wills. But it is a good that evil should exist. For Augustine says: *Although evil in so far as it is evil is not a good, yet it is good that not only good things should exist, but also evil things.*[26] Therefore God wills evil things.

Obj. 2. Further, Dionysius says: *Evil would conduce to the perfection of everything, i.e.,* the universe.[27] And Augustine says: *Out of all things is built up the admirable beauty of the universe, wherein even that which is called evil, properly ordered and disposed, commends the good the more evidently, so that the good be more pleasing and praiseworthy when contrasted with evil.*[28] But God wills all that pertains to the perfection and beauty of the universe, for this is what God desires above all things in His creatures. Therefore God wills evils.

Obj. 3. Further, that evil should exist, and should not exist, are contradictory opposites. But God does not will that evil should not exist; otherwise, since various evils do exist, God's will would not always be fulfilled. Therefore God wills that evils should exist.

On the contrary, Augustine says: *No wise man is the cause of another man becoming worse. Now God surpasses all men in wisdom. Much less therefore is God the cause of man becoming worse: and when He is said to be the cause of a thing, He is said to will it.*[29] Therefore it is not by God's will that man becomes worse. Now it is clear that every evil makes a thing worse. Therefore God does not will evils.

I answer that, Since the good and the appetible are the same in nature, as was said before,[30] and since evil is opposed to good, it is impossible that any evil, as such, should

[26] *Enchir.,* XCVI (PL 40, 276).   [27] *De Div. Nom.,* IV, 19 (PG 3, 717).   [28] *Enchir.,* X (PL 40, 236).   [29] *Lib. 83 Quaest.,* q. 3 (PL 40, 11).   [30] Q. 5, a. 1.

be sought for by the appetite, either natural, or animal, or
by the intellectual appetite which is the will. Nevertheless
evil may be sought accidentally, so far as it accompanies a
good, as appears in each of the appetites. For a natural
agent does not intend privation or corruption; he intends the
form to which is yet annexed the privation of some other
form, and the generation of one thing, which yet implies the
corruption of another. For when a lion kills a stag, his object
is food, which yet is accompanied by the killing of the animal. Similarly the fornicator has merely pleasure for his
object, which is yet accompanied by the deformity of sin.

Now the evil that accompanies one good is the privation
of another good. Never therefore would evil be sought after,
not even accidentally, unless the good that accompanies the
evil were more desired than the good of which the evil is the
privation. Now God wills no good more than He wills His
own goodness; yet He wills one good more than another.
Hence He in no way wills the evil of sin, which is the privation of right order towards the divine good. The evil of natural defect, or of punishment, He does will, by willing
the good to which such evils are attached. Thus, in willing
justice He wills punishment; and in willing the preservation
of the order of nature, He wills some things to be naturally
corrupted.

Reply Obj. 1. Some have said that although God does not
will evil, yet He wills that evil should be or be done, because,
although evil is not a good, yet it is good that evil should be
or be done.[31] This they said because things evil in themselves
are ordered to some good end; and this order they thought
was expressed in the words *that evil should be* or *be done*.
This, however, is not correct; since evil is not of itself
ordered to good, but accidentally. For it is outside the
intention of the sinner that any good should follow from his
sin; as it was outside the intention of tyrants that the
patience of the martyrs should shine forth from all their
persecutions. It cannot therefore be said that such an ordering to good is implied in the statement that it is a good
thing that evil should be or be done, since nothing is judged
by that which pertains to it accidentally, but by that which
belongs to it essentially.

[31] Hugh of St. Victor, *De Sacram.*, I, iv, 13 (PL 176, 239); *Summa
Sent.*, I, 13 (PL 176, 66).—Cf. Peter Lombard, *Sent.*, I, xlvi, 3 (I, 280).

Reply Obj. 2. Evil does not contribute towards the perfection and beauty of the universe, except accidentally, as was said above. Therefore, in saying that *evil would conduce to the perfection of the universe,* Dionysius draws this conclusion as the consequence of false premises.

Reply Obj. 3. The statements that evil comes to be and that it does not come to be are opposed as contradictories; yet the statements that anyone wills evil to be and that he wills it not to be, are not so opposed, since either is affirmative. God therefore neither wills evil to be done, nor wills it not to be done; but He wills to permit evil to be done, and this is a good.

Tenth Article

WHETHER GOD HAS FREE CHOICE?

We proceed thus to the Tenth Article:—

Objection 1. It seems that God has not free choice. For Jerome says, in a homily on the prodigal son: *God alone it is Who is not liable to sin, nor can be liable: all others, as having free choice, can be inclined to either side.*[32]

Obj. 2. Further, free choice is a faculty of the reason and will, by which good and evil are chosen. But God does not will evil, as has been said. Therefore there is not free choice in God.

On the contrary, Ambrose says: *The Holy Spirit divideth unto each one as He will, namely, according to the free choice of the will, not in obedience to necessity.*[33]

I answer that, We have free choice with respect to what we do not will of necessity, or by natural instinct. That we will to be happy does not pertain to free choice but to natural instinct. Hence other animals, that are moved to act by natural instinct, are not said to be moved by free choice. Since then God wills His own goodness necessarily, but other things not necessarily, as was shown above, He has free choice with respect to what He does not will necessarily.

Reply Obj. 1. Jerome seems to deny free choice to God, not absolutely, but not as regards the turning to sin.

Reply Obj. 2. Since the evil of sin consists in turning

---

[32] *Epist.* XXI (PL 22, 393).   [33] *De Fide,* II, 6 (PL 16, 592).

away from the divine goodness, by which God wills all
things, as was above shown, it is manifestly impossible for
Him to will the evil of sin; yet He can choose one of two
opposites, inasmuch as He can will a thing to be or not to be.
In the same way we ourselves can, without sin, will to sit
down and not will to sit down.

Question XXII

THE PROVIDENCE OF GOD

(*In Four Articles*)

HAVING considered all that relates to the will absolutely, we must now proceed to those things which have relation to both the intellect and the will, namely providence, in relation to all created things; predestination and reprobation, and all that is connected with them, in relation especially to man as ordered to his eternal salvation.[1] For in the science of morals, after the moral virtues themselves, comes the consideration of prudence, to which providence would seem to belong. Concerning God's providence there are four points of inquiry: (1) Whether providence is suitably assigned to God? (2) Whether everything comes under divine providence? (3) Whether divine providence is immediately concerned with all things? (4) Whether divine providence imposes any necessity upon what it foresees?

First Article

WHETHER PROVIDENCE CAN SUITABLY BE ATTRIBUTED TO GOD?

We proceed thus to the First Article:—

Objection 1. It seems that providence is not becoming to God. For providence, according to Tully, is a part of prudence.[2] But since, according to the Philosopher, prudence gives good counsel,[3] it cannot belong to God, Who never has any doubt for which He should take counsel. Therefore providence cannot belong to God.

Obj. 2. Further, whatever is in God is eternal. But providence is not anything eternal, *for it is concerned with existing things* that are not eternal, according to Damascene.[4] Therefore there is no providence in God.

Obj. 3. Further, there is nothing composite in God. But providence seems to be something composite, because it in-

[1] Q. 23.   [2] *De Invent.*, II, 53 (p. 147[b]).   [3] *Eth.*, VI, 5 (1140a 26).
[4] *De Fide Orth.*, II, 29 (PG 94, 964).

cludes both the intellect and the will. Therefore providence is not in God.

On the contrary, It is said (*Wis.* xiv. 3): *But Thou, Father, governeth all things by providence.*

I answer that, It is necessary to attribute providence to God. For all the good that is in things has been created by God, as was shown above.[5] Good is found in things not only as regards their substance, but also as regards their order towards an end and especially their last end, which, as was said above, is the divine goodness.[6] This good of order existing in created things is itself created by God. Now God is the cause of things by His intellect, and therefore it is necessary that the exemplar of every effect should pre-exist in Him, as is clear from what has gone before.[7] Hence, the exemplar of the order of things towards their end must necessarily pre-exist in the divine mind: and the exemplar of things ordered towards an end is, properly speaking, providence. For providence is the chief part of prudence, to which two other parts are directed—namely, remembrance of the past, and understanding of the present; inasmuch as from the remembrance of what is past and the understanding of what is present, we gather how to provide for the future. Now it belongs to prudence, according to the Philosopher, *to direct other things towards an end,*[8] whether in regard to oneself—as for instance, a man is said to be prudent, who orders well his acts towards the end of life—or in regard to others subject to him, in a family, city, or kingdom; in which sense it is said (*Matt.* xxiv. 45): a *faithful and wise servant, whom his lord hath appointed over his family.* In this second way prudence or providence may suitably be attributed to God. For in God Himself there can be nothing ordinable towards an end, since He is the last end. Hence, the very exemplar of the order of things towards an end is in God called providence. Whence Boethius says that *Providence is the divine reason itself which, seated in the Supreme Ruler, disposes all things;*[9] which disposition may refer either to the exemplar of the order of things towards an end, or to the exemplar of the order of parts in the whole.

Reply Obj. 1. According to the Philosopher, *Prudence, strictly speaking, commands all that 'eubulia' has rightly*

[5] Q. 6, a. 4.   [6] Q. 21, a. 4.   [7] Q. 19, a. 4.   [8] *Eth.,* VI, 12 (1144a 8).   [9] *De Consol.,* IV, prose 6 (PL 63, 814).

counselled and 'synesis' rightly judged.[10] Whence, though to take counsel may not be fitting to God, insofar as counsel is an inquiry into matters that are doubtful, nevertheless to give a command as to the ordering of things towards an end, the right reason of which He possesses, does belong to God, according to *Ps.* cxlviii. 6: *He hath made a decree, and it shall not pass away.* In this manner both prudence and providence belong to God. At the same time, it may also be said that the very exemplar of things to be done is called counsel in God; not because of any inquiry necessitated, but from the certitude of the knowledge, to which those who take counsel come by inquiry. Whence it is said: *Who worketh all things according to the counsel of His will* (*Ephes.* i. 11).

Reply Obj. 2. Two things pertain to the care of providence —namely, the *exemplar of order,* which is called providence and disposition; and the *execution of order,* which is termed government. Of these, the first is eternal, and the second is temporal.

Reply Obj. 3. Providence resides in the intellect; but it presupposes the act of willing the end. For no one gives a precept about things done for an end, unless he wills that end. Hence likewise prudence presupposes the moral virtues, by means of which the appetitive power is directed towards good, as the Philosopher says.[11] But even supposing that providence were equally related to the divine will and intellect, this would not affect the divine simplicity, since in God both the will and intellect are one and the same thing, as we have said above.[12]

Second Article

WHETHER EVERYTHING IS SUBJECT TO THE PROVIDENCE OF GOD?

We proceed thus to the Second Article:—

Objection 1. It seems that not everything is subject to divine providence. For nothing foreseen can happen by chance. If then everything has been foreseen by God, nothing will happen by chance. And thus chance and fortune disappear; which is against common opinion.

---

[10] *Eth.,* VI, 9 (1142b 31); 10 (1143b 8).   [11] Aristotle, *Eth.,* VI, 13 (1144b 32).   [12] Q. 19, a. 1; a. 4, ad 2.

Obj. 2. Further, a wise provider excludes any defect or evil, as far as he can, from those over whom he has a care. But we see many evils existing in things. Either, then, God cannot hinder these, and thus is not omnipotent; or else He does not have care for everything.

Obj. 3. Further, whatever happens of necessity does not require providence or prudence. Hence, according to the Philosopher: *Prudence is the right reason of contingent things concerning which there is counsel and choice.*[13] Since, then, many things happen from necessity, everything cannot be subject to providence.

Obj. 4. Further, whatsoever is left to itself cannot be subject to the providence of a governor. But men are left to themselves by God, in accordance with the words: *God made man from the beginning, and left him in the hand of his own counsel (Ecclus.* xv. 14). And particularly in reference to the wicked: *I let them go according to the desires of their heart (Ps.* lxxx. 13). Everything, therefore, cannot be subject to divine providence.

Obj. 5. Further, the Apostle says (*1 Cor.* ix. 9): *God doth not care for oxen;* and we may say the same of other irrational creatures. Thus everything cannot be under the care of divine providence.

On the contrary, It is said of divine wisdom: *She reacheth from end to end mightily, and ordereth all things sweetly (Wis.* viii. 1).

I answer that, Certain persons totally denied the existence of providence, as Democritus and the Epicureans,[14] maintaining that the world was made by chance. Others taught that incorruptible substances only were subject to providence, while corruptible substances were not in their individual being, but only according to their species; for in this respect they are incorruptible.[15] They are represented as saying (*Job* xxii. 14): *The clouds are His covert; and He doth not consider our things; and He walketh about the poles of heaven.* Rabbi Moses, however, excluded men from the gen-

---

[13] *Eth.,* VI, 5 (1140a 35); 7 (1141b 9); 13 (1144b 27).   [14] Cf. Nemesius, *De Nat. Hom.,* XLIV (PG 40, 795).   [15] According to St. Thomas himself (*In I Sent.,* d. xxxix, q. 2, a. 2), this opinion is attributed to Aristotle and expressly held by Averroes.—Cf. Maimonides, *Guide,* III, 17 (p. 282); Averroes, *In Metaph.,* XII, comm. 52 (VIII, 158v).

erality of corruptible things, because of the excellence of the
intellect which they possess, but in reference to all else that
suffers corruption he adhered to the opinion of the others.[16]

We must say, however, that all things are subject to divine
providence, not only in general, but even in their own individual being. This is made evident thus. For since every
agent acts for an end, the ordering of effects towards that
end extends as far as the causality of the first agent extends.
Whence it happens that in the effects of an agent something
takes place which has no reference towards the end, because
the effect comes from some other cause outside the intention
of the agent. But the causality of God, Who is the first agent,
extends to all beings not only as to the constituent principles
of species, but also as to the individualizing principles; not
only of things incorruptible, but also of things corruptible.
Hence all things that exist in whatsoever manner are necessarily directed by God towards the end; as the Apostle says:
Those things that are of God are well ordered (*Rom.* xiii. 1).
Since, therefore, the providence of God is nothing other than
the notion of the order of things towards an end, as we have
said, it necessarily follows that all things, inasmuch as they
participate being, must to that extent be subject to divine
providence. It has also been shown that God knows all
things, both universal and particular.[17] And since His knowledge may be compared to the things themselves as the
knowledge of art to the objects of art, as was said above,[18]
all things must of necessity come under His ordering; as all
things wrought by an art are subject to the ordering of that
art.

Reply Obj. 1. There is a difference between universal and
particular causes. A thing can escape the order of a particular cause, but not the order of a universal cause. For nothing
escapes the order of a particular cause, except through the
intervention and hindrance of some other particular cause;
as, for instance, wood may be prevented from burning by the
action of water. Since, then, all particular causes are included
under the universal cause, it is impossible that any effect
should escape the range of the universal cause. So far then
as an effect escapes the order of a particular cause, it is said

[16] *Guide*, III, 17 (p. 286).   [17] Q. 14, a. 11.   [18] Q. 14, a. 8.

to be by chance or fortuitous in respect to that cause; but if we regard the universal cause, outside whose range no effect can happen, it is said to be foreseen. Thus, for instance, the meeting of two servants, although to them it appears a chance circumstance, has been fully foreseen by their master, who has purposely sent them to meet at the one place, in such a way that the one has no knowledge of the other.

Reply Obj. 2. It is otherwise with one who is in charge of a particular thing, and one whose providence is universal, because a particular provider excludes all defects from what is subject to his care as far as he can; whereas one who provides universally allows some little defect to remain, lest the good of the whole should be hindered. Hence, corruption and defects in natural things are said to be contrary to some particular nature, yet they are in keeping with the plan of universal nature, inasmuch as the defect in one thing yields to the good of another, or even to the universal good: for the corruption of one is the generation of another, and through this it is that a species is kept in existence. Since God, then, provides universally for all being, it belongs to His providence to permit certain defects in particular effects, that the perfect good of the universe may not be hindered; for if all evil were prevented, much good would be absent from the universe. A lion would cease to live, if there were no slaying of animals; and there would be no patience of martyrs if there were no tyrannical persecution. Thus Augustine says: *Almighty God would in no wise permit evil to exist in His works, unless He were so almighty and so good as to produce good even from evil.*[19] It would appear that it was because of these two arguments to which we have just replied, that some were persuaded to consider corruptible things—*i.e.*, things in which chance and evil are found—as removed from the care of divine providence.

Reply Obj. 3. Man is not the author of nature; but he uses natural things for his own purposes in his works of art and virtue. Hence human providence does not reach to that which takes place in nature from necessity; but divine providence extends thus far, since God is the author of nature. Apparently it was this argument that moved those who withdrew the course of nature from the care of divine providence,

[19] *Enchir.*, XI (PL 40, 236).

attributing it rather to the necessity of matter, as did Democritus, and others of the ancients.[20]

Reply Obj. 4. When it is said that God left man to himself, this does not mean that man is exempt from divine providence, but merely that he has not a prefixed operating power determined to only the one effect; as in the case of natural things, which are only acted upon as though directed by another towards an end: for they do not act of themselves, as if they directed themselves towards an end, like rational creatures, through the possession of free choice, by which these are able to take counsel and make choices. Hence it is significantly said: *In the hand of his own counsel.* But since the very act of free choice is traced to God as to a cause, it necessarily follows that everything happening from the exercise of free choice must be subject to divine providence. For human providence is included under the providence of God as a particular cause under a universal cause. God, however, extends His providence over the just in a certain more excellent way than over the wicked, inasmuch as He prevents anything happening which would impede their final salvation. For *to them that love God, all things work together unto good* (*Rom.* viii. 28). But from the fact that He does not restrain the wicked from the evil of sin, He is said to abandon them. This does not mean that He altogether withdraws His providence from them; otherwise they would return to nothing, if they were not preserved in existence by His providence. This was the reason that had weight with Tully, who withdrew human affairs, concerning which we take counsel, from the care of divine providence.[21]

Reply Obj. 5. Since a rational creature has, through its free choice, control over its actions, as was said above,[22] it is subject to divine providence in an especial manner: something is imputed to it as a fault. or as a merit, and accordingly there is given to it something by way of punishment or reward. In this way the Apostle withdraws oxen from the care of God: not, however, that individual irrational creatures escape the care of divine providence, as was the opinion of the Rabbi Moses.[23]

[20] Cf. Aristotle, *Metaph.*, I, 3 (983b 7); 4 (985b 5).   [21] *De Divinat.*, II, 5 (p. 69).   [22] Ad 4, and q. 19, a. 10.   [23] *Guide*, III, 17 (p. 286).

Third Article

WHETHER GOD HAS IMMEDIATE PROVIDENCE OVER EVERYTHING?

We proceed thus to the Third Article:—

Objection 1. It seems that God has not immediate providence over all things. For whatever pertains to dignity must be attributed to God. But it belongs to the dignity of a king that he should have ministers, through whose mediation he provides for his subjects. Therefore much less has God Himself immediate providence over all things.

Obj. 2. Further, it belongs to providence to order all things to an end. Now the end of everything is its perfection and its good. But it pertains to every cause to bring its effect to good; and therefore every agent cause is a cause of the effect over which it has providence. If therefore God were to have immediate providence over all things, all secondary causes would be withdrawn.

Obj. 3. Further, Augustine says that, *It is better to be ignorant of some things than to know them, for example, ignoble things;* [24] and the Philosopher says the same. [25] But whatever is better must be attributed to God. Therefore He has not immediate providence over ignoble and wicked things.

On the contrary, It is said (*Job* xxxiv. 13): *What other hath He appointed over the earth? or whom hath He set over the world which He made?* On which passage Gregory says: *Himself He ruleth the world which He Himself hath made.* [26]

I answer that, Two things belong to providence—namely, the exemplar of the order of things foreordained towards an end, and the execution of this order, which is called government. As regards the first of these, God has immediate providence over everything, because he has in His intellect the exemplars of everything, even the smallest; and whatsoever causes He assigns to certain effects, He gives them the power to produce those effects. Whence it must be that He has precomprehended the order of those effects in His mind. As to the second, there are certain intermediaries of God's providence, for He governs things inferior by superior, not be-

[24] *Enchir.,* XVII (PL 40, 239).   [25] *Metaph.,* XI, 10 (1074b 32).
[26] *Moral.,* XXIV, 20 (PL 76, 314).

cause of any defect in His power, but by reason of the abundance of His goodness; so that the dignity of causality is imparted even to creatures. Thus Plato's opinion, as narrated by Gregory of Nyssa, is removed.[27] He taught a threefold providence. First, one which belongs to the supreme Deity, Who first and foremost has provision over spiritual things, and thus over the whole world as regards genus, species, and universal causes. The second providence, which is over the individuals of all that can be generated and corrupted, he attributed to the divinities who circulate in the heavens; that is, certain separate substances, which move corporeal things in a circular motion. The third providence, which is over human affairs, he assigned to demons, whom the Platonic philosophers placed between us and the gods, as Augustine tells us.[28]

Reply Obj. 1. It pertains to a king's dignity to have ministers who execute his providence. But the fact that he does not know the plans of what is done by them arises from a deficiency in himself. For every operative science is the more perfect, the more it considers the particular things where action takes place.

Reply Obj. 2. God's immediate provision over everything does not exclude the action of secondary causes, which are the executors of His order, as was said above.[29]

Reply Obj. 3. It is better for us not to know evil and ignoble things, insofar as by them we are impeded in our knowledge of what is better and higher (for we cannot understand many things simultaneously), and insofar as the thought of evil sometimes perverts the will towards evil. This does not hold true of God, Who sees everything simultaneously at one glance, and Whose will cannot turn in the direction of evil.

Fourth Article

WHETHER PROVIDENCE IMPOSES ANY NECESSITY ON WHAT IT FORESEES?

We proceed thus to the Fourth Article:—

Objection 1. It seems that divine providence imposes necessity upon what it foresees. For every effect that has an

---

[27] Cf. Nemesius, *De Nat. Hom.*, XLIV (PG 40, 794).   [28] *De Civit. Dei*, IX 1 (PL 41, 257); VIII, 14 (PL 41, 238).   [29] Q. 19, a. 5 and 8.

essential cause (present or past) which it necessarily follows, comes to be of necessity; as the Philosopher proves.[30] But the providence of God, since it is eternal, precedes its effect, and the effect flows from it of necessity; for divine providence cannot be frustrated. Therefore divine providence imposes a necessity upon what it foresees.

Obj. 2. Further, every provider makes his work as stable as he can, lest it should fail. But God is most powerful. Therefore He assigns the stability of necessity to things whose providence He is.

Obj. 3. Further, Boethius says: *Fate from the immutable source of providence binds together human acts and fortunes by the indissoluble connexion of causes.*[31] It seems therefore that providence imposes necessity upon what it foresees.

On the contrary, Dionysius says that *to corrupt nature is not the work of providence.*[32] But it is in the nature of some things to be contingent. Divine providence does not therefore impose any necessity upon things so as to destroy their contingency.

I answer that, Divine providence imposes necessity upon some things; not upon all, as some believed.[33] For to providence it belongs to order things towards an end. Now after the divine goodness, which is an extrinsic end to all things, the principal good in things themselves is the perfection of the universe; which would not be, were not all grades of being found in things. Whence it pertains to divine providence to produce every grade of being. And thus for some things it has prepared necessary causes, so that they happen of necessity; for others contingent causes, that they may happen by contingency, according to the disposition of their proximate causes.

Reply Obj. 1. The effect of divine providence is not only that things should happen *somehow*; but that they should happen either by necessity or by contingency. Therefore whatsoever divine providence ordains to happen infallibly and of necessity, happens infallibly and of necessity; and what the divine providence plans to happen contingently, happens contingently.

Reply Obj. 2. The order of divine providence is unchange-

[30] *Metaph.,* V, 3 (1027a 30).   [31] *De Consol.,* IV, prose 6 (PL 63, 817).   [32] *De Div. Nom.,* IV, 33 (PG 3, 733).   [33] The Stoics: cf. Nemesius, *De Nat. Hom.,* XXXVII (PG 40, 752).

able and certain, so far as all things foreseen happen as they have been foreseen, whether from necessity or from contingency.

Reply Obj. 3. The indissolubility and unchangeableness, of which Boethius speaks, pertain to the certainity of providence, which does not fail to produce its effect, and that in the way foreseen; but they do not pertain to the necessity of the effects. We must remember that, properly speaking, *necessary* and *contingent* are consequent upon being as such. Hence the mode both of necessity and of contingency falls under the foresight of God, Who provides universally for all being; not under the foresight of causes that provide only for some particular order of things.

THE POWER OF GOD

(*In Six Articles*)

AFTER considering the divine knowledge and will, and what pertains to them, it remains for us to consider the power of God. About this are six points of inquiry: (1) Whether there is power in God? (2) Whether His power is infinite? (3) Whether He is omnipotent? (4) Whether He could make the past not to have been? (5) Whether He could do what He does not, or not do what He does? (6) Whether what He makes He could make better?

First Article

WHETHER THERE IS POWER IN GOD?

We proceed thus to the First Article:—

Objection 1. It seems that power is not in God. For as primary matter is to power, so God, who is the first agent, is to act. But primary matter, considered in itself, is devoid of all act. Therefore, the first agent—namely, God—is devoid of power.

Obj. 2. Further, according to the Philosopher, better than every power is its act.[1] For form is better than matter, and action than active power, since it is its end. But nothing is better than what is in God; because whatsoever is in God, is God, as was shown above.[2] Therefore, there is no power in God.

Obj. 3. Further, power is the principle of operation. But the divine power is God's essence, since there is nothing accidental in God. But of the essence of God there is no principle. Therefore there is no power in God.

Obj. 4. Further, it was shown above that God's knowledge and will are the cause of things.[3] But *cause* and *principle* are identical. We ought not, therefore, to assign power to God, but only knowledge and will.

---

[1] *Metaph.*, VIII, 9 (1051a 4).   [2] Q. 3, a. 3.   [3] Q. 14, a. 8; q. 19, a. 4.

On the contrary, It is said: *Thou are mighty, O Lord, and Thy truth is round about Thee* (*Ps.* lxxxviii. 9).

I answer that, Power is twofold—namely, passive, which exists not at all in God; and active, which we must assign to Him in the highest degree. For it is manifest that everything, according as it is in act and is perfect, is the active principle of something; whereas everything is passive according as it is deficient and imperfect. Now it was shown above that God is pure act, absolutely and universally perfect, and completely without any imperfection.[4] Whence it most fittingly belongs to Him to be an active principle, and in no way whatsoever to be passive. On the other hand, the nature of active principle belongs to active power. For active power is the principle of acting upon something else; whereas passive power is the principle of being acted upon by something else, as the Philosopher says.[5] It remains, therefore, that in God there is active power in the highest degree.

Reply Obj. 1. Active power is not contrary to act, but is founded upon it, for everything acts according as it is actual; but passive power is contrary to act, for a thing is passive according as it is potential. Whence this potentiality is excluded from God, but not active power.

Reply Obj. 2. Whenever act, is distinct from power, act must be nobler than power. But God's action is not distinct from His power, for both are His divine essence; since neither is His being distinct from His essence. Hence it does not follow that there should be anything in God nobler than His power.

Reply Obj. 3. In creatures, power is the principle not only of action, but likewise of the effect of action. So in God the idea of power is retained in so far as it is the principle of an effect, not, however, so far as it is a principle of action, for this is the divine essence itself; except, perchance, according to our manner of understanding, inasmuch as the divine essence, which pre-contains in itself all perfection that exists in created things, can be understood either under the notion of action, or under that of power; just as it is also understood under the notion of a *suppositum* possessing nature, and under that of nature. Accordingly the nature of

[4] Q. 3, a. 1 and 2; q. 4, a. 1 and 2.   [5] *Metaph.,* IV, 12 (1019a 19).

power is retained in God in so far as it is the principle of an effect.

Reply Obj. 4. Power is predicated of God not as something really distinct from His knowledge and will, but as differing from them logically; inasmuch (namely) as power implies the notion of a principle putting into execution what the will commands and what knowledge directs; which three things in God are identified.—Or we may say that the knowledge or will of God, according as it is an effective principle, has the notion of power contained in it. Hence the consideration of the knowledge and will of God precedes the consideration of His power as the cause precedes operation and the effect.

Second Article

WHETHER THE POWER OF GOD IS INFINITE?

We proceed thus to the Second Article:—

Objection 1. It seems that the power of God is not infinite. For everything that is infinite is imperfect according to the Philosopher.[6] But the power of God is far from imperfect. Therefore it is not infinite.

Obj. 2. Further, every power is made known by its effect; otherwise it would be in vain. If, then, the power of God were infinite, it could produce an infinite effect, but this is impossible.

Obj. 3. Further, the Philosopher proves that if the power of any corporeal thing were infinite, it would cause movement instantaneously.[7] God, however, does not cause instantaneous movement, but *moves the spiritual creature in time, and the corporeal creature in place and time,* as Augustine says.[8] Therefore, His power is not infinite.

On the contrary, Hilary says, that *God's power is immeasurable. He is the living mighty One.*[9] Now everything that is immeasurable is infinite. Therefore the power of God is infinite.

I answer that, As was stated above, active power exists in God according to the measure in which He is actual. Now

---

[6] *Phys.*, III, 6 (207a 7).   [7] *Op. cit.*, VIII, 10 (266a 31).   [8] *De Genesi ad Litt.*, VIII, 20; 22 (PL 34, 388; 389).   [9] *De Trin.*, VIII, 24 (PL 10, 253).

His being is infinite, inasmuch as it is not limited by anything that receives it, as is clear from what was said when we discussed the infinity of the divine essence.[10] Therefore, it is necessary that the active power of God should be infinite. For in every agent we find that the more perfectly an agent has the form by which it acts, the greater its power to act. For instance, the hotter a thing is, the greater power has it to give heat; and it would have infinite power to give heat, were its own heat infinite. Whence, since the divine essence, through which God acts, is infinite, as was shown above,[11] it follows that His power likewise is infinite.

Reply Obj. 1. The Philosopher is here speaking of an infinity belonging to matter not limited by any form; and such infinity belongs to quantity. But the divine essence is not infinite in this way, as was shown above,[12] and consequently, neither is God's power. It does not follow, therefore, that it is imperfect.

Reply Obj. 2. The power of a univocal agent is wholly manifested in its effect. The generative power of man, for example, is not able to do more than beget man. But the power of a non-univocal agent does not wholly manifest itself in the production of its effect: as, for example, the power of the sun does not wholly manifest itself in the production of an animal generated from putrefaction. Now it is clear that God is not a univocal agent. For nothing agrees with Him either in species or in genus, as was shown above.[13] Whence it follows that His effect is always less than His power. It is not necessary, therefore, that the infinite power of God should be manifested in the production of an infinite effect. Yet even if it were to produce no effect, the power of God would not be in vain; because a thing is in vain if it is ordained towards an end to which it does not attain. But the power of God is not ordered towards its effect as towards an end; rather, it is the end of the effect produced by it.

Reply Obj. 3. The Philosopher proves that *if a body had infinite power, it would move in null time.*[14] And yet he shows that the power of the mover of heaven is infinite, because he can move in an infinite time.[15] It remains, there-

---

[10] Q. 7, a. 1.   [11] *Ibid.*   [12] *Ibid.*   [13] Q. 3, a. 5; q. 4, a. 3.
[14] *Phys.*, VIII, 10 (266a 29).   [15] *Ibid.* (267b 24).

fore, according to Aristotle's intention, that the infinite power of a body, if such existed, would move in null time; not, however, the power of an incorporeal mover. The reason for this is that one body moving another is a univocal agent; wherefore it follows that the whole power of the agent is made manifest in its motion. Since then the greater the power of a moving body, the more quickly does it move, the necessary conclusion is that, if its power were infinite, it would move with a speed incommensurably faster; and this is to move in null time. An incorporeal mover, however, is not a univocal agent; whence it is not necessary that the whole of its power should be manifested in motion, which would in fact be a motion in null time; especially since an incorporeal mover moves in accordance with the disposition of his will.

Third Article

WHETHER GOD IS OMNIPOTENT?

We proceed thus to the Third Article:—

Objection 1. It seems that God is not omnipotent. For movement and passiveness belong to everything. But this is impossible for God, since He is immovable, as was said above.[16] Therefore He is not omnipotent.

Obj. 2. Further, sin is an act of some kind. But God cannot sin, nor *deny Himself*, as it is said *2 Tim.* ii. 13. Therefore He is not omnipotent.

Obj. 3. Further, it is said of God that He manifests His omnipotence *especially by sparing and having mercy.*[17] Therefore the greatest act possible to the divine power is to spare and have mercy. There are things much greater, however, than sparing and having mercy; for example, to create another world, and the like. Therefore God is not omnipotent.

Obj. 4. Further, upon the text, *God hath made foolish the wisdom of this world* (*1 Cor.* i. 20), the *Gloss* says: *God hath made the wisdom of this world foolish* by showing those things to be possible which it judges to be impossible.[18] Whence it seems that nothing is to be judged pos-

---

[16] Q. 2, a. 3; q. 9, a. 1.   [17] *Collect* of Tenth Sunday after Pentecost.
[18] *Glossa ordin., super I Cor.* I, 20 (VI, 34E).—Cf. St. Ambrose, *In I Cor.,* super I, 20 (PL 17, 199).

sible or impossible in reference to inferior causes, as the
wisdom of this world judges them; but in reference to the
divine power. If God, then, were omnipotent, all things
would be possible; nothing, therefore, impossible. But if we
take away the impossible, then we destroy also the necessary; for what necessarily exists cannot possibly not exist.
Therefore, there would be nothing at all that is necessary in
things if God were omnipotent. But this is an impossibility.
Therefore God is not omnipotent.

On the contrary, It is said: *No word shall be impossible
with God (Luke* i. 37).

I answer that, All confess that God is omnipotent; but it
seems difficult to explain in what His omnipotence precisely
consists. For there may be a doubt as to the precise meaning
of the word "all" when we say that God can do all things.
If, however, we consider the matter aright, since power is
said in reference to possible things, this phrase, *God can do
all things,* is rightly understood to mean that God can do all
things that are possible; and for this reason He is said to
be omnipotent. Now according to the Philosopher a thing is
said to be possible in two ways.[19] First, in relation to some
power; thus whatever is subject to human power is said to
be possible to man. Now God cannot be said to be omnipotent through being able to do all things that are possible
to created nature; for the divine power extends farther than
that. If, however, we were to say that God is omnipotent because He can do all things that are possible to His power,
there would be a vicious circle in explaining the nature of
His power. For this would be saying nothing else but that
God is omnipotent because He can do all that He is able to
do.

It remains, therefore, that God is called omnipotent because he can do all things that are possible absolutely;
which is the second way of saying a thing is possible. For a
thing is said to be possible or impossible absolutely, according to the relation in which the very terms stand to one another: possible, if the predicate is not incompatible with the
subject, as that Socrates sits; and absolutely impossible
when the predicate is altogether incompatible with the subject, as, for instance, that a man is an ass.

[19] *Metaph.,* IV, 12 (1019b 34).

It must, however, be remembered that since every agent
produces an effect like itself, to each active power there corresponds a thing possible as its proper object according to
the nature of that act on which its active power is founded;
for instance, the power of giving warmth is related, as to its
proper object, to the being capable of being warmed. The
divine being, however, upon which the nature of power in
God is founded, is infinite; it is not limited to any class of
being, but possesses within itself the perfection of all being.
Whence, whatsoever has or can have the nature of being is
numbered among the absolute possibles, in respect of which
God is called omnipotent.

Now nothing is opposed to the notion of being except
non-being. Therefore, that which at the same time implies
being and non-being is repugnant to the notion of an absolute possible, which is subject to the divine omnipotence.
For such cannot come under the divine omnipotence; not
indeed because of any defect in the power of God, but because it has not the nature of a feasible or possible thing.
Therefore, everything that does not imply a contradiction in
terms is numbered among those possibles in respect of
which God is called omnipotent; whereas whatever implies
contradiction does not come within the scope of divine omnipotence, because it cannot have the aspect of possibility.
Hence it is more appropriate to say that such things cannot
be done, than that God cannot do them. Nor is this contrary
to the word of the angel, saying: *No word shall be impossible with God* (*Luke* i. 37). For whatever implies a contradiction cannot be a word, because no intellect can possibly conceive such a thing.

Reply Obj. 1. God is said to be omnipotent in respect to
active power, not to passive power, as was shown above.
Whence the fact that He is immovable or impassible is not
repugnant to His omnipotence.

Reply Obj. 2. To sin is to fall short of a perfect action;
hence to be able to sin is to be able to fall short in action,
which is repugnant to omnipotence. Therefore it is that God
cannot sin, because of His omnipotence. Now it is true that
the Philosopher says that *God can deliberately do what is
evil.*[20] But this must be understood either on a condition,
the antecedent of which is impossible—as, for instance, if

[20] *Top.*, IV, 5 (126a 34).

we were to say that God can do evil things if He will. For
there is no reason why a conditional proposition should not
be true, though both the antecedent and consequent are impossible: as if one were to say: *If man is an ass, he has four
feet.* Or he may be understood to mean that God can do
some things which now seem to be evil: which, however, if
He did them, would then be good. Or he is, perhaps, speaking after the common manner of the pagans, who thought
that men became gods, like Jupiter or Mercury.

Reply Obj. 3. God's omnipotence is particularly shown in
sharing and having mercy, because in this it is made manifest that God has supreme power, namely, that He freely
forgives sins. For it is not for one who is bound by laws of
a superior to forgive sins of his own free choice. Or, it is thus
shown because by sparing and having mercy upon men, He
leads them to the participation of an infinite good; which is
the ultimate effect of the divine power. Or it is thus shown
because, as was said above, the effect of the divine mercy is
the foundation of all the divine works.[21] For nothing is due
anyone, except because of something already given him
gratuitously by God. In this way the divine omnipotence is
particularly made manifest, because to it pertains the first
foundation of all good things.

Reply Obj. 4. The absolute possible is not so called in
reference either to higher causes, or to inferior causes, but
in reference to itself. But that which is called possible in
reference to some power is named possible in reference to its
proximate cause. Hence those things which it belongs to
God alone to do immediately—as, for example, to create,
to justify, and the like—are said to be possible in reference
to a higher cause. Those things, however, which are such as
to be done by inferior causes, are said to be possible in reference to those inferior causes. For it is according to the
condition of the proximate cause that the effect has contingency or necessity, as was shown above.[22] Thus it is that the
wisdom of the world is deemed foolish, because what is impossible to nature it judges to be impossible to God. So it is
clear that the omnipotence of God does not take away from
things their impossibility and necessity.

[21] Q. 21, a. 4.   [22] Q. 14, a. 13, ad 1.

CREATION

Question XLIV

THE PROCESSION OF CREATURES FROM GOD, AND THE FIRST CAUSE OF ALL THINGS

(*In Four Articles*)

AFTER treating of the procession of the divine persons, we must consider the procession of creatures from God. This consideration will be threefold: (1) the production of creatures; (2) the distinction of creatures;[1] (3) their preservation and government.[2] Concerning the first point there are three things to be considered: (1) the first cause of things; (2) the mode of procession of creatures from the first cause;[3] (3) the beginning of the duration of things.[4]

Under the first head there are four points of inquiry: (1) Whether God is the efficient cause of all beings? (2) Whether primary matter is created by God, or is an independent co-ordinate principle with Him? (3) Whether God is the exemplary cause of things, or whether there are other exemplary causes? (4) Whether He is the final cause of things?

First Article

WHETHER IT IS NECESSARY THAT EVERY BEING BE CREATED BY GOD?

We proceed thus to the First Article:—

Objection 1. It would seem that it is not necessary that every being be created by God. For there is nothing to prevent a thing from being without that which does not belong to its essence, as a man can be found without whiteness. But the relation of the thing caused to its cause does not appear

---

[1] Q. 47. [2] Q. 103. [3] Q. 45. [4] Q. 46.

to be essential to beings, for some beings can be understood without it. Therefore they can exist without it; and hence it is possible that some beings should not be created by God.

Obj. 2. Further, a thing requires an efficient cause in order to exist. Therefore whatever cannot not-be does not require an efficient cause. But no necessary thing can not-be, because whatever necessarily exists cannot not-be. Therefore as there are many necessary things in existence, it appears that not all beings are from God.

Obj. 3. Further, among whatever things there is a cause, there can be demonstration by that cause. But in mathematics demonstration is not made *by the efficient cause,* as appears from the Philosopher.[5] Therefore not all beings are from God as from their efficient cause.

On the contrary, It is said (*Rom.* xi. 36): *Of Him, and by Him, and in Him are all things.*

I answer that, It must be said that everything, that in any way is, is from God. For whatever is found in anything by participation must be caused in it by that to which it belongs essentially, as iron becomes heated by fire. Now it has been shown above, when treating of the divine simplicity, that God is self-subsisting being itself,[6] and also that subsisting being can be only one;[7] just as, if whiteness were self-subsisting, it would be one, since whiteness is multiplied by its recipients. Therefore all beings other than God are not their own being, but are beings by participation. Therefore, it must be that all things which are diversified by the diverse participation of being, so as to be more or less perfect, are caused by one First Being, Who possesses being most perfectly.

Hence Plato said that unity must come before multitude;[8] and Aristotle said that whatever is greatest in being and greatest in truth is the cause of every being and of every truth, just as *whatever is the greatest in heat is the cause of all heat.*[9]

Reply Obj. 1. Though relation to its cause is not part of the definition of a thing caused, still it follows as a result of what belongs to its nature. For, from the fact that a thing is being by participation, it follows that it is caused. Hence

[5] *Metaph.,* II, 2 (996a 29).   [6] Q. 3, a. 4.   [7] Q. 7, a. 1, ad 3; a. 2.
[8] Cf. St. Augustine, *De Civit. Dei,* VIII, 4 (PL 41, 231).   [9] *Metaph.,* Ia, 1 (993b 25).

such a being cannot be without being caused, just as man cannot be without having the faculty of laughing. But, since to be caused does not enter into the nature of being taken absolutely, that is why there exists a being that is uncaused.

Reply Obj. 2. This objection has led some to say that what is necessary has no cause.[10] But this is manifestly false in demonstrative sciences, where necessary principles are the causes of necessary conclusions. And therefore Aristotle says that there are some necessary things which have a cause of their necessity.[11] But the reason why an efficient cause is required is not merely because the effect can not-be, but because the effect would not be if the cause were not. For this conditional proposition is true, whether the antecedent and consequent be possible or impossible.

Reply Obj. 3. Although they are not abstract in reality, mathematicals are considered in abstraction by the reason. Now, it belongs to a thing to have an efficient cause according as it has being. And so, although mathematicals do have an efficient cause, it is not according to their relation to their efficient cause that they fall under the consideration of the mathematician. Therefore there is no demonstration by means of an efficient cause in mathematics.

Second Article

WHETHER PRIMARY MATTER IS CREATED BY GOD?

We proceed thus to the Second Article:—

Objection 1. It would seem that primary matter is not created by God. For whatever is made is composed of a subject and of something else.[12] But primary matter has no subject. Therefore primary matter cannot have been made by God.

Obj. 2. Further, action and passion are opposite members of a division. But just as the first active principle is God, so the first passive principle is matter. Therefore God and primary matter are two principles divided against each other, neither of which is from the other.

Obj. 3. Further, every agent produces its like, and thus, since every agent acts in proportion to its actuality, it fol-

[10] *Phys.*, VIII, 1 (252a 35).   [11] *Metaph.*, IV, 5 (1015b 9).   [12] Aristotle, *Phys.*, I, 7 (190b 1).

lows that everything made is in some degree actual. But primary matter, considered in itself, is only in potentiality. Therefore it is against the nature of primary matter to be a thing made.

On the contrary, Augustine says, *Two things hast Thou made, O Lord; one nigh unto Thyself*—viz., angels—*the other nigh unto nothing*—viz., primary matter.[13]

I answer that, The ancient philosophers gradually, and as it were step by step, advanced in the knowledge of truth.[14] At first, being rather undeveloped, they failed to realize that any beings existed except sensible bodies.[15] And those among them who admitted movement did not consider it except according to certain accidents,[16] for instance, according to rarefaction and condensation,[17] through union and separation.[18] And supposing, as they did, that corporeal substance itself was uncreated,[19] they assigned certain causes for these accidental changes, as for instance, friendship, discord,[20] intellect,[21] or something of that kind. An advance was made when they understood that there was a distinction between the substantial form and matter, which latter they held to be uncreated,[22] and when they perceived transmutation to take place in bodies in regard to essential forms. These transmutations they attributed to certain more universal causes, such as the oblique circle, according to Aristotle,[23] or the Ideas, according to Plato.[24]

But we must take into consideration that matter is contracted by its form to a determinate species, just as a substance belonging to a certain species is contracted by a supervening accident to a determinate mode of being, for instance, man by whiteness. Each of these opinions, therefore, considered *being* under some particular aspect, namely, either

---

[13] *Confess.*, XII, 7 (PL 32, 828).   [14] Cf. Aristotle, *Metaph.*, I, 3-4 (983b 6-985b 22).   [15] Cf. Aristotle, *Phys.*, IV, 6 (213a 29); *Metaph.*, II, 5 (1002a 8); St. Augustine, *De Civit. Dei*, VIII, 2 (PL 41, 225). [16] Cf. Aristotle, *De Gener.*, II, 9 (335b 24); *Phys.*, I, 4 (187a 30). [17] Cf. Aristotle, *Phys.*, I, 4 (187a 15).   [18] Cf. Aristotle, *De Gener.*, II, 9 (336a 4).   [19] Cf. Aristotle, *Phys.*, I, 8 (191a 27).   [20] Empedocles, according to Aristotle, *Metaph.*, I, 4 (985a 8); *Phys.*, I, 5 (188b 34). [21] Anaxagoras, according to Aristotle, *Phys.*, VIII, 1 (250b 24). [22] Plato, cf. above, q. 15, a. 3, ad 3; below, q. 46, a. 1, obj. 1 and ad 3. —Cf. also St. Thomas, *In Phys.*, I, lect. 15.   [23] *De Gener.*, II, 10 (336a 32).   [24] Cf. *ibid.*—Cf. also *Phaedo* (p. 96A).

as *this* being or as *such* a being; and so they assigned particular efficient causes to things.

Then others advanced further and raised themselves to the consideration of being as being, and who assigned a cause to things, not only according as they are *these* or *such,* but according as they are *beings.*[25] Therefore, whatever is the cause of things considered as beings, must be the cause of things, not only according as they are *such* by accidental forms, nor according as they are *these* by substantial forms, but also according to all that belongs to their being in any way whatever. And thus it is necessary to say that also primary matter is created by the universal cause of things.

Reply Obj. 1. The Philosopher is speaking of *becoming* in particular—that is, from form to form, either accidental or substantial.[26] But here we are speaking of things according to their coming forth from the universal principle of being. From this coming forth matter itself is not excluded, although it is excluded from the other mode of being made.

Reply Obj. 2. Passion is an effect of action. Hence it is reasonable that the first passive principle should be the effect of the first active principle, since every imperfect thing is caused by one perfect. For the first principle must be most perfect, as Aristotle says.[27]

Reply Obj. 3. The reason adduced does not show that matter is not created, but that it is not created without form; for though everything created is actual, still it is not pure act. Hence it is necessary that even what is potential in it should be created, if all that belongs to its being is created.

Third Article

WHETHER THE EXEMPLARY CAUSE IS ANYTHING OTHER THAN GOD?

We proceed thus to the Third Article:—

Objection 1. It would seem that the exemplary cause is something other than God. For the effect is like its exemplar. But creatures are far from being like God. Therefore God is not their exemplary cause.

[25] Cf. E. Gilson, *L'esprit de la phil. méd.* (Paris: J. Vrin, 1932) I, pp. 240-242.   [26] *Phys.,* I, 7 (190b 1).   [27] *Metaph.,* XI, 7 (1072b 29).

Obj. 2. Further, whatever is by participation is reduced to something self-existing, as a thing ignited is reduced to fire, as was stated above. But whatever exists in sensible things exists only by participation of some species. This appears from the fact that in all sensible things is found not only what belongs to the species, but also individuating principles added to the principles of the species. Therefore it is necessary to admit self-existing species, as, for instance, a *per se* man, and a *per se* horse, and the like, which are called exemplars. Therefore exemplary causes exist outside God.

Obj. 3. Further, sciences and definitions are concerned with species themselves, but not as these are in particular things, because there is no science or definition of particular things. Therefore there are some beings, which are beings or species not existing in singular things, and these are called exemplars. Therefore the same conclusion follows as above.

Obj. 4. Further, this likewise appears from Dionysius, who says that self-subsisting being is before self-subsisting life, and before self-subsisting wisdom.[28]

On the contrary, The exemplar is the same as the idea. But ideas, according to Augustine, are *the master forms which are contained in the divine intelligence.*[29] Therefore the exemplars of things are not outside God.

I answer that, God is the first exemplary cause of all things. In proof whereof we must consider that if for the production of anything an exemplar is necessary, it is in order that the effect may receive a determinate form. For an artificer produces a determinate form in matter by reason of the exemplar before him, whether it be the exemplar beheld externally, or the exemplar interiorly conceived in the mind. Now it is manifest that things made by nature receive determinate forms. This determination of forms must be reduced to the divine wisdom as its first principle, for divine wisdom devised the order of the universe residing in the distinction of things. And therefore we must say that in the divine wisdom are the models of all things, which we have called *ideas*—*i.e.,* exemplary forms existing in the divine mind.[30] And although these ideas are multiplied by their relations to things, nevertheless, they are not really distinct from the divine essence, inasmuch as the likeness of that es-

[28] *De Div. Nom.,* V, 5 (PG 3, 820).   [29] *Lib. 83 Quaest.,* q. 46 (PL 40, 30).   [30] Q. 15, a. 1.

sence can be shared diversely by different things. In this
manner, therefore, God Himself is the first exemplar of all
things. Moreover, in created things one may be called the
exemplar of another by the reason of its likeness to it either
in species, or by the analogy of some kind of imitation.

Reply Obj. 1. Although creatures are not so perfect as to
be specifically like God in nature, after the manner in which
a man begotten is like to the man begetting, still they do attain to likeness to Him, according to the representation in
the exemplar known by God; just as a material house is like
the house in the architect's mind.

Reply Obj. 2. It is of a man's nature to be in matter, and
so a man without matter is impossible. Therefore, although
this particular man is a man by participation of the species,
he cannot be reduced to anything self-existing in the same
species, but to a superior species, such as separate substances.
The same applies to other sensible things.

Reply Obj. 3. Although every science and definition is
concerned only with beings, still it is not necessary that a
thing should have the same way of being as the intellect has
of understanding. For through the power of the agent intellect we abstract universals from particular conditions; but
it is not necessary that universals should subsist outside the
particulars as their exemplars.

Reply Obj. 4. As Dionysius says, by *self-existing life and
self-existing wisdom* he sometimes denotes God Himself,
sometimes the powers given to things themselves;[31] but not
any self-subsisting things, as the ancients asserted.

Fourth Article

WHETHER GOD IS THE FINAL CAUSE OF ALL THINGS?

We proceed thus to the Fourth Article:—

Objection 1. It would seem that God is not the final cause
of all things. For to act for an end seems to imply need of
the end. But God needs nothing. Therefore it does not become Him to act for an end.

Obj. 2. Further, the end of generation, and the form of
the thing generated, and the agent cannot be identical, because the end of generation is the form of the thing gener-

[31] *De Div. Nom.,* XI, 6 (PG 3, 953).

ated.[32] But God is the first agent producing all things. Therefore He is not the final cause of all things.

Obj. 3. Further, all things desire their end. But all things do not desire God, for all do not even know Him. Therefore God is not the end of all things.

Obj. 4. Further, the final cause is the first of causes. If, therefore, God is the efficient cause and the final cause, it follows that *before* and *after* exist in Him; which is impossible.

On the contrary, It is said (*Prov.* xvi. 4): *The Lord has made all things for Himself.*

I answer that, Every agent acts for an end, or otherwise one thing would not follow more than another from the action of the agent, unless it were by chance. Now the end of the agent and of the patient considered as such is the same, but in a different way respectively. For the impression which the agent intends to produce, and which the patient intends to receive, are one and the same. Some things, however, are both agent and patient at the same time: these are imperfect agents, and to these it belongs to intend, even in acting, the acquisition of something. But it does not belong to the First Agent, Who is agent only, to act for the acquisition of some end: He intends only to communicate His perfection, which is His goodness; while every creature intends to acquire its own perfection, which is the likeness of the divine perfection and goodness. Therefore the divine goodness is the end of all things.

Reply Obj. 1. To act from need belongs only to an imperfect agent, which by its nature is both agent and patient. But this does not belong to God, and therefore He alone is the most perfectly liberal giver, because He does not act for His own profit, but only out of His own goodness.

Reply Obj. 2. The form of the thing generated is not the end of generation, except inasmuch as it is the likeness of the form of the generator, which intends to communicate its own likeness; otherwise the form of the thing generated would be more noble than the generator, since the end is more noble than the means to the end.

Reply Obj. 3. All things desire God as their end in desiring any particular good, whether this desire be intellectual or sensible, or natural, *i.e.*, without knowledge; for nothing is

[33] Aristotle, *Phys.*, II, 7 (198a 26).

good and desirable except inasmuch as it participates in the likeness to God.

Reply Obj. 4. Since God is the efficient, the exemplar and the final cause of all things, and since primary matter is from Him, it follows that the first principle of all things is one in reality. But this does not prevent us from thinking that, from the standpoint of our reason, there are many things in God, of which we come to know some before others.

THE MODE OF EMANATION OF THINGS FROM THE FIRST PRINCIPLE

(*In Eight Articles*)

THE next question concerns the mode of the emanation of things from the First Principle which is called creation. On creation there are eight points of inquiry: (1) What is creation? (2) Whether God can create anything? (3) Whether creation is a reality in things? (4) To what things it belongs to be created? (5) Whether it belongs to God alone to create? (6) Whether to create is common to the whole Trinity, or proper to any one Person? (7) Whether any trace of the Trinity is to be found in created things? (8) Whether the work of creation enters into the works of nature and of the will?

Fifth Article

WHETHER IT BELONGS TO GOD ALONE TO CREATE?

We proceed thus to the Fifth Article:—

Objection 1. It would seem that it does not belong to God alone to create. For according to the Philosopher, that is perfect which can make something like itself.[1] But immaterial creatures are more perfect than material creatures, which nevertheless can produce their like; for fire generates fire, and man begets man. Therefore an immaterial substance can make a substance like to itself. But immaterial substance can be made only by creation, since it has no matter from which to be made. Therefore a creature can create.

Obj. 2. Further, the greater the resistance on the part of the thing made, the greater power required in the maker. But a *contrary* resists more than *nothing*. Therefore it requires more power to make something from its contrary (which nevertheless a creature can do) than to make a thing from nothing. All the more therefore can a creature make something out of nothing.

Obj. 3. Further, the power of the maker is considered according to the measure of what is made. But created being is

[1] *Meteor.*, IV, 3 (380a 14); *De An.*, II, 4 (415a 26).

finite, as we proved above when treating of the infinity of God.[2] Therefore only a finite power is needed to produce a creature by creation. But to have a finite power is not contrary to the nature of a creature. Therefore it is not impossible for a creature to create.

On the contrary, Augustine says that neither good nor bad angels can create anything.[3] Much less therefore can any other creatures.

I answer that, It is sufficiently apparent at first glance, according to what has preceded, that to create can be the proper action of God alone.[4] For the more universal effects must be reduced to the more universal and prior causes. Now among all effects the most universal is being itself; and hence it must be the proper effect of the first and most universal cause, God. Hence we find it said that *neither intelligence nor the soul gives being, except inasmuch as it works by divine operation.*[5] Now to produce being absolutely, and not merely as this or that being, belongs to the nature of creation. Hence it is manifest that creation is the proper act of God alone.

It is possible, however, for something to participate in the proper action of another, not by its own power, but instrumentally, inasmuch as it acts by the power of another; as air can heat and ignite by the power of fire. And so some have supposed that although creation is the proper act of the universal cause, still some lesser cause, acting by the power of the first cause, can create. And thus Avicenna asserted that the first separate substance created by God created another separate substance after itself, then the substance of the heavens and its soul; and that the substance of the heavens creates the matter of the inferior bodies.[6] And in the same manner the Master of the *Sentences* says that God can communicate to a creature the power of creating, so that the creature can create as God's minister, and not by its own power.[7]

But such a thing cannot be, because the secondary instru-

---

[2] Q. 7, a. 2, 3 and 4.   [3] *De Trin.,* III, 8 (PL 42, 876).   [4] A. 1; q. 44, a. 1 and 2.   [5] *De Causis,* III (p. 163).   [6] *Metaph.,* IX, 4 (104vb).—Cf. Algazel, *Metaph.,* V (p. 119); Averroes, *Destruct. Destruct.,* III (IX, 23ra; 24rab); *De Causis,* III (p. 163).—Cf. also St. Albert, *Summa de Creatur.,* II, q. 61, a. 2 (XXXV, 524).   [7] Peter Lombard, *Sent.,* IV, v, 3 (II, 575).

mental cause does not share in the action of the superior cause, except inasmuch as by something proper to itself it acts dispositively in relation to the effect of the principal agent. If therefore it produced nothing by means of what is proper to itself, it would be set to work in vain; nor would there be any need for us to use special instruments for special actions. Thus we see that a saw, in cutting wood, which it does by the property of its own form, produces the form of a bench, which is the proper effect of the principal agent. But the proper effect of God creating is what is presupposed to all other effects, and that is being taken absolutely. Hence nothing else can act dispositively and instrumentally towards this effect, since creation does not depend on anything presupposed, which can be disposed by the action of the instrumental agent. So it is impossible for any creature to create, either by its own power, or instrumentally—that is, ministerially.

And above all it is absurd to suppose that a body can create, for no body acts except by touching or moving; and thus it requires in its action some pre-existing thing which can be touched or moved, which is contrary to the very idea of creation.

Reply Obj. 1. A perfect thing participating in any nature makes a likeness to itself, not by absolutely producing that nature, but by applying it to something else. For an individual man cannot be the cause of human nature absolutely, because he would then be the cause of himself; but he is the cause that human nature exists in the man begotten. And thus he presupposes in his action the determinate matter whereby he is an individual man. But just as an individual man participates in human nature, so every created being participates, so to speak, in the nature of being; for God alone is His own being, as we have said above.[8] Therefore no created being can produce a being absolutely, except inasmuch as it causes *being* in some particular subject; and so it is necessary to presuppose that whereby a thing is this particular thing as prior to the action whereby it produces its own like. But in an immaterial substance it is not possible to presuppose anything whereby it is this thing, because it is a *this* by its form, through which it has being. For an immaterial substance is a subsisting form. Therefore an imma-

[8] Q. 7, a. 1, ad 3; a. 2.

terial substance cannot produce another like immaterial substance as regards its being, but only as regards some added perfection; as we may say that a superior angel illumines an inferior, as Dionysius says.[9] In this sense we also speak of paternity in heaven, as the Apostle says (*Ephes.* iii. 15): *From whom all paternity in heaven and on earth is named.* From which it clearly appears that no created being can cause anything, unless something is presupposed; which is against the nature of creation.

Reply Obj. 2. A thing is made from its contrary accidentally; but properly it is made from the subject which is in potentiality.[10] And so the contrary resists the agent, inasmuch as it keeps the potentiality from the act to which the agent intends to reduce the matter; just as fire intends to reduce the matter of water to an act like to itself, but is impeded by the form and contrary dispositions, by which the potentiality of the water is as it were restrained from being reduced to act. But the more the potentiality is restrained, the more power is required in the agent to reduce the matter to act. Hence a much greater power is required in the agent when no potentiality pre-exists. Thus it appears that it is an act of much greater power to make a thing from nothing than from its contrary.

Reply Obj. 3. The power of the maker is reckoned not only from the substance of the thing made, but also from the mode of its being made; for a greater heat heats not only more, but also more quickly. Therefore, although to create a finite effect does not reveal an infinite power, yet to create it from nothing does reveal an infinite power. This appears from what has been said. For if a greater power is required in the agent in proportion to the distance of the potentiality from act, it follows that the power of that which produces something from no presupposed potentiality (which is how a creating agent produces) is infinite, because there is no proportion between *no potentiality* and the potentiality presupposed by the power of a natural agent, as there is no proportion between *non-being* and *being.* And because no creature has an absolutely infinite power, any more than it has an infinite being, as was proved above,[11] it follows that no creature can create.

[9] *De Cael. Hier.*, VIII, 2 (PG 3, 240).   [10] Aristotle, *Phys.*, I, 7 (190b 27).   [11] Q. 7, a. 2.

ON THE BEGINNING OF THE DURATION
OF CREATURES

(*In Three Articles*)

NEXT must be considered the beginning of the duration of creatures, about which there are three points for treatment: (1) Whether creatures always existed? (2) Whether that they began to exist is an article of Faith? (3) How God is said to have created heaven and earth in the beginning?

First Article

WHETHER THE UNIVERSE OF CREATURES ALWAYS EXISTED?

We proceed thus to the First Article:—

Objection 1. It would seem that the universe of creatures, which is now called the world, had no beginning, but existed from eternity. For everything which begins to be had, before being, the possibility of being: otherwise its coming to be would have been impossible. If therefore the world began to be, before it began to be it was possible for it to be. But *that which can be* is matter, which is in potentiality to being, which results from a form, and to non-being, which results from privation of form. If therefore the world began to be, matter must have existed before the world. But matter cannot be without form: and if the matter of the world is joined to form, that *is* the world. Therefore the world existed before it began to be: which is impossible.[1]

Obj. 2. Further, nothing which has power to be always, sometimes is and sometimes is not; because as far as the power of a thing lasts, so long does it exist. But every incorruptible thing has the power to be always, for its power does not extend to any determinate time. Therefore no incorruptible thing sometimes is, and sometimes is not. But everything, which has a beginning, at some time is, and at

[1] Argument of the Peripatetics, according to Maimonides, *Guide*, II, 14 (p. 174).—Cf. Averroes, *Destruct. Destruct.*, I (IX, 16ra); *In Phys.*, VIII, comm. 4 (IV, 155r).

some time is not. Therefore no incorruptible thing begins to be. But there are many incorruptible things in the world, as the celestial bodies and all intellectual substances. Therefore the world did not begin to be.[2]

Obj. 3. Further, what is ungenerated has no beginning. But the Philosopher proves that matter is ungenerated,[3] and also that the heavens are ungenerated.[4] Therefore the universe did not begin to be.[5]

Obj. 4. Further, there is a vacuum where there is not a body, but there could be. But if the world began to be, there was first no body where the body of the world now is; and yet it could be there, otherwise it would not be there now. Therefore before the world there was a vacuum; which is impossible.[6]

Obj. 5. Further, nothing begins anew to be moved except for the fact that either the mover or the thing moved is now otherwise than it was before. But what is now otherwise than it was before is moved. Therefore before every new motion there was a previous motion. Therefore motion always was; and therefore so also was the thing moved, because motion is only in a movable thing.[7]

Obj. 6. Further, every mover is either natural or voluntary. But neither begins to move except by some pre-existing motion. For nature always operates in the same manner: hence unless some change precede either in the nature of the mover, or in the movable thing, there cannot arise from the natural mover a motion which was not there before. As for the will, without itself being changed, it puts off doing what it proposes to do; but this can be only by some imagined change, even if it involves only the passage of time. Thus he who wills to make a house to-morrow, and not to-day, awaits something which will be to-morrow, but is not to-day. At the very least he awaits for to-day to pass, and for to-morrow to come; and this cannot be without change, because time is the number of motion. Therefore it remains that before every new mo-

---

[2] Aristotle, *De Caelo*, I, 12 (281b 18).—Averroes, *In De Caelo*, I, comm. 119 (V, 38r).   [3] *Phys.*, I, 9 (192a 28).   [4] *De Caelo*, I, 3 (270a 13).   [5] An argument of Aristotle, found in Maimonides, *Guide*, II, 13 (p. 173).   [6] Averroes, *In De Caelo*, III, comm. 29 (V, 92v-93r). [7] An argument of Aristotle, found in Maimonides, *Guide*, II, 14 (p. 174).—Cf. Averroes, *In Phys.*, VIII, comm. 7 (IV, 156r).

tion, there was a previous motion; and so the same conclusion follows as before.[8]

Obj. 7. Further, whatever is always in its beginning, and always in its end, cannot cease and cannot begin; because what begins is not in its end, and what ceases is not in its beginning. But time is always in its beginning and end, because no part of time exists except *now*, which is the end of the past and the beginning of the future. Therefore time cannot begin or end, and consequently neither can motion, of which time is the number.[9]

Obj. 8. Further, God is before the world either in the order of nature only, or also in duration. If in the order of nature only, therefore, since God is eternal, the world also is eternal. But if God is prior in duration, since what is prior and posterior in duration constitutes time, it follows that time existed before the world; which is impossible.[10]

Obj. 9. Further, if there is a sufficient cause, there is an effect; for a cause from which there is no effect is an imperfect cause, requiring something else to make the effect follow. But God is the sufficient cause of the world: He is the final cause, by reason of His goodness, the exemplary cause by reason of His wisdom, and the efficient cause by reason of His power, as appears from the above.[11] Since therefore God is eternal, the world also is eternal.[12]

Obj. 10. Further, He who has an eternal action also has an eternal effect. But the action of God is His substance, which is eternal. Therefore the world is eternal.[13]

On the contrary, It is said (*Jo.* xvii. 5), *Glorify Me, O Father, with Thyself with the glory which I had before the world was;* and (*Prov.* viii. 22), *The Lord possessed Me in the beginning of His ways, before He made anything from the beginning.*

I answer that, Nothing except God can be eternal. This

---

[8] Avicenna, *Metaph.*, IX, 1 (102ra).—Averroes, *In Phys.*, VIII, comm. 8 (IV, 156v); comm. 15 (IV, 158v ff.); *Destruct. Destruct.*, I (IX, 8rb).   [9] Aristotle, *Phys.*, VIII, 1 (251b 19).—Cf. Averroes, *In Phys.*, VIII, comm. 11 (IV, 157v).   [10] Avicenna, *Metaph.*, IX, 1 (101vab).—Cf. Averroes, *Destruct. Destruct.*, I (IX, 13ra).   [11] Q. 44, a. 1, 3 and 4.   [12] Avicenna, *Metaph.*, IX 1 (101vb).—Cf. Alex. of Hales, *Summa Theol.*, I, no. 64 (I, 93); St. Bonaventure, *In II Sent.*, d. 1, pt. 1, a. 1, q. 2 (II, 20).   [13] Avicenna, *Metaph.*, IX, 1 (101va).—Maimonides, *Guide*, II, 18 (p. 181).

statement is far from impossible. For it has been shown above that the will of God is the cause of things.[14] Therefore, things are necessary according as it is necessary for God to will them, since the necessity of the effect depends on the necessity of the cause.[15] Now it was shown above that, absolutely speaking, it is not necessary that God should will anything except Himself.[16] It is not therefore necessary for God to will that the world should always exist; but supposing an eternal world to exist, it exists to the extent that God wills it to exist, since the being of the world depends on the will of God as on its cause. It is not therefore necessary for the world to be always; hence neither can it be proved demonstratively.

Nor are Aristotle's arguments absolutely demonstrative, but only relatively—viz., as against the arguments of some of the ancients who asserted that the world began to be in some actually impossible ways. This appears in three ways.[17] First, because both in *Physics* viii.[18] and in *De Caelo* i.[19] he premises some opinions, such as those of Anaxagoras, Empedocles and Plato, and brings forward arguments to refute them. Secondly, because wherever he speaks of this subject, he quotes the testimony of the ancients, which is not the way of a demonstrator, but of one persuading of what is probable. Thirdly, because he expressly says that there are dialectical problems which we cannot solve demonstratively, as, *whether the world is eternal.*[20]

Reply Obj. 1. Before the world existed, it was possible for the world to be, not, indeed, according to the passive power which is matter, but according to the active power of God. The world was possible also, according as a thing is called absolutely possible, not in relation to any power, but from the sole relation of the terms which are not repugnant to each other; in which sense possible is opposed to impossible, as appears from the Philosopher.[21]

Reply Obj. 2. Whatever has the power always to be, from the fact of having that power cannot sometimes be and sometimes not-be. However, before it received that power, it did not exist. Hence this argument, which is given by Aristotle,[22]

[14] Q. 19, a. 4.   [15] Aristotle, *Metaph.*, IV, 5 (1015b 9).   [16] Q. 19, a. 3.   [17] Cf. Maimonides, *Guide*, II, 15 (p. 176).   [18] *Phys.*, VIII, 1 (250b 24; 251b 17).   [19] *De Caelo*, I, 10 (279b 4; 280a 30).   [20] *Top.*, I, 9 (104b 16).   [21] *Metaph.*, IV, 12 (1019b 19).   [22] *De Caelo*, I, 12 (281b 18).

does not prove absolutely that incorruptible beings never began to be; it proves that they did not begin according to the natural process by which generable and corruptible beings begin to be.

Reply Obj. 3. Aristotle proves that *matter is ungenerated* from the fact that *it has not a subject* from which to derive its existence;[23] and he proves that the heavens are ungenerated, because they have no contrary from which to be generated.[24] Hence it appears that no conclusion follows in either case, except that matter and the heavens did not begin by generation; as some said especially about the heavens.[25] But what we say is that matter and the heavens were produced into being by creation, as appears above.[26]

Reply Obj. 4. The notion of a vacuum is not only that *in which is nothing,* but also implies a space capable of holding a body and in which there is not a body, as appears from Aristotle.[27] But we hold that there was no place or space before the world was.

Reply Obj. 5. The first mover was always in the same state, but the first movable thing was not always so, because it began to be whereas hitherto it was not. This, however, was not through change, but by creation, which is not change, as was said above.[28] Hence it is evident that this argument, which Aristotle gives,[29] is valid against those who admitted the existence of eternal movable things, but not eternal motion, as appears from the opinions of Anaxagoras and Empedocles.[30] But we hold that motion always existed from the moment that movable things began to exist.

Reply Obj. 6. The first agent is a voluntary agent. And although He had the eternal will to produce some effect, yet He did not produce an eternal effect. Nor is it necessary for some change to be presupposed, not even because of imaginery time. For we must take into consideration the difference between a particular agent, that presupposes something and produces something else, and the universal agent, who produces the whole. The particular agent produces the form, and presupposes the matter; and hence it is necessary that it introduce the form in due proportion into a suitable mat-

---

[23] *Phys.*, I, 9 (192a 28).   [24] *De Caelo*, I, 3 (270a 13).   [25] Cf. *op. cit.*, I, 10 (279a 13).   [26] Q. 45, a. 2.   [27] *Phys.*, IV, 1 (208b 26).   [28] Q. 45, a. 2, ad 2.   [29] *Phys.*, VIII, 1 (251a 25).   [30] Cf. *ibid.* (250b 24).

ter. Hence it is logical to say that the particular agent introduces the form into such matter, and not into another, because of the different kinds of matter. But it is not logical to say so of God Who produces form and matter together; whereas it is logical to say of Him that He produces matter fitting to the form and to the end. Now a particular agent presupposes time just as it presupposes matter. Hence it is logically described as acting in a time *after* and not in a time *before,* according to an imaginary succession of time after time. But the universal agent, who produces both the thing and time, is not correctly described as acting now, and not before, according to an imaginary succession of time succeeding time, as if time were presupposed to His action; but He must be considered as giving time to His effect as much as and when He willed, and according to what was fitting to demonstrate His power. For the world leads more evidently to the knowledge of the divine creating power if it was not always, than if it had always been; since everything which was not always manifestly has a cause; whereas this is not so manifest of what always was.

Reply Obj. 7. As is stated in *Physics* iv., *before and after belong to time,* according as *they are found in motion.*[31] Hence beginning and end in time must be taken in the same way as in motion. Now, granted the eternity of motion, it is necessary that any given moment in motion be a beginning and an end of motion; which need not be if motion has a beginning. The same applies to the *now* of time. Thus it appears that the view of the instant *now,* as being always the begining and end of time, presupposes the eternity of time and motion. Hence Aristotle brings forward this argument against those who asserted the eternity of time, but denied the eternity of motion.[32]

Reply Obj. 8. God is prior to the world by priority of duration. But the word *prior* signifies priority, not of time, but of eternity.—Or we may say that it signifies the eternity of imaginary time, and not of time really existing; much as, when we say that above the heavens there is nothing, the word *above* signifies only an imaginary place, according as it is possible to imagine other dimensions beyond those of the body of the heavens.

[31] Aristotle, *op. cit.,* IV, 11 (219a 17).   [32] *Op. cit.,* VIII, 1 (251b 29).

Reply Obj. 9. Just as the effect of a cause that acts by nature follows from it according to the mode of its form, so likewise it follows from the voluntary agent according to the form preconceived and determined by the agent, as appears from what was said above.[33] Therefore, although God was from eternity the sufficient cause of the world, we may not hold that the world was produced by Him, except as pre-ordained by His will—that is, that it should have being after non-being, in order more manifestly to declare its author.

Reply Obj. 10. Given the action, the effect follows according to the requirement of the form which is the principle of action. But in agents acting by will, what is conceived and preordained is considered as the form which is the principle of action. Therefore, from the eternal action of God an eternal effect does not follow; there follows only such an effect as God has willed, an effect, namely, which has being after non-being.

Second Article

WHETHER IT IS AN ARTICLE OF FAITH THAT THE WORLD BEGAN?

We proceed thus to the Second Article:—

Objection 1. It would seem that it is not an article of faith but a demonstrable conclusion that the world began. For everything that is made has a beginning of its duration. But it can be proved demonstratively that God is the producing cause of the world; indeed this is asserted by the more approved philosophers.[34] Therefore it can be demonstratively proved that the world began.[35]

Obj. 2. Further, if it is necessary to say that the world was made by God, it must have been made from nothing, or from something. But it was not made from something, or otherwise the matter of the world would have preceded the world; and against this are the arguments of Aristotle who held that the heavens are ungenerated. Therefore it must be said that the world was made from nothing; and thus it has

---

[33] Q. 19, a. 4; q. 41, a. 2.   [34] Cf. above, q. 44, a. 2.   [35] Alex. of Hales, *Summa Theol.,* I, no. 64 (I, 95) ; St. Bonaventure, *In II Sent.,* d. 1, pt. 1, a. 1, q. 3 (II, 22).

being after non-being. Therefore it must have begun to be.[36]

Obj. 3. Further, *everything which works by intellect works from some principle*,[37] as is revealed in all works of human art. But God acts by intellect, and therefore His work has a principle, from which to begin. The world, therefore, which is His effect, did not always exist.

Obj. 4. Further, it appears manifestly that certain arts have developed, and certain parts of the world have begun to be inhabited at some fixed time. But this would not be the case if the world had always been in existence. Therefore it is manifest that the world did not always exist.

Obj. 5. Further, it is certain that nothing can be equal to God. But if the world had always been, it would be equal to God in duration. Therefore it is certain that the world did not always exist.[38]

Obj. 6. Further, if the world always was, the consequence is that an infinite number of days preceded this present day. But it is impossible to traverse what is infinite. Therefore we should never have arrived at this present day; which is manifestly false.[39]

Obj. 7. Further, if the world was eternal, generation also was eternal. Therefore one man was begotten of another in an infinite series. But the father is the efficient cause of the son.[40] Therefore in efficient causes there could be an infinite series; which however is disproved in *Metaph.* ii.[41]

Obj. 8. Further, if the world and generation always were, there have been an infinite number of men. But man's soul is immortal. Therefore an infinite number of human souls would now actually exist, which is impossible. Therefore it can be known with certainty that the world began: it is not held by faith alone.[42]

On the contrary, The articles of faith cannot be proved

---

[36] Alex. of Hales, *Summa Theol.*, I, no. 64 (I, 93).   [37] Aristotle, *Phys.*, III, 4 (203a 31).   [38] Alex. of Hales, *Summa Theol.*, I, no. 64 (I, 93).   [39] Argument of Algazel in Averroes, *Destruct. Destruct.*, I (IX, 9rb; 10rb); and of the Mutakallimin, found in Maimonides, *Guide*, I, 74 (p. 138).   [40] Aristotle, *Phys.*, II, 3 (194b 30).   [41] Aristotle, *Metaph.*, Ia, 2 (994a 5)—For the use of this argument, cf. the Mutakallimin in Averroes, *Destruct. Destruct.*, I (IX, 12vab).   [42] Argument of Algazel, found in Averroes, *Destruct. Destruct.*, I (IX, 12vab); and of the Mutakallimin in Maimonides, *Guide*, I, 73 (p. 132).

demonstratively, because faith is of things *that appear not*.
But that God is the Creator of the world in such a way that
the world began to be is an article of faith; for we say,
I believe in one God, etc.[43] And again, Gregory says that
Moses prophesied of the past, saying, *In the beginning God
created heaven and earth:* in which words the newness of
the world is stated.[44] Therefore the newness of the world is
known only by revelation, and hence it cannot be proved
demonstratively.

I answer that, That the world did not always exist we hold
by faith alone: it cannot be proved demonstratively; which
is what was said above of the mystery of the Trinity.[45] The
reason for this is that the newness of the world cannot be
demonstrated from the world itself. For the principle of demonstration is the essence of a thing. Now everything, considered in its species, abstracts from *here* and *now*; which
is why it is said that *universals are everywhere and always*.[46]
Hence it cannot be demonstrated that man, or the heavens,
or a stone did not always exist.

Likewise, neither can the newness of the world be demonstrated from the efficient cause, which acts by will. For the
will of God cannot be investigated by reason, except as regards those things which God must will of necessity; and
what He wills about creatures is not among these, as was
said above.[47] But the divine will can be manifested by revelation, on which faith rests. Hence that the world began to
exist is an object of faith, but not of demonstration or science.
And it is useful to consider this, lest anyone, presuming to
demonstrate what is of faith, should bring forward arguments that are not cogent; for this would give unbelievers
the occasion to ridicule, thinking that on such grounds we
believe the things that are of faith.

Reply Obj. 1. As Augustine says, the opinion of philosophers who asserted the eternity of the world was twofold.[48]
For some said that the substance of the world was not from
God, which is an intolerable error; and therefore it is refuted
by proofs that are cogent. Some, however, said that the world
was eternal, although made by God. *For they hold that the*

---

[43] *Symb. Nicaenum* (Denzinger, no. 54).   [44] *In Ezech.*, hom. 1, bk.
1 (PL 76, 786).   [45] Q. 32, a. 1.   [46] Aristotle, *Post. Anal.*, I, 31 (87b
33).   [47] Q. 19, a. 3.   [48] *De Civit. Dei*, XI, 4 (PL 41, 319).

*world has a beginning, not of time, but of creation; which
means that, in a scarcely intelligible way, it was always
made. And they try to explain their meaning thus: for just
as, if a foot were always in the dust from eternity, there
would always be a footprint which without doubt was caused
by him who trod on it, so also the world always was, because
its Maker always existed.*[49] To understand this we must consider that an efficient cause which acts by motion of necessity
precedes its effect in time; for the effect exists only in the
end of the action, and every agent must be the beginning of
action. But if the action is instantaneous and not successive,
it is not necessary for the maker to be prior in duration to
the thing made, as appears in the case of illumination. Hence
it is held that it does not follow necessarily that if God is the
active cause of the world, He must be prior to the world in
duration;[50] because creation, by which He produced the
world, is not a successive change, as was said above.[51]

Reply Obj. 2. Those who would hold that the world was
eternal would say that the world was made by God from
nothing; not that it was made after nothing, according to
what we understand by the term *creation,* but that it was
not made from anything. And so some of them even do not
reject the term creation, as appears from Avicenna.[52]

Reply Obj. 3. This is the argument of Anaxagoras as re-
ported in *Physics* iii.[53] But it does not lead to a necessary
conclusion, except as to that intellect which deliberates in
order to find out what should be done; which procedure is
like movement. Such is the human intellect, but not the
divine intellect.[54]

Reply Obj. 4. Those who hold the eternity of the world
hold that some region was changed an infinite number of
times from being uninhabitable to being inhabitable and *vice
versa.*[55] They also hold that the arts, by reason of various
corruptions and accidents, were subject to an infinite succession of discovery and decay.[56] Hence Aristotle says that

[49] *Op. cit.,* X, 31 (PL 41, 311).   [50] Cf. Averroes, *Destruct. Destruct.,* I (IX, 13rb).   [51] Q. 45, a. 2, ad 3.   [52] *Metaph.,* IX, 4
(104va).   [53] Aristotle, *Phys.,* III, 4 (203a 31); VIII, 1 (250b 24).
[54] Q. 14, a. 7.   [55] Cf. St. Augustine, *De Civit. Dei,* XII, 10 (PL 41,
358); Aristotle, *Meteor.,* I, 14 (351a 19).   [56] Cf. St. Augustine, *De
Civit. Dei,* XII, 10 (PL 41, 358); Averroes, *In Metaph.,* XII, comm.
50 (VIII, 156v).

it is absurd to base our opinion of the newness of the whole world on such particular changes.[57]

Reply Obj. 5. Even supposing that the world always was, it would not be equal to God in eternity, as Boethius says;[58] for the divine Being is all being simultaneously without succession, but with the world it is otherwise.

Reply Obj. 6. Passage is always understood as being from term to term. Whatever by-gone day we choose, from it to the present day there is a finite number of days which can be traversed. The objection is founded on the idea that, given two extremes, there is an infinite number of mean terms.

Reply Obj. 7. In efficient causes it is impossible to proceed to infinity *per se*. Thus, there cannot be an infinite number of causes that are *per se* required for a certain effect; for instance, that a stone be moved by a stick, the stick by the hand, and so on to infinity. But it is not impossible to proceed to infinity *accidentally* as regards efficient causes; for instance, if all the causes thus infinitely multiplied should have the order of only one cause, while their multiplication is accidental: *e.g.*, as an artificer acts by means of many hammers accidentally, because one after the other is broken. It is accidental, therefore, that one particular hammer should act after the action of another, and it is likewise accidental to this particular man as generator to be generated by another man; for he generates as a man, and not as the son of another man. For all men generating hold one grade in the order of efficient causes—viz., the grade of a particular generator. Hence it is not impossible for a man to be generated by man to infinity; but such a thing would be impossible if the generation of this man depended upon this man, and on an elementary body, and on the sun, and so on to infinity.

Reply Obj. 8. Those who hold the eternity of the world evade this argument in many ways. For some do not think it impossible for there to be an actual infinity of souls, as appears from the *Metaphysics* of Algazel, who says that such a thing is an accidental infinity.[59] But this was disproved above.[60] Some say that the soul is corrupted with the body.[61]

[57] *Meteor.*, I, 14 (352a 26; 351b 8).   [58] *De Consol.*, V, prose 6 (PL 63, 859).   [59] *Metaph.*, I, tr. 1, div. 6 (p. 40).—Cf. Averroes, *Destruct. Destruct.*, I (IX, 12vab).   [60] Q. 7, a. 4.   [61] Cf. Nemesius, *De Nat. Hom.*, II (PG 40, 537).

And some say that of all souls only one remains.[62] But others, as Augustine says, asserted on this account a circulation of souls—viz., that souls separated from their bodies again return thither after a course of time.[63] A fuller consideration of this matter will be given later.[64] But be it noted that this argument considers only a particular case. Hence one might say that the world was eternal, or at least some creature, as an angel, but not man. But we are considering the question in general, namely, whether any creature can exist from eternity.

Third Article

WHETHER THE CREATION OF THINGS WAS IN THE BEGINNING OF TIME?

We proceed thus to the Third Article:—

Objection 1. It would seem that the creation of things was not in the beginning of time. For whatever is not in time, is not in any part of time. But the creation of things was not in time, for by the creation the substance of things was brought into being; but time does not measure the substance of things, and especially of incorporeal things. Therefore, creation was not in the beginning of time.

Obj. 2. Further, the Philosopher proves that everything which is made, was being made.[65] Hence, to be made implies a *before* and *after*. But in the beginning of time, since it is indivisible, there is no *before* and *after*. Therefore, since to be created is a kind of *being made*, it appears that things were not created in the beginning of time.

Obj. 3. Further, even time itself is created. But time cannot be created in the beginning of time, since time is divisible, and the beginning of time is indivisible. Therefore, the creation of things was not in the beginning of time.

On the contrary, It is said (*Gen.* i. 1): *In the beginning God created heaven and earth.*

I answer that, The words of *Genesis, In the beginning God created heaven and earth,* are interpreted in a threefold sense

---

[62] Averroes, *Destruct. Destruct.,* I (IX, 10va).   [63] *Serm.* CCXLI, 4 (PL 38, 1135); *De Civit. Dei*, XII, 13 (PL 41, 361).—Cf. Plato *Timaeus* (p. 39a).   [64] Q. 75, a. 6; q. 76, a. 2; q. 118, a. 3.   [65] *Phys.,* VI, 6 (237b 10).

in order to exclude three errors. For some said that the world always was, and that time had no beginning;[66] and to exclude this the words *In the beginning* are interpreted to mean *the beginning of time.*

And some said that there are two principles of creation, one of good things and the other of evil things,[67] against which *In the beginning* is expounded—*in the Son.* For as the efficient principle is appropriated to the Father by reason of power, so the exemplary principle is appropriated to the Son by reason of wisdom; in order that, according to the words (*Ps.* ciii. 24), *Thou hast made all things in wisdom,* it may be understood that God made all things in the beginning— that is, in the Son. As it is said by the Apostle (*Col.* i. 16), *In Him*—viz., the Son—*were created all things.*

But others said that corporeal things were created by God through the medium of spiritual creatures;[68] and to exclude this the words of *Genesis* are interpreted thus: *In the beginning—i.e., before* all things—*God created heaven and earth.* For four things are stated to be created together—viz., the empyrean heavens, corporeal matter, by which is meant the earth, time, and the angelic nature.

Reply Obj. 1. Things are said to be created in the beginning of time, not as if the beginning of time were a measure of creation, but because together with time the heavens and earth were created.

Reply Obj. 2. This saying of the Philosopher is understood *of being made* by means of movement, or as the term of movement. For, since in every motion there is *before* and *after,* before any one point in a given motion—that is, while anything is in the process of being moved and made,—there is a *before* and also an *after,* because what is in the beginning of motion or in its term is not in the state of *being moved.* But creation is neither motion nor the term of motion, as was said above.[69] Hence a thing is created in such a way that it was not being created before.

Reply Obj. 3. Nothing is made except as it exists. But nothing of time exists except *now.* Hence time cannot be made except according to some *now*; not because there is time in the first *now,* but because from it time begins.

---

[66] Cf. St. Augustine, *De Civit. Dei,* X, 31; XI, 4; XII, 10 (PL 41, 311; 319; 357).   [67] Cf. below, q. 49, a. 3.   [68] Cf. above, q. 45, a. 5; below, q. 65, a. 4.   [69] Q. 45, a. 2, ad 3; a. 3.

ON THE DISTINCTION OF THINGS IN GENERAL

(*In Three Articles*)

AFTER considering the production of creatures, we must turn to the consideration of the distinction among them. This consideration will be threefold—first, the distinction of things in general; secondly, the distinction of good and evil;[1] thirdly, the distinction of spiritual and corporeal creatures.[2]

Under the first head there are three points of inquiry: (1) The multitude or distinction of things. (2) Their inequality. (3) The unity of the world.

First Article

WHETHER THE MULTITUDE AND DISTINCTION OF THINGS IS FROM GOD?

We proceed thus to the First Article:—

Objection 1. It would seem that the multitude and distinction of things does not come from God. For one naturally always makes one. But God is supremely one, as appears from what precedes.[3] Therefore He produces but one effect.

Obj. 2. Further, the representation is assimilated to its exemplar. But God is the exemplary cause of His effect, as was said above.[4] Therefore, as God is one, His effect is only one, and not diverse.

Obj. 3. Further, the means are proportioned to the end. But the end of the creature is one—viz., the divine goodness, as was shown above.[5] Therefore the effect of God is but one.

On the contrary, It is said (*Gen.* i. 4, 7) that God *divided the light from the darkness,* and *divided waters from waters.* Therefore the distinction and multitude of things is from God.

I answer that, The distinction of things has been ascribed to many causes. For some attributed the distinction to matter, either by itself or with the agent. Democritus, for instance, and all the ancient natural philosophers, who admitted

[1] Q. 48.   [2] Q. 50.   [3] Q. 11, a. 4.   [4] Q. 44, a. 3.   [5] Q. 44, a. 4.

no cause but matter, attributed it to matter alone;[6] and in their opinion the distinction of things comes from chance according to the motion of matter. Anaxagoras, however, attributed the distinction and multitude of things to matter and to the agent together; and he said that the intellect distinguishes things by separating what is mixed in the matter.[7]

But this cannot stand, for two reasons. First, because, as was shown above, even matter itself was created by God.[8] Hence we must reduce to a higher cause whatever distinction comes from matter. Secondly, because matter is for the sake of the form, and not the form for the matter, and the distinction of things comes from their proper forms. Therefore, the distinction of things is not for the sake of the matter; but rather, on the contrary, created matter is formless, in order that it may be accommodated to different forms.

Others have attributed the distinction of things to secondary agents, as did Avicenna, who said that God by understanding Himself, produced the first intelligence; in which, since it was not its own being, there is necessarily composition of potentiality and act,[9] as will appear later.[10] And so the first intelligence, inasmuch as it understood the first cause, produced the second intelligence; and in so far as it understood itself as in potentiality it produced the body of the heavens, which causes motion, and inasmuch as it understood itself as having actuality it produced the soul of the heavens.

But this opinion cannot stand, for two reasons. First, because it was shown above that to create belongs to God alone;[11] and hence whatever can be caused only by creation is produced by God alone—viz., all those things which are not subject to generation and corruption. Secondly, because, according to this opinion, the universe of things would not proceed from the intention of the first cause, but from the concurrence of many producing causes; and such an effect is an effect produced by chance. Therefore, the perfection of the universe, which consists of the diversity of things, would thus be a thing of chance; which is impossible.

Hence we must say that the distinction and multitude of

[6] Cf. Aristotle, *Phys.*, II, 2 (194a 20); II, 4 (196a 24); III, 4 (203a 34).   [7] Cf. *op. cit.*, III, 4 (203a 23).   [8] Q. 44, a. 2.   [9] *Metaph.*, IX, 4 (104va); cf. *op. cit.*, I, 7 (73rb).   [10] Q. 50, a. 2, ad 3.   [11] Q. 45, a. 5.

things is from the intention of the first cause, who is God.
For He brought things into being in order that His goodness
might be communicated to creatures, and be represented by
them. And because His goodness could not be adequately
represented by one creature alone, He produced many and
diverse creatures, so that what was wanting to one in the
representation of the divine goodness might be supplied by
another. For goodness, which in God is simple and uniform,
in creatures is manifold and divided; and hence the whole
universe together participates the divine goodness more perfectly, and represents it better, than any given single creature. And because the divine wisdom is the cause of the
distinction of things, therefore Moses said that things are
made distinct by the Word of God, which is the conception
of His wisdom; and this is what we read in *Genesis* (i. 3, 4):
*God said: Be light made. . . . And He divided the light
from the darkness.*

Reply Obj. 1. The natural agent acts by the form which
makes it what it is, and which is only one in one thing; and
therefore its effect is one only. But the voluntary agent, such
as God is, as was shown above, acts by an intellectual
form.[12] Since, therefore, it is not against God's unity and
simplicity to understand many things, as was shown above,[13]
it follows that, although He is one, He can make many things.

Reply Obj. 2. This argument would apply to the representation which perfectly represents the exemplar, and which
is multiplied only by reason of matter. Hence the uncreated
image, which is perfect, is only one. But no creature perfectly
represents the first exemplar, which is the divine essence;
and, therefore, it can be represented by many things. Still,
according as ideas are called exemplars, the plurality of ideas
corresponds in the divine mind to the plurality of things.

Reply Obj. 3. In speculative matters the means of demonstration, which demonstrates the conclusion perfectly, is only
one; whereas probable means of proof are many. Likewise
when operation is concerned, if the means be equal, so to
speak, to the end, only one is necessary. But the creature
is not so related to its end, which is God; and hence the
multiplication of creatures is necessary.

[12] Q. 19, a. 4.   [13] Q. 15, a. 2.

Second Article

WHETHER THE INEQUALITY OF THINGS IS FROM GOD?

We proceed thus to the Second Article:—

Objection 1. It would seem that the inequality of things is not from God. For it belongs to the best to produce the best. But among things that are best, one is not greater than another.Therefore, it belongs to God, Who is the Best, to make all things equal.

Obj. 2. Further, equality is the effect of unity.[14] But God is one. Therefore, He has made all things equal.

Obj. 3. Further, it is the part of justice to give unequal gifts to unequal things. But God is just in all His works. Since, therefore, no inequality of things is presupposed to the operation whereby He gives being to things, it seems that He has made all things equal.

On the contrary. It is said (*Ecclus.* xxxiii. 7): *Why does one day excel another, and one light another, and one year another year, one sun another sun? By the knowledge of the Lord they were distinguished.*

I answer that, When Origen wished to refute those who said that the distinction of things arose from the contrariety of the principles of good and evil, he said that in the beginning all things were created equal by God.[15] For he asserted that God first created only rational creatures, and all equal; and that inequality arose in them from free choice, since some turned to God more and some less, and others turned more and others less away from God. And so those rational creatures which were turned to God by free choice, were promoted to the various orders of angels according to the diversity of merits. Those however, who were turned away from God were bound to bodies according to the diversity of their sin; and this was the cause (he said) of the creation and diversity of bodies.

But according to this opinion, it would follow that the universe of bodily creatures would not be for the sake of the communication of the goodness of God to creatures, but for the sake of the punishment of sin; which is contrary to what

---

[14] Aristotle, *Metaph.*, IV, 15 (1021a 12).   [15] *Peri Archon,* I, 6; 8; II, 9 (PG 11, 166; 178; 229).

is said: *God saw all the things that He had made, and they were very good* (*Gen.* i. 31). And, as Augustine says: *What can be more stupid than to say that the divine Artist provided this one sun for the one world, not to be an ornament to its beauty, nor for the benefit of corporeal things, but that it happened through the sin of one soul; so that, if a hundred souls had sinned, there would be a hundred suns in the world?* [16]

Therefore it must be said that, just as the wisdom of God is the cause of the distinction of things, so the same wisdom is the cause of their inequality. This may be explained as follows. A twofold distinction is found in things: one is a formal distinction among things differing specifically; the other is a material distinction among things differing numerically only. And since matter is for the sake of form, material distinction exists for the sake of formal distinction. Hence we see that in incorruptible things there is only one individual of each species, for the species is sufficiently preserved in the one; whereas in generable and corruptible things there are many individuals of one species for the preservation of the species. Whence it appears that formal distinction is of greater consequence than the material. Now, formal distinction always requires inequality, because, as the Philosopher says,[17] the forms of things are like numbers in which species vary by the addition or subtraction of unity. Hence in natural things species seem to be arranged in a hierarchy: as the mixed things are more perfect than the elements, and plants than minerals, and animals than plants, and men than other animals; and in each of these one species is more perfect than others. Therefore, just as the divine wisdom is the cause of the distinction of things for the sake of the perfection of the universe, so is it the cause of inequality. For the universe would not be perfect if only one grade of goodness were found in things.

Reply Obj. 1. It is the part of the best cause to produce an effect which is best *as a whole*; but this does not mean that He makes every part of the whole the best absolutely, but in proportion to the whole. In the case of an animal, for instance, its goodness would be taken away if every part of it had the dignity of an eye. In the same way, God made

[16] *De Civit. Dei,* XI, 23 (PL 41, 337).   [17] Aristotle, *Metaph.,* VII, 3 (1043b 34).

the universe to be best as a whole, according to its requirement as a creature; whereas He did not make each single
creature best, but one better than another. And therefore we
find it said of each creature, *God saw the light that it was
good* (*Gen.* i. 4); and in like manner of each one of the rest.
But of all together it is said, *God saw all the things that He
had made, and they were very good* (*Gen.* i. 31).

Reply Obj. 2. The first effect of unity is equality, and then
comes multiplicity. Therefore from the Father, to Whom,
according to Augustine, unity is appropriated,[18] the Son proceeds, to Whom is appropriated equality; and then comes
the creature, to which belongs inequality. Nevertheless, creatures share also in a certain equality, namely, that of proportion.

Reply Obj. 3. This is the argument that persuaded
Origen;[19] but it holds only as regards the distribution of rewards, the inequality of which is due to unequal merits. But
in the constitution of things here is no inequality of parts
through any preceding inequality, either of merits or of the
disposition of the matter; but inequality comes from the
perfection of the whole. This appears also in works done by
art; for the roof of a house does not differ from the foundation because it is made of other material. But the builder
seeks different materials in order that the house may be perfect in its different parts. Indeed, he would make such materials if he could.

Third Article

WHETHER THERE IS ONLY ONE WORLD?

We proceed thus to the Third Article:—

Objection 1. It would seem that there is not only one world,
but many. Because, as Augustine says, it is unfitting to say
that God has created things without a reason.[20] But for the
same reason that He created one, He could create many,
since His power is not limited to the creation of one world,
but is infinite, as was shown above.[21] Therefore God has produced many worlds.

[18] *De Doct. Christ.,* I, 5 (PL 34, 21).   [19] *Peri Archon,* I, 6; 8; II,
9 (PG 11, 166; 178; 229).   [20] *Lib. 83 Quaest.,* q. 46 (PL 40, 30).
[21] Q. 25, a. 2.

Obj. 2. Further, nature does what is best, and much more does God. But it is better that there be many worlds than that there be one, because many good things are better than a few. Therefore many worlds have been made by God.

Obj. 3. Further, everything which has a form in matter can be multiplied in number, while the species remains the same, because multiplication in number comes from matter. But the world has form in matter. Thus, when I say *man*, I mean the form, and when I say *this man*, I mean the form in matter; so when we say *world*, the form is signified, and when we say *this world*, the form in matter is signified. Therefore there is nothing to prevent the existence of many worlds.

On the contrary, It is said (*Jo.* i. 10): *The world was made by Him,* where the world is named as one, as if only one existed.

I answer that, The very order of things created by God shows the unity of the world. For this world is called one by the unity of order, whereby some things are ordered to others. But whatever things come from God have relation of order to each other and to God Himself, as was shown above.[22] Hence it is necessary that all things should belong to one world. Therefore only those were able to assert the existence of many worlds who did not acknowledge any ordaining wisdom, but rather believed in chance; as did Democritus, who said that this world, besides an infinite number of other worlds, was made from a coming together of atoms.[23]

Reply Obj. 1. This argument proves that the world is one because all things must be arranged in one order, and to one end. Therefore from the unity of order in things Aristotle infers the unity of God governing all.[24] In the same way, Plato proves the unity of the world, as a sort of copy, from the unity of the exemplar.[25]

Reply Obj. 2. No agent intends material plurality as the end; for material multitude has no certain limit, but of itself tends to infinity, and the infinite is opposed to the notion of end. Now when it is said that many worlds are better than one, this has reference to material multitude. But the *best,*

[22] Q. 11, a. 3; q. 21, a. 1, ad 3.   [23] Cf. Aristotle, *De Caelo,* III, 4 (303a 4); Cicero, *De Nat. Deor.,* I, 26 (p. 28); St. Ambrose, *In Hexaëm.,* I, 1 (PL 14, 135).   [24] *Metaph.,* XI, 10 (1076a 4).   [25] Cf. St. Thomas, *In De Caelo,* I, lect. 19.—Cf. also Plato, *Timaeus* (p. 31a).

in this sense, is not the intention of the divine agent; since for the same reason it might be said that if He had made two worlds, it would be better if He had made three; and so on to infinity.

Reply Obj. 3. The world is composed of the whole of its matter. For it is not possible for there to be another earth than this one, since every earth would naturally be carried to this central one, wherever it was. The same applies to the other bodies which are parts of the world.

THE DISTINCTION OF THINGS IN PARTICULAR

(*In Six Articles*)

WE must now consider the distinction of things in particular. And firstly the distinction of good and evil; then the distinction of spiritual and corporeal creatures.[1]

Concerning the first, we inquire into evil and its cause.[2]

Concerning evil, six points are to be considered: (1) Whether evil is a nature? (2) Whether evil is found in things? (3) Whether good is the subject of evil? (4) Whether evil totally corrupts good? (5) The division of evil into pain [*poena*] and fault [*culpa*]. (6) Which has more the nature of evil, pain or fault?

Third Article

WHETHER EVIL IS IN GOOD AS IN ITS SUBJECT?

We proceed thus to the Third Article:—

Objection 1. It would seem that evil is not in good as its subject. For good is something that exists. But Dionysius says that *evil does not exist, nor is it in that which exists.*[3] Therefore, evil is not in good as its subject.

Obj. 2. Further, evil is not a being, whereas good is a being. But *non-being* does not require being as its subject. Therefore, neither does evil require good as its subject.

Obj. 3. Further, one contrary is not the subject of another. But good and evil are contraries. Therefore, evil is not in good as in its subject.

Obj. 4. Further, the subject of whiteness is called white. Therefore, also, the subject of evil is evil. If, therefore, evil is in good as in its subject, it follows that good is evil, against what is said (*Isa.* v. 20.): *Woe to you who call evil good, and good evil!*

On the contrary, Augustine says that *evil exists only in good.*[4]

[1] Q. 50.　　[2] Q. 49.　　[3] *De Div. Nom.,* IV, 33 (PG 3, 733).　　[4] *Enchir.,* XIV (PL 40, 238).

I answer that, As was said above, evil indicates the absence of good. But not every absence of good is evil. For absence of good can be taken in a privative and in a negative sense. Absence of good, taken negatively, is not evil; otherwise, it would follow that what does not exist is evil, and also that every thing would be evil because of not having the good belonging to something else. For instance, a man would be evil because he did not have the swiftness of the roe, or the strength of a lion. But the absence of good, taken in a privative sense, is an evil; as, for instance, the privation of sight is called blindness.

Now, the subject of privation and of form is one and the same—viz., being in potentiality, whether it be being in potentiality absolutely, as primary matter, which is the subject of the substantial form and of the privation of the opposite form; or whether it be being in potentiality relatively, and actuality absolutely, as in the case of a transparent body, which is the subject both of darkness and light. It is, however, manifest that the form which makes a thing actual is a perfection and a good. Hence, every actual being is a good; and likewise every potential being, as such, is a good, as having a relation to good. For as it has being in potentiality, so it has goodness in potentiality. Therefore, the subject of evil is good.

Reply Obj. 1. Dionysius means that evil is not in existing things as a part, or as a natural property of any existing thing.

Reply Obj. 2. *Non-being,* understood negatively, does not require a subject; but privation is negation in a subject, as the Philosopher says, and such a *non-being* is an evil.[5]

Reply Obj. 3. Evil is not in the good opposed to it as in its subject, but in some other good, for the subject of blindness is not *sight,* but *the animal.* Yet it appears, as Augustine says, that the rule of dialectic here fails, the rule, namely, which says that contraries cannot exist together.[6] But this is to be taken according to the universal meaning of good and evil, but not in reference to any particular good and evil. For white and black, sweet and bitter, and like contraries, are considered as contraries only in a special sense, because they exist in some determinate genera; whereas good enters into

[5] *Metaph.,* III, 2 (1004a 15).   [6] *Enchir.,* XIV (PL 40, 238).

every genus. Hence one good can coexist with the privation
of another good.

Reply Obj. 4. The prophet invokes woe to those who say
that good as such is evil. But this does not follow from what
is said above, as is clear from the explanation given.

Fourth Article

WHETHER EVIL CORRUPTS THE WHOLE GOOD?

We proceed thus to the Fourth Article:—

Objection 1. It would seem that evil corrupts the whole
good. For one contrary is wholly corrupted by another. But
good and evil are contraries. Therefore evil corrupts the
whole good.

Obj. 2. Further, Augustine says that *evil injures inasmuch
as it takes away good.*[7] But good is all of a piece and uniform. Therefore it is wholly taken away by evil.

Obj. 3. Further, evil, as long as it lasts, causes injury and
takes away good. But that from which something is always
being removed, is at some time consumed, unless it is infinite,
which cannot be said of any created good. Therefore evil
wholly consumes good.

On the contrary, Augustine says that *evil cannot wholly
consume good.*[8]

I answer that, Evil cannot wholly consume good. To prove
this we must consider that there is a threefold good. One kind
of good is wholly destroyed by evil, and this is the good
opposed to evil; as light is wholly destroyed by darkness, and
sight by blindness. Another kind of good is neither wholly
destroyed nor diminished by evil, and that is the good which
is the subject of evil; for by darkness the substance of the
air is not injured. And there is also a kind of good which is
diminished by evil, but is not wholly taken away; and this
good is the aptitude of a subject to some actuality.

The diminution, however, of this last kind of good is not
to be considered by way of subtraction, as is diminution in
quantity, but rather by way of remission, as is diminution in
qualities and forms. The remission of this aptitude is to be
taken as contrary to its intensity. For this kind of aptitude

---

[7] *Op. cit.,* XII (PL 40, 237); *De Mor. Eccl.,* II, 3 (PL 32, 1347).
[8] *Enchir.,* XII (PL 40, 237).

receives its intensity by the dispositions whereby the matter is prepared for actuality. The more they are multiplied in the subject, the more is it fitted to receive its perfection and form; and, on the contrary, it is decreased by contrary dispositions, whose greater multiplication in the matter, as well as greater intensity, weaken all the more the potentiality in relation to its act.

Therefore, if contrary dispositions cannot be multiplied and intensified to infinity, but only to a certain limit, neither is the aforesaid aptitude diminished or remitted infinitely. This appears in the active and passive qualities of the elements, for coldness and humidity, whereby the aptitude of matter to the form of fire is diminished or remitted, cannot be infinitely multiplied. But if the contrary dispositions can be infinitely multiplied, the aforesaid aptitude is also infinitely diminished or remitted. Nevertheless, it is not wholly taken away, because it always remains in its root, which is the substance of the subject. Thus, if opaque bodies were interposed to infinity between the sun and the air, the aptitude of the air for light would be infinitely diminished; but still it would never be wholly removed while the air remained, which in its very nature is transparent. In the same way, addition in sin can be made to infinitude, whereby the aptitude of the soul for grace is more and more lessened; and these sins are like obstacles interposed between us and God, according to *Isa.* lix. 2: *Our sins have divided between us and God.* Yet the aforesaid aptitude of the soul is not wholly taken away, for it belongs to its very nature.

Reply Obj. 1. The good which is opposed to evil is wholly taken away; but other goods are not wholly removed, as was said above.

Reply Obj. 2. The aforesaid aptitude is intermediate between subject and act. Hence, where it touches act, it is diminished by evil; but where it reaches the subject, it remains as it was. Therefore, although good is like to itself, yet, because of its relation to different things, it is not wholly, but only partially, taken away.

Reply Obj. 3. Some, imagining that the diminution of this kind of good is like the diminution of quantity, said that just as the continuous is infinitely divisible, if the division be made according to the same proportion (for instance, half of a half, or a third of a third), so is it in the present case.[9] But this explanation does not avail here. For when in a division we keep the same proportion, we continue to subtract less and less; for half of a half is less than half the whole. But a second sin does not necessarily diminish the above mentioned aptitude less than a preceding sin, but perchance either equally or more.

Therefore it must be said that, although this aptitude is a finite thing, still it may be so diminished infinitely, not *per se*, but accidentally, according as the contrary dispositions are also increased infinitely, as was explained.

[9] William of Auxerre, *Summa Aurea*, II, tr. 26, q. 5 (fol. 87a).

Question XLIX

THE CAUSE OF EVIL

(*In Three Articles*)

WE next inquire into the cause of evil. Concerning this there are three points of inquiry: (1) Whether good can be the cause of evil? (2) Whether the supreme good, God, is the cause of evil? (3) Whether there be any supreme evil, which is the first cause of all evils?

First Article

WHETHER GOOD CAN BE THE CAUSE OF EVIL?

We proceed thus to the First Article:—

Objection 1. It would seem that good cannot be the cause of evil. For it is said (*Matt.* vii. 18): *A good tree cannot bring forth evil fruit.*

Obj. 2. Further, one contrary cannot be the cause of another. But evil is the contrary to good. Therefore good cannot be the cause of evil.

Obj. 3. Further, a deficient effect can proceed only from a deficient cause. But supposing that evil has a cause, it is a deficient effect; and therefore it has a deficient cause. But everything deficient is an evil. Therefore the cause of evil can be only evil.

Obj. 4. Further, Dionysius says that evil has no cause.[1] Therefore good is not the cause of evil.

On the contrary, Augustine says: *There is no possible source of evil except good.*[2]

I answer that, It must be said that every evil in some way has a cause. For evil is the absence of the good which is natural and due to a thing. But that anything fall short of its natural and due disposition can come only from some cause drawing it out of its proper disposition. For a heavy thing is not moved upwards except by some impelling force; nor does an agent fail in its action except from some impediment. But only good can be a cause; because nothing can be a cause except inasmuch as it is a being, and every being, as such, is

---

[1] *Op. cit.,* IV, 30 (PG 3, 732).   [2] *Contra Julian.,* I, 9 (PL 44, 670).

good. And if we consider the special kinds of causes, we see that the agent, the form and the end imply some kind of perfection which belongs to the notion of good. Even matter, as a potentiality to good, has the nature of good.

Now that good is the cause of evil by way of the material cause was shown above.[3] For it was shown that good is the subject of evil. But evil has no formal cause, but is rather a privation of form. So, too, neither has it a final cause, but is rather a privation of order to the proper end; since it is not only the end which has the nature of good, but also the useful, which is ordered to the end. Evil, however, has a cause by way of an agent, not directly, but accidentally.

In proof of this, we must know that evil is caused in action otherwise than in the effect. In action, evil is caused by reason of the defect of some principle of action, either of the principal or the instrumental agent. Thus, the defect in the movement of an animal may happen by reason of the weakness of the motive power, as in the case of children, or by reason only of the ineptitude of the instrument, as in the lame. On the other hand, evil is caused in a thing, but not in the proper effect of the agent, sometimes by the power of the agent, sometimes by reason of a defect, either of the agent or of the matter. It is caused by reason of the power or perfection of the agent when there necessarily follows on the form intended by the agent the privation of another form; as, for instance, when on the form of fire there follows the privation of the form of air or of water. Therefore, as the more perfect the fire is in strength, so much the more perfectly does it impress its own form, so also the more perfectly does it corrupt the contrary. Hence that evil and corruption befall air and water comes from the perfection of the fire, but accidentally; because fire does not aim at the privation of the form of water, but at the introduction of its own form, though by doing this it also accidentally causes the other. But if there is a defect in the proper effect of the fire—as, for instance, that it fails to heat—this comes either by defect of the action, which implies the defect of some principle, as was said above, or by the indisposition of the matter, which does not receive the action of the fire acting on it. But the fact itself that it is a deficient being is accidental to good to which it belongs

[3] Q. 48, a. 3.

essentially to act. Hence it is true that evil in no way has any but an accidental cause. Thus good is the cause of evil.

Reply Obj. 1. As Augustine says, *The Lord calls an evil will an evil tree, and a good will a good tree.*[4] Now, a good will does not produce a morally bad act, since it is from the good will itself that a moral act is judged to be good. Nevertheless the movement itself of an evil will is caused by the rational creature, which is good; and thus good is the cause of evil.

Reply Obj. 2. Good does not cause that evil which is contrary to itself, but some other evil. Thus, the goodness of the fire causes evil to the water, and man, good in his nature, causes a morally evil act. Furthermore, as was explained above, this is by accident.[5] Moreover, it does happen sometimes that one contrary causes another by accident: for instance, the exterior surrounding cold heats inasmuch as the heat is confined by it.

Reply Obj. 3. Evil has a deficient cause in voluntary beings otherwise than in natural things. For the natural agent produces the same kind of effect as it is itself, unless it is impeded by some exterior thing; and this amounts to some defect in it. Hence evil never follows in the effect unless some other evil pre-exists in the agent or in the matter, as was said above. But in voluntary beings the defect of the action comes from an actually deficient will inasmuch as it does not actually subject itself to its proper rule. This defect, however, is not a fault; but fault follows upon it from the fact that the will acts with this defect.

Reply Obj. 4. Evil has no direct cause, but only an accidental cause, as was said above.

Second Article

WHETHER THE HIGHEST GOOD, GOD, IS THE CAUSE OF EVIL?

We proceed thus to the Second Article:—

Objection 1. It would seem that the highest good, God, is the cause of evil. For it is said (*Isa.* xlv. 5, 7): *I am the Lord, and there is no other God, forming the light, and creating darkness, making peace, and creating evil.* It is also said

---

[4] *Contra Julian.*, I, 9 (PL 44, 672).   [5] Q. 19, a. 9.

(*Amos* iii. 6), *Shall there be evil in a city, which the Lord hath not done?*

Obj. 2. Further, the effect of the secondary cause is reduced to the first cause. But good is the cause of evil, as was said above. Therefore, since God is the cause of every good, as was shown above,[6] it follows that also every evil is from God.

Obj. 3. Further, as is said by the Philosopher, the cause of both *the safety and danger of the ship* is the same.[7] But God is the cause of the safety of all things. Therefore He is the cause of all perdition and of all evil.

On the contrary, Augustine says that, *God is not the author of evil, because He is not the cause of tending to nonbeing.*[8]

I answer that, As appears from what was said, the evil which consists in the defect of action is always caused by the defect of the agent. But in God there is no defect, but the highest perfection, as was shown above.[9] Hence, the evil which consists in defect of action, or which is caused by defect of the agent, is not reduced to God as to its cause.

But the evil which consists in the corruption of some things is reduced to God as the cause. And this appears as regards both natural things and voluntary things. For it was said that some agent, inasmuch as it produces by its power a form which is followed by corruption and defect, causes by its power that corruption and defect. But it is manifest that the form which God chiefly intends in created things is the good of the order of the universe. Now, the order of the universe requires, as was said above, that there should be some things that can, and sometimes do, fail.[10] And thus God, by causing in things the good of the order of the universe, consequently and, as it were by accident, causes the corruptions of things, according to *1 Kings* ii: 6: *The Lord killeth and maketh alive.* But when we read that *God hath not made death* (*Wis.* i. 13), the sense is that God does not will death for its own sake. Nevertheless, the order of justice belongs to the order of the universe; and this requires that penalty should be dealt out to sinners. And so God is the author of the evil

---

[6] Q. 2, a. 3; q. 6, a. 1 and 4.   [7] Aristotle, *Phys.*, II, 3 (195a 3).
[8] *Lib. 83 Quaest.*, q. 21 (PL 40, 16).   [9] Q. 4, a. 1.   [10] Q. 22, a. 2, ad 2; q. 48, a. 2.

which is penalty, but not of the evil which is fault, by reason of what is said above.

Reply Obj. 1. These passages refer to the evil of penalty, and not to the evil of fault.

Reply Obj. 2. The effect of the deficient secondary cause is reduced to the first non-deficient cause as regards what it has of being and perfection, but not as regards what it has of defect; just as whatever there is of motion in the act of limping is caused by the motive power, whereas what is unbalanced in it does not come from the motive power, but from the curvature of the leg. So, too, whatever there is of being and action in a bad action is reduced to God as the cause; whereas whatever defect is in it is not caused by God, but by the deficient secondary cause.

Reply Obj. 3. The sinking of a ship is attributed to the sailor as the cause from the fact that he does not fulfill what the safety of the ship requires; but God does not fail in doing what is necessary for safety. Hence there is no parity.

Third Article

WHETHER THERE BE ONE HIGHEST EVIL WHICH IS THE CAUSE OF EVERY EVIL?

We proceed thus to the Third Article:—

Objection 1. It would seem that there is one highest evil which is the cause of every evil. For contrary effects have contrary causes. But contrariety is found in things, according to *Ecclus.* xxxiii. 15: *Good is set against evil, and life against death; so also is the sinner against a just man.* Therefore there are contrary principles, one of good, the other of evil.

Obj. 2. Further, if one contrary is in nature, so is the other, as it is said in *De Caelo*, ii.[11] But the highest good is in nature, and is the cause of every good, as was shown above.[12] Therefore, there is also a highest evil opposed to it as the cause of every evil.

Obj. 3. Further, as we find good and better things, so we find evil and worse. But good and better are so considered in

[11] Aristotle, *De Caelo*, II, 3 (286a 23).   [12] Q. 2, a. 3; q. 6, a. 2 and 4.

relation to what is best. Therefore evil and worse are so considered in relation to some highest evil.

Obj. 4. Further, everything participated is reduced to what is essentially so. But things which are evil among us are evil, not essentially, but by participation. Therefore it is possible to find some highest essential evil, which is the cause of every evil.

Obj. 5. Further, whatever is accidental is reduced to that which is *per se.* But good is the accidental cause of evil. Therefore, we must suppose some highest evil which is the *per se* cause of evils. Nor can it be said that evil has no *per se* cause, but only an accidental cause; for it would then follow that evil would not exist in the majority of cases, but only in a few.

Obj. 6. Further, the evil of the effect is reduced to the evil of the cause; because the deficient effect comes from the deficient cause, as was said above. But we cannot proceed to infinity in this matter. Therefore, we must posit one first evil as the cause of every evil.

On the contrary, The highest good is the cause of every being, as was shown above.[13] Therefore there cannot be any principle opposed to it as the cause of evils.

I answer that, It appears from what precedes that there is no one first principle of evil, as there is one first principle of good.

First, because the first principle of good is essentially good, as was shown above.[14] But nothing can be evil in its very essence. For it was shown above that every being, as such, is good,[15] and that evil can exist only in good as in its subject.[16]

Secondly, because the first principle of good is the highest and perfect good which pre-contains in itself all goodness, as was shown above.[17] But there cannot be a highest evil, for, as was shown above, although evil always lessens good, yet it never wholly consumes it;[18] and thus, since the good always survives, nothing can be wholly and perfectly evil. Therefore, the Philosopher says that *if the wholly evil could be, it would destroy itself.*[19] For if all good were destroyed (which is essential for something to be wholly evil), evil itself would be taken away, since its subject is good.

[13] Q. 2, a. 3; q. 6, a. 4.   [14] Q. 6, a. 3 and 4.   [15] Q. 5, a. 3.   [16] Q. 48, a. 3.   [17] Q. 6, a. 2.   [18] Q. 48, a. 4.   [19] *Eth.,* IV, 5 (1126a 12).

Thirdly, because the very nature of evil is against the idea of a first principle; both because every evil is caused by good, as was shown above, and because evil can be only an accidental cause, and thus it cannot be the first cause, for the accidental cause is subsequent to an essential cause, as appears in *Physics* ii.[20]

Those, however, who upheld two first principles, one good and the other evil, fell into this error from the same cause, whence also arose other strange notions of the ancients.[21] For they failed to consider the universal cause of all being, and considered only the particular causes of particular effects. Hence on that account, if they found a thing injurious to something by the power of its own nature, they thought that the very nature of that thing was evil; as, for instance, if one were to say that the nature of fire was evil because it burnt the house of some poor man. The judgment, however, of the goodness of anything does not depend upon its reference to any particular thing, but rather upon what it is in itself, and on its reference to the whole universe, wherein every part has its own perfectly ordered place, as was said above.[22] So, too, because they found two contrary particular causes of two contrary particular effects, they did not know how to reduce these contrary particular causes to a universal common cause; and therefore they extended the contrariety of causes even to the first principles. But since all contraries agree in something common, it is necessary to search for one common cause for them above their own contrary causes; just as above the contrary qualities of the elements there exists the power of the body of the heavens, and above all things that exist, no matter how, there exists one first principle of being, as was shown above.[23]

Reply Obj. 1. Contraries agree in one genus, and they also agree in the nature of being; and therefore, although they have contrary particular causes, nevertheless we must come at last to one first common cause.

Reply Obj. 2. Privation and habit belong naturally to the same subject. Now the subject of privation is a being in potentiality, as was said above.[24] Hence, since evil is privation of good, as appears from what was said above,[25] it is opposed

---

[20] Aristotle, *Phys.*, II, 6 (198a 8).   [21] Cf. St. Thomas, *C. G.*, II, 41; St. Augustine, *De Haeres.*, 14; 21; 46 (PL 42, 28; 29; 37).   [22] Q. 47, a. 2, ad 1.   [23] Q. 2, a. 3.   [24] Q. 48, a. 3.   [25] *Ibid.*

to that good which has some potentiality, but not to the highest good, who is pure act.

Reply Obj. 3. Increase in intensity is in proportion to the nature of a thing. And just as the form is a perfection, so privation removes a perfection. Hence every form, perfection, and good is intensified by approach to a perfect terminus, while privation and evil are intensified by receding from that term. Hence a thing is not said to be evil and worse by reason of access to the highest evil, in the same way as a thing is said to be good and better by reason of access to the highest good.

Reply Obj. 4. No being is called evil by participation, but by privation of participation. Hence it is not necessary to reduce it to any essential evil.

Reply Obj. 5. Evil can have only an accidental cause, as was shown above. Hence reduction to any *per se* cause of evil is impossible. Hence, to say that evil is in the majority of cases is absolutely false. For things which are generated and corrupted, in which alone there can be natural evil, are a very small part of the whole universe. Then again, defects in nature are found in every species only in a small number of cases. In man alone does evil manifest itself in the majority of cases. For the good of man as regards the senses of the body is not the good of man as man, but the good according to the reason. More men, however, follow the sense rather than the reason.

Reply Obj. 6. In the causes of evil we do not proceed to infinity, but reduce all evils to some good cause, whence evil follows accidentally.

MAN; HIS POWERS; HIS KNOWLEDGE

Question LXXV

ON MAN WHO IS COMPOSED OF A SPIRITUAL AND A CORPOREAL SUBSTANCE: AND FIRST, CONCERNING WHAT BELONGS TO THE ESSENCE OF THE SOUL

(*In Seven Articles*)

HAVING treated of the spiritual and of the corporeal creature, we now proceed to treat of man, who is composed of a spiritual and of a corporeal substance. We shall treat first of the nature of man, and secondly of his origin.[1] Now the theologian considers the nature of man in relation to the soul, but not in relation to the body, except in so far as the body has relation to the soul. Hence the first object of our consideration will be the soul. And since Dionysius says that three things are to be found in spiritual substances—essence, power and operation[2]—we shall treat first of what belongs to the essence of the soul; secondly, of what belongs to its power;[3] thirdly, of what belongs to its operation.[4]

Concerning the first, two points have to be considered; the first is the nature of the soul considered in itself; the second is the union of the soul with the body.[5] Under the first head there are seven points of inquiry.

(1) Whether the soul is a body? (2) Whether the human soul is something subsistent? (3) Whether the souls of brute animals are subsistent? (4) Whether the soul is man, or is man composed of soul and body? (5) Whether the soul is composed of matter and form? (6) Whether the soul is incorruptible? (7) Whether the soul is of the same species as an angel?

---

[1] Q. 90.   [2] *De Cael. Hier.*, XI, 2 (PG 3, 284).   [3] Q. 77.   [4] Q. 84.   [5] Q. 76.

First Article

WHETHER THE SOUL IS A BODY?

We proceed thus to the First Article:—

Objection 1. It would seem that the soul is a body. For the soul is the mover of the body. Nor does it move unless moved. First, because apparently nothing can move unless it is itself moved, since nothing gives what it has not. For instance, what is not hot does not give heat. Secondly, because if there be anything that moves and is itself not moved, it must be the cause of eternal and uniform movement, as we find proved *Physics* viii.[6] Now this does not appear to be the case in the movement of an animal, which is caused by the soul. Therefore the soul is a moved mover. But every moved mover is a body. Therefore the soul is a body.

Obj. 2. Further, all knowledge is caused by means of a likeness. But there can be no likeness of a body to an incorporeal thing. If, therefore, the soul were not a body, it could not have knowledge of corporeal things.

Obj. 3. Further, between the mover and the moved there must be contact. But contact is only between bodies. Since, therefore, the soul moves the body, it seems that the soul must be a body.

On the contrary, Augustine says that the soul *is simple in comparison with the body, inasmuch as it does not occupy space by any bulk.*[7]

I answer that, To seek the nature of the soul, we must premise that the soul is defined as the first principle of life in those things in our world which live; for we call living things *animate,* and those things which have no life, *inanimate.* Now life is shown principally by two activities, knowledge and movement. The philosophers of old, not being able to rise above their imagination, supposed that the principle of these actions was something corporeal;[8] for they asserted that only bodies were real things, and that what is not corporeal is nothing.[9] Hence they maintained that the soul is

---

[6] Aristotle, *Phys.,* VIII, 10 (267b 3).   [7] *De Trin.,* VI, 6 (PL 42, 929).   [8] Democritus and Empedocles, according to Aristotle, *De An.,* I, 2 (404a 1; b 11).   [9] Cf. above, q. 50, a. 1.

some sort of body.[10] This opinion can be proved in many ways to be false; but we shall make use of only one proof, which shows quite universally and certainly that the soul is not a body.

It is manifest that not every principle of vital action is a soul, for then the eye would be a soul, as it is a principle of vision; and the same might be applied to the other instruments of the soul. But it is the *first* principle of life which we call the soul. Now, though a body may be a principle of life, as the heart is a principle of life in an animal, yet no body can be the first principle of life. For it is clear that to be a principle of life, or to be a living thing, does not belong to a body as a body, since, if that were the case, every body would be a living thing, or a principle of life. Therefore a body is competent to be a living thing, or even a principle of life, as *such* a body. Now that it is actually such a body it owes to some principle which is called its act. Therefore the soul, which is the first principle of life, is not a body, but the act of a body; just as heat, which is the principle of calefaction, is not a body, but an act of a body.

Reply Obj. 1. Since everything which is moved must be moved by something else, a process which cannot be prolonged indefinitely, we must allow that not every mover is moved. For, since to be moved is to pass from potentiality to actuality, the mover gives what it has to the thing moved, inasmuch as it causes it to be in act. But, as is shown in *Physics* viii., there is a mover which is altogether immovable, and which is not moved either essentially or accidentally; and such a mover can cause an eternally uniform movement.[11] There is, however, another kind of mover, which, though not moved essentially, is moved accidentally; and for this reason it does not cause a uniform movement. Such a mover is the soul. There is, again, another mover, which is moved essentially—namely, the body. And because the philosophers of old believed that nothing existed but bodies, they maintained that every mover is moved, and that the soul is moved essentially, and is a body.[12]

Reply Obj. 2. It is not necessary that the likeness of the

[10] Cf. Macrobius, *In Somn. Scipion.*, I, 14 (p. 543); Nemesius, *De Nat. Hom.*, II (PG 40, 536); St. Augustine, *De Civit. Dei*, VIII, 5 (PL 41, 230).   [11] Aristotle, *Phys.*, VIII, 5 (258b 4); 6 (258b 15); 10 (267b 3).   [12] Cf. Aristotle, *De An.*, I, 2 (403b 29).

thing known be actually in the nature of the knower. But given a being which knows potentially, and afterwards knows actually, the likeness of the thing known must be in the nature of the knower, not actually, but only potentially; and thus color is not actually in the pupil of the eye, but only potentially. Hence it is necessary, not that the likeness of corporeal things be actually in the nature of the soul, but that there be a potentiality in the soul for such a likeness. But the ancient naturalists did not know how to distinguish between actuality and potentiality;[13] and so they held that the soul must be a body in order to have knowledge of a body, and that it must be composed of the principles of which all bodies are formed.

Reply Obj. 3. There are two kinds of contact, that of *quantity*, and that of *power*. By the former a body can be touched only by a body; by the latter a body can be touched by an incorporeal reality, which moves that body.

Second Article

WHETHER THE HUMAN SOUL IS SOMETHING SUBSISTENT?

We proceed thus to the Second Article:—

Objection 1. It would seem that the human soul is not something subsistent. For that which subsists is said to be *this particular thing.* Now *this particular thing* is said not of the soul, but of that which is composed of soul and body. Therefore the soul is not something subsistent.

Obj. 2. Further, everything subsistent operates. But the soul does not operate, for, as the Philosopher says, *to say that the soul feels or understands is like saying that the soul weaves or builds.*[14] Therefore the soul is not subsistent.

Obj. 3. Further, if the soul were something subsistent, it would have some operation apart from the body. But it has no operation apart from the body, not even that of understanding; for the act of understanding does not take place without a phantasm, which cannot exist apart from the body. Therefore the human soul is not something subsistent.

On the contrary, Augustine says: *Whoever understands that the nature of the mind is that of a substance and not that of a body, will see that those who maintain the cor-*

[13] Cf. Aristotle, *De Gener.*, I, 10 (327b 23).   [14] *De An.*, I, 4 (408b 11).

*poreal nature of the mind are led astray because they as-
sociate with the mind those things without which they are
unable to think of any nature—i.e.,* imaginary pictures of
corporeal things.[15] Therefore the nature of the human mind
is not only incorporeal, but it is also a substance, that is,
something subsistent.

I answer that, It must necessarily be allowed that the
principle of intellectual operation, which we call the soul of
man, is a principle both incorporeal and subsistent. For it is
clear that by means of the intellect man can know all corporeal things. Now whatever knows certain things cannot have
any of them in its own nature, because that which is in it
naturally would impede the knowledge of anything else. Thus
we observe that a sick man's tongue, being unbalanced by a
feverish and bitter humor, is insensible to anything sweet,
and everything seems bitter to it. Therefore, if the intellectual principle contained within itself the nature of any body,
it would be unable to know all bodies. Now every body has
its own determinate nature. Therefore it is impossible for
the intellectual principle to be a body. It is also impossible
for it to understand by means of a bodily organ, since the
determinate nature of that organ would likewise impede
knowledge of all bodies; as when a certain determinate color
is not only in the pupil of the eye, but also in a glass vase,
the liquid in the vase seems to be of that same color.

Therefore the intellectual principle, which we call the mind
or the intellect, has essentially an operation in which the
body does not share. Now only that which subsists in itself
can have an operation in itself. For nothing can operate but
what is actual, and so a thing operates according as it is; for
which reason we do not say that heat imparts heat, but that
what is hot gives heat. We must conclude, therefore, that the
human soul, which is called intellect or mind, is something
incorporeal and subsistent.

Reply Obj. 1. *This particular thing* can be taken in two
senses. Firstly, for anything subsistent; secondly, for that
which subsists and is complete in a specific nature. The former sense excludes the inherence of an accident or of a material form; the latter excludes also the imperfection of the
part, so that a hand can be called *this particular thing* in the
first sense, but not in the second. Therefore, since the human

[15] *De Trin.*, X, 7 (PL 42, 979).

soul is a part of human nature, it can be called *this particular thing* in the first sense, as being something subsistent; but not in the second, for in this sense the composite of body and soul is said to be *this particular thing*.

Reply Obj. 2. Aristotle wrote those words as expressing, not his own opinion, but the opinion of those who said that to understand is to be moved, as is clear from the context.[16] Or we may reply that to operate through itself belongs to what exists through itself. But for a thing to exist through itself, it suffices sometimes that it be not inherent, as an accident or a material form; even though it be part of something. Nevertheless, that is rightly said to subsist through itself which is neither inherent in the above sense, nor part of anything else. In this sense, the eye or the hand cannot be said to subsist through itself; nor can it for that reason be said to operate through itself. Hence the operation of the parts is through each part attributed to the whole. For we say that man sees with the eye, and feels with the hand, and not in the same sense as when we say that what is hot gives heat by its heat; for heat, strictly speaking, does not give heat. We may therefore say that the soul understands just as the eye sees; but it is more correct to say that man understands through the soul.

Reply Obj. 3. The body is necessary for the action of the intellect; not as its organ of action, but on the part of the object; for the phantasm is to the intellect what color is to the sight. Neither does such a dependence on the body prove the intellect to be non-subsistent, or otherwise it would follow that an animal is non-subsistent simply because it requires external sensibles for sensation.

Fourth Article

WHETHER THE SOUL IS MAN?

We proceed thus to the Fourth Article:—

Objection 1. It would seem that the soul is man. For it is written (2 *Cor.* iv. 16): *Though our outward man is corrupted, yet the inward man is renewed day by day.* But that which is within man is the soul. Therefore the soul is the inward man.

[16] *De An.,* I, 4 (408a 34).

Obj. 2. Further, the human soul is a substance. But it is not a universal substance. Therefore it is a particular substance. Therefore it is a *hypostasis* or a person; and it can be only a human person. Therefore the soul is a man, for a human person is a man.

On the contrary, Augustine commends Varro as holding *that man is not the soul alone, nor the body alone, but both soul and body.*[17]

I answer that, The assertion, *the soul is a man,* can be taken in two senses. First, that man is a soul, though this particular man (Socrates, for instance) is not a soul, but composed of soul and body. I say this, because some held that the form alone belongs to the species,[18] while matter is part of the individual, and not of the species. This cannot be true, for to the nature of the species belongs what the definition signifies, and in natural things the definition does not signify the form only, but the form and the matter. Hence, in natural things the matter is part of the species; not, indeed, signate matter, which is the principle of individuation, but common matter. For just as it belongs to the nature of this particular man to be composed of this soul, of this flesh, and of these bones, so it belongs to the nature of man to be composed of soul, flesh, and bones; for whatever belongs in common to the substance of all the individuals contained under a given species must belong also to the substance of the species.

That *the soul is a man* may also be understood in this sense, namely, that this soul is this man. Now this could be held if it were supposed that the operation of the sensitive soul were proper to it without the body; because in that case all the operations which are attributed to man would belong only to the soul. But each thing is that which performs its own operations, and consequently that is man which performs the operations of a man. But it has been shown above that sensation is not the operation of the soul alone. Since, then, sensation is an operation of man, but not proper to the soul, it is clear that man is not only a soul, but something composed of soul and body.—Plato, through supposing that

[17] *De Civit. Dei,* XIX, 3 (PL 41, 626).   [18] Averroes, *In Metaph.,* VII, comm. 21; comm. 24 (VIII, 80v; 82v).—Cf. St. Thomas, *In Metaph,* VII, lect. 9.

sensation was proper to the soul, could maintain man to be *a soul making use of a body*.[19]

Reply Obj. 1. According to the Philosopher, each thing seems to be chiefly what is most important in it.[20] Thus, what the governor of a state does, the state is said to do. In this way sometimes what is most important in man is said to be man: sometimes it is the intellectual part which, in accordance with truth, is called the *inward* man; and sometimes the sensitive part with the body is called man in the opinion of those who remain the slaves of sensible things. And this is called the *outward* man.

Reply Obj. 2. Not every particular substance is a hypostasis or a person, but that which has the complete nature of its species. Hence a hand, or a foot, is not called a hypostasis, or a person; nor, likewise, is the soul alone so called, since it is a part of the human species.

Sixth Article

WHETHER THE HUMAN SOUL IS CORRUPTIBLE?

We proceed thus to the Sixth Article:—

Objection 1. It would seem that the human soul is corruptible. For those things that have a like beginning and process seemingly have a like end. But the beginning of men, by generation, is like that of animals, for they are made from the earth. And the process of life is alike in both; because *all things breathe alike, and man hath nothing more than the beast*, as it is written (*Eccles*. iii. 19). Therefore, as the same text concludes, *the death of man and beast is one, and the condition of both is equal*. But the souls of brute animals are corruptible. Therefore the human soul too is corruptible.

Obj. 2. Further, whatever is out of nothing can return to nothingness, because the end should correspond to the beginning. But as it is written (*Wis*. ii. 2), *We are born of nothing;* and this is true, not only of the body, but also of the soul. Therefore, as is concluded in the same passage, *After this we shall be as if we had not been,* even as to our soul.

Obj. 3. Further, nothing is without its own proper opera-

---

[19] Cf. Nemesius, *De Nat. Hom.*, I (PG 40, 505).—Plato, *Alcib*. (p. 130c).   [20] *Eth.*, IX, 8 (1168b 31).

tion. But the operation proper to the soul, which is to understand through a phantasm, cannot be without the body. For the soul understands nothing without a phantasm, and *there is no phantasm without the body,* as the Philosopher says.[21] Therefore the soul cannot survive the dissolution of the body.

On the contrary, Dionysius says that human souls owe to divine goodness that they are *intellectual,* and that they have *an incorruptible substantial life.*[22]

I answer that, We must assert that the intellectual principle which we call the human soul is incorruptible. For a thing may be corrupted in two ways—in itself and accidentally. Now it is impossible for any subsistent being to be generated or corrupted accidentally, that is, by the generation or corruption of something else. For generation and corruption belong to a thing in the same way that being belongs to it, which is acquired by generation and lost by corruption. Therefore, whatever has being in itself cannot be generated or corrupted except in itself; while things which do not subsist, such as accidents and material forms, acquire being or lose it through the generation or corruption of composites. Now it was shown above that the souls of brutes are not self-subsistent, whereas the human soul is, so that the souls of brutes are corrupted, when their bodies are corrupted, while the human soul could not be corrupted unless it were corrupted in itself. This is impossible, not only as regards the human soul, but also as regards anything subsistent that is a form alone. For it is clear that what belongs to a thing by virtue of the thing itself is inseparable from it. But being belongs to a form, which is an act, by virtue of itself. And thus, matter acquires actual being according as it acquires form; while it is corrupted so far as the form is separated from it. But it is impossible for a form to be separated from itself; and therefore it is impossible for a subsistent form to cease to exist.

Granted even that the soul were composed of matter and form, as some pretend,[23] we should nevertheless have to maintain that it is incorruptible. For corruption is found only where there is contrariety, since generation and corruption are from contraries and into contraries. Therefore the heavenly bodies, since they have no matter subject to con-

[21] Aristotle, *De An.,* I, 1 (403a 9).   [22] *De Div. Nom.,* IV, 2 (PG 3, 696).   [23] Cf. above, a. 5 and q. 50, a. 2.

trariety, are incorruptible. Now there can be no contrariety
in the intellectual soul; for it is a receiving subject according
to the manner of its being, and those things which it receives
are without contrariety. Thus, the notions even of contraries
are not themselves contrary, since contraries belong to the
same science. Therefore it is impossible for the intellectual
soul to be corruptible.

Moreover we may take a sign of this from the fact that
everything naturally aspires to being after its own manner.
Now, in things that have knowledge, desire ensues upon
knowledge. The senses indeed do not know being, except under the conditions of *here* and *now*, whereas the intellect apprehends being absolutely, and for all time; so that everything that has an intellect naturally desires always to exist.
But a natural desire cannot be in vain. Therefore every intellectual substance is incorruptible.

Reply Obj. 1. Solomon reasons thus in the person of the
foolish, as expressed in the words of *Wis.* ii. Therefore the
saying that man and animals have a like beginning in generation is true of the body; for all animals alike are made of
earth. But it is not true of the soul. For while the souls of
brutes are produced by some power of the body, the human
soul is produced by God. To signify this, it is written of other
animals: *Let the earth bring forth the living soul* (*Gen.* i.
24); while of man it is written (*Gen.* ii. 7) that *He breathed
into his face the breath of life.* And so in the last chapter of
Ecclesiastes (xii. 7) it is concluded: *The dust returns into
its earth from whence it was; and the spirit returns to God
Who gave it.* Again, the process of life is alike as to the body,
concerning which it is written (*Eccles.* iii. 19): *All things
breathe alike*, and (*Wis.* ii. 2), *The breath in our nostrils is
smoke.* But the process is not alike in the case of the soul,
for man has understanding whereas animals do not. Hence
it is false to say: *Man has nothing more than beasts.* Thus
death comes to both alike as to the body, but not as to the
soul.

Reply Obj. 2. As a thing can be created, not by reason of
a passive potentiality, but only by reason of the active potentiality of the Creator, Who can produce something out of
nothing, so when we say that a thing can be reduced to nothing, we do not imply in the creature a potentiality to non-
being, but in the Creator the power of ceasing to sustain

being. But a thing is said to be corruptible because there is in it a potentiality to non-being.

Reply Obj. 3. To understand through a phantasm is the proper operation of the soul by virtue of its union with the body. After separation from the body, it will have another mode of understanding, similar to other substances separated from bodies, as will appear later on.[24]

[24] Q. 89, a. 1.

THE UNION OF BODY AND SOUL

(*In Eight Articles*)

WE NOW consider the union of the soul with the body, on which there are eight points for inquiry: (1) Whether the intellectual principle is united to the body as its form? (2) Whether the intellectual principle is multiplied numerically according to the number of bodies, or is there one intellect for all men? (3) Whether in a body, the form of which is an intellectual principle, there is some other soul? (4) Whether in that body there is any other substantial form? (5) Of the qualities required in the body of which the intellectual principle is the form? (6) Whether the intellectual soul is joined to the body by means of accidental dispositions? (7) Whether the intellectual soul is united to such a body by means of another body? (8) Whether the soul is wholly in each part of the body?

First Article

WHETHER THE INTELLECTUAL PRINCIPLE IS UNITED TO THE BODY AS ITS FORM?

We proceed thus to the First Article:—

Objection 1. It seems that the intellectual principle is not united to the body as its form. For the Philosopher says that *the intellect is separate,* and that it is not the act of any body.[1] Therefore it is not united to the body as its form.

Obj. 2. Further, every form is determined according to the nature of the matter of which it is the form; otherwise no proportion would be required between matter and form. Therefore if the intellect were united to the body as its form, since every body has a determinate nature, it would follow that the intellect has a determinate nature; and thus, it would not be capable of knowing all things, as is clear from what has been said.[2] This is contrary to the nature of the intellect. Therefore the intellect is not united to the body as its form.

Obj. 3. Further, whatever receptive power is an act of a

[1] *De An.,* III, 4 (429b 5). [2] Q. 75, a. 2.

body, receives a form materially and individually; for what is received must be received according to the condition of the receiver. But the form of the thing understood is not received into the intellect materially and individually, but rather immaterially and universally. Otherwise, the intellect would not be capable of knowing immaterial and universal objects, but only individuals, like the senses. Therefore the intellect is not united to the body as its form.

Obj. 4. Further, power and action have the same subject, for the same subject is what can, and does, act. But intellectual action is not the action of a body, as appears from the above.[3] Therefore neither is the intellectual power a power of the body. But a virtue or a power cannot be more abstract or more simple than the essence from which the virtue or power is derived. Therefore, neither is the substance of the intellect the form of a body.

Obj. 5. Further, whatever has being in itself is not united to the body as its form, because a form is that *by which* a thing exists; which means that the very being of a form does not belong to the form by itself. But the intellectual principle has being in itself and is subsistent, as was said above.[4] Therefore it is not united to the body as its form.

Obj. 6. Further, whatever exists in a thing by reason of its nature exists in it always. But to be united to matter belongs to the form by reason of its nature, because form is the act of matter, not by any accidental quality, but by its own essence; or otherwise matter and form would not make a thing substantially one, but only accidentally one. Therefore, a form cannot be without its own proper matter. But the intellectual principle, since it is incorruptible, as was shown above,[5] remains separate from the body, after the dissolution of the body. Therefore the intellectual principle is not united to the body as its form.

On the contrary, According to the Philosopher in *Metaph.* viii., difference is derived from the form.[6] But the difference which constitutes man is *rational*, which is said of man because of his intellectual principle. Therefore the intellectual principle is the form of man.

I answer that, We must assert that the intellect which is the principle of intellectual operation is the form of the human body. For that whereby primarily anything acts is a

[3] *Ibid.*   [4] *Ibid.*   [5] Q. 75, a. 6.   [6] *Metaph.*, VII, 2 (1043a 19).

form of the thing to which the act is attributed. For instance, that whereby a body is primarily healed is health, and that whereby the soul knows primarily is knowledge; hence health is a form of the body, and knowledge is a form of the soul. The reason for this is that nothing acts except so far as it is in act; and so, a thing acts by that whereby it is in act. Now it is clear that the first thing by which the body lives is the soul. And as life appears through various operations in different degrees of living things, that whereby we primarily perform each of all these vital actions is the soul. For the soul is the primary principle of our nourishment, sensation, and local movement; and likewise of our understanding. Therefore this principle by which primarily we understand, whether it be called the intellect or the intellectual soul, is the form of the body. This is the demonstration used by Aristotle.[7]

But if anyone say that the intellectual soul is not the form of the body,[8] he must explain how it is that this action of understanding is the action of this particular man; for each one is conscious that it is he himself who understands. Now an action may be attributed to anyone in three ways, as is clear from the Philosopher.[9] For a thing is said to move or act, either by virtue of its whole self, for instance, as a physician heals; or by virtue of a part, as a man sees by his eye; or through an accidental quality, as when we say that something that is white builds, because it is accidental to the builder to be white. So when we say that Socrates or Plato understands, it is clear that this is not attributed to him accidentally, since it is ascribed to him as man, which is predicated of him essentially. We must therefore say either that Socrates understands by virtue of his whole self, as Plato maintained, holding that man is an intellectual soul;[10] or that the intellect is a part of Socrates. The first cannot stand, as was shown above, because it is one and the same man who is conscious both that he understands and that he senses.[11] But one cannot sense without a body, and therefore the body must be some part of man. It follows therefore that the in-

---

[7] *De An.*, II, 2 (414a 12).   [8] Cf. St. Albert, *Summa de Creatur.*, II, q. 4, a. 1 (XXXV, 34).—Cf. also Avicenna, *De An.*, I, 1 (1rb); V, 4 (24va).   [9] *Phys.*, V, 1 (224a 31).   [10] Cf. above, q. 75, a. 4. [11] *Ibid.*

tellect by which Socrates understands is a part of Socrates, so that it is in some way united to the body of Socrates.

As to this union, the Commentator held that it is through the intelligible species,[12] as having a double subject, namely, the possible intellect and the phantasms which are in the corporeal organs. Thus, through the intelligible species, the possible intellect *is linked* to the body of this or that particular man. But this link or union does not sufficiently explain the fact that the act of the intellect is the act of Socrates. This can be clearly seen from comparison with the sensitive power, from which Aristotle proceeds to consider things relating to the intellect. For the relation of phantasms to the intellect is like the relation of colors to the sense of sight, as he says *De Anima* iii.[13] Therefore, just as the species of colors are in the sight, so the species of phantasms are in the possible intellect. Now it is clear that because the colors, the likenesses of which are in the sight, are on a wall, the action of seeing is not attributed to the wall; for we do not say that the wall sees, but rather that it is seen. Therefore, from the fact that the species of phantasms are in the possible intellect, it does not follow that Socrates, in whom are the phantasms, understands, but that he or his phantasms are understood.

Some,[14] however, have tried to maintain that the intellect is united to the body as its mover, and hence that the intellect and body form one thing in such a way that the act of the intellect could be attributed to the whole. This is, however, absurd for many reasons. First, because the intellect does not move the body except through the appetite, whose movement presupposes the operation of the intellect. The reason therefore why Socrates understands is not because he is moved by his intellect, but rather, contrariwise, he is moved by his intellect because he understands.—Secondly, because, since Socrates is an individual in a nature of one essence composed of matter and form, if the intellect be not the form, it follows that it must be outside the essence, and then the intellect is to the whole Socrates as a motor to the thing moved. But to understand is an action that remains in the agent, and does not pass into something else, as does the

[12] *In De An.*, III, comm. 5 (VI, 164v).   [13] Aristotle, *De An.*, III, 7 (431a 14).   [14] Cf. William of Auvergne, *De An.*, I, 7 (II, Suppl., 72); VI, 35 (II, Suppl., 194).

action of heating. Therefore the action of understanding cannot be attributed to Socrates for the reason that he is moved by his intellect.—Thirdly, because the action of a mover is never attributed to the thing moved, except as to an instrument, just as the action of a carpenter is attributed to a saw. Therefore, if understanding is attributed to Socrates as the action of his mover, it follows that it is attributed to him as to an instrument. This is contrary to the teaching of the Philosopher, who holds that understanding is not possible through a corporeal instrument.[15]—Fourthly, because, although the action of a part be attributed to the whole, as the action of the eye is attributed to a man, yet it is never attributed to another part, except perhaps accidentally; for we do not say that the hand sees because the eye sees. Therefore, if the intellect and Socrates are united in the above manner, the action of the intellect cannot be attributed to Socrates. If, however, Socrates be a whole composed of a union of the intellect with whatever else belongs to Socrates, but with the supposition that the intellect is united to the other parts of Socrates only as a mover, it follows that Socrates is not one absolutely, and consequently neither a being absolutely, for a thing is a being according as it is one.

There remains, therefore, no other explanation than that given by Aristotle—namely, that this particular man understands because the intellectual principle is his form.[16] Thus from the very operation of the intellect it is made clear that the intellectual principle is united to the body as its form.

The same can be clearly shown from the nature of the human species. For the nature of each thing is shown by its operation. Now the proper operation of man as man is to understand, for it is in this that he surpasses all animals. Whence Aristotle concludes that the ultimate happiness of man must consist in this operation as properly belonging to him.[17] Man must therefore derive his species from that which is the principle of this operation. But the species of each thing is derived from its form. It follows therefore that the intellectual principle is the proper form of man.

But we must observe that the nobler a form is, the more it rises above corporeal matter, the less it is subject to matter, and the more it excels matter by its power and its operation.

[15] De An., III, 4 (429a 26).   [16] Op. cit., II, 2 (414a 12).—Cf. C. G., II, 59.   [17] Eth., X, 7 (1177a 17).

Hence we find that the form of a mixed body has an operation not caused by its elemental qualities. And the higher we advance in the nobility of forms, the more we find that the power of the form excels the elementary matter; as the vegetative soul excels the form of the metal, and the sensitive soul excels the vegetative soul. Now the human soul is the highest and noblest of forms. Therefore, in its power it excels corporeal matter by the fact that it has an operation and a power in which corporeal matter has no share whatever. This power is called the intellect.

It is well to remark, furthermore, that if anyone held that the soul is composed of matter and form,[18] it would follow that in no way could the soul be the form of the body. For since form is an act, and matter is being only in potentiality, that which is composed of matter and form cannot in its entirety be the form of another. But if it is a form by virtue of some part of itself, then that part which is the form we call the soul, and that of which it is the form we call the *primary animate*, as was said above.[19]

Reply Obj. 1. As the Philosopher says,[20] the highest natural form (namely, the human soul) to which the consideration of the natural philosopher is directed is indeed separate, but it exists in matter. He proves this from the fact that *man and the sun generate man from matter.* It is separate according to its intellectual power, because an intellectual power is not the power of a corporeal organ, as the power of seeing is the act of the eye; for understanding is an act which cannot be performed by a corporeal organ, as can the act of seeing. But it exists in matter in so far as the soul itself, to which this power belongs, is the form of the body, and the term of human generation. And so the Philosopher says that *the intellect is separate,*[21] because it is not the power of a corporeal organ.

From this it is clear how to answer the Second and Third objections. For in order that man may be able to understand all things by means of his intellect, and that his intellect may understand all things immaterial and universal, it is sufficient that the intellectual power be not the act of the body.

Reply Obj. 4. The human soul, by reason of its perfection, is not a form immersed in matter, or entirely embraced by

[18] Cf. above, q. 75, a. 5; q. 50, a. 2.   [19] Q. 75, a. 5.   [20] *Phys.*, II, 2 (194b 12).   [21] *De An.*, III, 4 (429b 5).

matter. Therefore there is nothing to prevent some power of the soul from not being the act of the body, although the soul is essentially the form of the body.

Reply Obj. 5. The soul communicates that being in which it subsists to the corporeal matter, out of which and the intellectual soul there results one being; so that the being of the whole composite is also the being of the soul. This is not the case with other non-subsistent forms. For this reason the human soul retains its own being after the dissolution of the body; whereas it is not so with other forms.

Reply Obj. 6. To be united to the body belongs to the soul by reason of itself, just as it belongs to a light body by reason of itself to be raised up. And just as a light body remains light, when removed from its proper place, retaining meanwhile an aptitude and an inclination for its proper place, so the human soul retains its proper being when separated from the body, having an aptitude and a natural inclination to be united to the body.

Second Article

WHETHER THE INTELLECTUAL PRINCIPLE IS MULTIPLIED ACCORDING TO THE NUMBER OF BODIES?

We proceed thus to the Second Article:—

Objection 1. It would seem that the intellectual principle is not multiplied according to the number of bodies, but that there is one intellect in all men. For an immaterial substance is not multiplied numerically within one species. But the human soul is an immaterial substance, since it is not composed of matter and form, as was shown above.[22] Therefore there are not many human souls in one species. But all men are of one species. Therefore there is but one intellect in all men.

Obj. 2. Further, when the cause is removed, the effect is also removed. Therefore, if human souls were multiplied according to the number of bodies, it would follow that if the bodies were removed, the number of souls would not remain, but from all the souls there would be but a single remainder. This is heretical, for it would do away with the distinction of rewards and punishments.

Obj. 3. Further, if my intellect is distinct from your in-

[22] Q. 75, a. 5.

tellect, my intellect is an individual, and so is yours; for individuals are things which differ in number but agree in one species.[23] Now whatever is received into anything must be received according to the condition of the receiver. Therefore the species of things would be received individually into my intellect, and also into yours; which is contrary to the nature of the intellect, which knows universals.

Obj. 4. Further, the thing understood is in the intellect which understands. If, therefore, my intellect is distinct from yours, what is understood by me must be distinct from what is understood by you; and consequently it will be reckoned *as something individual, and be only potentially something understood.*[24] Hence, the common intention will have to be abstracted from both, since from things which are diverse something intelligible and common to them may be abstracted. But this is contrary to the nature of the intellect, for then the intellect would not seem to be distinct from the imagination. It seems to follow, therefore, that there is one intellect in all men.

Obj. 5. Further, when the disciple receives knowledge from the teacher, it cannot be said that the teacher's knowledge begets knowledge in the disciple, because then knowledge too would be an active form, such as heat is; which is clearly false. It seems, therefore, that the same individual knowledge which is in the teacher is communicated to the disciple.[25] This cannot be, unless there is one intellect in both. Seemingly, therefore, the intellect of the disciple and teacher is but one; and, consequently, the same applies to all men.

Obj. 6. Further, Augustine says: *If I were to say that there are many human souls, I should laugh at myself.*[26] But the soul seems to be one chiefly because of the intellect. Therefore there is one intellect of all men.

On the contrary, The Philosopher says that the relation of universal causes to what is universal is like the relation of particular causes to individuals.[27] But it is impossible that a soul, one in species, should belong to animals of different species. Therefore it is impossible that one individual intellectual soul should belong to several individuals.

[23] Cf. Averroes, *In De An.*, III, comm. 5 (VI, 166r).   [24] *Ibid.* (VI, 163v-164r).   [25] Cf. Averroes, *In De An.*, III, comm. 5 (VI, 166rv).   [26] *De Quant. An.*, XXXII (PL 32, 1073).   [27] *Phys.*, II, 3 (195b 26).

I answer that, It is absolutely impossible for one intellect to belong to all men. This is clear if, as Plato maintained, man is the intellect itself.[28] For if Socrates and Plato have one intellect, it would follow that Socrates and Plato are one man, and that they are not distinct from each other, except by something outside the essence of each. The distinction between Socrates and Plato would then not be other than that of one man with a tunic and another with a cloak; which is quite absurd.

It is likewise clear that this is impossible if, according to the opinion of Aristotle, it is supposed that the intellect is a part or a power of the soul which is the form of man.[29] For it is impossible for many distinct individuals to have one form, just as it is impossible for them to have one being. For the form is the principle of being.

Again, this is clearly impossible, whatever one may hold as to the manner of the union of the intellect to this or that man. For it is manifest that, if there is one principal agent, and two instruments, we can say without qualification that there is one agent but several actions; as when one man touches several things with his two hands, there will be one who touches, but two contacts. If, on the contrary, we suppose one instrument and several principal agents, we can say that there are several agents, but one act; for example, if there be many pulling a ship by means of a rope, those who pull will be many, but the pulling will be one. If, however, there is one principal agent, and one instrument, we say that there is one agent and one action; as when the smith strikes with one hammer, there is one striker and one stroke. Now it is clear that no matter how the intellect is united or joined to this or that man, the intellect has the primacy among all the other things which pertain to man, for the sensitive powers obey the intellect, and are at its service. So if we suppose two men to have two intellects and one sense,—for instance, if two men had one eye,—there would be two seers, but one seeing. But if the intellect is held to be one, no matter how diverse may be all those things which the intellect uses as instruments, it is in no way possible to say that Socrates and Plato are more than one understanding man. And if to this we add that to understand, which is the act of the intellect,

---

[28] Cf. above, q. 75, a. 4.   [29] *De An.*, II, 2 (414a 13); 3 (414a 32).

is not produced by any organ other than the intellect itself, it will further follow that there is but one agent and one action; in other words, all men are but one "understander," and have but one act of understanding,—I mean, of course, in relation to one and the same intelligible object.

Now, it would be possible to distinguish my intellectual action from yours by the distinction of the phantasms—because there is one phantasm of a stone in me, and another in you—if the phantasm itself, according as it is one thing in me and another in you, were a form of the possible intellect. For the same agent produces diverse actions through diverse forms. Thus, through the diverse forms in things in relation to the same eye, there are diverse "seeings." But the phantasm itself is not the form of the possible intellect; the intelligible species abstracted from phantasms is such a form. Now in one intellect, from different phantasms of the same species, only one intelligible species is abstracted; as appears in one man, in whom there may be different phantasms of a stone, and yet from all of them only one intelligible species of a stone is abstracted, by which the intellect of that one man, by one operation, understands the nature of a stone, notwithstanding the diversity of phantasms. Therefore, if there were one intellect for all men, the diversity of phantasms in this man and in that would not cause a diversity of intellectual operation in this man and that man, as the Commentator imagines.[30] It follows, therefore, that it is altogether impossible and inappropriate to posit one intellect for all men.

Reply Obj. 1. Although the intellectual soul, like the angel, has no matter from which it is produced, yet it is the form of a certain matter; in which it is unlike an angel. Therefore, according to the division of matter, there are many souls of one species; while it is quite impossible for many angels to be of one species.

Reply Obj. 2. Everything has unity in the same way that it has being, and consequently we must judge of the multiplicity of a thing as we judge of its being. Now it is clear that the intellectual soul is according to its very being united to the body as its form. And yet, after the dissolution of the body, the intellectual soul retains its own being. In like man-

---

[30] *In De An.*, III, comm. 5 (VI, 166v).

ner, the multiplicity of souls is in proportion to the multiplicity of bodies; and yet, after the dissolution of the bodies, the souls remain multiplied in their being.

Reply Obj. 3. The individuality of the understanding being, or of the species whereby it understands, does not exclude the understanding of universals; or otherwise, since separate intellects are subsistent substances, and consequently individual, they could not understand universals. But it is the materiality of the knower, and of the species whereby he knows, that impedes the knowledge of the universal. For as every action is according to the mode of the form by which the agent acts, as heating is according to the mode of the heat, so knowledge is according to the mode of the species by which the knower knows. Now it is clear that the common nature becomes distinct and multiplied by reason of the individuating principles which come from the matter. Therefore if the form, which is the means of knowledge, is material —that is, not abstracted from material conditions—its likeness to the nature of a species or genus will be according to the distinction and multiplication of that nature by means of individuating principles; so that the knowledge of the nature in its community will be impossible. But if the species be abstracted from the conditions of individual matter, there will be a likeness of the nature without those things which make it distinct and multiplied. And thus there will be knowledge of the universal. Nor does it matter, as to this particular point, whether there be one intellect or many; because, even if there were but one, it would necessarily be an individual intellect, and the species whereby it understands, an individual species.

Reply Obj. 4. Whether the intellect be one or many, what is understood is one. For what is understood is in the intellect, not in itself, but according to its likeness; for *the stone is not in the soul, but its likeness is,* as is said *De Anima* iii.[31] Yet it is the stone which is understood, not the likeness of the stone, except by a reflection of the intellect on itself. Otherwise, the objects of sciences would not be things, but only intelligible species. Now it is possible for different things, according to different forms, to be likened to the same thing. And since knowledge is begotten according to the

[31] Aristotle, *De An.*, III, 8 (431b 29).

assimilation of the knower to the thing known, it follows
that the same thing can be known by several knowers; as is
apparent in regard to the senses, for several see the same
color by means of diverse likenesses. In the same way several
intellects understand one thing. But there is this difference,
according to the opinion of Aristotle,[32] between the sense and
the intellect—that a thing is perceived by the sense according to that disposition which it has outside the soul—that is,
in its individuality; whereas, though the nature of the thing
understood is outside the soul, yet its mode of being outside
the soul is not the mode of being according to which it is
known. For the common nature is understood as apart from
the individuating principles; whereas such is not its mode of
being outside the soul. (But according to the opinion of Plato,
the thing understood exists outside the soul in the same way
as it is understood.[33] For Plato supposed that the natures
of things exist separate from matter.)

Reply Obj. 5. One knowledge exists in the disciple and another in the teacher. How it is caused will be shown later
on.[34]

Reply Obj. 6. Augustine denies such a plurality of souls as
would involve a denial of their communication in the one
nature of the species.

Third Article

WHETHER BESIDES THE INTELLECTUAL SOUL THERE ARE
IN MAN OTHER SOULS ESSENTIALLY DIFFERENT FROM
ONE ANOTHER?

We proceed thus to the Third Article:—
Objection 1. It would seem that besides the intellectual
soul there are in man other souls essentially different from
one another, namely, the sensitive soul and the nutritive soul.
For corruptible and incorruptible are not of the same substance. But the intellectual soul is incorruptible, whereas the
other souls, namely, the sensitive and the nutritive, are corruptible, as was shown above.[35] Therefore in man the essence
of the intellectual soul, the sensitive soul and the nutritive
soul cannot be the same.

[32] *Ibid.* (432a 2).   [33] Cf. above, q. 6, a. 4.   [34] Q. 117, a. 1.
[35] Q. 75, a. 6.

Obj. 2. Further, if it be said that the sensitive soul in man is incorruptible, against this is the dictum that the *corruptible and the incorruptible differ generically,* according to the Philosopher in *Metaph.* x.[36] But the sensitive soul in the horse, the lion, and other brute animals, is corruptible. If, therefore, in man it be incorruptible, the sensitive soul in man and brute animals will not be of the same *genus.* Now, an animal is so called because it has a sensitive soul; and, therefore, *animal* will not be one genus common to man and other animals, which is absurd.

Obj. 3. Further, the Philosopher says that the embryo is an animal before it is a man.[37] But this would be impossible if the essence of the sensitive soul were the same as that of the intellectual soul; for an animal is such by its sensitive soul, while a man is a man by the intellectual soul. Therefore in man the essence of the sensitive soul is not the same as the essence of the intellectual soul.

Obj. 4. Further, the Philosopher says in *Metaph.* viii., that the genus is taken from the matter, and difference from the form.[38] But *rational,* which is the difference constituting man, is taken from the intellectual soul; while he is called *animal* by reason of his having a body animated by a sensitive soul. Therefore the intellectual soul is compared to the body animated by a sensitive soul as form to matter. Therefore in man the intellectual soul is not essentially the same as the sensitive soul, but presupposes it as a material subject.

On the contrary, It is said in the book *De Ecclesiasticis Dogmatibus: Nor do we say that there are two souls in one man, as James and other Syrians write,—one, animal, by which the body is animated, and which is mingled with the blood; the other, spiritual, which obeys the reason; but we say that it is one and the same soul in man which both gives life to the body by being united to it, and orders itself by its own reason.*[39]

I answer that, Plato held that there were several souls in one body, distinct even according to organs. To these souls he referred the different vital actions, saying that the nutri-

[36] Aristotle, *Metaph.,* IX, 10 (1059a 10).   [37] *De Gener. Anim.,* II, 3 (736a 35).   [38] *Metaph.,* VII, 2 (1043a 5; a 19); cf. *op. cit.,* VI, 12 (1038a 6).   [39] Gennadius, *De Eccles. Dogm.,* XV (PL 58, 984).—Cf. Pseudo-Augustine (Alcher of Clairvaux), *De Spir. et An.,* 48 (PL 40, 814).

tive power is in the liver, the concupiscible in the heart, and the knowing power in the brain.[40] Which opinion is rejected by Aristotle with reference to those parts of the soul which use corporeal organs.[41] His reason is that in those animals which continue to live when they have been divided, in each part are observed the operations of the soul, such as those of sense and appetite. Now this would not be the case if the various principles of the soul's operations were essentially diverse in their distribution through the various parts of the body. But with regard to the intellectual part, Aristotle seems to leave it in doubt whether it be *only logically* distinct from the other parts of the soul, *or also locally*.

The opinion of Plato could be maintained if, as he held, the soul were united to the body, not as its form, but as its mover. For nothing incongruous is involved if the same movable thing be moved by several movers; and still less if it be moved according to its various parts. If we suppose, however, that the soul is united to the body as its form, it is quite impossible for several essentially different souls to be in one body. This can be made clear by three reasons.

In the first place, an animal in which there were several souls would not be absolutely one. For nothing is absolutely one except by one form, by which a thing has being; because a thing has both being and unity from the same source, and therefore things which are denominated by various forms are not absolutely one; as, for instance, *a white man*. If, therefore, man were *living* by one form, the vegetative soul, and *animal* by another form, the sensitive soul, and *man* by another form, the intellectual soul, it would follow that man is not absolutely one. Thus Aristotle argues in *Metaph.* viii., against Plato, that if the Idea of an animal is distinct from the Idea of a biped, then a biped animal is not absolutely one.[42] For this reason, against those who hold that there are several souls in the body, he asks, *what contains them?*— that is, what makes them one? [43] It cannot be said that they are united by the unity of the body; because it is rather the soul that contains the body and makes it one, than the reverse.

[40] Cf. Averroes, *In De An.*, I, comm. 90 (VI, 125v).—Cf. also Plato, *Timaeus* (p. 69e).   [41] *De An.*, II, 2 (413b 13).   [42] *Metaph.*, VII, 6 (1045a 14).   [43] *De An.*, I, 5 (411b 6).

Secondly, this is proved to be impossible by the mode in which one thing is predicated of another. Those things which are derived from various forms are predicated of one another either accidentally (if the forms are not ordered one to another, as when we say that something white is sweet), or essentially, in the second mode of essential predication (if the forms are ordered one to another, as when the subject enters into the definition of the predicate; and thus a surface is presupposed for color, so that if we say that a body with a surface is colored, we have the second mode of essential predication). Therefore, if we have one form by which a thing is an animal, and another form by which it is a man, it follows either that one of these two things could not be predicated of the other, except accidentally (supposing these two forms not to be ordered to one another), or that one would be predicated of the other according to the second mode of essential predication, if one soul be presupposed to the other. But both of these consequences are clearly false. For *animal* is predicated of man essentially and not accidentally, and man is not part of the definition of an animal, but the other way about. Therefore it is of necessity by the same form that a thing is animal and man. Otherwise man would not really be the being which is an animal, so that animal could be essentially predicated of man.

Thirdly, this is shown to be impossible by the fact that when one operation of the soul is intense it impedes another; which could never be the case unless the principle of such actions were essentially one.

We must therefore conclude that the sensitive soul, the intellectual soul and the nutritive soul are in man numerically one and the same soul. This can easily be explained, if we consider the differences of species and forms. For we observe that the species and forms of things differ from one another as the perfect and the less perfect; just as in the order of things, the animate are more perfect than the inanimate, animals more perfect than plants, and man more perfect than brute animals. Furthermore, in each of these genera there are various degrees. For this reason Aristotle compares the species of things to numbers, which differ in species by the addition or subtraction of unity.[44] He also compares the

---

[44] *Metaph.*, VII, 3 (1043b 34).

various souls to the species of figures, one of which contains another, as a pentagon contains and exceeds a tetragon.[45] Thus the intellectual soul contains virtually whatever belongs to the sensitive soul of brute animals, and to the nutritive soul of plants. Therefore, just as a surface which is of a pentagonal shape is not tetragonal by one shape, and pentagonal by another—since a tetragonal shape would be superfluous, as being contained in the pentagonal—so neither is Socrates a man by one soul, and an animal by another; but by one and the same soul he is both animal and man.

Reply Obj. 1. The sensitive soul is incorruptible, not by reason of its being sensitive, but by reason of its being intellectual. When, therefore, a soul is sensitive only, it is corruptible; but when the intellectual is joined to the sensitive, then the sensitive soul is incorruptible. For although the sensitive does not give incorruptibility, yet it cannot deprive the intellectual of its incorruptibility.

Reply Obj. 2. Not forms, but composites, are classified either generically or specifically. Now man is corruptible like other animals. And so the difference of corruptible and incorruptible which is on the part of the forms does not involve a generic difference between man and the other animals.

Reply Obj. 3. The embryo has first of all a soul which is merely sensitive, and when this is removed, it is supplanted by a more perfect soul, which is both sensitive and intellectual, as will be shown farther on.[46]

Reply Obj. 4. We must not base the diversity of natural things on the various logical notions or intentions which follow from our manner of understanding; for reason can apprehend one and the same thing in various ways. Therefore since, as we have said, the intellectual soul contains virtually what belongs to the sensitive soul, and something more, reason can consider separately what belongs to the power of the sensitive soul, as something imperfect and material. And because it observes that this is something common to man and to other animals, it forms thence the notion of the *genus*. On the other hand, that wherein the intellectual soul exceeds the sensitive soul, the reason takes as formal and perfecting; and thence it gathers the *difference* of man.

---

[45] *De An.,* II, 3 (414b 28).   [46] Q. 118, a. 2, ad 2.

Fourth Article

WHETHER IN MAN THERE IS ANOTHER FORM BESIDES THE INTELLECTUAL SOUL?

We proceed thus to the Fourth Article:—

Objection 1. It would seem that in man there is another form besides the intellectual soul. For the Philosopher says that *the soul is the act of a physical body which has life potentially.*[47] Therefore the soul is to the body as a form to matter. But the body has a substantial form by which it is a body. Therefore some other substantial form in the body precedes the soul.

Obj. 2. Further, man moves himself as every animal does. *Now everything that moves itself is divided into two parts, of which one moves, and the other is moved,* as the Philosopher proves.[48] But the part which moves is the soul. Therefore the other part must be such that it can be moved. But primary matter cannot be moved since it is a being only potentially,[49] while everything that is moved is a body. Therefore in man and in every animal there must be another substantial form, by which the body is constituted.

Obj. 3. Further, the order of forms depends on their relation to primary matter; for *before* and *after* apply by comparison to some beginning. Therefore, if there were not in man some other substantial form besides the rational soul, and if the rational soul inhered immediately to primary matter, it would follow that it ranks among the most imperfect forms which inhere to matter immediately.

Obj. 4. Further, the human body is a mixed body. Now mixture does not result from matter alone; for then we should have mere corruption. Therefore the forms of the elements must remain in a mixed body; and these are substantial forms. Therefore in the human body there are other substantial forms besides the intellectual soul.

On the contrary, Of one thing there is but one substantial being. But the substantial form gives substantial being. Therefore of one thing there is but one substantial form. But

---

[47] *De An.,* II, 1 (412a 28).   [48] Aristotle, *Phys.,* VIII, 5 (257b 12).
[49] *Op. cit.,* V, 1 (225a 25).

the soul is the substantial form of man. Therefore it is impossible that there be in man another substantial form besides the intellectual soul.

I answer that, If we supposed that the intellectual soul is not united to the body as its form, but only as its mover, as the Platonists maintain, it would necessarily follow that in man there is another substantial form by which the body is established in its being as movable by the soul.[50] If, however, the intellectual soul is united to the body as its substantial form, as we have said above, it is impossible for another substantial form besides the intellectual soul to be found in man.

In order to make this evident, we must consider that the substantial form differs from the accidental form in this, that the accidental form does not make a thing *to be absolutely,* but *to be such,* as heat does not make a thing to be absolutely, but only to be hot. Therefore by the coming of the accidental form a thing is not said to be made or generated absolutely, but to be made such, or to be in some particular disposition; and in like manner, when an accidental form is removed, a thing is said to be corrupted, not absolutely, but relatively. But the substantial form gives being absolutely, and hence by its coming a thing is said to be generated absolutely, and by its removal to be corrupted absolutely. For this reason, the old natural philosophers, who held that primary matter was some actual being—for instance, fire or air, or something of that sort—maintained that nothing is generated absolutely, or corrupted absolutely, but that *every becoming is nothing but an alteration,* as we read *Physics* i.[51] Therefore, if besides the intellectual soul there pre-existed in matter another substantial form by which the subject of the soul were made an actual being, it would follow that the soul does not give being absolutely, and consequently that it is not the substantial form; and so at the advent of the soul there would not be absolute generation, nor at its removal absolute corruption. All of which is clearly false.

Whence we must conclude that there is no other substantial form in man besides the intellectual soul; and that just as the soul contains virtually the sensitive and nutritive souls, so does it contain virtually all inferior forms, and does alone

[50] Cf. Alex. of Hales, *Summa Theol.,* II, I, no. 344 (II, 419).   [51] Aristotle, *Phys.,* I, 4 (187a 30).

whatever the imperfect forms do in other things. The same is to be said of the sensitive soul in brute animals, and of the nutritive soul in plants, and universally of all more perfect forms in relation to the imperfect.

Reply Obj. 1. Aristotle does not say that the soul is the act of a body only, but *the act of a physical organic body which has life potentially;* and that this potentiality *does not exclude the soul.*[52] Whence it is clear that in the being of which the soul is called the act, the soul itself is included; as when we say that heat is the act of what is hot, and light of what is lucid. And this means, not that the lucid is lucid in separation from light, but that it is lucid through light. In like manner, the soul is said to be the *act of a body,* etc., because it is by the soul that the body is a body, and is organic, and has life potentially. When the first act is said to be *in potentiality,* this is to be understood in relation to the second act, which is operation. Now such a potentiality *does not remove*—that is, does not exclude—the soul.

Reply Obj. 2. The soul does not move the body by its essence, as the form of the body, but by the motive power, whose act presupposes that the body is already actualized by the soul: so that the soul by its motive power is the part which moves; and the animate body is the part moved.

Reply Obj. 3. There are in matter various degrees of perfection, as *to be, to live, to sense, to understand.* Now what is added is always more perfect. Therefore that form which gives matter only the first degree of perfection is the most imperfect, while that form which gives the first, second, and third degree, and so on, is the most perfect: and yet it is present to matter immediately.

Reply Obj. 4. Avicenna held that the substantial forms of the elements remain entire in the mixed body, and that the mixture is made by the contrary qualities of the elements being reduced to an equilibrium.[53] But this is impossible. For the various forms of the elements must necessarily be in various parts of matter, and for the distinction of the parts we must suppose dimensions, without which matter cannot be divisible. Now matter subject to dimension is not to be found except in a body. But several distinct bodies cannot be in the same place. Whence it follows that the elements in the

[52] *De An.,* II, 2 (412a 27; b 25).   [53] Cf. Averroes, *In De Gener.,* I, comm. 90 (V, 167r).

mixed body would be distinct as to position. Hence, there would not be a real mixture which affects the whole, but only a mixture that seems so to the sense because of the juxtaposition of very small particles.

Averroes[54] maintained that the forms of elements, by reason of their imperfection, are between accidental and substantial forms, and so can be *more* or *less*; and therefore in the mixture they are modified and reduced to an equilibrium, so that one form emerges among them. But this is even more impossible. For the substantial being of each thing consists in something indivisible, and every addition and subtraction varies the species, as in numbers, according to *Metaph.* viii.[55] Consequently, it is impossible for any substantial form to receive *more* or *less*. Nor is it less impossible for anything to be between substance and accident.

Therefore we must say, in accordance with the Philosopher,[56] that the forms of the elements remain in the mixed body, not actually, but virtually. For the proper qualities of the elements remain, though modified; and in these qualities is the power of the elementary forms. This quality of the mixture is the proper disposition for the substantial form of the mixed body; for instance, the form of a stone, or of any sort of soul.

[54] *In De Caelo,* III, comm. 67 (v, 105r).   [55] Aristotle, *Metaph.,* VII, 3 (1044a 9).   [56] *De Gener.,* I, 10 (327b 22).

WHAT BELONGS TO THE POWERS OF THE SOUL IN GENERAL

(*In Eight Articles*)

WE PROCEED to consider those things which belong to the powers of the soul, first, in general, and secondly, in particular.[1] Under the first head there are eight points of inquiry: (1) Whether the essence of the soul is its power? (2) Whether there is one power of the soul, or several? (3) How the powers of the soul are distinguished from one another? (4) Of the order of the powers, one to another. (5) Whether the powers of the soul are in it as in their subject? (6) Whether the powers flow from the essence of the soul? (7) Whether one power rises from another? (8) Whether all the powers of the soul remain in the soul after death?

First Article

WHETHER THE ESSENCE OF THE SOUL IS ITS POWER?

We proceed thus to the First Article:—

Objection 1. It would seem that the essence of the soul is its power. For Augustine says that *mind, knowledge and love are in the soul substantially, or, what is the same thing, essentially;*[2] and that *memory, understanding and will are one life, one mind, one essence.*[3]

Obj. 2. Further, the soul is nobler than primary matter. But primary matter is its own potentiality. Much more therefore is the soul its own power.

Obj. 3. Further, the substantial form is simpler than the accidental form; a sign of which is that the substantial form is not intensified or relaxed, but is indivisible. But the accidental form is its own power. Much more therefore is that substantial form which is the soul.

Obj. 4. Further, we sense by the sensitive power and we understand by the intellectual power. But *that by which we*

[1] Q. 78.   [2] *De Trin.*, IX, 4 (PL 42, 963).   [3] *Op. cit.*, X, 11 (PL 42, 984).

first sense and understand is the soul, according to the Philosopher.[4] Therefore the soul is its power.

Obj. 5. Further, whatever does not belong to the essence is an accident. Therefore, if the power of the soul is something else beside the essence thereof, it is an accident; which is contrary to Augustine, who says that the foregoing [*i.e.*, the trinities mentioned in objection 1] *are not in the soul as in a subject, as color or shape, or any other quality, or quantity, is in a body; for such a thing does not exceed the subject in which it is, whereas the mind can love and know other things.*[5]

Obj. 6. Further, *a simple form cannot be a subject.*[6] But the soul is a simple form, since it is not composed of matter and form, as we have said above.[7] Therefore the power of the soul cannot be in it as in a subject.

Obj. 7. Further, an accident is not the principle of a substantial difference. But *sensitive* and *rational* are substantial differences; and they are taken from sense and reason, which are powers of the soul. Therefore the powers of the soul are not accidents; and so it would seem that the power of the soul is its own essence.

On the contrary, Dionysius says that *heavenly spirits are divided into essence, power, and operation.*[8] Much more, then, in the soul is the essence distinct from the virtue or power.

I answer that, It is impossible to admit that the power of the soul is its essence, although some have maintained it.[9] For the present purpose this may be proved in two ways. First, because, since potency and act divide being and every kind of being, we must refer a potency and its act to the same genus. Therefore, if the act be not in the genus of substance, the potency which is said in relation to that act cannot be in the genus of substance. Now the operation of the soul is not in the genus of substance, for this belongs to God alone, whose operation is His own substance. Therefore the divine potency or power which is the principle of His operation is the divine essence itself. This cannot be true either of the soul or of any creature, as we have said above when speaking

[4] *De An.,* II, 2 (414a 12).   [5] *De Trin.,* IX, 4 (PL 42, 963). [6] Boethius, *De Trin.,* II (PL 64, 1250).   [7] Q. 75, a. 5.   [8] *De Cael. Hier.,* XI, 2 (PG 3, 284).   [9] William of Auvergne, *De An.,* III, 4 (II, Suppl., 89).—Cf. Peter Lombard, *Sent.,* I, iii, 2 (I, 35).

of the angels.[10] Secondly, this may be also shown to be impossible in the soul. For the soul by its very essence is an act. Therefore, if the very essence of the soul were the immediate principle of operation, whatever has a soul would always have actual vital actions, as that which has a soul is always an actually living thing. For, as a form, the soul is not an act ordained to a further act; it is rather the ultimate term of generation. Therefore, for it to be in potentiality to another act does not belong to it according to its essence as a form, but according to its power. So the soul itself, as the subject of its power, is called the first act, with a further relation to the second act.[11] Now we observe that what has a soul is not always actual with respect to its vital operations. Hence it is also said in the definition of the soul that it is *the act of a body having life potentially;* which potentiality, however, *does not exclude the soul.*[12] Therefore it follows that the essence of the soul is not its power. For nothing is in potentiality by reason of an act, as act.

Reply Obj. 1. Augustine is speaking of the mind as it knows and loves itself. Thus knowledge and love, as referred to the soul as known and loved, are substantially or essentially in the soul, for the very substance or essence of the soul is known and loved. In the same way are we to understand what he says in the other passage, that those things are *one life, one mind, one essence.* Or, as some say,[13] this passage is true in the sense in which the potential whole is predicated of its parts, being midway between the universal whole and the integral whole. For the universal whole is in each part according to its entire essence and power, as animal in a man and in a horse; and therefore it is properly predicated of each part. But the integral whole is not in each part, either according to its whole essence, or according to its whole power. Therefore in no way can it be predicated of each part. Yet in a way it is predicated, though improperly, of all the parts together; as if we were to say that the wall, roof and foundations are a house. But the potential whole is in each part according to its whole essence, not, however, according to its whole power. Therefore it can in a way be predicated of each part, but not so properly as the universal

[10] Q. 54, a. 3.   [11] Aristotle, *De An.,* II, 1 (412a 27).   [12] *Ibid.* (412a 25).   [13] St. Albert, *In I Sent.,* d. iii, a. 34 (XXV, 140).

whole. In this sense, Augustine says that the memory, understanding and will are the one essence of the soul.

Reply Obj. 2. The act to which primary matter is in potentiality is the substantial form. Therefore the potentiality of matter is nothing else but its essence.

Reply Obj. 3. Action belongs to the composite, as does being; for to act belongs to what exists. Now the composite has being substantially through the substantial form; and it operates by the power which results from the substantial form. Hence an active accidental form is to the substantial form of the agent (for instance, heat compared to the form of fire) as the power of the soul is to the soul.

Reply Obj. 4. That the accidental form is a principle of action is due to the substantial form. Therefore the substantial form is the first principle of action, but not the proximate principle. In this sense the Philosopher says that *the soul is that whereby we understand and sense.*

Reply Obj. 5. If we take accident as meaning what is divided against substance, then there can be no medium between substance and accident; for they are divided by affirmation and negation, that is, according to being in a subject, and not being in a subject. In this sense, since the power of the soul is not its essence, it must be an accident. It belongs to the second species of accident, that of quality. But if we take accident as one of the five predicables, in this sense there is a medium between substance and accident. For the substance is all that belongs to the essence of a thing. But whatever is beyond the essence of a thing cannot be called accident in this sense; but only what is not caused by the essential principle of the species. For *property* does not belong to the essence of a thing, but is caused by the essential principles of the species; and hence it is a medium between the essence and accident thus understood. In this sense the powers of the soul may be said to be a medium between substance and accident, as being natural properties of the soul. When Augustine says that knowledge and love are not in the soul as accidents in a subject, this must be understood in the sense given above, inasmuch as they are compared to the soul, not as loving and knowing, but as loved and known. His argument holds good in this sense; for if love were in the soul loved as in a subject, it would follow that an accident tran-

scends its subject, since even other things are loved through
the soul.

Reply Obj. 6. Although the soul is not composed of matter
and form, yet it has an admixture of potentiality, as we have
said above,[14] and for this reason it can be the subject of an
accident. The statement quoted is verified in God, Who is
Pure Act; and it is in treating of this subject that Boethius
employs the phrase.

Reply Obj. 7. Rational and sensitive, as differences, are
not taken from the powers of sense and reason, but from the
sensitive and rational soul itself. But because substantial
forms, which in themselves are unknown to us, are known
by their accidents, nothing prevents us from sometimes sub-
stituting accidents for substantial differences.

Second Article

WHETHER THERE ARE SEVERAL POWERS OF THE SOUL?

We proceed thus to the Second Article:—

Objection 1. It would seem that there are not several
powers of the soul. For the intellectual soul approaches nearest to the likeness of God. But in God there is one simple
power. So, too, therefore, in the intellectual soul.

Obj. 2. Further, the higher a power is, the more unified it
is. But the intellectual soul excels all other forms in power.
Therefore above all others it has one virtue or power.

Obj. 3. Further, to operate belongs to what is in act. But
by the one essence of the soul, man has actual being in the
different degrees of perfection, as we have seen above.[15]
Therefore by the one power of the soul he performs operations of various degrees.

On the contrary, The Philosopher places several powers in
the soul.[16]

I answer that, Of necessity we must place several powers
in the soul. To make this evident, we observe that, as the
Philosopher says,[17] the lowest order of things cannot acquire
perfect goodness, but they acquire a certain imperfect goodness, by few movements. Those which belong to a higher
order acquire perfect goodness by many movements. Those

---

[14] Q. 75, a. 5, ad 4.   [15] Q. 76, a. 3 and 4.   [16] *De An.,* II, 3 (414a
31).   [17] *De Caelo,* II, 12 (292a 22).

yet higher acquire perfect goodness by few movements, and the highest perfection is found in those things which acquire perfect goodness without any movement whatever. Thus he is least of all disposed to health, who can only acquire imperfect health by means of a few remedies. Better disposed is he who can acquire perfect health by means of many remedies, and better still, he who can by few remedies; but best of all is he who has perfect health without any remedies. We conclude, therefore, that things which are below man acquire a certain limited goodness, and so have a few determinate operations and powers. But man can acquire universal and perfect goodness, because he can acquire beatitude. Yet he is in the lowest degree, according to his nature, of whose to whom beatitude is possible; and therefore the human soul requires many and various operations and powers. But to angels a smaller variety of powers is sufficient. In God, however, there is no power or action beyond His own Essence.

There is yet another reason why the human soul abounds in a variety of powers:—it is on the confines of spiritual and corporeal creatures, and therefore the powers of both meet together in the soul.

Reply Obj. 1. The intellectual soul approaches to the divine likeness, more than inferior creatures, in being able to acquire perfect goodness, although by many and various means; and in this it falls short of more perfect creatures.

Reply Obj. 2. A unified power is superior if it extends to equal things. But a multiform power is superior to it, if it is over many things.

Reply Obj. 3. One thing has one substantial being, but may have several operations. So there is one essence in the soul, but several powers.

Third Article

WHETHER THE POWERS ARE DISTINGUISHED BY THEIR ACTS AND OBJECTS?

We proceed thus to the Third Article:—

Objection 1. It would seem that the powers of the soul are not distinguished by acts and objects. For nothing is determined to its species by what is subsequent and extrinsic to it. But the act is subsequent to the power, and the object is extrinsic to it. Therefore the soul's powers are not specifically distinct by acts and objects.

Obj. 2. Further, contraries are what differ most from each other. Therefore if the powers are distinguished by their objects, it follows that the same power could not have contrary objects. This is clearly false in almost all the powers, for the power of vision extends to white and black, and the power of taste to sweet and bitter.

Obj. 3. Further, if the cause be removed, the effect is removed. Hence if the difference of powers came from the difference of objects, the same object would not come under different powers. This is clearly false, for the same thing is known by the cognitive power, and desired by the appetitive.

Obj. 4. Further, that which of itself is the cause of anything, is the cause thereof, wherever it is. But various objects which belong to various powers belong also to some one power; as sound and color belong to sight and hearing, which are different powers, yet come under the one power of common sense. Therefore the powers are not distinguished according to the difference of their objects.

On the contrary, Things that are subsequent are distinguished by what precedes. But the Philosopher says that *acts and operations precede the powers according to the reason; and these again are preceded by their opposites,*[18] that is, their objects. Therefore the powers are distinguished according to their acts and objects.

I answer that, A power as such is directed to an act. Therefore we must derive the nature of a power from the act to which it is directed; and consequently the nature of a power is diversified according as the nature of the act is diversified. Now the nature of an act is diversified according to the various natures of the objects. For every act is either of an active power or of a passive power. Now, the object is to the act of a passive power as the principle and moving cause; for color is the principle of vision, inasmuch as it moves the sight. On the other hand, to the act of an active power the object is a term and an end; just as the object of the power of growth is perfect quantity, which is the end of growth. Now, from these two things an act receives its species, namely, from its principle, or from its end or term. For the act of heating differs from the act of cooling in this, that the former pro-

[18] *De An.,* II, 4 (415a 18).

ceeds from something hot, which is the active principle, to
heat; while the latter proceeds from something cold, which
is the active principle, to cold. Therefore the powers are of
necessity distinguished by their acts and objects.

Nevertheless, we must observe that things which are accidental do not change the species. For since to be colored is
accidental to an animal, its species is not changed by a difference of color, but by a difference in that which belongs
to the nature of an animal, that is to say, by a difference in
the sensitive soul, which is sometimes found accompanied by
reason, and sometimes not. Hence *rational* and *irrational* are
differences dividing animal, constituting its various species.
In like manner, therefore, not any variety of objects diversifies the powers of the soul, but a difference in that to which
the power of its very nature is directed. Thus the senses of
their very nature are directed to the passive quality which of
itself is divided into color, sound, and the like, and therefore
there is one sensitive power with regard to color, namely,
sight, and another with regard to sound, namely, hearing.
But it is accidental to a passive quality, for instance, to something colored, to be a musician or a grammarian, great or
small, a man or a stone. Therefore by reason of such differences the powers of the soul are not distinguished.

Reply Obj. 1. Act, though subsequent in being to power,
is, nevertheless, prior to it in intention and logically; as the
end is with regard to the agent. And the object, although extrinsic, is, nevertheless, the principle or end of the action;
and the conditions which are intrinsic to a thing are proportionate to its principle and end.

Reply Obj. 2. If any power were to have one of two contraries as such for its object, the other contrary would belong
to another power. But the power of the soul does not regard
the nature of the contrary as such, but rather the common
aspect of both contraries; as sight does not regard white as
such, but as color. This is because, of two contraries, one, in
a manner, includes the nature of the other, since they are to
one another as perfect and imperfect.

Reply Obj. 3. Nothing prevents things which coincide in
subject from being considered under different aspects; and
therefore they can belong to various powers of the soul.

Reply Obj. 4. The higher power of itself regards a more
universal formality in its object than the lower power; be-

cause the higher a power is, to a greater number of things does it extend. Therefore many things are combined in the one formality of the object, which the higher power considers of itself; while they differ in the formalities regarded by the lower powers of themselves. Thus it is that various objects belong to various lower powers; which objects, however, are subject to one higher power.

Fifth Article

WHETHER ALL THE POWERS OF THE SOUL ARE IN THE SOUL AS THEIR SUBJECT?

We proceed thus to the Fifth Article:—

Objection 1. It would seem that all the powers of the soul are in the soul as their subject. For as the powers of the body are to the body, so the powers of the soul are to the soul. But the body is the subject of the corporeal powers. Therefore the soul is the subject of the powers of the soul.

Obj. 2. Further, the operations of the powers of the soul are attributed to the body by reason of the soul; because, as the Philosopher says, *the soul is that by which we sense and understand primarily.*[19] But the first principles of the operations of the soul are the powers. Therefore the powers are primarily in the soul.

Obj. 3. Further, Augustine says that the soul senses certain things, not through the body, but in fact, without the body, as fear and the like; and some things it senses through the body.[20] But if the sensitive powers were not in the soul alone as their subject, the soul could not sense anything without the body. Therefore the soul is the subject of the sensitive powers; and for a similar reason, of all the other powers.

On the contrary, The Philosopher says that *sensation belongs neither to the soul, nor to the body, but to the composite.*[21] Therefore the sensitive power is in the composite as its subject. Therefore the soul alone is not the subject of all the powers.

I answer that, The subject of operative power is that which is able to operate; for every accident denominates its proper subject. Now it is the same being which is able to operate,

---

[19] Aristotle, *op. cit.,* II, 2 (414a 12).   [20] *De Genesi ad Litt.,* XII, 7; 24 (PL 34, 459; 474).   [21] *De Somno,* I (454a 7).

and which does operate. Therefore the *subject of power* is of
necessity *the subject of operation,* as again the Philosopher
says in the beginning of *De Somno et Vigilia.*[22] Now, it is
clear from what we have said above that some operations of
the soul are performed without a corporeal organ, as to understand and to will.[23] Hence the powers of these operations
are in the soul as their subject. But some operations of the
soul are performed by means of corporeal organs, as seeing
by the eye, and hearing by the ear. And so it is with all the
other operations of the nutritive and sensitive parts. Therefore, the powers which are the principles of these operations
have their subject in the composite, and not in the soul alone.

Reply Obj. 1. All the powers are said to belong to the soul,
not as their subject, but as their principle; because it is by
the soul that the composite has the power to perform such
operations.

Reply Obj. 2. All such powers are in the soul before they
are in the composite; not, however, as in their subject, but
as in their principle.

Reply Obj. 3. Plato's opinion was that sensation is an operation proper to the soul, just as understanding is.[24] Now in
many things relating to philosophy, Augustine makes use of
the opinions of Plato, not asserting them as true, but report-
ing them. However, as far as the present question is concerned, when it is said that the soul senses some things with
the body, and some without the body, this can be taken in
two ways. Firstly, the words *with the body or without the
body* may determine the act of sense in its mode of proceeding from the one who senses. *Thus* the soul senses nothing
without the body, because the action of sensation cannot proceed from the soul except by a corporeal organ. Secondly,
they may be understood as determining the act of sense on
the part of the object sensed. *Thus* the soul senses some
things with the body, that is, things existing in the body, as
when it feels a wound or something of that sort; while it
senses some things without the body, that is, which do not
exist in the body, but only in the apprehension of the soul,
as when it feels sad or joyful on hearing something.

[22] *Ibid.* (454a 8).   [23] Q. 75, a. 2 and 3; q. 76, a. 1, ad 1.   [24] Cf.
above, q. 75, a. 3.

THE POWERS OF THE SOUL IN PARTICULAR

(*In Four Articles*)

WE NEXT treat of the powers of the soul in particular. The theologian, however, has only to inquire specifically concerning the intellectual and appetitive powers, in which the virtues reside. And since the knowledge of these powers depends to a certain extent on the other powers, our consideration of the powers of the soul in particular will be divided into three parts: first, we shall consider those powers which are a preamble to the intellect; secondly, the intellectual powers;[1] thirdly, the appetitive powers.[2]

Under the first head there are four points of inquiry: (1) The powers of the soul considered generally. (2) The species of powers in the vegetative part of the soul. (3) The exterior senses. (4) The interior senses.

First Article

WHETHER THERE ARE TO BE DISTINGUISHED FIVE GENERA OF POWERS IN THE SOUL?

We proceed thus to the First Article:—

Objection 1. It would seem that there are not to be distinguished five genera of powers in the soul—namely, vegetative, sensitive, appetitive, locomotive, and intellectual. For the powers of the soul are called its parts. But only three parts of the soul are commonly assigned—namely, the vegetative soul, the sensitive soul, and the rational soul. Therefore there are only three genera of powers in the soul, and not five.

Obj. 2. Further, the powers of the soul are the principles of its vital operations. Now, in four ways is a thing said to live. For the Philosopher says: *In several ways a thing is said to live, and even if only one of these is present, the thing is said to live; as intellect and sense, local movement and rest, and lastly, movement of decrease and increase due to nourishment.*[3] Therefore there are only four genera of powers of the soul, as the appetitive is excluded.

[1] Q. 79.　　[2] Q. 80.　　[3] *De An.*, II, 2 (413a 22).

Obj. 3. Further, a special kind of soul ought not to be assigned as regards what is common to all the powers. Now desire is common to each power·of the soul. For sight desires its appropriate visible object; whence we read (*Ecclus.* xl. 22): *The eye desireth favor and beauty, but more than these green sown fields.* In the same way, every other power desires its appropriate object. Therefore the appetitive power should not be made a special genus of the powers of the soul.

Obj. 4. Further, the moving principle in animals is sense, or intellect, or appetite, as the Philosopher says.[4] Therefore the motive power should not be added to the above as a special genus of soul.

On the contrary, The Philosopher says: *The powers are the vegetative, the sensitive, the appetitive, the locomotive, and the intellectual.*[5]

I answer that, There are five genera among the powers of the soul, as above numbered. Of these, three are called souls, and four are called modes of living. The reason of this diversity is that the various souls are distinguished according as the operation of the soul transcends the operation of the corporeal nature in various ways; for the whole corporeal nature is subject to the soul, and is related to it as its matter and instrument. There exists, therefore, an operation of the soul which so far exceeds the corporeal nature that it is not even performed by any corporeal organ; and such is the operation of the *rational soul.* Below this, there is another operation of the soul, which is indeed performed through a corporeal organ, but not through a corporeal quality, and this is the operation of the *sensitive soul.* For though hot and cold, wet and dry, and other such corporeal qualities are required for the work of the senses, yet they are not required in such a way that the operation of the senses takes place by the power of such qualities; but only for the proper disposition of the organ. The lowest of the operations of the soul is that which is performed by a corporeal organ and by the power of a corporeal quality. Yet this transcends the operation of the corporeal nature; because the movements of bodies are caused by an extrinsic principle, while these operations are from an intrinsic principle. For this is common to all the operations of the soul, since every animate thing, in some way, moves itself. Such is the operation of the *vegetative*

[4] *Op. cit.,* III, 10 (433a 9).   [5] *Op. cit.,* II, 3 (414a 31).

soul; for digestion, and what follows, is caused instrumentally by the action of heat, as the Philosopher says.[6]

Now the powers of the soul are distinguished generically by their objects. For the higher a power is, the more universal is the object to which it extends, as we have said above.[7] But the object of the soul's operation may be considered in a triple order. For in the soul there is a power whose object is only the body that is united to that soul; and the powers of this genus are called *vegetative*, for the vegetative power acts only on the body to which the soul is united. There is another genus in the powers of the soul which regards a more universal object—namely, every sensible body, and not only the body to which the soul is united. And there is yet another genus in the powers of the soul which regards a still more universal object—namely, not only the sensible body, but universally all being. Therefore it is evident that the latter two genera of the soul's powers have an operation in regard not merely to that which is united to them, but also to something extrinsic. Now, since whatever operates must in some way be united to the object in relation to which it operates, it follows of necessity that this something extrinsic, which is the object of the soul's operation, must be related to the soul in a twofold manner. First, inasmuch as this something extrinsic has a natural aptitude to be united to the soul, and to be by its likeness in the soul. In this way there are two kinds of powers—namely, the *sensitive*, in regard to the less common object, the sensible body; and the *intellectual*, in regard to the most common object, universal being. Secondly, inasmuch as the soul itself has an inclination and tendency to the external thing. And in this way there are again two kinds of powers in the soul: one—*the appetitive*—according to which the soul is referred to something extrinsic as to an end, which is first in the intention; the other—the *locomotive* power—according to which the soul is referred to something extrinsic as to the term of its operation and movement; for every animal is moved for the purpose of realizing its desires and intentions.

The modes of living, on the other hand, are distinguished according to the degrees of living things. There are some living things in which there exists only vegetative power, as

[6] Aristotle, *op. cit.*, II, 4 (416b 25).   [7] Q. 77, a. 3, ad 4.

plants. There are others in which along with the vegetative there exists also the sensitive, but not the locomotive, power; and such are immovable animals, as shellfish. There are others which, besides this, have locomotive powers, as do the perfect animals, which require many things for their life, and consequently need movement to seek necessaries of life from a distance. And there are some living things which along with these have intellectual power—namely, men. But the appetitive power does not constitute a degree of living things; because *wherever there is sense there is also appetite.*[8]

Thus the first two objections are hereby solved.

Reply Obj. 3. *Natural appetite* is that inclination which each thing has, of its own nature, for something; wherefore by its natural appetite each power desires what is suitable to itself. But *animal appetite* follows from the apprehended form. This sort of appetite requires a special power in the soul—apprehension alone does not suffice. For a thing is desired according as it exists in its own nature, whereas in the apprehensive power it exists, not according to its own nature, but according to its likeness. Whence it is clear that sight desires naturally a visible object for the purpose of its act only—namely, for the purpose of seeing; but the animal by its appetitive power desires the thing seen, not merely for the purpose of seeing it, but also for other purposes. But if the soul did not require the things perceived by the senses, except for the sake of the actions of the senses (that is, for the purpose of sensing them), there would be no need for a special genus of appetitive powers, since the natural appetite of the powers would suffice.

Reply Obj. 4. Although sense and appetite are principles of movement in perfect animals, yet sense and appetite, as such, are not sufficient to cause movement, unless another power be added to them; for immovable animals have sense and appetite, and yet they have not the power of motion. Now this motive power is not only in the appetite and sense as commanding the movement, but also in the parts of the body, to make them obey the appetite of the soul which moves them. Of this we have a sign in the fact that when the members are deprived of their natural disposition, they do not move in obedience to the appetite.

[8] Aristotle, *De An.*, II, 3 (414b 1).

Second Article

WHETHER THE PARTS OF THE VEGETATIVE SOUL ARE FITTINGLY ENUMERATED AS THE NUTRITIVE, AUGMENTATIVE, AND GENERATIVE?

We proceed thus to the Second Article:—

Objection 1. It would seem that the parts of the vegetative soul are not fittingly enumerated as the nutritive, augmentative, and generative. For these are called *natural* powers. But the powers of the soul are above the natural powers. Therefore we should not class the above powers as powers of the soul.

Obj. 2. Further, we should not assign a particular power of the soul to that which is common to living and non-living things. But generation is common to all things that can be generated and corrupted, whether living or not living. Therefore the generative power should not be classed as a power of the soul.

Obj. 3. Further, the soul is more powerful than the body. But the body by the same active power gives species and due quantity; much more, therefore, does the soul. Therefore the augmentative power of the soul is not ·distinct from the generative power.

Obj. 4. Further, everything is preserved in being by that whereby it has being. But the generative power is that whereby a living thing acquires being. Therefore by the same power the living thing is preserved. Now the nutritive power is directed to the preservation of the living thing, being *a power which is capable of preserving whatever receives it.*[9] Therefore we should not distinguish the nutritive power from the generative.

On the contrary, The Philosopher says that the operations of this soul are *generation, the use of food, and growth.*[10]

I answer that, The vegetative part has three powers. For the vegetative part, as we have said, has for its object the body itself, living by the soul; and for this body a triple operation of the soul is required. One is whereby it acquires being, and to this is directed the *generative* power. Another is whereby the living body acquires its due quantity, and to this

[9] Aristotle, *op. cit.,* II, 4 (416b 14).   [10] *Ibid.* (415a 25; b 23).

is directed the *augmentative* power. Another is whereby the body of a living thing is preserved in its being and in its due quantity, and to this is directed the *nutritive* power.

We must, however, observe a difference among these powers. The nutritive and the augmentative have their effect where they exist, since the body itself united to the soul grows and is preserved by the augmentative and nutritive powers which exist in one and the same soul. But the generative power has its effect, not in one and the same body, but in another; for a thing cannot generate itself. Therefore the generative power in a way approaches to the dignity of the sensitive soul, which has an operation extending to extrinsic things, although in a more excellent and more universal manner; for that which is highest in an inferior nature approaches to that which is lowest in the higher nature, as is made clear by Dionysius.[11] Therefore, of these three powers, the generative has the greater finality, nobility and perfection, as the Philosopher says, for it belongs to a thing which is already perfect *to produce another like unto itself.*[12] Furthermore, the generative power is served by the augmentative and nutritive powers; and the augmentative power by the nutritive.

Reply Obj. 1. Such powers are called natural, both because they produce an effect like that of nature, which also gives being, quantity and preservation (although the above powers accomplish these things in a more perfect way); and because these powers perform their actions instrumentally, through the active and passive qualities, which are the principles of natural actions.

Reply Obj. 2. Generation in inanimate things is entirely from an extrinsic source; whereas the generation of living things is in a higher way, through something in the living thing itself, which is the semen containing the formative principle of the body. Therefore, there must be in the living thing a power that prepares this semen; and this is the generative power.

Reply Obj. 3. Since the generation of living things is from a semen, it is necessary that in the beginning an animal of small size be generated. For this reason it must have a power

---

[11] *De Div. Nom.*, VII, 3 (PG 3, 872).   [12] Aristotle, *De·An.*, II, 4 (416b 24).

in the soul, whereby it is brought to its appropriate size. But the inanimate body is generated from determinate matter by an extrinsic agent; and therefore it receives at once its nature and its quantity, according to the condition of the matter.

Reply Obj. 4. As we have said above, the operation of the vegetative principle is performed by means of heat, the property of which is to consume humidity. Therefore, in order to restore the humidity thus lost, the nutritive power is required, whereby the food is changed into the substance of the body. This is also necessary for the action of the augmentative and generative powers.

Third Article

WHETHER THE FIVE EXTERIOR SENSES ARE PROPERLY DISTINGUISHED?

We proceed thus to the Third Article:—

Objection 1. It would seem inaccurate to distinguish five exterior senses. For sense can know accidents. But there are many kinds of accidents. Therefore, since powers are distinguished by their objects, it seems that the senses are multiplied according to the number of the kinds of accidents.

Obj. 2. Further, magnitude and shape, and other so-called *common sensibles*, are *not sensibles by accident*, but are contradistinguished from them by the Philosopher.[13] Now the diversity of the proper objects diversifies the powers. Since, therefore, magnitude and shape are further from color than sound is, it seems that there is much more need for another sensitive power that can grasp magnitude or shape than for that which grasps color or sound.

Obj. 3. Further, one sense regards one contrariety; as sight regards white and black. But the sense of touch grasps several contrarieties, such as hot or cold, moist or dry, and the like. Therefore, it is not a single sense but several. Therefore there are more than five senses.

Obj. 4. Further, a species is not divided against its genus. But taste is a kind of touch. Therefore it should not be classed as a distinct sense from touch.

On the contrary, The Philosopher says: *There is none other besides the five senses.*[14]

---

[13] Aristotle, *op. cit.*, II, 6 (418a 8).   [14] *Op. cit.*, III, 1 (424b 22).

I answer that, The reason of the distinction and number of the senses has been assigned by some on the basis of the organs, in which one or other of the elements preponderates, as water, air, or the like.[15] By others it has been assigned to the medium, which is either in conjunction or extrinsic, and is either water or air, or the like. Others[16] have ascribed it to the diverse natures of the sensible qualities, according as such quality belongs to a simple body or results from complexity.

But none of these explanations is apt. For the powers are not for the organs, but the organs for the powers, and therefore there are not various powers for the reason that there are various organs, but, on the contrary, for this has nature provided a variety of organs, that they might be suitable to the diversity of powers. In the same way, nature provided various mediums for the various senses, according to what suited the acts of the powers. Now to be cognizant of the natures of sensible qualities does not pertain to the senses, but to the intellect. The reason of the number and distinction of the exterior senses must therefore be ascribed to that which belongs to the senses properly and *per se.* Sense is a passive power, and is naturally immuted by the exterior sensible. Hence, the exterior cause of such immutation is what is *per se* perceived by the sense, and according to the diversity of that exterior cause are the sensitive powers diversified.

Now, immutation is of two kinds, one natural, the other spiritual. Natural immutation takes place when the form of that which causes the immutation is received, according to its natural being, into the thing immuted, as heat is received into the thing heated. But spiritual immutation takes place when the form of what causes the immutation is received, according to a spiritual mode of being, into the thing immuted, as the form of color is received into the pupil which does not thereby become colored. Now, for the operation of the senses, a spiritual immutation is required, whereby an intention of the sensible form is effected in the sensile organ. Otherwise, if a natural immutation alone sufficed for the sense's action, all natural bodies would have sensation when they undergo alteration.

[15] Cf. St. Albert, *Summa de Creatur.,* II, q. 34, a. 4 (XXXV, 304); Alex. of Hales, *Summa Theol.,* II, I, no. 356 (II, 432).   [16] Cf. St. Bonaventure, *Itin. Mentis In Deum,* II (V, 300).

But in some senses we find spiritual immutation only, as in *sight*, while in others we find not only a spiritual but also a natural immutation, and this either on the part of the object only, or likewise on the part of the organ. On the part of the object, we find local natural immutation in sound, which is the object of *hearing*; for sound is caused by percussion and commotion of the air. We find natural immutation by alteration in odor, which is the object of *smelling*; for in order to give off an odor, a body must be in a measure affected by heat. On the part of the organ, natural immutation takes place in *touch* and *taste*; for the hand that touches something hot becomes hot, while the tongue is moistened by the humidity of flavors. But the organs of smelling and hearing are not affected in their respective operations by any natural immutation, except accidentally.

Now, the sight, which is without natural immutation either in its organ or in its object, is the most spiritual, the most perfect, and the most universal of all the senses. After this comes the hearing and then the smell, which require a natural immutation on the part of the object; while local motion is more perfect than, and naturally prior to, the motion of alteration, as the Philosopher proves.[17] Touch and taste are the most material of all (of their distinction we shall speak later on). Hence it is that the three other senses are not exercised through a medium united to them, to obviate any natural immutation in their organ; as happens as regards these two senses.

Reply Obj. 1. Not every accident has in itself a power of immutation, but only qualities of the third species, according to which there can be alteration. Therefore only such qualities are the objects of the senses, because *the senses are affected by the same things whereby inanimate bodies are affected*, as is stated in *Physics* vii.[18]

Reply Obj. 2. Size, shape, and the like, which are called *common sensibles*, are midway between *accidental sensibles* and *proper sensibles*, which are the objects of the senses. For the proper sensibles first, and of their very nature, affect the senses, since they are qualities that cause alteration. But the common sensibles are all reducible to quantity. As to size

[17] Aristotle, *Phys.*, VIII, 7 (260a 28).   [18] *Op. cit.*, VII, 2 (244b 12).

and number, it is clear that they are species of quantity. Shape is a quality about quantity, since the nature of shape consists in fixing the bounds of magnitude. Movement and rest are sensed according as the subject is affected in one or more ways in the magnitude of the subject or of its local distance, as in the movement of growth or of locomotion, or again, according as it is affected in some sensible qualities, as in the movement of alteration; and thus to sense movement and rest is, in a way, to sense one thing and many. Now quantity is the proximate subject of the qualities that cause alteration, as surface is of color. Therefore the common sensibles do not move the senses first and of their own nature, but by reason of sensible quality; as the surface by reason of color. Yet they are not accidental sensibles, for they produce a certain diversity in the immutation of the senses. For sense is immuted differently by a large and by a small surface; since whiteness itself is said to be great or small, and therefore is divided according to its proper subject.

Reply Obj. 3. As the Philosopher seems to say, the sense of touch is generically one, but is divided into several specific senses, and for this reason it extends to various contrarieties.[19] These senses, however, are not separate from one another in their organ, but are spread together throughout the whole body, so that their distinction is not evident. But taste, which perceives the sweet and the bitter, accompanies touch in the tongue, but not in the whole body; so it is easily distinguished from touch. We might also say that all those contrarieties agree, each in some proximate genus, and all in a common genus, which is the common and formal object of touch. Such a common genus is, however, unnamed, just as the proximate genus of hot and cold is unnamed.

Reply Obj. 4. The sense of taste, according to a saying of the Philosopher, is a kind of touch existing only in the tongue.[20] It is not distinct from touch in general, but only from the species of touch distributed in the body. But if touch is only one sense, because of the common formality of its object, we must say that taste is distinguished from touch by reason of a different kind of immutation. For touch involves a natural, and not only a spiritual, immutation in its

[19] *De An.*, II, 11 (422b 17).   [20] *Op. cit.*, II, 9 (421a 18); 11 (423a 17).

organ, by reason of the quality which is its proper object. But the organ of taste is not necessarily immuted by a natural immutation according to the quality which is its proper object, so that the tongue itself becomes sweet or bitter, but according to the quality which is a preamble to, and on which is based, the flavor; which quality is moisture, the object of touch.

Fourth Article

WHETHER THE INTERIOR SENSES ARE SUITABLY DISTINGUISHED?

We proceed thus to the Fourth Article:—

Objection 1. It would seem that the interior senses are not suitably distinguished. For the common is not divided against the proper. Therefore the common sense should not be numbered among the interior sensitive powers, in addition to the proper exterior senses.

Obj. 2. Further, there is no need to assign an interior power of apprehension when the proper and exterior sense suffices. But the proper and exterior senses suffice for us to judge of sensible things; for each sense judges of its proper object. In like manner, they seem to suffice for the perception of their own actions; for since the action of the sense is, in a way, between the power and its object, it seems that sight must be much more able to perceive its own vision, as being nearer to it, than the color; and in like manner with the other senses. Therefore for this purpose there is no need to assign an interior power, called the common sense.

Obj. 3. Further, according to the Philosopher, the imagination and the memory are passions of the *first sensitive*.[21] But passion is not divided against its subject. Therefore memory and imagination should not be assigned as powers distinct from sense.

Obj. 4. Further, the intellect depends on the senses less than any power of the sensitive part. But the intellect knows nothing but what it receives from the senses; whence we read that *those who lack one sense lack one kind of knowledge*.[22] Therefore much less should we assign to the sensitive part a

---

[21] *De Mem. et Rem.*, I (450a 10).   [22] Aristotle, *Post. Anal.*, I, 18 (81a 38).

power, which they call the *estimative* power, for the perception of representations which the sense does not perceive.

Obj. 5. Further, the action of the *cogitative* power, which consists in comparing, uniting and dividing, and the action of the *reminiscence,* which consists in the use of a kind of syllogism for the sake of inquiry, are not less distant from the actions of the *estimative* and *memorative* powers, than the action of the estimative is from the action of the imagination. Therefore either we must add the cogitative and reminiscitive powers to the estimative and memorative powers, or the estimative and memorative powers should not be made distinct from the imagination.

Obj. 6. Further, Augustine describes three kinds of vision, namely, corporeal, which is an action of the sense; spiritual, which is an action of the imagination or phantasy; and intellectual, which is an action of the intellect.[23] Therefore there is no interior power between the sense and intellect, besides the imagination.

On the contrary, Avicenna assigns five interior sensitive powers, namely, *common sense, phantasy, imagination, the estimative and the memorative.*[24]

I answer that, As nature does not fail in necessary things, there must needs be as many actions of the sensitive soul as may suffice for the life of a perfect animal. If any of these actions cannot be reduced to one and the same principle, they must be assigned to diverse powers; since a power of the soul is nothing else than the proximate principle of the soul's operation.

Now we must observe that for the life of a perfect animal, the animal should apprehend a thing not only at the actual time of sensation, but also when it is absent. Otherwise, since animal motion and action follow apprehension, an animal would not be moved to seek something absent; the contrary of which we may observe especially in perfect animals, which are moved by progression, for they are moved towards something apprehended and absent. Therefore, through the sensitive soul an animal must not only receive the species of sensible things, when it is actually affected by them, but it must also retain and preserve them. Now to receive and re-

[23] *De Genesi ad Litt.,* XII, 6; 7; 24 (PL 34, 458; 459; 474).   [24] *De An.,* I, 5 (5rb); IV, 1 (17va).

tain are, in corporeal things, reduced to diverse principles; for moist things are apt to receive, but retain with difficulty, while it is the reverse with dry things. Therefore, since the sensitive power is the act of a corporeal organ, it follows that the power which receives the species of sensible things must be distinct from the power which preserves them.

Again, we must observe that if an animal were moved by pleasing and disagreeable things only as affecting the sense, there would be no need to suppose that an animal has a power besides the apprehension of those forms which the senses perceive, and in which the animal takes pleasure, or from which it shrinks with horror. But the animal needs to seek or to avoid certain things, not only because they are pleasing or otherwise to the senses, but also because of other advantages and uses, or disadvantages; just as the sheep runs away when it sees a wolf, not because of its color or shape, but as a natural enemy. So, too, a bird gathers together straws, not because they are pleasant to the sense, but because they are useful for building its nest. Animals, therefore, need to perceive such intentions, which the exterior sense does not perceive. Now some distinct principle is necessary for this, since the perception of sensible forms comes by an immutation caused by the sensible, which is not the case with the perception of the above intentions.

Thus, therefore, for the reception of sensible forms, the *proper sense* and the *common sense* are appointed. Of their distinction we shall speak later. But for the retention and preservation of these forms, the *phantasy* or *imagination* is appointed, being as it were a storehouse of forms received through the senses. Furthermore, for the apprehension of intentions which are not received through the senses, the *estimative* power is appointed: and for their preservation, the *memorative power*, which is a storehouse of such intentions. A sign of which we have in the fact that the principle of memory in animals is found in some such intention, for instance, that something is harmful or otherwise. And the very character of something as past, which memory observes, is to be reckoned among these intentions.

Now, we must observe that as to sensible forms there is no difference between man and other animals; for they are similarly immuted by external sensibles. But there is a difference as to the above intentions: for other animals perceive these intentions only by some sort of natural instinct, while man perceives them also by means of a certain comparison. Therefore the power which in other animals is called the *natural estimative* in man is called the *cogitative,* which by some sort of comparison discovers these intentions.[25] Therefore it is also called the *particular reason,* to which medical men assign a particular organ, namely, the middle part of the head;[26] for it compares individual intentions, just as the intellectual reason compares universal intentions. As to the memorative power, man has not only memory, as other animals have, in the sudden recollection of the past, but also *reminiscence,* by seeking syllogistically, as it were, for a recollection of the past by the application of individual intentions. Avicenna,[27] however, assigns between the estimative and the imaginative a fifth power, which combines and divides imaginary forms; as when from the imaginary form of gold, and the imaginary form of a mountain, we compose the one form of a golden mountain, which we have never seen. But this operation is not to be found in animals other than man, in whom the imaginative power suffices for this purpose. Averroes also attributes this action to the imagination, in his book *De sensu et sensibilibus.*[28] So there is no need to assign more than four interior powers of the sensitive part—namely, the common sense, the imagination, and the estimative and memorative powers.

Reply Obj. 1. The interior sense is called *common* not by predication, as if it were a genus, but as the common root and principle of the exterior senses.

Reply Obj. 2. The proper sense judges of the proper sensible by discerning it from other things which come under the same sense; for instance, by discerning white from black or green. But neither sight nor taste can discern white from sweet, because what discerns between two things must know both. Hence, the discerning judgment must be assigned to the common sense. To it, as to a common term, all apprehensions of the senses must be referred, and by it, again, all the intentions of the senses are perceived; as when someone sees that he sees. For this cannot be done by the proper sense,

[25] Cf. Alex. of Hales, *Summa Theol.,* II, I, no. 357 (II, 434).—Cf. also Averroes, *Colliget,* II, 20 (X, 17va).   [26] Avicenna, *De An.,* I, 5 (5rb) ; Averroes, *Colliget,* II, 20 (X, 17va).   [27] *De An.,* IV, 1 (17va). [28] *De Sensu et Sensibili* (VI, 193v).

which knows only the form of the sensible by which it is immuted. In this immutation the action of sight is completed, and from it follows another immutation in the common sense which perceives the act of seeing.

Reply Obj. 3. Just as one power arises from the soul by means of another, as we have seen above,[29] so likewise the soul is the subject of one power through another. In this way the imagination and the memory are called passions of the *first sensitive.*

Reply Obj. 4. Although the operation of the intellect has its origin in the senses, yet, in the thing apprehended through the senses, the intellect knows many things which the senses cannot perceive. In like manner does the estimative power, though in a less perfect way.

Reply Obj. 5. The cogitative and memorative powers in man owe their excellence not to that which is proper to the sensitive part, but to a certain affinity and proximity to the universal reason, which, so to speak, overflows into them. Therefore they are not distinct powers, but the same, yet more perfect than in other animals.

Reply Obj. 6. Augustine calls that vision spiritual which is effected by the images of bodies in the absence of bodies. Whence it is clear that it is common to all interior apprehensions.

[29] Q. 77, a. 7.

THE INTELLECTUAL POWERS

(*In Thirteen Articles*)

THE next question concerns the intellectual powers, under which head there are thirteen points of inquiry: (1) Whether the intellect is a power of the soul, or its essence? (2) If it is a power, whether it is a passive power? (3) If it is a passive power, whether there must be an agent intellect? (4) Whether it is something in the soul? (5) Whether the agent intellect is one in all? (6) Whether memory is in the intellect? (7) Whether the memory is distinct from the intellect? (8) Whether the reason is a distinct power from the intellect? (9) Whether the superior and inferior reason are distinct powers? (10) Whether intelligence is a power distinct from the intellect? (11) Whether the speculative and practical intellect are distinct powers? (12) Whether *synderesis* is some power of the intellectual part? (13) Whether the conscience is a power of the intellectual part?

First Article

WHETHER THE INTELLECT IS A POWER OF THE SOUL?

We proceed thus to the First Article:—

Objection 1. It would seem that the intellect is not a power of the soul, but the essence of the soul. For the intellect seems to be the same as the mind. Now the mind is not a power of the soul, but the essence; for Augustine says: *Mind and spirit are not names of relations, but denominate the essence.*[1] Therefore the intellect is the essence of the soul.

Obj. 2. Further, different genera of the soul's powers are not united in some one power, but only in the essence of the soul. Now the appetitive and the intellectual are different genera of the soul's powers, as the Philosopher says;[2] but they are united in the mind, for Augustine places the intelligence and will in the mind.[3] Therefore the mind and intellect of man is the very essence of the soul, and not a power.

[1] *De Trin.*, IX, 2 (PL 42, 962).   [2] Aristotle, *De An.*, II, 3 (414a 31).   [3] *De Trin.*, X, 11 (PL 42, 983).

Obj. 3. Further, according to Gregory, in a homily for the Ascension, *man understands with the angels.*[4] But angels are called *minds* and *intellects.* Therefore the mind and intellect of man is not a power of the soul, but the soul itself.

Obj. 4. Further, a substance is intellectual by the fact that it is immaterial. But the soul is immaterial through its essence. Therefore it seems that the soul must be intellectual through its essence.

On the contrary, The Philosopher assigns the intellect as a power of the soul.[5]

I answer that, In accordance with what has been already shown, it is necessary to say that the intellect is a power of the soul, and not the very essence of the soul.[6] For the essence of that which operates is then alone the immediate principle of operation, when operation itself is its being; for as power is related to operation as to its act, so is essence related to being. But in God alone is His act of understanding the same as His very Being. Hence, in God alone is His intellect His essence; while in other intellectual creatures, the intellect is a power.

Reply Obj. 1. Sense is sometimes taken for the power, and sometimes for the sensitive soul; for the sensitive soul takes its name from its chief power, which is sense. And in like manner the intellectual soul is sometimes called intellect, as from its chief power; and thus we read that the *intellect is a substance.*[7] And in this sense also Augustine says that the mind is spirit or essence.[8]

Reply Obj. 2. The appetitive and intellectual powers are different genera of powers in the soul, by reason of the different natures of their objects. But the appetitive power agrees partly with the intellectual power, and partly with the sensitive, in its mode of operation either through a corporeal organ or without it; for appetite follows apprehension. It is in this way that Augustine puts the will in the mind; and the Philosopher, in the reason.[9]

Reply Obj. 3. In the angels there is no other power besides the intellect and the will, which follows the intellect. This is the reason why an angel is called a *mind* or an *intellect,*

---

[4] *In Evang.,* II, hom. 29 (PL 76, 1214).   [5] *De An.,* II, 3 (414a 32).
[6] Q. 54, a. 3; q. 77, a. 1.   [7] Aristotle, *De An.,* I, 4 (408b 18).   [8] *De Trin.,* IX, 2; XIV, 16 (PL 42, 962; 1053).   [9] *De An.,* III, 9 (432b 5).

because his whole power consists in this. But the soul has many other powers, such as the sensitive and nutritive powers, and therefore the comparison fails.

Reply Obj. 4. The immateriality of a created intelligent substance is not its intellect; but rather through its immateriality it has the power of understanding. Therefore it follows, not that the intellect is the substance of the soul, but that it is its virtue and power.

Second Article

WHETHER THE INTELLECT IS A PASSIVE POWER?

We proceed thus to the Second Article:—

Objection 1. It would seem that the intellect is not a passive power. For everything is passive by its matter, and acts by its form. But the intellectual power results from the immateriality of the intelligent substance. Therefore it seems that the intellect is not a passive power.

Obj. 2. Further, the intellectual power is incorruptible, as we have said above.[10] But *if the intellect is passive, it is corruptible.*[11] Therefore the intellectual power is not passive.

Obj. 3. Further, the *agent is nobler than the patient,* as Augustine[12] and Aristotle[13] say. But all the powers of the vegetative part are active, and yet they are the lowest among the powers of the soul. Much more, therefore, are all the intellectual powers, which are the highest, active.

On the contrary, The Philosopher says that *to understand is in a way to be passive.*[14]

I answer that, To be passive may be taken in three ways. Firstly, in its most strict sense, when from a thing is taken something which belongs to it by virtue either of its nature, or of its proper inclination; as when water loses coolness by heating, and as when a man becomes ill or sad. Secondly, less strictly, a thing is said to be passive when something, whether suitable or unsuitable, is taken away from it. And in this way not only he who is ill is said to be passive, but also he who is healed; not only he that is sad, but also he that is joyful; or whatever way he be altered or moved.

---

[10] Q. 75, a. 6.　　[11] Aristotle, *De An.,* III, 5 (430a 24).　　[12] *De Genesi ad Litt.,* XII, 16 (PL 34, 467).　　[13] *De An.,* III, 5 (430a 18).　　[14] *Op. cit.,* III, 4 (429b 24).

Thirdly, in a wide sense a thing is said to be passive, from the very fact that what is in potentiality to something receives that to which it was in potentiality, without being deprived of anything. And accordingly, whatever passes from potentiality to act may be said to be passive, even when it is perfected. It is *thus* that to understand is to be passive. This is clear from the following reason. For the intellect, as we have seen above, has an operation extending to universal being.[15] We may therefore see whether an intellect is in act or potentiality by observing first of all the nature of the relation of the intellect to universal being. For we find an intellect whose relation to universal being is that of the act of all being; and such is the divine intellect, which is the essence of God, in which, originally and virtually, all being pre-exists as in its first cause. Therefore the divine intellect is not in potentiality, but is pure act. But no created intellect can be an act in relation to the whole universal being; for then it would needs be an infinite being. Therefore no created intellect, by reason of its very being, is the act of all things intelligible; but it is compared to these intelligible things as a potentiality to act.

Now, potentiality has a double relation to act. There is a potentiality which is always perfected by its act. Such is the case with the matter of the heavenly bodies.[16] And there is another potentiality which is not always in act, but proceeds from potentiality to act; as we observe in things that are corrupted and generated. Hence the angelic intellect is always in act as regards those things which it can understand, by reason of its proximity to the first intellect, which is pure act, as we have said above. But the human intellect, which is the lowest in the order of intellects and most remote from the perfection of the divine intellect, is in potentiality with regard to things intelligible, and is at first *like a clean tablet on which nothing is written,* as the Philosopher says.[17] This is made clear from the fact that at first we are only in potentiality towards understanding, and afterwards we are made to understand actually. And so it is evident that with us to understand is *in a way to be passive,* taking passion in the third sense. And consequently the intellect is a passive power.

Reply Obj. 1. This objection is verified of passion in the

---

[15] Q. 78, a. 1.   [16] Q. 58, a. 1.   [17] *De An.,* III, 4 (430a 1)

first and second senses, which belong to primary matter. But in the third sense, passion is in anything which is reduced from potentiality to act.

Reply Obj. 2. *Passive intellect* is the name given by some to the sensitive appetite, in which are the passions of the soul;[18] which appetite is also called *rational by participation,* because it *obeys the reason.*[19] Others give the name of passive intellect to the cogitative power, which is called the *particular reason.*[20] And in each case *passive* may be taken in the two first senses, since this so-called intellect is the act of a corporeal organ. But the intellect which is in potentiality to things intelligible, and which for this reason Aristotle calls the *possible intellect,*[21] is not passive except in the third sense; for it is not an act of a corporeal organ. Hence it is incorruptible.

Reply Obj. 3. The agent is nobler than the patient, if the action and the passion are referred to the same thing; but not always, if they refer to different things. Now the intellect is a passive power in regard to the whole universal being, while the vegetative power is active in regard to some particular thing, namely, the body as united to the soul. Therefore nothing prevents such a passive power being nobler than such an active one.

Third Article

WHETHER THERE IS AN AGENT INTELLECT?

We proceed thus to the Third Article:—

Objection 1. It would seem that there is no agent intellect. For as the senses are to things sensible, so is our intellect to things intelligible. But because sense is in potentiality to things sensible, there is not said to be an *agent sense,* but only a passive one. Therefore, since our intellect is in potentiality to things intelligible, it seems that we cannot say that there is an agent intellect, but only a passive one.[22]

Obj. 2. Further, if we say that also in the senses there is

---

[18] Themistius, *In De An.,* III, 5 (II, 186).—Cf. Averroes, *In De An.,* III, 20 (VI, 170v). [19] Aristotle, *Eth.,* I, 13 (1102b 25). [20] Cf. Averroes, *In De An.,* III, 20 (VI, 171r). [21] *De An.,* III, 4 (429a 22). [22] An argument of William of Auvergne, *De An.,* VII, 4 (II, Suppl., 207).

something active, such as light,[23] on the contrary, light is required for sight, inasmuch as it makes the medium to be actually luminous; for color of its own nature moves the luminous medium. But in the operation of the intellect there is no appointed medium that has to be brought into act. Therefore there is no necessity for an agent intellect.

Obj. 3. Further, the likeness of the agent is received into the patient according to the nature of the patient. But the possible intellect is an immaterial power. Therefore its immaterial nature suffices for forms to be received into it immaterially. Now a form is intelligible in act from the very fact that it is immaterial. Therefore there is no need for an agent intellect to make the species actually intelligible.[24]

On the contrary, The Philosopher says: *As in every nature, so in the soul, there is something by which it becomes all things, and something by which it makes all things.*[25] Therefore we must admit an agent intellect.

I answer that, According to the opinion of Plato, there is no need for an agent intellect in order to make things actually intelligible, but perhaps in order to provide intellectual light to the intellect, as will be explained farther on.[26] For Plato supposed that the forms of natural things subsisted apart from matter, and consequently that they are intelligible;[27] for a thing is actually intelligible from the very fact that it is immaterial. And he called such forms *species or ideas.* From a participation in these, he said that even corporeal matter was formed, in order that individuals might be naturally established in their proper genera and species,[28] and also that our intellect was formed by such participation in order to have knowledge of the genera and species of things.[29] But since Aristotle did not allow that the forms of natural things exist apart from matter, and since forms existing in matter are not actually intelligible,[30] it follows that the natures or forms of the sensible things which we understand are not actually intelligible. Now nothing is reduced from potentiality to act except by something in act; as the senses are made actual by what is actually sensible. We must

[23] Cf. *ibid.*   [24] Cf. *op. cit.,* VII, 5 (II, Suppl., 210).   [25] *De An.,* III, 5 (430a 10).   [26] A. 4; q. 84, a. 6.   [27] Cf. above, q. 6, a. 4. [28] Cf. Aristotle, *Metaph.,* I, 9 (991b 3); Plato, *Phaedo* (p. 100d).—Cf. above, q. 15, a. 3.   [29] Cf. below, q. 84, a. 1; a. 4.   [30] Cf. *Metaph.,* II, 4 (999b 18); VII, 3 (1043b 19).

therefore assign on the part of the intellect some power to make things actually intelligible, by the abstraction of the species from material conditions. And such is the necessity for positing an agent intellect.

Reply Obj. 1. Sensible things are found in act outside the soul; and hence there is no need for an agent sense. Therefore it is clear that, in the nutritive part, all the powers are active, whereas in the sensitive part all are passive; but in the intellectual part, there is something active and something passive.

Reply Obj. 2. There are two opinions as to the effect of light. For some say that light is required for sight, in order to make colors actually visible.[31] And according to this, the agent intellect is required for understanding in like manner and for the same reason as light is required for seeing. But in the opinion of others, light is required for sight, not for the colors to become actually visible, but in order that the medium may become actually luminous, as the Commentator says on *De Anima* ii.[32] And according to this, Aristotle's comparison of the agent intellect to light[33] is verified in this, that as it is required for understanding, so is light required for seeing; but not for the same reason.

Reply Obj. 3. If the agent pre-exist, it may well happen that its likeness is received variously into various things, because of their dispositions. But if the agent does not pre-exist, the disposition of the recipient has nothing to do with the matter. Now the intelligible in act is not something existing in nature, provided, of course, that we are thinking of the nature of sensible things, which do not subsist without matter. And therefore in order to understand them, the immaterial nature of the possible intellect would not suffice but for the presence of the agent intellect, which makes things actually intelligible by way of abstraction.

[31] Avempace: cf. Averroes, *In De An.*, II, comm. 67 (VI, 140r)
[32] *Ibid.*   [33] *De An.*, III, 5 (430a 15).—Cf. Averroes, *In De An.*, II, comm. 67 (VI, 140r); III, comm. 18 (VI, 169v).

Fourth Article

WHETHER THE AGENT INTELLECT IS SOMETHING IN THE SOUL?

We proceed thus to the Fourth Article:—

Objection 1. It would seem that the agent intellect is not something in the soul. For the effect of the agent intellect is to give light for the purpose of understanding. But this is done by something higher than the soul, according to *Jo.* i. 9, *He was the true light that enlighteneth every man coming into this world.* Therefore the agent intellect is not something in the soul.[34]

Obj. 2. Further, the Philosopher says of the agent intellect, *that it does not sometimes understand and sometimes not understand.*[35] But our soul does not always understand, but sometimes it understands, and sometimes it does not understand. Therefore the agent intellect is not something in our soul.[36]

Obj. 3. Further, agent and patient suffice for action. If, therefore, the possible intellect, which is a passive power, is something belonging to the soul; and also the agent intellect, which is an active power:—it follows that man would always be able to understand when he wished, which is clearly false. Therefore the agent intellect is not something in our soul.[37]

Obj. 4. Further, the Philosopher says that the agent intellect is *a substance in actual being.*[38] But nothing can be in potentiality and in act with regard to the same thing. If, therefore, the possible intellect, which is in potentiality to all things intelligible, is something in the soul, it seems impossible for the agent intellect to be also something in our soul.

Obj. 5. Further, if the agent intellect is something in the soul, it must be a power. For it is neither a passion nor a habit, since habits and passions do not have the nature of agents in regard to what the soul receives; but passion is rather the very action of the passive power, while habit is something which results from acts. Now every power flows

---

[34] Cf. William of Auvergne, *De An.*, VII, 6 (II, Suppl., 211).   [35] *De An.*, III, 5 (430a 22).   [36] Cf. William of Auvergne, *De An.*, VII, 3 (II, Suppl., 206).   [37] Cf. *op. cit.*, VII, 4 (II, Suppl., 208).   [38] *De An.*, III, 5 (430a 18).

from the essence of the soul. It would therefore follow that the agent intellect flows from the essence of the soul. And thus it would not be in the soul by way of participation from some higher intellect; which is unfitting. Therefore the agent intellect is not something in our soul.

On the contrary, The Philosopher says that *it is necessary for these differences,* namely, the possible and agent intellect, *to be in the soul.*[39]

I answer that, The agent intellect, of which the Philosopher speaks, is something in the soul. In order to make this evident, we must observe that above the intellectual soul of man we must needs suppose a superior intellect, from which the soul acquires the power of understanding. For what is such by participation, and what is movable, and what is imperfect, always requires the pre-existence of something essentially such, immovable and perfect. Now the human soul is called intellectual by reason of a participation in intellectual power, a sign of which is that it is not wholly intellectual but only in part. Moreover it reaches to the understanding of truth by reasoning, with a certain discursiveness and movement. Even more, it has an imperfect understanding, both because it does not understand everything, and because, in those things which it does understand, it passes from potentiality to act. Therefore there must needs be some higher intellect, by which the soul is helped to understand.

Therefore some held that this intellect, substantially separate, is the agent intellect,[40] which by lighting up the phantasms, as it were, makes them to be actually intelligible. But, even supposing the existence of such a separate agent intellect, it would still be necessary to assign to the human soul some power participating in that superior intellect, by which power the human soul makes things to be actually intelligible. Such is also the case in other perfect natural things, among which, besides the universal active causes, each one is endowed with its proper powers derived from those universal causes: for the sun alone does not generate man, but in man himself there is the power of begetting man; and in like manner with other perfect animals. Now among these

[39] *Op. cit.,* III, 5 (430a 13).   [40] Alexander of Aphrodisias, *De Intellectu et Intellecto* (p. 76); Averroes, *In De An.,* III, comm. 18 (VI, 169v); comm. 19 (VI, 170r); Avicenna, *De An.,* V, 5 (25rb); *Metaph.,* IX, 3 (104rb).

sublunary things nothing is more perfect than the human soul. Therefore we must say that in the soul is some power derived from a higher intellect, whereby it is able to illumine the phantasms.

And we know this by experience, since we perceive that we abstract universal forms from their particular conditions; which is to make them actually intelligible. Now no action belongs to anything except through some principle formally inherent therein, as we have said above of the possible intellect.[41] Therefore the power which is the principle of this action must be something in the soul. For this reason Aristotle compared the agent intellect to light, which is something received into the air,[42] while Plato compared the separate intellect, whose light touches the soul, to the sun, as Themistius says in his commentary on *De Anima* iii.[43]

.But the separate intellect, according to the teaching of our Faith, is God Himself, Who is the soul's Creator, and only beatitude; as will be shown later on.[44] Therefore the human soul derives its intellectual light from Him, according to *Ps.* iv. 7, *The light of Thy countenance, O Lord, is signed upon us.*

Reply Obj. 1. That true light illumines as a universal cause, from which the human soul derives a particular power, as we have explained.

Reply Obj. 2. The Philosopher says those words not of the agent intellect, but of the intellect in act; of which he had already said: *Knowledge in act is the same as the thing.*[45] Or, if we refer those words to the agent intellect, then they are said because it is not owing to the agent intellect that sometimes we do, and sometimes we do not understand, but to the intellect which is in potentiality.

Reply Obj. 3. If the relation of the agent intellect to the possible intellect were that of an active object to a power (as, for instance, of the visible in act to the sight), it would follow that we could understand all things instantly, since the agent intellect is not an object, rather is it that whereby the objects are made to be in act; and for this, besides the presence of the agent intellect, we require the presence of phantasms, the good disposition of the sensitive powers, and

⁴¹ Q. 76, a. 1.   ⁴² *De An.*, III, 5 (430a 15).   ⁴³ *In De An.*, III 5 (II, 191); cf. Plato, *Republic*, VI (p. 508).   ⁴⁴ Q. 90, a. 3; I-II, q. 3, a. 7.   ⁴⁵ *De An.*, III, 5 (430a 19).

practice in this sort of operation. For from one thing understood, other things come to be understood, as from terms propositions are made, and from first principles, conclusions. From this point of view, it matters not whether the agent intellect is something belonging to the soul, or something separate from the soul.

Reply Obj. 4. The intellectual soul is indeed actually immaterial, but it is in potentiality to the determinate species of things. On the contrary, phantasms are actual likenesses of certain species, but they are immaterial in potentiality. Therefore nothing prevents one and the same soul, inasmuch as it is actually immaterial, from having a power by which it makes things actually immaterial, by abstraction from the conditions of individual matter (this power is called the *agent intellect*), and another power, receptive of such species, which is called the *possible intellect* by reason of its being in potentiality to such species.

Reply Obj. 5. Since the essence of the soul is immaterial, created by the supreme intellect, nothing prevents the power which it derives from the supreme intellect, and whereby it abstracts from matter, from proceeding from the essence of the soul, in the same way as its other powers.

Fifth Article

WHETHER THE AGENT INTELLECT IS ONE IN ALL?

We proceed thus to the Fifth Article:—

Objection 1. It would seem that there is one agent intellect in all. For what is separate from the body is not multiplied according to the number of bodies. But the agent intellect is *separate,* as the Philosopher says.[46] Therefore it is not multiplied in the multitude of human bodies, but is one for all men.

Obj. 2. Further, the agent intellect is the cause of the universal, which is one in many. But that which is the cause of unity is still more itself one. Therefore the intellect is the same in all.

Obj. 3. Further, all men agree in the first intellectual concepts. But to these they assent by the agent intellect. Therefore all are united in one agent intellect.

[46] *Ibid.* (430a 17).

On the contrary, The Philosopher says that the agent intellect is as a light.[47] But light is not the same in the various
illuminated things. Therefore the same agent intellect is not
in various men.

I answer that, The truth about this question depends on
what we have already said. For if the agent intellect were
not something belonging to the soul, but were some separate
substance, there would be one agent intellect for all men.
And this is what they mean who hold that there is one agent
intellect for all. But if the agent intellect is something belonging to the soul, as one of its powers, we are bound to say
that there are as many agent intellects as there are souls,
which are multiplied according to the number of men, as we
have said above.[48] For it is impossible that one and the same
power belong to various substances.

Reply Obj. 1. The Philosopher proves that the agent intellect is separate by the fact that the possible intellect is separate; because, as he says, *the agent is more noble than the
patient.*[49] Now the possible intellect is said to be separate
because it is not the act of any corporeal organ. And in this
sense the agent intellect is also called *separate*; but not as a
separate substance.

Reply Obj. 2. The agent intellect is the cause of the universal, by abstracting it from matter. But for this purpose it
need not be one in all intelligent beings; but it must be one
in relation to all those things from which it abstracts the
universal, with respect to which things the universal is one.
And this befits the agent intellect inasmuch as it is immaterial.

Reply Obj. 3. All things which are of one species enjoy in
common the action which accompanies the nature of the
species, and consequently the power which is the principle of
such action; but not in such a way that the power be identical in all. Now to know the first intelligible principles is an
action belonging to the human species. Therefore all men enjoy in common the power which is the principle of this action; and this power is the agent intellect. But there is no
need for it to be identical in all; although it must be derived
by all from one principle. And thus the possession by all men
in common of first principles proves the unity of the separate

⁴⁷ *Ibid.* (430a 15).   ⁴⁸ Q. 76, a. 2.   ⁴⁹ *De An.,* III, 5 (430a 18).

intellect, which Plato compares to the sun, but not the unity of the agent intellect, which Aristotle compares to light.[50]

Eleventh Article

WHETHER THE SPECULATIVE AND PRACTICAL INTELLECTS ARE DISTINCT POWERS?

We proceed thus to the Eleventh Article:—

Objection 1. It would seem that the speculative and practical intellects are distinct powers. For the *apprehensive* and the *motive* are different kinds of powers, as is clear from *De Anima* ii.[51] But the speculative intellect is merely an apprehensive power; while the practical intellect is a motive power. Therefore they are distinct powers.

Obj. 2. Further, the different nature of the object differentiates the power. But the object of the speculative intellect is *truth*, and of the practical, *good*; which differ in nature. Therefore the speculative and practical intellects are distinct powers.

Obj. 3. Further, in the intellectual part, the practical intellect is compared to the speculative, as the estimative is compared to the imaginative power in the sensitive part. But the estimative differs from the imaginative as power from power, as we have said above.[52] Therefore so does the speculative intellect differ from the practical.

On the contrary, The speculative intellect by extension becomes practical.[53] But one power is not changed into another. Therefore the speculative and practical intellects are not distinct powers.

I answer that, The speculative and practical intellects are not distinct powers. The reason for this is, as we have said above, that what is accidental to the nature of the object of a power does not differentiate that power;[54] for it is accidental to a colored thing to be a man, or to be great or small. Hence all such things are apprehended by the same power of sight. Now, to a thing apprehended by the intellect, it is accidental whether it be directed to operation or not; but it is according to this that the speculative and practical intellects differ. For it is the speculative intellect which directs

[50] *Ibid.* (430a 15).   [51] Aristotle, *De An.*, II, 3 (414a 31).   [52] Q. 78, a. 4.   [53] Aristotle, *De An.*, III, 10 (433a 14).   [54] Q. 77, a. 3.

what it apprehends, not to operation, but to the sole consideration of truth; while the practical intellect is that which directs what it apprehends to operation. And this is what the Philosopher says, namely, that *the speculative differs from the practical in its end.*[55] Whence each is named from its end: the one speculative, the other practical—*i.e.,* operative.

Reply Obj. 1. The practical intellect is a motive power, not as executing movement, but as directing towards it; and this belongs to it according to its mode of apprehension.

Reply Obj. 2. Truth and good include one another; for truth is something good, or otherwise it would not be desirable, and good is something true, or otherwise it would not be intelligible. Therefore, just as the object of the appetite may be something true, as having the aspect of good (for example, when some one desires to know the truth), so the object of the practical intellect is the good directed to operation, under the aspect of truth. For the practical intellect knows truth, just as the speculative, but it directs the known truth to operation.

Reply Obj. 3. Many differences differentiate the sensitive powers, which do not differentiate the intellectual powers, as we have said above.[56]

[55] *De An.,* III, 10 (433a 14).   [56] A. 7, ad 2; q. 77, a. 3, ad 4.

THE APPETITIVE POWERS IN GENERAL

(*In Two Articles*)

NEXT we consider the appetitive powers, concerning which there are four heads of consideration: first, the appetitive powers in general; second, sensuality;[1] third, the will;[2] fourth, free choice.[3] Under the first there are two points of inquiry. (1) Whether the appetite should be considered a special power of the soul? (2) Whether the appetite is divided into intellectual and sensitive as distinct powers?

First Article

WHETHER THE APPETITE IS A SPECIAL POWER OF THE SOUL?

We proceed thus to the First Article:—

Objection 1. It would seem that the appetite is not a special power of the soul. For no power of the soul is to be assigned for those things which are common to animate and to inanimate beings. But appetite is common to animate and inanimate beings, since *all desire good,* as the Philosopher says.[4] Therefore the appetite is not a special power of the soul.

Obj. 2. Further, powers are differentiated by their objects. But what we desire is the same as what we know. Therefore the appetitive power is not distinct from the apprehensive power.

Obj. 3. Further, the common is not divided from the proper. But each power of the soul desires some particular desirable thing—namely, its own suitable object. Therefore, with regard to the object which is the desirable in general, we should not assign some particular power distinct from the others, called the appetitive power.

On the contrary, The Philosopher distinguishes the appetitive from the other powers.[5] Damascene also distinguishes the appetitive from the cognitive powers.[6]

---

[1] Q. 81.   [2] Q. 82.   [3] Q. 83.   [4] Aristotle, *Eth.,* I, 1 (1094a 3). [5] *De An.,* II, 3 (414a 31); cf. *op. cit.,* III, 10 (433a 9).   [6] *De Fide Orth.,* II, 22 (PG 94, 941).

I answer that, It is necessary to assign an appetitive power to the soul. To make this evident, we must observe that some inclination follows every form: for example, fire, by its form, is inclined to rise, and to generate its like. Now, the form is found to have a more perfect existence in those things which participate in knowledge than in those which lack knowledge. For in those which lack knowledge, the form is found to determine each thing only to its own being—that is, to the being which is natural to each. Now this natural form is followed by a natural inclination, which is called the natural appetite. But in those things which have knowledge, each one is determined to its own natural being by its natural form, but in such a manner that it is nevertheless receptive of the species of other things. For example, sense receives the species of all sensible things, and the intellect, of all intelligible things; so that the soul of man is, in a way, all things by sense and intellect. In this way, those beings that have knowledge approach, in a way, to a likeness to God, *in Whom all things pre-exist,* as Dionysius says.[7]

Therefore, just as in those beings that have knowledge forms exist in a higher manner and above the manner of natural forms, so there must be in them an inclination surpassing the natural inclination, which is called the natural appetite. And this superior inclination belongs to the appetitive power of the soul, through which the animal is able to desire what it apprehends, and not only that to which it is inclined by its natural form. And so it is necessary to assign an appetitive power to the soul.

Reply Obj. 1. Appetite is found in things which have knowledge, above the common manner in which it is found in all things, as we have said above. Therefore it is necessary to assign to the soul a particular power.

Reply Obj. 2. What is apprehended and what is desired are the same in reality, but differ in aspect; for a thing is apprehended as something sensible or intelligible, whereas it is desired as suitable or good. Now, it is diversity of aspect in the objects, and not material diversity, which demands a diversity of powers.

Reply Obj. 3. Each power of the soul is a form or nature, and has a natural inclination to something. Hence each power

[7] *De Div. Nom.,* V, 5 (PG 3, 820).

desires, by natural appetite, that object which is suitable to itself. Above this natural appetite is the animal appetite, which follows the apprehension, and by which something is desired, not as suitable to this or that power (such as sight for seeing, or sound for hearing), but as suitable absolutely to the animal.

Second Article

WHETHER THE SENSITIVE AND INTELLECTUAL APPETITES ARE DISTINCT POWERS?

We proceed thus to the Second Article:—

Objection 1. It would seem that the sensitive and intellectual appetites are not distinct powers. For powers are not differentiated by accidental differences, as we have seen above.[8] But it is accidental to the appetible object whether it be apprehended by the sense or by the intellect. Therefore the sensitive and intellectual appetites are not distinct powers.

Obj. 2. Further, intellectual knowledge is of universals, and is thereby distinguished from sensitive knowledge, which is of individuals. But there is no place for this distinction in the appetitive part. For since the appetite is a movement of the soul to individual things, every act of the appetite seems to be towards individual things. Therefore the intellectual appetite is not distinguished from the sensitive.

Obj. 3. Further, just as under the apprehensive power the appetitive is subordinate as a lower power, so also is the motive power. But the motive power which in man follows the intellect is not distinct from the motive power which in animals follows sense. Therefore, for a like reason, neither is there distinction in the appetitive part.

On the contrary, The Philosopher distinguishes a double appetite, and says that the higher appetite moves the lower.[9]

I answer that, We must needs say that the intellectual appetite is a distinct power from the sensitive appetite. For the appetitive power is a passive power, which is naturally moved by the thing apprehended. Therefore *the apprehended appetible is a mover which is not moved, while the appetite*

[8] Q. 77, a. 3.   [9] *De An.,* III, 9 (432b 5); 10 (433a 23); 11 (434a 12).

is a moved mover, as the Philosopher says in *De Anima* iii. and in *Metaph*. xii.[10] Now things passive and movable are differentiated according to the distinction of the corresponding active and motive principles, for the motive must be proportionate to the movable, and the active to the passive. Indeed, the passive power itself has its very nature from its relation to its active principle. Therefore, since what is apprehended by the intellect and what is apprehended by sense are generically different, consequently, the intellectual appetite is distinct from the sensitive.

Reply Obj. 1. It is not accidental to the thing desired to be apprehended by the sense or the intellect. On the contrary, this belongs to it by its nature, for the appetible does not move the appetite except as it is apprehended. Hence differences in the thing apprehended are of themselves differences in the appetible. And so the appetitive powers are distinguished according to the distinction of the things apprehended as according to their proper objects.

Reply Obj. 2. The intellectual appetite, though it tends to individual things which exist outside the soul, yet it tends to them as standing under the universal; as when it desires something because it is good. Therefore the Philosopher says that hatred can be of a universal, as when *we hate every kind of thief*.[11] In the same way, by the intellectual appetite we may desire the immaterial good, which is not apprehended by sense, such as knowledge, virtue and the like.

Reply Obj. 3. As the Philosopher says, a universal opinion does not move except by means of a particular opinion;[12] and in like manner the higher appetite moves by means of the lower. Therefore, there are not two distinct motive powers following the intellect and the sense.

[10] *Op. cit.*, III, 10 (433b 16); *Metaph.*, XI, 7 (1072a 26).   [11] *Rhetor.*, II, 4 (1382a 5).   [12] Aristotle, *De An.*, III, 11 (434a 16).

Question LXXXI

THE POWER OF SENSUALITY

(*In Three Articles*)

NEXT we have to consider the power of sensuality, concerning which there are three points of inquiry: (1) Whether sensuality is only an appetitive power? (2) Whether it is divided into *irascible* and *concupiscible* as distinct powers? (3) Whether the irascible and concupiscible powers obey reason?

First Article

WHETHER SENSUALITY IS ONLY APPETITIVE?

We proceed thus to the First Article:—

Objection 1. It would seem that sensuality is not only appetitive, but also cognitive. For Augustine says that *the sensual movement of the soul which is directed to the bodily senses is common to us and beasts.*[1] But the bodily senses belong to the apprehensive powers. Therefore sensuality is a cognitive power.

Obj. 2. Further, things which come under one division seem to be of one genus. But Augustine divides sensuality against the higher and lower reason, which belong to knowledge.[2] Therefore sensuality also is apprehensive.

Obj. 3. Further, in man's temptations sensuality stands in the place of the *serpent.* But in the temptation of our first parents, the serpent presented himself as one giving information and proposing sin, which belong to the cognitive power. Therefore sensuality is a cognitive power.

On the contrary, Sensuality is defined as *the appetite of things belonging to the body.*[3]

I answer that, The name *sensuality* seems to be taken from the sensual movement, of which Augustine speaks,[4] just as the name of a power is taken from its act, for instance, sight from seeing. Now the sensual movement is an appetite following sensible apprehension. For the act of the apprehensive

---

[1] *De Trin.*, XII, 12 (PL 42, 1007). [2] *Ibid.* [3] Cf. Peter Lombard, *Sent.*, II, xxiv, 4 (I, 421). [4] *De Trin.*, XII, 12; 13 (PL 42, 1007; 1009).

power is not so properly called a movement as the act of the appetite; since the operation of the apprehensive power is completed in the very fact that the thing apprehended is in the one that apprehends, while the operation of the appetitive power is completed in the fact that he who desires is borne towards the desirable thing. Hence it is that the operation of the apprehensive power is likened to rest; whereas the operation of the appetitive power is rather likened to movement. Therefore by sensual movement we understand the operation of the appetitive power. Thus, sensuality is the name of the sensitive appetite.

Reply Obj. 1. By saying that the sensual movement of the soul is directed to the bodily senses, Augustine does not give us to understand that the bodily senses are included in sensuality, but rather that the movement of sensuality is a certain inclination to the bodily senses, since we desire things which are apprehended through the bodily senses. And thus the bodily senses pertain to sensuality as a sort of gateway.

Reply Obj. 2. Sensuality is divided against higher and lower reason, as having in common with them the act of movement; for the apprehensive power, to which belong the higher and lower reason, is a motive power; as is appetite, to which sensuality pertains.

Reply Obj. 3. The serpent not only showed and proposed sin, but also incited to the commission of sin. And in this, sensuality is signified by the serpent.

Second Article

WHETHER THE SENSITIVE APPETITE IS DIVIDED INTO THE IRASCIBLE AND CONCUPISCIBLE AS DISTINCT POWERS?

We proceed thus to the Second Article:—

Objection 1. It would seem that the sensitive appetite is not divided into the irascible and concupiscible as distinct powers. For the same power of the soul regards both sides of a contrariety, as sight regards both black and white, according to the Philosopher.[5] But suitable and harmful are contraries. Since, then, the concupiscible power regards what is suitable, while the irascible is concerned with what is harm-

[5] Aristotle, *De An.*, II, 11 (422b 23).

ful, it seems that irascible and concupiscible are the same power in the soul.

Obj. 2. Further, the sensitive appetite regards only what is suitable according to the senses. But such is the object of the concupiscible power. Therefore there is no sensitive appetite differing from the concupiscible.

Obj. 3. Further, hatred is in the irascible part, for Jerome says on *Matt.* xiii. 33: *We ought to have the hatred of vice in the irascible power.*[6] But hatred is contrary to love, and is in the concupiscible part. Therefore the concupiscible and irascible are the same powers.

On the contrary, Gregory of Nyssa and Damascene assign two parts to the sensitive appetite, the irascible and the concupiscible.[7]

I answer that, The sensitive appetite is one generic power, and is called sensuality; but it is divided into two powers, which are species of the sensitive appetite—the irascible and the concupiscible. In order to make this clear, we must observe that in natural corruptible things there is needed an inclination not only to the acquisition of what is suitable and to the avoiding of what is harmful, but also to resistance against corruptive and contrary forces which are a hindrance to the acquisition of what is suitable, and are productive of harm. For example, fire has a natural inclination, not only to rise from a lower place, which is unsuitable to it, towards a higher place, which is suitable, but also to resist whatever destroys or hinders its action. Therefore, since the sensitive appetite is an inclination following sensitive apprehension (just as natural appetite is an inclination following the natural form), there must needs be in the sensitive part two appetitive powers:—one, through which the soul is inclined absolutely to seek what is suitable, according to the senses, and to fly from what is hurtful, and this is called the *concupiscible*; and another, whereby an animal resists the attacks that hinder what is suitable, and inflict harm, and this is called the *irascible*. Whence we say that its object is something arduous, because its tendency is to overcome and rise above obstacles.

Now these two inclinations are not to be reduced to one

---

[6] *In Matt.*, I, super XIII, 33 (PL 26, 94).   [7] Cf. Nemesius, *De Nat. Hom.*, XVI; XVII (PL 40, 672; 676); Damascene, *De Fide Orth.*, II, 12 (PG 94, 928).

principle. For sometimes the soul busies itself with unpleasant things, against the inclination of the concupiscible appetite, in order that, following the impulse of the irascible appetite, it may fight against obstacles. And so even the passions of the irascible appetite counteract the passions of the concupiscible appetite; since concupiscence, on being roused, diminishes anger, and anger, being roused, very often diminishes concupiscence. This is clear also from the fact that the irascible is, as it were, the champion and defender of the concupiscible, when it rises up against what hinders the acquisition of the suitable things which the concupiscible desires, or against what inflicts harm, from which the concupiscible flies. And for this reason all the passions of the irascible appetite rise from the passions of the concupiscible appetite and terminate in them. For instance, anger rises from sadness, and, having wrought vengeance, terminates in joy. For this reason also the quarrels of animals are about things concupiscible—namely, food and sex, as the Philosopher says.[8]

Reply Obj. 1. The concupiscible power regards both what is suitable and what is unsuitable. But the object of the irascible power is to resist the onslaught of the unsuitable.

Reply Obj. 2. Just as in the apprehensive powers of the sensitive part there is an estimative power, which perceives those things which do not impress the senses, as we have said above,[9] so also in the sensitive appetite there is an appetitive power which regards something as suitable, not because it pleases the senses, but because it is useful to the animal for self-defence. And this is the irascible power.

Reply Obj. 3. Hatred belongs absolutely to the concupiscible appetite, but by reason of the strife which arises from hatred it may belong to the irascible appetite.

Third Article

WHETHER THE IRASCIBLE AND CONCUPISCIBLE APPETITES OBEY REASON?

We proceed thus to the Third Article:—

Objection 1. It would seem that the irascible and concupiscible appetites do not obey reason. For irascible and concupiscible are parts of sensuality. But sensuality does not

[8] Aristotle, *Hist. Anim.*, VIII, 1 (589a 2).   [9] Q. 78, a. 2.

obey reason; which is why it is signified by the serpent, as Augustine says.[10] Therefore the irascible and concupiscible appetites do not obey reason.

Obj. 2. Further, what obeys a certain thing does not resist it. But the irascible and concupiscible appetites resist reason, according to the Apostle (*Rom.* vii. 23): *I see another law in my members fighting against the law of my mind.* Therefore the irascible and concupiscible appetites do not obey reason.

Obj. 3. Further, as the appetitive power is inferior to the rational part of the soul, so also is the sensitive power. But the sensitive part of the soul does not obey reason, for we neither hear nor see just when we wish. Therefore, in like manner, neither do the powers of the sensitive appetite, the irascible and concupiscible, obey reason.

On the contrary, Damascene says that *the part of the soul which is obedient and amenable to reason is divided into concupiscence and anger.*[11]

I answer that, In two ways do the irascible and concupiscible powers obey the higher part, in which are the intellect or reason, and the will: first, as to the reason, and secondly, as to the will. They obey the reason in their own acts, because in other animals the sensitive appetite is naturally moved by the estimated power; for instance, a sheep, esteeming the wolf as an enemy, is afraid. In man the estimated power, as we have said above, is replaced by the cogitative power, which is called by some *the particular reason,* because it compares individual intentions.[12] Hence, in man the sensitive appetite is naturally moved by this particular reason. But this same particular reason is naturally guided and moved according to the universal reason; and that is why in syllogisms particular conclusions are drawn from universal propositions. Therefore it is clear that the universal reason directs the sensitive appetite, which is divided into concupiscible and irascible, and that this appetite obeys it. But because to draw particular conclusions from universal principles is not the work of the intellect, as such, but of the reason, hence it is that the irascible and concupiscible are said to obey the reason rather than to obey the intellect. Anyone can experience this in himself; for by applying certain universal considerations, anger or fear or the like may be lessened or increased.

[10] *De Trin.,* XII, 12; 13 (PL 42, 1007; 1009).   [11] *De Fide Orth.,* II, 12 (PG 94, 928).   [12] Q. 78, a. 4.

To the will also is the sensitive appetite subject in execution, which is accomplished by the motive power. For in other animals movement follows at once the concupiscible and irascible appetites. For instance, the sheep, fearing the wolf, flies at once, because it has no superior counteracting appetite. On the contrary, man is not moved at once according to the irascible and concupiscible appetites; but he awaits the command of the will, which is the superior appetite. For wherever there is order among a number of motive powers, the second moves only by virtue of the first; and so the lower appetite is not sufficient to cause movement, unless the higher appetite consents. And this is what the Philosopher says, namely, that *the higher appetite moves the lower appetite, as the higher sphere moves the lower.*[13] In this way, therefore, the irascible and concupiscible are subject to reason.

Reply Obj. 1. Sensuality is signified by the serpent in what is proper to it as a sensitive power. But the irascible and concupiscible powers denominate the sensitive appetite rather on the part of the act, to which they are led by the reason, as we have said.

Reply Obj. 2. As the Philosopher says: *We observe in an animal a despotic and a politic principle; for the soul dominates the body by a despotic rule, but the intellect dominates the appetite by a politic and royal rule.*[14] For that rule is called despotic whereby a man rules his slaves, who have not the means to resist in any way the orders of the one that commands them, since they have nothing of their own. But that rule is called politic and royal by which a man rules over free subjects, who, though subject to the government of the ruler, have nevertheless something of their own, by reason of which they can resist the orders of him who commands. And so, the soul is said to rule the body by a despotic rule, because the members of the body cannot in any way resist the sway of the soul, but at the soul's command both hand and foot, and whatever member is naturally moved by voluntary movement, are at once removed. But the intellect or reason is said to govern the irascible and concupiscible by a politic rule because the sensitive appetite has something of its own, by virtue whereof it can resist the commands of reason. For the sensitive appetite is naturally moved, not only by the esti-

[13] *De An.*, III, 11 (434a 12).   [14] *Polit.*, I, 2 (1254b 2).

mative power in other animals, and in man by the cogitative power which the universal reason guides, but also by the imagination and the sense. Whence it is that we experience that the irascible and concupiscible powers do resist reason, inasmuch as we sense or imagine something pleasant, which reason forbids, or unpleasant, which reason commands. And so from the fact that the irascible and concupiscible resist reason in something, we must not conclude that they do not obey it.

Reply Obj. 3. The exterior senses require for their acts exterior sensible things by which to be immuted, whose presence does not lie in the power of the reason. But the interior powers, both appetitive and apprehensive, do not require exterior things. Therefore they are subject to the command of reason, which can not only incite or modify the affections of the appetitive power, but can also form the phantasms of the imagination.

Question LXXXII

THE WILL

(*In Five Articles*)

WE NEXT consider the will. Under this head there are five points of inquiry: (1) Whether the will desires something of necessity? (2) Whether it desires everything of necessity? (3) Whether it is a higher power than the intellect? (4) Whether the will moves the intellect? (5) Whether the will is divided into irascible and concupiscible?

First Article

WHETHER THE WILL DESIRES SOMETHING OF NECESSITY?

We proceed thus to the First Article:—

Objection 1. It would seem that the will desires nothing of necessity. For Augustine says that if anything is necessary, it is not voluntary.[1] But whatever the will desires is voluntary. Therefore nothing that the will desires is desired of necessity.

Obj. 2. Further, *the rational powers*, according to the Philosopher, *extend to opposite things.*[2] But the will is a rational power, because, as he says, *the will is in the reason.*[3] Therefore the will extends to opposite things, and hence is determined to nothing of necessity.

Obj. 3. Further, by the will we are masters of our own actions. But we are not masters of that which is of necessity. Therefore the act of the will cannot be necessitated.

On the contrary, Augustine says that *all desire happiness with one will.*[4] Now if this were not necessary, but contingent, there would at least be a few exceptions. Therefore the will desires something of necessity.

I answer that, The word *necessity* is employed in many ways. For that which must be is necessary. Now that a thing must be may belong to it by an intrinsic principle:—either material, as when we say that everything composed of contraries is of necessity corruptible;—or formal, as when we

[1] *De Civit. Dei,* V, 10 (PL 41, 152). [2] *Metaph.,* VIII, 2 (1046b 5). [3] Aristotle, *De An.,* III, 9 (432b 5). [4] *De Trin.,* XIII, 4 (PL 42, 1018).

say that it is necessary for the three angles of a triangle to be
equal to two right angles. And this is *natural* and *absolute
necessity*. In another way, that a thing must be belongs to it
by reason of something extrinsic, which is either the end or
the agent. The necessity is imposed on something by the end
when without it the end is not to be attained or so well attained: for instance, food is said to be necessary for life, and
a horse is necessary for a journey. This is called the *necessity
of the end,* and sometimes also *utility.* The necessity is imposed by the agent when someone is forced by some agent,
so that he is not able to do the contrary. This is called the
necessity of coercion.

Now this necessity of coercion is altogether repugnant to
the will. For we call *violent* that which is against the inclination of a thing. But the very movement of the will is an inclination to something. Therefore, just as a thing is called
natural because it is according to the inclination of nature, so
a thing is called *voluntary* because it is according to the inclination of the will. Therefore, just as it is impossible for a
thing to be at the same time violent and natural, so it is impossible for a thing to be absolutely coerced, or violent, and
voluntary.

But the necessity of the end is not repugnant to the will,
when the end cannot be attained except in one way; and thus
from the will to cross the sea arises in the will the necessity
to desire a ship.

In like manner, neither is natural necessity repugnant to
the will. Indeed, just as the intellect of necessity adheres to
first principles, so the will must of necessity adhere to the last
end, which is happiness; for the end is in practical matters
what the principle is in speculative matters, as is said in
Physics ii.[5] For what befits a thing naturally and immovably
must be the root and principle of all else pertaining thereto,
since the nature of a thing is the first in everything, and every
movement arises from something immovable.

Reply Obj. 1. The words of Augustine are to be understood
of the necessity of coercion. But natural necessity *does not
take away the liberty of the will,* as he himself says in the
same work.[6]

Reply Obj. 2. The will, so far as it desires a thing nat-

[5] Aristotle, *Phys.*, II, 9 (200a 21).   [6] *De Civit. Dei,* V, 10 (PL 41,
152).

urally, corresponds rather to the intellect of natural principles than to the reason, which extends to contraries. Hence, in this respect, it is rather an intellectual than a rational power.

Reply Obj. 3. We are masters of our own actions by reasons of our being able to choose this or that. But choice regards, not the end, but *the means to the end,* as the Philosopher says.[7] Consequently, the desire of the ultimate end is not among those actions of which we are masters.

Second Article

WHETHER THE WILL DESIRES OF NECESSITY WHATEVER IT DESIRES?

We proceed thus to the Second Article:—
Objection 1. It would seem that the will desires of necessity all that it desires. For Dionysius says that *evil is outside the scope of the will.*[8] Therefore the will tends of necessity to the good which is proposed to it.

Obj. 2. Further, the object of the will is compared to the will as the mover to the movable thing. But the movement of the movable necessarily follows the mover. Therefore it seems that the will's object moves it of necessity.

Obj. 3. Further, just as the thing apprehended by sense is the object of the sensitive appetite, so the thing apprehended by the intellect is the object of the intellectual appetite, which is called the will. But what is apprehended by the sense moves the sensitive appetite of necessity, for Augustine says that *animals are moved by things seen.*[9] Therefore it seems that whatever is apprehended by the intellect moves the will of necessity.

On the contrary, Augustine says that *it is the will by which we sin and live well.*[10] Thus, the will extends to opposites. Therefore it does not desire of necessity all things whatsoever it desires.

I answer that, The will does not desire of necessity whatsoever it desires. In order to make this evident we must observe that, just as the intellect naturally and of necessity adheres

---

[7] Aristotle, *Eth.,* III, 2 (111b 27).   [8] *De Div. Nom.,* IV, 32 (PG 3, 732).   [9] *De Genesi ad Litt.,* IX, 14 (PL 34, 402).   [10] *Retract.,* I, 9 (PL 32, 596); *De Civit. Dei,* V, 10 (PL 41, 152).

to first principles, so the will adheres to the last end, as we have said already. Now there are some intelligible things which have no necessary connection with first principles: *e.g.*, contingent propositions, the denial of which does not involve a denial of first principles. And to such the intellect does not assent of necessity. But there are some propositions which have a necessary connection with first principles, namely, demonstrable conclusions, a denial of which involves a denial of first principles. And to these the intellect assents of necessity, when once it is aware (by demonstration) of the necessary connection of these conclusions with the principles; but it does not assent of necessity until through the demonstration it recognizes the necessity of such a connection.

It is the same with the will. For there are certain particular goods which have not a necessary connection with happiness, because without them a man can be happy; and to such the will does not adhere of necessity. But there are some things which have a necessary connection with happiness, namely, those by means of which man adheres to God, in Whom alone true happiness consists. Nevertheless, until through the certitude produced by seeing God the necessity of such a connection be shown, the will does not adhere to God of necessity, nor to those things which are of God. But the will of the man who sees God in His essence of necessity adheres to God, just as now we desire of necessity to be happy. It is therefore clear that the will does not desire of necessity whatever it desires.

Reply Obj. 1. The will can tend to nothing except under the aspect of good. But because good is of many kinds, for this reason the will is not of necessity determined to one.

Reply Obj. 2. The mover of necessity causes movement in the movable thing only when the power of the mover exceeds the movable thing in such a way that its entire capacity is subject to the mover. But as the capacity of the will is for the universal and perfect good, it is not subjected to any particular good. And therefore it is not of necessity moved by it.

Reply Obj. 3. The sensitive power does not compare different things with each other, as reason does; but it apprehends simply some one thing. Therefore, according to that one thing, it moves the sensitive appetite in a determinate way. But the reason is a power that compares several things together. Therefore the intellectual appetite—that is, the will

—may be moved by several things, but not of necessity by one thing.

Fourth Article

WHETHER THE WILL MOVES THE INTELLECT?

We proceed thus to the Fourth Article:—

Objection 1. It would seem that the will does not move the intellect. For what moves excels and precedes what is moved, because what moves is an agent, and *the agent is nobler than the patient*, as Augustine says,[11] and the Philosopher.[12] But the intellect excels and precedes the will, as we have said above. Therefore the will does not move the intellect.

Obj. 2. Further, what moves is not moved by what is moved, except perhaps accidentally. But the intellect moves the will, because the good apprehended by the intellect moves without being moved; whereas the appetite is a moved mover. Therefore the intellect is not moved by the will.

Obj. 3. Further, we can will nothing but what we understand. If, therefore, in order to understand, the will moves by willing to understand, that act of the will must be preceded by another act of the intellect, and this act of the intellect by another act of the will, and so on indefinitely, which is impossible. Therefore the will does not move the intellect.

On the contrary, Damascene says: *It is in our power to learn an art or not, as we will.*[13] But a thing is in our power by the will, and we learn an art by the intellect. Therefore the will moves the intellect.

I answer that, A thing is said to move in two ways: First, as an end, as when we say that the end moves the agent. In this way the intellect moves the will, because the understood good is the object of the will, and moves it as an end. Secondly, a thing is said to move as an agent, as what alters moves what is altered, and what impels moves what is impelled. In this way the will moves the intellect, and all the powers of the soul, as Anselm says.[14] The reason is, because wherever we have order among a number of active powers, that power which is related to the universal end moves the

[11] *De Genesi ad Litt.,* XII, 16 (PL 34, 467).   [12] *De An.,* III, 5 (430a 18).   [13] *De Fide Orth.,* II, 26 (PG 94, 960).   [14] Eadmer, *De Similit.,* II (PL 159, 605).

powers which refer to particular ends. And we may observe this both in nature and in political things. For the heavens, which aims at the universal preservation of things subject to generation and corruption, moves all inferior bodies, each of which aims at the preservation of its own species or of the individual. So, too, a king, who aims at the common good of the whole kingdom, by his rule moves all the governors of cities, each of whom rules over his own particular city. Now the object of the will is the good and the end in general, whereas each power is directed to some suitable good proper to it, as sight is directed to the perception of color, and the intellect to the knowledge of truth. Therefore the will as an agent moves all the powers of the soul to their respective acts, except the natural powers of the vegetative part, which are not subject to our choice.

Reply Obj. 1. The intellect may be considered in two ways: as apprehensive of universal being and truth, and as a reality and a particular power having a determinate act. In like manner also the will may be considered in two ways: according to the common nature of its object—that is to say, as appetitive of universal good—and as a determinate power of the soul having a determinate act. If, therefore, the intellect and will be compared with one another according to the universality of their respective objects, then, as we have said above, the intellect is absolutely higher and nobler than the will. If, however, we take the intellect in relation to the common nature of its object and the will as a determinate power, then again the intellect is higher and nobler than the will, because under the notion of being and truth is contained both the will itself, its act, and its object. Therefore the intellect understands the will, its act, and its object, just as it understands other species of things, as stone or wood, which are contained in the common notion of being and truth. But if we consider the will in relation to the common nature of its object, which is good, and the intellect as a reality and a special power, then the intellect itself, its act, and its object, which is the true, each of which is some species of good, are contained under the common notion of good. And in this way the will is higher than the intellect, and can move it. From this we can easily understand why these powers include one another in their acts, because the intellect understands that the will wills, and the will wills the intellect to understand. In the same way, the good is contained under the true, inasmuch as it is an understood truth, and the true under the good, inasmuch as it is a desired good.

Reply Obj. 2. The intellect moves the will in one sense, and the will moves the intellect in another, as we have said above.

Reply Obj. 3. There is no need to go on indefinitely, but we must stop at the intellect as preceding all the rest. For every movement of the will must be preceded by apprehension, whereas every apprehension is not preceded by an act of the will; but the principle of counselling and understanding is an intellectual principle higher than our intellect—namely, God; as Aristotle also says, explaining in this way that there is no need to proceed indefinitely.[15]

[15] *Eth. Eudem.,* VII, 14 (1248a 26).

FREE CHOICE

(*In Four Articles*)

WE NOW inquire concerning free choice. Under this head there are four points of inquiry: (1) Whether man has free choice? (2) What is free choice—a power, an act, or a habit? (3) If it is a power, is it appetitive or cognitive? (4) If it is appetitive, is it the same power as the will, or distinct?

First Article

WHETHER MAN HAS FREE CHOICE?

We proceed thus to the First Article:—

Objection 1. It would seem that man has not free choice. For whoever has free choice does what he wills. But man does not what he wills, for it is written (*Rom.* vii. 19): *For the good which I will I do not, but the evil which I will not, that I do.* Therefore man has not free choice.

Obj. 2. Further, whoever has free choice has in his power to will or not to will, to do or not to do. But this is not in man's power, for it is written (*Rom.* ix. 16): *It is not of him that willeth*—namely, to will—*nor of him that runneth*—namely, to run. Therefore man has not free choice.

Obj. 3. Further, he is free who is his own master, as the Philosopher says.[1] Therefore what is moved by another is not free. But God moves the will, for it is written (*Prov.* xxi. 1): *The heart of the king is in the hand of the Lord; whithersoever He will He shall turn it;* and (*Phil.* ii. 13): *It is God Who worketh in you both to will and to accomplish.* Therefore man has not free choice.

Obj. 4. Further, whoever has free choice is master of his own actions. But man is not master of his own actions, for it is written (*Jer.* x. 23): *The way of a man is not his, neither is it in a man to walk.* Therefore man has not free choice.

Obj. 5. Further, the Philosopher says: *According as each one is, such does the end seem to him.*[2] But it is not in our power to be such as we are, for this comes to us from nature.

---

[1] Aristotle, *Metaph.*, I, 2 (982b 26).   [2] *Eth.*, III, 5 (1114a 32).

Therefore it is natural to us to follow some particular end, and therefore we are not free in so doing.

On the contrary, It is written (*Ecclus.* xv. 14): *God made man from the beginning, and left him in the hand of his own counsel;* and the *Gloss* adds: *That is, in the liberty of choice.*[3]

I answer that, Man has free choice, or otherwise counsels, exhortations, commands, prohibitions, rewards and punishments would be in vain. In order to make this evident, we must observe that some things act without judgment, as a stone moves downwards; and in like manner all things which lack knowledge. And some act from judgment, but not a free judgment; as brute animals. For the sheep, seeing the wolf, judges it a thing to be shunned, from a natural and not a free judgment; because it judges, not from deliberation, but from natural instinct. And the same thing is to be said of any judgment in brute animals. But man acts from judgment, because by his apprehensive power he judges that something should be avoided or sought. But because this judgment, in the case of some particular act, is not from a natural instinct, but from some act of comparison in the reason, therefore he acts from free judgment and retains the power of being inclined to various things. For reason in contingent matters may follow opposite courses, as we see in dialectical syllogisms and rhetorical arguments. Now particular operations are contingent, and therefore in such matters the judgment of reason may follow opposite courses, and is not determinate to one. And in that man is rational, it is necessary that he have free choice.

Reply Obj. 1. As we have said above, the sensitive appetite, though it obeys the reason, yet in a given case can resist by desiring what the reason forbids.[4] This is therefore the good which man does not when he wishes—namely, *not to desire against reason,* as Augustine says.[5]

Reply Obj. 2. Those words of the Apostle are not to be taken as though man does not wish or does not run of his free choice, but because free choice is not sufficient thereto unless it be moved and helped by God.

Reply Obj. 3. Free choice is the cause of its own move-

---

[3] *Glossa interl.* (III, 401v); cf. *Glossa ordin.* (III, 401E).   [4] Q. 81, a. 3, ad 2.   [5] *Glossa interl.,* super *Rom.,* VII, 19 (VI, 171).—Cf. St. Augustine, *Serm. ad Popul.,* serm. CLIV, 3 (PL 38, 834).

ment, because by his free choice man moves himself to act. But it does not of necessity belong to liberty that what is free should be the first cause of itself, as neither for one thing to be cause of another need it be the first cause. God, therefore, is the first cause, Who moves causes both natural and voluntary. And just as by moving natural causes He does not prevent their actions from being natural, so by moving voluntary causes He does not deprive their actions of being voluntary; but rather is He the cause of this very thing in them, for He operates in each thing according to its own nature.

Reply Obj. 4. *Man's way* is said *not to be his* in the execution of his choice, wherein he may be impeded, whether he will or not. The choice itself, however, is in us, but presupposes the help of God.

Reply Obj. 5. Quality in man is of two kinds: natural and adventitious. Now the natural quality may be in the intellectual part, or in the body and its powers. From the very fact, therefore, that man is such by virtue of a natural quality which is in the intellectual part, he naturally desires his last end, which is happiness. This desire is, indeed, a natural desire, and is not subject to free choice, as is clear from what we have said above.[6] But on the part of the body and its powers, man may be such by virtue of a natural quality, inasmuch as he is of such a temperament or disposition due to any impression whatever produced by corporeal causes, which cannot affect the intellectual part, since it is not the act of a corporeal organ. And such as a man is by virtue of a corporeal quality, such also does his end seem to him, because from such a disposition a man is inclined to choose or reject something. But these inclinations are subject to the judgment of reason, which the lower appetite obeys, as we have said.[7] Therefore this is in no way prejudicial to free choice.

The adventitious qualities are habits and passions, by virtue of which a man is inclined to one thing rather than to another. And yet even these inclinations are subject to the judgment of reason. Such qualities, too, are subject to reason, as it is in our power either to acquire them, whether by causing them or disposing ourselves to them, or to reject them. And so there is nothing in this that is repugnant to free choice.

[6] Q. 82, a. 1 and 2.   [7] Q. 81, a. 3.

Second Article

WHETHER FREE CHOICE IS A POWER?

We proceed thus to the Second Article:—

Objection 1. It would seem that free choice is not a power. For free choice is nothing but a free judgment. But judgment denominates an act, not a power. Therefore free choice is not a power.

Obj. 2. Further, free choice is defined as *the faculty of the will and reason.*[8] But faculty denominates the facility of power, which is due to a habit. Therefore free choice is a habit. Moreover Bernard says that free choice is *the soul's habit of disposing of itself.*[9] Therefore it is not a power.

Obj. 3. Further, no natural power is forfeited through sin. But free choice is forfeited through sin, for Augustine says that *man, by abusing free choice, loses both it and himself.*[10] Therefore free choice is not a power.

On the contrary, Nothing but a power, seemingly, is the subject of a habit. But free choice is the subject of grace, by the help of which it chooses what is good. Therefore free choice is a power.

I answer that, Although *free choice,* in its strict sense, denotes an act, in the common manner of speaking we call free choice that which is the principle of the act by which man judges freely. Now in us the principle of an act is both power and habit; for we say that we know something both by science and by the intellectual power. Therefore free choice must be either a power,[11] or a habit,[12] or a power with a habit.[13] That it is neither a habit nor a power together with a habit can be clearly proved in two ways. First of all, because, if it is a habit, it must be a natural habit; for it is natural to man to have free choice. But there is no natural habit in us with respect to those things which come under free choice, for we are naturally inclined to those things of which we have natural habits, for instance, to assent to first principles. Now those things to which we are naturally inclined are not sub-

---

[8] Peter Lombard, *Sent.,* II, xxiv, 3 (I, 421).   [9] St. Bernard, *De Gratia et Libero Arbitrio,* I (PL 182, 1002).   [10] *Enchir.,* XXX (PL 40, 246).   [11] St. Albert, *Summa de Creatur.,* II, q. 70, a. 2 (XXXV, 575).   [12] St. Bonaventure, *In II Cent.,* d. xxv, pt. 1, a. 1, q. 4 (II, 601).   [13] Alex. of Hales, *Summa Theol.,* II, I, no. 390 (II, 486).

ject to free choice, as we have said in the case of the desire of happiness.[14] Therefore it is against the very notion of free choice that it should be a natural habit; and that it should be a non-natural habit is against its nature. Therefore in no sense is it a habit.

Secondly, this is clear because habits are defined as that *by reason of which we are well or ill disposed with regard to actions and passions.*[15] For by temperance we are well-disposed as regards concupiscences, and by intemperance ill-disposed; and by science we are well-disposed to the act of the intellect when we know the truth, and by the contrary habit ill-disposed. But free choice is indifferent to choosing well or ill, and therefore it is impossible that it be a habit. Therefore it is a power.

Reply Obj. 1. It is not unusual for a power to be named from its act. And so from this act, which is a free judgment, is named the power which is the principle of this act. Otherwise, if free choice denominated an act, it would not always remain in man.

Reply Obj. 2. *Faculty* sometimes denominates a power ready for operation, and in this sense faculty is used in the definition of free choice. But Bernard takes habit, not as divided against power, but as signifying any aptitude by which a man is somehow disposed to an act.[16] This may be both by a power and by a habit, for by a power man is, as it were, empowered to do the action, and by the habit he is apt to act well or ill.

Reply Obj. 3. Man is said to have lost free choice by falling into sin, not as to natural liberty, which is freedom from coercion, but as regards freedom from fault and unhappiness. Of this we shall treat later in the treatise on Morals in the second part of this work.[17]

Third Article

WHETHER FREE CHOICE IS AN APPETITIVE POWER?

We proceed thus to the Third Article:—
Objection 1. It would seem that free choice is not an appetitive, but a cognitive power. For Damascene says that *free*

[14] Q. 82, a. 1 and 2.   [15] Aristotle, *Eth.*, II, 5 (1105b 25).   [16] *De Grat. et Lib. Arb.*, I (PL 182, 1002).   [17] *S.T.*, I-II, q. 85; q. 109.

choice straightway accompanies the rational power.[18] But reason is a cognitive power. Therefore free choice is a cognitive power.

Obj. 2. Further, free choice is so called as though it were a free judgment. But to judge is an act of a cognitive power. Therefore free choice is a cognitive power.

Obj. 3. Further, the principal function of free choice is election. But election seems to belong to knowledge, because it implies a certain comparison of one thing to another; which belongs to the cognitive power. Therefore free choice is a cognitive power.

On the contrary, The Philosopher says that election is *the desire of those things which are in our power.*[19] But desire is an act of the appetitive power. Therefore election is also. But free choice is that by which we elect. Therefore free choice is an appetitive power.

I answer that, The proper act of free choice is election, for we say that we have a free choice because we can take one thing while refusing another; and this is to elect. Therefore we must consider the nature of free choice by considering the nature of election. Now two things concur in election: one on the part of the cognitive power, the other on the part of the appetitive power. On the part of the cognitive power, counsel is required, by which we judge one thing to be preferred to another; on the part of the appetitive power, it is required that the appetite should accept the judgment of counsel. Therefore Aristotle leaves it in doubt whether election belongs principally to the appetitive or the cognitive power: since he says that election is either *an appetitive intellect or an intellectual appetite.*[20] But he inclines to its being an intellectual appetite when he describes election as *a desire proceeding from counsel.*[21] And the reason of this is because the proper object of election is the means to the end. Now the means, as such, has the nature of that good which is called *useful*; and since the good, as such, is the object of the appetite, it follows that election is principally an act of an appetitive power. And thus free choice is an appetitive power.

Reply Obj. 1. The appetitive powers accompany the apprehensive, and in this sense Damascene says that free choice straightway accompanies the rational power.

[18] *De Fide Orth.,* II, 27 (PG 94, 949).   [19] *Eth.,* III, 3 (1113a 11). [20] *Op. cit.,* VI, 2 (1139b 4).   [21] *Op. cit.,* III, 3 (1113a 11).

Reply Obj. 2. Judgment, as it were, concludes and terminates counsel. Now counsel is terminated, first, by the judgment of reason; secondly, by the acceptation of the appetite. Hence the Philosopher says that, *having formed a judgment by counsel, we desire in accordance with that counsel.*[22] And in this sense election itself is a judgment from which free choice takes its name.

Reply Obj. 3. This comparison which is implied in the term election belongs to the preceding counsel, which is an act of reason. For though the appetite does not make comparisons, yet inasmuch as it is moved by the apprehensive power which does compare, it has some likeness of comparison, by choosing one in preference to another.

Fourth Article

WHETHER FREE CHOICE IS A POWER DISTINCT FROM
THE WILL?

We proceed thus to the Fourth Article:—

Objection 1. It would seem that free choice is a power distinct from the will.[23] For Damascene says that θέλησις is one thing and βούλησις another.[24] But θέλησις is will, while βούλησις seems to be free choice, because βούλησις, according to him, is the will as concerning an object by way of comparison between two things. Therefore it seems that free choice is a power distinct from the will.

Obj. 2. Further, powers are known by their acts. But election, which is the act of free choice, is distinct from the will, because *the will regards the end, whereas choice regards the means to the end.*[25] Therefore free choice is a power distinct from the will.

Obj. 3. Further, the will is the intellectual appetite. But on the part of the intellect there are two powers—agent and possible. Therefore, also on the part of the intellectual appetite there must be another power besides the will. And this, seemingly, can be only free choice. Therefore free choice is a power distinct from the will.

[22] *Ibid.*   [23] Cf. St. Albert, *Summa de Creatur.*, II, q. 70, a. 2 (XXXV, 577).   [24] *De Fide Orth.*, XXII (PG 94, 944).   [25] Aristotle, *Eth.*, III, 2 (1111b 26).

On the contrary, Damascene says free choice is nothing else than the will.[26]

I answer that, The appetitive powers must be proportionate to the apprehensive powers, as we have said above.[27] Now, as on the part of intellectual apprehension we have intellect and reason, so on the part of the intellectual appetite we have will and free choice, which is nothing else but the power of election. And this is clear from their relations to their respective objects and acts. For the act of *understanding* implies the simple acceptation of something, and hence we say that we understand first principles, which are known of themselves without any comparison. But to *reason*, properly speaking, is to come from one thing to the knowledge of another, and so, properly speaking, we reason about conclusions, which are known from the principles. In like manner, on the part of the appetite, to *will* implies the simple appetite for something, and so the will is said to regard the end, which is desired for itself. But to *elect* is to desire something for the sake of obtaining something else, and so, properly speaking, it regards the means to the end. Now in appetitive matters, the end is related to the means, which is desired for the end, in the same way as, in knowledge, principles are related to the conclusion to which we assent because of the principles. Therefore it is evident that as *intellect* is to *reason*, so *will* is to the *elective power*, which is free choice. But it has been shown above that it belongs to the same power both to understand and to reason,[28] even as it belongs to the same power to be at rest and to be in movement. Hence it belongs also to the same power to will and to elect. And on this account will and the free choice are not two powers, but one.

Reply Obj. 1. βούλησις is distinct from θέλησις because of a distinction, not of powers, but of acts.

Reply Obj. 2. Election and will—that is, the act of willing —are different acts, yet they belong to the same power, as do *to understand* and *to reason*, as we have said.

Reply Obj. 3. The intellect is compared to the will as moving the will. And therefore there is no need to distinguish in the will an *agent* and a *possible* will.

[26] *De Fide Orth.,* XIV (PG 94, 1037).   [27] Q. 64, a. 2; q. 80, a. 2.
[28] Q. 79, a. 8.

Question LXXXIV

HOW THE SOUL WHILE UNITED TO THE BODY UNDERSTANDS CORPOREAL THINGS BENEATH IT

(*In Eight Articles*)

WE NOW have to consider the acts of the soul in regard to the intellectual and the appetitive powers, for the other powers of the soul do not come directly under the consideration of the theologian. Now the acts of the appetitive part of the soul come under the consideration of the science of morals, and so we shall treat of them in the second part of this work, to which the consideration of moral matters belongs. But of the acts of the intellectual part we shall treat now. In treating of these acts, we shall proceed in the following order. First, we shall inquire how the soul understands when united to the body; secondly, how it understands when separated from the body.[1]

The former of these inquiries will be threefold: (1) How the soul understands bodies, which are beneath it. (2) How it understands itself and things contained in itself.[2] (3) How it understands immaterial substances, which are above it.[3]

In treating of the knowledge of corporeal things, there are three points to be considered: (1) Through what does the soul know them? (2) How and in what order does it know them? [4] (3) What does it know in them? [5]

Under the first head there are eight points of inquiry: (1) Whether the soul knows bodies through the intellect? (2) Whether it understands them through its essence, or through any species? (3) If through some species, whether the species of all things intelligible are naturally innate in the soul? (4) Whether these species are derived by the soul from certain separate immaterial forms? (5) Whether our soul sees in the eternal exemplars all that it understands? (6) Whether it acquires intellectual knowledge from the senses? (7) Whether the intellect can, through the species of which it is possessed, actually understand, without turning to the phantasms? (8) Whether the judgment of the intellect is hindered by an obstacle in the sensitive powers?

[1] Q. 89.   [2] Q. 87.   [3] Q. 88.   [4] Q. 85.   [5] Q. 86.

First Article

WHETHER THE SOUL KNOWS BODIES THROUGH THE INTELLECT?

We proceed thus to the First Article:—

Objection 1. It would seem that the soul does not know bodies through the intellect. For Augustine says that *bodies cannot be understood by the intellect: nor indeed anything corporeal unless it can be perceived by the senses.*[6] He says also that intellectual vision is of those things that are in the soul by their essence.[7] But such are not bodies. Therefore the soul cannot know bodies through the intellect.

Obj. 2. Further, as sense is to the intelligible, so is the intellect to the sensible. But the soul can by no means, through the senses, understand spiritual things, which are intelligible. Therefore by no means can it, through the intellect, know bodies, which are sensible.

Obj. 3. Further, the intellect is concerned with things that are necessary and unchangeable. But all bodies are movable and changeable. Therefore the soul cannot know bodies through the intellect.

On the contrary, Science is in the intellect. If, therefore, the intellect does not know bodies, it follows that there is no science of bodies; and thus perishes the science of nature, which treats of movable bodies.

I answer, In order to elucidate this question, that the early philosophers, who inquired into the natures of things, thought there was nothing in the world save bodies.[8] And because they observed that all bodies are subject to motion, and considered them to be ever in a state of flux, they were of the opinion that we can have no certain knowledge of the reality of things. For what is in a continual state of flux cannot be grasped with any degree of certitude, for it passes away before the mind can form a judgment on it. As Heraclitus said, *it is not possible to touch the water in a passing stream twice* (as the Philosopher relates[9]).

After these came Plato, who, wishing to save the certitude of our knowledge of truth through the intellect, maintained

---

[6] *Solil.,* II, 4 (PL 32, 888).   [7] *De Genesi ad Litt.,* XII, 24 (PL 34, 474).   [8] Cf. above, q. 44, a. 2.   [9] *Metaph.,* III, 5 (1010a 14).

that, besides these corporeal things, there is another genus of beings, separate from matter and movement, which he called *species* or *ideas*, by participation in which each one of these singular and sensible things is said to be either a man, or a horse, or the like.[10] And so, he said that sciences and definitions, and whatever pertains to the act of the intellect, is not referred to these sensible bodies, but to those immaterial and separate beings;[11] so that, according to this, the soul does not understand these corporeal things, but their separated species.

Now this is clearly false for two reasons. First, because, since those species are immaterial and immovable, knowledge of movement and matter (which is proper to natural philosophy) would be excluded from among the sciences, and likewise all demonstration through moving and material causes. Secondly, because it seems ridiculous, when we seek for knowledge of things which are to us manifest, to introduce other beings, which cannot be the substances of the things with which we began, since they differ from them in being. Hence, granted that we have a knowledge of those separate substances, we cannot for that reason claim to form judgments concerning these sensible things.

Now it seems that Plato strayed from the truth because, having observed that all knowledge takes place through some kind of similitude,[12] he thought that the form of the thing known must of necessity be in the knower in the same manner as in the thing known itself. But it was his opinion that the form of the thing understood is in the intellect under conditions of universality, immateriality, and immobility; which is apparent from the very operation of the intellect, whose act of understanding is universal, and characterized by a certain necessity; for the mode of action corresponds to the mode of the agent's form. Therefore he concluded that the things which we understand must subsist in themselves under the same conditions of immateriality and immobility.

But there is no necessity for this. For even in sensible things it is to be observed that the form is otherwise in one sensible than in another. For instance, whiteness may be of great intensity in one, and of a less intensity in another; in

[10] Cf. Aristotle, *op. cit.*, I, 6 (987b 6; b 7); I, 9 (992b 7).—Cf. also Plato, *Theaetet.* (p. 156a).   [11] Cf. Avicenna, *Metaph.*, VII, 2 (96ra). [12] Cf. *ibid.* (96rb).—Cf. also, Aristotle, *De An.*, I, 2 (404b 17).

one we find whiteness with sweetness, in another without sweetness. In the same way, the sensible form is in one way in the thing which is external to the soul, and in another way in the senses, which receive the forms of sensible things without receiving matter, such as the color of gold without receiving gold. So, too, the intellect, according to its own mode, receives under conditions of immateriality and immobility the species of material and movable bodies; for the received is in the receiver according to the mode of the receiver. We must conclude, therefore, that the soul knows bodies through the intellect by a knowledge which is immaterial, universal and necessary.

Reply Obj. 1. These words of Augustine are to be understood as referring to the medium of intellectual knowledge, and not to its object. For the intellect knows bodies by understanding them, not indeed through bodies, nor through material and corporeal likenesses, but through immaterial and intelligible species, which can be in the soul by their own essence.

Reply Obj. 2. As Augustine says, it is not correct to say that as the sense knows only bodies so the intellect knows only spiritual things;[13] for it would follow that God and the angels would not know bodies. The reason for this diversity is that the lower power does not extend to those things that belong to the higher power; whereas the higher power accomplishes in a more excellent manner what belongs to the lower power.

Reply Obj. 3. Every movement presupposes something immovable. For when a change of quality occurs, the substance remains unmoved; and when there is a change of substantial form, matter remains unmoved. Moreover, mutable things have immovable dispositions; for instance, though Socrates be not always sitting, yet it is an immovable truth that whenever he does sit he remains in one place. For this reason there is nothing to hinder our having an immovable science of movable things.

[13] *De Civit. Dei,* XXII, 29 (PL 41, 800).

Second Article

WHETHER THE SOUL UNDERSTANDS CORPOREAL THINGS THROUGH ITS ESSENCE?

We proceed thus to the Second Article:—

Objection 1. It would seem that the soul understands corporeal things through its essence. For Augustine says that the soul *collects and lays hold of the images of bodies which are formed in the soul and of the soul; for in forming them it gives them something of its own substance.*[14] But the soul understands bodies by the likenesses of bodies. Therefore the soul knows bodies through its essence, which it employs for the formation of such likenesses, and from which it forms them.

Obj. 2. Further, the Philosopher says that *the soul, after a fashion, is everything.*[15] Since, therefore, like is known by like, it seems that the soul knows corporeal things through itself.

Obj. 3. Further, the soul is superior to corporeal creatures. Now lower things are in higher things in a more eminent way than in themselves, as Dionysius says.[16] Therefore all corporeal creatures exist in a more excellent way in the essence of the soul than in themselves. Therefore the soul can know corporeal creatures through its essence.

On the contrary, Augustine says that *the mind gathers the knowledge of corporeal things through the bodily senses.*[17] But the soul itself cannot be known through the bodily senses. Therefore it does not know corporeal things through itself.

I answer that, The ancient philosophers held that the soul knows bodies through its essence. For it was universally admitted that *like is known by like.*[18] But they thought that the form of the thing known is in the knower in the same way as in the thing known. The Platonists however were of a contrary opinion. For Plato, having observed that the intellectual soul has an immaterial nature,[19] and an immaterial

---

[14] *De Trin.,* X, 5 (PL 42, 977).   [15] *De An.,* III, 8 (431b 21).
[16] *De Cael. Hier.,* XII, 2 (PG 3, 293).   [17] *De Trin.,* IX, 3 (PL 42, 963).   [18] Cf. Aristotle, *De An.,* I, 5 (409b 24).   [19] Cf. Nemesius, *De Nat. Hom.,* II (PG 40, 572); St. Augustine, *De Civit. Dei.* VIII, 5 (PL 41, 230).

mode of knowing,[20] held that the forms of the things known subsist immaterially. But the earlier natural philosophers, observing that the things known are corporeal and material, held that they must exist materially even in the soul that knows them. And therefore, in order to ascribe to the soul a knowledge of all things, they held that it has the same nature in common with all.[21] And because the nature of an effect is determined by its principles, they ascribed to the soul the nature of a principle.[22] Hence it is that those who thought fire to be the principle of all, held that the soul had the nature of fire,[23] and in like manner as to air[24] and water.[25] Lastly, Empedocles, who held the existence of four material elements and two principles of movement,[26] said that the soul was composed of these.[27] Consequently, since they held that things existed in the soul materially, they maintained that all the soul's knowledge is material, thus failing to distinguish intellect from sense.[28]

But this opinion will not hold. First, because in the material principle of which they were speaking, effects do not exist save in potentiality. But a thing is not known according as it is in potentiality, but only according as it is in act, as is shown in *Metaph.* ix.;[29] therefore neither is a power known except through its act. It was therefore insufficient to ascribe to the soul the nature of the principles of things in order to guarantee to the soul a knowledge of all things; it was further necessary to admit in the soul the natures and forms of each individual effect, for instance, of bone, flesh, and the like. Thus does Aristotle argue against Empedocles.[30] Secondly, because if it were necessary for the thing known to exist materially in the knower, there would be no reason why things which have a material existence outside the soul should be devoid of knowledge; why, for instance, if by fire

---

[20] Cf. Aristotle, *Metaph.*, I, 6 (987b 6).   [21] Cf. Aristotle, *De An.*, I, 5 (409b 24).   [22] Cf. *op. cit.*, I, 2 (404b 110).   [23] A theory of Democritus, according to Aristotle, *De An.*, I, 2 (405a 5).   [24] A theory of Diogenes, according to Aristotle, *ibid.* (405a 21); and of Anaximenes, according to Macrobius, *In Somn. Scipion.*, I, 14 (p. 543). [25] A theory of Hippo, according to Aristotle, *De An.*, I, 2 (405b 1). [26] Cf. Aristotle, *De Gener.*, I, 1 (314a 16).   [27] Cf. Aristotle, *De An.*, I, 5 (410a 3); I, 4 (408a 19).   [28] Cf. *op. cit.*, III, 3 (427a 21). [29] Aristotle, *Metaph.*, VIII, 9 (1051a 29).   [30] *De An.*, I, 5 (409b 23).

the soul knows fire, that fire also which is outside the soul should not have knowledge of fire.

We must conclude, therefore, that the material things known must needs exist in the knower, not materially, but rather immaterially. The reason for this is that the act of knowledge extends to things outside the knower; for we know even the things that are outside us. Now by matter the form of a thing is determined to some one thing. Therefore it is clear that knowledge is in inverse ratio to materiality. Consequently, things that are not receptive of forms, save materially, have no power of knowledge whatever—such as plants, as the Philosopher says.[31] But the more immaterially a being receives the form of the thing known, the more perfect is its knowledge. Therefore the intellect, which abstracts the species not only from matter, but also from the individuating conditions of matter, knows more perfectly than the senses, which receive the form of the thing known, without matter indeed, but subject to material conditions. Moreover, among the senses themselves, sight has the most perfect knowledge, because it is the least material, as we have remarked above.[32] So, too, among intellects, the more perfect is the more immaterial.

It is therefore clear from the foregoing, that if there be an intellect which knows all things by its essence, then its essence must needs have all things in itself immaterially; much as the early philosophers held that the essence of the soul must be composed actually of the principles of all material things in order to know all things. Now it is proper to God that His essence comprise all things immaterially, as effects pre-exist virtually in their cause. God alone, therefore, understands all things through His essence; but neither the human soul nor the angels can do so.

Reply Obj. 1. Augustine in that passage is speaking of an imaginary vision, which takes place through the images of bodies. To the formation of such images the soul gives part of its substance, just as a subject is given in order to be informed by some form. In this way the soul makes such images from itself; not that the soul or some part of the soul be turned into this or that image, but just as we say that a body is made into something colored because of its being in-

---

[31] *Op. cit.*, II, 12 (424a 32).   [32] Q. 78, a. 3.

formed with color. That this is the sense is clear from the sequel. For he says that the soul *keeps something*—namely, not informed with such an image—*which is able freely to judge of the species of these images,* and that this is the *mind* or *intellect*.[33] And he says that the part which is informed with these images—namely, the imagination—is *common to us and beasts.*

Reply Obj. 2. Aristotle did not hold that the soul was actually composed of all things, as did the earlier naturalists; he said that the soul is all things, *after a fashion,* inasmuch as it is in potentiality to all—through the senses, to all sensible things; through the intellect, to all intelligible things.

Reply Obj. 3. Every creature has a finite and determinate being. Therefore, although the essence of a higher creature has a certain likeness to a lower creature, inasmuch as they share in a common genus, yet it has not a complete likeness thereof, because it is determined to a certain species other than the species of the lower creature. But the divine essence is a perfect likeness of all that may be found to exist in things created, being the universal principle of all.

Third Article

WHETHER THE SOUL UNDERSTANDS ALL THINGS THROUGH INNATE SPECIES?

We proceed thus to the Third Article:—

Objection 1. It would seem that the soul understands all things through innate species. For Gregory says, in a homily for the Ascension, that *man has understanding in common with the angels.*[34] But angels understand all things through innate species: wherefore in the *Book of Causes* it is said that *every intelligence is full of forms.*[35] Therefore the soul also has innate species of things, by means of which it understands corporeal things.

Obj. 2. Further, the intellectual soul is more excellent than corporeal primary matter. But primary matter was created by God under the forms to which it has potentiality. Therefore much more is the intellectual soul created by God with

---

[33] *De Trin.,* X, 5 (PL 42, 977).   [34] *In Evang.,* II, hom. 29 (PL 76, 1214).   [35] *De Causis,* X (p. 170).

intelligible species. And so the soul understands corporeal things through innate species.

Obj. 3. Further, no one can answer the truth except concerning what he knows. But even a person untaught, and devoid of acquired knowledge, answers the truth to every question if put to him in orderly fashion, as we find related in the *Meno* of Plato concerning a certain individual.[36] Therefore we have some knowledge of things even before we acquire knowledge; which would not be the case unless we had innate species. Therefore the soul understands corporeal things through innate species.

On the contrary, The Philosopher, speaking of the intellect, says that it is like *a tablet on which nothing is written.*[37]

I answer that, Since form is the principle of action, a thing must be related to the form which is the principle of an action in the same way as it is to that action. For instance, if upward motion is from lightness, then that which moves upwards only potentially must needs be only potentially light, but that which actually moves upwards must needs be actually light. Now we observe that man sometimes is only a potential knower, both as to sense and as to intellect. And he is reduced from such potentiality to act:—through the action of sensible objects on his senses, to the act of sensation; by instruction or discovery, to the act of understanding. Therefore we must say that the cognitive soul is in potentiality both to the likenesses which are the principles of sensing, and to the likenesses which are the principles of understanding. For this reason Aristotle held that the intellect by which the soul understands has no innate species, but is at first in potentiality to all such species.[38]

But since that which actually has a form is sometimes unable to act according to that form because of some hindrance (as a light thing may be hindered from moving upwards), for this reason Plato held that man's intellect is naturally filled with all intelligible species, but that, by being united to the body, it is hindered from the realization of its act.[39] But this seems to be unreasonable. First, because, if the soul has a natural knowledge of all things, it seems impossible for the soul so far to forget the existence of such knowledge as

[36] *Meno* (p. 82b).—Cf. St. Augustine, *De Trin.*, II, 15 (PL 42, 1011). [37] *De An.*, III, 4 (430a 1). [38] *Ibid.* (429b 30). [39] Cf. Aristotle, *Metaph.*, I, 9 (993a 1).

not to know itself to be possessed of it. For no man forgets what he knows naturally, *e.g.*, that every whole is larger than its part, and the like. And especially unreasonable does this seem if we suppose that it is natural to the soul to be united to the body, as we have established above;[40] for it is unreasonable that the natural operation of a thing be totally hindered by that which belongs to it naturally. Secondly, the falseness of this opinion is clearly proved from the fact that if a sense be wanting, the knowledge of what is apprehended through that sense is also wanting. For instance, a man who is born blind can have no knowledge of colors. This would not be the case if the soul had innate likenesses of all intelligible things. We must therefore conclude that the soul does not know corporeal things through innate species.

Reply Obj. 1. Man indeed has understanding in common with the angels, but not in the same degree of perfection; just as the lower grades of bodies, which merely exist, according to Gregory, have not the same degree of perfection as the higher bodies. For the matter of the lower bodies is not totally completed by its form, but is in potentiality to forms which it has not; whereas the matter of the heavenly bodies is totally completed by its form, so that it is not in potentiality to any other form, as we have said above.[41] In the same way the angelic intellect is perfected by intelligible species, in accordance with its nature; whereas the human intellect is in potentiality to such species.

Reply Obj. 2. Primary matter has substantial being through its form, and consequently it had need to be created under some form; for otherwise it would not be in act. But when once it exists under one form it is in potentiality to others. On the other hand, the intellect does not receive substantial being through the intelligible species; and therefore there is no comparison.

Reply Obj. 3. If questions be put in an orderly fashion, they proceed from universal self-evident principles to what is particular. Now by such a process knowledge is produced in the soul of the learner. Therefore, when he answers the truth to a subsequent question, this is not because he had knowledge previously, but because he then acquires such knowledge for the first time. For it matters not whether the teacher proceed from universal principles to conclusions by

[40] Q. 76, a. 1.   [41] Q. 66, a. 2.

questioning or by asserting; for in either case the intellect of the listener is assured of what follows by that which preceded.

Fourth Article

WHETHER THE INTELLIGIBLE SPECIES ARE DERIVED BY THE SOUL FROM CERTAIN SEPARATE FORMS?

We proceed thus to the Fourth Article:—

Objection 1. It would seem that the intelligible species are derived by the soul from some separate forms. For whatever is such by participation is caused by what is such essentially; for instance, that which is on fire is reduced to fire as its cause. But the intellectual soul, in so far as it is actually understanding, participates in the intelligibles themselves; for, in a manner, the intellect in act is the thing understood in act. Therefore that which in itself and in its essence is understood in act, is the cause that the intellectual soul actually understands. Now that which in its essence is actually understood is a form existing without matter. Therefore the intelligible species, by which the soul understands, are caused by some separate forms.

Obj. 2. Further, the intelligible is to the intellect as the sensible is to the sense. But the sensible species which are in the senses, and by which we sense, are caused by the sensible things which exist actually outside the soul. Therefore the intelligible species, by which our intellect understands, are caused by some things actually intelligible, existing outside the soul. But these can be nothing else than forms separate from matter. Therefore the intelligible forms of our intellect are derived from some separate substances.

Obj. 3. Further, whatever is in potentiality is reduced to act by something actual. If, therefore, our intellect, previously in potentiality, afterwards actually understands, this must needs be caused by some intellect which is always in act. But this is a separate intellect. Therefore the intelligible species, by which we actually understand, are caused by some separate substances.

On the contrary, If this were true, we should not need the senses in order to understand. And this is proved to be false especially from the fact that if a man be wanting in a sense, he cannot have any knowledge of the sensibles corresponding to that sense.

I answer that, Some have held that the intelligible species of our intellect are derived from certain separate Forms or substances. And this in two ways. For Plato, as we have said, held that the forms of sensible things subsist by themselves without matter: *e.g.*, the Form of a man which he called man-in-himself, and the Form or Idea of a horse which he called horse-in-itself, and so forth. He said therefore that these Forms are participated both by our soul and by corporeal matter: by our soul, for knowledge,[42] and by corporeal matter for being;[43] so that, just as corporeal matter, by participating the Idea of a stone, becomes an individual stone, so our intellect, by participating the Idea of a stone, is made to understand a stone. Now the participation of an Idea takes place by some likeness of the Idea in the participator, in the way that a model is participated by a copy.[44] So just as he held that the sensible forms, which are in corporeal matter, are derived from the Ideas as certain likenesses of them, so he held that the intelligible species of our intellect are likenesses of the Ideas, derived therefrom.[45] And for this reason, as we have said above, he referred sciences and definitions to those Ideas.

But since it is contrary to the nature of sensible things that their forms should subsist without matter, as Aristotle proves in many ways,[46] Avicenna, setting this opinion aside, held that the intelligible species of all sensible things, instead of subsisting in themselves without matter, pre-exist immaterially in some separate intellects.[47] From the first of these intellects, said he, such species are derived by a second, and so on to the last separate intellect, which he called the *agent intellect*. From the agent intellect, according to him, intelligible species flow into our souls, and sensible species into corporeal matter.[48] And so Avicenna agrees with Plato in this, that the intelligible species of our intellect are derived from certain separate Forms; but these Plato held to subsist of them-

[42] Cf. St. Augustine, *Lib. 83 Quaest.*, q. 46 (PL 40, 30).   [43] Cf. Aristotle, *Metaph.*, I, 9 (991b 3).—Plato, *Phaedo* (p. 100d).   [44] Cf. Aristotle, *Metaph.*, I, 9 (991a 21).—Plato, *Timaeus* (pp. 28a, 30c).   [45] Cf. Avicenna, *De An.*, V, 5 (25rb); *Metaph.*, IX, 4 (105ra).   [46] *Metaph.*, VI, 14 (1039a 24).   [47] *De An.*, V, 5 (25rb); *Metaph.*, IX, 4 (105ra).   [48] *De An.*, V, 6 (26rb); *Metaph.*, IX, 5 (105rb).

selves, while Avicenna placed them in the agent intellect.
They differ, too, in this respect, that Avicenna held that the
intelligible species do not remain in our intellect after it has
ceased actually to understand, and that it needs to turn [to
the agent intellect] in order to receive them anew.[49] Consequently, he does not hold that the soul has innate knowledge,
as Plato, who held that the participations of the Ideas remain immovably in the soul.[50]

But in this opinion no sufficient reason can be assigned
for the soul being united to the body. For it cannot be said
that the intellectual soul is united to the body for the sake
of the body, since neither is form for the sake of matter, nor
is the mover for the sake of the thing moved, but rather the
reverse. Especially does the body seem necessary to the intellectual soul for the latter's proper operation, which is to
understand; since as to its being, the soul does not depend
on the body. But if the soul by its very nature had an inborn
aptitude for receiving intelligible species only through the
influence of certain separate principles, and were not to receive them from the senses, it would not need the body in
order to understand. Hence, it would be united to the body
to no purpose.

But if it be said that our soul needs the senses in order to
understand, in that it is in some way awakened by them to
the consideration of those things whose intelligible species
it receives from the separate principles,[51] even this seems an
insufficient explanation. For this awakening does not seem
necessary to the soul, except in as far as it is overcome by
sleep, as the Platonists expressed it, and by forgetfulness,
through its union with the body;[52] and thus the senses would
be of no use to the intellectual soul except for the purpose
of removing the obstacle which the soul encounters through
its union with the body.[53] Consequently, the reason for the
union of the soul with the body still remains unexplained.

And if it be said, with Avicenna, that the senses are necessary to the soul because by them it is roused to turn to the
agent intellect from which it receives the species,[54] neither

[49] De An., V, 6 (26rb).—Cf. C. G., II, 74.   [50] Cf. Aristotle, Metaph.,
I, 7 (988b 3); Top., II, 7 (113a 27).   [51] Cf. William of Auvergne, De
Univ., IIa IIae, 76 (I, pt. II, 929); IIIa IIae, 3 (I, pt. II, 1018).
[52] Pseudo-Augustine (Alcher of Clairvaux), De Spir. et An., I (PL 40,
781).   [53] Cf. below, q. 89, a. 1.   [54] De An., V, 5 (25rb).

is this a sufficient explanation. Because if it is natural for the soul to understand through species derived from the agent intellect, it would follow that the soul can turn to the agent intellect from the inclination of its very nature, or through being roused by another sense to turn to the agent intellect, and receive the species of those sensible things for which we are missing a sense. And thus a man born blind could have knowledge of colors; which is clearly untrue. We must therefore conclude that the intelligible species, by which our soul understands, are not derived from separate forms.

Reply Obj. 1. The intelligible species which are participated by our intellect are reduced, as to their first cause, to a first principle which is by its essence intelligible—namely, God. But they proceed from that principle by way of the forms of sensible and material things, from which we gather knowledge, as Dionysius says.[55]

Reply Obj. 2. Material things, as to the being which they have outside the soul, may be actually sensible, but not actually intelligible. Therefore there is no comparison between sense and intellect.

Reply Obj. 3. Our possible intellect is reduced from potentiality to act by some being in act, that is, by the agent intellect, which is a power of the soul, as we have said;[56] and not by any separate intellect, as a proximate cause, although perchance as a remote cause.

Fifth Article

WHETHER THE INTELLECTUAL SOUL KNOWS MATERIAL THINGS IN THE ETERNAL EXEMPLARS?

We proceed thus to the Fifth Article:—

Objection 1. It would seem that the intellectual soul does not know material things in the eternal exemplars. For that in which anything is known must itself be known more and antecedently. But the intellectual soul of man, in the present state of life, does not know the eternal exemplars, for it does not know God in Whom the eternal exemplars exist, but is *united to God as to the unknown*, as Dionysius says.[57] Therefore the soul does not know all in the eternal exemplars.

[55] *De Div. Nom.*, VII, 2 (PG 3, 886).   [56] Q. 79, a. 4.   [57] *De Myst. Theol.*, I, 3 (PG 3, 1001); cf. *De Div. Nom.*, I, 1 (PG 3, 585).

Obj. 2. Further, it is written (*Rom.* i. 20) that *the invisible things of God are clearly seen . . . by the things that are made.* But among the invisible things of God are the eternal exemplars. Therefore the eternal exemplars are known through creatures, and not the converse.

Obj. 3. Further, the eternal exemplars are nothing else but ideas, for Augustine says that *ideas are permanent exemplars existing in the divine mind.*[58] If therefore we say that the intellectual soul knows all things in the eternal exemplars, we come back to the opinion of Plato who said that all knowledge is derived from them.

On the contrary, Augustine says: *If we both see that what you say is true, and if we both see that what I say is true, where do we see this, I pray? Neither do I see it in you, nor do you see it in me; but we both see it in the unchangeable truth which is above our minds.*[59] Now the unchangeable truth is contained in the eternal exemplars. Therefore the intellectual soul knows all truths in the eternal exemplars.

I answer that, As Augustine says: *If those who are called philosophers said by chance anything that was true and consistent with our faith, we must claim it from them as from unjust possessors. For some of the doctrines of the pagans are spurious imitations or superstitious inventions, which we must be careful to avoid when we renounce the society of the pagans.*[60] Consequently whenever Augustine, who was imbued with the doctrines of the Platonists, found in their teaching anything consistent with faith, he adopted it; and those things which he found contrary to faith he amended. Now Plato held, as we have said above, that the forms of things subsist of themselves apart from matter. These he called Ideas, and he said that our intellect knows all things by participation in them; so that just as corporeal matter, by participating in the Idea of a stone, becomes a stone, so our intellect, by participating in the same Idea, has knowledge of a stone. But it seems contrary to faith that the forms of things should subsist of themselves without matter outside the things themselves, as the Platonists held, asserting that *life-in-itself* and *wisdom-in-itself* are certain creative substances, as Dionysius relates.[61] Therefore, in the place of the

[58] *Lib. 83 Quaest.,* q. 46 (PL 40, 30).   [59] *Confess.,* XII, 25 (PL 32, 840).   [60] *De Doc. Christ.,* II, 40 (PL 34, 63).   [61] *De Div. Nom.,* XI, 6 (PG 3, 956).

Ideas defended by Plato, Augustine said that the exemplars of all creatures existed in the divine mind. It is according to these that all things are formed, as well as that the human soul knows all things.[62]

When, therefore, the question is asked: Does the human soul know all things in the eternal exemplars? we must reply that one thing is said to be known in another in two ways. First, as in an object itself known; as one may see in a mirror the images of the things reflected therein. In this way the soul, in the present state of life, cannot see all things in the eternal exemplars; but thus the blessed, who see God and all things in Him, know all things in the eternal exemplars. Secondly, one thing is said to be known in another as in a principle of knowledge; and thus we might say that we see in the sun what we see by the sun. And thus we must needs say that the human soul knows all things in the eternal exemplars, since by participation in these exemplars we know all things. For the intellectual light itself, which is in us, is nothing else than a participated likeness of the uncreated light, in which are contained the eternal exemplars. Whence it is written (*Ps.* iv. 6, 7), *Many say: who showeth us good things?* which question the Psalmist answers, *The light of Thy countenance, O Lord, is signed upon us;* as though to say: By the seal of the divine light in us, all things are made known to us.

But since besides the intellectual light which is in us, intelligible species, which are derived from things, are required in order that we may have knowledge of material things, therefore this knowledge is not due merely to a participation of the eternal exemplars, as the Platonists held, maintaining that the mere participation in the Ideas sufficed for knowledge.[63] Therefore Augustine says: *Although the philosophers prove by convincing arguments that all things occur in time according to the eternal exemplars, were they able to see in the eternal exemplars, or to find out from them, how many kinds of animals there are and the origin of each? Did they not seek for this information from the story of times and places?* [64]

Now that Augustine did not understand all things to be

[62] *Lib. 83 Quaest.*, q. 46 (PL 40, 30).   [63] Cf. below, q. 87, a. 1.— Cf. also, St. Bonaventure, *Quaest. Disp. de Scientia Christi*, q. 4 (V, 17).   [64] *De Trin.*, IV, 16 (PL 42, 902).

known in their *eternal exemplars* or in *the unchangeable truth*, as though the eternal exemplars themselves were seen, is clear from what he says, viz., that *not each and every rational soul can be said to be worthy of that vision*, namely, of the eternal exemplars, *but only those that are holy and pure*,[65] such as the souls of the blessed.

From what has been said the objections are easily solved.

Sixth Article

WHETHER INTELLECTUAL KNOWLEDGE IS DERIVED FROM SENSIBLE THINGS?

We proceed thus to the Sixth Article:—

Objection 1. It would seem that intellectual knowledge is not derived from sensible things. For Augustine says that *we cannot expect to acquire the pure truth from the senses of the body*.[66] This he proves in two ways. First, because, *whatever the bodily senses reach is continually being changed; and what is never the same cannot be perceived*. Secondly, because, *whatever we perceive by the body, even when not present to the senses, may be present in their images, as when we are asleep or angry; yet we cannot discern by the senses whether what we perceive be the sensible things themselves, or their deceptive images. Now nothing can be perceived which cannot be distinguished from its counterfeit*. And so he concludes that we cannot expect to learn the truth from the senses. But intellectual knowledge apprehends the truth. Therefore intellectual knowledge cannot be conveyed by the senses.

Obj. 2. Further, Augustine says: *We must not think that the body can make any impression on the spirit, as though the spirit were to subject itself like matter to the body's action; for that which acts is in every way more excellent than that which it acts on*.[67] Whence he concludes that *the body does not cause its image in the spirit, but the spirit itself causes it in itself*. Therefore intellectual knowledge is not derived from sensible things.

Obj. 3. Further, an effect does not surpass the power of its cause. But intellectual knowledge extends beyond sensible

[65] *Lib. 83·Quaest.*, q. 46 (PL 40, 30).   [66] *Op. cit.*, q. 9 (PL 40, 13)
[67] *De Genesi ad Litt.*, XII, 16 (PL 34, 467).

things, for we understand some things which cannot be perceived by the senses. Therefore intellectual knowledge is not derived from sensible things.

On the contrary, The Philosopher proves that the origin of knowledge is from the senses.[68]

I answer that, On this point the philosophers held three opinions. For Democritus held that *all knowledge is caused by images issuing from the bodies we think of and entering into our souls,* as Augustine says in his letter to Dioscorus.[69] And Aristotle says that Democritus held that knowledge is caused by a *discharge of images.*[70] And the reason for this opinion was that both Democritus and the other early philosophers did not distinguish between intellect and sense, as Aristotle relates.[71] Consequently, since the sense is immuted by the sensible, they thought that all our knowledge is caused merely by an immutation from sensible things. This immutation Democritus held to be caused by a discharge of images.

Plato, on the other hand, held that the intellect differs from sense, and that it is an immaterial power not making use of a corporeal organ for its action.[72] And since the incorporeal cannot be affected by the corporeal, he held that intellectual knowledge is not brought about by sensible things immuting the intellect, but by the participation in separate intelligible forms by the intellect, as we have said above. Moreover he held that sense is a power operating through itself. Consequently not even the sense itself, since it is a spiritual power, is affected by sensible things; but the sensible organs are affected by the sensible, with the result that the soul is in a way roused to form within itself the species of the sensible. Augustine seems to touch on this opinion where he says that the *body feels not, but the soul through the body, which it makes use of as a kind of messenger, for reproducing within itself what is announced from without.*[73] Thus according to Plato, neither does intellectual knowledge proceed from sensible knowledge, nor does sensible knowledge itself come entirely from sensible things; but these rouse the sensible soul to sensation, and the senses likewise rouse the intellect to the act of understanding.

[68] *Metaph.,* I, 1 (981a 2); *Post. Anal.,* II, 15 (100a 3).   [69] *Epist.* CXVIII, 4 (PL 33, 446).   [70] *De Divinat.,* II (464a 5).   [71] *De An.,* III, 3 (427a 17).   [72] Cf. above, q. 75, a. 3.   [73] *De Genesi ad Litt.,* XII, 24 (PL 34, 475).

Aristotle chose a middle course. For with Plato he agreed that intellect and sense are different.[74] But he held that the sense has not its proper operation without the cooperation of the body; so that *to sense is not an act of the soul alone,* but of the *composite*.[75] And he held the same in regard to all the operations of the sensitive part. Since, therefore, it is not incongruous that the sensible things which are outside the soul should produce some effect in the *composite,* Aristotle agreed with Democritus in this, that the operations of the sensitive part are caused by the impression of the sensible on the sense; not indeed by a discharge, as Democritus said, but by some kind of operation. Democritus, it must be remembered, maintained that every action is by way of a discharge of atoms, as we gather from *De Gener.* i.[76] But Aristotle held that the intellect has an operation in which the body does not share.[77] Now nothing corporeal can make an impression on the incorporeal. And therefore, in order to cause the intellectual operation, according to Aristotle, the impression caused by sensible bodies does not suffice, but something more noble is required, *for the agent is more noble than the patient,* as he says.[78] Not, be it observed, in the sense that the intellectual operation is effected in us by the mere impression of some superior beings, as Plato held; but that the higher and more noble agent which he calls the agent intellect, of which we have spoken above,[79] causes the phantasms received from the senses to be actually intelligible, by a process of abstraction.

According to this opinion, then, on the part of the phantasms, intellectual knowledge is caused by the senses. But since the phantasms cannot of themselves immute the possible intellect, but require to be made actually intelligible by the agent intellect, it cannot be said that sensible knowledge is the total and perfect cause of intellectual knowledge, but rather is in a way the matter of the cause.

Reply Obj. 1. These words of Augustine mean that truth is not entirely from the senses. For the light of the agent intellect is needed, through which we know the truth of changeable things unchangeably, and discern things themselves from their likenesses.

[74] *De An.,* III, 3 (427b 6).   [75] *De Somno,* I (454a 7).   [76] Aristotle, *De Gener.,* I, 8 (324b 25).   [77] *De An.,* III, 4 (492a 24).   [78] *Op. cit.,* III, 5 (430a 18).   [79] Q. 79, a. 3 and 4.

Reply Obj. 2. In this passage Augustine speaks not of intellectual but of imaginary knowledge. And since, according to the opinion of Plato, the imagination has an operation which belongs to the soul only, Augustine, in order to show that corporeal images are impressed on the imagination, not by bodies but by the soul, uses the same argument as Aristotle does in proving that the agent intellect must be separate, namely, because *the agent is more noble than the patient.*[80] And without doubt, according to the above opinion, in the imagination there must needs be not only a passive but also an active power. But if we hold, according to the opinion of Aristotle,[81] that the action of the imaginative power is an action of the *composite,* there is no difficulty; because the sensible body is more noble than the organ of the animal, in so far as it is compared to it as a being in act to a being in potentiality; even as the object actually colored is compared to the pupil which is potentially colored. Now, although the first immutation of the imagination is through the agency of the sensible, since *the phantasm is a movement produced in accordance with sensation,*[82] nevertheless, it may be said that there is in man an operation which by division and composition forms images of various things, even of things not perceived by the senses. And Augustine's words may be taken in this sense.

Reply Obj. 3. Sensitive knowledge is not the entire cause of intellectual knowledge. And therefore it is not strange that intellectual knowledge should extend beyond sensitive knowledge.

Seventh Article

WHETHER THE INTELLECT CAN UNDERSTAND ACTUALLY THROUGH THE INTELLIGIBLE SPECIES OF WHICH IT IS POSSESSED, WITHOUT TURNING TO THE PHANTASMS?

We proceed thus to the Seventh Article:—

Objection 1. It would seem that the intellect can understand actually through the intelligible species of which it is possessed, without turning to the phantasms. For the intellect is made actual by the intelligible species by which it is informed. But if the intellect is in act, it understands. There-

---

[80] *De An.,* III, 5 (430a 18).   [81] *Op. cit.,* I, 1 (403a 5).   [82] *Op. cit.,* III, 3 (429a 1).

fore the intelligible species suffices for the intellect to understand actually, without turning to the phantasms.

Obj. 2. Further, the imagination is more dependent on the senses than the intellect on the imagination. But the imagination can actually imagine in the absence of the sensible. Therefore much more can the intellect understand without turning to the phantasms.

Obj. 3. There are no phantasms of incorporeal things, for the imagination does not transcend time and space. If, therefore, our intellect cannot understand anything actually without turning to the phantasms, it follows that it cannot understand anything incorporeal. Which is clearly false, for we understand truth, and God, and the angels.

On the contrary, The Philosopher says that *the soul understands nothing without a phantasm.*[83]

I answer that, In the state of the present life, in which the soul is united to a corruptible body, it is impossible for our intellect to understand anything actually, except by turning to phantasms. And of this there are two indications. First of all because the intellect, being a power that does not make use of a corporeal organ, would in no way be hindered in its act through the lesion of a corporeal organ, if there were not required for its act the act of some power that does make use of a corporeal organ. Now sense, imagination and the other powers belonging to the sensitive part make use of a corporeal organ. Therefore it is clear that for the intellect to understand actually, not only when it acquires new knowledge, but also when it uses knowledge already acquired, there is need for the act of the imagination and of the other powers. For when the act of the imagination is hindered by a lesion of the corporeal organ, for instance, in a case of frenzy, or when the act of the memory is hindered, as in the case of lethargy, we see that a man is hindered from understanding actually even those things of which he had a previous knowledge. Secondly, anyone can experience this of himself, that when he tries to understand something, he forms certain phantasms to serve him by way of examples, in which as it were he examines what he is desirous of understanding. For this reason it is that when we wish to help someone to understand something, we lay examples before him, from which he can form phantasms for the purpose of understanding.

[83] *Op. cit.,* III, 7 (431a 16).

Now the reason for this is that the power of knowledge is proportioned to the thing known. Therefore the proper object of the angelic intellect, which is entirely separate from a body, is an intelligible substance separate from a body. Whereas the proper object of the human intellect, which is united to a body, is the quiddity or nature existing in corporeal matter; and it is through these natures of visible things that it rises to a certain knowledge of things invisible. Now it belongs to such a nature to exist in some individual, and this cannot be apart from corporeal matter; for instance, it belongs to the nature of a stone to be in an individual stone, and to the nature of a horse to be in an individual horse, and so forth. Therefore the nature of a stone or any material thing cannot be known completely and truly, except in as much as it is known as existing in the individual. Now we apprehend the individual through the sense and the imagination. And, therefore, for the intellect to understand actually its proper object, it must of necessity turn to the phantasms in order to perceive the universal nature existing in the individual. But if the proper object of our intellect were a separate form, or if, as the Platonists say, the natures of sensible things subsisted apart from the individual, there would be no need for the intellect to turn to the phantasms whenever it understands.

Reply Obj. 1. The species preserved in the possible intellect exist there habitually when it does not understand them actually, as we have said above.[84] Therefore for us to understand actually, the fact that the species are preserved does not suffice; we need further to make use of them in a manner befitting the things of which they are the species, which things are natures existing in individuals.

Reply Obj. 2. Even the phantasm is the likeness of an individual thing; and so the imagination does not need any further likeness of the individual, whereas the intellect does.

Reply Obj. 3. Incorporeal beings, of which there are no phantasms, are known to us by comparison with sensible bodies of which there are phantasms. Thus we understand truth by considering a thing in which we see the truth; and God, as Dionysius says,[85] we know as cause, by way of excess and by way of remotion. Other incorporeal substances we know, in the state of the present life, only by way of remotion

[84] Q. 79, a. 6.   [85] *De Div. Nom.*, I, 5 (PG 3, 593).

or by some comparison to corporeal things. Hence, when we understand something about these beings, we need to turn to the phantasms of bodies, although there are no phantasms of these beings themselves.

Eighth Article

WHETHER THE JUDGMENT OF THE INTELLECT IS HINDERED THROUGH SUSPENSION OF THE SENSITIVE POWERS?

We proceed thus to the Eighth Article:—

Objection 1. It would seem that the judgment of the intellect is not hindered by suspension of the sensitive powers. For the superior does not depend on the inferior. But the judgment of the intellect is higher than the senses. Therefore the judgment of the intellect is not hindered through suspension of the senses.

Obj. 2. Further, to syllogize is an act of the intellect. But during sleep the senses are suspended, as is said in *De Somno et Vigilia*,[86] and yet it sometimes happens to us to syllogize while asleep. Therefore the judgment of the intellect is not hindered through suspension of the senses.

On the contrary, What a man does while asleep, against the moral law, is not imputed to him as a sin, as Augustine says.[87] But this would not be the case if man, while asleep, had free use of his reason and intellect. Therefore the judgment of the intellect is hindered by suspension of the senses.

I answer that, As we have said above, our intellect's proper and proportionate object is the nature of a sensible thing. Now a perfect judgment concerning anything cannot be formed, unless all that pertains to that thing be known; especially if that be ignored which is the term and end of judgment. For the Philosopher says that *as the end of practical science is a work, so the end of the science of nature is that which is perceived principally through the senses.*[88] For the smith does not seek the knowledge of a knife except for the purpose of producing this individual knife; and in like manner the natural philosopher does not seek to know the nature of a stone and of a horse, save for the purpose of knowing

[86] Aristotle, *De Somno*, I (454b 13).   [87] *De Genesi ad Litt.*, XII, 15 (PL 34, 466).   [88] *De Caelo*, III, 7 (306a 16).

the essential properties of those things which he perceives
with his senses. Now it is clear that a smith cannot judge
perfectly of a knife unless he knows what making this particular knife means; and in like manner the natural philosopher cannot judge perfectly of natural things, unless he
knows sensible things. But in the present state of life, whatever we understand we know by comparison with natural
sensible things. Consequently it is not possible for our intellect to form a perfect judgment while the senses are suspended, through which sensible things are known to us.

Reply Obj. 1. Although the intellect is superior to the
senses, nevertheless in a manner it receives from the senses,
and its first and principal objects are founded in sensible
things. Hence, suspension of the senses necessarily involves
a hindrance to the judgment of the intellect.

Reply Obj. 2. The senses are suspended in the sleeper
through certain evaporations and the escape of certain ex-
halations, as we read in *De Somno et Vigilia.*[89] And, therefore, according to the disposition of such evaporation, the
senses are more or less suspended. For when the movement
of the vapors is very agitated, not only are the senses suspended, but also the imagination, so that there are no phantasms; as happens especially when a man falls asleep after
much eating and drinking. If, however, the movement of the
vapors be somewhat less violent, phantasms appear, but dis-
torted and without sequence; as happens in a case of fever.
And if the movement be still more attenuated, the phantasms
will have a certain sequence; as happens especially towards
the end of sleep, and in sober men and those who are gifted
with a strong imagination. If the movement be very slight,
not only does the imagination retain its freedom, but even
the common sense is partly freed; so that sometimes while
asleep a man may judge that what he sees is a dream, discerning, as it were, between things and their images. Nevertheless, the common sense remains partly suspended, and
therefore, although it discriminates some images from reality,
yet it is always deceived in some particular. Therefore, while
a man is asleep, according as sense and imagination are free,
so is the judgment of his intellect unfettered, though not entirely. Consequently, if a man syllogizes while asleep, when
he wakes up he invariably recognizes a flaw in some respect.

[89] Aristotle, *De Somno,* III (456b 17).

THE MODE AND ORDER OF UNDERSTANDING

(*In Eight Articles*)

WE COME now to consider the mode and order of understanding. Under this head there are eight points of inquiry: (1) Whether our intellect understands by abstracting species from the phantasms? (2) Whether the intelligible species abstracted from the phantasms are what our intellect understands, or that whereby it understands? (3) Whether our intellect naturally first understands the more universal? (4) Whether our intellect can know many things at the same time? (5) Whether our intellect understands by composition and division? (6) Whether the intellect can err? (7) Whether one intellect can understand the same thing better than another? (8) Whether our intellect understands the indivisible before the divisible?

First Article

WHETHER OUR INTELLECT UNDERSTANDS CORPOREAL AND MATERIAL THINGS BY ABSTRACTION FROM PHANTASMS?

We proceed thus to the First Article:—

Objection 1. It would seem that our intellect does not understand corporeal and material things by abstraction from the phantasms. For the intellect is false if it understands a thing otherwise than as it is. Now the forms of material things do not exist in abstraction from the particular things represented by the phantasms. Therefore, if we understand material things by the abstraction of species from phantasms, there will be error in the intellect.

Obj. 2. Further, material things are those natural things which include matter in their definition. But nothing can be understood apart from that which enters into its definition. Therefore material things cannot be understood apart from matter. Now matter is the principle of individuation. Therefore material things cannot be understood by the abstraction of the universal from the particular; and this is to abstract intelligible species from the phantasm.

Obj. 3. Further, the Philosopher says that the phantasm is to the intellectual soul what color is to the sight.[1] But seeing is not caused by abstraction of species from color, but by color impressing itself on the sight. Therefore neither does the act of understanding take place by the abstraction of something from the phantasms, but by the phantasms impressing themselves on the intellect.

Obj. 4. Further, the Philosopher says that there are two things in the intellectual soul—the possible intellect and the agent intellect.[2] But it does not belong to the possible intellect to abstract the intelligible species from the phantasm, but to receive them already abstracted. Neither does it seem to be the function of the agent intellect, which is related to phantasms as light is to colors; since light does not abstract anything from colors, but rather acts on them. Therefore in no way do we understand by abstraction from phantasms.

Obj. 5. Further, the Philosopher says that *the intellect understands the species in the phantasms;*[3] and not, therefore, by abstraction.

On the contrary, The Philosopher says that *things are intelligible in proportion as they are separable from matter.*[4] Therefore material things must needs be understood according as they are abstracted from matter and from material images, namely, phantasms.

I answer that, As stated above, the object of knowledge is proportionate to the power of knowledge.[5] Now there are three grades of the cognitive powers. For one cognitive power, namely, the sense, is the act of a corporeal organ. And therefore the object of every sensitive power is a form as existing in corporeal matter; and since such matter is the principle of individuation, therefore every power of the sensitive part can have knowledge only of particulars. There is another grade of cognitive power which is neither the act of a corporeal organ, nor in any way connected with corporeal matter. Such is the angelic intellect, the object of whose cognitive power is therefore a form existing apart from matter; for though angels know material things, yet they do not know them save in something immaterial, namely, either in themselves or in God. But the human intellect holds a middle

[1] Aristotle, *De An.,* III, 7 (431a 14).   [2] *Op. cit.,* III, 5 (430a 14).
[3] *Op. cit.,* III, 7 (431b 2).   [4] *Op. cit.,* III, 4 (429b 21).   [5] Q. 84, a. 7.

place; for it is not the act of an organ, and yet it is a power of the soul, which is the form of the body, as is clear from what we have said above.[6] And therefore it is proper to it to know a form existing individually in corporeal matter, but not as existing in this individual matter. But to know what is in individual matter, yet not as existing in such matter, is to abstract the form from individual matter which is represented by the phantasms. Therefore we must needs say that our intellect understands material things by abstracting from phantasms; and that through material things thus considered we acquire some knowledge of immaterial things, just as, on the contrary, angels know material things through the immaterial.

But Plato, considering only the immateriality of the human intellect, and not that it is somehow united to the body, held that the objects of the intellect are separate Ideas, and that we understand, not by abstraction, but rather by participating in abstractions, as was stated above.[7]

Reply Obj. 1. Abstraction may occur in two ways. First, by way of composition and division, and thus we may understand that one thing does not exist in some other, or that it is separate from it. Secondly, by way of a simple and absolute consideration; and thus we understand one thing without considering another. Thus, for the intellect to abstract one from another things which are not really abstract from one another, does, in the first mode of abstraction, imply falsehood. But, in the second mode of abstraction, for the intellect to abstract things which are not really abstract from one another, does not involve falsehood, as clearly appears in the case of the senses. For if we said that color is not in a colored body, or that it is separate from it, there would be error in what we thought or said. But if we consider color and its properties, without reference to the apple which is colored, or if we express in word what we thus understand, there is no error in such an opinion or assertion; for an apple is not essential to color, and therefore color can be understood independently of the apple. In the same way, the things which belong to the species of a material thing, such as a stone, or a man, or a horse, can be thought without the individual principles which do not belong to the notion of the species.

[6] Q. 76, a. 1.   [7] Q. 84, a. 1.

This is what we mean by abstracting the universal from the particular, or the intelligible species from the phantasm; in other words, this is to consider the nature of the species apart from its individual principles represented by the phantasms. If, therefore, the intellect is said to be false when it understands a thing otherwise than as it is, that is so, if the word *otherwise* refers to the thing understood; for the intellect is false when it understands a thing to be otherwise than as it is. Hence, the intellect would be false if it abstracted the species of a stone from its matter in such a way as to think that the species did not exist in matter, as Plato held.[8] But it is not so, if the word *otherwise* be taken as referring to the one who understands. For it is quite true that the mode of understanding, in one who understands, is not the same as the mode of a thing in being; since the thing understood is immaterially in the one who understands, according to the mode of the intellect, and not materially, according to the mode of a material thing.

Reply Obj. 2. Some have thought that the species of a natural thing is a form only, and that matter is not part of the species.[9] If that were so, matter would not enter into the definition of natural things. Therefore we must disagree and say that matter is twofold, common and *signate*, or individual: common, such as flesh and bone; individual, such as this flesh and these bones. The intellect therefore abstracts the species of a natural thing from the individual sensible matter, but not from the common sensible matter. For example, it abstracts the species of *man* from *this flesh and these bones,* which do not belong to the species as such, but to the individual,[10] and need not be considered in the species. But the species of man cannot be abstracted by the intellect from *flesh and bones.*

Mathematical species, however, can be abstracted by the intellect not only from individual sensible matter, but also from common sensible matter. But they cannot be abstracted from common intelligible matter, but only from individual intelligible matter. For sensible matter is corporeal matter as subject to sensible qualities, such as being cold or hot, hard or soft, and the like; while intelligible matter is sub-

---

[8] Cf. above, q. 84, a. 4.   [9] Averroes, *In Metaph.,* VII, comm. 21 (VIII, 80v; 81r) ; comm. 34 (VIII, 87r).—Cf. St. Thomas, *In Metaph.,* VII, lect. 9.   [10] Aristotle, *Metaph.,* VI, 10 (1035b 28).

stance as subject to quantity. Now it is manifest that quantity is in substance before sensible qualities are. Hence quantities, such as number, dimension, and figures, which are the terminations of quantity, can be considered apart from sensible qualities, and this is to abstract them from sensible matter. But they cannot be considered without understanding the substance which is subject to the quantity, for that would be to abstract them from common intelligible matter. Yet they can be considered apart from this or that substance, and this is to abstract them from individual intelligible matter.

But some things can be abstracted even from common intelligible matter, such as *being, unity, potency, act,* and the like, all of which can exist without matter, as can be verified in the case of immaterial substances. And because Plato failed to consider the twofold kind of abstraction, as above explained, he held that all those things which we have stated to be abstracted by the intellect, are abstract in reality.[11]

Reply Obj. 3. Colors, as being in individual corporeal matter, have the same mode of being as the power of sight; and therefore they can impress their own image on the eye. But phantasms, since they are images of individuals, and exist in corporeal organs, have not the same mode of being as the human intellect, as is clear from what we have said, and therefore they have not the power of themselves to make an impression on the possible intellect. But through the power of the agent intellect, there results in the possible intellect a certain likeness produced by the turning of the agent intellect toward the phantasms. This likeness represents what is in the phantasms, but includes only the nature of the species. It is thus that the intelligible species is said to be abstracted from the phantasm; not that the identical form which previously was in the phantasm is subsequently in the possible intellect, as a body transferred from one place to another.

Reply Obj. 4. Not only does the agent intellect illumine phantasms, it does more; by its power intelligible species are abstracted from phantasms. It illumines phantasms because, just as the sensitive part acquires a greater power by its conjunction with the intellectual part, so through the power of the agent intellect phantasms are made more fit for the abstraction of intelligible intentions from them. Now the agent

[11] Cf. above, q. 84, a. 1; cf. also q. 50, a. 2.

intellect abstracts intelligible species from phantasms inasmuch as by its power we are able to take into our consideration the natures of species without individual conditions. It is in accord with their likenesses that the possible intellect is informed.

Reply Obj. 5. Our intellect both abstracts the intelligible species *from* phantasms, inasmuch as it considers the natures of things universally, and yet understands these natures *in* the phantasms, since it cannot understand the things, of which it abstracts the species, without turning to phantasms, as we have said above.[12]

Second Article

WHETHER THE INTELLIGIBLE SPECIES ABSTRACTED FROM PHANTASMS ARE RELATED TO OUR INTELLECT AS THAT WHICH IS UNDERSTOOD?

We proceed thus to the Second Article:—

Objection 1. It would seem that the intelligible species abstracted from phantasms are related to our intellect as that which is understood. For the understood in act is in the one who understands: since the understood in act is the intellect itself in act. But nothing of what is understood is in the actually understanding intellect save the abstracted intelligible species. Therefore this species is what is actually understood.

Obj. 2. Further, what is actually understood must be in something; or else it would be nothing. But it is not in something outside the soul; for, since what is outside the soul is material, nothing therein can be actually understood. Therefore what is actually understood is in the intellect. Consequently it can be nothing else than the aforesaid intelligible species.

Obj. 3. Further, the Philosopher says that *words are signs of the passions in the soul*.[13] But words signify the things understood, for we express by word what we understand. Therefore these passions of the soul, viz., the intelligible species, are what is actually understood.

On the contrary, The intelligible species is to the intellect what the sensible species is to the sense. But the sensible species is not *what* is perceived, but rather that *by which*

[12] Q. 84, a. 7.   [13] *Perih.,* I, 1 (16a 3).

the sense perceives. Therefore the intelligible species is not what is actually understood, but that by which the intellect understands.

I answer that, Some[14] have asserted that our intellectual powers know only the impressions made on them; as, for example, that sense is cognizant only of the impression made on its own organ. According to this theory, the intellect understands only its own impressions, namely, the intelligible species which it has received.

This is, however, manifestly false for two reasons. First, because the things we understand are also the objects of science. Therefore, if what we understand is merely the intelligible species in the soul, it would follow that every science would be concerned, not with things outside the soul, but only with the intelligible species within the soul; just as, according to the teaching of the Platonists, all the sciences are about Ideas, which they held to be that which is actually understood.[15] Secondly, it is untrue, because it would lead to the opinion of the ancients who maintained that *whatever seems, is true,*[16] and that consequently contradictories are true simultaneously. For if a power knows only its own impressions, it can judge only of them. Now a thing *seems* according to the impression made on the cognitive power. Consequently the cognitive power will always judge of its own impression as such; and so every judgment will be true. For instance, if taste perceived only its own impression, when anyone with a healthy taste perceives that honey is sweet, he would judge truly, and if anyone with a corrupt taste perceives that honey is bitter, this would be equally true; for each would judge according to the impression on his taste. Thus every opinion, in fact, every sort of apprehension, would be equally true.

Therefore it must be said that the intelligible species is related to the intellect as that by which it understands. Which is proved thus. Now action is twofold, as it is said in *Metaph.* ix:[17] one which remains in the agent (for instance, to see and to understand), and another which passes into an external object (for instance, to heat and to cut).

---

[14] The reference seems to be to Protagoras and to Heraclitus: cf. Aristotle, *Metaph.*, VIII, 3 (1047a 6); III, 3 (1005b 25).   [15] Q. 84, a. 1 and 4.   [16] Cf. Aristotle, *Metaph.*, III, 5 (1009a 8).   [17] *Op. cit.*, VIII, 8 (1050a 23).

Each of these actions proceeds in virtue of some form. And just as the form from which proceeds an act tending to something external is the likeness of the object of the action, as heat in the heater is a likeness of the thing heated, so the form from which proceeds an action remaining in the agent is a likeness of the object. Hence that by which the sight sees is the likeness of the visible thing; and the likeness of the thing understood, that is, the intelligible species, is the form by which the intellect understands. But since the intellect reflects upon itself, by such reflection it understands both its own act of understanding, and the species by which it understands. Thus the intelligible species is secondarily that which is understood; but that which is primarily understood is the thing, of which the species is the likeness.

This also appears from the opinion of the ancient philosophers, who said that *like is known by like*.[18] For they said that the soul knows the earth outside itself by the earth within itself; and so of the rest. If, therefore, we take the species of the earth instead of the earth, in accord with Aristotle who says *that a stone is not in the soul, but only the likeness of the stone*,[19] it follows that by means of its intelligible species the soul knows the things which are outside it.

Reply Obj. 1. The thing understood is in the knower by its own likeness. It is in this sense that we say that the thing actually understood is the intellect in act, because the likeness of the thing understood is the form of the intellect, just as the likeness of a sensible thing is the form of the sense in act. Hence it does not follow that the abstracted intelligible species is what is actually understood; but rather that it is the likeness thereof.

Reply Obj. 2. In these words *the thing actually understood* there is a double meaning:—the thing which is understood, and the fact that it is understood. In like manner, the words *abstract universal* mean two things, the nature of a thing and its abstraction or universality. Therefore the nature itself which suffers the act of being understood, or the act of being abstracted, or the intention of universality, exists only in individuals; but that it is understood, abstracted or considered as universal is in the intellect. We see something

[18] The opinion of Empedocles, according to Aristotle, *De An.*, I, 5 (409b 26); and of Plato: cf. *op. cit.*, I, 2 (404b 17).   [19] *Op. cit.*, III, 8 (431b 29).

similar to this in the senses. For the sight sees the color of the apple apart from its smell. If therefore it be asked where is the color which is seen apart from the smell, it is quite clear that the color which is seen is only in the apple; but that it be perceived apart from the smell, this is owing to the sight, inasmuch as sight receives the likeness of color and not of smell. In like manner, the humanity which is understood exists only in this or that man; but that humanity be apprehended without the conditions of individuality, that is, that it be abstracted and consequently considered as universal, befalls humanity inasmuch as it is perceived by the intellect, in which there is a likeness of the specific nature, but not of the individual principles.

Reply Obj. 3. There are two operations in the sensitive part. One is limited to immutation, and thus the operation of the senses takes place when the senses are impressed by the sensible. The other is formation, inasmuch as the imagination forms for itself an image of an absent thing, or even of something never seen. Both of these operations are found in the intellect. For in the first place there is the passion of the possible intellect as informed by the intelligible species; and then the possible intellect, as thus informed, then forms a definition, or a division, or a composition, which is expressed by language. And so, the notion signified by a *term* is a definition; and a *proposition* signifies the intellect's division or composition. Words do not therefore signify the intelligible species themselves; but that which the intellect forms for itself for the purpose of judging of external things.

Third Article

WHETHER THE MORE UNIVERSAL IS FIRST IN OUR INTELLECTUAL COGNITION?

We proceed thus to the Third Article:—

Objection 1. It would seem that the more universal is not first in our intellectual cognition. For what is first and more known in its own nature is secondarily and less known in relation to ourselves. But universals come first as regards their nature, because *that is first which does not involve the existence of its correlative.* Therefore universals are secondarily known by our intellect.

Obj. 2. Further, the composite precedes the simple in relation to us. But universals are the more simple. Therefore they are known secondarily by us.

Obj. 3. Further, the Philosopher says that the object defined comes in our knowledge before the parts of its definition.[20] But the more universal is part of the definition of the less universal, as *animal* is part of the definition of *man*. Therefore universals are secondarily known by us.

Obj. 4. Further, we know causes and principles by their effects. But universals are principles. Therefore universals are secondarily known by us.

On the contrary, We must proceed from the universal to the singular.[21]

I answer that, In our knowledge there are two things to be considered. First, that intellectual knowledge in some degree arises from sensible knowledge. Now because sense has singular and individual things for its object, and intellect has the universal for its object, it follows that our knowledge of the former comes before our knowledge of the latter. Secondly, we must consider that our intellect proceeds from a state of potentiality to a state of actuality; and that every power thus proceeding from potentiality to actuality comes first to an incomplete act, which is intermediate between potentiality and actuality, before accomplishing the perfect act. The perfect act of the intellect is complete knowledge, when the object is distinctly and determinately known; whereas the incomplete act is imperfect knowledge, when the object is known indistinctly, and as it were confusedly. A thing thus imperfectly known is known partly in act and partly in potentiality. Hence the Philosopher says that *what is manifest and certain is known to us at first confusedly; afterwards we know it by distinguishing its principles and elements.*[22] Now it is evident that to know something that comprises many things, without a proper knowledge of each thing contained in it, is to know that thing confusedly. In this way we can have knowledge not only of the universal whole, which contains parts potentially, but also of the integral whole; for each whole can be known confusedly, without its parts being known distinctly. But to know distinctly what is contained in the universal whole is to know the less common;

---

[20] *Phys.,* I, 1 (184b 11).   [21] *Ibid.* (184a 23).   [22] *Ibid.* (184a 21).

and thus to know *animal* indistinctly is to know it as *animal*, whereas to know *animal* distinctly is to know it as *rational* or *irrational animal,* that is, to know a man or a lion. And so our intellect knows *animal* before it knows man; and the same reason holds in comparing any more universal concept with the less universal.

Moreover, as sense, like the intellect, proceeds from potentiality to act, the same order of knowledge appears in the senses. For by sense we judge of the more common before the less common, in reference both to place and time. In reference to place, when a thing is seen afar off it is seen to be a body before it is seen to be an animal, and to be an animal before it is seen to be a man, and to be a man before it is seen to be Socrates or Plato. The same is true as regards time, for a child can distinguish man from not-man before he distinguishes this man from that, and therefore *children at first call all men fathers, and later on distinguish each one from the others.*[23] The reason of this is clear: he who knows a thing indistinctly is in a state of potentiality as regards its principle of distinction; just as he who knows *genus* is in a state of potentiality as regards *difference.* Thus it is evident that indistinct knowledge is midway between potentiality and act.

We must therefore conclude that knowledge of the singular and individual is prior, as regards us, to the knowledge of the universal, just as sensible knowledge is prior to intellectual knowledge. But in both sense and intellect the knowledge of the more common precedes the knowledge of the less common.

Reply Obj. 1. The universal can be considered in two ways. First, the universal nature may be considered together with the intention of universality. And since the intention of universality—viz., the relation of one and the same to many—is due to intellectual abstraction, the universal thus considered is subsequent in our knowledge. Hence it is said that the *universal animal is either nothing or something subsequent.*[24] But according to Plato, who held that universals are subsistent, the universal considered thus would be prior to the particular, for the latter, according to him, are mere participations in the subsistent universals which he called Ideas.[25]

[23] *Ibid.* (184b 12).   [24] Aristotle, *De An.,* I, 1 (402b 7).   [25] Cf. above, q. 84, a. 1.

Secondly, the universal can be considered according to the nature itself (for instance, *animality* or *humanity*) as existing in the individual. And thus we must distinguish two orders of nature: one, by way of generation and time; and thus the imperfect and the potential come first. In this way the more common comes first in the order of nature. This appears clearly in the generation of man and animal; for *the animal is generated before man,* as the Philosopher says.[26] The other order is the order of perfection or of the intention of nature. For instance, act considered absolutely is naturally prior to potentiality, and the perfect to the imperfect; and thus the less common comes naturally before the more common, as man comes before animal. For the intention of nature does not stop at the generation of animal, but aims at the generation of man.

Reply Obj. 2. The more common universal may be compared to the less common as a whole, and as a part. As a whole, inasmuch as in the more universal there is potentially contained not only the less universal, but also other things; as in *animal* is contained not only *man* but also *horse*. As a part, inasmuch as the less common universal contains in its notion not only the more common, but also more; as *man* contains not only *animal* but also *rational*. Therefore *animal* considered in itself is in our knowledge before *man*; but *man* comes before *animal* considered as a part of the notion of man.

Reply Obj. 3. A part can be known in two ways. First, absolutely considered in itself; and thus nothing prevents the parts from being known before the whole, as stones are known before a house is known. Secondly, as belonging to a certain whole; and thus we must needs know the whole before its parts. For we know a house confusedly before we know its different parts. So, likewise, that which defines is known before the thing defined is known; otherwise the thing defined would not be made known by the definition. But as parts of the definition they are known after. For we know man confusedly as man before we know how to distinguish all that belongs to human nature.

Reply Obj. 4. The universal, as understood with the intention of universality, is, in a certain manner, a principle

of knowledge, in so far as the intention of universality results from the mode of understanding, which is by way of
abstraction. But that which is a principle of knowledge is
not of necessity a principle of being, as Plato thought, since
at times we know a cause through its effect, and substance
through accidents. Therefore the universal thus considered,
according to the opinion of Aristotle, is neither a principle of
being, nor a substance, as he makes clear.[27] But if we consider
the generic or specific nature itself as existing in the singular, thus in a way it has the character of a formal principle
in regard to singulars; for the singular is the result of matter,
while the nature of the species is from the form. But the
generic nature is compared to the specific nature rather after
the fashion of a material principle, because the generic nature
is taken from that which is material in a thing, while the
nature of the species is taken from that which is formal.
Thus the notion of animal is taken from the sensitive part,
whereas the notion of man is taken from the intellectual
part. Thus it is that the ultimate intention of nature is towards the species and not the individual, or the genus; because the form is the end of generation, while matter is for
the sake of the form. Neither is it necessary that the knowledge of any cause or principle should be subsequent in relation to us, since through sensible causes we sometimes
become acquainted with unknown effects, and sometimes
conversely.

Fourth Article

WHETHER WE CAN UNDERSTAND MANY THINGS AT THE SAME TIME?

We proceed thus to the Fourth Article:—
Objection 1. It would seem that we can understand many
things at the same time. For intellect is above time, whereas
the succession of before and after belongs to time. Therefore
the intellect does not understand different things in succession, but at the same time.

Obj. 2. Further, there is nothing to prevent different forms
not opposed to each other from actually being in the same
subject, as, for instance, color and smell are in the apple.

[27] Aristotle, *Metaph.*, VI, 13 (1038b 8).

But intelligible species are not opposed to each other. Therefore there is nothing to prevent the same intellect from being in act as regards different intelligible species. Thus it can understand many things at the same time.

Obj. 3. Further, the intellect understands a whole at the same time, such as a man or a house. But a whole contains many parts. Therefore the intellect understands many things at the same time.

Obj. 4. Further, we cannot know the difference between two things unless we know both at the same time;[28] and the same is to be said of any other comparison. But our intellect knows the difference between one thing and another. Therefore it knows many things at the same time.

On the contrary, It is said that *understanding is of one thing only, science is of many.*[29]

I answer that, The intellect can, indeed, understand many things as one, but not as many, that is to say, by *one* but not by *many* intelligible species. For the mode of every action follows the form which is the principle of that action. Therefore whatever things the intellect can understand under one species, it can understand together. Hence it is that God sees all things at the same time, because He sees all in one, that is, in His essence. But whatever things the intellect understands under different species, it does not understand at the same time. The reason for this is that it is impossible for one and the same subject to be perfected at the same time by many forms of one genus and diverse species, just as it is impossible for one and the same body at the same time to have different colors or different shapes. Now all intelligible species belong to one genus, because they are the perfections of one intellectual power even though the things which the species represent belong to different genera. Therefore it is impossible for one and the same intellect to be perfected at the same time by different intelligible species so as actually to understand different things.

Reply Obj. 1. The intellect is above that time which is the measure of the movement of corporeal things. But the multitude itself of intelligible species causes a certain succession of intelligible operations, according as one operation is prior to another. And this succession is called time by

[28] Aristotle, *De An.,* III, 2 (426b 22).   [29] Aristotle, *Top.,* II, 10 (114b 34).

Augustine, who says that *God moves the spiritual creature through time*.[30]

Reply Obj. 2. Not only is it impossible for opposite forms to exist at the same time in the same subject, but neither can any forms belonging to the same genus, although they be not opposed to one another, as is clear from the examples of colors and shapes.

Reply Obj. 3. Parts can be understood in two ways. First, in a confused way, as existing in the whole; and thus they are known through the one form of the whole, and so are known together. In another way, they are known distinctly; and thus each is known by its species, and hence they are not understood at the same time.

Reply Obj. 4. If the intellect sees the difference or comparison between one thing and another, it knows both in relation to their difference or comparison; just as it knows the parts in the whole, as we said above.

Fifth Article

WHETHER OUR INTELLECT UNDERSTANDS BY COMPOSITION AND DIVISION?

We proceed thus to the Fifth Article:—

Objection 1. It would seem that our intellect does not understand by composition and division. For composition and division are only of many, whereas the intellect cannot understand many things at the same time. Therefore it cannot understand by composition and division.

Obj. 2. Further, every composition and division implies past, present, or future time. But the intellect abstracts from time, as also from other particular conditions. Therefore the intellect does not understand by composition and division.

Obj. 3. Further, the intellect understands things by an assimilation to them. But composition and division are not in things; for nothing is in things but the thing which is signified by the predicate and the subject, and which is one and the same thing, provided that the composition be true; for *man* is truly what *animal* is. Therefore the intellect does not act by composition and division.

On the contrary, Words signify the conceptions of the in-

[30] *De Genesi ad Litt.*, VIII, 20; 22 (PL 34, 388; 389).

tellect, as the Philosopher says.[31] But in words we find composition and division, as appears in affirmative and negative propositions. Therefore the intellect acts by composition and division.

I answer that, The human intellect must of necessity understand by composition and division. For since the intellect passes from potentiality to act, it has a likeness to generable things, which do not attain to perfection all at once but acquire it by degrees. In the same way, the human intellect does not acquire perfect knowledge of a thing by the first apprehension; but it first apprehends something of the thing, such as its quiddity, which is the first and proper object of the intellect; and then it understands the properties, accidents, and various dispositions affecting the essence. Thus it necessarily relates one thing with another by composition or division; and from one composition and division it necessarily proceeds to another, and this is *reasoning*.

But the angelic and the divine intellects, like all incorruptible beings, have their perfection at once from the beginning. Hence the angelic and the divine intellect have the entire knowledge of a thing at once and perfectly; and hence, in knowing the quiddity of a thing, they know at once whatever we can know by composition, division and reasoning. Therefore the human intellect knows by composition, division and reasoning. But the divine and the angelic intellects have a knowledge of composition, division, and reasoning, not by the process itself, but by understanding the simple essence.

Reply Obj. 1. Composition and division of the intellect are made by differentiating and comparing. Hence the intellect knows many things by composition and division, by knowing the difference and comparison of things.

Reply Obj. 2. Although the intellect abstracts from phantasms, it does not understand actually without turning to the phantasms, as we have said.[32] And in so far as the intellect turns to phantasms, composition and division involve time.

Reply Obj. 3. The likeness of a thing is received into the intellect according to the mode of the intellect, not according to the mode of the thing. Hence, although something on the part of the thing corresponds to the composition and division of the intellect, still, it does not exist in the same way in the

[31] *Perih.,* I, 1 (16a 3).   [32] A. 1; q. 84, a. 7.

intellect and in the thing. For the proper object of the human intellect is the quiddity of a material thing, which is apprehended by the senses and the imagination. Now in a material thing there is a twofold composition. First, there is the composition of form with matter. To this corresponds that composition of the intellect whereby the universal whole is predicated of its part: for the genus is derived from common matter, while the difference that completes the species is derived from the form, and the particular from individual matter. The second composition is of accident with subject; and to this composition corresponds that composition of the intellect whereby accident is predicated of subject, as when we say *the man is white*. Nevertheless, the composition of the intellect differs from the composition of things; for the components in the thing are diverse, whereas the composition of the intellect is a sign of the identity of the components. For the above composition of the intellect was not such as to assert that *man is whiteness*; but the assertion, *the man is white*, means that *the man is something having whiteness*. In other words, *man* is identical in subject with the *being having whiteness*. It is the same with the composition of form and matter. For *animal* signifies that which has a sensitive nature; *rational*, that which has an intellectual nature; *man*, that which has both; and *Socrates*, that which has all these things together with individual matter. And so, according to this kind of identity our intellect composes one thing with another by means of predication.

Sixth Article

WHETHER THE INTELLECT CAN BE FALSE?

We proceed thus to the Sixth Article:—

Objection 1. It would seem that the intellect can be false, for the Philosopher says that *truth and falsehood are in the mind*.[33] But the *mind* and *intellect* are the same, as is shown above.[34] Therefore falsehood may be in the intellect.

Obj. 2. Further, opinion and reasoning belong to the intellect. But falsehood exists in both. Therefore falsehood can be in the intellect.

Obj. 3. Further, sin is in the intellectual part. But sin in-

---

[33] *Metaph.*, V, 4 (1027b 27).   [34] Q. 72.

volves falsehood, for *those err that work evil* (*Prov.* xiv. 22).
Therefore falsehood can be in the intellect.

On the contrary, Augustine says that *everyone who is deceived, does not rightly understand that wherein he is deceived.*[35] And the Philosopher says that *the intellect is always
true.*[36]

I answer that, The Philosopher compares the intellect with
the sense on this point.[37] For the sense is not deceived in its
proper object (as sight in regard to color), save accidentally,
through some hindrance to the sensible organ. For example,
the taste of a fever-stricken person judges a sweet thing to be
bitter, because his tongue is vitiated by ill humors. The sense,
however, may be deceived as regards common sensible objects, as size or figure; as when, for example, it judges the sun
to be only a foot in diameter, whereas in reality it exceeds the
earth in size. Much more is the sense deceived concerning accidental sensible objects; as when it judges that vinegar is
honey because the color is similar. The reason of this is evident. Every power, as such, is essentially directed to its
proper object; and things of this kind are always uniform.
Hence, so long as the power exists, its judgment concerning
its own proper object does not fail. Now the proper object of
the intellect is the *quiddity* in a thing. Hence, properly
speaking, the intellect is not in error concerning this quiddity; whereas it may go astray as regards the accompani-
ments of the essence or quiddity in the thing, either in referring one thing to another, in what concerns composition or
division, or also in the process of reasoning. That is why it is
also true that the intellect cannot err in regard to those
propositions which are understood as soon as their terms are
understood. Such is the case with first principles, from which
there also arises infallible truth in the certitude of science
with respect to its conclusions.

The intellect, however, may be accidentally deceived in the
quiddity of composite things, not by the defect of its organ,
for the intellect is a power that is independent of an organ,
but on the part of the composition affecting the definition.
This may happen, for instance, when the definition of a thing
is false in relation to something else, as the definition of a

[35] *Lib. 83 Quaest.*, q. 32 (PL 40, 22).   [36] *De An.*, III, 10 (433a 26).
[37] *Op. cit.*, III, 6 (430b 29).

circle predicated of a triangle; or when a definition is false in itself as involving the composition of things incompatible, as, for instance, to describe anything as *a rational winged animal*. Hence as regards simple things, in whose definitions there is no composition, we cannot be deceived; but if we fail, we fail completely in understanding them, as is said in *Metaph*. ix.[38]

Reply Obj. 1. The Philosopher says that falsehood is in the intellect in regard to composition and division. The same answer applies to the *second objection* concerning opinion and reasoning; as well as to the *third objection,* concerning the error of the sinner, who errs in the practical judgment of the appetible object. But in the absolute consideration of the quiddity of a thing, and of those things which are known thereby, the intellect is never deceived. In this sense are to be understood the authorities quoted in proof of the opposite conclusion.

Seventh Article

WHETHER ONE PERSON CAN UNDERSTAND ONE AND THE SAME THING BETTER THAN ANOTHER CAN?

We proceed thus to the Seventh Article:—

Objection 1. It would seem that one person cannot understand on and the same thing better than another can. For Augustine says: *Whoever understands a thing otherwise than as it is, does not understand it at all. Hence it is clear that there is a perfect understanding, than which none other is more perfect; and therefore there are not infinite degrees of understanding a thing, nor can one person understand a thing better than another can.*[39]

Obj. 2. Further, the intellect is true in its act of understanding. But truth, being a certain equality between thought and thing, is not subject to more or less; for a thing cannot be said to be more or less equal. Therefore a thing cannot be more or less understood.

Obj. 3. Further, the intellect is that which most pertains to the form in man. But different forms cause different species.

[38] Aristotle, *Metaph.*, VIII, 10 (1052a 1).   [39] *Lib. 83 Quaest.*, q. 32 (PL 40, 22).

Therefore if one man understands better than another, it would seem that they do not belong to the same species.

On the contrary, Experience shows that some understand more profoundly than do others; as one who carries a conclusion to its first principles and ultimate causes understands it better than the one who reduces it only to its proximate causes.

I answer that, To say that a thing is understood more by one than by another may be taken in two senses. First, so that the word *more* be taken as determining the act of understanding as regards the thing understood; and thus, one cannot understand the same thing more than another, because to understand it otherwise than as it is, either better or worse, would be to be deceived rather than to understand, as Augustine argues. In another sense, the word *more* can be taken as determining the act of understanding on the part of the one who understands. In this way, one may understand the same thing better than someone else, through having a greater power of understanding; just as a man may see a thing better with his bodily sight, whose power is greater, and whose sight is more perfect. The same applies to the intellect in two ways. First, as regards the intellect itself, which is more perfect. For it is plain that the better the disposition of a body, the better the soul allotted to it; which clearly appears in things of different species. The reason for this is that act and form are received into matter according to the capacity of matter; and thus because some men have bodies of better disposition, their souls have a greater power of understanding. Hence, it is said that *those who have soft flesh are of apt mind.*[40] Secondly, this occurs in regard to the lower powers of which the intellect needs its operation; for those in whom the imaginative, cogitative and memorative powers are of better disposition, are better disposed to understand.

The reply to the first objection is clear from the above; and likewise the reply to the second, for the truth of the intellect consists in this, that the intellect understands a thing as it is.

Reply Obj. 3. The difference of form which is due only to the different disposition of matter causes, not a specific, but only a numerical, difference: for different individuals have

---

[40] Aristotle, *De An.,* II, 9 (421a 25).

different forms, diversified according to the diversity of matter.

Eighth Article

WHETHER THE INTELLECT UNDERSTANDS THE INDIVISIBLE BEFORE THE DIVISIBLE?

We proceed thus to the Eighth Article:—

Objection 1. It would seem that the intellect understands the indivisible before the divisible. For the Philosopher says that we *understand and know from the knowledge of principles and elements.*[41] But indivisibles are the principles and elements of divisible things. Therefore the indivisible is known to us before the divisible.

Obj. 2. Further, the definition of a thing contains what is known antecedently, for a definition *proceeds from the first and more known,* as is said *Topic.* vi.[42] But the indivisible is included in the definition of the divisible, as a point comes into the definition of a line; for, as Euclid says, *a line is length without breadth, the extremities of which are two points.*[43] So, too, unity comes into the definition of number, for *number is multitude measured by one,* as is said in *Metaph.* x.[44] Therefore our intellect understands the indivisible before the divisible.

Obj. 3. Further, *Like is known by like.* But the indivisible is more like to the intellect than is the divisible, because *the intellect is simple.*[45] Therefore our intellect first knows the indivisible.

On the contrary, It is said that *the indivisible is made known as a privation.*[46] But privation is known secondarily. Therefore so is the indivisible.

I answer that, The object of our intellect in its present state is the quiddity of a material thing, which it abstracts from phantasms, as was stated above.[47] And since that which is known first and of itself by our cognitive power is its proper object, we must consider its relationship to that quiddity in order to discover in what order the indivisible is

---

[41] *Phys.,* I, 1 (184a 12).   [42] Aristotle, *Top.,* VI, 4 (141a 32).
[43] *Geometria,* trans. Boethius, I (PL 63, 1307).   [44] Aristotle, *Metaph.,* IX, 6 (1057a 3).   [45] Aristotle, *De An.,* III, 4 (429a 18; b 23).
[46] *Op. cit.,* III, 6 (430b 21).   [47] A. 1; q. 84, a. 7.

known. Now the indivisible is threefold, as is said in *De Anima* iii.[48] First, the continuous is indivisible, since it is actually undivided, although potentially divisible. This indivisible is known to us before its division, which is a division into parts, because confused knowledge is prior to distinct knowledge, as we have said above. Secondly, there is the indivisible in species, as man's nature is something indivisible. This way, also, the indivisible is understood before its division into the parts of the nature, as we have said above; and also before the intellect composes and divides by affirmation and negation. The reason of this priority is that both these kinds of indivisible are understood by the intellect of itself as its proper object. The third kind of indivisible is what is altogether indivisible, as a point and unity, which cannot be divided either actually or potentially. And this indivisible is known secondarily, through the privation of divisibility. Therefore a point is defined by way of privation *as that which has no parts;*[49] and in like manner the notion of *one* is that it is *indivisible,* as is stated in *Metaph.* x.[50] And the reason for this posteriority is that this indivisible has a certain opposition to a corporeal being, the quiddity of which is the primary and proper object of the intellect.

But if our intellect understood by participation in certain separate indivisibles, as the Platonists maintained,[51] it would follow that such an indivisible is prior in the understanding, for, according to the Platonists, it is first in being participated by things.[52]

Reply Obj. 1. In the acquisition of knowledge, principles and elements are not always first; for sometimes from sensible effects we arrive at the knowledge of principles and intelligible causes. But in perfect knowledge, the knowledge of effects always depends on the knowledge of principles and elements; for, as the Philosopher says in the same passage, *Then do we consider that we know, when we can resolve principles into their causes.*[53]

Reply Obj. 2. A point is not included in the definition of a line in general; for it is manifest that in a line of indefinite length, and also in a circular line, there is no point, save po-

[48] Aristotle, *De An.,* III, 6 (430b 6).   [49] Euclid, *Geometria,* I (PL 63, 1307).   [50] Aristotle, *Metaph.,* IX, 1 (1052b 16).   [51] Cf. above, q. 84, a. 1 and 4.   [52] Cf. *De Causis,* I (p. 161).   [53] *Phys.,* I, 1 (184a 12).

tentially. Euclid defines a straight line of definite length, and therefore he includes a point in the definition as the limit in the definition of that which is limited.[54]—Unity, however, is the measure of number: wherefore it is included in the definition of a measured number. But it is not included in the definition of the divisible, but rather conversely.

Reply Obj. 3. The likeness through which we understand is the species of the thing known in the knower. Hence, a thing is prior in being known, not according to the likeness of its nature to the knowing power, but according to its agreement with the proper object of that power. Otherwise, sight would perceive hearing rather than color.

[54] *Geometria,* I (PL 63, 1307).

Question LXXXVI

WHAT OUR INTELLECT KNOWS IN MATERIAL THINGS

(In Four Articles)

WE NOW have to consider what our intellect knows in material things. Under this head there are four points of inquiry: (1) Whether it knows singulars? (2) Whether it knows infinite things? (3) Whether it knows contingent things? (4) Whether it knows future things?

First Article

WHETHER OUR INTELLECT KNOWS SINGULARS?

We proceed thus to the First Article:—

Objection 1. It would seem that our intellect knows singulars. For whoever knows a composition, knows the terms of composition. But our intellect knows this composition: *Socrates is a man,* for the intellect can form a proposition to this effect. Therefore our intellect knows this singular, *Socrates.*

Obj. 2. Further, the practical intellect directs to action. But action has relation to singular things. Therefore the intellect knows the singular.

Obj. 3. Further, our intellect understands itself. But in itself it is a singular, or otherwise it would have no action of its own; for actions belong to singulars. Therefore our intellect knows singulars.

Obj. 4. Further, a superior power can do whatever is done by an inferior power. But sense knows the singular. Much more, therefore, can the intellect know it.

On the contrary, The Philosopher says that *the universal is known by reason, and the singular is known by sense.*[1]

I answer that, Our intellect cannot know the singular in material things directly and primarily. The reason for this is that the principle of singularity in material things is individual matter; whereas our intellect, as we have said above,[2] understands by abstracting the intelligible species from such matter. Now what is abstracted from individual matter is

[1] *Phys.,* I, 5 (189a 5).   [2] Q. 85, a. 1.

423

universal. Hence our intellect knows directly only universals. But indirectly, however, and as it were by a kind of reflexion, it can know the singular, because, as we have said above,[3] even after abstracting the intelligible species, the intellect, in order to understand actually, needs to turn to the phantasms in which it understands the species, as is said in *De Anima* iii.[4] Therefore it understands the universal directly through the intelligible species, and indirectly the singular represented by the phantasm. And thus it forms the proposition, *Socrates is a man.*

Therefore the reply to the first objection is clear.

Reply Obj. 2. The choice of a particular thing to be done is as the conclusion of a syllogism formed by the practical intellect, as is said in *Ethics* vii.[5] But a singular proposition cannot be directly concluded from a universal proposition, except through the medium of a singular proposition. Therefore the universal principle of the practical intellect does not move save through the medium of the particular apprehension of the sensitive part, as is said in *De Anima* iii.[6]

Reply Obj. 3. Intelligibility is incompatible with the singular not as such, but as material; for nothing can be understood otherwise than immaterially. Therefore if there be an immaterial singular such as the intellect, there is no reason why it should not be intelligible.

Reply Obj. 4. The higher power can do what the lower power can, but in a more eminent way. And so, what the sense knows materially and concretely, which is to know the singular directly, the intellect knows immaterially and in the abstract, which is to know the universal.

[3] Q. 84, a. 7. [4] Aristotle, *De An.*, III, 7 (431b 2). [5] Aristotle, *Eth.*, VII, 3 (1147a 28). [6] Aristotle, *De An.*, III, 11 (434a 16).

HOW THE INTELLECTUAL SOUL KNOWS ITSELF AND ALL THAT IS WITHIN ITSELF

(*In Four Articles*)

WE HAVE now to consider how the intellectual soul knows itself and all that is within itself. Under this head there are four points of inquiry: (1) Whether the soul knows itself by its own essence? (2) Whether it knows its own habits? (3) How does the intellect know its own act? (4) How does it know the act of the will?

First Article

WHETHER THE INTELLECTUAL SOUL KNOWS ITSELF BY ITS ESSENCE?

We proceed thus to the First Article:—

Objection 1. It would seem that the intellectual soul knows itself by its own essence. For Augustine says that *the mind knows itself by itself, because it is incorporeal.*[1]

Obj. 2. Further, both angels and human souls belong to the genus of intellectual substance. But an angel understands himself by his own essence. Therefore so does the human soul.

Obj. 3. Further, *in things without matter, the intellect and that which is understood are the same.*[2] But the human mind is without matter, not being the act of a body, as was stated above.[3] Therefore the intellect and its object are the same in the human mind; and therefore the human mind understands itself by its own essence.

On the contrary, It is said that the *intellect understands itself in the same way as it understands other things.*[4] But it understands other things, not by their essence, but by their likenesses. Therefore it does not understand itself by its own essence.

I answer that, Everything is knowable so far as it is in act,

[1] *De Trin.,* IX, 3 (PL 42, 963). [2] Aristotle, *De An.,* III, 4 (430a 3). [3] Q. 76, a. 1. [4] Aristotle, *De An.,* III, 4 (430a 2).

and not so far as it is in potentiality;[5] for a thing is a being, and is true, and therefore knowable, according as it is actual. This is quite clear as regards sensible things, for the eye does not see what is potentially, but what is actually, colored. In like manner, it is clear that the intellect, so far as it knows material things, does not know save what is in act; and hence it does not know primary matter except as proportionate to form, as is stated *Physics* i.[6] Consequently immaterial substances are intelligible by their own essence, according as each one is actual by its own essence.

Therefore it is that the essence of God, the pure and perfect act, is absolutely and perfectly in itself intelligible; and hence God by His own essence knows Himself, and all other things also. The angelic essence belongs, indeed, to the genus of intelligible things as *act*, but not as a *pure act*, nor as a *complete act*; and hence the angel's act of intelligence is not completed by his essence. For, although an angel understands himself by his own essence, still he cannot understand all other things by his own essence; he rather knows things other than himself by their likenesses. Now the human intellect is only potential in the genus of intelligible beings, just as primary matter is potential in the genus of sensible beings; and hence it is called *possible*.[7] Therefore in its essence the human intellect is potentially understanding. Hence it has in itself the power to understand, but not to be understood, except as it is made actual. For even the Platonists asserted that an order of intelligible beings existed above the order of intellects, since the intellect understands only by participation in the intelligible;[8] for that which participates is below what it participates.

If, therefore, the human intellect, as the Platonists held, became actual by participating in separate intelligible Forms, it would understand itself by such a participation in incorporeal beings. But as in this life our intellect has material and sensible things for its proper object, as was stated above,[9] it understands itself according as it is made actual by the species abstracted from sensible things, through the light of the agent intellect, which not only actualizes the intelligibles

[5] Aristotle, *Metaph.*, VIII, 9 (1051a 29).   [6] Aristotle, *Phys.*, I, 7 (191a 8).   [7] Aristotle, *De An.*, III, 4 (428a 22).   [8] Cf. Dionysius, *De Div. Nom.*, IV, 1 (PG 3, 693); *De Causis*, IX (p. 169). Cf. also Proclus, *Elem. of Theol.*, prop. 163 and 164 (p. 142).   [9] Q. 84, a. 7.

themselves, but also, by their instrumentality, actualizes the possible intellect. Therefore the intellect knows itself, not by its essence, but by its act. This happens in two ways: In the first place, singularly, as when Socrates or Plato perceives that he has an intellectual soul because he perceives that he understands. In the second place, universally, as when we consider the nature of the human mind from a knowledge of the intellectual act. It is true, however, that the judgment and power of this knowledge, by which we know the nature of the soul, comes to us according to the derivation of our intellectual light from the divine truth which contains the exemplars of all things, as was stated above.[10] Hence Augustine says: *We gaze on the inviolable truth whence we can as perfectly as possible define, not what each man's mind is, but what it ought to be in the light of the eternal exemplars.*[11] There is, however, a difference between these two kinds of knowledge, and it consists in this that the mere presence of the mind suffices for the first; since the mind itself is the principle of action whereby it perceives itself, and hence it is said to know itself by its own presence. But as regards the second kind of knowledge, the mere presence of the mind does not suffice, but there is further required a careful and subtle inquiry. Hence many are ignorant of the soul's nature, and many have erred about it. So Augustine says concerning such mental inquiry: *Let the mind strive not to see itself as if it were absent, but to discern itself as present* [12]—*i.e.*, to know how it differs from other things; which is to know its essence and nature.

Reply Obj. 1. The mind knows itself by means of itself, because at length it arrives at a knowledge of itself, though led thereto by its own act:—because it is itself that it knows, since it loves itself, as Augustine says in the same passage. Now a thing can be called self-evident in two ways, either because we can know it by nothing else except itself, as first principles are called self-evident; or because it is not accidentally knowable, as color is visible of itself, whereas substance is visible accidentally.

Reply Obj. 2. The essence of an angel is as an act in the genus of intelligible beings, and therefore it is both intellect and the thing understood. Hence an angel apprehends his

<hr/>

[10] Q. 84, a. 5.   [11] *De Trin.,* IX, 6 (PL 42, 966).   [12] *Op. cit.,* X, 9 (PL 42, 980).

own essence through himself; not so the human intellect, which is either altogether in potentiality to intelligible things, —as is the possible intellect,—or is the act of the intelligible abstracted from the phantasms,—as is the agent intellect.

Reply Obj. 3. This saying of the Philosopher is universally true in every kind of intellect. For as the sense in act is the sensible in act, by reason of the sensible likeness which is the form of the sense in act, so likewise the intellect in act is the object understood in act, by reason of the likeness of the thing understood, which is the form of the intellect in act. So the human intellect, which becomes actual by the species of the thing understood, is itself understood by the same species as by its own form. Now to say that in *things without matter the intellect and what is understood are the same,* is equal to saying that *as regards things actually understood the intellect and what is understood are the same.* For a thing is actually understood in that it is immaterial. But a distinction must be drawn, since the essences of some things are immaterial, as the separate substances called angels, each of which is understood and understands; whereas there are other things whose essences are not without matter but only their abstract likenesses. Hence the Commentator says that the proposition quoted is true only of separate substances;[13] because in a sense it is verified in their regard, and not in regard to other substances, as was already stated.

[13] *In De An.,* III, comm. 15 (VI 169r).

THE END OF MAN

THE SUMMA CONTRA GENTILES

THIRD BOOK

CHAPTER II

THAT EVERY AGENT ACTS FOR AN END

ACCORDINGLY we must first show that every agent, by its action, intends an end.

For in those things which clearly act for an end, we declare the end to be that towards which the movement of the agent tends; for when this is reached, the end is said to be reached, and to fail in this is to fail in the end intended. This may be seen in the physician who aims at health, and in a man who runs towards an appointed goal. Nor does it matter, as to this, whether that which tends to an end be endowed with knowledge or not; for just as the target is the end of the archer, so is it the end of the arrow's flight. Now the movement of every agent tends to something determinate, since it is not from any force that any action proceeds, but heating proceeds from heat, and cooling from cold; and therefore actions are differentiated by their active principles. Action sometimes terminates in something made, as for instance building terminates in a house, and healing in health; while sometimes it does not so terminate, as for instance, in the case of understanding and sensation. And if action terminates in something made, the movement of the agent tends by that action towards the thing made; while if it does not terminate in something made, the movement of the agent tends to the action itself. It follows therefore that every agent intends an end while acting, which end is sometimes the action itself, sometimes a thing made by the action.

Again. In all things that act for an end, that is said to be the last end beyond which the agent seeks nothing further; and thus the physician's action goes as far as health, and when this is attained, his efforts cease. But in the action of every agent, a point can be reached beyond which the agent does not desire to go; or else actions would tend to infinity, which is impossible, for since *it is not possible to pass through an infinite medium*,[1] the agent would never begin to act, because nothing moves towards what it cannot reach. Therefore every agent acts for an end.

Moreover. If the actions of an agent proceed to infinity, these actions must needs result either in something made, or not. If the result is something made, the being of that thing made, will follow after an infinity of actions. But that which presupposes an infinity of things cannot possibly be, since *an infinite medium cannot be passed through*. Now impossibility of being argues impossibility of becoming, and that which cannot become, it is impossible to make. Therefore it is impossible for an agent to begin to make a thing for the making of which an infinity of actions is presupposed.— If, however, the result of such actions be not something made, the order of these actions must be either according to the order of active powers (for instance, if a man feels that he may imagine, and imagines that he may understand, and understands that he may will), or according to the order of objects (for instance, I consider the body that I may consider the soul, which I consider in order to consider a separate substance, which again I consider so that I may consider God). Now it is not possible to proceed to infinity, either in active powers (as neither is this possible in the forms of things, as is proved in *Metaph.* ii,[2] since the form is the principle of activity), or in objects (as neither is this possible in beings, since there is one first being, as we have proved above).[3] Therefore it is not possible for agents to proceed to infinity, and consequently there must be something, upon whose attainment the efforts of the agent cease. Therefore every agent acts for an end.

Further. In things that act for an end, whatsoever comes between the first agent and the last end, is an end in respect to what precedes, and an active principle in respect of what follows. Hence if the effort of the agent does not tend to

[1] Aristotle, *Post. Anal.*, I, 22 (82b 38). [2] Aristotle, *Metaph.*, Ia, 2 (994, 6). • [3] *C. G.* I, 42.

something determinate, and if its action, as stated, proceeds to infinity, the active principles must needs proceed to infinity; which is impossible, as we have shown above. Therefore the effort of the agent must of necessity tend to something determinate.

Again. Every agent acts either by nature or by intellect. Now there can be no doubt that those which act by intellect act for an end, since they act *with* an intellectual preconception of what they attain by their action, and they act *through* such a preconception; for this is to act by intellect. Now just as in the preconceiving intellect there exists the entire likeness of the effect that is attained by the action of the intellectual being, so in the natural agent there pre-exists the likeness of the natural effect, by virtue of which the action is determined to the appointed effect; for fire begets fire, and an olive produces an olive. Therefore, even as that which acts by intellect tends by its action to a definite end, so also does that which acts by nature. Therefore every agent acts for an end.

Moreover. Fault is not found save in those things which are for an end, for we do not find fault with one who fails in that to which he is not appointed; and thus we find fault with a physician if he fail to heal, but not with a builder or a grammarian. But we find fault in things done according to art, as when a grammarian fails to speak correctly, and in things that are ruled by nature, as in the case of monstrosities. Therefore every agent, whether according to nature, or according to art, or acting of set purpose, acts for an end.

Again. Were an agent not to act for a definite effect, all effects would be indifferent to it. Now that which is indifferent to many effects does not produce one rather than another. Therefore, from that which is indifferent to either of two effects, no effect results, unless it be determined by something to one of them. Hence it would be impossible for it to act. Therefore every agent tends to some definite effect, which is called its end.

There are, however, certain actions which would seem not to be for an end, such as playful and contemplative actions, and those which are done without attention, such as scratching one's beard, and the like. Whence some might be led to think that there is an agent that acts not for an end.—But we must observe that contemplative actions are not for another end, but are themselves an end. Playful actions are sometimes an end, when one plays for the mere pleasure of play; and sometimes they are for an end, as when we play that afterwards we may study better. Actions done without attention do not proceed from the intellect, but from some sudden act of the imagination, or some natural principle; and thus a disordered humor produces an itching sensation and is the cause of a man scratching his beard, which he does without his intellect attending to it. Such actions do tend to an end, although outside the order of the intellect. Hereby is excluded the error of certain natural philosophers of old, who maintained that all things happen by the necessity of matter, thus utterly banishing the final cause from things.[4]

[4] Cf. Aristotle, *Phys.*, II, 8 (198b 12).

CHAPTER III

THAT EVERY AGENT ACTS FOR A GOOD

HENCE we must go on to prove that every agent acts for a good.

For that every agent acts for an end clearly follows from the fact that every agent tends to something definite. Now that to which an agent tends definitely must needs be befitting to that agent, since the agent would not tend to it save because of some fittingness thereto. But that which is befitting to a thing is good for it. Therefore every agent acts for a good.

Further. The end is that wherein the appetite of the agent or mover comes to rest, as also the appetite of that which is moved. Now it is the very notion of good to be the term of appetite, since *good is the object of every appetite.*[1] Therefore all action and movement is for a good.

Again. All action and movement would seem to be directed in some way to being, either for the preservation of being in the species or in the individual, or for the acquisition of being. Now this itself, namely, being, is a good; and for this reason all things desire being. Therefore all action and movement is for a good.

Furthermore. All action and movement is for some perfection. For if the action itself be the end, it is clearly a second

[1] Aristotle, *Eth.*, I, 1 (1094a 1).

perfection of the agent. And if the action consist in the transformation of external matter, clearly the mover intends to induce some perfection into the thing moved, towards which perfection the movable also tends, if the movement be natural. Now we say that this is to be good, namely, to be perfect. Therefore every action and movement is for a good.

Also. Every agent acts according as it is actual. Now by acting it tends to something similar to itself. Therefore it tends to an act. But an act has the nature of good, since evil is not found save in a potentiality lacking act. Therefore every action is for a good.

Moreover. The intellectual agent acts for an end, as determining for itself its end; whereas the natural agent, though it acts for an end, as was proved above,[2] does not determine its end for itself, since it knows not the nature of end, but is moved to the end determined for it by another. Now an intellectual agent does not determine the end for itself except under the aspect of good; for the intelligible object does not move except it be considered as a good, which is the object of the will. Therefore the natural agent also is not moved, nor does it act for an end, except in so far as this end is a good, since the end is determined for the natural agent by some appetite. Therefore every agent acts for a good.

Again. To shun evil and to seek good are of the same nature, even as movement downward and upward are of the same nature. Now we observe that all things shun evil, for intellectual agents shun a thing for the reason that they apprehend it as evil, and all natural agents, in proportion to their strength, resist corruption which is the evil of everything. Therefore all things act for a good.

Again. That which results from the agent's action outside his intention is said to happen by chance or luck. Now we observe in the works of nature that either always or more often that happens which is best: thus in plants the leaves are so placed as to protect the fruit; and the parts of an animal are so disposed as to conduce to the animal's safety. Therefore, if this happens outside the intention of the natural agent, it will be the result of chance or luck. But that is impossible, because things that happen always, or frequently, are not by chance or fortuitous, but those which occur seldom.[3] Therefore the natural agent tends to that which is best; and much more evidently is this so with the intellectual agent. Therefore every agent intends a good in acting.

Moreover. Whatever is moved is brought to the term of movement by the mover and agent. Therefore mover and moved tend to the same term. Now that which is moved, since it is in potentiality, tends to an act, and consequently to perfection and goodness; for by its movement it passes from potentiality to act. Therefore mover and agent by moving and acting always intend a good.

Hence the philosophers in defining the good said: *The good is the object of every appetite;* and Dionysius says that *all things desire the good and the best.*[4]

[3] Cf. Aristotle, *Phys.,* II, 5 (196b 11).   [4] *De Div. Nom.,* IV, 4 (PG 3, 699).

CHAPTER XVI

THAT THE END OF EVERYTHING IS A GOOD

ACCORDINGLY if every agent acts for some good, as we have shown above,[1] it follows that good is the end of each thing. For everything is directed by its action to some end; for either the action itself is an end, or the end of the action is also the end of the agent: and this is its good.

Again. The end of a thing is the term of its appetite. Now the appetite of a thing terminates in a good, for the philosophers define good as *the object of all appetite.*[2] Therefore the end of everything is a good.

Moreover. That toward which a thing tends while it is without it, and wherein it rests when it has it, is its end. Now anything that is without its proper perfection is moved towards it, as far as in it lies; and if it have that perfection, it rests therein. Therefore the end of a thing is its perfection. But the perfection of a thing is its good. Therefore every thing is directed to good as its end.

Further. Things that know the end and things that do not know the end are equally directed to the end; although those which know the end are moved thereto *per se,* whereas those which do not know it tend thereto as directed by another, as may be seen in the archer and the arrow. Now those that know the end are always directed to a good as their end; be-

[1] Ch. 3.   [2] *E.g.,* Aristotle, *Eth.,* I, 1 (1094a 2).

cause the will, which is the appetite of a previously known end, does not tend towards a thing except under the aspect of good, which is its object. Therefore those things also that do not know the end are directed to a good as their end. Therefore the end of all is a good.

CHAPTER XVII

THAT ALL THINGS ARE DIRECTED TO ONE END, WHICH IS GOD

FROM the foregoing it is clear that all things are directed to one good as their last end.

For if nothing tends to something as its end, except in so far as this is good, it follows that good, as such, is an end. Consequently that which is the supreme good is supremely the end of all. Now there is but one supreme good, namely God, as we have shown in the First Book.[1] Therefore all things are directed to the highest good, namely God, as their end.

Again. *That which is supreme in any genus is the cause of everything in that genus.*[2] Thus fire which is supremely hot is the cause of heat in other bodies. Therefore the supreme good, namely God, is the cause of goodness in all things good. Therefore He is the cause of every end being an end, since whatever is an end is such in so far as it is good. Now *the cause that a thing is so is itself more so.*[3] Therefore God is supremely the end of all things.

Further. In every genus of causes, the first cause is more a cause than the second cause, since the second cause is not a cause save through the first. Therefore that which is the first cause in the order of final causes must needs be more the final cause of each thing than the proximate final cause. Now God is the first cause in the order of final causes, for He is supreme in the order of good things. Therefore He is the end of each thing more even than any proximate end.

Moreover. In all ordered ends the last must needs be the end of each preceding end. Thus if a potion be mixed to be given to a sick man, and is given to him that he may be purged, and he be purged that he may be lowered, and low-

[1] *C. G.*, I, 42.   [2] Aristotle, *Metaph.*, Ia, 1 (993b 22).   [3] Aristotle, *Post. Anal.*, I, 2 (72a 28).

ered that he may be healed, it follows that health is the end of the lowering, and of the purging, and of those that precede. Now all things are ordered in various degrees of goodness to the one supreme good, which is the cause of all goodness; and so, since good has the nature of an end, all things are ordered under God as preceding ends under the last end. Therefore God must be the end of all.

Furthermore. The particular good is directed to the common good as its end, for the being of the part is for the sake of the being of the whole.[4] So it is that *the good of the nation is more godlike than the good of one man.*[5] Now the supreme good, namely God, is the common good, since the good of all things depends on Him; and the good, whereby each thing is good, is the particular good of that thing, and of those that depend thereon. Therefore all things are directed to one good, namely God, as their end.

Again. Order among ends is consequent on the order among agents. For just as the supreme agent moves all second agents, so all the ends of second agents must be directed to the end of the supreme agent, since whatever the supreme agent does, it does for its own end. Now the supreme agent is the active principle of the actions of all inferior agents, by moving all to their actions, and consequently to their ends. Hence it follows that all the ends of second agents are ordered by the first agent to its own end. Now the first agent in all things is God, as we proved in the Second Book.[6] And His will has no other end but His own goodness, which is Himself, as we showed in the First Book.[7] Therefore all things, whether they were made by Him immediately, or by means of secondary causes, are ordered to God as their end. But this applies to all things, for, as we proved in the Second Book,[8] there can be nothing that has not its being from Him. Therefore all things are ordered to God as their end.

Moreover. The last end of every maker, as such, is himself, for what we make we use for our own sake; and if at any time a man make a thing for the sake of something else, it is referred to his own good, whether his use, his pleasure, or his virtue. Now God is the producing cause of all things: of some immediately, of others by means of other causes, as we have explained above.[9] Therefore He is the end of all things.

[4] Aristotle, *Polit.*, I, 4 (1254a 9).   [5] Aristotle, *Eth.*, I, 2 (1094b 9).
[6] *C. G.*, II, 15.   [7] *C. G.*, I, 74.   [8] *C. G.*, II, 15.   [9] *Ibid.*

And again. The end holds the primary place among causes, and it is from it that all other causes derive their actual causality; since the agent does not act except for the end, as was proved.[10] Now it is due to the agent that the matter is brought to the actuality of the form, and therefore the matter is made actually the matter, and the form is made the form, of this particular thing, through the agent's action, and consequently through the end. The later end also is the cause that the preceding end is intended as an end; for a thing is not moved towards a proximate end except for the sake of the last end. Therefore the last end is the first cause of all. Now it must necessarily befit the First Being, namely God, to be the first cause of all, as we proved above.[11] Therefore God is the last end of all.

Hence it is written (*Prov.* xvi. 4): *The Lord hath made all things for himself;* and (*Apoc.* xxii. 13), *I am Alpha and Omega, the first and the last.*

[10] Ch. 2.   [11] *C. G.,* II, 15.

CHAPTER XVIII

HOW GOD IS THE END 'OF THINGS

IT REMAINS to ask how God is the end of all things. This will be made clear from what has been said.

For He is the end of all things, yet so as to precede all in being.[1] Now there is an end which, though it holds the first place in causing in so far as it is in the intention, is nevertheless last in execution. This applies to any end which the agent establishes by his action. Thus the physician by his action establishes health in the sick man, which is nevertheless his end. There is also an end which, just as it precedes in causing, so also does it precede in being. Thus, that which one intends to acquire by one's motion or action is said to be one's end. For instance, fire seeks to reach a higher place by its movement, and the king seeks to take a city by fighting. Accordingly, God is the end of things as something to be obtained by each thing in its own way.

Again. God is at once the last end of things and the first agent, as we have shown.[2] Now the end effected by the agent's action cannot be the first agent, but rather is it the

[1] *C. G.,* I, 13.   [2] Ch. 17.

agent's effect. God, therefore, cannot be the end of things as though He were something effected, but only as something already existing and to be acquired.

Further. If a thing act for the sake of something already in existence, and if by its action some result ensue, then something through the agent's action must accrue to the thing for the sake of which it acts; and thus soldiers fight for the cause of their captain, to whom victory accrues, which the soldiers bring about by their actions. Now nothing can accrue to God from the action of anything whatever, since His goodness is perfect in every way, as we proved in the First Book.[3] It follows, then, that God is the end of things, not as something made or effected by them, nor as though He obtained something from things, but in this way alone, that He is obtained by them.

Moreover. The effect must tend to the end in the same way as the agent acts for the end. Now God, who is the first agent of all things, does not act as though He gained something by His action, but as bestowing something thereby; since He is not in potentiality so that He can acquire something, but solely in perfect actuality, whereby He is able to bestow. Things therefore are not ordered to God as to an end to which something will be added; they are ordered to Him to obtain God Himself from Him according to their measure, since He is their end.

[3] *C. G.*, I, 37ff.

CHAPTER XIX

THAT ALL THINGS TEND TO BE LIKE UNTO GOD

From the fact that they acquire the divine goodness, creatures are made like unto God. Therefore, if all things tend to God as their last end, so as to acquire His goodness,[1] it follows that the last end of things is to become like unto God.

Moreover. The agent is said to be the end of the effect in so far as the effect tends to be like the agent; and hence it is that *the form of the generator is the end of the act of generation.*[2] Now God is the end of things in such wise as to be also their first producing cause. Therefore all things tend to a likeness to God, as their last end.

[1] Ch. 18.   [2] Aristotle, *Phys.*, II, 7 (198a 26).

Again. Things give evidence that *they naturally desire to be*;[3] so that if any are corruptible, they naturally resist corruptives, and tend to where they can be safeguarded, as the fire tends upwards and earth downwards. Now all things have being in so far as they are like God, Who is self-subsistent being, since they are all beings only by participation. Therefore all things desire as their last end to be like God.

Further. All creatures are images of the first agent, namely God, since *the agent produces its like*.[4] Now the perfection of an image consists in representing the original by a likeness to it, for this is why an image is made. Therefore all things exist for the purpose of acquiring a likeness to God, as for their last end.

Again. Each thing by its movement or action tends to some good as its end, as was proved above.[5] Now a thing partakes of good in so far as it is like to the first goodness, which is God. Therefore all things, by their movements and actions, tend to a likeness to God as to their last end.

[3] Aristotle, *Eth.*, IX, 7 (1168a 5); 9 (1170a 26).   [4] Aristotle, *De Gener.*, I, 7 (324a 11).   [5] Ch. 16.

CHAPTER XX

HOW THINGS IMITATE THE DIVINE GOODNESS

FROM what has been said it is clear that the last end of all things is to become like God. Now, that which has properly the nature of an end is the good. Therefore, properly speaking, things tend to become like to God inasmuch as He is good.

Now, creatures do not acquire goodness in the way in which it is in God, even though each thing imitates the divine goodness according to its own manner. For the divine goodness is simple, being, as it were, all in one. For the divine being contains the whole fullness of perfection, as we proved in the First Book.[1] Therefore, since a thing is good so far as it is perfect, God's being is His perfect goodness; for in God, to be, to live, to be wise, to be happy, and whatever else is seen to pertain to perfection and goodness, are one and the same in God, as though the sum total of His goodness were God's very being. Again, the divine being is the substance of

[1] *C. G.*, I, 28.

the existing God.[2] But this cannot be so in other things. For it was proved in the Second Book that no created substance is its own being.[3] Therefore, if a thing is good so far as it is, and if no creature is its own being, none is its own goodness, but each one is good by participating in goodness, even as by participating in being it is a being.

Also. All creatures are not placed on the same level of goodness. For in some the substance is both form and actuality: such, namely, as are competent, by the mere fact that they exist, to be actually and to be good. But in others, the substance is composed of matter and form, and such are competent to be actually and to be good, though it is by some part of their being, namely, their form. Accordingly, God's substance is His goodness, whereas a simple substance participates in goodness by the very fact that it exists, and a composite substance participates in goodness by some part of itself.

In this third degree of substances, diversity is to be found again in respect of being. For in some substances composed of matter and form, the form fills the entire potentiality of matter, in such a way that the matter retains no potentiality to another form, and consequently neither is there in any other matter a potentiality to this same form. Such are the heavenly bodies, which exhaust their entire matter.—In others, the form does not fill the whole potentiality of matter, so that the matter retains a potentiality to another form, and in another part of matter there remains potentiality to this form; for instance in the elements and their compounds. Since, then, privation is the absence in substance of what can be in substance, it is clear that, together with this form which does not fill the whole potentiality of matter, there is associated the privation of a form, which privation cannot be associated with a substance whose form fills the whole potentiality of matter, nor with that which is a form essentially, and much less with that one whose essence is its very being. And seeing that it is clear that there can be no movement where there is no potentiality to something else, for movement is *the act of that which is in potentiality*,[4] and since evil is the privation of good, it is clear that in this last order of

---

[2] *C. G.*, I, 21ff.   [3] *C. G.*, II, 15.   [4] Aristotle, *Phys.*, III, 1 (201a 10).

substances, good is changeable, and has an admixture of the opposite evil; which cannot occur in the higher orders of substances. Therefore the substance answering to this last description stands lowest both in being and in goodness.

We find degrees of goodness also among the parts of the substance composed of matter and form. For since matter considered in itself is being in potentiality, and since form is its act; and, again, since a composite substance has actual existence through its form, it follows that the form is, in itself, good, the composite substance is good as having its form actually, and the matter is good as being in potentiality to the form. And although a thing is good in so far as it is a being, it does not follow that matter, which is being only potentially, is only a potential good. For being is predicated absolutely, while good is founded on order, for a thing is said to be good, not merely because it is an end, or possesses the end; but even though it has not attained the end, so long as it is directed to the end, for this very reason it is said to be good. Accordingly, matter cannot be called a being absolutely, in so far as it is a potential being, whereby it is shown to have an order towards being; but this suffices for it to be called a good absolutely, because of this very order. This shows that the good, in a sense, extends further than being; for which reason Dionysius says that *the good includes both existing and non-existing things*.[5] For even non-existent things (namely, matter, considered as subject to privation) seek a good, namely, to exist. Hence it follows that matter is also good, for nothing but the good seeks the good.

In yet another way the creature's goodness falls short of that of God. For, as we have stated, God, in His very being, contains the supreme perfection of goodness. But the creature has its perfection, not in one thing but in many, because what is united in the highest is manifold in the lowest. Therefore, in respect of one and the same thing, virtue, wisdom and operation are predicated of God; but of creatures, they are predicated in respect of different things, and the further a creature is from the first goodness, the more does the perfection of its goodness require to be manifold. And if it be unable to attain to perfect goodness, it will reach to imperfect goodness in a few respects. Hence it is that, although the first and highest good is utterly simple, and although the

[5] *De Div. Nom.*, IV, 7 (PG 3, 704).

substances nearest to it in goodness approach likewise thereto in simplicity, yet the lowest substances are found to be more simple than some that are higher. Elements, for instance, are simpler than animals and men, because they are unable to reach the perfection of knowledge and understanding, to which animals and men attain.

From what has been said, it is evident that, although God possesses His perfect and entire goodness according to the manner of His simple being, creatures nevertheless do not attain to the perfection of their goodness through their being alone, but through many things. Therefore, although each one is good inasmuch as it exists, it cannot be called good absolutely if it lack other things that are required for its goodness. Thus a man who, being despoiled of virtue, is addicted to vice, is said indeed to be good in a restricted sense, namely, as a being, and as a man; but he is not said to be good absolutely, but rather evil. Accordingly, in every creature to be and to be good are not the same absolutely, although each one is good inasmuch as it exists; whereas in God to be and to be good are absolutely one and the same.

If, then, each thing tends to a likeness to God's goodness as its end; and if a thing is like God's goodness in respect of whatever belongs to its goodness; and if furthermore the goodness of a thing consists not merely in its being, but in whatever is required for its perfection, as we have proved: it is clear that things are directed to God as their end, not only in respect of their substantial being, but also in respect of such things as are accidental thereto and belong to its perfection, as well as in respect of their proper operation, which also belongs to a thing's perfection.

CHAPTER XXV

THAT TO KNOW GOD IS THE END OF EVERY INTELLECTUAL SUBSTANCE

Now, seeing that all creatures, even those that are devoid of reason, are directed to God as their last end, and that all reach this end in so far as they have some share of a likeness to Him, the intellectual creature attains to Him in a special way, namely, through its proper operation, by understanding

Him. Consequently this must be the end of the intellectual creature, namely, to understand God.

For, as we have shown above,[1] God is the end of each thing, and hence, as far as it is possible to it, each thing intends to be united to God as its last end. Now a thing is more closely united to God by reaching in a way to the very substance of God; which happens when it knows something of the divine substance, rather than when it reaches to a divine likeness. Therefore the intellectual substance tends to the knowledge of God as its last end.

Again. The operation proper to a thing is its end, for it is its second perfection; so that when a thing is well conditioned for its proper operation it is said to be fit and good. Now understanding is the proper operation of the intellectual substance, and consequently is its end. Therefore, whatever is most perfect in this operation is its last end; and especially in those operations which are not directed to some product, such as understanding and sensation. And since operations of this kind take their species from their objects, by which also they are known, it follows that the more perfect the object of any such operation, the more perfect is the operation. Consequently to understand the most perfect intelligible, namely God, is the most perfect in the genus of the operation which consists in understanding. Therefore to know God by an act of understanding is the last end of every intellectual substance.

Someone, however, might say that the last end of an intellectual substance consists indeed in understanding the best intelligible object, but that what is the best intelligible for this or that intellectual substance is not absolutely the best intelligible; and that the higher the intellectual substance, the higher is its best intelligible. So that possibly the supreme intellectual substance has for its best intelligible object that which is best absolutely, and its happiness will consist in understanding God; whereas the happiness of any lower intellectual substance will consist in understanding some lower intelligible object, which however will be the highest thing understood by that substance. Especially would it seem not to be in the power of the human intellect to understand that which is absolutely the best intelligible, because of its weak-

[1] Ch. 17.

ness; for it is as much adapted for knowing the supreme intelligible *as the owl's eye for seeing the sun*.[2]

Nevertheless it is evident that the end of any intellectual substance, even the lowest, is to understand God. For it has been shown above that God is the last end towards which all things tend.[3] And the human intellect, although the lowest in the order of intelligent substances, is superior to all that are devoid of understanding. Since then a more noble substance has not a less noble end, God will be the end also of the human intellect. Now every intelligent being attains to its last end by understanding it, as we have proved. Therefore the human intellect attains to God as its end, by understanding Him.

Again. Just as things devoid of intellect tend to God as their end by way of assimilation, so do intellectual substances by way of knowledge, as clearly appears from what has been said. Now, although things devoid of reason tend towards a likeness to their proximate causes, the intention of nature does not rest there, but has for its end a likeness to the highest good, as we have proved,[4] although they are able to attain to this likeness in a most imperfect manner. Therefore, however little be the knowledge of God to which the intellect is able to attain, this will be the intellect's last end, rather than a perfect knowledge of lower intelligibles.

Moreover. Everything desires most of all its last end. Now the human intellect desires, loves and enjoys the knowledge of divine things, although it can grasp but little about them, more than the perfect knowledge which it has of the lowest things. Therefore man's last end is to understand God in some way.

Further. Everything tends to a divine likeness as its own end. Therefore a thing's last end is that whereby it is most of all like God. Now the intellectual creature is especially likened to God in that it is intellectual, since this likeness belongs to it above other creatures, and includes all other likenesses. And in this particular kind of likeness it is more like God in understanding actually than in understanding habitually or potentially, because God is always actually understanding, as we proved in the First Book.[5] Furthermore, in understanding actually, the intellectual creature is espe-

[2] Aristotle, *Metaph.*, Ia, 1 (993b 9).   [3] Ch. 17.   [4] Ch. 19.   [5] *C. G.*, I, 56.

cially like God in understanding God; for by understanding
Himself God understand all other things, as we proved in
the First Book.[6] Therefore the last end of every intellectual
substance is to understand God.

Again. That which is lovable only because of another is
for the sake of that which is lovable for its own sake alone;
because we cannot go on indefinitely in the appetite of nature, since then nature's desire would be in vain, for it is impossible to pass through an infinite number of things. Now
all practical sciences, arts and powers are lovable only for
the sake of something else, since their end is not knowledge,
but work. But speculative sciences are lovable for their own
sake, for their end is knowledge itself. Nor can we find any
action in human life that is not directed to some other end,
with the exception of speculative consideration. For even
playful actions, which seem to be done without any purpose,
have some end due to them, namely that the mind may be
relaxed, and that thereby we may afterwards become more
fit for studious occupations; or otherwise we should always
have to be playing, if play were desirable for its own sake,
and this is unreasonable. Accordingly, the practical arts are
directed to the speculative arts, and again every human
operation, to intellectual speculation, as its end. Now, in all
sciences and arts that are mutually ordered, the last end
seems to belong to the one from which others take their
rules and principles. Thus the art of sailing, to which belongs
the ship's purpose, namely its use, provides rules and principles to the art of ship-building. And such is the relation of
first philosophy to other speculative sciences, for all others
depend thereon, since they derive their principles from it,
and are directed by it in defending those principles; and
moreover first philosophy is wholly directed to the knowledge
of God as its last end, and is consequently called the *divine
science*.[7] Therefore the knowledge of God is the last end of
all human knowledge and activity.

Furthermore. In all mutually ordered agents and movers,
the end of the first agent and mover must be the end of all,
even as the end of the commander-in-chief is the end of all
who are soldiering under him. Now of all the parts of man
the intellect is the highest mover, for it moves the appetite,

[6] *C. G.*, I, 49.　　[7] Aristotle, *Metaph.*, I, 2 (983a 6).

by proposing its object to it; and the intellective appetite, or will, moves the sensitive appetites, namely the irascible and concupiscible. Hence it is that we do not obey the concupiscence, unless the will command; while the sensitive appetite, when the will has given its consent, moves the body. Therefore the end of the intellect is the end of all human actions. *Now the intellect's end and good are the true*,[8] and its last end is the first truth. Therefore the last end of the whole man, and of all his deeds and desires, is to know the first truth, namely, God.

Moreover. Man has a natural desire to know the causes of whatever he sees; and so through wondering at what they saw, and not knowing its cause, men first began to philosophize, and when they had discovered the cause they were at rest. Nor do they cease inquiring until they come to the first cause; and *then do we deem ourselves to know perfectly when we know the first cause*.[9] Therefore man naturally desires, as his last end, to know the first cause. But God is the first cause of all things. Therefore man's last end is to know God.

Besides. Man naturally desires to know the cause of any known effect. But the human intellect knows universal being. Therefore it naturally desires to know its cause, which is God alone, as we proved in the Second Book.[10] Now one has not attained to one's last end until the natural desire is at rest. Therefore the knowledge of any intelligible object is not enough for man's happiness, which is his last end, unless he know God also, which knowledge terminates his natural desire as his last end. Therefore this very knowledge of God is man's last end.

Further. A body that tends by its natural appetite to its place is moved all the more vehemently and rapidly the nearer it approaches its end. Hence Aristotle proves that a natural straight movement cannot be towards an indefinite point, because it would not be more moved afterwards than before.[11] Hence that which tends more vehemently to a thing afterwards than before is not moved towards an indefinite point but towards something fixed. Now this we find in the desire of knowledge, for the more one knows, the greater one's desire to know. Consequently, man's natural desire in

[8] Aristotle, *Eth.*, VI, 2 (1139a 27).   [9] Aristotle, *Metaph.*, I, 3 (983a 25).   [10] *C. G.*, II, 15.   [11] *De Caelo*, I, 8 (277a 18).

knowledge tends to a definite end. This can be none other than the highest thing knowable, which is God. Therefore the knowledge of God is man's last end.

Now the last end of man and of any intelligent substance is called *happiness* or *beatitude*, for it is this that every intellectual substance desires as its last end, and for its own sake alone. Therefore the last beatitude or happiness of any intellectual substance is to know God.

Hence it is said (*Matt.* v. 8): *Blessed are the clean of heart, for they shall see God;* and (*Jo.* xvii. 3): *This is eternal life, that they may know thee, the only true God.* Aristotle himself agrees with this judgment when he says that man's ultimate happiness is *speculative, and this with regard to the highest object of speculation.*[12]

[12] *Eth.*, X, 7 (1177a 18).

CHAPTER XXVI

DOES HAPPINESS CONSIST IN AN ACT OF THE WILL?

SINCE the intellectual substance attains to God by its operation, not only by an act of understanding but also by an act of the will, through desiring and loving Him, and through delighting in Him, someone might think that man's last end and ultimate happiness consists, not in knowing God, but in loving Him, or in some other act of the will towards Him; [1] especially since the object of the will is the good, which has the nature of an end, whereas the true, which is the object of the intellect, has not the nature of an end except in so far as it also is a good. Therefore, seemingly, man does not attain to his last end by an act of his intellect, but rather by an act of his will.

[2] Further. The ultimate perfection of operation is delight, *which perfects operation as beauty perfects youth,* as the Philosopher says.[1] Hence, if the last end be a perfect operation, it would seem that it must consist in an act of the will rather than of the intellect.

[3] Again. Delight apparently is desired for its own sake, so that it is never desired for the sake of something else; for it is silly to ask of anyone why he seeks to be delighted. Now this is a condition of the ultimate end, namely, that it be

[1] *Eth.*, X, 4 (1174b 31).

sought for its own sake. Therefore, seemingly, the last end consists in an act of the will rather than of the intellect.

[4] Moreover. All agree in their desire of the last end, for it is a natural desire. But more people seek delight than knowledge. Therefore delight would seem to be the last end rather than knowledge.

[5] Furthermore. The will is seemingly a higher power than the intellect, for the will moves the intellect to its act; since when a person wills, his intellect considers by an act what he holds by a habit. Therefore, seemingly, the action of the will is more noble than the action of the intellect. Therefore, it would seem that the last end, which is beatitude, consists in an act of the will rather than of the intellect.

But this can be clearly shown to be impossible.

For since happiness is the proper good of the intellectual nature, it must needs become the intellectual nature according to that which is proper thereto. Now appetite is not proper to the intellectual nature, but is in all things, although it is found diversely in diverse things. This diversity, however, arises from the fact that things are diversely related to knowledge. For things wholly devoid of knowledge have only a natural appetite; those that have a sensitive knowledge have also a sensitive appetite, under which the irascible and concupiscible appetites are comprised; and those which have intellectual knowledge have also an appetite proportionate to that knowledge, namely, the will. The will, therefore, in so far as it is an appetite, is not proper to the intellectual nature, but only in so far as it is dependent on the intellect. On the other hand, the intellect is in itself proper to the intellectual nature. Therefore, beatitude or happiness consists principally and essentially in an act of the intellect, rather than in an act of the will.

Again. In all powers that are moved by their objects, the object is naturally prior to the acts of those powers, even as the mover is naturally prior to the movable being moved. Now the will is such a power, for the appetible object moves the appetite. Therefore the will's object is naturally prior to its act, and consequently its first object precedes its every act. Therefore an act of the will cannot be the first thing willed. But this is the last end, which is beatitude. Therefore beatitude or happiness cannot be the very act of the will.

Besides. In all those powers which are able to reflect on their acts, their act must first bear on some other object, and afterwards the power is brought to bear on its own act. For if the intellect understands that it understands, we must suppose first that it understands some particular thing, and that afterwards it understands that it understands; for this very act of understanding, which the intellect understands, must have an object. Hence either we must go on forever, or if we come to some first thing understood, this will not be an act of understanding, but some intelligible thing. In the same way, the first thing willed cannot be the very act of willing, but must be some other good. Now the first thing willed by an intellectual nature is beatitude or happiness; because it is for its sake that we will whatever we will. Therefore happiness cannot consist in an act of the will.

Further. The truth of a thing's nature is derived from those things which constitute its substance; for a true man differs from a man in a picture by the things which constitute man's substance. Now false happiness does not differ from true in an act of the will; because, whatever be proposed to the will as the supreme good, whether truly or falsely, it makes no difference to the will in its desiring, loving, or enjoying that good: the difference is on the part of the intellect, as to whether the good proposed as supreme be truly so or not. Therefore beatitude or happiness consists essentially in an act of the intellect rather than of the will.

Again. If an act of the will were happiness itself, this act would be an act either of desire, or love, or delight. But desire cannot possibly be the last end. For desire implies that the will is tending to what it has not yet; and this is contrary to the very notion of the last end.—Nor can love be the last end. For a good is loved not only while it is in our possession, but even when it is not, because it is through love that we seek by desire what we have not; and if the love of a thing we possess is more perfect, this arises from the fact that we possess the good we love. It is one thing, therefore, to possess the good which is our end, and another to love it; for love was imperfect before we possessed the end, and perfect after we obtained possession.—Nor again is delight the last end. For it is possession of the good that causes delight, whether we are conscious of possessing it actually, or call to mind our previous possession, or hope to possess it in the future. Therefore delight is not the last end.—Therefore no act of the will can be happiness itself essentially.

Furthermore. If delight were the last end, it would be desirable for its own sake. But this is not true. For the desirability of a delight depends on what gives rise to the delight, since that which arises from good and desirable operations is itself good and desirable, but that which arises from evil operations is itself evil and to be avoided. Therefore its goodness and desirability are from something else, and consequently it is not itself the last end or happiness.

Moreover. The right order of things agrees with the order of nature, for in the natural order things are ordered to their end without any error. Now, in the natural order delight is for the sake of operation, and not conversely. For it is to be observed that nature has joined delight with those animal operations which are clearly ordered to necessary ends: for instance, to the use of food that is ordered to the preservation of the individual, and to sexual matters, that are appointed for the preservation of the species; since were there no pleasure, animals would abstain from the use of these necessary things. Therefore delight cannot be the last end.

Again. Delight, seemingly, is nothing else than the quiescence of the will in some becoming good, just as desire is the inclining of the will towards the attaining of some good. Now just as by his will a man is inclined towards an end, and rests in it, so too natural bodies have a natural inclination to their respective ends, and are at rest when they have once attained their end. Now it is absurd to say that the end of the movement of a heavy body is not to be in its proper place, but that it is the quiescence of the inclination towards that place. For if it were nature's chief intent that this inclination should be quiescent, it would not give such an inclination; but it gives the inclination so that the body may tend towards its proper place, and when it has arrived there, as though it were its end, quiescence of the inclination follows. Hence this quiescence is not the end, but accompanies the end. Neither therefore is delight the ultimate end, but accompanies it. Much less therefore is happiness any act of the will.

Besides. If a thing have something extrinsic for its end, the operation whereby it first obtains that thing will be called its last end. Thus, for those whose end is money possession is said to be their end, but not love or desire. Now the last end of the intellectual substance is God. Hence that operation of man whereby he first obtains God is essentially his happiness or beatitude. And this is understanding, since we cannot will what we do not understand. Therefore man's ultimate happiness is essentially to know God by the intellect; it is not an act of the will.

From what has been said we can now solve the arguments that were objected in the contrary sense. For it does not necessarily follow that happiness is essentially the very act of the will, from the fact that it is the object of the will, through being the highest good, as the *first argument* reasoned. On the contrary, the fact that it is the first object of the will shows that it is not an act of the will, as appears from what we have said.

Nor does it follow that whatever perfects a thing in any way whatever must be the end of that thing, as the *second objection* argued. For a thing perfects another in two ways: first, it perfects a thing that has its species; secondly, it perfects a thing that it may have its species. Thus the perfection of a house, considered as already having its species, is that to which the species "house" is directed, namely to be a dwelling; for one would not build a house but for that purpose, and consequently we must include this in the definition of a house, if the definition is to be perfect. On the other hand, the perfection that conduces to the species of a house is both that which is directed to the completion of the species, for instance, its substantial principles; and also that which conduces to the preservation of the species, for instance, the buttresses which are made to support the building; as well as those things which make the house more fit for use, for instance, the beauty of the house. Accordingly, that which is the perfection of a thing, considered as already having its species, is its end; as the end of a house is to be a dwelling. Likewise, the operation proper to a thing, its use, as it were, is its end. On the other hand, whatever perfects a thing by conducing to its species is not the end of that thing; in fact, the thing itself is its end, for matter and form are for the sake of the species. For although the form is the end of generation, it is not the end of the thing already generated and having its species, but is required in order that the species be complete. Again, whatever preserves the thing in its species, such as health and the nutritive power, although it perfects the animal, is not the animal's end, but vice versa. And again, whatever adapts a thing for the perfection of its proper specific operations, and for the easier attainment of its proper end, is not the end of that thing, but vice versa; for instance, a man's comeliness and bodily strength, and the like, of which the Philosopher says that they *conduce to happiness instrumentally*.[2]—Now delight is a perfection of operation, not as though operation were directed thereto in respect of its species, for thus it is directed to other ends (thus, eating, in respect of its species, is directed to the preservation of the individual); but it is like a perfection that is conducive to a thing's species, since for the sake of the delight we perform more attentively and becomingly an operation we delight in. Hence the Philosopher says that *delight perfects operation as beauty perfects youth*,[3] for beauty is for the sake of the one who has youth and not *vice versa*.

Nor is the fact that men seek delight not for the sake of something else but for its own sake a sufficient indication that delight is the last end, as the *third objection* argued. Because delight, though it is not the last end, nevertheless accompanies the last end, since delight arises from the attainment of the end.

Nor do more people seek the pleasure that comes from knowledge than knowledge itself. But more there are who seek sensible delights than intellectual knowledge and the delight consequent thereto; because those things that are outside us are better known to the majority, in that human knowledge takes its beginning from sensible objects.

The suggestion put forward by the *fifth argument*, that the will is a higher power than the intellect, as being the latter's motive power, is clearly untrue. Because the intellect moves the will first and *per se*, for the will, as such, is moved by its object, which is the apprehended good; whereas the will moves the intellect accidentally as it were, in so far, namely, as the act of understanding is itself apprehended as a good, and on that account is desired by the will, with the result that the intellect understands actually. Even in this, the intellect precedes the will, for the will would never desire understanding, did not the intellect first apprehend its

[2] *Eth.*, I, 8 (1099b 2); 9 (1099b 28).   [3] *Op. cit.*, X, 4 (1174b 31).

understanding as a good.—And again, the will moves the intellect to actual operation in the same way as an agent is said to move; whereas the intellect moves the will in the same way as the end moves, for the good understood is the end of the will. Now the agent in moving presupposes the end, for the agent does not move except for the sake of the end. It is therefore clear that the intellect is higher than the will absolutely, while the will is higher than the intellect accidentally and in a restricted sense.

CHAPTER XXXVII

THAT MAN'S ULTIMATE HAPPINESS CONSISTS IN CONTEMPLATING GOD

ACCORDINGLY, if man's ultimate happiness does not consist in external things, which are called goods of fortune; nor in goods of the body; nor in goods of the soul, as regards the sensitive part; nor as regards the intellectual part, in terms of the life of moral virtue; nor in terms of the intellectual virtues which are concerned with action, namely, art and prudence:—it remains for us to conclude that man's ultimate happiness consists in the contemplation of truth.

For this operation alone is proper to man, and it is in it that none of the other animals communicates.

Again. This is not directed to anything further as to its end, since the contemplation of the truth is sought for its own sake.

Again. By this operation man is united to beings above him, by becoming like them; because of all human actions this alone is both in God and in the separate substances. Also, by this operation man comes into contact with those higher beings, through knowing them in any way whatever.

Besides, man is more self-sufficing for this operation, seeing that he stands in little need of the help of external things in order to perform it.

Further. All other human operations seem to be ordered to this as to their end. For perfect contemplation requires that the body should be disencumbered, and to this effect are directed all the products of art that are necessary for life. Moreover, it requires freedom from the disturbance caused by the passions, which is achieved by means of the moral virtues and of prudence; and freedom from external disturbance, to which the whole governance of the civil life is directed. So that, if we consider the matter rightly, we shall see that all human occupations appear to serve those who contemplate the truth.

Now, it is not possible that man's ultimate happiness consist in contemplation based on the understanding of first principles; for this is most imperfect, as being most universal, containing potentially the knowledge of things. Moreover, it is the beginning and not the end of human inquiry, and comes to us from nature, and not through the pursuit of the truth. Nor does it consist in contemplation based on the sciences that have the lowest things for their object, since happiness must consist in an operation of the intellect in relation to the most noble intelligible objects. It follows then that man's ultimate happiness consists in wisdom, based on the consideration of divine things.

It is therefore evident also by way of induction that man's ultimate happiness consists solely in the contemplation of God, which conclusion was proved above by arguments.[1]

[1] Ch. 25.

CHAPTER XXXVIII

THAT HUMAN HAPPINESS DOES NOT CONSIST IN THE KNOWLEDGE OF GOD WHICH IS POSSESSED GENERALLY BY THE MAJORITY

IT REMAINS for us to inquire in what kind of knowledge of God the ultimate happiness of an intellectual substance consists. For there is a certain general and confused knowledge of God, which is in almost all men, whether from the fact that, as some think, the existence of God, like other principles of demonstration, is self-evident, as we have stated in the First Book,[1] or, as seems nearer to the truth, because by his natural reason man is able at once to arrive at some knowledge of God. For seeing that natural things run their course according to a fixed order, and since there cannot be order without a cause of order, men, for the most part, perceive that there is one who orders the things that we see.

[1] C. G., I, 10.

But who or of what kind this cause of order may be, or whether there be but one, cannot be gathered from this general consideration; just as, when we see a man in motion, and performing other works, we perceive that in him there is some cause of these operations which is not in other things, and we give this cause the name of *soul*, but without knowing yet what the soul is, whether it be a body, or how it brings about operations in question.

Now, this knowledge of God cannot possibly suffice for happiness.

For the activity of the happy man must be without any defect; but this knowledge of God is subject to an admixture of many errors. Thus, some believed that there was no other governor of mundane things than the heavenly bodies; and so they said that the heavenly bodies were gods.—Some ascribed this order to the elements and to the things generated from them; as though they thought that their movements and natural operations were not introduced into them by an external governor, but that the order in other things was caused by them.—And some, deeming human acts not to be subject to any but a human rule, declared that men who cause order in other men were gods.—Evidently *this* knowledge of God is not sufficient for happiness.

Moreover. Happiness is the end of human acts. But human acts are not directed to the aforesaid knowledge as to their end; indeed, it is in everyone almost right from the very beginning. Therefore happiness does not consist in this kind of knowledge of God.

Again. No one appears to be blamed for lacking happiness; nay, those who lack it and seek it are praised. But he who lacks the aforesaid knowledge of God is seemingly very much to be blamed, since it is a very clear sign of a man's dullness of perception if he fail to perceive such evident signs of God; even as a man would be deemed dull who, seeing man, understood not that he has a soul. Hence it is said in the Psalm (xiii. 1: lii. 1): *The fool hath said in his heart: There is no God.* Therefore it is not this knowledge of God which suffices for happiness.

Further. Knowledge of a thing in general only, and not in terms of what is proper to it, is most imperfect. Such is the knowledge which is had of man from the fact that he is moved; for this is a knowledge whereby a thing is known only potentially, because the proper is only potentially contained in the common. Now happiness is a perfect operation: and man's highest good must needs be in terms of what exists actually, and not in terms of what exists only potentially; since potentiality perfected by act has the character of a good. Therefore the aforesaid knowledge of God is not sufficient for our happiness.

CHAPTER XXXIX

THAT MAN'S HAPPINESS DOES NOT CONSIST IN THE KNOWLEDGE OF GOD ACQUIRED BY DEMONSTRATION

THERE is also another knowledge of God, higher than the one just mentioned, which is acquired by means of a demonstration, and which approaches nearer to a proper knowledge of Him; for by means of a demonstration many things are removed from Him, so that in consequence we understand Him as something apart from other things. For demonstration proves that God is immovable, eternal, incorporeal, utterly simple, one, and the like, as we have shown in the First Book. Now we arrive at the proper knowledge of a thing not only by affirmations, but also by negations. For just as it is proper to man to be a rational animal, so is it proper to him not to be inanimate or irrational. Yet there is this difference between these two modes of proper knowledge, that when we have proper knowledge of a thing by affirmations we know what that thing is, and how it is distinguished from others; whereas when we have proper knowledge of a thing by negations, we know that it is distinct from others, but remain ignorant of what it is. Such is the proper knowledge of God that can be obtained by demonstrations. But neither does this suffice for man's ultimate happiness.

For things belonging to one species for the most part attain to the end of that species, because nature achieves its purpose always or nearly always, and fails in a few instances because of some corruption. Now happiness is the end of the human species, since all men naturally desire it. Therefore happiness is a common good that can be attained by all men, unless some obstacle occur to some whereby they be deprived of it.[1] Few, however, attain to the possession of the

---

[1] Cf. Aristotle, *Eth.*, I, 9 (1099b 18).

aforesaid knowledge of God by way of demonstration, because of the obstacles to this knowledge mentioned at the beginning of this work.[2] Therefore this knowledge is not essentially man's happiness.

Again. To be actual is the end of that which exists potentially, as was made clear above.[3] Therefore happiness, which is the last end, is an act free of any potentiality to a further act. Now this knowledge of God that is acquired by way of demonstration is still in potentiality to a further knowledge of God, or to the same knowledge, but by a better way: because those who came afterwards endeavored to add something to the knowledge of God besides that which they found handed down to them by those who preceded them. Therefore such knowledge is not man's ultimate happiness.

Further. Happiness excludes all unhappiness, for no man can be at the same time happy and unhappy. Now deception and error have a large place in unhappiness, since all naturally avoid them. But the aforesaid knowledge of God is subject to the admixture of many errors, as evidenced by many who knew some truths about God through demonstration, yet, following their own opinions, when they lacked proof, fell into many errors. And if there were some who by the way of demonstration discovered the truth about divine things, without any admixture of error in their opinions, it is evident that they were very few. This fact is not in keeping with happiness, which is the common end. Therefore man's ultimate happiness is not seated in such knowledge as this.

Moreover. Happiness consists in a perfect operation. Now perfect knowledge requires certitude, and that is why we cannot be said to know unless we know what cannot be otherwise, as is stated in *Post. Anal.* 1.[4] But the aforesaid knowledge is beset with uncertainty, as is clear from the diversity among sciences about divine things elaborated by those who endeavored to discover something about God by the way of demonstration. Therefore ultimate happiness does not consist in such knowledge.

Besides. When the will has obtained its last end, its desire is at rest. Now the ultimate end of all human knowledge is happiness. Therefore happiness is essentially that knowledge of God the possession of which leaves no knowledge to be

[2] *C. G.*, I, 4.   [3] Ch. 20, 22.   [4] Aristotle, *Post. Anal.*, I, 2 (72a 17).

desired of anything knowable. Such, however, is not the knowledge which the philosophers were able to have about God by the way of demonstration; because even when we have this knowledge, we still desire to know other things— things that we do not yet know by means of this knowledge. Therefore happiness does not consist in such a knowledge of God.

Furthermore. The end of everything that exists in potentiality is that it be brought to actuality; for to this does it tend by means of the movement with which it is moved to its end. Now every potential being tends to becoming actualized as far as possible. For there are things in potentiality whose whole potentiality is reducible to act: the end of such things is that they be wholly actualized. Thus, a heavy body that is outside its medium is in potentiality to its proper place. There are also things whose potentiality cannot be actualized all at once,—for instance primary matter: so that by its movement it seeks actualization by various forms in succession, which cannot be in the matter at the same time because of their diversity. Furthermore, our intellect is in potentiality to all intelligibles, as was stated in the Second Book.[5] Now it is possible for two intelligible objects to be in the possible intellect at the same time according to the first act which is *science,* although perhaps not in respect of the second act which is *consideration.* Accordingly, it is clear that the whole potentiality of the possible intellect can be actualized at one time; and consequently this is required for its ultimate end, which is happiness. But the aforesaid knowledge, which can be acquired about God by the way of demonstration, does not accomplish this, since when we have it we still are ignorant of many things. Therefore such a knowledge of God does not suffice for ultimate happiness.

[5] *C. G.,* II, 47.

CHAPTER XL

THAT MAN'S HAPPINESS DOES NOT CONSIST IN THE KNOWLEDGE OF GOD BY FAITH

THERE is yet another knowledge of God, in one respect superior to the knowledge we have been discussing, namely, that

whereby God is known by men through faith. Now this
knowledge surpasses the knowledge of God through demonstration in this respect, namely, that by faith we know certain
things about God which are so sublime that reason cannot
reach them by means of demonstration, as we have stated at
the beginning of this work.[1] But not even in this knowledge
of God can man's ultimate happiness consist.

For happiness is the intellect's perfect operation, as was
already declared.[2] But in knowledge by faith, the operation
of the intellect is found to be most imperfect as regards the
contribution of the intellect, although it is most perfect on
the part of the object; for the intellect in believing does not
grasp the object of its assent. Therefore neither does man's
happiness consist in this knowledge of God.

Again. It has been shown that ultimate happiness does not
consist chiefly in an act of the will.[3] Now in knowledge by
faith, the will has the leading place; for the intellect assents
by faith to things proposed to it, because it so wills, and not
through being constrained by the evidence of their truth.
Therefore man's final happiness does not consist in this
knowledge.

Besides. A believer assents to things proposed to him by
another, but not seen by himself; so that the knowledge of
faith resembles hearing rather than seeing. Now a man would
not believe in what is unseen by him, and proposed to him by
another, unless he thought this other to have a more perfect
knowledge of the things proposed than he himself has
who sees not. Either therefore the judgment of the believer
is wrong, or the proposer must have more perfect knowledge
of the things proposed. And if the latter also knows these
things only through hearing them from another, we cannot
proceed thus indefinitely, for then the assent of faith would
be without foundation or certitude, since we should not come
to some first principle certain in itself, to give certitude to
the faith of believers. Now, in reality, it is not possible that
the assent of faith be false and without foundation, as is clear
from what we have said at the beginning of this work;[4] and
yet if it were false and baseless, happiness could not consist
in such knowledge. There is therefore some knowledge of God
that is higher than the knowledge of faith, whether he who

[1] *C. G.,* I, 5.   [2] Ch. 25.   [3] Ch. 26.   [4] *C. G.,* I, 7.

proposes faith sees the truth immediately, as when we believe Christ, or whether he receives the truth from him who sees it immediately, as when we believe the Apostles and Prophets. Since, then, man's happiness consists in the highest knowledge of God, it cannot consist in the knowledge of faith.

Moreover. Since happiness is the last end, the natural desire is set at rest thereby. But the knowledge of faith does not set the desire at rest, but inflames it; for everyone desires to see what he believes. Therefore man's ultimate happiness does not consist in the knowledge of faith.

Further. The knowledge of God has been declared to be the end inasmuch as it unites us to the last end of all, namely, God. Now the knowledge of faith does not make the thing believed to be perfectly present to the intellect, since faith is of absent, and not present, things. Hence the Apostle says (*2 Cor.* v. 6, 7) that *so long as we walk by faith, we are pilgrims from the Lord*. Yet faith makes God to be present to love, since the believer assents to God voluntarily, according to the saying of *Ephes.* iii. 17: *That Christ may dwell by faith in our hearts*. Therefore the knowledge of faith cannot be man's ultimate happiness.

CHAPTER XLVII

THAT IN THIS LIFE WE ARE UNABLE TO SEE GOD IN HIS ESSENCE

IF, in this life, we are unable to understand separate substances by reason of our intellect's connatural relation to phantasms, much less can we see the divine essence in this life, since it is far above all separate substances.

We may take it as a sign of this, that the more our mind is raised to the contemplation of spiritual things, the more it is withdrawn from sensible things. Now the divine substance is the ultimate term to which contemplation can reach, and hence the mind that sees the divine substance must be wholly freed from the corporeal senses, either by death or by rapture. Therefore it is said in God's person (*Exod.* xxxiii. 20): *Man shall not see me, and live*.

If it is stated in Holy Scripture that some have seen God, we must understand this to have been either through an imaginary vision—or even a bodily vision, when the presence of the divine power is shown by corporeal species, whether appearing externally, or formed internally in the imagination, or by gathering some intellectual knowledge of God from His spiritual effects.

A difficulty, however, arises through some words of Augustine which would seem to imply that we are able to understand God in this life. For he says that *with the sight of the soul we see in the eternal truth, from which all temporal things have been made, the form according to which we are and according to which we effect something, in ourselves or in bodies, with a true and right reason; and it is from the same source that we conceive and possess a true knowledge of things.*[1] Again he says: *If we both see that what you say is true, and that what I say is true, where, I ask, do we see this? Surely, neither I in you, nor you in me, but both of us in the immutable truth itself which transcends our minds.*[2] Again, he says that *we judge of all things according to the divine truth,*[3] and again: *We must first know the truth by which other things can be known,*[4] referring, it would seem, to the divine truth. It would seem, then, from his words, that we see God Himself Who is His own truth, and that through Him we know other things.

Other words of his would seem to point to the same conclusion. In *De Trin.* xii he says: *It is the office of reason to judge of these corporeal things according to the incorporeal and eternal ideas which, unless they were above the human mind, would surely not be unchangeable.*[5] Now unchangeable and eternal ideas cannot be elsewhere than in God, since, according to the teaching of Faith, God alone is eternal. Accordingly it would seem to follow that we can see God in this life, and that, through seeing Him and the ideas of things in Him, we judge of other things.

Yet it is not to be believed that Augustine, by these words, meant that we are able in this life to see God in His essence. We must therefore inquire how, in this life, we see that *unchangeable truth,* or these *eternal ideas,* and how we judge of other things according to this truth.

---

[1] *De Trin.,* IX, 7 (PL 42, 967).   [2] *Confess.,* XII, 25 (PL 32, 840).
[3] *De Vera Relig.,* XXXI (PL 34, 148).   [4] *Solil.,* I, 15 (PL 32, 883).
[5] *De Trin.,* XII, 2 (PL 42, 999).

Augustine allows that truth is in the soul,[6] and therefore it is that he proves the immortality of the soul from the eternity of truth. Now truth is in the soul not only in the same way as God is said to be in all things by His essence, or as He is in all things by His likeness (in so far, namely, as a thing is true according as it approaches to a likeness of God), for then the soul would not be higher than other things in this respect. It is therefore in the soul in a special way, inasmuch as the soul knows truth. Accordingly, just as the soul and other things are said to be true in their nature according as they are likened to that supreme nature, which is truth itself, since it is its own understood being, so too, that which is known by the soul is true so far as it contains a likeness to that divine truth which God knows. Therefore a *Gloss* on *Ps.* xi. 2, *Truths are decayed from among the children of men*, says that *as from one man's face many likenesses are reflected in a mirror, so many truths are reflected from the one divine truth*.[7] Now although different things are known, and different things believed to be true, by different people, yet some truths there are in which all men agree, such as the first principles both of the speculative and of the practical intellect, inasmuch as a kind of image of the divine truth is reflected in the minds of all men. Consequently, when a mind knows with certitude anything at all, and by tracing it back to the principles by which we judge of everything, comes to see it in those principles, it is said to see all such things in the divine truth or in the eternal ideas and to judge of all things according to them. This explanation is confirmed by Augustine's words: *The speculations of the sciences are seen in the divine truth, even as these visible things are seen in the light of the sun*.[8] For it is evident that these things are not seen in the body of the sun, but by the light, which is a likeness of the solar brilliance reflected in the air, and cast upon such bodies.

Therefore, from these words of Augustine we cannot conclude that God is seen in His essence in this life, but only as in a mirror; and to this the Apostle witnesses as regards the knowledge of this life (*1 Cor.* xiii. 12): *We see now through a glass in a dark manner.*

[6] *Solil.*, II, 19 (PL 32, 901).   [7] Cf. St. Augustine, *Enarr. in Psalm*, super XI, 2 (PL 36, 138); Peter Lombard, *In Psalm.*, super XI, 2 (PL 191, 155).   [8] *Solil.*, I, 8 (PL 32, 877).

And though this mirror, which is the human mind, reflects the likeness of God in a higher way than creatures of lower degree, yet the knowledge of God that can be gathered from the human mind does not transcend the genus of the knowledge gathered from sensible things; since even the soul knows what it itself is through understanding the natures of sensible things, as we have already stated.[9] Consequently, even in this way God is not known in higher manner than the cause is known from its effect.

[9] Ch. 45, 46.

CHAPTER XLVIII

THAT MAN'S ULTIMATE HAPPINESS IS NOT IN THIS LIFE

SEEING, then, that man's ultimate happiness does not consist in that knowledge of God whereby He is known by all or many in a vague kind of opinion, nor again in that knowledge of God whereby He is known in the speculative sciences through demonstration, nor in that knowledge whereby He is known through faith, as we have proved above;[1] and seeing that it is not possible in this life to arrive at a higher knowledge of God in His essence, or at least so that we understand other separate substances, and thus know God through that which is nearest to Him, so to say, as we have proved;[2] and since we must place our ultimate happiness in some kind of knowledge of God, as we have shown:[3]—it is impossible for man's happiness to be in this life.

Again. Man's last end is the term of his natural appetite, so that when he has obtained it, he desires nothing more; because if he still has a movement towards something, he has not yet reached an end wherein to be at rest. Now this cannot happen in this life, since the more man understands, the more is the desire to understand increased in him (for this is natural to man), unless perhaps there be someone who understands all things. Now in this life this never did nor can happen to anyone that was a mere man, seeing that in this life we are unable to know separate substances which in themselves are most intelligible, as we have proved.[4] Therefore man's ultimate happiness cannot possibly be in this life.

Besides. Whatever is in motion towards an end has a nat-

[1] Ch. 38ff.   [2] Ch. 45.   [3] Ch. 37.   [4] Ch. 45.

ural desire to be established and at rest therein. Hence a
body does not move away from the place towards which it
has a natural movement, except by a violent movement which
is contrary to that appetite. Now happiness is the last end
which man naturally desires. Therefore it is his natural desire to be established in happiness. Consequently, unless together with happiness he acquires a state of immobility, he
is not yet happy, since his natural desire is not yet at rest.
When, therefore, a man acquires happiness, he also acquires
stability and rest; so that all agree in conceiving stability as
a necessary condition of happiness. Hence the Philosopher
says: *We do not look upon the happy man as a kind of
chameleon.*[5] Now in this life there is no sure stability, since,
however happy a man may be, sickness and misfortune may
come upon him, so that he is hindered in the operation, whatever it be, in which happiness consists. Therefore man's ultimate happiness cannot be in this life.

Moreover. It would seem unfitting and unreasonable for
a thing to take a long time in becoming, and to have but a
short time in being; for it would follow that for a longer
duration of time nature would be deprived of its end. Hence
we see that animals which live but a short time are perfected
in a short time. But if happiness consists in a perfect operation according to perfect virtue,[6] whether intellectual or
moral, it cannot possibly come to man except after a long
time. This is most evident in speculative matters, wherein
man's ultimate happiness consists, as we have proved;[7] for
hardly is man able to arrive at perfection in the speculations
of science, even though he reach the last stage of life, and
then, in the majority of cases, but a short space of life remains to him. Therefore man's ultimate happiness cannot be
in this life.

Further. All admit that happiness is a perfect good, or else
it would not bring rest to the appetite. Now perfect good is
that which is wholly free from any admixture of evil; just
as that which is perfectly white is that which is entirely free
from any admixture of black. But man cannot be wholly free
from evils in this state of life, and not only from evils of the
body, such as hunger, thirst, heat, cold and the like, but also
from evils of the soul. For there is no one who at times is

[5] *Eth.,* I, 10 (1100b 5).   [6] *Op. cit.,* X, 7 (1177a 11).   [7] Ch. 37.

not disturbed by inordinate passions; who sometimes does not go beyond the mean, wherein virtue consists,[8] either in excess or in deficiency; who is not deceived in some thing or another; or who at least is not ignorant of what he would wish to know, or does not feel doubtful about an opinion of which he would like to be certain. Therefore no man is happy in this life.

Again. Man naturally shuns death, and is sad about it, not only shunning it at the moment when he feels its presence, but also when he thinks about it. But man, in this life, cannot obtain not to die. Therefore it is not possible for man to be happy in this life.

Besides. Ultimate happiness consists, not in a habit, but in an operation, since habits are for the sake of actions. But in this life it is impossible to perform any action continuously. Therefore man cannot be entirely happy in this life.

Further. The more a thing is desired and loved, the more does its loss bring sorrow and pain. Now happiness is most desired and loved. Therefore its loss brings the greatest sorrow. But if there be ultimate happiness in this life, it will certainly be lost, at least by death. Nor is it certain that it will last till death, since it is possible for every man in this life to encounter sickness, whereby he is wholly hindered from the operation of virtue, e.g., madness and the like, which hinder the use of reason. Such happiness therefore always has sorrow naturally connected with it, and consequently it will not be perfect happiness.

But someone might say that, since happiness is a good of the intellectual nature, perfect and true happiness is for those in whom the intellectual nature is perfect, namely, in separate substances, and that in man it is imperfect, and by a kind of participation. For man can arrive at a full understanding of the truth only by a sort of movement of inquiry; and he fails entirely to understand things that are by nature most intelligible, as we have proved. Therefore neither is happiness, in its perfect nature, possible to man; but he has a certain participation of it, even in this life. This seems to have been Aristotle's opinion about happiness. Hence, inquiring whether misfortunes destroy happiness, he shows that happiness seems especially to consist in deeds of virtue, which seem to be

[8] Cf. Aristotle, Eth., II, 6 (1106b 24).

most stable in this life, and concludes that those who in this life attain to this perfection are happy *as men,* as though not attaining to happiness absolutely, but in a human way.[9]

We must now show that this explanation does not remove the foregoing arguments. For although man is below the separate substances according to the order of nature, he is above irrational creatures, and so he attains his ultimate end in a more perfect way than they. Now these attain their last end so perfectly that they seek nothing further. Thus a heavy body rests when it is in its own proper place, and when an animal enjoys sensible pleasure, its natural desire is at rest. Much more, therefore, when man has obtained his last end, must his natural desire be at rest. But this cannot happen in this life. Therefore in this life man does not obtain happiness considered as his proper end, as we have proved. Therefore he must obtain it after this life.

Again. Natural desire cannot be empty, since *nature does nothing in vain.*[10] But nature's desire would be empty if it could never be fulfilled. Therefore man's natural desire can be fulfilled. But not in this life, as we have shown. Therefore it must be fulfilled after this life. Therefore man's ultimate happiness is after this life.

Besides. As long as a thing is in motion towards perfection, it has not reached its last end. Now in the knowledge of truth all men are always in motion and tending towards perfection; because those who follow make discoveries in addition to those made by their predecessors, as is also stated in *Metaph.* ii.[11] Therefore in the knowledge of truth man is not situated as though he had arrived at his last end. Since, then, as Aristotle himself shows,[12] man's ultimate happiness in this life consists apparently in speculation, whereby he seeks the knowledge of truth, we cannot possibly allow that man obtains his last end in this life.

Moreover. Whatever is in potentiality tends to become actual, so that as long as it is not wholly actual, it has not reached its last end. Now our intellect is in potentiality to the knowledge of all the forms of things, and it becomes actual when it knows any one of them. Consequently, it will not be wholly actual, nor in possession of its last end, except

[9] *Op. cit.,* I, 10 (1101a 18). [10] Aristotle, *De Caelo,* II, 11 (291b 13). [11] Aristotle, *Metaph.,* Ia, 1 (993a 31). [12] *Eth.,* X, 7 (1177a 18).

when it knows all things, at least all these material things. But man cannot obtain this through the speculative sciences, by which we know truth in this life. Therefore man's ultimate happiness cannot be in this life.

For these and like reasons, Alexander and Averroes held that man's ultimate happiness does not consist in that human knowledge obtained through the speculative sciences, but in that which results from a union with a separate substance, which union they deemed possible to man in this life.[13] But as Aristotle realized that man has no knowledge in this life other than that which he obtains through the speculative sciences, he maintained that man attains to a happiness which is not perfect, but a human one.

Hence it becomes sufficiently clear how these great minds suffered from being so straitened on every side. We, however, shall be freed from these straits if we hold, in accordance with the foregoing arguments, that man is able to reach perfect happiness after this life, since man has an immortal soul; and that in that state his soul will understand in the same way as separate substances understand, as we proved in the Second Book.[14]

Therefore man's ultimate happiness will consist in that knowledge of God which the human mind possesses after this life, a knowledge similar to that by which separate substances know him. Hence our Lord promises us a *reward . . . in heaven* (*Matt.* v. 12) and states (*Matt.* xxii. 30) that the saints *shall be as the angels,* who always see God in heaven (*Matt.* xviii. 10).

[13] Cf. ch. 42, 43.   [14] *C. G.,* II, 81.

CHAPTER LI

HOW GOD MAY BE SEEN IN HIS ESSENCE

SINCE, then, it is impossible for a natural desire to be empty (and it would be, were it impossible to arrive at understanding the divine substance, for all minds desire this naturally), we must conclude that it is possible for the divine substance to be seen through the intellect, both by separate intellectual substances, and by our souls.

It is sufficiently clear, from what has been said, what man-

ner of vision this is. For we have proved that the divine substance cannot be seen by the intellect by means of any
created species.[1] Therefore, if God's essence is to be seen at
all, it must be that the intellect sees it through the divine
essence itself; so that in that vision the divine essence is both
the object and the medium of vision.

Since, however, the intellect is unable to understand any
particular substance unless it be actualized by a species in-
forming it, which is the likeness of the thing understood,
someone might deem it impossible for a created intellect to
seè the very substance of God through the divine essence as
an intelligible species. For the divine essence is self-subsistent, and we have proved in the First Book that God cannot be the form of anything.[2]

In order to understand this truth, we must note that a self-
subsisting substance is either a form alone, or a composite of
matter and form. Accordingly, that which is composed of
matter and form cannot be the form of something else, because the form therein is already confined to that matter, so
that it cannot be the form of another thing. But that which
so subsists that it is yet a form alone, can be the form of
something else, provided its being be such that some other
thing can participate in it, as we have proved concerning the
human soul in the Second Book.[3] If, however, its being cannot be participated in by another, it cannot be the form of
anything, because by its very being it is determined in itself,
just as material things are determined by their matter. Now
we must consider this as being the case not only with regard
to substantial or natural being, but also as regards intelligible
being. For, since truth is the perfection of the intellect, that
intelligible which is truth itself will be a pure form in the
genus of intelligible things. This applies solely to God, for,
since truth is consequent upon being,[4] that alone is its own
truth, which is its own being; and this belongs to God alone,
as we have proved in the Second Book.[5] Consequently, other
subsistent intelligibles are not pure forms in the genus of intelligible things, but have a form in a subject; for each of
them is a true thing, but not the truth, even as it is a being,
but not being itself. It is therefore clear that the divine essence can be compared to the created intellect as an intelligible

[1] Ch. 49. [2] *C. G.*, I, 26ff. [3] *C. G.*, II, 68. [4] Cf. Aristotle,
Metaph., Ia, 1 (993b 30). [5] *C. G.*, II, 15.

species by which it understands; which cannot be said of the essence of any separate substance. And yet it cannot be the form of another thing through its natural being. For it would follow that, once united to another being, it would constitute one nature; which is impossible, since the divine essence is in itself perfect in its own nature. But an intelligible species, in its union with the intellect, does not constitute a nature, but perfects the intellect for understanding; and this is not inconsistent with the perfection of the divine essence.

This immediate vision of God is promised to us in Holy Scripture (*1 Cor.* xiii. 12): *We see now through a glass in a dark manner; but then face to face.* It would be impious to understand this in a material way, and imagine a material face in the Godhead; for we have proved that God is not a body.[6] Nor is it possible for us to see God with a bodily face, since the eyes of the body, which are situated in the face, can see only bodily things. Thus then shall we see God face to face, because we shall see Him immediately, even as a man whom we see face to face.

It is through this vision that we become most like God, and participators of His blessedness, since God understands His substance through His essence, and this is His blessedness. Therefore it is said (*1 John* iii. 2): *When He shall appear, we shall be like to Him; because we shall see Him as He is.* Again, our Lord said (*Luke* xxii. 29, 30): *I dispose to you, as My Father hath disposed to Me, a banquet, that you may eat and drink at My table in My kingdom.* Now these words cannot be understood as referring to bodily food and drink, but to that which is taken from the table of Wisdom, of which Wisdom says (*Prov.* ix. 5): *Eat my bread and drink the wine which I have mingled for you.* Accordingly, to eat and drink at God's table is to enjoy the same blessedness as that which makes God happy, and to see God as He sees Himself.

[6] *C. G.,* I, 27.

CHAPTER LII

THAT NO CREATED SUBSTANCE CAN BY ITS NATURAL POWER ARRIVE AT SEEING GOD IN HIS ESSENCE

HOWEVER, it is not possible for any created substance to attain, by its own power, to this way of seeing God.

For that which is proper to the higher nature cannot be acquired by a lower nature, except through the action of the higher nature to which it properly belongs. Thus water cannot become hot except through the action of heat. Now to see God through His essence is proper to the divine nature, since to operate through his own form is proper to each operator. Therefore no intellectual substance can see God through the divine essence, unless God Himself bring this about.

Again. A form proper to A does not become B's except through A's agency, because an agent produces its like by communicating its form to another. Now it is impossible to see the divine substance unless the divine essence itself become the form by which the intellect understands, as we have proved.[1] Therefore no created substance can attain to that vision, except through the divine agency.

Besides. If any two things have to be united together so that one be formal and the other material, their union must be completed by an action on the part of the one that is formal, and not by the action of the one that is material; for the form is the principle of action, whereas matter is the passive principle. Now in order that the created intellect see God's substance, the divine essence itself must be united to the intellect as an intelligible form, as we have proved. Therefore no created intellect can attain to this vision except through the divine agency.

Further. *What is so of itself is the cause of what is so through another.*[2] Now the divine intellect sees through itself the divine substance, for the divine intellect is the divine essence itself, by means of which God's substance is seen, as we proved in the First Book.[3] But the created intellect sees the divine substance through the divine essence as through something other than itself. Therefore this vision cannot be acquired by the created intellect, except through the action of God.

Moreover. Whatever exceeds the limits of a given nature, cannot be acquired by that nature except through the agency of another; and thus water does not flow upwards unless it be moved by something else. Now it is beyond the limits of any created nature to see God's substance, because it is proper to every created intellectual nature to understand ac-

---

[1] Ch. 51.   [2] Cf. Aristotle, *Phys.*, VIII, 5 (257a 31).   [3] *C. G.*, I. 45.

cording to the mode of its substance. But the divine substance cannot be thus understood, as we proved above.[4] Therefore no created intellect can possibly attain to a vision of the divine substance except by the agency of God, Who surpasses all creatures.

Hence it is said (*Rom.* vi. 23): *The grace of God is life everlasting.* For we have proved that man's happiness consists in seeing God, which is called life everlasting.[5] Now we are said to obtain this by God's grace alone, because that vision surpasses the ability of every creature, and it is impossible to attain thereto except by God's gift; and when such things are obtained by a creature, it is put down to God's grace. And so our Lord says (*Jo.* xiv. 21): *I will manifest myself to him.*

[4] Ch. 49.   [5] Ch. 50.

CHAPTER LIII

THAT THE CREATED INTELLECT NEEDS THE ASSISTANCE OF THE DIVINE LIGHT IN ORDER TO SEE GOD IN HIS ESSENCE

To so sublime a vision the created intellect needs to be raised by some kind of outpouring of the divine goodness. For it is impossible that the proper form of anything become the form of another, unless this other bear some resemblance to the thing to which that form properly belongs. Thus light does not actualize a body which has nothing in common with the diaphanous. Now the divine essence is the proper intelligible form of the divine intellect, and is proportionate to it; for these three, *understanding, means of understanding* and *object understood* are one in God. Therefore that same essence cannot become the intelligible form of a created intellect, except because the created intellect participates in some divine likeness. Therefore this participation in a divine likeness is necessary in order that the divine substance be seen.

Again. Nothing can receive a higher form unless it be raised through some disposition to the capacity for this form; for every act is realized in its proper potency. Now the divine essence is a higher form than any created intellect. Therefore, in order that the divine essence become the intelligible species of a created intellect, which is requisite in order that the divine substance be seen, the created intellect needs to be raised to that capacity by some higher disposition.

Besides. If two things, after not being united, become united, this must be either because both are changed, or only one. Now if we suppose that some created intellect begins to see the divine essence, it follows, from what we have said,[1] that the divine essence comes to be united to that intellect as an intelligible species. But it is impossible that the divine essence be changed, as we have proved.[2] Therefore this union must begin through a change in the created intellect, and this change can consist only in the fact that the created intellect acquires some new disposition.—The same conclusion follows if we suppose some created intellect to be endowed from the outset of its creation with such a vision. For if, as we have proved,[3] this vision exceeds the ability of nature, it is possible to conceive any created intellect as complete in the species of its nature without its seeing God's substance. Consequently, whether it see God from the beginning, or begin to see Him afterwards, its nature needs something to be added to it.

Further. Nothing can be raised to a higher operation except through its power being strengthened. Now a power may be strengthened in two ways. First, by a mere intensifying of its power. Thus, the active power of a hot thing is increased by the intensity of the heat, so that it is capable of a more vehement action of the same species. Secondly, by the addition of a new form. Thus the power of a diaphanous body is strengthened so that it can give light, through its being made actually lucid by receiving the form of light anew. This increase of power is necessary in order to accomplish an operation of another species. Now the natural power of the created intellect is not sufficient for the vision of the divine substance, as we have shown.[4] Therefore its power needs to be increased in order that it attain to that vision. But increase through intensification of the natural power is insufficient, because that vision is not of the same kind as the natural vision of the created intellect; which is clear from the distance separating the things seen. Therefore there must be an increase of the intellectual power through its receiving a new disposition.

[1] Ch. 51.   [2] *C. G.*, I, 13.   [3] Ch. 52.   [4] *Ibid.*

Now, owing to the fact that we derive our knowledge of intelligible beings from sensible things, we transfer the terms employed in sensible knowledge to our intellectual knowledge; especially those terms that pertain to the sight, which of all the senses is the highest and most spiritual, and therefore most akin to the intellect. It is for this reason that intellectual knowledge is called *sight* [*visio*]. And because bodily sight is not effected without light, those things which serve for the perfection of intellectual vision are called *light*; and so Aristotle compares the agent intellect to light, because the agent intellect makes things actually intelligible, even as light somehow makes things to be actually visible.[5] Accordingly, the disposition whereby the created intellect is raised to the intellectual vision of the divine substance is rightly called the *light of glory*; not indeed because it makes the object actually intelligible, as the light of the agent intellect does, but because it makes the intellect able to understand actually.

This is the light of which it is said (*Ps.* xxxv. 10): *In Thy light we shall see light*, *i.e.*, the light of the divine substance. Again it is said (*Apoc.* xxii. 5 [cf. xxi. 23]): *The city,* namely of the Blessed, *hath no need of the sun, nor of the moon . . . for the glory of God hath enlightened it.* Again it is said (*Isa.* lx. 19): *Thou shalt no more have the sun for thy light by day, neither shall the brightness of the moon enlighten thee; but the Lord shall be unto thee for an everlasting light, and thy God for thy glory.*—For this reason, too, since in God to be is the same as to understand, and because He is to all the cause of their understanding, He is said to be *the light* (*Jo.* i. 9): *That was the true light which enlighteneth every man that cometh into this world;* and (*1 John* i. 5): *God is light.* Again (*Ps.* ciii. 2): *Thou . . . art clothed with light as with a garment.*—For this reason, too, both God and the angels are described in Holy Scripture in figures of fire, because of the splendor of fire (*Exod.* xxiv. 17; *Acts* ii. 3; *Ps.* ciii. 4).

[5] *De An.,* III, 5 (430a 15).

CHAPTER LIV

ARGUMENTS THAT WOULD SEEM TO PROVE THAT GOD CAN-
NOT BE SEEN IN HIS ESSENCE, AND THEIR SOLUTION

SOMEONE will object against the foregoing:

[1] No additional light can help the sight to see things
that surpass the natural ability of corporeal sight, since the
sight can see only colored things. Now the divine substance
surpasses every capacity of a created intellect, more even
than the intellect surpasses the senses' capacity. Therefore no
additional light can raise the created intellect to see the divine substance.

[2] Again. This light, that is received into the created intellect, is something created. Therefore it also is infinitely
distant from God, and consequently such a light cannot help
the created intellect to see the divine substance.

[3] Besides. If the aforesaid light can do this for the reason that it is a likeness of the divine substance, since every
intellectual substance, for the very reason that it is intellectual, bears a likeness to God, the nature itself of an intellectual substance will suffice for it to see God.

[4] Further. If this light is created, since there is no reason why that which is created should not be connatural to
some creature, there might possibly be a creature that would
see the divine substance through its connatural light. But the
contrary of this has been proved.[1]

[5] Moreover. *The infinite, as such, is unknown.*[2] Now we
proved in the First Book that God is infinite.[3] Therefore the
divine substance cannot be seen through the light in question.

[6] Again. There should be a proportion between the one
understanding and the thing understood. But there is no proportion between the created intellect, even perfected by this
light, and the divine substance; for there still remains an infinite distance between them. Therefore the created intellect
cannot be raised by any light to see the divine substance.

By these and like arguments some have been induced to
maintain that the divine substance is never seen by a created

[1] Ch. 52.   [2] Aristotle, *Phys.*, I, 4 (187b 7).   [3] *C. G.*, I, 43.

intellect. This opinion both destroys the rational creature's true happiness, which can consist in nothing but the vision of the divine substance, as we have proved,[4] and is contrary to the authority of Holy Scripture, as appears from what we have said.[5] Therefore it should be rejected as false and heretical.

Now it is not difficult to answer the above arguments. For the divine substance is not so outside the range of the created intellect, as to be absolutely beyond its reach, as sound is to the sight, or an immaterial substance to the senses. For the divine substance is the first intelligible, and the principle of all intellectual knowledge. Rather, it is outside the range of the created intellect as exceeding its power, just as the highest sensibles are outside the range of the senses. Therefore the Philosopher says that *our intellect stands in relation to the most evident things as the owl's eye does in relation to the sun*.[6] Therefore the created intellect needs to be strengthened by some divine light in order to be able to see the divine substance. This solves the *first argument*.

Moreover, this light raises the created intellect to the vision of God, not because of its affinity to the divine substance, but because of the power which it receives from God to produce such an effect; even though in its being it is infinitely distant from God, as the *second argument* stated. For this light unites the created intellect to God, not in being, but only in understanding.

Since, however, it belongs to God Himself to understand His substance perfectly, the light in question is a likeness of God in this that it perfects the intellect for seeing the divine substance. Now no intellectual substance can be like God in this way. For since no created substance's simplicity is equal to the divine simplicity, it is impossible for the created substance to have its entire perfection in one subject: for this is proper to God, as we proved in the First Book,[7] Who is *being, understanding* and *blessed* in respect of the same reality. Consequently, in the intellectual substance, the created light through which it is raised to the beatific vision of God differs from any light whereby it is perfected in its specific nature and understands proportionately to its substance. Hence the reply to the *third argument* is clear.

[4] Ch. 50.   [5] Ch. 51.   *Metaph.*, Iα, 1 (993b 9).   [7] *C. G.*, I, 28.

The *fourth argument* is solved thus. The vision of the divine substance surpasses all natural power, as was shown. Consequently the light whereby the created intellect is perfected in order to see the divine substance must needs be supernatural.

Nor can the fact that God is infinite be an obstacle to the vision of the divine substance, as the *fifth objection* argued. For He is not said to be infinite by way of privation, as is quantity. The infinite of this kind is quite logically unknown, because it is like matter devoid of form, which is the principle of knowledge. But God is said to be infinite negatively, as a *per se* subsistent form that is not limited by being received into matter. Therefore, that which is infinite in this way is in itself most knowable.

There is, furthermore, a proportion between the created intellect and understanding God, a proportion not of a common measure, but of a relation of one thing to another, such as of matter to form, or cause to effect. In this way there is no reason against there being in the creature a proportion to God, consisting in the relation of the one understanding to the thing understood, as well as of an effect to its cause. Therefore the solution of the *sixth objection* is clear.

CHAPTER LXI

THAT BY SEEING GOD A MAN IS MADE A PARTAKER OF ETERNAL LIFE

IT FOLLOWS that by the aforesaid vision the created intellect is made a partaker of eternal life.

For eternity differs from time in that the latter has its being in a kind of succession, whereas the former is all simultaneously.[1] Now it has already been proved that there is no succession in the vision in question,[2] and that whatsoever is seen in it, is seen at once and at a glance. Therefore this vision takes place in a kind of participation of eternity. Moreover this vision is a kind of life, because the act of the intellect is a kind of life.[3] Therefore by that vision the created intellect becomes a partaker of eternal life.

[1] Cf. Boethius, *De Consol.*, V, prose 6 (PL 63, 858).   [2] Ch. 60.
[3] *Eth.*, IX, 9 (1170a 18).

Again. Actions take their species from their objects. Now the object of the aforesaid vision is the divine substance in its very being, and not in some created likeness, as we have shown.[4] But the being of the divine substance is in eternity, or rather is eternity itself. Therefore the aforesaid vision consists in a participation of eternity.

Besides. If an action takes place in time, this is either because the principle of the action is in time (for instance, the actions of natural things are temporal), or because of the term of the action (for instance, the actions which spiritual substances, which are above time, exercise on things subject to time). Now the vision in question is not subject to time on the part of the thing seen, since this is an eternal substance; nor on the part of the medium of vision, which is also the eternal substance; nor on the part of the seer, namely the intellect, whose being is independent of time because it is incorruptible, as we have proved.[5] Therefore this vision is according to a participation of eternity, as altogether transcending time.

Further. The intellectual soul is created *on the border line between eternity and time*, as is stated in the *Book of Causes*,[6] and was explained above,[7] because it is the last in order among intellects, and yet its substance stands above corporeal matter, and is independent thereof. On the other hand, its action, in respect of which it comes into conjunction with lower and temporal things, is itself temporal. Consequently, its action, by reason of which it comes into conjunction with higher things that are above time, partakes of eternity. Especially does this apply to the vision in which it sees the divine substance. Therefore by this vision it enters into a participation of eternity; and for the same reason, so too does any other created intellect that sees God.

For this reason our Lord says (*Jo.* xvii. 3): *This is eternal life, that they may know Thee, the only true God*.

---

[4] Ch. 50.   [5] *C. G.*, II, 55, 79.   [6] *De Causis*, II (p. 162).
[7] *C. G.*, II, 68.

HUMAN ACTS

THE SUMMA THEOLOGICA

FIRST PART OF THE SECOND PART

Question VI

ON THE VOLUNTARY AND THE INVOLUNTARY

(*In Eight Articles*)

SINCE therefore happiness is to be gained by means of certain acts, we must as a consequence consider human acts in order to know by what acts we may obtain happiness, and by what acts we are prevented from obtaining it. But because operations and acts are concerned with what is singular, consequently, all practical knowledge is incomplete unless it take account of things in the particular. The study of Morals, therefore, since it treats of human acts, should consider, first, what is universal; and, secondly, what pertains to the particular.[1]

In treating of what is universal in human acts, the points that offer themselves for our consideration are (1) human acts themselves; (2) their principles.[2] Now of human acts some are proper to man, while others are common to man and animals. And since happiness is man's proper good, those acts which are proper to man have a closer connection with happiness than have those which are common to man and the other animals. First, then, we must consider those acts which are proper to man; secondly, those acts which are common to man and the other animals, and are called passions of the soul.[3] The first of these points offers a twofold consideration: (1) What makes a human act? (2) What distinguishes human acts?[4]

[1] *S. T.*, II-II. [2] Q. 49. [3] Q. 22. [4] Q. 18.

And since those acts are properly called human which are voluntary, because the will is the rational appetite, which is proper to man, we must consider acts in so far as they are voluntary.

First, then, we must consider the voluntary and involuntary in general; secondly, those acts which are voluntary, as being elicited by the will, and as issuing from the will immediately;[5] thirdly, those acts which are voluntary, as being commanded by the will, which issue from the will through the medium of the other powers.[6]

Furthermore, because voluntary acts have certain circumstances, according to which we form our judgment concerning them, we must first consider the voluntary and the involuntary, and afterwards, the circumstances of those acts which are found to be voluntary or involuntary.[7] Under the first head there are eight points of inquiry: (1) Whether there is anything voluntary in human acts? (2) Whether in irrational animals? (3) Whether there can be voluntariness without any act? (4) Whether violence can be done to the will? (5) Whether violence causes involuntariness? (6) Whether fear causes involuntariness? (7) Whether concupiscence causes involuntariness? (8) Whether ignorance causes involuntariness?

First Article

WHETHER THERE IS ANYTHING VOLUNTARY IN HUMAN ACTS?

We proceed thus to the First Article:—

Objection 1. It would seem that there is nothing voluntary in human acts. For that is voluntary *which has its principle within itself,* as Gregory of Nyssa,[8] Damascene[9] and Aristotle[10] declare. But the principle of human acts is not in man himself, but outside him, since man's appetite is moved to act by the appetible object which is outside him, and which is as a *mover unmoved.*[11] Therefore there is nothing voluntary in human acts.

Obj. 2. Further, the Philosopher proves that in animals no

---

[5] Q. 8.   [6] Q. 17.   [7] Q. 7.   [8] Cf. Nemesius, *De Nat. Hom.,* XXXII (PG 40, 728).   [9] *De Fide Orth.,* II, 24 (PG 94, 953).   [10] *Eth.,* III, 1 (1111a 23).   [11] Aristotle, *De An.,* III, 10 (433b 11).

new movement arises that is not preceded by another and exterior motion.[12] But all human acts are new, since none is eternal. Consequently, the principle of all human acts is from outside man, and therefore there is nothing voluntary in them.

Obj. 3. Further, he that acts voluntarily can act of himself. But this is not true of man, for it is written (*Jo.* xv. 5): *Without Me you can do nothing.* Therefore there is nothing voluntary in human acts.

On the contrary, Damascene says that *the voluntary is an act consisting in a rational operation.*[13] Now such are human acts. Therefore there is something voluntary in human acts.

I answer that, There must needs be something voluntary in human acts. In order to make this clear, we must take note that the principle of some acts is within the agent, or in that which is moved; whereas the principle of some movements or acts is outside. For when a stone is moved upwards, the principle of this movement is outside the stone; whereas, when it is moved downwards, the principle of this movement is in the stone. Now of those things that are moved by an intrinsic principle, some move themselves, some not. For since every agent or thing moved acts or is moved for an end, as was stated above,[14] those are perfectly moved by an intrinsic principle whose intrinsic principle is one not only of movement but of movement for an end. Now in order that a thing be done for an end, some knowledge of the end is necessary. Therefore, whatever so acts or is so moved by an intrinsic principle that it has some knowledge of the end, has within itself the principle of its act, so that it not only acts, but acts for an end. On the other hand, if a thing has no knowledge of the end, even though it have an intrinsic principle of action or movement, nevertheless, the principle of acting or being moved for an end is not in that thing, but in something else, by which the principle of its action towards an end is imprinted on it. Therefore such things are not said to move themselves, but to be moved by others. But those things which have a knowledge of the end are said to move themselves because there is in them a principle by which they not only act but also act for an end. And, consequently, since both are from an intrinsic principle, *i.e.*, that they act and that they act for

[12] *Phys.*, VIII, 2 (253a 11).   [13] *De Fide Orth.*, II, 24 (PG 94, 953).
[14] Q. 1, a. 2.

an end, the movements and acts of such things are said to be voluntary; for the term *voluntary* signifies that their movements and acts are from their own inclination. Hence it is that, according to the definitions of Aristotle,[15] Gregory of Nyssa[16] and Damascene,[17] the voluntary is defined not only as having *a principle within* the agent, but also as implying *knowledge*. Therefore, since man especially knows the end of his work, and moves himself, in his acts especially is the voluntary to be found.

Reply Obj. 1. Not every principle is a first principle. Therefore, although it is of the nature of the voluntary act that its principle be within the agent, nevertheless, it is not contrary to the nature of the voluntary act that this intrinsic principle be caused or moved by an extrinsic principle; for it is not of the nature of the voluntary act that its intrinsic principle be a first principle.—Nevertheless, it must be observed that a principle of movement may happen to be first in a genus, but not first absolutely. Thus, in the genus of things subject to alteration, the first principle of alteration is the body of the heavens, which nevertheless is not the first mover absolutely, but is moved locally by a higher mover. And so the intrinsic principle of the voluntary act, *i.e.*, the cognitive and appetitive power, is the first principle in the genus of appetitive movement, although it is moved by an extrinsic principle according to other species of movement.

Reply Obj. 2. New movements in animals are indeed preceded by a motion from without; and this in two respects. First, in so far as by means of an extrinsic motion an animal's senses are confronted with something sensible, which, on being apprehended, moves the appetite. Thus a lion, on seeing the approach of the stag through its movement, begins to be moved towards the stag.—Secondly, in so far as some extrinsic motion produces a physical change in an animal's body, for example, through cold or heat; and when the body is thus affected by the motion of an exterior body, the sensitive appetite likewise, which is the power of a bodily organ, is moved accidentally. Thus, it happens that through some alteration in the body the appetite is roused to the desire of something. But this is not contrary to the nature of volun-

[15] *Eth.*, III, 1 (1111a 23).   [16] Cf. Nemesius, *De Nat. Hom.*, XXXII (PG 40, 728).   [17] *De Fide Orth.*, II, 24 (PG 94, 953).

tariness, as was stated above, for such movements caused by an extrinsic principle are of another genus of movement.

Reply Obj. 3. God moves man to act, not only by proposing the appetible to the senses, or by effecting a change in his body, but also by moving the will itself; for every movement both of the will and of nature proceeds from God as the First Mover. And just as it is not incompatible with nature that the movement of nature be from God as the First Mover, inasmuch as nature is an instrument of God moving it, so it is not contrary to the character of a voluntary act that it proceed from God, inasmuch as the will is moved by God. Nevertheless, both natural and voluntary movements have this in common, that it belongs to the nature of both that they should proceed from a principle within the agent.

Second Article

WHETHER THERE IS ANYTHING VOLUNTARY IN IRRATIONAL ANIMALS?

We proceed thus to the Second Article:—

Objection 1. It would seem that there is nothing voluntary in irrational animals. For *voluntary* is so called from *voluntas* [*will*]. Now since the will is in the reason,[18] it cannot be in irrational animals. Therefore neither is there anything voluntary in them.

Obj. 2. Further, according as human acts are voluntary, man is said to be master of his actions. But irrational animals are not masters of their actions; for *they act not, but rather are they acted upon,* as Damascene says.[19] Therefore there is no voluntary act in irrational animals.

Obj. 3. Further, Damascene says that *voluntary acts lead to praise and blame.*[20] But neither praise nor blame befits the acts of irrational animals. Therefore such acts are not voluntary.

On the contrary, The Philosopher says that *both children and irrational animals participate in the voluntary.*[21] The same is said by Gregory of Nyssa[22] and Damascene.[23]

---

[18] Aristotle, *De An.,* III, 9 (432b 5).   [19] *De Fide Orth.,* II, 27 (PG 94, 960).   [20] *Op. cit.,* II, 24 (PG 94, 953).   [21] *Eth.,* III, 2 (1111b 8).   [22] Cf. Nemesius, *De Nat. Hom.,* XXXII (PG 40, 729).   [23] *De Fide Orth.,* II, 24 (PG 94, 956).

I answer that, As was stated above, it is of the nature of a voluntary act that its principle be within the agent, together with some knowledge of the end. Now knowledge of the end is twofold, perfect and imperfect. Perfect knowledge of the end consists in not only apprehending the thing which is the end, but also in knowing it under the aspect of end, and the relationship of the means to that end. And such a knowledge of the end belongs to none but the rational nature.—But imperfect knowledge of the end consists in a mere apprehension of the end, without knowing it under the aspect of end, or the relationship of an act to the end. Such a knowledge of the end is exercised by irrational animals, through their senses and their natural estimative power.

Consequently, perfect knowledge of the end is accompanied by the voluntary in its perfect nature, inasmuch as, having apprehended the end, a man can, from deliberating about the end and the means thereto, be moved, or not, to gain that end.—But imperfect knowledge of the end is accompanied by the voluntary in its imperfect nature, inasmuch as the agent apprehends the end, but does not deliberate, and is moved to the end at once. Therefore the voluntary in its perfection belongs to none but the rational nature, whereas the imperfect voluntary belongs also to irrational animals.

Reply Obj. 1. The will is the name of the rational appetite, and consequently it cannot be in beings devoid of reason. But the term *voluntary* is derived from *voluntas* [*will*], and can be extended to those things in which there is some participation of will, by way of likeness thereto. It is thus that voluntary action is attributed to irrational animals, in so far as they are moved to an end, through some kind of knowledge.

Reply Obj. 2. The fact that man is master of his actions is due to his being able to deliberate about them; for since the deliberating reason is indifferently disposed to opposites, the will can proceed to either. But it is not thus that voluntariness is in irrational animals, as was stated above.

Reply Obj. 3. Praise and blame attach to the voluntary act according to the perfect notion of the voluntary, which is not to be found in irrational animals.

Third Article

WHETHER THERE CAN BE VOLUNTARINESS WITHOUT ANY ACT?

We proceed thus to the Third Article:—

Objection 1. It would seem that voluntariness cannot be without any act. For that is voluntary which proceeds from the will. But nothing can proceed from the will, except through some act, at least an act of the will itself. Therefore there cannot be voluntariness without act.

Obj. 2. Further, just as one is said to will by an act of the will, so when the act of the will ceases, one is said not to will. But not to will causes involuntariness, which is contrary to voluntariness. Therefore there can be nothing voluntary when the act of the will ceases.

Obj. 3. Further, knowledge is part of the nature of the voluntary, as was stated above. But knowledge involves an act. Therefore voluntariness cannot be without some act.

On the contrary, The term *voluntary* is applied to that of which we are masters. Now we are masters in respect of to act and not to act, to will and not to will. Therefore, just as to act and to will are voluntary, so also are not to act and not to will.

I answer that, Voluntary is what proceeds from the will. Now one thing proceeds from another in two ways. First, directly, in which sense something proceeds from another inasmuch as this other acts: *e.g.,* heating from heat. Secondly, indirectly, in which sense something proceeds from another through the fact that this other does not act. Thus the sinking of a ship is attributed to the helmsman, from his having ceased to steer.—But we must take note that the cause of what follows from the failure to act is not always the agent as not acting, but only when the agent can and ought to act. For if the helmsman were unable to steer the ship, or if the ship's helm were not entrusted to him, the sinking of the ship would not be attributed to him, although it might be due to his absence from the helm.

Since, then, by willing and acting, the will is able, and sometimes ought, to hinder not-willing and not-acting, this not-willing and not-acting is imputed to the will as though proceeding from it. And thus it is that we can have the voluntary without an act, and this sometimes without an outward act, but with an interior act, for instance, when one wills not to act, and sometimes without even an interior act, as when one does not will to act.

Reply Obj. 1. We apply the term *voluntary* not only to that which proceeds from the will directly, as from its agent, but also to that which proceeds from it indirectly as from its non-agent.

Reply Obj. 2. *Not to will* is said in two senses. First, as though it were one word, and the infinitive of *I-do-not-will*. Consequently, just as when I say *I do not will to read,* the sense is, *I will not to read,* so *not to will to read* is the same as *to will not to read;* and in this sense *not to will* causes involuntariness.—Secondly it is taken as a sentence, and then no act of the will is affirmed. And in this sense *not to will* does not cause involuntariness.

Reply Obj. 3. Voluntariness requires an act of knowledge in the same way as it requires an act of will, namely, in order that it be in one's power to consider, to will and to act. And then, just as not to will and not to act, when it is time to will and to act, is voluntary, so is it voluntary not to consider.

Fourth Article

WHETHER VIOLENCE CAN BE DONE TO THE WILL?

We proceed thus to the Fourth Article:—

Objection 1. It would seem that violence can be done to the will. For everything can be compelled by that which is more powerful. But there is something, namely, God, that is more powerful than the human will. Therefore it can be compelled, at least by Him.

Obj. 2. Further, every passive subject is compelled by its active principle, when it is changed by it. But the will is a passive power, for it is a *moved mover.*[24] Therefore, since it is sometimes moved by its active principle, it seems that it is sometimes compelled.

Obj. 3. Further, violent movement is that which is contrary to nature. But the movement of the will is sometimes contrary to nature, as is clear of the will's movement to sin,

---

[24] Aristotle, *De An.*, III, 10 (433a 9; b 16).

which is contrary to nature, as Damascene says.[25] Therefore the movement of the will can be compelled.

On the contrary, Augustine says that what is done voluntarily is not done of necessity.[26] Now whatever is done under compulsion is done of necessity, and consequently what is done by the will cannot be compelled. Therefore the will cannot be compelled to act.

I answer that, The act of the will is twofold: one is its immediate act, as it were, elicited by it, namely, *to will;* the other is an act of the will commanded by it, and put into execution by means of some other power: *e.g., to walk* and *to speak,* which are commanded by the will to be executed by means of the power of locomotion.

As regards the commanded acts of the will, then, the will can suffer violence, in so far as violence can prevent the exterior members from executing the will's command. But as to the will's own proper act, violence cannot be done to the will. The reason for this is that the act of the will is nothing else than an inclination proceeding from an interior knowing principle, just as the natural appetite is an inclination proceeding from an interior principle without knowledge. Now what is compelled or violent is from an exterior principle. Consequently, it is contrary to the nature of the will's own act that it should be subject to compulsion or violence; just as it is also contrary to the nature of the natural inclination or the movement of a stone to be moved upwards. For a stone may have an upward movement from violence, but that this violent movement be from its natural inclination is impossible. In like manner, a man may be dragged by force, but it is contrary to the very notion of violence that he be thus dragged of his own will.

Reply Obj. 1. God, Who is more powerful than the human will, can move the will of man, according to *Prov.* xxi. 1: *The heart of the king is in the hand of the Lord; whithersoever He will He shall turn it.* But if this were by compulsion, it would no longer be by an act of the will, nor would the will itself be moved, but something else against the will.

Reply Obj. 2. It is not always a violent movement when a passive subject is moved by its active principle, but only then when this is done against the interior inclination of the

[25] *De Fide Orth.,* IV, 20 (PG 94, 1196).   [26] *De Civit. Dei,* V, 10 (PL 41, 152).

passive subject. Otherwise, every alteration and generation of simple bodies would be unnatural and violent; whereas they are natural by reason of the natural interior aptitude of the matter or subject to such a disposition. In like manner, when the will is moved, according to its own inclination, by the appetible object, this movement is not violent but voluntary.

Reply Obj. 3. That to which the will tends by sinning, although in reality it is evil and contrary to the rational nature, is nevertheless apprehended as something good and suitable to nature, in so far as it is suitable to man by reason of some pleasurable sensation or some vicious habit.

Fifth Article

WHETHER VIOLENCE CAUSES INVOLUNTARINESS?

We proceed thus to the Fifth Article:—

Objection 1. It would seem that violence does not cause involuntariness. For we speak of voluntariness and involuntariness in terms of the will. But violence cannot be done to the will, as was shown above. Therefore violence cannot cause involuntariness.

Obj. 2. Further, that which is done involuntarily is done with grief, as Damascene[27] and the Philosopher[28] say. But sometimes a man suffers compulsion without being grieved thereby. Therefore violence does not cause involuntariness.

Obj. 3. Further, what is from the will cannot be involuntary. But some violent actions proceed from the will, for instance, when a man with a heavy body goes upwards, or when a man contorts his members in a way contrary to their natural flexibility. Therefore violence does not cause involuntariness.

On the contrary, The Philosopher[29] and Damascene[30] say that *things done under compulsion are involuntary.*

I answer that, Violence is directly opposed to the voluntary, as likewise to the natural. For the voluntary and the natural have this in common, that both are from an intrinsic principle, whereas the violent is from an extrinsic principle. And for this reason, just as in things devoid of knowledge

---

[27] *De Fide Orth.,* II, 24 (PG 94, 953).   [28] *Eth.,* III, 1 (1111a 20).
[29] *Ibid.* (1109b 35).   [30] *De Fide Orth.,* II, 24 (PG 94, 953).

violence effects something against nature, so in things endowed with knowledge it effects something against the will. Now that which is against nature is said to be *unnatural*, and, in like manner, that which is against the will is said to be *involuntary*. Therefore violence causes involuntariness.

Reply Obj. 1. The involuntary is opposed to the voluntary. Now it has been said that not only the act which proceeds immediately from the will is called voluntary, but also the act commanded by the will. Consequently, as to the act which proceeds immediately from the will, violence cannot be done to the will, as was stated above. But as to the commanded act, the will can suffer violence, and consequently in this respect violence causes involuntariness.

Reply Obj. 2. Just as that is said to be natural which is according to the inclination of nature, so that is said to be voluntary which is according to the inclination of the will. Now a thing is said to be natural in two ways. First, because it is from nature as from an active principle: *e.g.*, it is natural for fire to produce heat. Secondly, according to a passive principle, because, namely, there is in nature an inclination to receive an action from an extrinsic principle. Thus, the movement of the heavens is said to be natural by reason of the natural aptitude in the body of the heavens to receive such movement, although the cause of that movement is a voluntary agent. In like manner, an act is said to be voluntary in two ways. First, in regard to action, for instance, when one wills to act; secondly, in regard to passion, as when one wills to receive an action from another. Hence, when action is inflicted by an extrinsic agent, as long as the will to suffer that action remains in the passive subject, this is not violent absolutely; for although the patient does nothing by way of action, he does something by being willing to suffer. Consequently this cannot be called involuntary.

Reply Obj. 3. As the Philosopher says,[31] the movement of an animal, whereby at times an animal is moved against the natural inclination of the body, although it is not natural to the body, is nevertheless in a way natural to the animal, to which it is natural to be moved according to its appetite. Accordingly this is violent, not absolutely, but relatively.— The same remark applies in the case of one who contorts his

[31] *Phys.*, VIII, 4 (254b 14).

members in a way that is contrary to their natural disposition. For this is violent relatively, *i.e.*, as to that particular
member; but not absolutely, *i.e.*, as to the man himself.

Sixth Article

WHETHER FEAR CAUSES WHAT IS INVOLUNTARY ABSOLUTELY?

We proceed thus to the Sixth Article:—

Objection 1. It would seem that fear causes what is involuntary absolutely. For just as violence regards that which
is contrary to the will in the present, so fear regards a future
evil which is repugnant to the will. But violence causes what
is involuntary absolutely. Therefore fear too causes what is
involuntary absolutely.

Obj. 2. Further, that which is of itself such, remains such,
whatever be added to it. Thus what is of itself hot, as long
as it remains, is still hot, whatever be added to it. But that
which is done through fear is involuntary in itself. Therefore,
even with the addition of fear it is involuntary.

Obj. 3. Further, that which is such, subject to a condition,
is such in a certain respect; whereas what is such, without
any condition, is such absolutely. Thus, what is necessary,
subject to a condition, is necessary in some respect, but what
is necessary without qualification is necessary absolutely. But
that which is done through fear is involuntary absolutely;
and it is not voluntary, save under a condition, namely, in
order that the evil feared may be avoided. Therefore that
which is done through fear is involuntary absolutely.

On the contrary, Gregory of Nyssa[32] and the Philosopher[33]
say that such things as are done through fear are *voluntary
rather than involuntary*.

I answer that, As the Philosopher says,[34] and likewise
Gregory of Nyssa in his book *On Man*,[35] such things as are
done through fear *are of a mixed character*, being partly
voluntary and partly involuntary. For that which is done
through fear, considered in itself, is not voluntary; but it
becomes voluntary in this particular case, in order, namely,
to avoid the evil feared.

---

[32] Cf. Nemesius, *De Nat. Hom.*, XXX (PG 40, 721).   [33] *Eth.*, III,
1 (1110a 12).   [34] *Ibid.*   [35] Cf. Nemesius, *De Nat. Hom.*, XXX
(PG 40, 721).

But if the matter be considered rightly, such things are voluntary rather than involuntary; for they are voluntary absolutely, but involuntary in a certain respect. For a thing is said to be absolutely according as it is in act; but according as it is only in the apprehension, it is not so absolutely, but in a certain respect. Now that which is done through fear is in act in so far as it is done. For, since acts are concerned with singulars, and since the singular, as such, is here and now, that which is done is in act in so far as it is here and now and under other individuating circumstances. Hence that which is done through fear is voluntary, inasmuch as it is here and now, that is to say, in so far as, under the circumstances, it hinders a greater evil which was feared; and thus, the throwing of the cargo into the sea becomes voluntary during the storm, through fear of danger, and so it is clear that it is voluntary absolutely. And hence it is that what is done out of fear has the nature of what is voluntary, because its principle is within.—But if we consider what is done through fear, as outside this particular case, and inasmuch as it is repugnant to the will, this exists only according to our consideration of things; and consequently it is involuntary, considered in that respect, that is to say, outside the actual circumstances of this or that particular case.

Reply Obj. 1. Things done through fear and compulsion differ not only according to present and future time, but also in this, that the will does not consent, but is moved entirely counter to that which is done through compulsion; whereas what is done through fear becomes voluntary because the will is moved towards it, although not for its own sake, but because of something else, that is, in order to avoid an evil which is feared. For the conditions of a voluntary act are satisfied, if it be done because of something else voluntary; since the voluntary is not only what we will for its own sake as an end, but also that we will for the sake of something else as an end. It is clear therefore that in what is done from compulsion, the will does nothing inwardly, whereas in what is done through fear, the will does something. Accordingly, as Gregory of Nyssa says,[36] in order to exclude things done through fear, a violent action is defined not only as one *whose principle is from the outside,* but with the addition,

[36] *Ibid.* (PG 40, 720).

in which he that suffers violence concurs not at all; for the will of him that is in fear does concur somewhat in that which he does through fear.

Reply Obj. 2. Things that are such absolutely, remain such, whatever be added to them: *e.g.,* a cold thing, or a white thing; but things that are such relatively vary according as they are compared with different things. For what is big in comparison with one thing is small in comparison with another. Now a thing is said to be voluntary, not only for its own sake, as it were, absolutely; but also for the sake of something else, as it were, relatively. Accordingly, nothing prevents a thing, which was not voluntary in comparison with one thing, from becoming voluntary when compared with another.

Reply Obj. 3. That which is done through fear is voluntary without any condition, that is to say, according as it is actually done; but it is involuntary under a certain condition, that is to say, if such a fear were not threatening. Consequently, this argument proves rather the opposite.

Seventh Article

WHETHER CONCUPISCENCE CAUSES INVOLUNTARINESS?

We proceed thus to the Seventh Article:—

Objection 1. It would seem that concupiscence causes involuntariness. For just as fear is a passion, so is concupiscence. But fear causes involuntariness to a certain extent. Therefore concupiscence does so too.

Obj. 2. Further, just as the timid man through fear acts counter to that which he proposed, so does the incontinent, through concupiscence. But fear causes involuntariness to a certain extent. Therefore concupiscence does so also.

Obj. 3. Further, knowledge is necessary for voluntariness. But concupiscence impairs knowledge, for the Philosopher says that *delight,* or the lust of pleasure, *destroys the judgment of prudence.*[37] Therefore concupiscence causes involuntariness.

On the contrary, Damascene says: *The involuntary act deserves mercy or indulgence, and is done with regret.*[38] But neither of these can be said of that which is done out of

---

[37] *Eth.,* VI, 5 (1140b 12).   [38] *De Fide Orth.,* II, 24 (PG 94, 953).

concupiscence. Therefore concupiscence does not cause involuntariness.

I answer that, Concupiscence does not cause involuntariness, but, on the contrary, makes something to be voluntary. For a thing is said to be voluntary from the fact that the will is moved to it. Now concupiscence inclines the will to desire the object of concupiscence. Therefore the effect of concupiscence is to make something to be voluntary rather than involuntary.

Reply Obj. 1. Fear has reference to evil, but concupiscence has reference to good. Now evil of itself is counter to the will, whereas good harmonizes with the will. Therefore fear has a greater tendency than concupiscence to cause involuntariness.

Reply Obj. 2. He who acts from fear retains the repugnance of the will to that which he does, considered in itself. But he that acts from concupiscence, *e.g.*, an incontinent man, does not retain his former will whereby he repudiated the object of his concupiscence; rather his will is changed so that he desires that which previously he repudiated. Accordingly, that which is done out of fear is involuntary, to a certain extent, but that which is done from concupiscence is in no way involuntary. For the man who yields to concupiscence acts counter to that which he purposed at first, but not counter to that which he desires now; whereas the timid man acts counter to that which in itself he desires now.

Reply Obj. 3. If concupiscence were to destroy knowledge altogether, as happens with those whom concupiscence has rendered mad, it would follow that concupiscence would take away voluntariness. And yet, properly speaking, it would not make the act involuntary, because in beings bereft of reason there is neither voluntary nor involuntary. But sometimes in those actions which are done from concupiscence, knowledge is not completely destroyed, because the power of knowing is not taken away entirely, but only the actual consideration in some particular possible act. Nevertheless, this itself is voluntary, according as by voluntary we mean that which is in the power of the will, for example, *not to act* or *not to will*, and in like manner *not to consider*; for the will can resist the passion, as we shall state later on.[39]

[39] Q. 10, a. 3; q. 77, a. 7.

Eighth Article

WHETHER IGNORANCE CAUSES INVOLUNTARINESS?

We proceed thus to the Eighth Article:—

Objection 1. It would seem that ignorance does not cause involuntariness. For *the involuntary act deserves pardon,* as Damascene says.[40] But sometimes that which is done through ignorance does not deserve pardon, according to *1 Cor.* xiv. 38: *If any man know not, he shall not be known.* Therefore ignorance does not cause involuntariness.

Obj. 2. Further, every sin implies ignorance, according to *Prov.* xiv. 22: *They err, that work evil.* If, therefore, ignorance causes involuntariness, it would follow that every sin is involuntary; which is opposed to the saying of Augustine, that *every sin is voluntary.*[41]

Obj. 3. Further, *involuntariness is not without sadness,* as Damascene says.[42] But some things are done out of ignorance, but without sadness. For instance, a man may kill a foe, whom he wishes to kill, thinking at the time that he is killing a stag. Therefore ignorance does not cause involuntariness.

On the contrary, Damascene[43] and the Philosopher[44] say that *what is done through ignorance is involuntary.*

I answer that, If ignorance cause involuntariness, it is in so far as it deprives one of knowledge, which is a necessary condition of voluntariness, as was declared above. But it is not every ignorance that deprives one of this knowledge. Accordingly, we must take note that ignorance has a threefold relationship to the act of the will: in one way, *concomitantly;* in another, *consequently;* in a third way, *antecedently. Concomitantly,* when there is ignorance of what is done, but so that even if it were known, it would be done. For then ignorance does not induce one to will this to be done, but it just happens that a thing is at the same time done and not known. Thus, in the example given, a man did indeed will to kill his foe, but killed him in ignorance, thinking to kill a stag. And ignorance of this kind, as the Philosopher states,[45] does not cause involuntariness, since it is

[40] *De Fide Orth.,* II, 24 (PG 94, 953).   [41] *De Vera Relig.,* XIV (PL 34, 133).   [42] *De Fide Orth.,* II, 24 (PG 94, 953).   [43] *Ibid.* [44] *Eth.,* III, 1 (1110a 1).   [45] *Ibid.* (1110b 25).

not the cause of anything that is repugnant to the will; but it causes *non-voluntariness*, since that which is unknown cannot be actually willed.

Ignorance is *consequent* to the act of the will, in so far as ignorance itself is voluntary; and this happens in two ways in accordance with the two aforesaid modes of the voluntary. First, because the act of the will is brought to bear on the ignorance, as when a man wills not to know, that he may have an excuse for sin, or that he may not be withheld from sin, according to *Job* xxi. 14: *We desire not the knowledge of Thy ways.* And this is called *affected ignorance.*—Secondly, ignorance is said to be voluntary, when it regards that which one can and ought to know, for in this sense *not to act* and *not to will* are said to be voluntary, as was stated above. And ignorance of this kind happens either when one does not actually consider what one can and ought to consider (this is called *ignorance of evil choice,* and arises from some passion or habit), or when one does not take the trouble to acquire the knowledge which one ought to have; in which sense, ignorance of the general principles of law, which one ought to know, is voluntary, as being due to negligence.

Accordingly, if in either of these ways ignorance is voluntary, it cannot cause what is involuntary absolutely. Nevertheless it causes involuntariness in a certain respect, inasmuch as it precedes the movement of the will towards the act, which movement would not be, if there were knowledge.

Ignorance is *antecedent* to the act of the will when it is not voluntary, and yet is the cause of man's willing what he would not will otherwise. Thus a man may be ignorant of some circumstance of his act, which he was not bound to know, with the result that he does that which he would not do if he knew of that circumstance. For instance, a man, after taking proper precaution, may not know that someone is coming along the road, so that he shoots an arrow and slays a passer-by. Such ignorance causes what is involuntary absolutely.

From this may be gathered the solution of the objections. For the first objection deals with ignorance of what a man is bound to know. The second, with ignorance of choice, which is voluntary to a certain extent, as was stated above. The third, with that ignorance which is concomitant with the act of the will.

ON THE WILL, IN REGARD TO WHAT IT WILLS

(*In Three Articles*)

WE MUST now consider the different acts of the will, and in the first place, those acts which belong to the will itself immediately, as being elicited by the will; secondly, those acts which are commanded by the will.[1]

Now the will is moved to the end, and to the means to the end. We must therefore consider (1) those acts of the will whereby it is moved to the end; and (2) those whereby it is moved to the means.[2] And since it seems that there are three acts of the will in reference to the end: viz., *volition, enjoyment* and *intention,* we must consider (1) volition; (2) enjoyment;[3] (3) intention.[4]—Concerning the first, three things must be considered: (1) Of what things is the will? (2) By what is the will moved?[5] (3) How is it moved?[6]

Under the first head there are three points of inquiry: (1) Whether the will is of good only? (2) Whether it is of the end only, or also of the means? (3) If in any way it be of the means, whether it be moved to the end and to the means by the same movement?

Second Article

WHETHER VOLITION IS OF THE END ONLY, OR ALSO OF THE MEANS?

We proceed thus to the Second Article:—

Objection 1. It would seem that volition is not of the means, but of the end only. For the Philosopher says that *volition is of the end, while choice is of the means.*[7]

Obj. 2. Further, *For objects differing in genus there are corresponding different powers of the soul.*[8] Now the end and the means are in different genera of good, because the end, which is a good either of rectitude or of pleasure, is in the genus *quality,* or *action,* or *passion;* whereas the good which is useful, and is directed to an end, is in the genus

---

[1] Q. 17.   [2] Q. 13.   [3] Q. 11.   [4] Q. 12.   [5] Q. 9.   [6] Q. 10.
[7] *Op. cit.,* III, 2 (1111b 26).   [8] *Op. cit.,* VI, 1 (1139a 8).

relation.[9] Therefore, if volition is of the end, it is not of the means.

Obj. 3. Further, habits are proportioned to powers, since they are their perfections. But in those habits which are called practical arts, the end belongs to one, and the means to another art. Thus the use of a ship, which is its end, belongs to the art of the helmsman; whereas the building of the ship, which is directed to the end, belongs to the art of the shipwright. Therefore, since volition is of the end, it is not of the means.

On the contrary, In natural things, it is by the same power that a thing passes through the middle ground and arrives at the terminus. But the means are a kind of middle ground through which one arrives at the end or terminus. Therefore, if volition is of the end, it is also of the means.

I answer that, The term *voluntas* [*will*] sometimes designates the power of the will, sometimes its act [*volition*]. Accordingly, if we speak of the will as a power, thus it extends both to the end and to the means. For every power extends to those things in which the nature of its object may be found in any way whatever. Thus the sight extends to all things whatsoever that are in any way colored. Now the nature of good, which is the object of the power of will, may be found not only in the end, but also in the means.

If, however, we speak of will in so far as it is properly the name of an act, then, strictly speaking, it is of the end only. For every act denominated from a power designates the simple act of that power. Thus, *to understand* designates the simple act of the understanding. Now the simple act of a power is referred to that which is in itself the object of that power. But that which is good and willed in itself is the end. Therefore volition, properly speaking, is of the end itself. On the other hand, the means are good and willed, not in themselves, but as referred to the end. Therefore the will is directed to them only in so far as it is directed to the end; so that what it wills in them, is the end. So, too, to understand is properly directed to things that are known in themselves, *i.e.*, first principles; but we do not speak of understanding with regard to things known through first principles, except in so far as we see the principles in those things. Now in

[9] *Op. cit.*, I, 6 (1096a 26).

morals the end is what principles are in speculative matters.[10]

Reply Obj. 1. The Philosopher is speaking of the will as signifying the simple act of the will, not as signifying the power of the will.[11]

Reply Obj. 2. There are different powers for objects that differ in genus and are mutually independent. For instance, sound and color are different genera of sensibles, to which are referred hearing and sight. But the useful and the righteous are not mutually independent, but are as that which is of itself and that which is in relation to another. Now such objects are always referred to the same power. For instance, the power of sight perceives both color and the light by which color is seen.

Reply Obj. 3. Not everything that diversifies habits diversifies the powers, since habits are certain determinations of powers to certain special acts. Moreover, every practical art considers both the end and the means. For the art of the helmsman does indeed consider the end, as that which it effects; and the means, as that which it commands. On the other hand, the ship-building art considers the means as that which it effects; but it considers that which is the end as that to which it refers what it effects. And again, in every practical art there is an end proper to it and the means that belong properly to that art.

[10] *Op. cit.*, VII, 8 (1151a 16).   [11] *Op. cit.*, III, 2 (1111b 26).

Question IX

ON THAT WHICH MOVES THE WILL

(*In Six Articles*)

WE MUST now consider what moves the will, and under this head there are six points of inquiry: (1) Whether the will is moved by the intellect? (2) Whether it is moved by the sensitive appetite? (3) Whether the will moves itself? (4) Whether it is moved by an extrinsic principle? (5) Whether it is moved by a heavenly body? (6) Whether the will is moved by God alone as by an extrinsic principle?

First Article

WHETHER THE WILL IS MOVED BY THE INTELLECT?

We proceed thus to the First Article:—

Objection 1. It would seem that the will is not moved by the intellect. For Augustine says on *Ps.* cxviii. 20 (*My soul hath coveted to long for Thy justifications*): *The intellect flies ahead, the desire follows sluggishly or not at all; we know what is good, but deeds delight us not.*[1] But it would not be so, if the will were moved by the intellect; for the movement of the movable results from the motion of the mover. Therefore the intellect does not move the will.

Obj. 2. Further, the intellect, in presenting the appetible object to the will, stands in relation to the will as the imagination in representing the appetible object to the sensitive appetite. But the imagination, in presenting the appetible object, does not move the sensitive appetite; indeed sometimes our imagination affects us no more than what is set before us in a picture, and moves us not at all.[2] Therefore neither does the intellect move the will.

Obj. 3. Further, the same is not mover and moved in respect of the same thing. But the will moves the intellect, for we exercise the intellect when we will. Therefore the intellect does not move the will.

On the contrary, The Philosopher says that *the appetible is a mover not moved, whereas the will is a mover moved.*[3]

[1] *Enarr. in Psalm.*, super CXVIII, 20, serm. VIII (PL 37, 1552).
[2] Aristotle, *De An.*, III, 3 (427b 23).   [3] *Op. cit.*, III, 6 (433b 10; b 16).

498

I answer that, A thing requires to be moved by something in so far as it is in potentiality to several things. For that which is in potentiality needs to be reduced to act by something actual; and to do this is to move. Now a power of the soul is found to be in potentiality to different things in two ways: first, with regard to acting and not acting; secondly, with regard to this or that action. Thus, the sight sometimes sees actually, and sometimes sees not; and sometimes it sees white, and sometimes black. It needs therefore a mover in two respects: viz., as to the exercise or use of the act, and as to the determination of the act. The first of these is on the part of the subject, which is sometimes acting, sometimes not acting; while the other is on the part of the object, by reason of which the act is specified.

The motion of the subject itself is due to some agent. And since every agent acts for an end, as was shown above,[4] the principle of this motion lies in the end. Hence it is that the art, which is concerned with the end, by its command moves the art which is concerned with the means; just as the *art of sailing commands the art of shipbuilding.*[5] Now the good in general, which has the nature of an end, is the object of the will. Consequently, in this respect, the will moves the other powers of the soul to their acts, for we make use of the other powers when we will. For the ends and the perfections of every other power are included under the object of the will as particular goods; and the art or power, to which the universal end belongs, always moves to their acts the arts or powers to which belong the particular ends included in the universal end. Thus the leader of an army, who intends the common good—*i.e.,* the order of the whole army—by his command moves one of the captains, who intends the order of one company.

On the other hand, the object moves, by determining the act, after the manner of a formal principle, whereby in natural things actions are specified, as heating by heat. Now the first formal principle is universal *being* and *truth,* which is the object of the intellect. And therefore by this kind of motion the intellect moves the will, as presenting its object to it.

Reply Obj. 1. The passage quoted proves, not that the intellect does not move, but that it does not move of necessity.

[4] Q. 1, a. 2.   [5] Aristotle, *Phys.,* II, 2 (194b 5).

Reply Obj. 2. Just as the imagination of a form without estimation of fitness or harmfulness does not move the sensitive appetite, so neither does the apprehension of the true without the aspect of goodness and desirability. Hence it is not the speculative intellect that moves, but the practical intellect.[6]

Reply Obj. 3. The will moves the intellect as to the exercise of its act, since even the true itself, which is the perfection of the intellect, is included in the universal good as a particular good. But as to the determination of the act, which the act derives from the object, the intellect moves the will; for the good itself is apprehended under a special aspect as contained in the universal true. It is therefore evident that the same is not mover and moved in the same respect.

Second Article

WHETHER THE WILL IS MOVED BY THE SENSITIVE APPETITE?

We proceed thus to the Second Article:—

Objection 1. It would seem that the will cannot be moved by the sensitive appetite. For *to move and to act is more excellent than to be passive,* as Augustine says.[7] But the sensitive appetite is less excellent than the will which is the intellectual appetite, just as sense is less excellent than intellect. Therefore, the sensitive appetite does not move the will.

Obj. 2. Further, no particular power can produce a universal effect. But the sensitive appetite is a particular power, because it follows the particular apprehension of sense. Therefore, it cannot cause the movement of the will, which movement is universal, as following the universal apprehension of the intellect.

Obj. 3. Further, as is proved in *Physics* viii., the mover is not moved by that which it moves, in such a way that there be reciprocal motion.[8] But the will moves the sensitive appetite, inasmuch as the sensitive appetite obeys the reason. Therefore the sensitive appetite does not move the will.

On the contrary, It is written (*Jas.* i. 14): *Every man is tempted by his own concupiscence, being drawn away and*

---

[6] Aristotle, *De An.,* III, 9 (432b 26); 10 (433a 17).   [7] *De Genesi ad Litt.,* XII, 16 (PL 34, 467).   [8] Aristotle, *Phys.,* VIII, 5 (257b 23).

allured. But man would not be drawn away by his concupiscence, unless his will were moved by the sensitive appetite, wherein concupiscence resides. Therefore the sensitive appetite moves the will.

I answer that, As we have stated above, that which is apprehended under the nature of what is good and befitting moves the will as an object. Now that a thing appear to be good and fitting happens from two causes, namely, from the condition either of the thing proposed, or of the one to whom it is proposed. For fitness is spoken of by way of relation, and hence it depends on both extremes. And hence it is that taste, according as it is variously disposed, takes to a thing in various ways, as being fitting or unfitting. Therefore as the Philosopher says: *According as a man is, such does the end seem to him.*[9]

Now it is evident that according to a passion of the sensitive appetite man is changed to a certain disposition. Therefore, according as man is affected by a passion, something seems to him fitting, which does not seem so when he is not so affected; and thus that seems good to a man when angered, which does not seem good when he is calm. It is in this way that the sensitive appetite moves the will, on the part of the object.

Reply Obj. 1. Nothing hinders that which is better absolutely and in itself from being less excellent in a certain respect. Accordingly, the will is absolutely more excellent than the sensitive appetite; but in respect of the man in whom a passion is predominant, in so far as he is subject to that passion, the sensitive appetite is more excellent.

Reply Obj. 2. Men's acts and choices are concerned with singulars. Therefore, from the very fact that the sensitive appetite is a particular power, it has great influence in disposing man so that something seems to him such or otherwise, in particular cases.

Reply Obj. 3. As the Philosopher says,[10] the reason, in which resides the will, moves the irascible and concupiscible powers by its command, not, indeed, *by a despotic rule,* as a slave is moved by his master, but by a *royal and political rule,* as free men are ruled by their governor, and can nevertheless act counter to his commands. Hence both the irascible

[9] *Eth.,* III, 5 (1114a 32).   [10] *Polit.,* I, 2 (1254b 5).

and concupiscible parts can move counter to the will, and, accordingly, nothing hinders the will from being moved by them at times.

Third Article

WHETHER THE WILL MOVES ITSELF?

We proceed thus to the Third Article:—

Objection 1. It would seem that the will does not move itself. For every mover, as such, is in act, whereas what is moved is in potentiality; for *movement is the act of that which is in potentiality, in so far as it is in potentiality.*[11] Now the same is not in potentiality and in act in respect of the same. Therefore nothing moves itself. Neither, therefore, can the will move itself.

Obj. 2. Further, the movable is moved when the mover is present. But the will is always present to itself. If, therefore it moved itself, it would always be moved, which is clearly false.

Obj. 3. Further, the will is moved by the intellect, as was stated above. If, therefore, the will moves itself, it would follow that the same thing is at once moved immediately by two movers; which seems unreasonable. Therefore the will does not move itself.

On the contrary, The will is mistress of its own act, and to it belongs to will and not to will. But this would not be so, had it not the power to move itself to will. Therefore it moves itself.

I answer that, As was stated above, it belongs to the will to move the other powers, by reason of the end which is the will's object. Now, as we have stated above, the end is in the order of appetibles what a principle is in the order of intelligibles.[12] But it is evident that the intellect, through its knowledge of a principle, reduces itself from potentiality to act as to its knowledge of conclusions; and thus it moves itself. And, in like manner, the will, through its volition of the end, moves itself to will the means.

Reply Obj. 1. It is not in the same respect that the will moves itself and is moved, and so neither is it in act and in potentiality in the same respect. But in so far as it actually

---

[11] Aristotle, *Phys.*, III, 1 (201a 10).   [12] Q. 8, a. 2.

wills the end, it reduces itself from potentiality to act concerning the means, so as to will them actually.

Reply Obj. 2. The power of the will is always actually present to itself; but the act of the will, by which it wills an end, is not always in the will. But it is by this act that it moves itself. Accordingly, it does not follow that it is always moving itself.

Reply Obj. 3. The will is moved in the same way by the intellect and by itself. By the intellect it is moved on the part of the object, whereas it is moved by itself, as to the exercise of its act, in respect of the end.

Fourth Article

WHETHER THE WILL IS MOVED BY AN EXTERIOR PRINCIPLE?

We proceed thus to the Fourth Article:—

Objection 1. It would seem that the will is not moved by anything exterior. For the movement of the will is voluntary. But it is of the nature of the voluntary act that it be from an intrinsic principle, just as it is of the nature of the natural act. Therefore the movement of the will is not from anything exterior.

Obj. 2. Further, the will cannot suffer violence, as was shown above.[13] But the violent act is one *the principle of which is outside the agent*.[14] Therefore the will cannot be moved by anything exterior.

Obj. 3. Further, that which is sufficiently moved by one mover needs not to be moved by another. But the will moves itself sufficiently. Therefore it is not moved by anything exterior.

On the contrary, The will is moved by the object, as was stated above. But the object of the will can be something exterior, offered to the sense. Therefore the will can be moved by something exterior.

I answer that, As far as the will is moved by the object, it is evident that it can be moved by something exterior. But in so far as it is moved in the exercise of its act, we must likewise hold it to be moved by some exterior principle. For everything that is at one time an agent actually, and at an-

[13] Q. 6, a. 4.   [14] Aristotle, *Eth.*, III, 1 (1110a 1).

other time an agent in potentiality, needs to be moved by a mover. Now it is evident that the will begins to will something, which previously it did not will. Therefore it must, of necessity, be moved by something to will it. And, indeed, it moves itself, as was stated above, in so far as through willing the end it reduces itself to the act of willing the means. Now it cannot do this without the aid of counsel. For when a man wills to be healed, he begins to reflect how this can be attained, and through this reflection he comes to the conclusion that he can be healed by a physician; and this he wills. But since he did not always actually will to have health, he must, of necessity, have begun, through something moving him, to will to be healed. And if the will moved itself to will this, it must, of necessity, have done this with the aid of counsel following some previous volition. But this process could not go on to infinity. Therefore we must, of necessity, suppose that the will advanced to its first movement in virtue of the instigation of some exterior mover, as Aristotle concludes in a chapter of the *Eudemian Ethics*.[15]

Reply Obj. 1. It is of the nature of the voluntary act that its principle be within the agent; but it is not necessary that this inward principle be a first principle unmoved by another. Therefore, though the voluntary act has an inward proximate principle, nevertheless, its first principle is from the outside. Thus, too, the first principle of natural movement, namely, that which moves nature, is from the outside.

Reply Obj. 2. For an act to be violent it is not enough that its principle be extrinsic, but we must add, *without the concurrence of him that suffers violence*. This does not happen when the will is moved by an exterior principle; for it is the will that wills, though moved by another. But this movement would be violent, if it were counter to the movement of the will; which in the present case is impossible, since then the will would will and not will the same thing.

Reply Obj. 3. The will moves itself sufficiently in one respect, and in its own order, that is to say, as a proximate agent; but it cannot move itself in every respect, as we have shown. Therefore it needs to be moved by another as first mover.

[15] *Eth. Eudem.*, VII, 14 (1248a 14).

Fifth Article

WHETHER THE WILL IS MOVED BY A HEAVENLY BODY?

We proceed thus to the Fifth Article:—

Objection 1. It would seem that the human will is moved by a heavenly body. For all various and multiform movements are reduced, as to their cause, to a uniform movement which is that of the heavens, as is proved by *Physics* viii.[16] But human movements are various and multiform, since they begin to be, when previously they were not. Therefore they are reduced, as to their cause, to the movement of the heavens, which is uniform according to its nature.

Obj. 2. Further, according to Augustine *the lower bodies are moved by the higher*.[17] But the movements of the human body, which are caused by the will, could not be reduced to the movement of the heavens, as to their cause, unless the will too were moved by the heavens. Therefore the heavens move the human will.

Obj. 3. Further, by observing the heavenly bodies astrologers foretell the truth about future human acts, which are caused by the will. But this would not be so if the heavenly bodies could not move man's will. Therefore the human will is moved by a heavenly body.

On the contrary, Damascene says that *the heavenly bodies are not the causes of our acts.*[18] But they would be, if the will, which is the principle of human acts, were moved by the heavenly bodies. Therefore the will is not moved by the heavenly bodies.

I answer that, It is evident that the will can be moved by the heavenly bodies in the same way as it is moved by its exterior object, that is to say, in so far as exterior bodies, which move the will through being offered to the senses, and also the organs themselves of the sensitive powers, are subject to the movements of the heavenly bodies.

But some have maintained that heavenly bodies have an influence directly on the human will, in the same way as

[16] Aristotle, *Phys.*, VIII, 9 (265a 27); cf. *op. cit.*, IV, 14 (223b 18).
[17] *De Trin.*, III, 4 (PL 42, 873).   [18] *De Fide Orth.*, II, 7 (PG 94, 893).

some exterior agent moves the will, as to the exercise of its act.[19] But this is impossible. For the *will,* as is stated in *De Anima* iii., *is in the reason.*[20] Now the reason is a power of the soul not bound to a bodily organ, and so it follows that the will is a power absolutely incorporeal and immaterial. But it is evident that no body can act on what is incorporeal, but rather the reverse; for things incorporeal and immaterial have a power that is more formal and more universal than any corporeal things. Therefore it is impossible for a heavenly body to act directly on the intellect or the will. For this reason Aristotle ascribed to those who held that intellect differs not from the sense,[21] the theory that *such is the will of men, as is the day which the father of men and of gods brings on*[22] (referring to Jupiter, by whom they understand the entire heavens). For all the sensitive powers, since they are acts of bodily organs, can be moved accidentally by the heavenly bodies—*i.e.,* when those bodies are moved, whose acts they are.

But since it has been stated that the intellectual appetite is moved, in a fashion, by the sensitive appetite, the movements of the heavenly bodies have an indirect bearing on the will, in so far, namely, as the will happens to be moved by the passions of the sensitive appetite.

Reply Obj. 1. The multiform movements of the human will are reduced to some uniform cause, which, however, is above the intellect and will. This can be said, not of any body, but of some superior immaterial substance. Therefore there is no need for the movement of the will to be reduced to the movement of the heavens as to its cause.

Reply Obj. 2. The movements of the human body are reduced, as to their cause, to the movement of a heavenly body, in so far as the disposition suitable to a particular movement is somewhat due to the influence of heavenly bodies;—also, in so far as the sensitive appetite is stirred by the influence of heavenly bodies;—and again, in so far as exterior bodies are moved in accordance with the movement of heavenly bodies, at whose presence, the will begins to will or not to will something: *e.g.,* when the body is chilled, we

---

[19] Cf. H. Denifle, *Chartularium,* no. 432, error 4 (I, 487).   [20] Aristotle, *De An.,* III, 9 (432b 5).   [21] *E.g.,* Empedocles: cf. Aristotle, *De An.,* III, 3 (427a 21).   [22] *Ibid.* (427a 25).—Homer, *Odyss.,* XVIII, 136.

begin to wish to make the fire. But this movement of the will is on the part of the object offered from the outside, not on the part of an inward instigation.

Reply Obj. 3. As was stated above, the sensitive appetite is the act of a bodily organ.[23] Therefore there is no reason why man should not be prone to anger or concupiscence, or some like passion, by reason of the influence of heavenly bodies, just as by reason of his natural temperament. Now the majority of men are led by the passions, which the wise alone resist. Consequently, in the majority of cases predictions about human acts, gathered from the observation of the heavenly bodies, are fulfilled. Nevertheless, as Ptolemy says, *the wise man governs the stars,*[24] as though to say that by resisting his passions, he opposes his will, which is free and in no way subject to the movement of the heavens, to such effects of the heavenly bodies.

Or, as Augustine says: *We must confess that when the truth is foretold by astrologers, this is due to some most hidden inspiration, to which the human mind is subject without knowing it. And since this is done in order to deceive man, it must be the work of the lying spirits.*[25]

Sixth Article

WHETHER THE WILL IS MOVED BY GOD ALONE, AS EXTERIOR PRINCIPLE?

We proceed thus to the Sixth Article:—

Objection 1. It would seem that the will is not moved by God alone as exterior principle. For it is natural that the inferior be moved by its superior; and thus the lower bodies are moved by the heavenly bodies. But there is something which is higher than the will of man and below God, namely, the angel. Therefore man's will can be moved by an angel also, as exterior principle.

Obj. 2. Further, the act of the will follows the act of the intellect. But man's intellect is reduced to act, not by God alone, but also by the angel who illumines it, as Dionysius

[23] *S. T.,* I, q. 84, a. 6 and 7.   [24] *Centiloquium,* verba 4-8.—Cf. also St. Albert, *In II Sent.,* d. xv, a. 4 (XXVII, 276).   [25] *De Genesi ad Litt.,* II, 17 (PL 34, 278).

says.[26] For the same reason, therefore, the will is moved by an angel.

Obj. 3. Further, God is not cause of other than good things, according to *Gen.* i. 31: *God saw all the things that He had made, and they were very good.* If, therefore, man's will were moved by God alone, it would never be moved to evil; and yet it is the will by which *we sin and by which we do the right,* as Augustine says.[27]

On the contrary, It is written (*Phil.* ii. 13): *It is God Who worketh in us both to will and to accomplish.*

I answer that, The movement of the will is from within, as is also natural movement. Now although it is possible for something to move a natural thing, without being the cause of the nature of the thing moved, yet that alone which is in some way the cause of a thing's nature can cause a natural movement in that thing. For a stone is moved upwards by a man, who is not the cause of the stone's nature, but this movement is not natural to the stone; but the natural movement of the stone is caused by none other than the cause of its nature. Therefore it is said in *Physics* viii. that the generator moves locally heavy and light things.[28] Accordingly, man endowed with a will is sometimes moved by something that is not his cause; but that his voluntary movement be from an exterior principle which is not the cause of his will, is impossible.

But the cause of the will can be none other than God. And this is evident for two reasons. First, because the will is a power of the rational soul, which is caused by God alone through creation, as was stated in the First Part.[29] Secondly, it is evident from the fact that the will is ordained to the universal good. Therefore nothing else can be the cause of the will, except God Himself, Who is the universal good, while every other good is good by participation, and is some particular good; and a particular cause does not give a universal inclination. Hence, neither can primary matter, which is in potentiality to all forms, be created by some particular agent.

Reply Obj. 1. An angel is not above man in such a way as to be the cause of his will, as the heavenly bodies are the

---

[26] *De Cael. Hier.,* IV, 2 (PG 3, 180).   [27] *Retract.,* I, 9 (PL 32, 596).
[28] Aristotle, *Phys.,* VIII, 4 (255b 35).   [29] *S. T.,* I, q. 90, a. 2 and 3.

causes of natural forms, from which result the natural movements of natural bodies.

Reply Obj. 2. Man's intellect is moved by an angel, on the part of the object, which by the power of the angelic light is proposed to man's knowledge. And in this way the will also can be moved by a creature from the outside, as was stated above.

Reply Obj. 3. God moves man's will, as the Universal Mover, to the universal object of the will, which is the good. And without this universal motion man cannot will anything. But man determines himself by his reason to will this or that, which is a true or apparent good. Nevertheless, sometimes God moves some specially to the willing of something determinate, which is good; as in the case of those whom He moves by grace, as we shall state later on.[30]

[30] Q. 109, a. 2.

ON INTENTION

(*In Five Articles*)

WE MUST now consider intention, concerning which there are five points of inquiry: (1) Whether intention is an act of the intellect or of the will? (2) Whether it is only of the last end? (3) Whether one can intend two things at the same time? (4) Whether the intention of the end is the same act as the volition of the means to the end? (5) Whether intention befits irrational animals?

First Article

WHETHER INTENTION IS AN ACT OF THE INTELLECT OR OF THE WILL?

We proceed thus to the First Article:—

Objection 1. It would seem that intention is an act of the intellect, and not of the will. For it is written (*Matt.* vi. 22): *If thy eye be single, thy whole body shall be lightsome,* where, according to Augustine, the eye signifies intention.[1] But since the eye is the organ of sight, it signifies the apprehensive power. Therefore intention is not an act of the appetitive power, but of the apprehensive power.

Obj. 2. Further, Augustine says that Our Lord spoke of intention as a light, when He said (*Matt.* vi. 23): *If the light that is in thee be darkness,* etc.[2] But light pertains to knowledge. Therefore intention does too.

Obj. 3. Further, intention signifies a kind of ordaining to an end. But to ordain is an act of reason. Therefore intention belongs, not to the will, but to the reason.

Obj. 4. Further, an act of the will is either of the end or of the means. But the act of the will in respect of the end is called volition, or enjoyment, and with regard to the means, it is called choice. Intention is distinct from these. Therefore it is not an act of the will.

On the contrary, Augustine says that *the intention of the will unites the sight to the seen body; and likewise it unites*

---

[1] *De Serm. Dom.,* II, 13 (PL 34, 1289).   [2] *Ibid.*

*an image existing in the memory to the gaze of the soul
thinking within itself.*[3] Therefore intention is an act of the
will.

I answer that, Intention, as the very term denotes, signifies, *to tend to something.* Now both the action of the mover
and the movement of the thing moved tend to something.
But that the movement of the thing moved tends to anything
is due to the action of the mover. Consequently, intention
belongs first and principally to that which moves to the
end; and so we say that an architect, or anyone who is in
authority, moves others by his command to that which he
intends. Now it is the will that moves all the other powers
of the soul to the end, as was shown above.[4] Therefore it
is evident that intention, properly speaking, is an act of the
will.

Reply Obj. 1. The eye designates intention figuratively,
not because intention has reference to knowledge, but because it presupposes knowledge, which proposes to the will
the end to which the latter moves. So, too, we see ahead
with the eye whither we should tend with our bodies.

Reply Obj. 2. Intention is called a light because it is manifest to him who intends. Therefore works are called darkness
because a man knows what he intends, but knows not what
the result may be, as Augustine expounds in the same reference.

Reply Obj. 3. The will does not ordain, but tends to something according to the order of reason. Consequently, this
term *intention* indicates an act of the will, presupposing the
act by which the reason orders something to the end.

Reply Obj. 4. Intention is an act of the will in relation to
the end. Now the will stands in a threefold relation to the
end. First, absolutely, and thus we have *volition,* by which
we will absolutely to have health and so forth. Secondly, it
considers the end as its place of rest, and thus *enjoyment*
regards the end. Thirdly, it considers the end as the term
towards which something is ordained; and thus *intention*
regards the end. For when we speak of intending to have
health, we mean not only that we will to have it, but that
we will to reach it by means of something else.

[3] *De Trin.,* XI, 4; 8; 9 (PL 42, 990; 994; 996).   [4] Q. 9, a. 1.

Second Article

WHETHER INTENTION IS ONLY OF THE LAST END?

We proceed thus to the Second Article:—

Objection 1. It would seem that intention is only of the last end. For it is said in the book of Prosper's *Sentences: The intention of the heart is a cry to God.*[5] But God is the last end of the human heart. Therefore intention always regards the last end.

Obj. 2. Further, intention regards the end as the terminus, as was stated above. But a terminus is something last. Therefore intention always regards the last end.

Obj. 3. Further, just as intention regards the end, so does enjoyment. But enjoyment is always of the last end. Therefore intention is too.

On the contrary, There is but one last end of human volition, viz., happiness, as was stated above.[6] If, therefore, intentions were only of the last end, men would not have different intentions; which is evidently false.

I answer that, As we have stated above, intention regards the end as a terminus of the movement of the will. Now a terminus of movement may be taken in two ways. First, the very last terminus, when the movement comes to a stop; and this is the terminus of the whole movement. Secondly, some point midway, which is the beginning of one part of the movement and the end or terminus of the other. Thus, in the movement from A to C through B, C is the last terminus, while B is a terminus, but not the last. And intention can be of both. Consequently, though intention is always of the end, it need not always be of the last end.

Reply Obj. 1. The intention of the heart is called a cry to God, not because God is always the object of intention, but because He sees our intention.—Or because, when we pray, we direct our intention to God, which intention has the force of a cry.

Reply Obj. 2. A terminus is something last, not always in respect of the whole, but sometimes in respect of a part.

Reply Obj. 3. Enjoyment signifies rest in the end; and this belongs to the last end alone. But intention signifies movement towards an end, not rest. Therefore the comparison does not hold.

[5] Prosper of Aquitaine, *Sent.* C (PL 51, 441).   [6] Q. 1, a. 7.

ON CHOICE, WHICH IS AN ACT OF THE WILL IN RELATION TO THE MEANS TO THE END

(*In Six Articles*)

WE MUST now consider the acts of the will which are related to the means to the end. There are three of them: *to choose*, *to consent* and *to use*. Now choice is preceded by counsel. First of all, then, we must consider choice; secondly, counsel;[1] thirdly, consent;[2] fourthly, use.[3]

Concerning choice there are six points of inquiry: (1) Of what power is it the act, whether of the will or of the reason? (2) Whether choice is to be found in irrational animals? (3) Whether choice is only of the means to the end, or sometimes also of the end? (4) Whether choice is only of things that we do ourselves? (5) Whether choice is only of possible things? (6) Whether man chooses of necessity or freely?

First Article

WHETHER CHOICE IS AN ACT OF THE WILL OR OF THE REASON?

Objection 1. It would seem that choice is an act, not of the will, but of the reason. For choice expresses a certain comparison, whereby one thing is preferred to another. But to compare is an act of reason. Therefore choice is an act of reason.

Obj. 2. Further, it belongs to the same power to form a syllogism and to draw the conclusion. But, in practical matters, it is the reason that forms syllogisms. Since, therefore, choice is a kind of conclusion in practical matters, as is stated in *Ethics* vii.,[4] it seems that it is an act of reason.

Obj. 3. Further, ignorance does not belong to the will but to the cognitive power. Now there is an *ignorance attending choice,* as is stated in *Ethics* iii.[5] Therefore it seems that choice does not belong to the will but to the reason.

On the contrary, The Philosopher says that choice is *the*

[1] Q. 14.   [2] Q. 15.   [3] Q. 16.   [4] Cf. Aristotle, *Eth.*, III, 3 (1113a 4; a 11).   [5] *Op. cit.*, III, 1 (1110b 31).

desire of things which are in our power.[6] But desire is an act of will. Therefore choice is too.

I answer that, The term *choice* expresses something belonging to the reason or intellect, and something belonging to the will; for the Philosopher says that choice is either *intellect influenced by appetite or appetite influenced by intellect.*[7] Now whenever two things concur to make one, one of them is as a form in relation to the other. Hence Gregory of Nyssa says that choice *is neither desire only, nor counsel only, but a combination of the two. For just as we say that an animal is composed of soul and body, and that it is neither only the body, nor only the soul, but both, so is it with choice.*[8]

Now we must observe, as regards the acts of the soul, that an act belonging essentially to some power or habit receives its form or species from a higher power or habit, according as the inferior is ordered by the superior. For if a man were to perform an act of fortitude for the love of God, that act is materially an act of fortitude, but formally, an act of charity. Now it is evident that, in a sense, reason precedes the will and directs its act, namely, in so far as the will tends to its object according to the order of reason; for the apprehensive power presents to the appetite its object. Accordingly, that act whereby the will tends to something proposed to it as being good, through being ordained to the end by the reason, is materially an act of the will, but formally an act of the reason. Now in such matters, the substance of the act is as the matter in comparison to the order imposed by the higher power. Therefore, choice is substantially, not an act of the reason, but of the will; for choice is accomplished in a certain movement of the soul towards the good which is chosen. Consequently, it is evidently an act of the appetitive power.

Reply Obj. 1. Choice implies a previous comparison, but not that it consists in the comparison itself.

Reply Obj. 2. It is quite true that it is for the reason to draw the conclusion of a practical syllogism; and it is called *a decision* or *judgment,* to be followed by *choice.* And for this reason the conclusion seems to belong to the act of choice, as to that which results from it.

Reply Obj. 3. In speaking *of ignorance attending choice,*

---

[6] *Op. cit.,* III, 3 (1113a 9).   [7] *Op. cit.,* VI, 2 (1139b 4).   [8] Cf. Nemesius, *De Nat. Hom.,* XXXIII (PG 40, 733).

we do not mean that choice itself is a sort of knowledge, but that there is ignorance of what ought to be chosen.

Third Article

WHETHER CHOICE IS ONLY OF THE MEANS TO THE END OR SOMETIMES ALSO OF THE END?

We proceed thus to the Third Article:—

Objection 1. It would seem that choice is not only of the means to the end. For the Philosopher says that *virtue makes us choose rightly; but it is not the part of virtue, but of some other power, to direct rightly those things which are to be done for its sake.*[9] But that for the sake of which something is done is the end. Therefore choice is of the end.

Obj. 2. Further, choice signifies preference of one thing to another. But just as there can be preference of means, so can there be preference of ends. Therefore choice can be of ends, just as it can be of means.

On the contrary, The Philosopher says that *volition is of the end, but choice of the means.*[10]

I answer that, As we have already stated, choice follows the decision or judgment which is, as it were, the conclusion of a practical syllogism. Hence that which is the conclusion of a practical syllogism is the matter of choice. Now in practical things the end stands in the position of a principle, not of a conclusion, as the Philosopher says.[11] Therefore the end, as such, is not a matter of choice.

But just as in speculative matters nothing hinders the principle of one demonstration or of one science from being the conclusion of another demonstration or science (although the first indemonstrable principle cannot be the conclusion of any demonstration or science), so, too, that which is the end in one operation may be ordained to something as an end. And in this way it is a matter of choice. Thus in the work of a physician health is the end, and so it is not a matter of choice for a physician, but a matter of principle. But the health of the body is ordained to the good of the soul, and, consequently, with one who has charge of the soul's health, health or sickness may be a matter of choice; for the Apostle

[9] *Eth.,* VI, 12 (1144a 20).   [10] *Op. cit.,* III, 2 (1111b 26).
[11] *Phys.,* II, 9 (200a 20).

says (*2 Cor.* xii. 10): *For when I am weak, then am I power-ful.* But the last end is in no way a matter of choice.

Reply Obj. 1. The proper ends of the virtues are ordained to happiness as to their last end. And thus it is that they can be a matter of choice.

Reply Obj. 2. As was stated above, there is but one last end.[12] Accordingly, wherever there are several ends, they can be the subject of choice, in so far as they are ordained to a further end.

Fourth Article

WHETHER CHOICE IS OF THOSE THINGS ONLY THAT ARE DONE BY US?

We proceed thus to the Fourth Article:—

Objection 1. It would seem that choice is not only in re-spect of human acts. For choice is of the means. Now, not only acts, but also the organs, are means.[13] Therefore choice is not concerned only with human acts.

Obj. 2. Further, action is distinct from contemplation. But choice has a place even in contemplation, in so far, namely, as one opinion is preferred to another. Therefore choice is not concerned with human acts alone.

Obj. 3. Further, men are chosen for certain posts, whether secular or ecclesiastical, by those who exercise no action in their regard. Therefore choice is not concerned with human acts alone.

On the contrary, The Philosopher says that *no man chooses save what he thinks he can do himself.*[14]

I answer that, Just as intention regards the end, so choice regards the means. Now the end is either an action or a thing. And when the end is a thing, some human action must inter-vene, and this either in so far as man produces the thing which is the end, as the physician produces health (and so the production of health is said to be the end of the physi-cian), or in so far as man, in some fashion, uses or enjoys the thing which is the end: *e.g.,* for the miser, money or the possession of money is the end. The same is to be said of the

[12] Q. 1, a. 5.   [13] Aristotle, *Phys.,* II, 3 (195a 1).   [14] *Eth.,* III, 2 (1111b 25).

means. For the means must needs be either an action, or a thing, with some action intervening whereby man either makes the thing which is the means, or puts it to some use. And thus it is that choice is always in regard to human acts.

Reply Obj. 1. The organs are ordained to the end inasmuch as man makes use of them for the sake of the end.

Reply Obj. 2. In contemplation itself there is the act of the intellect assenting to this or that opinion. It is exterior action that is put in contradistinction to contemplation.

Reply Obj. 3. When a man chooses someone for a bishopric or some high position in the state, he chooses to name that man to that post. Otherwise, if he had no right to act in the appointment of the bishop or prince, he would have no right to choose. Likewise, whenever we speak of one thing being chosen in preference to another, it is in conjunction with some action of the chooser.

Fifth Article

WHETHER CHOICE IS ONLY OF POSSIBLE THINGS?

We proceed thus to the Fifth Article:—

Objection 1. It would seem that choice is not only of possible things. For choice is an act of the will, as was stated above. Now *there is a willing of the possible and the impossible.*[15] Therefore there is also a choice of them.

Obj. 2. Further, choice is of things done by us, as was stated above. Therefore it matters not, as far as the act of choosing is concerned, whether one choose that which is impossible in itself, or that which is impossible to the chooser. Now it often happens that we are unable to accomplish what we choose, so that this proves to be impossible to us. Therefore choice is of the impossible.

Obj. 3. Further, to try to do a thing is to choose to do it. But the Blessed Benedict says that, if the superior command what is impossible, it should be attempted.[16] Therefore choice can be of the impossible.

On the contrary, The Philosopher says that *there is no choice of the impossible.*[17]

---

[15] *Ibid.* (1111b 22).   [16] *Reg. ad Mon.,* LXVIII (PL 66, 917).
[17] *Eth.,* III, 2 (1111b 20).

I answer that, As was stated above, our choice is always concerned with our actions. Now whatever is done by us is possible to us. Therefore we must needs say that choice is only of possible things.

Moreover, the reason for choosing a thing is that we may gain the end through it, or that it conduces to an end. But what is impossible cannot conduce to an end. A sign of this is that when men, in taking counsel together, come to something that is impossible to them, they depart, as being unable to proceed with the business.

Again, this is evident if we examine the preceding process of the reason. For the means, which are the object of choice, are to the end as the conclusion is to the principle. Now it is clear that an impossible conclusion does not follow from a possible principle. Therefore an end cannot be possible unless the means be possible. Now no one is moved to the impossible. Consequently, no one would tend to the end, save for the fact that the means appear to be possible. Therefore the impossible is not the object of choice.

Reply Obj. 1. The will stands between the intellect and the external action; for the intellect proposes to the will its object, and the will causes the external action. Hence the principle of the movement in the will is to be found in the intellect, which apprehends something as a universal good; but the term or perfection of the will's act is to be observed in its relation to the action by which a man tends to the attainment of a thing, for the movement of the will is from the soul to the thing. Consequently, the perfection of the act of the will is in respect of something that is good for one to do. Now this cannot be something impossible. Therefore, perfect willing is only in respect of what is possible and good for him that wills. But imperfect willing is in respect of the impossible; and by some it is called *velleity*, because, namely, one would will [*vellet*] such a thing, were it possible. But choice is an act of the will already fixed on something to be done by the chooser. And therefore it is by no means of anything but what is possible.

Reply Obj. 2. Since the object of the will is the apprehended good, we must judge of the object of the will according as it is apprehended. And so, just as sometimes the will tends to something which is apprehended as good, and yet is not really good, so choice is sometimes made of something apprehended as possible to the chooser, and yet impossible to him.

Reply Obj. 3. The reason for this is that the subject should not rely on his own judgment to decide whether a certain thing is possible; but in each case should stand by his superior's judgment.

ON THE GOODNESS AND MALICE OF HUMAN ACTS, IN GENERAL

(*In Eleven Articles*)

WE MUST now consider the goodness and malice of human acts. First, we must consider how a human act is good or evil; secondly, what results from the goodness or malice of a human act, as merit or demerit, sin and guilt.[1]

Under the first head there will be a threefold consideration: the first will be of the goodness and malice of human acts, in general; the second, of the goodness and malice of internal acts;[2] the third, of the goodness and malice of external acts.[3]

Concerning the first there are eleven points of inquiry: (1) Whether every human action is good, or are there evil actions? (2) Whether the good or evil of a human act is derived from its object? (3) Whether it is derived from a circumstance? (4) Whether it is derived from the end? (5) Whether a human action is good or evil in its species? (6) Whether an act has the species of good or evil from its end? (7) Whether the species derived from the end is contained under the species derived from the object, as under its genus, or conversely? (8) Whether any act is indifferent in its species? (9) Whether an individual act can be indifferent? (10) Whether a circumstance places a moral act in a species of good or evil? (11) Whether every circumstance that makes an act better or worse places the moral act in a species of good or evil?

First Article

WHETHER EVERY HUMAN ACTION IS GOOD, OR ARE THERE EVIL ACTIONS?

We proceed thus to the First Article:—

Objection 1. It would seem that every human action is good, and that none is evil. For Dionysius says that evil acts not, save by the power of the good.[4] But no evil is done by the power of the good. Therefore no action is evil.

[1] Q. 21.   [2] Q. 19.   [3] Q. 20.   [4] *De Div. Nom.*, IV, 20 (PG 3, 717).

Obj. 2. Further, nothing acts except in so far as it is in act. Now a thing is evil, not according as it is in act, but according as its potentiality is deprived of act; whereas in so far as its potentiality is perfected by act, it is good, as is stated in *Metaph.* ix.[5] Therefore nothing acts in so far as it is evil, but only according as it is good. Therefore every action is good, and none is evil.

Obj. 3. Further, evil cannot be a cause, save accidentally, as Dionysius declares.[6] But every action has some effect which is proper to it. Therefore no action is evil, but every action is good.

On the contrary, Our Lord said (*Jo.* iii. 20): *Every one that doth evil, hateth the light.* Therefore some actions of man are evil.

I answer that, We must speak of good and evil in actions as of good and evil in things, because such as everything is, such is the act that it produces. Now in things, each one has so much good as it has being, for good and being are convertible, as was stated in the First Part.[7] But God alone has the whole fullness of His Being in a manner which is one and simple, whereas every other thing has its proper fullness of being in a certain multiplicity. Therefore it happens with some things, that they have being in some respect, and yet they are lacking in the fullness of being due to them. Thus the fullness of human being requires a composite of soul and body, having all the powers and instruments of knowledge and movement; and so if any man be lacking in any of these, he is lacking in something due to the fullness of his being. Hence, as much as he has of being, so much has he of goodness, while so far as something is lacking in the fullness of its being, so far does this fall short of goodness, and is said to be evil. Thus a blind man is possessed of goodness inasmuch as he lives, and of evil, inasmuch as he lacks sight. That, however, which has nothing of being or goodness, could not be said to be either evil or good. But since this same fullness of being is of the very notion of good, if a thing be lacking in its due fullness of being, it is not said to be good absolutely, but in a certain respect, inasmuch as it is a being;

[5] Aristotle, *Metaph.*, VIII, 9 (1051a 4; a 29).   [6] *De Div. Nom.*, IV, 20; 32 (PG 3, 717; 732).   [7] *S. T.*, I, q. 5, a. 1 and 3; q. 17, a. 4, ad 2.

although it can be called a being absolutely, and a non-being in a certain respect, as was stated in the First Part.[8]

We must therefore say that every action has goodness in so far as it has being, whereas it is lacking in goodness in so far as it is lacking in something that is due to its fullness of being; and thus it is said to be evil, for instance, if it lacks the measure determined by reason, or its due place, or something of the kind.

Reply Obj. 1. Evil acts in the power of a deficient good. For if there were nothing of good there, there would be neither being nor possibility of action. On the other hand, if good were not deficient, there would be no evil. Consequently, the action done is a deficient good, which is good in a certain respect, but evil absolutely.

Reply Obj. 2. Nothing hinders a thing from being in act in a certain respect, so that it can act, and in a certain respect deficient in act, so as to cause a deficient act. Thus, a blind man has actually the power of walking, whereby he is able to walk; but inasmuch as he is deprived of sight, he suffers a defect in walking by stumbling when he walks.

Reply Obj. 3. An evil action can have a proper effect, according to the goodness and being that it has. Thus, adultery is the cause of human generation, inasmuch as it implies union of male and female, but not inasmuch as it lacks the order of reason.

Second Article

WHETHER THE GOOD OR EVIL OF A MAN'S ACTION IS DERIVED FROM ITS OBJECT?

We proceed thus to the Second Article:—

Objection 1. It would seem that the good or evil of an action is not derived from its object. For the object of any action is a thing. But *evil is not in things, but in the sinner's use of them,* as Augustine says.[9] Therefore the good or evil of a human action is not derived from its object.

Obj. 2. Further, the object is compared to the action as its matter. But the goodness of a thing is not from its matter, but rather from the form, which is an act. Therefore good and evil in actions is not derived from their object.

[8] *S. T.,* I, q. 5, a. 1, ad 1. [9] *De Doct. Christ.,* III, 12 (PL 34, 73).

Obj. 3. Further, the object of an active power is compared to the action as effect to cause. But the goodness of a cause does not depend on its effect; rather is it the reverse. Therefore good or evil in actions is not derived from their object.

On the contrary, It is written (*Osee* ix. 10): *They became abominable as those things which they loved.* Now man becomes abominable to God because of the malice of his action. Therefore the malice of his action is according to the evil objects that man loves. And the same applies to the goodness of his action.

I answer that, As was stated above, the good or evil of an action, as of other things, depends on its fullness of being or its lack of that fullness. Now the first thing that belongs to the fullness of being seems to be that which gives a thing its species. And just as a natural thing has its species from its form, so an action has its species from its object, just as does movement from its term. Therefore, just as the primary goodness of a natural thing is derived from its form, which gives it its species, so the primary goodness of a moral action is derived from its suitable object; and so some call such an action *good in its genus,*[10] *e.g.,* to make use of what is one's own. And just as, in natural things, the primary evil is when a generated thing does not realize its specific form (for instance, if instead of a man, something else be generated), so the primary evil in moral actions is that which is from the object, for instance, *to take what belongs to another.* Furthermore, this action is said to be *evil in its genus* (genus here stands for species, just as we apply the term *mankind* [*humanum genus*] to the whole human species).

Reply Obj. 1. Although external things are good in themselves, nevertheless, they have not always a due proportion to this or that action. And so, inasmuch as they are considered as objects of such actions, they have not the nature of a good.

Reply Obj. 2. The object is not the matter *out of which,* but the matter *about which,* and stands in relation to the act as its form, as it were, through giving it its species.

Reply Obj. 3. The object of human action is not always the object of an active power. For the appetitive power is in a way passive, in so far as it is moved by the appetible ob-

---

[10] Cf. Peter Lombard, *Sent.,* II, xxxvi, 6 (I, 504).

ject; and yet it is a principle of human actions.—Nor again have the objects of the active powers always the nature of an effect, but only when they are already transformed. Thus food, when transformed, is the effect of the nutritive power, whereas food, before being transformed, stands in relation to the nutritive power as the matter about which it exercises its operation. Now since the object is in some way the effect of the active power, it follows that it is the term of its action, and consequently that it gives it its form and species, since movement derives its species from its terms.—Moreover, although the goodness of an action is not caused by the goodness of its effect, yet an action is said to be good from the fact that it can produce a good effect. Consequently, the very proportion of an action to its effect is the measure of its goodness.

Third Article

WHETHER MAN'S ACTION IS GOOD OR EVIL FROM A CIRCUMSTANCE?

We proceed thus to the Third Article:—

Objection 1. It would seem that an action is not good or evil from a circumstance. For circumstances stand around [*circumstant*] an action, as being outside it, as was stated above.[11] But *good and evil are in things themselves,* as is stated in *Metaph.* vi.[12] Therefore an action does not derive goodness or malice from a circumstance.

Obj. 2. Further, the goodness or malice of an action is considered principally in the doctrine of morals. But since circumstances are accidents of actions, it seems that they are outside the scope of an art, because *no art takes notice of what is accidental.*[13] Therefore the goodness or malice of an action is not taken from a circumstance.

Obj. 3. Further, that which belongs to a thing through its substance is not attributed to it through an accident. But good and evil belong to an action in its substance, for an action can be good or evil in its genus, as was stated above. Therefore an action is not good or evil from a circumstance.

On the contrary, The Philosopher says that a virtuous man

---

[11] Q. 7, a. 1.   [12] Aristotle, *Metaph.,* V, 4 (1027b 25).   [13] *Op. cit.,* V, 2 (1026b 4).

acts as he should, and when he should, and so on, according to the other circumstances.[14] Therefore, on the other hand, the vicious man, in the matter of each vice, acts when he should not, or where he should not, and so on with the other circumstances. Therefore human actions are good or evil according to circumstances.

I answer that, In natural things, it is to be noted that the whole fullness of perfection due to a thing is not from the mere substantial form, that gives it its species, for a thing derives much from supervening accidents, as man does from shape, color and the like; and if any one of these accidents be out of due proportion, evil is the result. So it is with action. For the fullness of its goodness does not consist wholly in its species, but also in certain additions which accrue to it by reason of certain accidents; and such are its due circumstances. Therefore, if something be wanting that is requisite as a due circumstance, the action will be evil.

Reply Obj. 1. Circumstances are outside an action inasmuch as they are not part of its essence; but they are in an action as its accidents. So, too, accidents in natural substances are outside the essence.

Reply Obj. 2. Every accident is not accidentally in its subject; for some are proper accidents, and of these every art takes notice. And thus it is that the circumstances of actions are considered in the doctrine of morals.

Reply Obj. 3. Since good and being are convertible, according as being is predicated substantially and accidentally, so good is predicated of a thing both in respect of its essential being, and in respect of its accidental being; and this, both in natural things and in moral actions.

Fourth Article

WHETHER A HUMAN ACTION IS GOOD OR EVIL FROM ITS END?

We proceed thus to the Fourth Article:—

Objection 1. It would seem that the good and evil in human actions are not from the end. For Dionysius says that *nothing acts with a view to evil.*[15] If, therefore, an action were good

---

[14] *Eth.,* II, 3 (1104b 26).   [15] *De Div. Nom.,* IV, 19; 31 (PG 3, 716; 732).

or evil from its end, no action would be evil. Which is clearly false.

Obj. 2. Further, the goodness of an action is something in the action. But the end is an extrinsic cause. Therefore an action is not said to be good or evil according to its end.

Obj. 3. Further, a good action may happen to be ordered to an evil end, as when a man gives an alms from vainglory; and conversely, an evil action may happen to be ordered to a good end, as a theft committed in order to give something to the poor. Therefore an action is not good or evil from its end.

On the contrary, Boethius says that *if the end is good, the thing is good,* and if the end be evil, the thing also is evil.[16]

I answer that, The disposition of things as to goodness is the same as their disposition as to being. But in some things the being does not depend on another, and in these it suffices to consider their being absolutely. But there are things the being of which depends on something else, and hence concerning them we must consider their being in its relation to the cause on which it depends. Now just as the being of a thing depends on the agent and the form, so the goodness of a thing depends on its end. Hence in the divine Persons, Whose goodness does not depend on another, the measure of goodness is not taken from the end. But human actions, and other things, the goodness of which depends on something else, have a measure of goodness from the end on which they depend, in addition to that goodness which is in them absolutely.

Accordingly, a fourfold goodness may be considered in a human action. First, that goodness which, as an action, it derives from its genus; since, as much as it has of action and being, so much has it of goodness, as was stated above. Secondly, it has goodness according to its species, which is derived from its befitting object. Thirdly, it has goodness from its circumstances,—its accidents, as it were. Fourthly, it has goodness from its end, to which it is compared as to the cause of its goodness.

Reply Obj. 1. The good in view of which one acts is not always a true good; but sometimes it is a true good, sometimes an apparent good. And in the latter event, an evil action results from the end in view.

Reply Obj. 2. Although the end is an extrinsic cause, never-

[16] *De Differ. Top.,* II (PL 64, 1189).

theless, a due proportion to the end and a relation to it are inherent in the action.

Reply Obj. 3. Nothing hinders an action that is good in one of the ways mentioned above from lacking goodness in another way. And thus it may happen that an action which is good in its species or in its circumstances is ordained to an evil end, or vice versa. However, an action is not good absolutely, unless it is good in all those ways; for *evil results from any single defect, but good from the complete cause,* as Dionysius says.[17]

Fifth Article

WHETHER A HUMAN ACTION IS GOOD OR EVIL IN ITS SPECIES?

We proceed thus to the Fifth Article:—

Objection 1. It would seem that good and evil in moral actions do not make a difference of species. For the existence of good and evil in actions is in conformity with their existence in things, as was stated above. But good and evil do not make a specific difference in things, for a good man is specifically the same as a bad man. Therefore neither do they make a specific difference in actions.

Obj. 2. Further, since evil is a privation, it is a non-being. But non-being cannot be a difference, according to the Philosopher.[18] Since, therefore, the difference constitutes the species, it seems that an action is not constituted in a species through being evil. Consequently, good and evil do not diversify the species of human actions.

Obj. 3. Further, acts that differ in species produce different effects. But the same specific effect results from a good and from an evil action; and thus a man is born of adulterous or of lawful wedlock. Therefore good and evil actions do not differ in species.

Obj. 4. Further, actions are sometimes said to be good or bad from a circumstance, as was stated above. But since a circumstance is an accident, it does not give an action its species. Therefore human actions do not differ in species because of their goodness or malice.

On the contrary, According to the Philosopher, *like habits*

[17] *De Div. Nom.,* IV, 30 (PG 3, 729).   [18] *Metaph.,* II, 3 (998b 22).

produce like actions.[19] But a good and a bad habit differ in species, as liberality and prodigality. Therefore good and evil actions likewise differ in species.

I answer that, Every action derives its species from its object, as we have stated above. Hence it follows that a difference of object causes a diversity of species in our actions. Now it must be observed that a difference of objects causes a diversity of species in our actions according as our actions are referred to one active principle, which does not cause a difference in actions, according as they are referred to another active principle. For nothing accidental constitutes a species, but only that which is essential; and a difference of object may be essential in reference to one active principle, and accidental in reference to another. Thus, to know color and to know sound differ essentially in reference to sense, but not in reference to the intellect.

Now in human actions, good and evil are predicated in relation to the reason, because, as Dionysius says, the good of man is to be in accordance with reason, *and evil is to be against reason.*[20] For that is good for a thing which suits it according to its form; and evil, that which is against the order of its form. It is therefore evident that the difference of good and evil, considered in reference to the object, is an essential difference in relation to reason, *i.e.,* according as the object is suitable or unsuitable to reason. Now certain actions are called human or moral inasmuch as they proceed from the reason. Consequently, it is evident that good and evil diversify the species in human actions, since essential differences cause a diversity in species.

Reply Obj. 1. Even in natural things, good and evil, inasmuch as something is according to nature, and something against nature, diversify the natural species; for a dead body and a living body are not of the same species. In like manner, good, inasmuch as it is in accord with reason, and evil, inasmuch as it is against reason, diversify the moral species.

Reply Obj. 2. Evil signifies privation, not an absolute one, but one affecting some potentiality. For an action is said to be evil in its species, not because it has no object at all, but because it has an object in disaccord with reason, for instance, to appropriate another's property. Therefore, in so

---

[19] *Eth.,* II, 1 (1103b 21).   [20] *De Div. Nom.,* IV, 32 (PG 3, 732).

far as the object is something positive, it can constitute the species of an evil act.

Reply Obj. 3. The conjugal act and adultery, as compared to reason, differ specifically and have effects specifically different; for the one deserves praise and reward, the other, blame and punishment. But as compared to the generative power, they do not differ in species, and thus they have one specific effect.

Reply Obj. 4. A circumstance is sometimes taken as the essential difference of the object, according as it is related to the reason; and then it can specify a moral act. And it must needs be so whenever a circumstance transforms an action from good to evil, for a circumstance would not make an action evil, except through being repugnant to reason.

Sixth Article

WHETHER AN ACT HAS THE SPECIES OF GOOD OR EVIL FROM ITS END?

We proceed thus to the Sixth Article:—

Objection 1. It would seem that the good and evil which are from the end do not diversify the species of acts. For acts derive their species from the object. But the end is outside the nature of the object. Therefore the good and evil which are from the end do not diversify the species of an act.

Obj. 2. Further, that which is accidental does not constitute the species, as was stated above. But it is accidental to an act to be ordained to some particular end, for instance, to give alms from vainglory. Therefore acts are not diversified in species, according to the good and evil which are from the end.

Obj. 3. Further, acts that differ in species can be ordained to the same end; and thus to the end of vainglory, actions of various virtues and vices can be ordained. Therefore the good and evil which are taken from the end do not diversify the species of action.

On the contrary, It has been shown above that human acts derive their species from the end.[21] Therefore good and evil in respect of the end diversify the species of acts.

I answer that, Certain acts are called human inasmuch as

[21] Q. 1, a. 3.

they are voluntary, as we have stated above.[22] Now, in a voluntary act, there is a twofold act, viz., the interior act of the will, and the external act; and each of these acts has its object. The end is properly the object of the interior act of the will, while the object of the external action is that on which the action is brought to bear. Therefore, just as the external act takes its species from the object on which it bears, so the interior act of the will takes its species from the end, as from its own proper object.

Now that which is on the part of the will is as form in relation to that which is on the part of the external act, because the will uses the members to act as its instruments; nor have external acts any measure of morality, save in so far as they are voluntary. Consequently, the species of a human act is considered formally with regard to the end, but materially with regard to the object of the external action. Hence the Philosopher says that *he who steals that he may commit adultery is, strictly speaking, more adulterer than thief.*[23]

Reply Obj. 1. The end also has the nature of an object, as we have stated above.

Reply Obj. 2. Although it is accidental to the external act to be ordered to some particular end, it is not accidental to the interior act of the will, which is compared to the external act as form to matter.

Reply Obj. 3. When many acts, differing in species, are ordered to the same end, there is indeed a diversity of species on the part of the external acts; but there is a unity of species on the part of the interior act.

Seventh Article

WHETHER THE SPECIES DERIVED FROM THE END IS CONTAINED UNDER THE SPECIES DERIVED FROM THE OBJECT AS UNDER ITS GENUS OR CONVERSELY?

We proceed thus to the Seventh Article:—

Objection 1. It would seem that the species of goodness derived from the end is contained under the species of goodness derived from the object as a species is contained under its genus: *e.g.,* when a man wills to steal in order to give an alms. For an act takes its species from its object, as was stated

---

[22] Q. 1, a. 1.   [23] *Eth.,* V, 2 (1130a 24).

above. But it is impossible for a thing to be contained under another species, if this species be not contained under the proper species of that thing; for the same thing cannot be contained in different species if there is no subalternation among them. Therefore the species which is taken from the end is contained under the species which is taken from the object.

Obj. 2. Further, the last difference always constitutes the lowest species. But the difference derived from the end seems to come after the difference derived from the object, because the end is something last. Therefore the species derived from the end is contained under the species derived from the object as its lowest species.

Obj. 3. Further, the more formal a difference is, the more specific it is, because difference is compared to genus as form to matter. But the species derived from the end is more formal than that which is derived from the object, as was stated above. Therefore the species derived from the end is contained under the species derived from the object as the lowest species is contained under the subaltern genus.

On the contrary, Each genus has its determinate differences. But an act of one and the same species, on the part of its object, can be ordered to an infinite number of ends: *e.g.,* theft can be ordered to an infinite number of good and bad ends. Therefore the species derived from the end is not contained under the species derived from the object as under its genus.

I answer that, The object of the external act can stand in a twofold relation to the end of the will: first, as being essentially ordered to it: *e.g.,* to fight well is of itself ordained to victory; secondly, as being ordained to it accidentally: *e.g.,* to take what belongs to another is ordered accidentally to the giving of alms. Now the differences that divide a genus and constitute the species of that genus must, as the Philosopher says, divide that genus essentially.[24] But if they divide it accidentally, the division is incorrect. Such would be the case if one were to say: *Animals are divided into rational and irrational, and the irrational into animals with wings and animals without wings;* for *winged* and *wingless* are not essential determinations of *irrational*. But the following division would

---

[24] *Metaph.,* VI, 12 (1038a 9).

be correct: *Some animals have feet, some have no feet, and of those that have feet, some have two feet, some four, some many;* for these are essential determinations of the prior difference. Accordingly, when the object is not essentially ordered to the end, the specific difference derived from the object is not an essential determination of the species derived from the end, nor is the reverse the case. Hence one of these species is not under the other; but then the moral action is contained under two species that are disparate, as it were. Consequently, we say that he that commits theft for the sake of adultery is guilty of a twofold malice in one action.—On the other hand, if the object be essentially ordered to the end, one of these differences is an essential determination of the other. Therefore one of these species will be contained under the other.

It remains to be considered which of the two is contained under the other. In order to make this clear, we must first of all observe that the more particular the form is from which a difference is taken, the more specific is the difference; secondly, that the more universal an agent is, the more universal a form does it cause; thirdly, that the more remote an end is, the more universal the agent to which it corresponds (*e.g.,* victory, which is the last end of the army, is the end intended by the commander in chief, while the right ordering of this or that regiment is the end intended by one of the lower officers). From all this it follows that the specific difference derived from the end is more general; and that the difference derived from an object which is essentially ordered to that end is a specific difference in relation to the former. For the will, the proper object of which is the end, is the universal mover in respect of all the powers of the soul, the proper objects of which are the objects of their particular acts.

Reply Obj. 1. One and the same thing, considered in its substance, cannot be in two species, one of which is not subordinate to the other. But in respect of those things which are superadded to the substance, one thing can be contained under diverse species. Thus, one and the same fruit, as to its color, is contained under one species, *i.e.,* a white thing; and, as to its odor, under the species of sweet-smelling things. In like manner, an act which, as to its substance, is in one natural species, considered in respect to the moral conditions that are added to it can belong to two species, as was stated above.[25]

Reply Obj. 2. The end is last in execution, but first in the intention of the reason, according to which moral actions receive their species.

Reply Obj. 3. Difference is compared to genus as form to matter, inasmuch as it actualizes the genus. On the other hand, the genus is considered as more formal than the species, inasmuch as it is something more absolute and less contracted. So, too, the parts of a definition are reduced to the genus of formal cause, as is stated in the *Physics*.[26] And in this sense the genus is the formal cause of the species; and so much the more formal, as it is more universal.

Eighth Article

WHETHER ANY ACT IS INDIFFERENT IN ITS SPECIES?

We proceed thus to the Eighth Article:—

Objection 1. It would seem that no action is indifferent in its species. For evil is the privation of good, according to Augustine.[27] But privation and habit are immediate contraries, according to the Philosopher.[28] Therefore, there is no such thing as an action that is indifferent in its species, as though it were between good and evil.

Obj. 2. Further, human acts derive their species from their end or object, as was stated above.[29] But every end and every object is either good or evil. Therefore every human act is good or evil according to its species. None, therefore, is indifferent in its species.

Obj. 3. Further, as was stated above, an act is said to be good when it has its due complement of goodness, and evil, when it lacks that complement. But every act must needs either have the entire fullness of its goodness, or lack it in some respect. Therefore every act must needs be either good or evil in its species, and none is indifferent.

On the contrary, Augustine says that *there are certain deeds of a middle kind, which can be done with a good or evil*

[25] Q. 1, a. 3, ad 3.   [26] Aristotle, *Phys.*, II, 3 (194b 26).   [27] *Enchir.*, XI (PL 40, 236).   [28] *Cat.*, X (12a 2; b 27).   [29] A. 6; q. 1, a. 3.

mind, of which it is rash to form a judgment.[30] Therefore some acts are indifferent according to their species.

I answer that, As we have stated above, every act takes its species from its object, and the human act, which is called the moral act, takes its species from the object as related to the principle of human acts, which is the reason. Therefore, if the object of an act includes something in accord with the order of reason, it will be a good act according to its species (for instance, to give alms to a person in want). On the other hand, if it includes something repugnant to the order of reason, it will be an evil act according to its species (for instance, to steal, which is to appropriate what belongs to another). But it may happen that the object of an act does not include something pertaining to the order of reason (for instance, to pick up a straw from the ground, to walk in the fields, and the like), and such acts are indifferent according to their species.

Reply Obj. 1. Privation is twofold. One is privation *as a result* [*privatum esse*], and this leaves nothing, but takes all away: *e.g.,* blindness takes away sight altogether; darkness, light; and death, life. Between this privation and the contrary habit, there can be no medium in respect of the proper subject.—The other is privation *in process* [*privari*]: *e.g.,* sickness is privation of health; not that it takes health away altogether, but that it is a kind of road to the entire loss of health, brought about by death. And since this sort of privation leaves something, it is not always the immediate contrary of the opposite habit. It is in this way that evil is a privation of good, as Simplicius says in his commentary on the *Categories*;[31] for it does not take away all good, but leaves some. Consequently, there can be something intermediate between good and evil.

Reply Obj. 2. Every object or end has some goodness or malice, at least that of its nature; but an object or an end does not always imply moral goodness or malice, which is considered in relation to the reason, as we have stated above. And it is of this that we are here treating.

Reply Obj. 3. Not everything belonging to an act belongs also to its species. Therefore, although according to the nature of its species an act may not contain all that belongs to the full complement of its goodness, it is not therefore an act

[30] *De Serm. Dom.,* II, 18 (PL 34, 1296).   [31] *In Cat.,* X (p. 388[7]).

specifically bad; nor is it specifically good. Thus, man, according to his species, is neither virtuous nor vicious.

Ninth Article

WHETHER AN INDIVIDUAL ACT CAN BE INDIFFERENT?

We proceed thus to the Ninth Article:—

Objection 1. It seems that an individual act can be indifferent. For there is no species that does not, or cannot, contain an individual. But an act can be indifferent in its species, as was stated above. Therefore an individual act can be indifferent.

Obj. 2. Further, individual acts are the causes of like habits, as is stated in *Ethics* ii.[32] But a habit can be indifferent, for the Philosopher says that those who are of an even temper and prodigal disposition are not evil;[33] and yet it is evident that they are not good, since they depart from virtue. And thus, they are indifferent in respect of a habit. Therefore some individual acts are indifferent.

Obj. 3. Further, moral good belongs to virtue, while moral evil belongs to vice. But it happens sometimes that a man fails to ordain a specifically indifferent act to a vicious or virtuous end. Therefore an individual act may happen to be indifferent.

On the contrary, Gregory says in a homily: *An idle word is one that lacks either the usefulness of rectitude or the motive of just necessity or pious utility.*[34] But an idle word is an evil, because *men . . . shall render an account of it in the day of judgment* (*Matt.* xii. 36); while if it does not lack the motive of just necessity or pious utility, it is good. Therefore every word is either good or evil. For the same reason, every other act is either good or evil. Therefore no individual act is indifferent.

I answer that, It sometimes happens that an act is indifferent in its species, which yet is good or evil, considered in the individual. And the reason for this is because a moral act, as we have stated above, derives its goodness not only from the object which specifies it, but also from the circumstances, which are its accidents, as it were. So, too, something belongs

---

[32] Aristotle, *Eth.*, II, 1 (1103b 21).   [33] *Op. cit.*, IV, 1 (1121a 26).
[34] *In Evang.*, I, hom. 6 (PL 76, 1098).

to a man by reason of his individual accidents, which does
not belong to him by reason of his species. And every individual act must needs have some circumstance that makes
it good or evil, at least in respect of the intention of the end.
For since it belongs to the reason to direct, if an act that proceeds from deliberate reason be not directed to the due end,
it is, by that fact alone, repugnant to reason, and has the
character of evil. But if it be directed to a due end, it is in
accord with the order of reason, and hence it has the character of good. Now it must needs be either directed or not directed to a due end. Consequently, every human act that
proceeds from deliberate reason, if it be considered in the
individual, must be good or evil.

If, however, it does not proceed from deliberate reason,
but from some act of the imagination, as when a man strokes
his beard, or moves his hand or foot, such an act, properly
speaking, is not moral or human, since an act has the character of being moral or human from the reason. Hence it will
be indifferent, as standing outside the genus of moral acts.

Reply Obj. 1. For an act to be indifferent in its species can
happen in several ways. First, in such a way that its species
demands that it remain indifferent; and the objection proceeds on this line. But no act can be specifically indifferent
thus, since no object of a human act is such that it cannot
be directed to good or evil, either through its end or through
a circumstance.—Secondly, the specific indifference of an act
may be due to the fact that, as far as its species is concerned,
it is neither good nor evil. Therefore it can be made good or
evil by something else. In the same way, man, as far as his
species is concerned, is neither white nor black, nor is it a
condition of his species that he should not be black or white;
but blackness or whiteness can be superadded to man by
other principles than those of his species.

Reply Obj. 2. The Philosopher states that a man is evil,
properly speaking, if he is injurious to others.[35] Accordingly,
he says that the prodigal is not evil, because he injures none
save himself.[36] And the same applies to all others who are
not injurious to other men. But here we are calling evil, in
general, all that is repugnant to right reason. And in this
sense every individual act is either good or evil, as we have
stated above.

[35] *Eth.,* IV, 1 (1121a 29).   [36] *Ibid.* (1121a 26).

Reply Obj. 3. Whenever an end is intended by deliberate reason, it belongs either to the good of some virtue, or to the evil of some vice. Thus, if a man's act is directed to the support or repose of his body, it is also directed to the good of virtue, provided he direct his body itself to the good of virtue. The same clearly applies to other acts.

Tenth Article

WHETHER A CIRCUMSTANCE PLACES A MORAL ACT IN A SPECIES OF GOOD OR EVIL?

We proceed thus to the Tenth Article:—

Objection 1. It would seem that a circumstance cannot place a moral act in a species of good or evil. For the species of an act is taken from its object. But circumstances differ from the object. Therefore circumstances do not give an act its species.

Obj. 2. Further, circumstances are as accidents in relation to the moral act, as was stated above.[37] But an accident does not constitute a species. Therefore a circumstance does not constitute a species of good or evil.

Obj. 3. Further, one thing is not in several species. But one act has several circumstances. Therefore a circumstance does not place a moral act in a species of good or evil.

On the contrary, Place is a circumstance. But place makes a moral act to be in a certain species of evil; for theft of a thing from a holy place is a sacrilege. Therefore a circumstance places a moral act in some species of good or evil.

I answer that, Just as the species of natural things are constituted by their natural forms, so the species of moral acts are constituted by forms as conceived by the reason, as is evident from what was said above. But since nature is determined to one course of action, and a process of nature cannot go on to infinity, there must needs be some ultimate form, giving a specific difference, after which no further specific difference is possible. Hence it is that, in natural things, that which is accidental to a thing cannot be taken as a difference constituting the species. But the process of reason is not fixed to one particular term, for at any point it can still proceed further. Consequently that which, in one act, is taken

[37] Q. 7, a. 1.

as a circumstance added to the object that specifies the act,
can again be taken, by the directing reason, as the principal
condition of the object that determines the species of the act.
Thus, to appropriate another's property is specified by the
character of being *another's*, for this is why it is placed in
the species of theft; and if we further consider the notion
of place or time, then this will be an additional circumstance.
But since the reason can direct as to place, time, and the like,
it may happen that the condition as to place, in relation to
the object, is considered as being in disaccord with reason:
for instance, reason forbids damage to be done to a holy
place. Consequently, to steal from a holy place has an additional repugnance to the order of reason. And thus place,
which was first of all considered as a circumstance, is considered here as the principal condition of the object, and as
itself repugnant to reason. In this way, whenever a circumstance has a special relation to reason, either for or against,
it must needs specify the moral act, whether good or evil.

Reply Obj. 1. A circumstance, in so far as it specifies an
act, is considered as a condition of the object, as we have
stated above, and as being, as it were, a specific difference of
the object.

Reply Obj. 2. A circumstance, so long as it is but a circumstance, does not specify an act, since thus it is a mere
accident; but when it becomes a principal condition of the
object, then it does specify the act.

Reply Obj. 3. It is not every circumstance that places the
moral act in a species of good or evil, for not every circumstance implies accord or disaccord with reason. Consequently,
although one act may have many circumstances, it does not
follow that it is in many species. Nevertheless, there is no
reason why one act should not be in several, even disparate,
moral species, as we have said above.[38]

Eleventh Article

WHETHER EVERY CIRCUMSTANCE THAT MAKES AN ACT BET-
TER OR WORSE PLACES A MORAL ACTION IN A SPECIES
OF GOOD OR EVIL?

We proceed thus to the Eleventh Article:—
Objection 1. It would seem that every circumstance relat-
[38] A. 7, ad 1; q. 1, a. 3, ad 3.

ing to good or evil specifies an act. For good and evil are
specific differences in moral acts. Therefore, that which
causes a difference in the goodness or malice of a moral act
causes a specific difference, which is the same as to make it
differ in species. Now that which makes an act better or
worse makes it differ in goodness and malice. Therefore it
causes it to differ in species. Therefore every circumstance
that makes an act better or worse constitutes a species.

Obj. 2. Further, an additional circumstance either has in
itself some character of goodness or malice, or it has not.
If not, it cannot make the act better or worse, because what
is not good, cannot make a greater good, and what is not evil
cannot make a greater evil. But if it has in itself the character of good or evil, for this very reason it has a certain
species of good or evil. Therefore, every circumstance that
makes an action better or worse constitutes a new species of
good or evil.

Obj. 3. Further, according to Dionysius, *evil is caused by
each single defect.*[39] Now every circumstance that increases
malice has a special defect. Therefore every such circumstance adds a new species of sin. And for the same reason,
every circumstance that increases goodness seems to add a
new species of goodness; just as every unity added to a number makes a new species of number, for the good consists in
number, weight and measure.

On the contrary, *More*-and-*less* does not change a species.
But *more*-and-*less* is a circumstance of additional goodness
or malice. Therefore, not every circumstance that makes a
moral act better or worse, places it in a species of good or
evil.

I answer that, As we have stated above, a circumstance
gives the species of good or evil to a moral act in so far as it
refers to a special order of reason. Now it happens sometimes
that a circumstance does not refer to a special order of reason
in 'respect of good or evil, except on the supposition of another previous circumstance, from which the moral act takes
its species of good or evil. Thus, to take something in a large
or small quantity does not concern the order of reason in respect of good or evil, except a certain other condition be presupposed, from which the act takes its malice or goodness.
Suppose, for instance, that what is taken belongs to another,

[39] *De Div. Nom.,* IV, 30 (PG 3, 729).

which makes the act to be discordant with reason. Therefore, to take what belongs to another in a large or small quantity does not change the species of the sin. Nevertheless it can aggravate or diminish the sin. The same applies to other evil or good acts. Consequently, not every circumstance that makes a moral act better or worse changes its species.

Reply Obj. 1. In things which can be more or less intense, the difference of more or less does not change the species. Thus, by differing in whiteness through being more or less white, a thing is not changed in its species of color. In like manner, that which makes an act to be more or less good or evil does not make the act differ in species.

Reply Obj. 2. A circumstance that aggravates a sin or adds to the goodness of an act sometimes has no goodness or malice in itself, but in relation to some other condition of the act, as was stated above. Consequently, it does not add a new species, but adds to the goodness or malice derived from this other condition of the act.

Reply Obj. 3. A circumstance does not always involve a distinct defect of its own; sometimes it causes a defect in reference to something else. In like manner, a circumstance does not always add further perfection, except in reference to something else. And, in so far as it does, although it may add to the goodness or malice, it does not always change the species of good or evil.

ON THE GOODNESS AND MALICE OF EXTERNAL HUMAN ACTS

(*In Six Articles*)

WE MUST next consider goodness and malice as to external acts, under which head there are six points of inquiry: (1) Whether goodness and malice are first in the act of the will, or in the external act? (2) Whether the whole goodness or malice of the external act depends on the goodness of the will? (3) Whether the goodness and malice of the interior act are the same as those of the external act? (4) Whether the external act adds any goodness or malice to that of the interior act? (5) Whether the consequences of an external act increase its goodness or malice? (6) Whether one and the same external act can be both good and evil?

Fourth Article

WHETHER THE EXTERNAL ACT ADDS ANY GOODNESS OR MALICE TO THAT OF THE INTERIOR ACT?

We proceed thus to the Fourth Article:—

Objection 1. It would seem that the external act does not add any goodness or malice to that of the interior act. For Chrysostom says: *It is the will that is rewarded for doing good, or punished for doing evil.*[1] Now works are the witnesses of the will. Therefore God seeks for works not on His own account, in order to know how to judge, but for the sake of others, that all may understand how just He is. But good or evil is to be estimated according to God's judgment rather than according to the judgment of man. Therefore the external act adds no goodness or malice to that of the interior act.

Obj. 2. Further, the goodness and malice of the interior and external acts are one and the same, as was stated above. But increase is the addition of one thing to another. Therefore the external act does not add to the goodness or malice of the interior act.

[1] *In Matt.*, hom. XIX (PG 57, 274).

Obj. 3. Further, the entire goodness of created things does not add to the divine goodness, because it is entirely derived therefrom. But sometimes the entire goodness of the external act is derived from the goodness of the interior act, and sometimes conversely, as was stated above. Therefore, neither of them adds to the goodness or malice of the other.

On the contrary, Every agent intends to attain good and avoid evil. If, therefore, by the external act no further goodness or malice be added, it is to no purpose that he who has a good or an evil will does a good deed or refrains from an evil deed. Which is unreasonable.

I answer that, If we speak of the goodness which the external act derives from the will tending to the end, then the external act adds nothing to this goodness, unless it happens that the will in itself is made better in good things, or worse in evil things. This, it seems, may happen in three ways. First in point of number. If, for instance, a man wishes to do something with a good or an evil end in view, and does not do it then, but afterwards wills and does it, the act of his will is doubled, and a double good or a double evil is the result.—Secondly, in point of extension. Suppose, for instance, that a man wishes to do something for a good or an evil end, and is hindered by some obstacle, whereas another man perseveres in the movement of the will until he accomplish it in deed. In such a case, it is evident that the will of the latter is more lasting in good or evil, and, in this respect, is better or worse.—Thirdly, in point of intensity. For there are certain external acts which, in so far as they are pleasurable or painful, are such as naturally to make the will more intense or less so; and it is evident that the more intensely the will tends to good or evil, the better or worse it is.

On the other hand, if we speak of the goodness which the external act derives from its matter and due circumstances, thus it stands in relation to the will as its term and end. And in this way it adds to the goodness or malice of the will, because every inclination or movement is perfected by attaining its end or reaching its term. Therefore the will is not perfect, unless it be such that, given the opportunity, it realizes the operation. But if this prove impossible, as long as the will is perfect, so as to realize the operation if it could, the lack of the perfection derived from the external action is absolutely involuntary. Now just as the involuntary deserves neither punishment nor reward in the accomplishment of good or evil deeds, so neither does it lessen reward or punishment, if a man through absolute involuntariness fail to do good or evil.

Reply Obj. 1. Chrysostom is speaking of the case where a man's will is completed and does not refrain from the act save through the impossibility of achievement.

Reply Obj. 2. This argument applies to that goodness which the external act derives from the will as tending to the end. But the goodness which the external act takes from its matter and circumstances is distinct from that which it derives from the end; but it is not distinct from that which it has from the very act willed, to which it stands in the relation of measure and cause, as was stated above.

From this the reply to the Third Objection is evident.

HABITS AND VIRTUES

Question XLIX

ON HABITS IN GENERAL, AS TO THEIR SUBSTANCE

(*In Four Articles*)

AFTER treating of human acts and passions, we now pass on to the consideration of the principles of human acts. And first we must consider intrinsic principles; secondly, the extrinsic principles.[1] The intrinsic principle is power and habit, but as we have treated of powers in the First Part,[2] it remains for us to consider habits. We shall first consider them in general; in the second place we shall consider virtues and vices and other like habits, which are the principles of human acts.[3]

Concerning habits in general there are four points to be considered: First, the substance of habits; second, their subject;[4] third, the cause of their generation, increase and corruption;[5] fourth, how they are distinguished from one another.[6]

Under the first head, there are four points of inquiry: (1) Whether habit is a quality? (2) Whether it is a distinct species of quality? (3) Whether habit implies an order to an act? (4) The necessity of habit.

Fourth Article

WHETHER HABITS ARE NECESSARY?

We proceed thus to the Fourth Article:—

Objection 1. It would seem that habits are not necessary. For by habits we are well or ill disposed in respect of something, as was stated above. But a thing is well or ill disposed by its form, for it is according to its form that a thing is

[1] Q. 90.   [2] QQ. 77-83.   [3] Q. 55.   [4] Q. 50.   [5] Q. 51.   [6] Q. 54.

good, even as it is a being. Therefore there is no necessity
for habits.

Obj. 2. Further, habit implies relation to an act. But power
implies sufficiently a principle of act, for even the natural
powers, without any habits, are principles of acts. Therefore
there was no necessity for habits.

Obj. 3. Further, as power is related to good and evil, so
also is habit, and as power does not always act, so neither
does habit. Given, therefore, the powers, habits become superfluous.

On the contrary, Habits are perfections.[7] But perfection
is of the greatest necessity to a thing, since it is in the nature
of an end. Therefore it was necessary that there should be
habits.

I answer that, As we have said above, habit implies a disposition in relation to a thing's nature, and to its operation
or end, by reason of which disposition a thing is well or ill
disposed thereto. Now for a thing to need to be disposed to
something else, three conditions are necessary. The first condition is that that which is disposed should be distinct from
that to which it is disposed, and that it should be related to
it as potentiality is to act. Whence, if there is a being whose
nature is not composed of potentiality and act, whose substance is its own operation, and which exists for itself, we
can find no room in such a thing for habit and disposition, as
is clearly the case in God.

The second condition is, that that which is in a state of
potentiality in regard to something else, be capable of determination in several ways and to various things. Whence, if
something be in a state of potentiality in regard to something
else, but in regard to that only, we find no room in such a
thing for disposition and habit; for such a subject has of its
own nature a proper relation to such an act. Therefore if a
heavenly body be composed of matter and form, since that
matter is not in a state of potentiality to another form, as
we said in the First Part,[8] there is no need for disposition or
habit in relation to form, or even in relation to operation,
since the nature of the heavenly body is not in a state of
potentiality to more than one fixed movement.

The third condition is that in disposing the subject to one

---

[7] Aristotle, *Phys.*, VII, 3 (246a 11).   [8] *S. T.*, I, q. 66, a. 2.

of those things to which it is in potentiality, several things should occur, capable of being adjusted in various ways, so as to dispose the subject well or ill to its form or to its operation. Therefore the simple qualities of the elements, which suit the natures of the elements in one single fixed way, are not called dispositions or habits, but *simple qualities*. But we call dispositions or habits such things as *health, beauty,* and so forth, which imply the adjustment of several things which may vary in their relative adjustability. For this reason the Philosopher says that *habit is a disposition*,[9] and *disposition is the order of that which has parts either as to place, or as to potentiality, or as to species*,[10] as we have said above. Therefore, since there are many things for whose natures and operations several things must concur which may vary in their relative adjustability, it follows that habit is necessary.

Reply Obj. 1. By the form the nature of a thing is perfected; yet the subject needs to be disposed in regard to the form itself by some disposition. But the form itself is further ordained to operation, which is either the end, or a means to the end. And if the form is limited to one fixed operation, no further disposition, besides the form itself, is needed for the operation. But if the form be such that it can operate in diverse ways, as is the soul, it needs to be disposed to its operations by means of habits.

Reply Obj. 2. Power sometimes has a relation to many things, and then it needs to be determined by something else. But if a power has not a relation to many things, it does not need a habit to determine it, as we have said. For this reason natural forces do not perform their operations by means of habits, because they are of themselves determined to one mode of operation.

Reply Obj. 3. The same habit has not a relation to good and evil, as will be made clear further on,[11] but the same power has a relation to good and evil. Hence it is that habits are necessary that powers be determined to good.

[9] *Metaph.*, IV, 20 (1022b 10).   [10] *Op. cit.*, IV, 19 (1022b 1).
[11] Q. 54, a. 3.

ON THE CAUSE OF HABITS, AS TO THEIR FORMATION

(*In Four Articles*)

WE MUST next consider the cause of habits. And firstly, as to their formation; secondly, as to their increase;[1] thirdly, as to their diminution and corruption.[2] Under the first head there are four points of inquiry: (1) Whether any habit is from nature? (2) Whether any habit is caused by acts? (3) Whether a habit can be generated by one act? (4) Whether any habits are infused in man by God?

First Article

WHETHER ANY HABIT IS FROM NATURE?

We proceed thus to the First Article:—

Objection 1. It would seem that no habit is from nature. For the use of those things which are from nature does not depend on the will. But habit *is that which we use when we will*, as the Commentator says on *De Anima* iii.[3] Therefore habit is not from nature.

Obj. 2. Further, nature does not employ two where one is sufficient. But the powers of the soul are from nature. If, therefore, the habits of the powers were from nature, habit and power would be one.

Obj. 3. Further, nature does not fail in the necessaries. But habits are necessary in order to act well, as we have stated above.[4] If, therefore, any habits were from nature, it seems that nature would not fail to cause all necessary habits. But this is clearly false. Therefore habits are not from nature.

On the contrary, In *Ethics* vi.[5] among other habits place is given to the *understanding of first principles*, which habit is from nature. Hence, too, first principles are said to be known naturally.[6]

I answer that, One thing can be natural to another in two

---

[1] Q. 52. [2] Q. 53. [3] Averroes, *In De Anima*, III, comm. 18 (VI, 169v). [4] Q. 49, a. 4. [5] Aristotle, *Eth.*, VI, 6 (1141a 5). [6] Cf. a text of St. Albert, *Summa de Bono,* quoted by O. Lottin, *Le droit naturel,* p. 117.

ways. First, in respect of the specific nature, as the ability to laugh is natural to man, and to have an upward tendency is natural to fire. Secondly, in respect of the individual nature, as it is natural to Socrates or Plato to be prone to sickness or inclined to health, in accordance with their respective temperaments.—Again, in respect of both natures, something may be called natural in two ways: first, because it is entirely from the nature; secondly, because it is partly from nature, and partly from an extrinsic principle. For instance, when a man is healed by himself, his health is entirely from nature; but when a man is healed by means of medicine, health is partly from nature, partly from an extrinsic principle.

Therefore, if we speak of habit as a disposition of the subject in relation to form or nature, it may be natural in either of the foregoing ways. For there is a certain natural disposition demanded by the human species, so that no man can be without it. And this disposition is natural in respect of the specific nature. But since such a disposition has a certain latitude, it happens that different grades of this disposition are becoming to different men in respect of the individual nature. And this disposition may be either entirely from nature, or partly from nature, and partly from an extrinsic principle, as we have said of those who are healed by means of art.

But the habit which is a disposition to operation, and whose subject is a power of the soul, as was stated above,[7] may be natural both in respect of the specific nature and in respect of the individual nature:—in respect of the specific nature, on the part of the soul itself, which, since it is the form of the body, is the specific principle; but in respect of the individual nature, on the part of the body, which is the material principle. Yet in neither way does it happen that there are natural habits in man, so that they be entirely from nature. In the angels, indeed, this does happen, since they have intelligible species naturally impressed on them; which does not belong to human nature, as we said in the First Part.[8]

There are, therefore, in man certain natural habits, owing their existence partly to nature, and partly to some extrinsic principle. They exist in one way, indeed, in the apprehensive

[7] Q. 50, a. 2.   [8] S. T., I, q. 55, a. 2; q. 84, a. 3.

powers; in another, in the appetitive powers. For in the apprehensive powers there may be a natural habit by way of a beginning, both in respect of the specific nature and in respect of the individual nature. This happens with regard to the specific nature, on the part of the soul itself. Thus the *understanding of first principles* is called a natural habit.[9] For it is owing to the very nature of the intellectual soul that man, having once grasped what is a whole and what is a part, should at once perceive that every whole is larger than its part. And the same is the case in like manner with regard to other such instances. Yet what is a whole, and what is a part, this he cannot know except through the intelligible species which he has received from phantasms. For this reason, the Philosopher at the end of the *Posterior Analytics* shows that the knowledge of principles comes to us from the senses.[10]

But in respect of the individual nature, a habit of knowledge is natural as to its beginning, in so far as one man, from the disposition of his organs of sense, is more apt than another to understand well, since we need the sensitive powers for the operation of the intellect.

In the appetitive powers, however, no habit is natural in its beginning, on the part of the soul itself, as to the substance of the habit; but only as to certain of its principles, as, for instance, the principles of common law are called *the seeds of the virtues*.[11] The reason for this is because the inclination to its proper objects, which seems to be the beginning of a habit, does not belong to the habit, but rather to the very nature of the powers.

But on the part of the body, in respect of the individual nature, there are some appetitive habits by way of natural beginnings. For some are disposed from their own bodily temperament to chastity or meekness or the like.

Reply Obj. 1. This objection takes nature as divided against reason and will; whereas reason itself and will belong to the nature of man.

Reply Obj. 2. Something may be added even naturally to

---

[9] For the opinions of Alexander of Hales and John of Rochelle on the "understanding of first principles," cf. O. Lottin, "La syndérèse chez les premiers maîtres franciscains de Paris" (*Revue néoscolastique de philosophie*, XXIX [1927], pp. 269, 273, 277).   [10] *Post. Anal.*, II, 15 (100a 3).   [11] Cf. the texts of St. Albert, *Summa de Bono*, as quoted by O. Lottin, *Le droit naturel*, p. 117.

the nature of a power, although it cannot belong to the power itself. For instance, with regard to the angels, it cannot belong to the intellective power itself to be of itself capable of knowing all things; for thus it would have to be the act of all things, which belongs to God alone. Evidently, that by which something is known must needs be the actual likeness of the thing known. Hence, if the power of the angel knew all things by itself, it would follow that it was the likeness and act of all things. Therefore there must needs be added to the angels' intellective power some intelligible species, which are likenesses of things understood; for it is by participation in the divine wisdom, and not by their own essence that their intellects can be actually those things which they understand. And so it is clear that not everything belonging to a natural habit can belong to the power.

Reply Obj. 3. Nature is not equally inclined to cause all the various kinds of habits, since some can be caused by nature, and some not, as we have said above. And so it does not follow that, because some habits are natural, therefore all are natural.

Second Article

WHETHER ANY HABIT IS CAUSED BY ACTS?

We proceed thus to the Second Article:—

Objection 1. It would seem that no habit is caused by acts. For habit is a quality, as we have said above.[12] Now every quality is caused in a subject according as the subject is receptive of something. Since, then, the agent, inasmuch as it acts, does not receive but rather gives, it seems impossible for a habit to be caused in an agent by its own acts.

Obj. 2. Further, the thing wherein a quality is caused is moved to that quality, as may be clearly seen in that which is heated or cooled; whereas that which produces the act that causes the quality, moves, as may be seen in that which heats or cools. If, therefore, habits were caused in anything by its own act, it would follow that the same would be mover and moved, active and passive; which is impossible, as is stated in *Physics* vii.[13]

Obj. 3. Further, the effect cannot be more noble than its

[12] Q. 49, a. 1.   [13] Aristotle, *Phys.*, VII, 1 (241b 24).

cause. But a habit is more noble than the act which precedes
the habit, as is clear from the fact that habit makes an act
to be more perfect. Therefore a habit cannot be caused by an
act which precedes the habit.

On the contrary, The Philosopher teaches that habits of
virtue and vice are caused by acts.[14]

I answer that, In the agent there is sometimes only the
active principle of its act. For instance, in fire there is only
the active principle of heating. In such an agent a habit cannot be caused by its own act; for which reason natural things
cannot become accustomed or unaccustomed, as is stated in
Ethics ii.[15] But there is an agent in which there is both the
active and the passive principle of its act, as we see in human
acts. For the acts of the appetitive power proceed from that
same power according as it is moved by the apprehensive
power presenting the object; and further, the intellective
power, according as it reasons about conclusions, has, as it
were, an active principle in a self-evident proposition. Therefore by such acts habits can be caused in their agents; not
indeed with regard to the first active principle, but with regard to that principle of the act which is a moved mover. For
everything that is passive and moved by another is disposed
by the action of the agent; and therefore if the acts be multiplied, a certain quality is formed in the power which is passive and moved, which quality is called a habit; just as the
habits of the moral virtues are caused in the appetitive powers, according as they are moved by the reason, and as the
habits of science are caused in the intellect, according as it is
moved by first propositions.

Reply Obj. 1. The agent, as agent, does not receive anything. But in so far as it moves through being moved by another, it receives something from that which moves it; and
thus a habit is caused.

Reply Obj. 2. The same thing, and in the same respect,
cannot be mover and moved; but nothing prevents a thing
from being moved by itself as to different respects, as is
proved in *Physics* viii.[16]

Reply Obj. 3. The act which precedes the habit, in so far
as it comes from an active principle, proceeds from a more
excellent principle than is the habit caused thereby; just as

[14] *Eth.,* II, 1 (1103a 31).   [15] *Ibid.* (1103a 19).   [16] Aristotle, *Phys.,*
VIII, 5 (257a 31).

the reason is a more excellent principle than the habit of
moral virtue produced in the appetitive power by repeated
acts, and as the understanding of first principles is a more
excellent principle than the science of conclusions.

Third Article

WHETHER A HABIT CAN BE CAUSED BY ONE ACT?

We proceed thus to the Third Article:—

Objection 1. It would seem that a habit can be caused by
one act. For demonstration is an act of reason. But science,
which is the habit of one conclusion, is caused by one demonstration. Therefore habit can be caused by one act.

Obj. 2. Further, as acts happen to increase by multiplication, so do they happen to increase by intensity. But a habit
is caused by multiplication of acts. So, too, if an act be very
intense, it can be the generating cause of a habit.

Obj. 3. Further, health and sickness are habits. But it happens that a man is healed or becomes ill by one act. Therefore one act can cause a habit.

On the contrary, The Philosopher says: *As neither does
one swallow nor one day make spring, so neither does one day
nor a short time make a man blessed and happy.*[17] But *happiness is an operation according to a habit of perfect virtue.*[18]
Therefore a habit of virtue, and for the same reason, other
habits, is not caused by one act.

I answer that, As we have said already, habit is caused by
act, in so far as a passive power is moved by an active principle. But in order that some quality be caused in that which
is passive, the active principle must entirely overcome the
passive. Whence we see that because fire cannot at once overcome the combustible, it does not enkindle it at once, but
gradually expels contrary dispositions, so that, by overcom-
ing it entirely, it may impress its likeness on it. Now it is
clear that the active principle which is reason cannot entirely
overcome the appetitive power in one act. For the appetitive
power is inclined variously, and to many things, while the
reason judges, in a single act, what should be willed in the
light of various conditions and circumstances. Therefore the
appetitive power is not thereby entirely overcome, so as to

---

[17] *Eth.,* I, 7 (1098a 18).   [18] *Ibid.* (1098a 16); 13 (1102a 5).

be inclined naturally to the same thing in the majority of cases; which inclination belongs to the habit of virtue. Therefore a habit of virtue cannot be caused by one act, but only by many.

But in the apprehensive powers, we must observe that there are two passive principles: one is the possible intellect itself; the other is the intellect which Aristotle calls *passive*,[19] and is the particular reason, that is, the cogitative power, with memory and imagination.[20] With regard then to the former passive principle, it is possible for a certain active principle to overcome entirely, by one act, the power of its passive principle. Thus one self-evident proposition convinces the intellect, so that it gives a firm assent to the conclusion; but a probable proposition cannot do this. Therefore a habit of opinion needs to be caused by many acts of the reason, even on the part of the possible intellect; whereas a habit of science can be caused by a single act of the reason, so far as the possible intellect is concerned. But with regard to the lower apprehensive powers, the same acts need to be repeated many times for anything to be firmly impressed on the memory. And so the Philosopher says that *meditation strengthens memory*.[21] Bodily habits, however, can be caused by one act, if the active principle is of great power. Sometimes, for instance, a powerful medicine restores health at once.

Hence the solutions to the objections are clear.

Fourth Article

WHETHER ANY HABITS ARE INFUSED IN MAN BY GOD?

We proceed thus to the Fourth Article:—

Objection 1. It would seem that no habit is infused in man by God. For God treats all equally. If, therefore, He infuses habits into some, He would infuse them into all; which is clearly untrue.

Obj. 2. Further, God works in all things according to the mode which is suitable to their nature; for *it belongs to the divine providence to preserve nature,* as Dionysius says.[22] But habits are naturally caused in man by acts, as we have

[19] *De An.,* III, 5 (430a 24).   [20] Cf. *S. T.,* I, q. 78, a. 4.   [21] *De Memor.,* I (451a 12).   [22] *De Div. Nom.,* IV, 33 (PG 3, 733).

said above. Therefore God does not cause habits to be in man except by acts.

Obj. 3. Further, if any habit be infused into man by God, man can by that habit perform many acts. But *from those acts a like habit is caused.*[23] Consequently, there will be two habits of the same species in the same man, one acquired, the other infused. Now this seems impossible, for two forms of the same species cannot be in the same subject. Therefore a habit is not infused into man by God.

On the contrary, It is written (*Ecclus.* xv. 5): *God filled him with the spirit of wisdom and understanding.* Now wisdom and understanding are habits. Therefore some habits are infused into man by God.

I answer that, Some habits are infused by God into man, for two reasons.

The first reason is because there are some habits by which man is disposed to an end which exceeds the proportion of human nature, namely, the ultimate and perfect happiness of man, as was stated above.[24] And since habits need to be in proportion with that to which man is disposed by them, therefore it is necessary that those habits, which dispose to this end, likewise exceed the proportion of human nature. Therefore such habits can never be in man except by divine infusion, as is the case with all gratuitous virtues.

The other reason is, because God can produce the effects of second causes without second causes themselves, as we have said in the First Part.[25] Just as, therefore, in order to show His power, God sometimes causes health, without its natural cause, but which nature could have caused, so also, at times, for the manifestation of His power, He infuses into man even those habits which can be caused by a natural power. Thus He gave to the apostles the science of the Scriptures and of all tongues, which men can acquire by study or by custom, though not so perfectly.

Reply Obj. 1. God, considered in His nature, is the same to all; but, considered according to the order of His wisdom, for some fixed motive, He gives certain things to some, which He does not give to others.

Reply Obj. 2. That God works in all according to their mode, does not hinder God from doing what nature cannot

[23] Aristotle, *Eth.*, II, 1 (1103b 21).   [24] Q. 5, a. 5.   [25] *S. T.*, I, q. 105, a. 6.

do; rather it follows from this that He does nothing contrary to that which is suitable to nature.

Reply Obj. 3. Acts produced by an infused habit do not cause a habit, but strengthen an already existing habit; just as the remedies of medicine given to a man who is naturally healthy do not cause a kind of health, but give new strength to the health he had before.

ON THE DISTINCTION OF HABITS

(*In Four Articles*)

WE HAVE now to consider the distinction of habits. Under this head there are four points of inquiry: (1) Whether many habits can be in one power? (2) Whether habits are distinguished by their objects? (3) Whether habits are divided into good and bad? (4) Whether one habit may be made up of many habits?

Second Article

WHETHER HABITS ARE DISTINGUISHED BY THEIR OBJECTS?

We proceed thus to the Second Article:—

Objection 1. It would seem that habits are not distinguished by their objects. For contraries differ in species. Now the same habit of science regards contraries. Thus medicine regards the healthy and the unhealthy. Therefore habits are not distinguished by objects specifically distinct.

Obj. 2. Further, different sciences are different habits. But the same scientific truth belongs to different sciences. Thus, both the natural philosopher and the astronomer prove the earth to be round, as is stated in *Physics* ii.[1] Therefore habits are not distinguished by their objects.

Obj. 3. Further, wherever the act is the same, the object is the same. But the same act can belong to different habits of virtue, if it be directed to different ends. Thus, to give money to anyone, if it be done for God's sake, is an act of charity; while, if it be done in order to pay a debt, it is an act of justice. Therefore the same object can also belong to different habits. Therefore diversity of habits does not follow diversity of objects.

On the contrary, Acts differ in species according to the diversity of their objects, as was stated above.[2] But habits are dispositions to acts. Therefore habits also are distinguished according to the diversity of objects.

I answer that, A habit is both a form and a habit. Hence the specific distinction of habits may be taken in the ordinary

---

[1] Aristotle, *Phys.*, II, 2 (193b 25).   [2] Q. 18, a. 5.

way in which forms differ specifically, or according to that mode of distinction which is proper to habits. Now forms are distinguished from one another in reference to the diversity of their active principles, since every agent produces its like in species. Habits, however, imply order to something, and all things that imply order to something are distinguished according to the distinction of the things to which they are ordained. Now a habit is a disposition implying a twofold order: viz., to nature, and to an operation consequent to nature. Accordingly, habits are specifically distinct in respect of three things. First, in respect of the active principles of such dispositions; secondly, in respect of nature; thirdly, in respect of specifically different objects, as will appear from what follows.

Reply Obj. 1. In distinguishing powers, or also habits, we must consider the object, not in its material aspect, but in its formal aspect, which may differ in species or even in genus. And though the distinction between specific contraries is a real distinction, yet they are both known under one aspect, since one is known through the other. And, consequently, in so far as they concur in the one aspect of cognoscibility, they belong to one cognitive habit.

Reply Obj. 2. The natural philosopher proves the earth to be round by one means, the astronomer by another. For the latter proves this by means of mathematics, *e.g.*, by the shapes of eclipses, or something of the sort; while the former proves it by means of physics, *e.g.*, by the movement of heavy bodies towards the center, and so forth. Now the whole force of a demonstration, which is *a syllogism producing science*, as is stated in *Posterior Analytics* i.,[3] depends on the means. And consequently various means are as so many active principles according to which the habits of science are distinguished.

Reply Obj. 3. As the Philosopher says, the end is, in practical matters, what a principle is in demonstrative matters.[4] Consequently, a diversity of ends demands a diversity of virtues, even as a diversity of active principles does.—Moreover, the ends are objects of the internal acts, with which, above all, the virtues are concerned, as is evident from what has been said.[5]

[3] Aristotle, *Post. Anal.*, I, 2 (71b 18).   [4] *Phys.*, II, 9 (200a 15); *Eth.*, VII, 8 (1151a 16).   [5] Q. 18, a. 6; q. 19, a. 2, ad 1; q. 34, a. 4.

Third Article

WHETHER HABITS ARE DIVIDED INTO GOOD AND BAD?

We proceed thus to the Third Article:—

Objection 1. It would seem that habits are not divided into good and bad. For good and bad are contraries. Now the same habit regards contraries, as was stated above. Therefore habits are not divided into good and bad.

Obj. 2. Further, good is convertible with being, so that, since it is common to all, it cannot be accounted a specific difference, as the Philosopher declares.[6] Again, evil, since it is a privation and a non-being, cannot differentiate any being. Therefore habits cannot be specifically divided into good and evil.

Obj. 3. Further, there can be different evil habits about one and the same object: for instance, intemperance and insensibility about matters of concupiscence; and in like manner there can be several good habits: for instance, human virtue and heroic or godlike virtue, as the Philosopher clearly states.[7] Therefore, habits are not divided into good and bad.

On the contrary, A good habit is contrary to a bad habit, as virtue to vice. Now contraries are distinct specifically. Therefore habits are divided specifically into good and bad habits.

I answer that, As was stated above, habits are specifically distinct not only in respect of their objects and active principles, but also in their relation to nature. Now this happens in two ways. First, by reason of their suitableness or unsuitableness to nature. In this way a good habit is specifically distinct from a bad habit. For a good habit is one which disposes to an act suitable to the agent's nature, while a bad habit is one which disposes to an act unsuitable to nature. Thus, acts of virtue are suitable to human nature, since they are according to reason, whereas acts of vice are opposed to human nature, since they are against reason. Hence it is clear that habits are distinguished specifically by the difference of good and bad.

Secondly, habits are distinguished in relation to nature from the fact that one habit disposes to an act that is suitable

---

[6] *Top.,* IV, 6 (127a 26).   [7] *Eth.,* VII, 1 (1145a 15).

to a lower nature, while another habit disposes to an act befitting a higher nature. And thus human virtue, which disposes to an act befitting human nature, is distinct from godlike or heroic virtue, which disposes to an act befitting some
higher nature.

Reply Obj. 1. The same habit may be about contraries in
so far as contraries agree in one common aspect. Never, however, does it happen that contrary habits are in one species,
since contrariety of habits follows contrariety of aspect. Accordingly, habits are divided into good and bad, namely, inasmuch as one habit is good, and another bad; but not because one habit is about something good, and another about
something bad.

Reply Obj. 2. It is not the good which is common to every
being that is a difference constituting the species of a habit;
it is rather some determinate good, by reason of a suitability
to some determinate, viz., human, nature. In like manner,
the evil that constitutes a difference of habits is not a pure
privation, but something determinate repugnant to a determinate nature.

Reply Obj. 3. Several good habits about one and the same
specific thing are distinguished according to their suitability
to various natures, as was stated above. But several bad
habits in respect of one action are distinguished according to
their diverse repugnance to that which is in keeping with
nature. Thus, various vices about one and the same matter
are contrary to one virtue.

ON THE VIRTUES, AS TO THEIR ESSENCE

(*In Four Articles*)

WE COME now to a particular consideration of habits. And since habits, as we have said, are divided into good and bad,[1] we must speak in the first place of good habits, which are virtues, and of other matters connected with them, namely, the Gifts, Beatitudes and Fruits;[2] in the second place, of bad habits, namely, of vices and sins.[3] Now five things must be considered about virtues: (1) the essence of virtue; (2) its subject;[4] (3) the division of the virtues;[5] (4) the cause of virtue;[6] (5) certain properties of virtue.[7]

Under the first head, there are four points of inquiry: (1) Whether human virtue is a habit? (2) Whether it is an operative habit? (3) Whether it is a good habit? (4) The definition of virtue.

First Article

WHETHER HUMAN VIRTUE IS A HABIT?

We proceed thus to the First Article:—

Objection 1. It would seem that human virtue is not a habit. For virtue is *the peak of power*.[8] But the peak of anything is reducible to the genus of that of which it is the peak, as a point is reducible to the genus of line. Therefore virtue is reducible to the genus of power, and not to the genus of habit.

Obj. 2. Further, Augustine says that *virtue is good use of free choice*.[9] But use of free choice is an act. Therefore virtue is not a habit, but an act.

Obj. 3. Further, we do not merit by our habits, but by our actions, or otherwise a man would merit continually, even while asleep. But we do merit by our virtues. Therefore virtues are not habits, but acts.

Obj. 4. Further, Augustine says that *virtue is the order of*

---

[1] Q. 54, a. 3.   [2] Q. 68.   [3] Q. 71.   [4] Q. 56.   [5] Q. 57.   [6] Q. 63.   [7] Q. 64.   [8] Aristotle, *De Caelo*, I, 11 (281a 14; a 18).—Cf. St. Thomas, *In De Caelo*, I, lect. 25.   [9] *De Lib. Arb.*, II, 19 (PL 32, 1268); *Retract.*, I, 9 (PL 32, 598).

love,[10] and that *the ordering which is called virtue consists in enjoying what we ought to enjoy, and using what we ought to use.*[11] Now order, or ordering, denominates either an action or a relation. Therefore virtue is not a habit, but an action or a relation.

Obj. 5. Further, just as there are human virtues, so there are natural virtues. But natural virtues are not habits, but powers. Neither therefore are human virtues habits.

On the contrary, The Philosopher says that *science **and** virtue are habits.*[12]

I answer that, Virtue denotes a certain perfection of a power. Now a thing's perfection is considered chiefly in relation to its end. But the end of power is act. Therefore power is said to be perfect according as it is determined to its act. Now there are some powers which of themselves are determined to their acts, for instance, the active natural powers. And therefore these natural powers are in themselves called virtues. But the rational powers, which are proper to man, are not determined to one particular action, but are inclined indifferently to many; but they are determined to acts by means of habits, as is clear from what we have said above.[13] Therefore human virtues are habits.

Reply Obj. 1. Sometimes we give the name of a virtue to that to which the virtue is directed, namely, either to its object or to its act. For instance, we give the name faith to that which we believe, or to the act of believing, as also to the habit by which we believe. When therefore we say that *virtue is the peak of power,* virtue is taken for the object of virtue. For the highest point to which a power can reach is said to be its virtue: for instance, if a man can carry a hundredweight and not more, his virtue [*i.e.,* his strength] is put at a hundredweight, and not at sixty. But the objection takes virtue as being essentially the peak of power.

Reply Obj. 2. Good use of free choice is said to be a virtue in the same sense as above, that is to say, because it is that to which virtue is directed as to its proper act. For an act of virtue is nothing else than the good use of free choice.

Reply Obj. 3. We are said to merit by something in two ways. First, as by merit itself, just as we are said to run by running; and thus we merit by acts. Secondly, we are said

[10] *De Mor. Eccl.,* I, 15 (PL 32, 1322).   [11] *Lib. 83 Quaest.,* q. 30 (PL 40, 19).   [12] *Cat.,* VIII (8b 29).   [13] Q. 49, a. 4.

to merit by something as by the principle whereby we merit, as we are said to run by the power of locomotion; and thus are we said to merit by virtues and habits.

Reply Obj. 4. When we say that virtue is the order or ordering of love, we refer to the end to which virtue is ordered; because in us love is set in order by virtue.

Reply Obj. 5. Natural powers are of themselves determined to one act; not so the rational powers. Hence there is no comparison, as we have said.

Fourth Article

WHETHER VIRTUE IS SUITABLY DEFINED?

We proceed thus to the Fourth Article:—

Objection 1. It would seem that the definition usually given of virtue (namely, *Virtue is a good quality of the mind, by which we live righteously, of which no one can make bad use, which God works in us without us*[14]) is not suitable. For virtue is man's goodness, since it is virtue that makes its subject good. But goodness does not seem to be good, as neither is whiteness white. It is therefore unsuitable to describe virtue as a *good quality.*

Obj. 2. Further, no difference is more common than its genus, since it is that which divides the genus. But *good* is more common than quality, since it is convertible with being. Therefore *good* should not be put in the definition of virtue, as a difference of quality.

Obj. 3. Further, as Augustine says: *When we come across anything that is not common to us and the beasts of the field, it is something pertaining to the mind.*[15] But there are virtues even of the irrational parts, as the Philosopher says.[16] Every virtue, therefore, is not a good quality *of the mind.*

Obj. 4. Further, righteousness seems to belong to justice; whence the righteous are called just. But justice is a species of virtue. It is therefore unsuitable to put *righteous* in the definition of virtue, when it is said that virtue is that *by which we live righteously.*

Obj. 5. Further, whoever is proud of a thing, makes bad use of it. But many are proud of virtue, for Augustine says in

---

[14] Cf. Peter Lombard, *Sent., II,* xxvii, 5 (I, 446).   [15] *De Trin.,* XII, 8 (PL 42, 1005).   [16] *Eth.,* III, 10 (1117b 23).

his *Rule,* that *pride lies in wait for good works in order to slay them.*[17] It is untrue, therefore, *that no one can make bad use of virtue.*

Obj. 6. Further, man is justified by virtue. But Augustine, commenting on *Jo.* xiv. 12 (*He shall do greater things than these*) says: *He who created thee without thee will not justify thee without thee.*[18] It is therefore unsuitable to say that *God works virtue in us without us.*

On the contrary, We have the authority of Augustine, from whose words this definition is gathered, and principally in *De Libero Arbitrio* ii.[19]

I answer that, This definition comprises perfectly the whole essential notion of virtue. For the perfect nature of anything is gathered from all its causes. Now the above definition comprises all the causes of virtue. For the formal cause of virtue, as of everything, is gathered from its genus and difference, when it is defined as *a good quality;* for *quality* is the genus of virtue, and the difference, *good.* To be sure, the definition would be more suitable if for *quality* we substitute *habit,* which is the proximate genus.

Now virtue has no matter *out of which* it is formed, as neither has any other accident; but it has the matter *about which* it is concerned, and the matter *in which* it exists, namely, the subject. The matter about which virtue is concerned is its object, and this could not be included in the above definition because the object fixes the virtue to a certain species, and here we are giving the definition of virtue in general. And so for the material cause we have the subject, which is mentioned when it is said that virtue is a good quality *of the mind.*

The end of virtue, since it is an operative habit, is operation itself. But it must be observed that some operative habits are always referred to evil, as are vicious habits. Others are sometimes referred to good, sometimes to evil. For instance, opinion is referred both to the true and to the untrue. But virtue is a habit which is always referred to good. Hence the distinction of virtue from those habits which are always referred to evil is expressed in the words *by which we live righteously;* and its distinction from those habits which are

[17] *Epist.,* CCXI (PL 33, 960).   [18] *Serm.,* CLXIX, 11 (PL 38, 923); *Tract.* LXXII, super *Ioann.,* XIV, 12 (PL 35, 1823).   [19] *De Lib. Arb.,* II, 19 (PL 32, 1268).

sometimes directed to good, and sometimes to evil, is expressed in the words, *of which no one makes bad use.*

Lastly, God is the efficient cause of infused virtue, to which this definition applies; and this is expressed in the words *which God works in us without us.* If we omit this phrase, the remainder of the definition will apply to all virtues in general, whether acquired or infused.

Reply Obj. 1. That which first falls in the intellect is *being*, and therefore everything that we apprehend we consider as being, and consequently as *one*, and as *good*, which are convertible with being. Hence we say that *essence is being* and *one* and *good*; and that *oneness is being* and *one* and *good*; and in like manner *goodness*. But this is not the case with specific forms, as whiteness and health, for everything that we apprehend is not apprehended with the notion of white and healthy. We must, however, observe that, as accidents and non-subsistent forms are called beings, not as if they themselves had being, but because things are by them, so also are they called good or one, not by some distinct goodness or oneness, but because by them something is good or one. So also is virtue called good, because by it something is good.

Reply Obj. 2. The good which is put in the definition of virtue is not the good in general which is convertible with being, and which extends further than quality, but the good as fixed by reason, with regard to which Dionysius says *that the good of the soul is to be in accord with reason.*[20]

Reply Obj. 3. Virtue cannot be in the irrational part of the soul, except in so far as this participates in the reason.[21] Therefore reason, or the mind, is the proper subject of virtue.

Reply Obj. 4. Justice has a righteousness of its own by which it puts those outward things right which come into human use, and which are the proper matter of justice, as we shall show further on.[22] But the righteousness which denotes order to a due end and to the divine law, which is the rule of the human will, as was stated above,[23] is common to all virtues.

Reply Obj. 5. One can make bad use of a virtue considered as an object, for instance, by having evil thoughts about it,

[20] *De Div. Nom.*, IV, 32 (PG 3, 733).   [21] Aristotle, *Eth.*, I, 13 (1102b 13; 1103 a 3).   [22] Q. 60, a. 2; II-II, q. 58, a. 8.   [23] Q. 19, a. 4.

e.g., by hating it, or by being proud of it; but one cannot make bad use of virtue as principle of action, so that an act of virtue be evil.

Reply Obj. 6. Infused virtue is caused in us by God without any action on our part, but not without our consent. This is the sense of the words, *which God works in us without us.* As to those things which are done by us, God causes them in us, yet not without action on our part, for He works in every will and in every nature.

Question LVI

ON THE SUBJECT OF VIRTUE

(*In Six Articles*)

WE HAVE now to consider the subject of virtue, about which there are six points of inquiry: (1) Whether virtue is in a power of the soul as in a subject? (2) Whether one virtue can be in several powers? (3) Whether the intellect can be a subject of virtue? (4) Whether the irascible and concupiscible powers can be a subject of virtue? (5) Whether the sensitive powers of apprehension can be a subject of virtue? (6) Whether the will can be a subject of virtue?

First Article

WHETHER VIRTUE IS IN A POWER OF THE SOUL AS IN A SUBJECT?

We proceed thus to the First Article:—

Objection 1. It would seem that the subject of virtue is not a power of the soul. For Augustine says that *virtue is that by which we live righteously.*[1] But we live by the essence of the soul, and not by a power of the soul. Therefore virtue is not in a power, but in the essence of the soul.

Obj. 2. Further, the Philosopher says that *virtue is that which makes its possessor good, and his work good likewise.*[2] But as a work is established by a power, so he that has a virtue is established by the essence of the soul. Therefore virtue does not belong to the power, any more than to the essence of the soul.

Obj. 3. Further, power is in the second species of quality. But virtue is a quality, as we have said above,[3] and quality is not the subject of quality. Therefore a power of the soul is not the subject of virtue.

On the contrary, Virtue is the peak of power.[4] But the peak is in that of which it is the peak. Therefore virtue is in a power of the soul.

---

[1] *De Lib. Arb.,* II, 19 (PL 32, 1268).   [2] *Eth.,* II, 6 (1106a 15).
[3] Q. 55, a. 4.   [4] Aristotle, *De Caelo,* I, 11 (281a 14; a 18).—Cf. St. Thomas, *In De Caelo,* I, lect. 25.

I answer that, It can be proved in three ways that virtue belongs to a power of the soul. First, from the very nature of virtue, which implies the perfection of a power; for perfection is in that which it perfects.—Secondly, from the fact that virtue is an operative habit, as we have said above.[5] Now all operation proceeds from the soul through a power.— Thirdly, from the fact that virtue disposes to that which is best; and the best is the end, which is either a being's operation, or something acquired by an operation proceeding from the being's power. Therefore a power of the soul is the subject of virtue.

Reply Obj. 1. *To live* may be taken in two ways. Sometimes it is taken for the very being of the living thing, and thus it belongs to the essence of the soul, which is the principle of being in the living thing. But sometimes *to live* is taken for the operation of the living thing, and in this sense we live righteously by virtue inasmuch as by virtue we perform righteous actions.

Reply Obj. 2. Good is either the end, or something referred to the end. Therefore, since the good of the worker consists in the work, this fact also, that virtue makes the worker good, is referred to the work, and consequently, to the power.

Reply Obj. 3. One accident is said to be the subject of another, not as though one accident could uphold another, but because one accident inheres in a substance by means of another, as color in a body by means of the surface; so that surface is said to be the subject of color. In this way a power of the soul is said to be the subject of virtue.

[5] Q. 55, a. 2.

ON THE DISTINCTION OF THE INTELLECTUAL VIRTUES

(*In Six Articles*)

WE NOW have to consider the distinction of the virtues, which are (1) the intellectual virtues; (2) the moral virtues;[1] (3) the theological virtues.[2] Concerning the first there are six points of inquiry: (1) Whether the habits of the speculative intellect are virtues? (2) Whether they are three, namely, *wisdom, science* and *understanding?* (3) Whether the intellectual habit *art* is a virtue? (4) Whether *prudence* is a virtue distinct from art? (5) Whether prudence is a virtue necessary to man? (6) Whether *eubulia, synesis* and *gnome* are virtues annexed to prudence?

Second Article

WHETHER THERE ARE ONLY THREE HABITS OF THE SPECULATIVE INTELLECT, VIZ., *WISDOM, SCIENCE* AND *UNDERSTANDING?*

We proceed thus to the Second Article:—

Objection 1. It would seem unfitting to distinguish three virtues of the speculative intellect, viz., *wisdom, science* and *understanding.* For a species should not be co-divided with its genus. But wisdom is a science, as is stated in *Ethics* vi.[3] Therefore wisdom should not be co-divided with science among the intellectual virtues.

Obj. 2. Further, in differentiating powers, habits and acts in respect of their objects, we consider chiefly the formal aspect of these objects, as we have already explained.[4] Therefore habits are diversified, not according to their material objects, but according to the formal aspect of their objects. Now the principle of a demonstration is the cause of having a science of conclusions. Therefore the understanding of principles should not be set down as a habit or virtue distinct from the science of conclusions.

---

[1] Q. 58.   [2] Q. 62.   [3] Aristotle, *Eth.,* VI, 7 (1141a 19).   [4] Q. 54, a. 2, ad 1; I, q. 77, a. 3.

Obj. 3. Further, an intellectual virtue is one which resides in the essentially rational part of the soul. Now even the speculative reason employs the dialectical syllogism in its reasoning, just as it employs the demonstrative syllogism. Therefore, just as science, which is the result of a demonstrative syllogism, is considered to be an intellectual virtue, so also should opinion be.

On the contrary, The Philosopher reckons these three alone as being intellectual virtues, viz., *wisdom, science* and *understanding.*[5]

I answer that, As has already been stated, the virtues of the speculative intellect are those which perfect the speculative intellect for the consideration of truth; for this is its good work. Now truth is subject to a twofold consideration, namely, as known in itself, and as known through another. What is known in itself is as a *principle,* and is at once understood by the intellect; and that is why the habit that perfects the intellect for the consideration of such truth is called *understanding,* which is the *habit of principles.*

On the other hand, a truth which is known through another is understood by the intellect, not at once, but by means of the reason's inquiry, and is as a *term.* This may happen in two ways: first, so that it is the last in some particular genus; secondly, so that it is the ultimate term of all human knowledge. And, since *things that are later knowable in relation to us are knowable first and chiefly in their nature,*[6] hence it is that that which is last with respect to all human knowledge is that which is knowable first and chiefly in its nature. And about these truths is *wisdom,* which considers the highest causes, as is stated in *Metaph.* i.[7] Therefore it rightly judges and orders all truths, because there can be no perfect and universal judgment except by resolution to first causes.—But in regard to that which is last in this or that genus of knowable truths, it is *science* that perfects the intellect. Therefore, according to the diverse genera of knowable truths, there are diverse habits of the sciences; whereas there is but one wisdom.

Reply Obj. 1. Wisdom is a science, in so far as it has that which is common to all the sciences: viz., to demonstrate conclusions from principles. But since it has something

[5] *Eth.,* VI, 7 (1141a 19); 3 (1139b 16).   [6] Aristotle, *Phys.,* I, 1 (184a 18).   [7] Aristotle, *Metaph.,* I, 1 (981b 28); 2 (982b 9).

proper to itself above the other sciences, inasmuch as it
judges of them all, not only as to their conclusions, but also
as to their first principles, therefore it is a more perfect virtue than science.

Reply Obj. 2. When the formal aspect of the object is referred to a power or habit by one and the same act, there is
no distinction of habit or power in relation to the formal aspect and the material object. Thus, it belongs to the same
power of sight to see both color and light, which is the formal
aspect under which color is seen, and is seen at the same time
as the color. On the other hand, the principles of demonstration can be considered by themselves, without the conclusion
being considered at all. They can also be considered together
with the conclusions, in so far as the principles are extended
to lead to the conclusions. Accordingly, to consider principles
in this second way belongs to *science*, which considers the
conclusions also; while to consider principles in themselves
belongs to *understanding*.

Consequently, if we consider the point rightly, these three
virtues are not distinguished as being on a par with one another, but in a certain order. The same is to be observed in
potential wholes, wherein one part is more perfect than another: *e.g.*, the rational soul is more perfect than the sensitive soul, and the sensitive, than the vegetative soul. For it is
thus that *science* depends on *understanding* as on a virtue of
higher degree. So, too, both of these depend on *wisdom* as
obtaining the highest place; for it contains beneath itself
both understanding and science, as judging both of the conclusions of sciences and of the principles on which they are
based.

Reply Obj. 3. As was stated above, a virtuous habit has a
fixed relation to good, and is in no way referable to evil.[8]
Now the good of the intellect is truth, and falsehood is its
evil. Therefore those habits alone are called intellectual virtues, whereby we express the truth and never a falsehood.
But opinion and surmise can be about both truth and falsehood; and so, as is stated in *Ethics* vi.,[9] they are not intellectual virtues.

[8] Q. 55, a. 3 and 4.   [9] Aristotle, *Eth.*, VI, 3 (1139b 17).

Third Article

WHETHER THE INTELLECTUAL HABIT *ART* IS A VIRTUE?

We proceed thus to the Third Article:—

Objection 1. It would seem that art is not an intellectual virtue. For Augustine says that *no one makes bad use of virtue.*[10] But one may make bad use of art, for a craftsman can work badly according to the science of his art. Therefore art is not a virtue.

Obj. 2. Further, there is no virtue of a virtue. But *there is a virtue of art,* according to the Philosopher.[11] Therefore art is not a virtue.

Obj. 3. Further, the liberal arts excel the mechanical arts. But just as the mechanical arts are practical, so the liberal arts are speculative. Therefore, if art were an intellectual virtue, it would have to be reckoned among the speculative virtues.

On the contrary, The Philosopher says that art is a virtue.[12] However, he does not reckon it among the speculative virtues, which, according to him, reside in the scientific part of the soul.

I answer that, Art is nothing else but *the right reason about certain works to be made.* And yet the good of these things depends, not on the disposition of man's appetite, but on the goodness of the work done. For a craftsman as such is commendable, not for the will with which he does a work, but for the quality of the work. Art, therefore, properly speaking, is an operative habit. And yet it has something in common with the speculative habits, since the disposition of the things considered by them is a matter of concern to the speculative habits also, although they are not concerned with the disposition of the appetite towards their objects. For as long as the geometrician demonstrates the truth, it matters not how his appetite is disposed, whether he be joyful or angry; even as neither does this matter in a craftsman, as we have observed. And so art has the nature of a virtue in the same way as the speculative habits, in so far, namely, as neither art nor a speculative habit makes a good work as regards the use of

---

[10] *De Lib. Arb.,* II, 18; 19 (PL 32, 1267; 1268).   [11] Aristotle, *Eth.,* VI, 5 (1140b 22).   [12] *Op. cit.,* VI, 3 (1139b 16); 7 (1141a 19).

the habit, which is distinctive of a virtue that perfects the appetite, but only as regards the ability to work well.

Reply Obj. 1. When anyone endowed with an art produces bad workmanship, this is not the work of that art; in fact, it is contrary to the art. In the same way, when a man lies, while knowing the truth, his words are not in accord with what he knows, but contrary thereto. Therefore, just as science has always a relation to good, as was stated above, so it is with art; and it is for this reason that it is called a virtue. And yet it falls short of being a perfect virtue, because it does not make its possessor to use it well; for which purpose something further is requisite, even though there cannot be a good use without the art.

Reply Obj. 2. In order that a man may make good use of the art he has, he needs a good will, which is perfected by moral virtue; and for this reason the Philosopher says there is a virtue of art, namely, a moral virtue, in so far as the good use of art requires a moral virtue. For it is evident that a craftsman is inclined by justice, which rectifies his will, to do his work faithfully.

Reply Obj. 3. Even in speculative matters there is something by way of work: *e.g.*, the making of a syllogism or of a fitting speech, or the work of counting or measuring. Hence whatever habits are ordained to such works of the speculative reason are, by a kind of comparison, called arts indeed, but *liberal* arts, in order to distinguish them from those arts that are ordained to works done by the body; for these arts are, in a fashion, servile, inasmuch as the body is in servile subjection to the soul, and man, as regards his soul, is free [*liber*]. On the other hand, those sciences which are not ordained to any such work are called sciences absolutely, and not arts. Nor, if the liberal arts be more excellent, does it follow that the notion of art is more applicable to them.

Fourth Article

WHETHER PRUDENCE IS A DISTINCT VIRTUE FROM ART?

We proceed thus to the Fourth Article:—

Objection 1. It would seem that prudence is not a distinct virtue from art. For art is right reason about certain works. But diversity of works does not make a habit cease to be an

art, since there are various arts about works widely different.
Since, therefore, prudence is also right reason about works, it
seems that it too should be reckoned an art.

Obj. 2. Further, prudence has more in common with art
that the speculative habits have, for they are both *about contingent matters that may be otherwise than they are.*[13] Now
some speculative habits are called arts. Much more, therefore,
should prudence be called an art.

Obj. 3. Further, it belongs to prudence *to be of good counsel.*[14] But counselling takes place in certain arts also, as is
stated in *Ethics* iii.,[15] *e.g.*, in the arts of warfare, of seamanship and of medicine. Therefore prudence is not distinct from
art.

On the contrary, The Philosopher distinguishes prudence
from art.[16]

I answer that, Where the nature of virtue differs, there is
a different kind of virtue. Now it has been stated above that
some habits have the nature of virtue, through merely conferring ability for a good work; while some habits are virtues,
not only through conferring ability for a good work, but also
through conferring the use.[17] But art confers the mere ability
for good work, since it does not regard the appetite, whereas
prudence confers not only ability for a good work, but also
the use, for it regards the appetite, since it presupposes the
rectitude of the appetite.

The reason for this difference is that art is the *right reason
of things to be made,* whereas prudence is the *right reason of
things to be done.* Now *making* and *doing* differ, as is stated
in *Metaph.* ix.,[18] in that *making* is an action passing into external matter, *e.g.*, *to build, to saw,* and so forth; whereas
doing is an action abiding in the agent, *e.g.*, *to see, to will,*
and the like. Accordingly, prudence stands in the same relation to such human actions, consisting in the use of powers
and habits, as art does to external makings; since each is the
perfect reason about the things with which it is concerned.
But perfection and rectitude of reason in speculative matters
depend on the principles from which reason argues; just as
we have said above that science depends on and presupposes

---

[13] Aristotle, *Eth.*, VI, 6 (1140b 35).   [14] *Op. cit.*, VI, 5 (1140a 25).
[15] *Op. cit.*, III, 3 (1112b 3).   [16] *Op. cit.*, VI, 3 (1139b 16); 5 (1140b
2; b 21).   [17] A. 1; q. 56, a. 3.   [18] Aristotle, *Metaph.*, VIII, 8
(1050a 30).

understanding, which is the habit of principles. *Now in human acts ends are what principles are in speculative matters,* as is stated in *Ethics* vii.[19] Consequently, it is requisite for prudence, which is right reason about things to be done, that man be well disposed with regard to ends; and this depends on the rectitude of his appetite. Therefore, for prudence there is need of moral virtue, which rectifies the appetite. On the other hand, the good of things made by art is not the good of man's appetite, but the good of the artificial things themselves, and hence art does not presuppose rectitude of the appetite. The consequence is that more praise is given to a craftsman who is at fault willingly, than to one who is unwillingly; whereas it is more contrary to prudence to sin willingly than unwillingly, since rectitude of the will is essential to prudence, but not to art.—Accordingly, it is evident that prudence is a virtue distinct from art.

Reply Obj. 1. The various kinds of things made by art are all external to man, and therefore there is no diversification in the nature of virtue. But prudence is right reason about human acts themselves, and hence it is a distinct kind of virtue, as was stated above.

Reply Obj. 2. Prudence has more in common with art than a speculative habit has, if we consider their subject and matter; for they are both in the part of the soul that does not deal with necessary truths, as well as about things that may be otherwise than they are. But if we consider them as virtues, then art has more in common with the speculative habits than with prudence, as is clear from what has been said.

Reply Obj. 3. Prudence is of good counsel about matters regarding man's entire life, and the last end of human life. But in some arts there is counsel about matters concerning the ends proper to those arts. Hence some men, in so far as they are good counsellors in matters of warfare, or seamanship, are said to be prudent officers or pilots, but not prudent absolutely; for only those are prudent absolutely who give good counsel about what concerns man's entire life.

[19] Aristotle, *Eth.*, VII, 8 (1151a 16).

Fifth Article

WHETHER PRUDENCE IS A VIRTUE NECESSARY TO MAN?

We proceed thus to the Fifth Article:—

Objection 1. It would seem that prudence is not a virtue necessary for a good life. For as art is to things that are made, of which it is the right reason, so prudence is to things that are done, in respect of which we judge of a man's life; for prudence is the right reason about these things, as is stated in *Ethics* vi. [20] Now art is not necessary in things that are made, save in order that they be made, but not after they have been made. Neither, therefore, is prudence necessary to man for a good life, after he has become virtuous, but perhaps only in order that he may become virtuous.

Obj. 2. Further, *It is by prudence that we are of good counsel,* as is stated in *Ethics* vi. [21] But man can act not only from his own good counsel, but also from another's. Therefore a man does not deem prudence for a good life, but it is enough that he follow the counsel of prudent men.

Obj. 3. Further, an intellectual virtue is one by which one always expresses the truth, and never what is false. But this does not seem to be the case with prudence, for it is not human never to err in taking counsel about what is to be done, since human actions are about things that may be otherwise than they are. Hence it is written (*Wis.* ix. 14): *The thoughts of mortal men are fearful, and our counsels uncertain.* Therefore it seems that prudence should not be reckoned an intellectual virtue.

On the contrary, It is reckoned with other virtues necessary for human life, when it is written (*Wis.* viii. 7) of divine Wisdom: *She teacheth temperance and prudence and justice and fortitude, which are such things as men can have nothing more profitable in life.*

I answer that, Prudence is a virtue most necessary for human life. For a good life consists in good deeds. Now in order to do good deeds, it matters not only what a man does, but also how he does it; in other words, it matters that he do it from right choice and not merely from impulse or passion. Now since choice is about means to the end, rectitude of

---

[20] *Op. cit.,* VI, 5 (1140b 3).   [21] *Ibid.* (1140a 25); 7 (1141b 9).

choice requires two things, namely, the due end, and that which is suitably ordained to that due end. Now man is suitably directed to his due end by a virtue which perfects the soul in the appetitive part, the object of which is the good and the end. But to that which is suitably ordained to the due end man needs to be rightly disposed by a habit in his reason, because counsel and choice, which are about means ordained to the end, are acts of the reason. Consequently an intellectual virtue is needed in the reason, to perfect the reason and make it suitably affected towards means ordained to the end; and this virtue is prudence. Consequently prudence is a virtue necessary for a good life.

Reply Obj. 1. The good of an art is to be found, not in the craftsman, but in the product of the art, since art is right reason about things to be made. For, since making passes into external matter, it is not a perfection of the maker, but of the thing made, even as movement is the act of the thing moved. Now art is concerned with the making of things. On the other hand, the good of prudence is in the agent himself, whose perfection consists in action itself; for prudence is right reason about things to be done, as was stated above. Consequently, art does not require of the craftsman that his act be a good act, but that his work be good. Rather would it be necessary for the thing made to act well (*e.g.*, that a knife should carve well, or that a saw should cut well), if it were proper to such things to act, rather than to be acted on, because they have not dominion over their actions. Therefore the craftsman needs art, not that he may live well, but that he may produce a good work of art, and an enduring one; whereas prudence is necessary to man that he may lead a good life, and not merely that he may become a good man.

Reply Obj. 2. When a man does a good deed, not of his own counsel, but moved by that of another, his operation is not yet quite perfect, as regards his reason in directing him and his appetite in moving him. Therefore, if he do a good deed, he does not do well absolutely; and yet this is required in order that he may lead a good life.

Reply Obj. 3. As is stated in *Ethics* vi.,[22] truth is not the same for the practical as for the speculative intellect. For the

---

[20] Aristotle, *Eth.*, VI, 2 (1139a 26).

truth of the speculative intellect depends on the conformity
of the intellect to the thing. And since the intellect cannot be
infallibly in conformity with things in contingent matters,
but only in necessary matters, therefore no speculative habit
about contingent things is an intellectual virtue, but only
such as is about necessary things.—On the other hand, the
truth of the practical intellect depends on conformity with
right appetite. This conformity has no place in necessary
matters, which are not effected by the human will, but only
in contingent matters which can be effected by us, whether
they be matters of interior action or the products of external
work. Hence it is only about contingent matters that an intellectual virtue is assigned to the practical intellect, viz.,
art, as regards things to be made, and *prudence,* as regards
things to be done.

ON THE DIFFERENCE BETWEEN MORAL AND INTELLECTUAL VIRTUES

(*In Five Articles*)

WE MUST now consider the moral virtues. We shall speak (1) of the difference between them and the intellectual virtues; (2) of their distinction, one from another, in respect of their proper matter;[1] (3) of the difference between the chief or cardinal virtues and the others.[2]

Under the first head there are five points of inquiry: (1) Whether every virtue is a moral virtue? (2) Whether moral virtue differs from intellectual virtue? (3) Whether virtue is adequately divided into moral and intellectual virtue? (4) Whether there can be moral virtue without intellectual virtue? (5) Whether, on the other hand, there can be intellectual virtue without moral virtue?

First Article

WHETHER EVERY VIRTUE IS A MORAL VIRTUE?

We proceed thus to the First Article:—

Objection 1. It would seem that every virtue is a moral virtue. For moral virtue is so called from the Latin *mos, i.e.,* custom. Now, we can accustom ourselves to the acts of all the virtues. Therefore every virtue is a moral virtue.

Obj. 2. Further, the Philosopher says that moral virtue is *a habit of choosing this rational mean*.[3] But every virtue is a habit of choosing, since the acts of any virtue can be done from choice. And, moreover, every virtue consists in following the rational mean in some way, as we shall explain further on.[4] Therefore every virtue is a moral virtue.

Obj. 3. Further, Cicero says that *virtue is a habit after the manner of a nature, in accord with reason*.[5] But since every human virtue is directed to man's good, it must be in accord with reason; for man's good *consists in being in accord with reason,* as Dionysius states.[6] Therefore every virtue is a moral virtue.

[1] Q. 59.   [2] Q. 61.   [3] *Eth.,* II, 6 (1106b 36).   [4] Q. 64, a. 1, 2 and 3.   [5] *De Invent.,* II, 53 (p. 147b).   [6] *De Div. Nom.,* IV, 32 (PG 3, 733).

On the contrary, The Philosopher says: *When we speak of a man's morals, we do not say that he is wise or intelligent, but that he is gentle or sober.*[7] Accordingly, then, wisdom and understanding are not moral virtues; and yet they are virtues, as was stated above.[8] Therefore, not every virtue is a moral virtue.

I answer that, In order to answer this question clearly, we must consider the meaning of the Latin word *mos,* for thus we shall be able to discover what *moral* virtue is. Now *mos* has a twofold meaning. For sometimes it means custom, in which sense we read (*Acts* xv. 1): *Except you be circumcised after the manner* [*morem*] *of Moses, you cannot be saved;* sometimes it means a natural or quasi-natural inclination to do some particular action, in which sense the word is applied to brute animals. Thus we read (2 *Macc.* xi. 11) that *rushing violently upon the enemy, like lions* [*leonum more*], *they slew them.* The word is used in the same sense in *Ps.* lxvii. 7, where we read: *Who maketh men of one manner* [*moris*] *to dwell in a house.* For both these significations there is but one word in Latin; but in Greek there is a distinct word for each, for the word *ethos,* which signifies the same as the Latin *mos,* is written sometimes with a long *e,* and is written η, and sometimes with a short *e,* and is written ε.

Now *moral* virtue is so called from *mos* in the sense of a natural or quasi-natural inclination to do some particular action. And the other meaning of *mos, i.e.,* custom, is akin to this, because custom somehow becomes a nature, and produces an inclination similar to a natural one. But it is evident that inclination to an action belongs properly to the appetitive power, whose function it is to move all the powers to their acts, as was explained above.[9] Therefore not every virtue is a moral virtue, but only those that are in the appetitive power.

Reply Obj. 1. This argument takes *mos* in the sense of *custom.*

Reply Obj. 2. Every act of virtue can be done from choice, but no virtue makes us choose rightly, save that which is in the appetitive part of the soul; for it has been stated above that choice is an act of the appetitive part.[10] Therefore a

---

[7] *Eth.,* I, 13 (1103a 7).   [8] Q. 57, a. 2.   [9] Q. 9, a. 1.   [10] Q. 13, a. 1.

habit of choosing, *i.e.*, a habit which is the principle whereby we choose, is that habit alone which perfects the appetitive power; although the acts of other habits also may be a matter of choice.

Reply Obj. 3. *Nature is the principle of movement.*[11] Now to move to act is the proper function of the appetitive power. Consequently, to become like nature in the point of consenting to the reason is proper to those virtues which are in the appetitive power.

Second Article

WHETHER MORAL VIRTUE DIFFERS FROM INTELLECTUAL VIRTUE?

We proceed thus to the Second Article:—

Objection 1. It would seem that moral virtue does not differ from intellectual virtue. For Augustine says *that virtue is the art of living rightly.*[12] But art is an intellectual virtue. Therefore moral and intellectual virtue do not differ.

Obj. 2. Further, some authors put science in the definition of the moral virtues. Thus some define perseverance as a *science or habit regarding those things to which we should hold or not hold;* and holiness as *a science which makes man to be faithful and to do his duty to God.*[13] Now science is an intellectual virtue. Therefore moral virtue should not be distinguished from intellectual virtue.

Obj. 3. Further, Augustine says that *virtue is the rectitude and perfection of reason.*[14] But this belongs to intellectual virtue, as is stated in *Ethics* vi.[15] Therefore moral virtue does not differ from intellectual virtue.

Obj. 4. Further, a thing does not differ from that which is included in its definition. But intellectual virtue is included in the definition of moral virtue; for the Philosopher says that *moral virtue is a habit of choosing the mean appointed by reason as a prudent man would appoint it.*[16] Now this right reason, that fixes the mean of moral virtue, belongs to

[11] Aristotle, *Phys.*, II, 1 (192b 21).   [12] *De Civit. Dei*, IV, 21 (PL 41, 128).   [13] Cf. St. Thomas, *S. T.*, II-II, q. 137, a. 1, sed contra, and for Andronicus, cf. J. von Arnim, *Stoicorum Veterum Fragmenta*, III, p. 66.   [14] *Solil.*, I, 6 (PL 32, 876).   [15] Aristotle, *Eth.*, VI, 13 (1144b 21).   [16] *Op. cit.*, II, 6 (1106b 36).

intellectual virtue, as is stated in *Ethics* vi.[17] Therefore moral virtue does not differ from intellectual virtue.

On the contrary, It is stated in *Ethics* i. that *there are two kinds of virtue: some we call intellectual, some, moral.*[18]

I answer that, Reason is the first principle of all human acts, and whatever other principles of human acts may be found, they obey reason in some way, but diversely. For some obey reason instantaneously and without any contradiction whatever. Such are the members of the body, provided they be in a healthy condition, for as soon as reason commands, the hand or the foot proceeds to action. Hence the Philosopher says that *the soul rules the body with a despotic rule,*[19] *i.e.,* as a master rules his slave, who has no right to rebel. Accordingly, some held that all the active principles in man are subordinate to reason in this way. If this were true, for a man to act well it would suffice that his reason be perfect. Consequently, since virtue is a habit perfecting man in view of his doing good actions, it would follow that virtue existed only in the reason, so that there would be none but intellectual virtues. This was the opinion of Socrates, who said *every virtue is a kind of prudence,* as is stated in *Ethics* vi.[20] Hence he maintained that as long as a man was in possession of knowledge, he could not sin, and that every one who sinned did so through ignorance.[21]

Now this is based on a false supposition. For the appetitive part obeys the reason, not instantaneously, but with a certain power of opposition; and so the Philosopher says that *reason commands the appetitive part by a political rule,*[22] whereby a man rules over subjects that are free, having a certain right of opposition. Hence Augustine says on *Ps.* cxviii. that *sometimes the intellect marks the way, while desire lags, or follows not at all;*[23] so much so, that sometimes the habits or passions of the appetitive part cause the use of reason to be impeded in some particular action. And in this way, there is some truth in the saying of Socrates that so long as a man is in possession of knowledge he does not sin: provided, however, that this knowledge is made to include the use of reason in this individual act of choice.

[17] *Op. cit.,* VI, 13 (1144b 21).   [18] *Op. cit.,* I, 13 (1103a 3). [19] *Polit.,* I, 2 (1254b 4).   [20] Aristotle, *Eth.,* VI, 13 (1144b 19).   [21] Cf. *op. cit.,* VII, 2 (1145b 23).—Cf. also Plato, *Protag.* (pp. 352B; 355A; 357B).   [22] *Polit.,* I, 5 (1254b 4).

Accordingly, for a man to do a good deed, it is requisite not only that his reason be well disposed by means of a habit of intellectual virtue, but also that his appetite be well disposed by means of a habit of moral virtue. And so moral differs from intellectual virtue, even as the appetite differs from the reason. Hence, just as the appetite is the principle of human acts, in so far as it partakes of reason, so moral habits are to be considered human virtues in so far as they are in conformity with reason.

Reply Obj. 1. Augustine usually applies the term *art* to any form of right reason; in which sense art includes prudence, which is the right reason about things to be done, even as art is the right reason about things to be made. Accordingly, when he says that *virtue is the art of right conduct*, this applies to prudence essentially; but to other virtues, by participation, in so far as they are directed by prudence.

Reply Obj. 2. All such definitions, by whomsoever given, have been based on the Socratic theory, and should be explained according to what we have said about art.

The same applies to the Third Objection.

Reply Obj. 4. Right reason in matters of prudence is included in the definition of moral virtue, not as part of its essence, but as something belonging by way of participation to all the moral virtues, in so far as they are all under the direction of prudence.

Question LX

HOW THE MORAL VIRTUES ARE DISTINGUISHED FROM ONE ANOTHER

(*In Five Articles*)

WE MUST now consider how the moral virtues are distinguished from one another. Under this head there are five points of inquiry: (1) Whether there is only one moral virtue? (2) Whether those moral virtues which are about operations are distinguished from those which are about passions? (3) Whether there is but one moral virtue about operations? (4) Whether there are different moral virtues about different passions? (5) Whether the moral virtues are distinguished according to the various objects of the passions?

First Article

WHETHER THERE IS ONLY ONE MORAL VIRTUE?

We proceed thus to the First Article:—

Objection 1. It would seem that there is only one moral virtue. For just as the direction of moral actions belongs to reason, which is the subject of the intellectual virtues, so their inclination belongs to the appetitive power, which is the subject of moral virtues. But there is only one intellectual virtue to direct all moral acts, viz., prudence. Therefore, there is also but one moral virtue to give all moral acts their respective inclinations.

Obj. 2. Further, habits differ, not in respect of their material objects, but according to the formal aspects of their objects. Now the formal aspect of the good to which moral virtue is directed is one, viz., the mean defined by reason. Therefore it appears that there is but one moral virtue.

Obj. 3. Further, moral matters are specified by the end, as was stated above.[1] Now there is but one common end of all the moral virtues, viz., happiness, while the proper and proximate ends are infinite in number. But the moral virtues themselves are not infinite in number. Therefore it seems that there is but one.

On the contrary, One habit cannot be in several powers, as

[1] Q. 1, a. 3.

was stated above.[2] But the subject of the moral virtues is the appetitive part of the soul, which is distinguished into several powers, as was stated in the First Part.[3] Therefore there cannot be only one moral virtue.

I answer that, As was stated above, the moral virtues are habits of the appetitive part of the soul.[4] Now habits differ specifically according to the specific differences of their objects, as was stated above.[5] Now the species of the object of appetite, as of anything, depends on its specific form which it receives from the agent. But we must observe that the matter of the receptive subject bears a twofold relation to the agent. For sometimes it receives the form of the agent in the same manner as the agent has that form, as happens with all univocal agents, so that if the agent be one specifically, the matter must of necessity receive a form that is specifically one. Thus, the univocal effect of fire is of necessity something in the species of fire.—Sometimes, however, the matter receives the form from the agent, but not in the same manner as the agent, as is the case with non-univocal causes of generation. Thus an animal is generated by the sun. In this case, the forms received into matter from one and the same agent are not of one species, but vary according to the adaptability of the matter to receive the action of the agent. For instance, we see that owing to the one action of the sun, animals of various species are produced by putrefaction according to the various adaptability of matter.

Now it is evident that in moral matters the reason holds the place of commander and mover, while the appetitive power is commanded and moved. But the appetite does not receive the action of reason univocally, so to say; for it is rational, not essentially, but by participation.[6] Consequently, appetible objects are established in various species according to the movement of reason, by having various relations to reason; so that it follows that moral virtues are of various species and are not one only.

Reply Obj. 1. The object of the reason is the true. Now in all moral matters, which are contingent matters of action, there is but one kind of truth. Consequently, there is but one virtue to direct all such matters, viz., prudence.—On the other hand, the object of the appetitive power is the ap-

[2] Q. 56, a. 2.   [3] *S. T.,* I, q. 80, a. 2; q. 81, a. 2.   [4] Q. 58, a. 1, 2 and 3.   [5] Q. 54, a. 2.   [6] Aristotle, *Eth.,* I, 13 (1102b 13; b 26).

petible good, which varies in kind according to its various relations to reason, the directing power.

Reply Obj. 2. This formal element is one generically because of the unity of the agent; but it varies in species because of the various relations of the receiving subjects, as was explained above.

Reply Obj. 3. Moral matters do not receive their species from the last end, but from their proximate ends; and these, although they be infinite in number, are not infinite in species.

Question LXI

THE CARDINAL VIRTUES

(*In Five Articles*)

WE MUST now consider the cardinal virtues. Under this head there are five points of inquiry: (1) Whether the moral virtues should be called cardinal or principal virtues? (2) Of their number. (3) Which are they? (4) Whether they differ from one another? (5) Whether they are fittingly divided into political, perfecting, perfect, and exemplar virtues?

First Article

WHETHER THE MORAL VIRTUES SHOULD BE CALLED CARDINAL OR PRINCIPAL VIRTUES?

We proceed thus to the First Article:—

Objection 1. It would seem that moral virtues should not be called cardinal or principal virtues. For *the opposed members of a division are by nature simultaneous,*[1] so that one is not principal rather than another. Now all the virtues are opposed members of the division of the genus *virtue*. Therefore none of them should be called principal.

Obj. 2. Further, the end is superior to the means. But the theological virtues are about the end, while the moral virtues are about the means. Therefore the theological virtues, rather than the moral virtues, should be called principal or cardinal.

Obj. 3. Further, that which is essentially so is superior to that which is so by participation. But the intellectual virtues belong to that which is essentially rational, whereas the moral virtues belong to that which is rational by participation, as was stated above.[2] Therefore the intellectual virtues are principal, rather than the moral virtues.

On the contrary, Ambrose, in explaining the words *Blessed are the poor in spirit* (*Luke* vi. 20) says: *We know that there are four cardinal virtues, viz., temperance, justice, prudence and fortitude.*[3] But these are moral virtues. Therefore the moral virtues are cardinal virtues.

---

[1] Aristotle, *Cat.*, XIII (14b 33).   [2] Q. 56, a. 6, ad 2; q. 58, a. 3; q. 59, a. 4, obj. 2.   [3] *In Luc.*, V, super VI, 20 (PL 15, 1738).

I answer that, When we speak without qualification of virtue, we are understood to speak of human virtue. Now human virtue, as was stated above, is virtue according to its perfect nature if it requires the rectitude of the appetite;[4] for such a virtue not only confers the ability to do well, but also causes the use of the good work. On the other hand, a virtue is so called according to the imperfect notion of virtue, when it does not require rectitude of the appetite, because it merely confers the ability of doing well without causing the use of the good work. Now it is evident that the perfect is principal as compared to the imperfect; and so those virtues which contain rectitude of the appetite are called principal virtues. Such are the moral virtues, and among the intellectual virtues prudence alone is such, for it is also in a way a moral virtue with respect to its subject matter, as was shown above.[5] Consequently, those virtues which are called principal or cardinal are fittingly found among the moral virtues.

Reply Obj. 1. When a univocal genus is divided into its species, the members of the division are on a par in the point of the generic notion; although considered according to reality, one species may surpass another in rank and perfection, as man surpasses the other animals. But when we divide an analogous notion, which is applied to several things, but to one before it is applied to another, nothing hinders one from ranking before another, even with respect to the common notion; as the notion of being is applied to substance more principally than to accident. Such is the division of virtue into the various genera of virtue, since the good defined by reason is not found in the same way in all things.

Reply Obj. 2. The theological virtues are above man, as was stated above.[6] Hence they should properly be called not human, but *super-human* or divine virtues.

Reply Obj. 3. Although the intellectual virtues, except prudence, rank before the moral virtues, in the point of their subject, they do not rank before them according to the nature of virtue; for a virtue, as such, has reference to the good, which is the object of the appetite.

[4] Q. 56, a. 3.   [5] Q. 57, a. 4.   [6] Q. 58, a. 3, ad 3.

Second Article

WHETHER THERE ARE FOUR CARDINAL VIRTUES?

We proceed thus to the Second Article:—

Objection 1. It would seem that there are not four cardinal virtues. For prudence is the directing principle of the other moral virtues, as is clear from what has been said above.[7] But that which directs others ranks before them. Therefore prudence alone is a principal virtue.

Obj. 2. Further, the principal virtues are, in a way, moral virtues. Now we are directed to moral works both by the practical reason and by a right appetite, as is stated in *Ethics* vi.[8] Therefore there are only two cardinal virtues.

Obj. 3. Further, even among the other virtues one ranks higher than another. But in order that a virtue be principal, it need not rank above all the others, but above some. Therefore it seems that there are many more principal virtues.

On the contrary, Gregory says: *The entire structure of good works is built on four virtues.*[9]

I answer that, Things may be numbered either in respect of their formal principles, or according to the subjects in which they are; and in either way we find that there are four cardinal virtues.

For the formal principle of the virtue of which we speak now is the good as defined by reason. This good can be considered in two ways. First, as existing in the consideration itself of reason, and thus we have one principal virtue called *prudence.*—Secondly, according as the reason puts its order into something else, and this either into operations, and then we have *justice,* or into passions, and then we need two virtues. For the need of putting the order of reason into the passions is due to their thwarting reason; and this occurs in two ways. First, when the passions incite to something against reason, and then they need a curb, which we thus call *temperance;* secondly, when the passions withdraw us from following the dictate of reason, *e.g.,* through fear of danger or toil, and then man needs to be strengthened for that which reason dictates, lest he turn back, and to this end there is *fortitude.*

[7] Q. 58, a. 4.   [8] Aristotle, *Eth.,* VI, 2 (1139a 24).   [9] *Moral.,* II, 49 (PL 75, 592).

In like manner, we find the same number if we consider the subjects of virtue. For there are four subjects of the virtue of which we now speak, viz., the power which is rational in its essence, and this is perfected by *prudence*; and that which is rational by participation, and is threefold, the will, subject of *justice,* the concupiscible power, subject of *temperance,* and the irascible power, subject of *fortitude.*

Reply Obj. 1. Prudence is absolutely the principal of all the virtues. The others are principal, each in its own genus.

Reply Obj. 2. That part of the soul which is rational by participation is threefold, as was stated above.

Reply Obj. 3. All the other virtues, among which one ranks before another, are reducible to the above four, both as to the subject and as to the formal principles.

Question LXII

THE THEOLOGICAL VIRTUES

(*In Four Articles*)

WE MUST now consider the Theological Virtues. Under this head there are four points of inquiry: (1) Whether there are theological virtues? (2) Whether the theological virtues are distinguished from the intellectual and moral virtues? (3) How many, and which are they? (4) Of their order.

First Article

WHETHER THERE ARE THEOLOGICAL VIRTUES?

We proceed thus to the First Article:—

Objection 1. It would seem that there are not any theological virtues. For according to *Physics* vii., *virtue is the disposition of a perfect thing to that which is best; and by perfect I mean that which is disposed according to nature.*[1] But that which is divine is above man's nature. Therefore the theological virtues are not the virtues of a man.

Obj. 2. Further, theological virtues are quasi-divine virtues. But the divine virtues are exemplars, as was stated above,[2] which are not in us but in God. Therefore the theological virtues are not the virtues of man.

Obj. 3. Further, the theological virtues are so called because they direct us to God, Who is the first cause and last end of all things. But by the very nature of his reason and will, man is directed to his first cause and last end. Therefore there is no need for any habits of theological virtue to direct the reason and the will to God.

On the contrary, The precepts of law are about acts of virtue. But the divine law contains precepts about the acts of faith, hope and charity: for it is written (*Ecclus.* ii. 8, seqq.): *Ye that fear the Lord believe Him,* and again, *hope in Him,* and again, *love Him.* Therefore faith, hope and charity are virtues directing us to God. Therefore they are theological virtues.

---

[1] Aristotle, *Phys.*, VII, 3 (246b 23).—Cf. *ibid.* (246a 13).   [2] Q. 61, a. 5.

I answer that, Man is perfected by virtue for those actions by which he is directed to happiness, as was explained above.[3] Now man's happiness or felicity is twofold, as was also stated above.[4] One is proportioned to human nature, a happiness, namely, which man can obtain by means of the principles of his nature. The other is a happiness surpassing man's nature, and which man can obtain by the power of God alone, by a kind of participation of the Godhead; and thus it is written (*2 Pet.* i. 4) that by Christ we are made *partakers of the divine nature.* And because such happiness surpasses the power of human nature, man's natural principles, which enable him to act well according to his power, do not suffice to direct man to this same happiness. Hence it is necessary for man to receive from God some additional principles, by which he may be directed to supernatural happiness, even as he is directed to his connatural end by means of his natural principles, albeit not without the divine assistance. Such principles are called *theological virtues.*[5] They are so called, first, because their object is God, inasmuch as they direct us rightly to God; secondly, because they are infused in us by God alone; thirdly, because these virtues are not made known to us, save by divine revelation, contained in Holy Scripture.

Reply Obj. 1. A certain nature may be ascribed to a certain thing in two ways. First, essentially, and thus these theological virtues surpass the nature of man. Secondly, by participation, as kindled wood partakes of the nature of fire, and thus, after a fashion, man becomes a partaker of the divine nature, as was stated above. Hence these virtues befit man according to the nature of which he is made a partaker.

Reply Obj. 2. These virtues are called divine, not as though God were virtuous by reason of them, but because by them God makes us virtuous, and directs us to Himself. Hence they are not exemplar virtues but copies.

Reply Obj. 3. The reason and the will are naturally directed to God, inasmuch as He is the cause and the end of nature, but according to the ability of nature. But the reason and the will, according to their nature, are not sufficiently directed to Him in so far as He is the object of supernatural happiness.

[3] Q. 5, a. 7.   [4] Q. 5, a. 5.   [5] Cf. William of Auxerre, *Summa Aurea,* III, tr. 2, ch. 2 (fol. 130ra).

Second Article

WHETHER THE THEOLOGICAL VIRTUES ARE DISTINGUISHED
FROM THE INTELLECTUAL AND MORAL·VIRTUES?

We proceed thus to the Second Article:—

Objection 1. It would seem that the theological virtues are
not distinguished from moral and intellectual virtues. For the
theological virtues, if they be in a human soul, must needs
perfect it either as to the intellectual part or as to the appetitive part. Now the virtues which perfect the intellectual part
are called intellectual, and the virtues which perfect the appetitive part are called moral. Therefore the theological virtues are not distinguished from the moral and intellectual
virtues.

Obj. 2. Further, the theological virtues are those which direct us to God. Now among the intellectual virtues there is
one which directs us to God, namely, wisdom, which is about
divine things, since it considers the highest cause. Therefore
the theological virtues are not distinguished from the intellectual virtues.

Obj. 3. Further, Augustine shows how the four cardinal
virtues are the *order of love.*[6] Now love is charity, which is a
theological virtue. Therefore the moral virtues are not distinct from the theological.

On the contrary, That which is above man's nature is distinguished from that which is according to his nature. But
the theological virtues are above man's nature, while the intellectual and moral virtues are proportioned to his nature,
as was shown above.[7] Therefore they are distinguished from
one another.

I answer that, As was stated above, habits are distinguished specifically from one another according to the formal
difference of their objects.[8] Now the object of the theological
virtues is God Himself, Who is the last end of all, as surpassing the knowledge of our reason. On the other hand, the
object of the intellectual and moral virtues is something
comprehensible to human reason. Therefore the theological
virtues are distinguished specifically from the moral and intellectual virtues.

[6] *De Mor. Eccl.,* I, 15 (PL 32, 1322).   [7] Q. 58, a. 3.   [8] Q. 54,
a. 2, ad 1.

Reply Obj. 1. The intellectual and moral virtues perfect man's intellect and appetite according to the power of human nature; the theological virtues, supernaturally.

Reply Obj. 2. The wisdom which the Philosopher reckons as an intellectual virtue considers divine things so far as they are open to the investigation of human reason.[9] Theological virtue, on the other hand, is about these same things so far as they surpass human reason.

Reply Obj. 3. Though charity is love, yet love is not always charity. When, then, it is stated that every virtue is the *order of love,* this can be understood either of love in the general sense, or of the love of charity. If it be understood of love commonly so called, then each virtue is stated to be the order of love in so far as each cardinal virtue requires an ordered affection. Now love is the root and cause of every affection, as was stated above.[10] If, however, it be understood of the love of charity, it does not mean that every other virtue is charity essentially, but that all other virtues depend on charity in some way, as we shall show further on.[11]

Third Article

WHETHER FAITH, HOPE AND CHARITY ARE FITTINGLY RECKONED AS THEOLOGICAL VIRTUES?

We proceed thus to the Third Article:—

Objection 1. It would seem that faith, hope and charity are not fittingly reckoned as three theological virtues. For the theological virtues are in relation to divine happiness just as the inclination of nature is in relation to the connatural end. Now among the virtues directed to the connatural end there is but one natural virtue, viz., the understanding of principles. Therefore there should be but one theological virtue.

Obj. 2. Further, the theological virtues are more perfect than the intellectual and moral virtues. Now faith is not reckoned among the intellectual virtues, but is something less than a virtue, since it is imperfect knowledge. Likewise, hope is not reckoned among the moral virtues, but is something less than a virtue, since it is a passion. Much less therefore should they be reckoned as theological virtues.

Obj. 3. Further, the theological virtues direct man's soul to

[9] *Eth.,* VI, 3 (1139b 17).   [10] Q. 27, a. 4; q. 28, a. 6, ad 2; q. 41, a. 2, ad 1.   [11] Q. 65, a. 2 and 4; II-II, q. 23, a. 7.

God. Now man's soul cannot be directed to God save through the intellectual part, in which are intellect and will. Therefore there should be only two theological virtues, one perfecting the intellect, the other, the will.

On the contrary, The Apostle says (*1 Cor.* xiii. 13): *Now there remain faith, hope, charity, these three.*

I answer that, As was stated above, the theological virtues direct man to supernatural happiness in the same way as by the natural inclination man is directed to his connatural end. Now the latter direction happens in two respects. First, according to the reason or intellect, in so far as it contains the first universal principles which are known to us through the natural light of the intellect, and which are reason's starting-point, both in speculative and in practical matters. Secondly, through the rectitude of the will tending naturally to the good as defined by reason.

But these two fall short of the order of supernatural happiness, according to *1 Cor.* ii. 9: *The eye hath not seen, nor ear heard, neither hath it entered into the heart of man, what things God hath prepared for them that love Him.* Consequently, in relation to both intellect and will, man needed to receive in addition something supernatural to direct him to a supernatural end. First, as regards the intellect, man receives certain supernatural principles, which are held by means of a divine light; and these are the things which are to be believed, about which is *faith.*—Secondly, the will is directed to this end, both as to the movement of intention, which tends to that end as something attainable,—this pertains to *hope* —and as to a certain spiritual union, whereby the will is, in a way, transformed into that end—and this belongs to *charity.* For the appetite of a thing is naturally moved and tends towards its connatural end and this movement is due to a certain conformity of the thing with its end.

Reply Obj. 1. The intellect requires intelligible species whereby to understand, and consequently there is need of a natural habit in addition to the power. But the very nature of the will suffices for it to be directed naturally to the end, both as to the intention of the end and as to its conformity with the end. But in relation to the things which are above nature, the nature itself of the power is insufficient. Consequently there was need for an additional supernatural habit in both respects.

Reply Obj. 2. Faith and hope imply a certain imperfection, since faith is of things unseen, and hope of things not possessed. Hence to have faith and hope in things that are subject to human power falls short of the nature of virtue. But to have faith and hope in things which are above the ability of human nature surpasses every virtue that is proportioned to man, according to *1 Cor.* i. 25: *The weakness of God is stronger than men.*

Reply Obj. 3. Two things pertain to the appetite, viz., movement to the end, and conformity with the end by means of love. Hence there must needs be two theological virtues in the human appetite, namely, hope and charity.

Fourth Article

WHETHER FAITH PRECEDES HOPE, AND HOPE CHARITY?

We proceed thus to the Fourth Article:—

Objection 1. It would seem that the order of the theological virtues is not that faith precedes hope, and hope charity. For the root precedes that which grows from it. Now charity is the root of all virtues, according to *Ephes.* iii. 17: *Being rooted and founded in charity.* Therefore charity precedes the others.

Obj. 2. Further, Augustine says: *A man cannot love what he does not believe to exist. But if he believes and loves, by doing good works he ends in hoping.*[12] Therefore it seems that faith precedes charity, and charity hope.

Obj. 3. Further, love is the principle of all our affections, as was stated above. Now hope is a kind of affection, since it is a passion, as was stated above.[13] Therefore charity, which is love, precedes hope.

On the contrary, The Apostle enumerates them thus (*1 Cor.* xiii. 13): *Now there remain faith, hope, charity.*

I answer that, There is a twofold order, namely, that of generation, and that of perfection. According to the order of generation, in which matter precedes form, and the imperfect precedes the perfect, in one and the same subject faith precedes hope, and hope charity, as to their acts; for the habits are infused together. For the movement of the appetite cannot tend to anything, either by hoping or loving, unless that

---

[12] *De Doct. Christ.,* I, 37 (PL 34, 35).   [13] Q. 23, a. 4.

thing be apprehended by the sense or by the intellect. Now it
is by faith that the intellect apprehends what it hopes for and
loves. Hence, in the order of generation, faith must precede
hope and charity. In like manner, a man loves a thing because he apprehends it as his good. Now from the very fact
that a man hopes to be able to obtain some good from someone, he looks on the man in whom he hopes as a good of his
own. Hence, for the very reason that a man bases his hopes in
someone, he proceeds to love him; so that in the order of
generation, hope precedes charity as regards their respective
acts.

But in the order of perfection, charity precedes faith and
hope, because both faith and hope are quickened by charity,
and receive from charity their full complement as virtues.
For thus charity is the mother and the root of all the virtues,
inasmuch as it is the form of them all, as we shall state
further on.[14]

This suffices for the Reply to the First Objection.

Reply Obj. 2. Augustine is speaking of that hope by which
a man hopes to obtain beatitude through the merits which
he has already; and this belongs to hope quickened by, and
following, charity. But it is possible for a man, before having
charity, to hope through merits not already possessed, but
which he hopes to possess.

Reply Obj. 3. As was stated above in treating of the passions, hope has reference to two things.[15] One is its principal
object, viz., the good hoped for. With regard to this, love
always precedes hope, for a good is never hoped for unless it
be desired and loved.—Hope also regards the person from
whom a man hopes to be able to obtain some good. With regard to this, hope precedes love at first, though afterwards
hope is increased by love. Because, from the fact that a man
thinks that he can obtain a good through someone, he begins
to love him; and from the fact that he loves him, he then
hopes all the more in him.

[14] *S. T.*, II-II, q. 23, a. 8.   [15] Q. 40, a. 7.

THE CAUSE OF THE VIRTUES

(*In Four Articles*)

WE MUST now consider the cause of the virtues. Under this head there are four points of inquiry: (1) Whether virtue is in us by nature? (2) Whether any virtue is caused in us by habituation from our acts? (3) Whether any moral virtues are in us by infusion? (4) Whether virtue acquired by habituation is of the same species as infused virtue?

First Article

WHETHER VIRTUE IS IN US BY NATURE?

We proceed thus to the First Article:—

Objection 1. It would seem that virtue is in us by nature. For Damascene says: *Virtues are natural to us and are equally in all of us.*[1] And Anthony says in a sermon to the monks: *If the will contradicts nature, it is perverse, if it follow nature, it is virtuous.*[2] Moreover, the *Gloss* on *Matt.* iv. 23 (*Jesus went about,* etc.) says: *He taught them natural virtues, i.e., chastity, justice, humility, which man possesses naturally.*[3]

Obj. 2. Further, the good of virtue is to be in accord with reason, as was shown above.[4] But that which is in accord with reason is natural to man, since reason is man's nature. Therefore virtue is in man by nature.

Obj. 3. Further, that which is in us from birth is said to be natural to us. Now virtues are in some from birth, for it is written (*Job* xxxi. 18): *From my infancy mercy grew up with me, and it came out with me from my mother's womb.* Therefore virtue is in man by nature.

On the contrary, Whatever is in man by nature is common to all men, and is not taken away by sin, since even in the demons natural gifts remain, as Dionysius states.[5] But virtue is not in all men, and is cast out by sin. Therefore it is not in man by nature.

I answer that, With regard to corporeal forms, it has been

[1] *De Fide Orth.,* III, 14 (PG 94, 1045).   [2] Cf. St. Athanasius, *Vita S. Antonii.* trans. Evagrius (PG 26, 873).   [3] *Glossa ordin.* (V. 17E).
[4] Q. 55, a. 4, ad 2.   [5] *De Div. Nom.,* IV, 23 (PG 3, 725).

maintained by some that they are wholly from within. It was so held, for instance, by those who upheld the theory of *latent forms*.[6] Others held that forms are entirely from the outside, those, for instance, who thought that corporeal forms originated from some separate cause.[7] Others, however, esteemed that they are partly from within, in so far as they pre-exist potentially in matter, and partly from the outside, in so far as they are reduced to act by an agent.[8]

In like manner, with regard to the sciences and the virtues, some held that they are wholly from within,[9] so that all virtues and sciences pre-exist in the soul naturally, but that the hindrances to science and virtue, which befall the soul because of the burden of the body, are removed by study and practice, even as iron is made bright by being polished. This was the opinion of the Platonists. Others said that they are wholly from the outside, being due to the action of the agent intellect, as Avicenna maintained.[10] Others, again, said that the sciences and the virtues are in us by nature, so far as we possess the ability to acquire them, but not in their perfection. This is the teaching of the Philosopher,[11] and is nearer the truth.

To make this clear, it must be observed that there are two ways in which something is said to be natural to a man. One is according to his specific nature, the other according to his individual nature. And, since each thing derives its species from its form, and its individuation from matter; furthermore, since the form of man is the rational soul, while the matter is the body, hence it is that whatever belongs to man according to the rational soul is natural to him according to his specific nature, while whatever belongs to him according to the particular temperament of his body is natural to him according to his individual nature. For whatever is natural to man because of his body, considered as part of his species, in a way is to be referred to the soul, in so far as this particular body is proportioned to this particular soul.

In both these ways virtue is natural to man inchoately. It is natural to man according to the specific nature, in so far as in man's reason there are to be found naturally present certain naturally known principles of both knowledge and

[6] Cf. *S. T.*, I, q. 45, a. 8.   [7] Cf. *ibid*.   [8] Cf. *ibid*.   [9] Cf. *S. T.*, I, q. 84, a. 3, obj. 3.   [10] *De An.*, V, 5 (25 rb).   [11] *Eth.*, II, 1 (1103a 25).

action, which are the seeds of intellectual and moral virtues, and in so far as there is in the will a natural appetite for the good which is in accord with reason. Again, it is natural to man according to the individual nature, in so far as, by reason of a disposition in the body, some are disposed either well or ill to certain virtues. This happens according as certain sensitive powers are acts of certain parts of the body, whose disposition helps or hinders these powers in the exercise of their acts, and, in consequence, the rational powers also, which such sensitive powers assist. In this way, one man has a natural aptitude for science, another for fortitude, another for temperance. This is the manner in which both the intellectual and the moral virtues are in us naturally, namely, according to an inchoateness which consists in our ability to acquire them. But their completion is not present naturally, since nature is determined to one course of action, while the completion of these virtues does not depend on one particular mode of action; rather does the completion vary according to the various matters which constitute the sphere of action of the virtues, and according to the variety of circumstances.

It is therefore evident that all virtues are in us by nature aptitudinally and inchoately, but not according to perfection, except the theological virtues, which are entirely from the outside.

This suffices for the Replies to the Objections. For the first two argue about the seeds of virtue which are in us by nature, inasmuch as we are rational beings.—The third objection must be taken in the sense that, owing to the natural disposition which the body has from birth, one has an aptitude for pity, another for living temperately, another for some other virtue.

Second Article

WHETHER ANY VIRTUE IS CAUSED IN US BY HABITUATION FROM OUR ACTS?

We proceed thus to the Second Article:—

Objection 1. It would seem that virtues cannot be caused in us by habituation from our acts. For the *Gloss* of Augustine, commenting on *Rom.* xiv. 23 (*All that is not of faith is sin*) says: *The whole life of an unbeliever is a sin, and there*

*is no good without the highest good. Where knowledge of the
truth is lacking, virtue is a mockery even in the most excellent behavior.*[12] Now faith cannot be acquired by means of
works, but is caused in us by God, according to *Ephes.* ii. 8:
By grace you are saved through faith. Therefore no virtue
can be acquired by us through habituation from our acts.

Obj. 2. Further, sin and virtue are contraries, so that they
are incompatible. Now man cannot avoid sin except by the
grace of God, according to *Wis.* viii. 21: *I knew that I could
not otherwise be continent, except God gave it.* Therefore
neither can any virtues be caused in us by habituation from
our acts, but only by the gift of God.

Obj. 3. Further, actions which are without virtue lack the
perfection of virtue. But an effect cannot be more perfect
than its cause. Therefore a virtue cannot be caused by actions
that precede it.

On the contrary, Dionysius says that good is more efficacious than evil.[13] But vicious habits are caused by evil acts.
Much more, therefore, can virtuous habits be caused by good
acts.

I answer that, We have spoken already in a general way
about the generation of habits from acts.[14] Speaking now in
a special way of this matter in relation to virtue, we must
take note that, as was stated above, man's virtue perfects him
in relation to good.[15] But since the notion of good consists in
mode, species and order, as Augustine states,[16] or in *number,
weight and measure,* according to *Wis.* xi. 21, man's good
must needs be appraised with respect to some rule. Now this
rule is twofold, as was stated above, viz., human reason and
divine law.[17] And since divine law is the higher rule, it extends to more things, so that whatever is ruled by human
reason is ruled by the divine law too; but the converse does
not hold.

It follows that human virtue, directed to the good which is
defined according to the rule of human reason, can be caused
by human acts; for such acts proceed from reason, by whose
power and rule the good in question is established. On the
other hand, virtue which directs man to good as defined by
the divine law, and not by human reason, cannot be caused

[12] *Glossa ordin.* (VI, 30B).   [13] *De Div. Nom.,* IV, 20; 32 (PG 3,
717; 732).   [14] Q. 51, a. 2 and 3.   [15] Q. 55, a. 3 and 4.   [16] *De Nat.
Boni,* III (PL 42, 553).   [17] Q. 19, a. 3 and 4.

by human acts, whose principle is reason, but is produced in us by the divine operation alone. Hence Augustine, in giving the definition of this virtue, inserts the words, *which God works in us without us*.[18] It is also of this virtue that the First Objection holds good.

Reply Obj. 2. Mortal sin is incompatible with divinely infused virtue, especially if this virtue be considered in its perfect nature. But actual sin, even mortal, is compatible with humanly acquired virtue, because the use of a habit in us is subject to our will, as was stated above,[19] and one sinful act does not destroy a habit of acquired virtue, since it is not an act but a habit that is directly contrary to a habit. Therefore, though man cannot avoid mortal sin without grace, so as never to sin mortally, yet he is not hindered from acquiring a habit of virtue, whereby he may abstain from evil in the majority of cases, and chiefly in matters most opposed to reason. —There are also certain mortal sins which man can in no way avoid without grace, those, namely, which are directly opposed to the theological virtues, which are in us through the gift of grace. This, however, will be more fully explained later.[20]

Reply Obj. 3. As was stated above, certain seeds or principles of the acquired virtues pre-exist in us by nature.[21] These principles are more excellent than the virtues acquired through their power. Thus, the understanding of speculative principles is more excellent than the science of conclusions, and the natural rectitude of the reason is more excellent than the rectification of the appetite which takes place through participation in the reason. This rectification belongs to moral virtue. Accordingly, human acts, in so far as they proceed from higher principles, can cause acquired human virtues.

Third Article

WHETHER ANY MORAL VIRTUES ARE IN US BY INFUSION?

We proceed thus to the Third Article:—

Objection 1. It would seem that no virtues besides the theological virtues are infused in us by God. For God does not

[18] Cf. above, q. 55, a. 4, obj. 1.   [19] Q. 49, a. 3.   [20] Q. 109, a. 4.
[21] A. 1; q. 51, a. 1.

do by Himself, save perhaps sometimes miraculously, those things that can be done by second causes; because, as Dionysius says, *it is God's rule to bring about extremes through the mean.*[22] Now intellectual and moral virtues can be caused in us by our acts, as was stated above. Therefore it is not fitting that they should be caused in us by infusion.

Obj. 2. Further, much less superfluity is found in God's works than in the works of nature. But the theological virtues suffice to direct us to the supernatural good. Therefore there are no other supernatural virtues requiring to be caused in us by God.

Obj. 3. Further, nature does not employ two means where one suffices. Much less does God. But God sowed the seeds of virtue in our souls, according to the *Gloss* on *Heb.* i. 6.[23] Therefore it is unfitting for Him to cause in us other virtues by means of infusion.

On the contrary, It is written (*Wis.* viii. 7): *She teacheth temperance and prudence and justice and fortitude.*

I answer that, Effects must needs be proportioned to their causes and principles. Now all virtues, intellectual and moral, that are acquired by our actions, arise from certain natural principles pre-existing in us, as was stated above.[24] In the place of these natural principles, God bestows on us the theological virtues, by which we are directed to a supernatural end, as was stated above.[25] Therefore we need to receive from God other habits annexed proportionately to the theological virtues, which are to the theological virtues what the moral and intellectual virtues are to the natural principles of the virtues.

Reply Obj. 1. Some moral and intellectual virtues can be caused in us by our actions, but they are not proportioned to the theological virtues. Therefore it was necessary for us to receive, from God immediately, others that are proportioned to those virtues.

Reply Obj. 2. The theological virtues direct us sufficiently to our supernatural end in an inchoate way, that is, in so far as it is to God Himself immediately. But the soul needs further to be perfected by infused virtues in regard to other things, yet in relation to God.

Reply Obj. 3. The power of those naturally instilled prin-

[22] *De Cael Hier.,* IV, 3 (PG 3, 181).   [23] *Glossa ordin.* (VI, 79E).
[24] A. 1; q. 51, a. 1.   [25] Q. 62, a. 1.

ciples does not extend beyond the capability of nature. Consequently man needs in addition to be perfected by other principles in relation to his supernatural end.

Fourth Article

WHETHER VIRTUE ACQUIRED BY HABITUATION FROM OUR ACTS BELONGS TO THE SAME SPECIES AS INFUSED VIRTUE?

We proceed thus to the Fourth Article:—

Objection 1. It would seem that the infused virtues do not differ in species from the acquired virtues. For acquired and infused virtues, according to what has been said, do not seem to differ save in relation to the last end. Now human habits and acts are specified, not by their last end, but by their proximate end. Therefore the infused moral or intellectual virtues do not differ specifically from the acquired virtues.

Obj. 2. Further, habits are known by their acts. But the act of infused and acquired temperance is the same, viz., to moderate desires of touch. Therefore they do not differ in species.

Obj. 3. Further, acquired and infused virtue differ as that which is wrought by God immediately, and that which is wrought by a creature. But the man whom God made is of the same species as a man begotten naturally; and the eye which He gave to the man born blind, as one produced by the power of generation. Therefore it seems that acquired and infused virtue belong to the same species.

On the contrary, Any change introduced into the difference expressed in a definition involves a difference of species. But the definition of infused virtue contains the words, *which God works in us without us,* as was stated above.[26] Therefore acquired virtue, to which these words cannot apply, is not of the same species as infused virtue.

I answer that, There is a twofold specific difference among habits. The first, as was stated above, is taken from the special and formal aspects of their objects.[27] Now the object of every virtue is a good considered as in that virtue's proper matter. Thus, the object of temperance is a good in relation to the pleasures connected with the concupiscence of touch. The formal aspect of this object is from reason, which fixes

[26] A. 2; q. 55, a. 4.   [27] Q. 54, a. 2; q. 56, a. 2; q. 60, a. 1.

the mean in these concupiscences; while the material element is something on the part of the concupiscences. Now it is evident that the mean that is appointed, in such concupiscences, according to the rule of human reason is of a different nature than the mean which is fixed according to the divine rule. For instance, in the consumption of food, the mean fixed by human reason is that food should not harm the health of the body, nor hinder the use of reason; whereas, according to the divine rule, it behooves man to *chastise* his *body, and bring it into subjection* (*1 Cor.* ix. 27), by abstinence in food, drink and the like. It is therefore evident that infused and acquired temperance differ in species; and the same applies to the other virtues.

The other specific difference among habits is taken from the things to which they are directed. For the health of a man and a horse is not of the same species, because of the diverse natures to which the health of the man and the health of the horse are directed. In the same sense, the Philosopher says that citizens have diverse virtues according as they are well directed to diverse forms of government.[28] In the same way, too, those infused moral virtues, by which men behave well in relation to their being *fellow-citizens with the saints, and of the household of God* (*Ephes.* ii. 19), differ from the acquired virtues by which man behaves well in relation to human affairs.

Reply Obj. 1. Infused and acquired virtue differ not only in relation to the ultimate end, but also in relation to their proper objects, as has been said.

Reply Obj. 2. Both acquired and infused temperance moderate desires for pleasures of touch, but for different reasons, as was stated, and therefore their respective acts are not identical.

Reply Obj. 3. God gave the man born blind an eye for the same act as the act for which other eyes are formed naturally, and consequently it was of the same species. It would be the same if God wished to give a man miraculously virtues such as those that are acquired by acts. But the case is not so in the question before us, as has been said.

[28] *Polit.*, III, 2 (1276b 31).

Question LXIV

ON THE MEAN OF VIRTUE

(*In Four Articles*)

WE MUST now consider the properties of virtues. We must consider (1) the mean of virtue; (2) the connection among the virtues;[1] (3) the equality of the virtues;[2] (4) the duration of the virtues.[3] Under the first head there are four points of inquiry: (1) Whether the moral virtues consist in a mean? (2) Whether the mean of moral virtue is a real mean or a mean of reason? (3) Whether the intellectual virtues consist in a mean? (4) Whether the theological virtues do?

First Article

WHETHER THE MORAL VIRTUES CONSIST IN A MEAN?

We proceed thus to the First Article:—

Objection 1. It would seem that moral virtue does not consist in a mean. For the nature of a mean is incompatible with that which is extreme. Now the nature of virtue is to be something extreme; for it is stated in *De Caelo* i. that *virtue is the peak of power*.[4] Therefore moral virtue does not consist in a mean.

Obj. 2. Further, the maximum is not a mean. Now some moral virtues tend to a maximum: for instance, magnanimity to very great honors, and magnificence to very large expenditures, as is stated in *Ethics* iv.[5] Therefore not every moral virtue consists in a mean.

Obj. 3. Further, if it is essential to a moral virtue to consist in a mean, it follows that a moral virtue is not perfected, but on the contrary corrupted, through tending to something extreme. Now some moral virtues are perfected by tending to something extreme. Thus virginity, which abstains from all sexual pleasure, observes the extreme, and is the most perfect chastity. In the same way, to give all to the poor is the most perfect mercy or liberality. Therefore it seems that it is not essential to moral virtue that it should consist in a mean.

---

[1] Q. 65.　　[2] Q. 66.　　[3] Q. 67.　　[4] Aristotle, *De Caelo*, I, 11 (281a 11; a 18).—Cf. St. Thomas, *In De Caelo*, I, lect. 25.　　[5] Aristotle, *Eth.*, IV, 2 (1122a 18); 3 (1123a 34).

On the contrary, The Philosopher says that *moral virtue is an elective habit consisting in the mean.*[6]

I answer that, As has already been explained, the nature of virtue is that it should direct man to good.[7] Now moral virtue is properly a perfection of the appetitive part of the soul in regard to some determinate matter; and the measure and rule of the appetitive movement in relation to appetible objects is the reason. But the good of that which is measured or ruled consists in its conformity with its rule; and, thus, the good of things made by art is that they follow the rule of art. Consequently, in things of this sort, evil consists in discordance from their rule or measure. Now this may happen either by their exceeding the measure or by their falling short of it; as we may clearly observe in all things ruled or measured. Hence it is evident that the good of moral virtue consists in conformity with the rule of reason. Now it is clear that between excess and deficiency the mean is equality or conformity. Therefore it is evident that moral virtue consists in a mean.

Reply Obj. 1. Moral virtue derives its goodness from the rule of reason, while its matter consists in passions or operations. If, therefore, we compare moral virtue to reason, then, if we look at that which it has of reason, it holds the position of one extreme, viz., conformity; while excess and defect take the position of the other extreme, viz., deformity. But if we consider moral virtue in respect of its matter, then it has the nature of a mean, in so far as it makes the passion conform to the rule of reason. Hence the Philosopher says that *virtue, as to its essence, is a mean,* in so far as the rule of virtue is imposed on its proper matter; *but it is an extreme in reference to the "best" and "the excellent,"* viz., as to its conformity with reason.[8]

Reply Obj. 2. In actions and passions, the mean and the extremes depend on various circumstances. Hence nothing hinders something from being extreme in a particular virtue according to one circumstance, while the same thing is a mean according to other circumstances, through its conformity with reason. This is the case with magnanimity and magnificence. For if we look at the absolute quantity of the respective objects of these virtues, we shall call it an extreme

[6] *Op. cit.,* II, 6 (1106b 36).   [7] Q. 55, a. 3.   [8] *Eth.,* II, 6 (1107a 7).

and a maximum; but if we consider the quantity in relation to other circumstances, then it has the character of a mean, since these virtues tend to this maximum in accordance with the rule of reason, *i.e., where* it is right, *when* it is right, and for an *end* that is right. There will be excess, if one tends to this maximum *when* it is not right, or *where* it is not right, or for an undue *end*; and there will be deficiency if one fails to tend thereto *where* one ought, and *when* one ought. This agrees with the saying of the Philosopher that the *magnanimous man observes the extreme in quantity, but the mean in the right mode of his action.*[9]

Reply Obj. 3. The same is to be said of virginity and poverty as of magnanimity. For virginity abstains from all sexual matters, and poverty from all wealth, for a right end, and in a right manner, *i.e.,* according to God's commandment, and for the sake of eternal life. But if this be done in an undue manner, *i.e.,* out of unlawful superstition, or again for vainglory, it will be in excess. And if it be not done when it ought to be done, or as it ought to be done, it is a vice by deficiency; as for instance, in those who break their vows of virginity or poverty.

Second Article

WHETHER THE MEAN OF MORAL VIRTUE IS A REAL MEAN, OR A MEAN OF REASON?

We proceed thus to the Second Article:—

Objection 1. It would seem that the mean of moral virtue is not the mean of reason, but a real mean. For the good of moral virtue consists in a mean. Now good, as is stated in *Metaph.* vi, is in things themselves.[10] Therefore the mean of moral virtue is a real mean.

Obj. 2. Further, the reason is a power of apprehension. But moral virtue does not observe a mean between apprehensions, but rather a mean between operations and passions. Therefore the mean of moral virtue is not the mean of reason, but a real mean.

Obj. 3. Further, a mean that is observed according to arithmetical or geometrical proportion is a real mean. Now

[9] *Op. cit.,* IV, 3 (1123b 13).   [10] Aristotle, *Metaph.,* VI, 4 (1027b 26).

such is the mean of justice, as is stated in *Ethics* v.[11] Therefore the mean of moral virtue is not the mean of reason, but
a real mean.

On the contrary, The Philosopher says that *moral virtue
observes the mean in relation to us, that is set by reason.*[12]

I answer that, The mean of reason can be understood in
two ways. First, according as the mean is found in the act itself of reason, as though the very act of reason were reduced
to a mean. In this sense, since moral virtue perfects, not the
act of reason, but the act of the appetitive power, the mean
of moral virtue is not the mean of reason. Secondly, the mean
of reason may be considered as that which the reason establishes in some particular matter. In this sense, every mean of
moral virtue is a mean of reason; for, as was stated above,
moral virtue is said to consist in a mean through conformity
with right reason.

But it happens sometimes that the mean of reason is also
a real mean, and in that case the mean of moral virtue is the
real mean (for instance, in justice). On the other hand, sometimes the mean of reason is not the real mean, but is established in relation to us. Such is the mean in all the other
moral virtues. The reason for this is that justice is about
operations, which deal with external things, wherein the right
has to be established absolutely and in itself, as was stated
above.[13] Hence the mean of reason in justice is the same as
the real mean, in so far, namely, as justice gives to each one
his due, neither more nor less. But the other moral virtues
deal with interior passions, wherein the right cannot be established in the same way, since men vary in their relations to
their passions. Hence the rectitude of reason has to be established in the passions with reference to us, who are influenced
through the passions.

This suffices for the Replies to the Objections. For the first
two arguments take the mean of reason as being in the very
act of reason, while the third argues from the mean of justice.

[11] Aristotle, *Eth.,* V, 4 (1132a 2); 3 (1131b 13); II, 6 (1106a 28).
[12] *Op. cit.,* II, 6 (1106b 36).   [13] Q. 60, a. 2.

LAW

Question XC

ON THE ESSENCE OF LAW

(*In Four Articles*)

WE HAVE now to consider the extrinsic principles of acts. Now the extrinsic principle inclining to evil is the devil, of whose temptations we have spoken in the First Part.[1] But the extrinsic principle moving to good is God, Who both instructs us by means of His Law, and assists us by His Grace. Therefore, in the first place, we must speak of law; in the second place, of grace.[2]

Concerning law, we must consider (1) law itself in general; (2) its parts.[3] Concerning law in general three points offer themselves for our consideration: (1) its essence; (2) the different kinds of law;[4] (3) the effects of law.[5]

Under the first head there are four points of inquiry: (1) Whether law is something pertaining to reason? (2) Concerning the end of law. (3) Its cause. (4) The promulgation of law.

First Article

WHETHER LAW IS SOMETHING PERTAINING TO REASON?

We proceed thus to the First Article:—

Objection 1. It would seem that law is not something pertaining to reason. For the Apostle says (*Rom.* vii. 23): *I see another law in my members,* etc. But nothing pertaining to reason is in the members, since the reason does not make use of a bodily organ. Therefore law is not something pertaining to reason.

Obj. 2. Further, in the reason there is nothing else but

---

[1] *S. T.,* I, q. 114.   [2] Q. 109.   [3] Q. 93.   [4] Q. 91.   [5] Q. 92.

power, habit and act. But law is not the power itself of reason. In like manner, neither is it a habit of reason, because the habits of reason are the intellectual virtues, of which we have spoken above.[6] Nor again is it an act of reason, because then law would cease when the act of reason ceases, for instance, while we are asleep. Therefore law is nothing pertaining to reason.

Obj. 3. Further, the law moves those who are subject to it to act rightly. But it belongs properly to the will to move to act, as is evident from what has been said above.[7] Therefore law pertains, not to the reason, but to the will, according to the words of the Jurist:[8] *Whatsoever pleaseth the sovereign has the force of law.*

On the contrary, It belongs to the law to command and to forbid. But it belongs to reason to command, as was stated above.[9] Therefore law is something pertaining to reason.

I answer that, Law is a rule and measure of acts, whereby man is induced to act or is restrained from acting; for *lex* [*law*] is derived from *ligare* [*to bind*], because it binds one to act. Now the rule and measure of human acts is the reason, which is the first principle of human acts, as is evident from what has been stated above.[10] For it belongs to the reason to direct to the end, which is the first principle in all matters of action, according to the Philosopher.[11] Now that which is the principle in any genus is the rule and measure of that genus: for instance, unity in the genus of numbers, and the first movement in the genus of movements. Consequently, it follows that law is something pertaining to reason.

Reply Obj. 1. Since law is a kind of rule and measure, it may be in something in two ways. First, as in that which measures and rules; and since this is proper to reason, it follows that, in this way, law is in the reason alone.—Secondly, as in that which is measured and ruled. In this way, law is in all those things that are inclined to something because of some law; so that any inclination arising from a law may be called a law, not essentially, but by participation as it were. And thus the inclination of the members to concupiscence is called *the law of the members.*[12]

Reply Obj. 2. Just as, in external acts, we may consider the

[6] Q. 57.   [7] Q. 9, a. 1.   [8] *Dig.,* I, iv, 1 (I, 35a).   [9] Q. 17, a. 1.
[10] Q. 1, a. 1, ad 3.   [11] *Phys.,* II, 9 (200a 22); *Eth.,* VII, 8 (1151a 16).
[12] Peter Lombard, *Sent.,* II, xxx, 8 (I, 464).

work and the work done, for instance, the work of building
and the house built, so in the acts of reason, we may consider
the act itself of reason, *i.e.*, to understand and to reason, and
something produced by this act. With regard to the speculative reason, this is first of all the definition; secondly, the
proposition; thirdly, the syllogism or argument. And since
the practical reason also makes use of the syllogism in operable matters, as we have stated above[13] and as the Philosopher teaches,[14] hence we find in the practical reason something that holds the same position in regard to operations as,
in the speculative reason, the proposition holds in regard to
conclusions. Such universal propositions of the practical reason that are directed to operations have the nature of law.
And these propositions are sometimes under our actual consideration, while sometimes they are retained in the reason
by means of a habit.

Reply Obj. 3. Reason has its power of moving from the
will, as was stated above;[15] for it is due to the fact that one
wills the end, that the reason issues its commands as regards
things ordained to the end. But in order that the volition of
what is commanded may have the nature of law, it needs to
be in accord with some rule of reason. And in this sense is to
be understood the saying that the will of the sovereign has
the force of law; or otherwise the sovereign's will would savor
of lawlessness rather than of law.

Second Article

WHETHER LAW IS ALWAYS DIRECTED TO THE
COMMON GOOD?

We proceed thus to the Second Article:—

Objection 1. It would seem that law is not always directed
to the common good as to its end. For it belongs to law to
command and to forbid. But commands are directed to certain individual goods. Therefore the end of law is not always
the common good.

Obj. 2. Further, law directs man in his actions. But human actions are concerned with particular matters. Therefore law is directed to some particular good.

[13] Q. 13, a. 3; q. 76, a. 1; q. 77, a. 2, ad 4.   [14] *Eth.*, VII, 3 (1147a
24).   [15] Q. 17, a. 1.

Obj. 3. Further, Isidore says: *If law is based on reason,
whatever is based on reason will be a law.*[16] But reason is the
foundation not only of what is ordained to the common good,
but also of that which is directed to private good. Therefore
law is not directed only to the good of all, but also to the
private good of an individual.

On the contrary, Isidore says that *laws are enacted for no
private profit, but for the common benefit of the citizens.*[17]

I answer that, As we have stated above, law belongs to that
which is a principle of human acts, because it is their rule and
measure. Now as reason is a principle of human acts, so in
reason itself there is something which is the principle in respect of all the rest. Hence to this principle chiefly and
mainly law must needs be referred. Now the first principle in
practical matters, which are the object of the practical reason,
is the last end: and the last end of human life is happiness or
beatitude, as we have stated above.[18] Consequently, law must
needs concern itself mainly with the order that is in beatitude. Moreover, since every part is ordained to the whole as
the imperfect to the perfect, and since one man is a part of
the perfect community, law must needs concern itself properly
with the order directed to universal happiness. Therefore the
Philosopher, in the above definition of legal matters, mentions both happiness and the body politic, since he says that
we call those legal matters *just which are adapted to produce
and preserve happiness and its parts for the body politic.*[19]
For the state is a perfect community, as he says in *Politics* i.[20]

Now, in every genus, that which belongs to it chiefly is the
principle of the others, and the others belong to that genus
according to some order towards that thing. Thus fire, which
is chief among hot things, is the cause of heat in mixed
bodies, and these are said to be hot in so far as they have a
share of fire. Consequently, since law is chiefly ordained to
the common good, any other precept in regard to some individual work must needs be devoid of the nature of a law,
save in so far as it regards the common good. Therefore every
law is ordained to the common good.

Reply Obj. 1. A command denotes the application of a

[16] *Etymol.*, II, 10; V, 3 (PL 82, 130; 199).   [17] *Op. cit.*, V, 21 (PL
82, 203).   [18] Q. 2, a. 7; q. 3, a. 1; q. 69, a. 1.   [19] *Eth.*, V, 1
(1129b 17).   [20] Aristotle, *Polit.*, I, 1 (1252a 5).

law to matters regulated by law. Now the order to the common good, at which law aims, is applicable to particular ends. And in this way commands are given even concerning particular matters.

Reply Obj. 2. Actions are indeed concerned with particular matters, but those particular matters are referable to the common good, not as to a common genus or species, but as to a common final cause, according as the common good is said to be the common end.

Reply Obj. 3. Just as nothing stands firm with regard to the speculative reason except that which is traced back to the first indemonstrable principles, so nothing stands firm with regard to the practical reason, unless it be directed to the last end which is the common good. Now whatever stands to reason in this sense has the nature of a law.

Third Article

WHETHER THE REASON OF ANY MAN IS COMPETENT TO MAKE LAWS?

We proceed thus to the Third Article:—

Objection 1. It would seem that the reason of any man is competent to make laws. For the Apostle says (*Rom.* ii. 14) that *when the Gentiles, who have not the law, do by nature those things that are of the law,* . . . *they are a law to themselves.* Now he says this of all in general. Therefore anyone can make a law for himself.

Obj. 2. Further, as the Philosopher says, *the intention of the lawgiver is to lead men to virtue.*[21] But every man can lead another to virtue. Therefore the reason of any man is competent to make laws.

Obj. 3. Further, just as the sovereign of a state governs the state, so every father of a family governs his household. But the sovereign of a state can make laws for the state. Therefore every father of a family can make laws for his household.

On the contrary, Isidore says, and the *Decretals* repeat: *A law is an ordinance of the people, whereby something is sanctioned by the Elders together with the Commonalty.*[22] Therefore not everyone can make laws.

[21] *Eth.,* II, 1 (1103b 3).   [22] *Etymol.,* V, 10 (PL 82, 200); Gratian, *Decretum,* I, ii, 1 (I, 3).

I answer that, A law, properly speaking, regards first and foremost the order to the common good. Now to order anything to the common good belongs either to the whole people, or to someone who is the vicegerent of the whole people. Hence the making of a law belongs either to the whole people or to a public personage who has care of the whole people; for in all other matters the directing of anything to the end concerns him to whom the end belongs.

Reply Obj. 1. As was stated above, a law is in a person not only as in one that rules, but also, by participation, as in one that is ruled. In the latter way, each one is a law to himself, in so far as he shares the direction that he receives from one who rules him. Hence the same text goes on: *Who show the work of the law written in their hearts* (*Rom.* ii. 15).

Reply Obj. 2. A private person cannot lead another to virtue efficaciously; for he can only advise, and if his advice be not taken, it has no coercive power, such as the law should have, in order to prove an efficacious inducement to virtue, as the Philosopher says.[23] But this coercive power is vested in the whole people or in some public personage, to whom it belongs to inflict penalties, as we shall state further on.[24] Therefore the framing of laws belongs to him alone.

Reply Obj. 3. As one man is a part of the household, so a household is a part of the state; and the state is a perfect community, according to *Politics* i.[25] Therefore, just as the good of one man is not the last end, but is ordained to the common good, so too the good of one household is ordained to the good of a single state, which is a perfect community. Consequently, he that governs a family can indeed make certain commands or ordinances, but not such as to have properly the nature of law.

Fourth Article

WHETHER PROMULGATION IS ESSENTIAL TO LAW?

We proceed thus to the Fourth Article:—

Objection 1. It would seem that promulgation is not essential to law. For the natural law, above all, has the character of law. But the natural law needs no promulgation. Therefore it is not essential to law that it be promulgated.

[23] *Eth.*, X, 9 (1180a 20). [24] Q. 92, a. 2, ad 3; II-II, q. 64, a. 3. [25] Aristotle, *Polit.*, I, 1 (1252a 5).

Obj. 2. Further, it belongs properly to law to bind one to do or not to do something. But the obligation of fulfilling a law touches not only those in whose presence it is promulgated, but also others. Therefore promulgation is not essential to law.

Obj. 3. Further, the binding force of law extends even to the future, since *laws are binding in matters of the future,* as the jurists say.[26] But promulgation concerns those who are present. Therefore it is not essential to law.

On the contrary, It is laid down in the *Decretals* that *laws are established when they are promulgated.*[27]

I answer that, As was stated above, a law is imposed on others as a rule and measure. Now a rule or measure is imposed by being applied to those who are to be ruled and measured by it. Therefore, in order that a law obtain the binding force which is proper to a law, it must needs be applied to the men who have to be ruled by it. But such application is made by its being made known to them by promulgation. Therefore promulgation is necessary for law to obtain its force.

Thus, from the four preceding articles, the definition of law may be gathered. Law is nothing else than an ordinance of reason for the common good, promulgated by him who has the care of the community.

Reply Obj. 1. The natural law is promulgated by the very fact that God instilled it into man's mind so as to be known by him naturally.

Reply Obj. 2. Those who are not present when a law is promulgated are bound to observe the law, in so far as it is made known or can be made known to them by others, after it has been promulgated.

Reply Obj. 3. The promulgation that takes place in the present extends to future time by reason of the durability of written characters, by which means it is continually promulgated. Hence Isidore says that *lex* [law] *is derived from legere* [to read] *because it is written.*[28]

[26] *Codex Justinianus,* I, xiv, 7 (II, 68a).   [27] Gratian, *Decretum,* I, iv, 3 (I, 6).   [28] *Etymol.,* II, 10 (PL 82, 130).

Question XCI

ON THE VARIOUS KINDS OF LAW

(*In Six Articles*)

WE MUST now consider the various kinds of law, under which head there are six points of inquiry: (1) Whether there is an eternal law? (2) Whether there is a natural law? (3) Whether there is a human law? (4) Whether there is a divine law? (5) Whether there is one divine law, or several? (6) Whether there is a law of sin?

First Article

WHETHER THERE IS AN ETERNAL LAW?

We proceed thus to the First Article:—

Objection 1. It would seem that there is no eternal law. For every law is imposed on someone. But there was not someone from eternity on whom a law could be imposed, since God alone was from eternity. Therefore no law is eternal.

Obj. 2. Further, promulgation is essential to law. But promulgation could not be from eternity, because there was no one to whom it could be promulgated from eternity. Therefore no law can be eternal.

Obj. 3. Further, law implies order to an end. But nothing ordained to an end is eternal, for the last end alone is eternal. Therefore no law is eternal.

On the contrary, Augustine says: *That Law which is the Supreme Reason cannot be understood to be otherwise than unchangeable and eternal.*[1]

I answer that, As we have stated above, law is nothing else but a dictate of practical reason emanating from the ruler who governs a perfect community.[2] Now it is evident, granted that the world is ruled by divine providence, as was stated in the First Part,[3] that the whole community of the universe is governed by the divine reason. Therefore the very notion of the government of things in God, the ruler of the

---

[1] *De Lib. Arb.*, I, 6 (PL 32, 1229).   [2] Q. 90, a. 1, ad 2; a. 3 and 4.   [3] *S. T.*, I, q. 22, a. 1, ad 2.

universe, has the nature of a law. And since the divine reason's conception of things is not subject to time, but is eternal, according to *Prov.* viii. 23, therefore it is that this kind of law must be called eternal.

Reply Obj. 1. Those things that do not exist in themselves exist in God, inasmuch as they are known and preordained by Him, according to *Rom.* iv. 17: *Who calls those things that are not, as those that are.* Accordingly, the eternal concept of the divine law bears the character of an eternal law in so far as it is ordained by God to the government of things foreknown by Him.

Reply Obj. 2. Promulgation is made by word of mouth or in writing, and in both ways the eternal law is promulgated, because both the divine Word and the writing of the Book of Life are eternal. But the promulgation cannot be from eternity on the part of the creature that hears or reads.

Reply Obj. 3. Law implies order to the end actively, namely, in so far as it directs certain things to the end; but not passively,—that is to say, the law itself is not ordained to the end, except accidentally, in a governor whose end is extrinsic to him, and to which end his law must needs be ordained. But the end of the divine government is God Himself, and His law is not something other than Himself. Therefore the eternal law is not ordained to another end.

Second Article

WHETHER THERE IS IN US A NATURAL LAW?

We proceed thus to the Second Article:—

Objection 1. It would seem that there is no natural law in us. For man is governed sufficiently by the eternal law, since Augustine says that *the eternal law is that by which it is right that all things should be most orderly.*[4] But nature does not abound in superfluities as neither does she fail in necessaries. Therefore man has no natural law.

Obj. 2. Further, by the law man is directed, in his acts, to the end, as was stated above.[5] But the directing of human acts to their end is not a function of nature, as is the case in irrational creatures, which act for an end solely by their nat-

---

[4] *De Lib. Arb.*, I, 6 (PL 32, 1229).   [5] Q. 90, a. 2.

ural appetite; whereas man acts for an end by his reason and will. Therefore man has no natural law.

Obj. 3. Further, the more a man is free, the less is he under the law. But man is freer than all the animals because of his free choice, with which he is endowed in distinction from all other animals. Since, therefore, other animals are not subject to a natural law, neither is man subject to a natural law.

On the contrary, The *Gloss* on *Rom.* ii. 14 (*When the Gentiles, who have not the law, do by nature those things that are of the law*) comments as follows: *Although they have no written law, yet they have the natural law, whereby each one knows, and is conscious of, what is good and what is evil.*[6]

I answer that, As we have stated above,[7] law, being a rule and measure, can be in a person in two ways: in one way, as in him that rules and measures; in another way, as in that which is ruled and measured, since a thing is ruled and measured in so far as it partakes of the rule or measure. Therefore, since all things subject to divine providence are ruled and measured by the eternal law, as was stated above, it is evident that all things partake in some way in the eternal law, in so far as, namely, from its being imprinted on them, they derive their respective inclinations to their proper acts and ends. Now among all others, the rational creature is subject to divine providence in a more excellent way, in so far as it itself partakes of a share of providence, by being provident both for itself and for others. Therefore it has a share of the eternal reason, whereby it has a natural inclination to its proper act and end; and this participation of the eternal law in the rational creature is called the natural law. Hence the Psalmist, after saying (*Ps.* iv. 6): *Offer up the sacrifice of justice,* as though someone asked what the works of justice are, adds: *Many say, Who showeth us good things?* in answer to which question he says: *The light of Thy countenance, O Lord, is signed upon us.* He thus implies that the light of natural reason, whereby we discern what is good and what is evil, which is the function of the natural law, is nothing else than an imprint on us of the divine light. It is therefore evident that the natural law is nothing else than the rational creature's participation of the eternal law.

Reply Obj. 1. This argument would hold if the natural law

---

[6] *Glossa ordin.* (VI, 7E) ; Peter Lombard, *In Rom.,* super II, 14 (PL 191, 1345).   [7] Q. 90, a. 1, ad 1.

were something different from the eternal law; whereas it is nothing but a participation thereof, as we have stated above.

Reply Obj. 2. Every act of reason and will in us is based on that which is according to nature, as was stated above.[8] For every act of reasoning is based on principles that are known naturally, and every act of appetite in respect of the means is derived from the natural appetite in respect of the last end. Accordingly, the first direction of our acts to their end must needs be through the natural law.

Reply Obj. 3. Even irrational animals partake in their own way of the eternal reason, just as the rational creature does. But because the rational creature partakes thereof in an intellectual and rational manner, therefore the participation of the eternal law in the rational creature is properly called a law, since a law is something pertaining to reason, as was stated above.[9] Irrational creatures, however, do not partake thereof in a rational manner, and therefore there is no participation of the eternal law in them, except by way of likeness.

Third Article

WHETHER THERE IS A HUMAN LAW?

We proceed thus to the Third Article:—

Objection 1. It would seem that there is not a human law. For the natural law is a participation of the eternal law, as was stated above. Now through the eternal law *all things are most orderly*, as Augustine states.[10] Therefore the natural law suffices for the ordering of all human affairs. Consequently there is no need for a human law.

Obj. 2. Further, law has the character of a measure, as was stated above.[11] But human reason is not a measure of things, but *vice versa*, as is stated in *Metaph.* x.[12] Therefore no law can emanate from the human reason.

Obj. 3. Further, a measure should be most certain, as is stated in *Metaph.* x.[13] But the dictates of the human reason in matters of conduct are uncertain, according to *Wis.* ix. 14: *The thoughts of mortal men are fearful, and our counsels uncertain.* Therefore no law can emanate from the human reason.

[8] Q. 10, a. 1.   [9] Q. 90, a. 1.   [10] *De Lib. Arb.*, I, 6 (PL 32, 1229).
[11] Q. 90, a. 1.   [12] Aristotle, *Metaph.*, IX, 1 (1053a 31).   [13] *Ibid.*

On the contrary, Augustine distinguishes two kinds of law, the one eternal, the other temporal, which he calls human.[14]

I answer that, As we have stated above, a law is a dictate of the practical reason.[15] Now it is to be observed that the same procedure takes place in the practical and in the speculative reason, for each proceeds from principles to conclusions, as was stated above.[16] Accordingly, we conclude that, just as in the speculative reason, from naturally known indemonstrable principles we draw the conclusions of the various sciences, the knowledge of which is not imparted to us by nature, but acquired by the efforts of reason, so too it is that from the precepts of the natural law, as from common and indemonstrable principles, the human reason needs to proceed to the more particular determination of certain matters. These particular determinations, devised by human reason, are called human laws, provided that the other essential conditions of law be observed, as was stated above.[17] Therefore Tully says in his *Rhetoric* that *justice has its source in nature; thence certain things came into custom by reason of their utility; afterwards these things which emanated from nature, and were approved by custom, were sanctioned by fear and reverence for the law.*[18]

Reply Obj. 1. The human reason cannot have a full participation of the dictate of the divine reason, but according to its own mode, and imperfectly. Consequently, just as on the part of the speculative reason, by a natural participation of divine wisdom, there is in us the knowledge of certain common principles, but not a proper knowledge of each single truth, such as that contained in the divine wisdom, so, too, on the part of the practical reason, man has a natural participation of the eternal law, according to certain common principles, but not as regards the particular determinations of individual cases, which are, however, contained in the eternal law. Hence the need for human reason to proceed further to sanction them by law.

Reply Obj. 2. Human reason is not, of itself, the rule of things. But the principles impressed on it by nature are the general rules and measures of all things relating to human conduct, of which the natural reason is the rule and measure, although it is not the measure of things that are from nature.

[14] *De Lib. Arb.,* I, 6 (PL 32, 1229).   [15] Q. 90, a. 1, ad 2.   [16] *Ibid.*
[17] Q. 90.   [18] *De Invent.,* II, 53 (p. 148b).

Reply Obj. 3. The practical reason is concerned with operable matters, which are singular and contingent, but not with necessary things, with which the speculative reason is concerned. Therefore human laws cannot have that inerrancy that belongs to the demonstrated conclusions of the sciences. Nor is it necessary for every measure to be altogether unerring and certain, but according as it is possible in its own particular genus.

Fourth Article

WHETHER THERE WAS ANY NEED FOR A DIVINE LAW?

We proceed thus to the Fourth Article:—

Objection 1. It would seem that there was no need for a divine law. For, as was stated above, the natural law is a participation in us of the eternal law. But the eternal law is the divine law, as was stated above. Therefore there is no need for a divine law in addition to the natural law and to human laws derived therefrom.

Obj. 2. Further, it is written (*Ecclus.* xv. 14) that *God left man in the hand of his own counsel.* Now counsel is an act of reason, as was stated above.[19] Therefore man was left to the direction of his reason. But a dictate of human reason is a human law, as was stated above. Therefore there is no need for man to be governed also by a divine law.

Obj. 3. Further, human nature is more self-sufficing than irrational creatures. But irrational creatures have no divine law besides the natural inclination impressed on them. Much less, therefore, should the rational creature have a divine law in addition to the natural law.

On the contrary, David prayed God to set His law before him, saying (*Ps.* cxviii. 33): *Set before me for a law the way of Thy justifications, O Lord.*

I answer that, Besides the natural and the human law it was necessary for the directing of human conduct to have a divine law. And this for four reasons. First, because it is by law that man is directed how to perform his proper acts in view of his last end. Now if man were ordained to no other end than that which is proportionate to his natural ability, there would be no need for man to have any further direction,

[19] Q. 14, a. 1.

on the part of his reason, in addition to the natural law and humanly devised law which is derived from it. But since man is ordained to an end of eternal happiness which exceeds man's natural ability, as we have stated above,[20] therefore it was necessary that, in addition to the natural and the human law, man should be directed to his end by a law given by God.

Secondly, because, by reason of the uncertainty of human judgment, especially on contingent and particular matters, different people form different judgments on human acts; whence also different and contrary laws result. In order, therefore, that man may know without any doubt what he ought to do and what he ought to avoid, it was necessary for man to be directed in his proper acts by a law given by God, for it is certain that such a law cannot err.

Thirdly, because man can make laws in those matters of which he is competent to judge. But man is not competent to judge of interior movements, that are hidden, but only of exterior acts which are observable; and yet for the perfection of virtue it is necessary for man to conduct himself rightly in both kinds of acts. Consequently, human law could not sufficiently curb and direct interior acts, and it was necessary for this purpose that a divine law should supervene.

Fourthly, because, as Augustine says,[21] human law cannot punish or forbid all evil deeds, since, while aiming at doing away with all evils, it would do away with many good things, and would hinder the advance of the common good, which is necessary for human living. In order, therefore, that no evil might remain unforbidden and unpunished, it was necessary for the divine law to supervene, whereby all sins are forbidden.

And these four causes are touched upon in *Ps*. cxviii. 8, where it is said: *The law of the Lord is unspotted*, *i.e.*, allowing no foulness of sin; *converting souls*, because it directs not only exterior, but also interior, acts; *the testimony of the Lord is faithful*, because of the certainty of what is true and right; *giving wisdom to little ones*, by directing man to an end supernatural and divine.

Reply Obj. 1. By the natural law the eternal law is participated proportionately to the capacity of human nature. But to his supernatural end man needs to be directed in a yet

---

[20] Q. 5, a. 5.   [21] *De Lib. Arb.*, I, 5 (PL 32, 1228).

higher way. Hence the additional law given by God, whereby man shares more perfectly in the eternal law.

Reply Obj. 2. Counsel is a kind of inquiry, and hence must proceed from some principles. Nor is it enough for it to proceed from principles imparted by nature, which are the precepts of the natural law, for the reasons given above; but there is need for certain additional principles, namely, the precepts of the divine law.

Reply Obj. 3. Irrational creatures are not ordained to an end higher than that which is proportionate to their natural powers. Consequently the comparison fails.

Fifth Article

WHETHER THERE IS BUT ONE DIVINE LAW?

We proceed thus to the Fifth Article:—

Objection 1. It would seem that there is but one divine law. For, where there is one king in one kingdom, there is but one law. Now the whole of mankind is compared to God as to one king, according to *Ps.* xlvi. 8: *God is the King of all the earth.* Therefore there is but one divine law.

Obj. 2. Further, every law is directed to the end which the lawgiver intends for those for whom he makes the law. But God intends one and the same thing for all men, since according to *1 Tim.* ii. 4: *He will have all men to be saved, and to come to the knowledge of the truth.* Therefore there is but one divine law.

Obj. 3. Further, the divine law seems to be more akin to the eternal law, which is one, than the natural law, according as the revelation of grace is of a higher order than natural knowledge. But natural law is one for all men. Therefore much more is the divine law but one.

On the contrary, The Apostle says (*Heb.* vii. 12): *The priesthood being translated, it is necessary that a translation also be made of the law.* But the priesthood is twofold, as stated in the same passage, viz., the levitical priesthood, and the priesthood of Christ. Therefore the divine law is twofold, namely, the Old Law and the New Law.

I answer that, As we have stated in the First Part, distinction is the cause of number.[22] Now things may be distin-

[22] *S. T.,* I, q. 30, a. 3.

guished in two ways. First, as those things that are altogether specifically different, *e.g.*, a horse and an ox. Secondly, as perfect and imperfect in the same species, *e.g.*, a boy and a man; and in this way the divine law is distinguished into Old and New. Hence the Apostle (*Gal.* iii. 24, 25) compares the state of man under the Old Law to that of a child *under a pedagogue*; but the state under the New Law, to that of a full grown man, who is *no longer under a pedagogue*.

Now the perfection and imperfection of these two laws is to be taken in connection with the three conditions pertaining to law, as was stated above. For, in the first place, it belongs to law to be directed to the common good as to its end, as was stated above.[23] This good may be twofold. It may be a sensible and earthly good, and to this man was directly ordained by the Old Law. Hence it is that, at the very outset of the Law, the people were invited to the earthly kingdom of the Chananæans (*Exod.* iii. 8, 17). Again it may be an intelligible and heavenly good, and to this, man is ordained by the New Law. Therefore, at the very beginning of His preaching, Christ invited men to the kingdom of heaven, saying (*Matt.* iv. 17): *Do penance, for the kingdom of heaven is at hand.* Hence Augustine says that *promises of temporal goods are contained in the Old Testament, for which reason it is called old; but the promise of eternal life belongs to the New Testament.*[24]

Secondly, it belongs to law to direct human acts according to the order of justice; wherein also the New Law surpasses the Old Law, since it directs our internal acts, according to *Matt.* v. 20: *Unless your justice abound more than that of the Scribes and Pharisees, you shall not enter into the kingdom of heaven.* Hence the saying that *the Old Law restrains the hand, but the New Law controls the soul.*[25]

Thirdly, it belongs to law to induce men to observe its commandments. This the Old Law did by the fear of punishment, but the New Law, by love, which is poured into our hearts by the grace of Christ, bestowed in the New Law, but foreshadowed in the Old. Hence Augustine says that *there is little difference between the Law and the Gospel—fear* [timor] *and love* [amor].[26]

[23] Q. 90, a. 2. [24] *Contra Faust.*, IV, 2 (PL 42, 217). [25] Cf. Peter Lombard, *Sent.*, III, xl, 1 (II, 734). [26] *Contra Adimant.*, XVII (PL 42, 159).

Reply Obj. 1. As the father of a family issues different commands to the children and to the adults, so also the one King, God, in His one kingdom, gave one law to men while they were yet imperfect, and another more perfect law when, by the preceding law, they had been led to a greater capacity for divine things.

Reply Obj. 2. The salvation of man could not be achieved otherwise than through Christ, according to *Acts* iv. 12: *There is no other name . . . given to men, whereby we must be saved.* Consequently, the law that brings all to salvation could not be given until after the coming of Christ. But before His coming it was necessary to give to the people, of whom Christ was to be born, a law containing certain rudiments of justice unto salvation, in order to prepare them to receive Him.

Reply Obj. 3. The natural law directs man by way of certain general precepts, common to both the perfect and the imperfect. Hence it is one and the same for all. But the divine law directs man also in certain particular matters, to which the perfect and imperfect do not stand in the same relation. Hence the necessity for the divine law to be twofold, as we have already explained.

Sixth Article

WHETHER THERE IS A LAW IN THE *FOMES* OF SIN?

We proceed thus to the Sixth Article:—

Objection 1. It would seem that there is no law of the 'fomes' of sin.[27] For Isidore says that the *law is based on reason*.[28] But the 'fomes' of sin is not based on reason, but deviates from it. Therefore the 'fomes' has not the nature of a law.

Obj. 2. Further, every law is binding, so that those who do not obey it are called transgressors. But man is not called a transgressor from not following the instigations of the 'fomes,' but rather from his following them. Therefore the 'fomes' has not the nature of a law.

Obj. 3. Further, law is ordained to the common good, as

---

[27] Cf. Peter Lombard, *Sent.*, II, xxx, 8 (I, 464) ; St. John Damascene, *De Fide Orth.*, IV, 22 (PG 94, 1200).   [28] *Etymol.*, V, 3 (PL 82, 199).

was stated above.[29] But the 'fomes' inclines us, not to the common good, but to our own private good. Therefore the 'fomes' has not the nature of law.

On the contrary, The Apostle says (*Rom.* vii. 23): *I see another law in my members, fighting against the law of my mind.*

I answer that, As we have stated above, law, as to its essence, resides in him that rules and measures, but, by way of participation, in that which is ruled and measured;[30] so that every inclination or ordination which may be found in things subject to law is called a law by participation, as was stated above.[31] Now those who are subject to law may receive a twofold inclination from the lawgiver. First, in so far as he directly inclines his subjects to something. According to this, he directs different subjects to different acts; and in this way we may say that there is a military law and a mercantile law. Secondly, indirectly, and thus by the very fact that a lawgiver deprives a subject of some dignity, the latter passes into another order, so as to be under another law, as it were. For example, if a soldier be turned out of the army, he will become a subject of rural or of mercantile legislation.

Accordingly, under the divine Lawgiver, various creatures have various natural inclinations, so that what is, as it were, a law for one, is against the law for another. Thus, I might say that fierceness is, in a way, the law of a dog, but against the law of a sheep or another meek animal. And so the law of man, which, by the divine ordinance, is allotted to him according to his proper natural condition, is that he should act in accordance with reason; and this law was so effective in man's first state, that nothing either outside or against reason could take man unawares. But when man turned his back on God, he fell under the influence of his sensual impulses. In fact, this happens to each one individually, according as he has the more departed from the path of reason; so that, after a fashion, he is likened to the beasts that are led by the impulse of sensuality, according to *Ps.* xlviii. 21: *Man, when he was in honor, did not understand: he hath been compared to senseless beasts, and made like to them.*

Accordingly, then, this very inclination of sensuality, which is called the 'fomes,' in other animals has absolutely

---

[29] Q. 90, a. 2.   [30] A. 2; q. 90, a. 1, ad 1.   [31] *Ibid.*

the nature of law, yet only in so far as we may consider as law what is an inclination subject to law. But in man, it has not the nature of law in this way; rather is it a deviation from the law of reason. But since, by the just sentence of God, man is deprived of original justice, and his reason bereft of its vigor, this impulse of sensuality, whereby he is led, has the nature of a law in so far as it is a penalty following from the divine law depriving man of his proper dignity.

Reply Obj. 1. This argument considers the 'fomes' in itself as an incentive to evil. It is not thus that it has the nature of a law, as we have stated above, but according as it results from the justice of the divine law; much as though we were to say that it is a law that a nobleman should be made subject to menial labor because of some misdeed.

Reply Obj. 2. This argument considers law in the light of a rule or measure; for it is in this sense that those who deviate from the law become transgressors. But the 'fomes' is not a law in this respect, but by a kind of participation, as was stated above.

Reply Obj. 3. This argument considers the 'fomes' as to its proper inclination, and not as to its origin. And yet if the inclination of sensuality be considered as it is in other animals, thus it is ordained to the common good, namely, to the preservation of nature in the species or in the individual. This is true in man also, in so far as sensuality is subject to reason. But it is called the 'fomes' in so far as it departs from the order of reason.

Question XCIII

THE ETERNAL LAW

(*In Six Articles*)

WE MUST now consider each law by itself: (1) the eternal law; (2) the natural law;[1] (3) the human law;[2] (4) the Old Law;[3] (5) the New Law, which is the law of the Gospel.[4] Of the sixth law, which is the law of the 'fomes,' what we have said when treating of original sin must suffice.[5]

Concerning the first there are six points of inquiry: (1) What is the eternal law? (2) Whether it is known to all? (3) Whether every law is derived from it? (4) Whether necessary things are subject to the eternal law? (5) Whether natural contingents are subject to the eternal law? (6) Whether all human things are subject to it?

First Article

WHETHER THE ETERNAL LAW IS A SUPREME EXEMPLAR EXISTING IN GOD?

We proceed thus to the First Article:—

Objection 1. It would seem that the eternal law is not a supreme exemplar existing in God. For there is only one eternal law. But there are many exemplars of things in the divine mind, for Augustine says that God *made each thing according to its exemplar*.[6] Therefore the eternal law does not seem to be the same as an exemplar existing in the divine mind.

Obj. 2. Further, it is of the nature of a law that it be promulgated by word, as was stated above.[7] But *Word* is a Personal name in God, as was stated in the First Part,[8] whereas *exemplar* refers to the essence. Therefore the eternal law is not the same as a divine exemplar.

Obj. 3. Further, Augustine says: *We see a law above our minds, which is called truth*.[9] But the law which is above our minds is the eternal law. Therefore truth is the eternal

[1] Q. 94. [2] Q. 95. [3] Q. 98. [4] Q. 106. [5] Q. 81, 82, 83.
[6] *Lib. 83 Quaest.*, q. 46 (PL 40, 30). [7] Q. 90, a. 4; q. 91, a. 1, ad 2.
[8] *S. T., I*, q. 34, a. 1. [9] *De Vera Relig.*, XXX (PL 34, 147).

law. But the notion of truth is not the same as the notion of an exemplar. Therefore the eternal law is not the same as the supreme exemplar.

On the contrary, Augustine says that *the eternal law is the supreme exemplar to which we must always conform.*[10]

I answer that, Just as in every artificer there pre-exists an exemplar of the things that are made by his art, so too in every governor there must pre-exist the exemplar of the order of those things that are to be done by those who are subject to his government. And just as the exemplar of the things yet to be made by an art is called the art or model of the products of that art, so, too, the exemplar in him who governs the acts of his subjects bears the character of a law, provided the other conditions be present which we have mentioned above as belonging to the nature of law.[11] Now God, by His wisdom, is the Creator of all things, in relation to which He stands as the artificer to the products of his art, as was stated in the First Part.[12] Moreover, He governs all the acts and movements that are to be found in each single creature, as was also stated in the First Part.[13] Therefore, just as the exemplar of the divine wisdom, inasmuch as all things are created by it, has the character of an art, a model or an idea, so the exemplar of divine wisdom, as moving all things to their due end, bears the character of law. Accordingly, the eternal law is nothing else than the exemplar of divine wisdom, as directing all actions and movements.

Reply Obj. 1. Augustine is speaking in that passage of the ideal exemplars which refer to the proper nature of each single thing; and consequently in them there is a certain distinction and plurality, according to their different relations to things, as was stated in the First Part.[14] But law is said to direct human acts by ordaining them to the common good, as was stated above.[15] Now things which are in themselves diverse may be considered as one, according as they are ordained to something common. Therefore the eternal law is one since it is the exemplar of this order.

Reply Obj. 2. With regard to any sort of word, two points may be considered: viz., the word itself, and that which is expressed by the word. For the spoken word is something

[10] *De Lib. Arb.,* I, 6 (PL 32, 1229).   [11] Q. 90.   [12] *S. T.,* I, q. 14, a. 8.   [13] *S. T.,* I, q. 103, a. 5.   [14] *S. T.,* I, q. 15, a. 2.   [15] Q. 90, a. 2.

uttered by the mouth of man, and expresses that which is signified by the human word. The same applies to the human mental word, which is nothing else than something conceived by the mind, by which man expresses mentally the things of which he is thinking. So, too, in God, therefore, the Word conceived by the intellect of the Father is the name of a Person; but all things that are in the Father's knowledge, whether they refer to the essence or to the Persons, or to the works of God, are expressed by this Word, as Augustine declares.[16] But among other things expressed by this Word, the eternal law itself is expressed thereby. Nor does it follow that the eternal law is a Personal name in God. Nevertheless, it is appropriated to the Son, because of the suitability of *exemplar* to *word*.

Reply Obj. 3. The exemplars of the divine intellect do not stand in the same relation to things as do the exemplars of the human intellect. For the human intellect is measured by things, so that a human concept is not true by reason of itself, but by reason of its being consonant with things, since *an opinion is true or false according as things are or are not.* But the divine intellect is the measure of things, since each thing has truth in it in so far as it is like the divine intellect, as was stated in the First Part.[17] Consequently the divine intellect is true in itself, and its exemplar is truth itself.

Second Article

WHETHER THE ETERNAL LAW IS KNOWN TO ALL?

We proceed thus to the Second Article:—

Objection 1. It would seem that the eternal law is not known to all. For, as the Apostle says (*1 Cor.* ii. 11), *the things that are of God no man knoweth, but the Spirit of God.* But the eternal law is an exemplar existing in the divine mind. Therefore it is unknown to all save God alone.

Obj. 2. Further, as Augustine says, *the eternal law is that by which it is right that all things should be most orderly.*[18] But all do not know how all things are most orderly. Therefore all do not know the eternal law.

Obj. 3. Further, Augustine says that *the eternal law is not*

---

[16] *De Trin.*, XV, 14 (PL 42, 1076).   [17] *S. T.*, I, q. 16, a. 1.   [18] *De Lib. Arb.*, I, 6 (PL 32, 1229).

subject to the judgment of man.[19] But according to *Ethics* i., *any man can judge well of what he knows.*[20] Therefore the eternal law is not known to us.

On the contrary, Augustine says that *knowledge of the eternal law is imprinted on us.*[21]

I answer that, A thing may be known in two ways: first, in itself; secondly, in its effect, in which some likeness of that thing is found: *e.g.,* someone, not seeing the sun in its substance, may know it by its rays. Hence we must say that no one can know the eternal law as it is in itself, except God and the blessed who see God in His essence. But every rational creature knows it according to some reflection, greater or less. For every knowledge of truth is a kind of reflection and participation of the eternal law, which is the unchangeable truth, as Augustine says.[22] Now all men know the truth to a certain extent, at least as to the common principles of the natural law. As to the other truths, they partake of the knowledge of truth, some more, some less; and in this respect they know the eternal law in a greater or lesser degree.

Reply Obj. 1. We cannot know the things that are of God as they are in themselves; but they are made known to us in their effects, according to *Rom.* i. 20: *The invisible things of God . . . are clearly seen, being understood by the things that are made.*

Reply Obj. 2. Although each one knows the eternal law according to his own capacity, in the way explained above, yet none can comprehend it, for it cannot be made perfectly known by its effects. Therefore it does not follow that anyone who knows the eternal law, in the aforesaid way, knows also the whole order of things whereby they are most orderly.

Reply Obj. 3. To judge of a thing may be understood in two ways. First, as when a cognitive power judges of its proper object, according to *Job* xii. 11: *Doth not the ear discern words, and the palate of him that eateth, the taste?* It is to this kind of judgment that the Philosopher alludes when he says that *anyone judges well of what he knows,*[23] by judging, namely, whether what is put forward is true. In another way, we speak of a superior judging of a subordinate by a kind of practical judgment, as to whether he should be

---

[19] *De Vera Relig.,* XXXI (PL 34, 148).   [20] Aristotle, *Eth.,* I, 3 (1094b 27).   [21] *De Lib. Arb.,* I, 6 (PL 32, 1229).   [22] *De Vera Relig.,* XXXI (PL 34, 147).   [23] *Eth.,* I, 3 (1094b 27).

such and such or not. And thus none can judge of the eternal law.

Third Article

WHETHER EVERY LAW IS DERIVED FROM THE ETERNAL LAW?

We proceed thus to the Third Article:—

Objection 1. It would seem that not every law is derived from the eternal law. For there is a law of the 'fomes,' as was stated above,[24] which is not derived from that divine law which is the eternal law, since to it pertains the *prudence of the flesh,* of which the Apostle says (*Rom.* viii. 7) that *it cannot be subject to the law of God.* Therefore, not every law is derived from the eternal law.

Obj. 2. Further, nothing unjust can be derived from the eternal law, because, as was stated above, *the eternal law is that according to which it is right that all things should be most orderly.* But some laws are unjust, according to *Isa.* x. 1: *Woe to them that make wicked laws.* Therefore, not every law is derived from the eternal law.

Obj. 3. Further, Augustine says that *the law which is framed for ruling the people rightly permits many things which are punished by the divine providence.*[25] But the exemplar of the divine providence is the eternal law, as was stated above. Therefore not even every good law is derived from the eternal law.

On the contrary, Divine Wisdom says (*Prov.* viii. 15): *By Me kings reign, and lawgivers decree just things.* But the exemplar of divine Wisdom is the eternal law, as was stated above. Therefore all laws proceed from the eternal law.

I answer that, As was stated above, law denotes a kind of plan directing acts towards an end.[26] Now wherever there are movers ordained to one another, the power of the second mover must needs be derived from the power of the first mover, since the second mover does not move except in so far as it is moved by the first. Therefore we observe the same in all those who govern, namely, that the plan of government is derived by secondary governors from the governor in chief. Thus the plan of what is to be done in a state flows from the

[24] Q. 91, a. 6.   [25] *De Lib. Arb.,* I, 5 (PL 32, 1228).   [26] Q. 90, a. 1 and 2.

king's command to his inferior administrators; and again in things of art the plan of whatever is to be done by art flows from the chief craftsman to the under-craftsmen who work with their hands. Since, then, the eternal law is the plan of government in the Chief Governor, all the plans of government in the inferior governors must be derived from the eternal law. But these plans of inferior governors are all the other laws which are in addition to the eternal law. Therefore all laws, in so far as they partake of right reason, are derived from the eternal law. Hence Augustine says that *in temporal law there is nothing just and lawful but what man has drawn from the eternal law.*[27]

Reply Obj. 1. The 'fomes' has the nature of law in man in so far as it is a punishment resulting from the divine justice; and in this respect it is evident that it is derived from the eternal law. But in so far as it denotes a proneness to sin, it is contrary to the divine law, and has not the nature of law, as was stated above.[28]

Reply Obj. 2. Human law has the nature of law in so far as it partakes of right reason; and it is clear that, in this respect, it is derived from the eternal law. But in so far as it deviates from reason, it is called an unjust law, and has the nature, not of law, but of violence. Nevertheless, even an unjust law, in so far as it retains some appearance of law, through being framed by one who is in power, is derived from the eternal law; for all power is from the Lord God, according to *Rom.* xiii. 1.

Reply Obj. 3. Human law is said to permit certain things, not as approving of them, but as being unable to direct them. And many things are directed by the divine law, which human law is unable to direct, because more things are subject to a higher than to a lower cause. Hence the very fact that human law does not concern itself with matters it cannot direct comes under the ordination of the eternal law. It would be different, were human law to sanction what the eternal law condemns. Consequently, it does not follow that human law is not derived from the eternal law; what follows is rather that it is not on a perfect equality with it.

[27] *De Lib. Arb.,* I, 6 (PL 32, 1229).   [28] Q. 91, a. 6.

Question XCIV

THE NATURAL LAW

(In Six Articles)

WE MUST now consider the natural law, concerning which there are six points of inquiry: (1) What is the natural law? (2) What are the precepts of the natural law? (3) Whether all the acts of the virtues are prescribed by the natural law? (4) Whether the natural law is the same in all? (5) Whether it is changeable? (6) Whether it can be abolished from the mind of man?

First Article

WHETHER THE NATURAL LAW IS A HABIT?

We proceed thus to the First Article:—

Objection 1. It would seem that the natural law is a habit. For, as the Philosopher says, *there are three things in the soul, power, habit and passion.*[1] But the natural law is not one of the soul's powers, nor is it one of the passions, as we may see by going through them one by one. Therefore the natural law is a habit.

Obj. 2. Further, Basil says that the *conscience or synderesis is the law of our mind;*[2] which can apply only to the natural law. But *synderesis* is a habit, as was shown in the First Part.[3] Therefore the natural law is a habit.

Obj. 3. Further, the natural law abides in man always, as will be shown further on. But man's reason, which the law regards, does not always think about the natural law. Therefore the natural law is not an act, but a habit.

On the contrary, Augustine says that *a habit is that whereby something is done when necessary.*[4] But such is not the natural law, since it is in infants and in the damned who cannot act by it. Therefore the natural law is not a habit.

I answer that, A thing may be called a habit in two ways. First, properly and essentially, and thus the natural law is not a habit. For it has been stated above that the natural law is something appointed by reason, just as a proposition is a

---

[1] *Eth.*, II, 5 (1105b 20). [2] Cf. *In Hexaëm.*, hom. VII (PG 29, 158); St. John Damascene, *De Fide Orth.*, IV, 22 (PG 94, 1200). [3] *S. T.*, I, q. 79, a. 12. [4] *De Bono Coniug.*, XXI (PL 40, 390).

work of reason.[5] Now that which a man does is not the same as that whereby he does it, for he makes a becoming speech by the habit of grammar. Since, then, a habit is that by which we act, a law cannot be a habit properly and essentially.

Secondly, the term habit may be applied to that which we hold by a habit. Thus *faith* may mean *that which we hold by faith*. Accordingly, since the precepts of the natural law are sometimes considered by reason actually, while sometimes they are in the reason only habitually, in this way the natural law may be called a habit. So, too, in speculative matters, the indemonstrable principles are not the habit itself whereby we hold these principles; they are rather the principles of which we possess the habit.

Reply Obj. 1. The Philosopher proposes there to discover the genus of virtue;[6] and since it is evident that virtue is a principle of action, he mentions only those things which are principles of human acts, viz., powers, habits and passions. But there are other things in the soul besides these three: *e.g.*, acts, as *to will* is in the one that wills; again, there are things known in the knower; moreover its own natural properties are in the soul, such as immortality and the like.

Reply Obj. 2. *Synderesis* is said to be the law of our intellect because it is a habit containing the precepts of the natural law, which are the first principles of human actions.

Reply Obj. 3. This argument proves that the natural law is held habitually; and this is granted.

To the argument advanced in the contrary sense we reply that sometimes a man is unable to make use of that which is in him habitually, because of some impediment. Thus, because of sleep, a man is unable to use the habit of science. In like manner, through the deficiency of his age, a child cannot use the habit of the understanding of principles, or the natural law, which is in him habitually.

Second Article

WHETHER THE NATURAL LAW CONTAINS SEVERAL PRECEPTS, OR ONLY ONE?

We proceed thus to the Second Article:—
Objection 1. It would seem that the natural law contain

[5] Q. 90, a. 1, ad 2.   [6] *Eth.*, II, 5 (1105b 20).

not several precepts, but only one. For law is a kind of precept, as was stated above.[7] If therefore there were many precepts of the natural law, it would follow that there are also many natural laws.

Obj. 2. Further, the natural law is consequent upon human nature. But human nature, as a whole, is one, though, as to its parts, it is manifold. Therefore, either there is but one precept of the law of nature because of the unity of nature as a whole, or there are many by reason of the number of parts of human nature. The result would be that even things relating to the inclination of the concupiscible power would belong to the natural law.

Obj. 3. Further, law is something pertaining to reason, as was stated above.[8] Now reason is but one in man. Therefore there is only one precept of the natural law.

On the contrary, The precepts of the natural law in man stand in relation to operable matters as first principles do to matters of demonstration. But there are several first indemonstrable principles. Therefore there are also several precepts of the natural law.

I answer that, As was stated above, the precepts of the natural law are to the practical reason what the first principles of demonstrations are to the speculative reason, because both are self-evident principles.[9] Now a thing is said to be self-evident in two ways: first, in itself; secondly, in relation to us. Any proposition is said to be self-evident in itself, if its predicate is contained in the notion of the subject; even though it may happen that to one who does not know the definition of the subject, such a proposition is not self-evident. For instance, this proposition, *Man is a rational being,* is, in its very nature, self-evident, since he who says *man,* says *a rational being*; and yet to one who does not know what a man is, this proposition is not self-evident. Hence it is that, as Boethius says,[10] certain axioms or propositions are universally self-evident to all; and such are the propositions whose terms are known to all, as, *Every whole is greater than its part,* and, *Things equal to one and the same are equal to one another.* But some propositions are self-evident only to the wise, who understand the meaning of the terms of such propositions. Thus to one who under-

[7] Q. 92, a. 2.   [8] Q. 90, a. 1.   [9] Q. 91, a. 3.   [10] *De Hebdom.* (PL 64, 1311).

stands that an angel is not a body, it is self-evident that an angel is not circumscriptively in a place. But this is not evident to the unlearned, for they cannot grasp it.

Now a certain order is to be found in those things that are apprehended by men. For that which first falls under apprehension is *being*, the understanding of which is included in all things whatsoever a man apprehends. Therefore the first indemonstrable principle is that *the same thing cannot be affirmed and denied at the same time*, which is based on the notion of *being* and *not-being*: and on this principle all others are based, as is stated in *Metaph.* iv.[11] Now as *being* is the first thing that falls under the apprehension absolutely, so *good* is the first thing that falls under the apprehension of the practical reason, which is directed to action (since every agent acts for an end, which has the nature of good). Consequently, the first principle in the practical reason is one founded on the nature of good, viz., that *good is that which all things seek after*. Hence this is the first precept of law, that *good is to be done and promoted, and evil is to be avoided*. All other precepts of the natural law are based upon this; so that all the things which the practical reason naturally apprehends as man's good belong to the precepts of the natural law under the form of things to be done or avoided.

Since, however, good has the nature of an end, and evil, the nature of the contrary, hence it is that all those things to which man has a natural inclination are naturally apprehended by reason as being good, and consequently as objects of pursuit, and their contraries as evil, and objects of avoidance. Therefore, the order of the precepts of the natural law is according to the order of natural inclinations. For there is in man, first of all, an inclination to good in accordance with the nature which he has in common with all substances, inasmuch, namely, as every substance seeks the preservation of its own being, according to its nature; and by reason of this inclination, whatever is a means of preserving human life, and of warding off its obstacles, belongs to the natural law. Secondly, there is in man an inclination to things that pertain to him more specially, according to that nature which he has in common with other animals; and in virtue of this inclination, those things are said to belong to the natural law *which*

[11] Aristotle, *Metaph.*, III, 3 (1005b 29).

nature has taught to all animals,[12] such as sexual intercourse, the education of offspring and so forth. Thirdly, there is in man an inclination to good according to the nature of his reason, which nature is proper to him. Thus man has a natural inclination to know the truth about God, and to live in society; and in this respect, whatever pertains to this inclination belongs to the natural law: *e.g.*, to shun ignorance, to avoid offending those among whom one has to live, and other such things regarding the above inclination.

Reply Obj. 1. All these precepts of the law of nature have the character of one natural law, inasmuch as they flow from one first precept.

Reply Obj. 2. All the inclinations of any parts whatsoever of human nature, *e.g.*, of the concupiscible and irascible parts, in so far as they are ruled by reason, belong to the natural law, and are reduced to one first precept, as was stated above. And thus the precepts of the natural law are many in themselves, but they are based on one common foundation.

Reply Obj. 3. Although reason is one in itself, yet it directs all things regarding man; so that whatever can be ruled by reason is contained under the law of reason.

Third Article

WHETHER ALL THE ACTS OF THE VIRTUES ARE PRESCRIBED BY THE NATURAL LAW?

We proceed thus to the Third Article:—

Objection 1. It would seem that not all the acts of the virtues are prescribed by the natural law. For, as was stated above, it is of the nature of law that it be ordained to the common good.[13] But some acts of the virtues are ordained to the private good of the individual, as is evident especially in regard to acts of temperance. Therefore, not all the acts of the virtues are the subject of natural law.

Obj. 2. Further, every sin is opposed to some virtuous act. If therefore all the acts of the virtues are prescribed by the natural law, it seems to follow that all sins are against nature; whereas this applies to certain special sins.

---

[12] *Dig.*, I, i, 1 (I, 29a).—Cf. O. Lottin, *Le droit naturel*, pp. 34, 78.
[13] Q. 90, a. 2.

Obj. 3. Further, those things which are according to nature are common to all. But the acts of the virtues are not common to all, since a thing is virtuous in one, and vicious in another. Therefore, not all the acts of the virtues are prescribed by the natural law.

On the contrary, Damascene says that *virtues are natural.*[14] Therefore virtuous acts also are subject to the natural law.

I answer that, We may speak of virtuous acts in two ways: first, in so far as they are virtuous; secondly, as such and such acts considered in their proper species. If, then, we are speaking of the acts of the virtues in so far as they are virtuous, thus all virtuous acts belong to the natural law. For it has been stated that to the natural law belongs everything to which a man is inclined according to his nature. Now each thing is inclined naturally to an operation that is suitable to it according to its form: *e.g.,* fire is inclined to give heat. Therefore, since the rational soul is the proper form of man, there is in every man a natural inclination to act according to reason; and this is to act according to virtue. Consequently, considered thus, all the acts of the virtues are prescribed by the natural law, since each one's reason naturally dictates to him to act virtuously. But if we speak of virtuous acts, considered in themselves, *i.e.,* in their proper species, thus not all virtuous acts are prescribed by the natural law. For many things are done virtuously, to which nature does not primarily incline, but which, through the inquiry of reason, have been found by men to be conducive to well-living.

Reply Obj. 1. Temperance is about the natural concupiscences of food, drink and sexual matters, which are indeed ordained to the common good of nature, just as other matters of law are ordained to the moral common good.

Reply Obj. 2. By human nature we may mean either that which is proper to man, and in this sense all sins, as being against reason, are also against nature, as Damascene states;[15] or we may mean that nature which is common to man and other animals, and in this sense, certain special sins are said to be against nature: *e.g.,* contrary to sexual intercourse, which is natural to all animals, is unisexual lust, which has received the special name of the unnatural crime.

[14] *De Fide Orth.,* III, 14 (PG 94, 1045).   [15] *Op. cit.,* II, 4; 30; IV, 20 (PG 94, 876; 976; 1196).

Reply Obj. 3. This argument considers acts in themselves. For it is owing to the various conditions of men that certain acts are virtuous for some, as being proportioned and becoming to them, while they are vicious for others, as not being proportioned to them.

Fourth Article

WHETHER THE NATURAL LAW IS THE SAME IN ALL MEN?

We proceed thus to the Fourth Article:—

Objection 1. It would seem that the natural law is not the same in all. For it is stated in the *Decretals* that *the natural law is that which is contained in the Law and the Gospel.*[16] But this is not common to all men, because, as it is written (*Rom.* x. 16), *all do not obey the gospel.* Therefore the natural law is not the same in all men.

Obj. 2. Further, *Things which are according to the law are said to be just,* as is stated in *Ethics* v.[17] But it is stated in the same book that nothing is so just for all as not to be subject to change in regard to some men.[18] Therefore even the natural law is not the same in all men.

Obj. 3. Further, as was stated above, to the natural law belongs everything to which a man is inclined according to his nature. Now different men are naturally inclined to different things,—some to the desire of pleasures, others to the desire of honors, and other men to other things. Therefore, there is not one natural law for all.

On the contrary, Isidore says: *The natural law is common to all nations.*[19]

I answer that, As we have stated above, to the natural law belong those things to which a man is inclined naturally; and among these it is proper to man to be inclined to act according to reason. Now it belongs to the reason to proceed from what is common to what is proper, as is stated in *Physics* i.[20] The speculative reason, however, is differently situated, in this matter, from the practical reason. For, since the speculative reason is concerned chiefly with necessary things, which cannot be otherwise than they are, its proper

---

[16] Gratian, *Decretum,* I, i. prol. (I, 1).   [17] Aristotle, *Eth.,* V, 1 (1129b 12).   [18] *Op. cit.,* V, 7 (1134b 32).   [19] *Etymol.,* V, 4 (PL 82, 199).   [20] Aristotle, *Phys.,* I, 1 (184a 16).

conclusions, like the universal principles, contain the truth without fail. The practical reason, on the other hand, is concerned with contingent matters, which is the domain of human actions; and, consequently, although there is necessity in the common principles, the more we descend towards the particular, the more frequently we encounter defects. Accordingly, then, in speculative matters truth is the same in all men, both as to principles and as to conclusions; although the truth is not known to all as regards the conclusions, but only as regards the principles which are called *common notions*.[21] But in matters of action, truth or practical rectitude is not the same for all as to what is particular, but only as to the common principles; and where there is the same rectitude in relation to particulars, it is not equally known to all.

It is therefore evident that, as regards the common principles whether of speculative or of practical reason, truth or rectitude is the same for all, and is equally known by all. But as to the proper conclusions of the speculative reason, the truth is the same for all, but it is not equally known to all. Thus, it is true for all that the three angles of a triangle are together equal to two right angles, although it is not known to all. But as to the proper conclusions of the practical reason, neither is the truth or rectitude the same for all, nor, where it is the same, is it equally known by all. Thus, it is right and true for all to act according to reason, and from this principle it follows, as a proper conclusion, that goods entrusted to another should be restored to their owner. Now this is true for the majority of cases. But it may happen in a particular case that it would be injurious, and therefore unreasonable, to restore goods held in trust; for instance, if they are claimed for the purpose of fighting against one's country. And this principle will be found to fail the more, according as we descend further towards the particular, *e.g.*, if one were to say that goods held in trust should be restored with such and such a guarantee, or in such and such a way; because the greater the number of conditions added, the greater the number of ways in which the principle may fail, so that it be not right to restore or not to restore.

Consequently, we must say that the natural law, as to the first common principles, is the same for all, both as to rectitude and as to knowledge. But as to certain more particular

[21] Boethius, *De Hebdom.* (PL 64, 1311).

aspects, which are conclusions, as it were, of those common principles, it is the same for all in the majority of cases, both as to rectitude and as to knowledge; and yet in some few cases it may fail, both as to rectitude, by reason of certain obstacles (just as natures subject to generation and corruption fail in some few cases because of some obstacle), and as to knowledge, since in some the reason is perverted by passion, or evil habit, or an evil disposition of nature. Thus at one time theft, although it is expressly contrary to the natural law, was not considered wrong among the Germans, as Julius Cæsar relates.[22]

Reply Obj. 1. The meaning of the sentence quoted is not that whatever is contained in the Law and the Gospel belongs to the natural law, since they contain many things that are above nature; but that whatever belongs to the natural law is fully contained in them. Therefore Gratian, after saying that *the natural law is what is contained in the Law and the Gospel,* adds at once, by way of example, *by which everyone is commanded to do to others as he would be done by.*[23]

Reply Obj. 2. The saying of the Philosopher is to be understood of things that are naturally just, not as common principles, but as conclusions drawn from them, having rectitude in the majority of cases, but failing in a few.[24]

Reply Obj. 3. Just as in man reason rules and commands the other powers, so all the natural inclinations belonging to the other powers must needs be directed according to reason. Therefore it is universally right for all men that all their inclinations should be directed according to reason.

Fifth Article

WHETHER THE NATURAL LAW CAN BE CHANGED?

We proceed thus to the Fifth Article:—

Objection 1. It would seem that the natural law can be changed. For on *Ecclus.* xvii. 9 (*He gave them instructions, and the law of life*) the *Gloss* says: *He wished the law of the letter to be written, in order to correct the law of nature.*[25] But that which is corrected is changed. Therefore the natural law can be changed.

[22] Caesar, *De Bello Gallico,* VI, 23 (I, 348).   [23] *Decretum,* I, i, prol. (I, 1).   [24] *Eth.,* V, 1 (1129b 12).   [25] *Glossa ordin.* (III, 403E).

Obj. 2. Further, the slaying of the innocent, adultery and theft are against the natural law. But we find these things changed by God: as when God commanded Abraham to slay his innocent son (*Gen.* xxii. 2); and when He ordered the Jews to borrow and purloin the vessels of the Egyptians (*Exod.* xii. 35); and when He commanded Osee to take to himself *a wife of fornications* (*Osee* i. 2). Therefore the natural law can be changed.

Obj. 3. Further, Isidore says that *the possession of all things in common, and universal freedom, are matters of natural law.*[26] But these things are seen to be changed by human laws. Therefore it seems that the natural law is subject to change.

On the contrary, It is said in the *Decretals: The natural law dates from the creation of the rational creature. It does not vary according to time, but remains unchangeable.*[27]

I answer that, A change in the natural law may be understood in two ways. First, by way of addition. In this sense, nothing hinders the natural law from being changed, since many things for the benefit of human life have been added over and above the natural law, both by the divine law and by human laws.

Secondly, a change in the natural law may be understood by way of subtraction, so that what previously was according to the natural law, ceases to be so. In this sense, the natural law is altogether unchangeable in its first principles. But in its secondary principles, which, as we have said, are certain detailed proximate conclusions drawn from the first principles, the natural law is not changed so that what it prescribes be not right in most cases. But it may be changed in some particular cases of rare occurrence, through some special causes hindering the observance of such precepts, as was stated above.

Reply Obj. 1. The written law is said to be given for the correction of the natural law, either because it supplies what was wanting to the natural law, or because the natural law was so perverted in the hearts of some men, as to certain matters, that they esteemed those things good which are naturally evil; which perversion stood in need of correction.

Reply Obj. 2. All men alike, both guilty and innocent, die

[26] *Etymol.,* V, 4 (PL 82, 199).   [27] Gratian, *Decretum,* I, v, prol. (I, 7).

the death of nature; which death of nature is inflicted by
the power of God because of original sin, according to *1
Kings* ii. 6: *The Lord killeth and maketh alive.* Consequently, by the command of God, death can be inflicted on
any man, guilty or innocent, without any injustice whatever.—In like manner, adultery is intercourse with another's
wife; who is allotted to him by the law emanating from God.
Consequently intercourse with any woman, by the command
of God, is neither adultery nor fornication.—The same applies to theft, which is the taking of another's property. For
whatever is taken by the command of God, to Whom all
things belong, is not taken against the will of its owner,
whereas it is in this that theft consists.—Nor is it only in
human things that whatever is commanded by God is right;
but also in natural things, whatever is done by God is, in
some way, natural, as was stated in the First Part.[28]

Reply Obj. 3. A thing is said to belong to the natural law
in two ways. First, because nature inclines thereto: *e.g.*, that
one should not do harm to another. Secondly, because nature did not bring with it the contrary. Thus, we might say
that for man to be naked is of the natural law, because nature did not give him clothes, but art invented them. In this
sense, *the possession of all things in common and universal
freedom* are said to be of the natural law, because, namely,
the distinction of possessions and slavery were not brought
in by nature, but devised by human reason for the benefit of
human life. Accordingly, the law of nature was not changed
in this respect, except by addition.

Sixth Article

WHETHER THE NATURAL LAW CAN BE ABOLISHED
FROM THE HEART OF MAN?

We proceed thus to the Sixth Article:—
Objection 1. It would seem that the natural law can be
abolished from the heart of man. For on *Rom.* ii. 14 (*When
the Gentiles who have not the law,* etc.) the *Gloss* says that
*the law of justice, which sin had blotted out, is graven on the
heart of man when he is restored by grace.*[29] But the law of

---

[28] *S. T.,* I, q. 105, a. 6, ad 1.   [29] *Glossa ordin.* (VI, 7E); Peter
Lombard, *In Rom.,* super II, 14 (PL 191, 1345).

justice is the law of nature. Therefore the law of nature can be blotted out.

Obj. 2. Further, the law of grace is more efficacious than the law of nature. But the law of grace is blotted out by sin. Much more, therefore, can the law of nature be blotted out.

Obj. 3. Further, that which is established by law is proposed as something just. But many things are enacted by men which are contrary to the law of nature. Therefore the law of nature can be abolished from the heart of man.

On the contrary, Augustine says: *Thy law is written in the hearts of men, which iniquity itself effaces not.*[30] But the law which is written in men's hearts is the natural law. Therefore the natural law cannot be blotted out.

I answer that, As we have stated above, there belong to the natural law, first, certain most common precepts that are known to all; and secondly, certain secondary and more particular precepts, which are, as it were, conclusions following closely from first principles. As to the common principles, the natural law, in its universal meaning, cannot in any way be blotted out from men's hearts. But it is blotted out in the case of a particular action, in so far as reason is hindered from applying the common principle to the particular action because of concupiscence or some other passion, as was stated above.[31]—But as to the other, *i.e.*, the secondary precepts, the natural law can be blotted out from the human heart, either by evil persuasions, just as in speculative matters errors occur in respect of necessary conclusions; or by vicious customs and corrupt habits, as, among some men, theft, and even unnatural vices, as the Apostle states (*Rom.* i. 24), were not esteemed sinful.

Reply Obj. 1. Sin blots out the law of nature in particular cases, not universally, except perchance in regard to the secondary precepts of the natural law, in the way stated above.

Reply Obj. 2. Although grace is more efficacious than nature, yet nature is more essential to man, and therefore more enduring.

Reply Obj. 3. This argument is true of the secondary precepts of the natural law, against which some legislators have framed certain enactments which are unjust.

[30] *Confess.,* II, 4 (PL 32, 678).   [31] Q. 77, a. 2.

HUMAN LAW

(*In Four Articles*)

WE MUST now consider human law, and (1) concerning this law considered in itself; (2) its power;[1] (3) its mutability.[2] Under the first head there are four points of inquiry: (1) Its utility. (2) Its origin. (3) Its quality. (4) Its division.

First Article

WHETHER IT WAS USEFUL FOR LAWS TO BE FRAMED BY MEN?

We proceed thus to the First Article:—

Objection 1. It would seem that it was not useful for laws to be framed by men. For the purpose of every law is that man be made good thereby, as was stated above.[3] But men are more to be induced to be good willingly by means of admonitions, than against their will, by means of laws. Therefore there was no need to frame laws.

Obj. 2. Further, As the Philosopher says, *men have recourse to a judge as to animate justice.*[4] But animate justice is better than inanimate justice, which is contained in laws. Therefore it would have been better for the execution of justice to be entrusted to the decision of judges than to frame laws in addition.

Obj. 3. Further, every law is framed for the direction of human actions, as is evident from what has been stated above.[5] But since human actions are about singulars, which are infinite in number, matters pertaining to the direction of human actions cannot be taken into sufficient consideration except by a wise man, who looks into each one of them. Therefore it would have been better for human acts to be directed by the judgment of wise men, than by the framing of laws. Therefore there was no need of human laws.

On the contrary, Isidore says: *Laws were made that in fear thereof human audacity might be held in check, that innocence might be safeguarded in the midst of wickedness,*

[1] Q. 96. [2] Q. 97. [3] Q. 92, a. 1. [4] *Eth.,* V, 4 (1132a 22).
[5] Q. 90, a. 1 and 2.

and that the dread of punishment might prevent the wicked from doing harm.[6] But these things are most necessary to mankind. Therefore it was necessary that human laws should be made.

I answer that, As we have stated above, man has a natural aptitude for virtue; but the perfection of virtue must be acquired by man by means of some kind of training.[7] Thus we observe that a man is helped by diligence in his necessities, for instance, in food and clothing. Certain beginnings of these he has from nature, viz., his reason and his hands; but he has not the full complement, as other animals have, to whom nature has given sufficiently of clothing and food. Now it is difficult to see how man could suffice for himself in the matter of this training, since the perfection of virtue consists chiefly in withdrawing man from undue pleasures, to which above all man is inclined, and especially the young, who are more capable of being trained. Consequently a man needs to receive this training from another, whereby to arrive at the perfection of virtue. And as to those young people who are inclined to acts of virtue by their good natural disposition, or by custom, or rather by the gift of God, paternal training suffices, which is by admonitions. But since some are found to be dissolute and prone to vice, and not easily amenable to words, it was necessary for such to be restrained from evil by force and fear, in order that, at least, they might desist from evil-doing, and leave others in peace, and that they themselves, by being habituated in this way, might be brought to do willingly what hitherto they did from fear, and thus become virtuous. Now this kind of training, which compels through fear of punishment, is the discipline of laws. Therefore, in order that man might have peace and virtue, it was necessary for laws to be framed; for, as the Philosopher says, *as man is the most noble of animals if he be perfect in virtue, so he is the lowest of all, if he be severed from law and justice.*[8] For man can use his reason to devise means of satisfying his lusts and evil passions, which other animals are unable to do.

Reply Obj. 1. Men who are well disposed are led willingly to virtue by being admonished better than by coercion; but

---

[6] *Etymol.,* V, 20 (PL 82, 202).   [7] Q. 63, a. 1; q. 94, a. 3.
[8] *Polit.,* I, 1 (1253a 31).

men whose disposition is evil are not led to virtue unless they are compelled.

Reply Obj. 2. As the Philosopher says, *it is better that all things be regulated by law, than left to be decided by judges.*[9] And this for three reasons. First, because it is easier to find a few wise men competent to frame right laws, than to find the many who would be necessary to judge rightly of each single case.—Secondly, because those who make laws consider long beforehand what laws to make, whereas judgment on each single case has to be pronounced as soon as it arises; and it is easier for man to see what is right, by taking many instances into consideration, than by considering one solitary instance.—Thirdly, because lawgivers judge universally and about future events, whereas those who sit in judgment judge of things present, towards which they are affected by love, hatred, or some kind of cupidity; and thus their judgment becomes perverted.

Since, then, the animated justice of the judge is not found in every man, and since it can be bent, therefore it was necessary, whenever possible, for the law to determine how to judge, and for very few matters to be left to the decision of men.

Reply Obj. 3. Certain individual facts which cannot be covered by the law *have necessarily to be committed to judges,* as the Philosopher says in the same passage: *e.g., concerning something that has happened or not happened,* and the like.[10]

Second Article

WHETHER EVERY HUMAN LAW IS DERIVED FROM THE NATURAL LAW?

We proceed thus to the Second Article:—

Objection 1. It would seem that not every human law is derived from the natural law. For the Philosopher says that *the legal just is that which originally was a matter of indifference.*[11] But those things which arise from the natural law are not matters of indifference. Therefore the enactments of human laws are not all derived from the natural law.

[9] *Rhetor.,* I, 1 (1354a 31).   [10] *Ibid.* (1354b 13).   [11] *Eth.,* V, 7 (1134b 20).

Obj. 2. Further, positive law is divided against natural law, as is stated by Isidore[12] and the Philosopher.[13] But those things which flow as conclusions from the common principles of the natural law belong to the natural law, as was stated above.[14] Therefore that which is established by human law is not derived from the natural law.

Obj. 3. Further, the law of nature is the same for all, since the Philosopher says that *the natural just is that which is equally valid everywhere.*[15] If therefore human laws were derived from the natural law, it would follow that they too are the same for all; which is clearly false.

Obj. 4. Further, it is possible to give a reason for things which are derived from the natural law. But *it is not possible to give the reason for all the legal enactments of the lawgivers,* as the Jurist says.[16] Therefore not all human laws are derived from the natural law.

On the contrary, Tully says: *Things which emanated from nature, and were approved by custom, were sanctioned by fear and reverence for the laws.*[17]

I answer that, As Augustine says, *that which is not just seems to be no law at all.*[18] Hence the force of a law depends on the extent of its justice. Now in human affairs a thing is said to be just from being right, according to the rule of reason. But the first rule of reason is the law of nature, as is clear from what has been stated above.[19] Consequently, every human law has just so much of the nature of law as it is derived from the law of nature. But if in any point it departs from the law of nature, it is no longer a law but a perversion of law.

But it must be noted that something may be derived from the natural law in two ways: first, as a conclusion from principles; secondly, by way of a determination of certain common notions. The first way is like to that by which, in the sciences, demonstrated conclusions are drawn from the principles; while the second is likened to that whereby, in the arts, common forms are determined to some particular. Thus, the craftsman needs to determine the common form of a house to the shape of this or that particular house. Some

---

[12] *Etymol.,* V, 4 (PL 82, 199).   [13] *Eth.,* V, 7 (1134b 18).   [14] Q. 94, a. 4.   [15] *Eth.,* V, 7 (1134b 19).   [16] *Dig.,* I, iii, 20 (I, 34a).
[17] *De Invent.,* II, 53 (p. 148[b]).   [18] *De Lib. Arb.,* I, 5 (PL 32, 1227).
[19] Q. 91, a. 2, ad 2.

things are therefore derived from the common principles of the natural law by way of conclusions: *e.g.*, that *one must not kill* may be derived as a conclusion from the principle that *one should do harm to no man;* while some are derived therefrom by way of determination: *e.g.*, the law of nature has it that the evil-doer should be punished, but that he be punished in this or that way is a determination of the law of nature.

Accordingly, both modes of derivation are found in the human law. But those things which are derived in the first way are contained in human law, not as emanating therefrom exclusively, but as having some force from the natural law also. But those things which are derived in the second way have no other force than that of human law.

Reply Obj. 1. The Philosopher is speaking of those enactments which are by way of determination or specification of the precepts of the natural law.

Reply Obj. 2. This argument holds for those things that are derived from the natural law by way of conclusion.

Reply Obj. 3. The common principles of the natural law cannot be applied to all men in the same way because of the great variety of human affairs; and hence arises the diversity of positive laws among various people.

Reply Obj. 4. These words of the Jurist are to be understood as referring to the decisions of rulers in determining particular points of the natural law; and to these determinations the judgment of expert and prudent men is related as to its principles, in so far, namely, as they see at once what is the best thing to decide. Hence the Philosopher says that, in such matters, *we ought to pay as much attention to the undemonstrated sayings and opinions of persons who surpass us in experience, age and prudence, as to their demonstrations.*[20]

[20] *Eth.*, VI, 11 (1143b 11).

GRACE

Question CIX

ON THE EXTERIOR PRINCIPLE OF HUMAN ACTS NAMELY, THE GRACE OF GOD

(*In Ten Articles*)

WE MUST now consider the exterior principle of human acts, *i.e.*, God, in so far as, through grace, we are helped by Him to do the right. First, we must consider the grace of God; secondly, its cause;[1] thirdly, its effects.[2]

The first point of consideration will be threefold, for we shall consider (1) the necessity of grace; (2) grace itself, as to its essence;[3] (3) its division.[4]

Under the first head there are ten points of inquiry (1) Whether without grace man can know any truth? (2) Whether without God's grace man can do or will any good? (3) Whether without grace man can love God above all things? (4) Whether without grace man can keep the commandments of the Law through his natural powers? (5) Whether without grace he can merit eternal life? (6) Whether without grace man can prepare himself for grace? (7) Whether without grace he can rise from sin? (8) Whether without grace man can avoid sin? (9) Whether man, having received grace, can do good and avoid sin without any further divine help? (10) Whether he can of himself persevere in good?

First Article

WHETHER WITHOUT GRACE MAN CAN KNOW ANY TRUTH?

We proceed thus to the First Article:—

Objection 1. It would seem that without grace man can know no truth. For on *1 Cor.* xii. 3 (*No man can say, the*

[1] Q. 112.   [2] Q. 113.   [3] Q. 110.   [4] Q. 111.

Lord Jesus, but by the Holy Ghost) the *Gloss* of Ambrose says: *Every truth, by whomsoever spoken, is from the Holy Ghost*.[5] Now the Holy Ghost dwells in us by grace. Therefore we cannot know truth without grace.

Obj. 2. Further, Augustine says that *the most certain sciences are like things lit up by the sun so as to be seen. Now God Himself is He Who illumines, while reason is in the mind as sight is in the eye, and the eyes of the mind are the senses of the soul*.[6] Now the bodily senses, however pure, cannot see any visible thing without the sun's light. Therefore the human mind, however perfect, cannot, by reasoning, know any truth without divine light; and this pertains to the aid of grace.

Obj. 3. Further, the human mind can understand truth only by thinking, as is clear from Augustine.[7] But the Apostle says (*2 Cor.* iii. 5): *Not that we are sufficient to think anything of ourselves, as of ourselves; but our sufficiency is from God.* Therefore man cannot, of himself, know truth without the help of grace.

On the contrary, Augustine says *I do not approve having said in the prayer: O God, Who dost wish the sinless alone to know the truth; for it may be answered that many who are not sinless know many truths*.[8] Now man is cleansed from sin by grace, according to *Ps.* l. 12: *Create a clean heart in me, O God, and renew a right spirit within my bowels.* Therefore without grace man of himself can know truth.

I answer that, To know truth is a certain use or act of intellectual light, since, according to the Apostle (*Ephes.* v. 13): *All that is made manifest is light.* Now every use implies some movement, taking movement broadly, so as to call thinking and willing movements, as is clear from the Philosopher.[9] But in corporeal things we see that for movement there is required not merely the form which is the principle of the movement or action, but also the motion of the first mover. Now the first mover in the order of corporeal things is the body of the heavens. Hence no matter how perfectly fire has heat, it would not bring about alteration, except by

[5] Peter Lombard, *In I Cor.*, super XII, 3 (PL 191, 1651); cf. *Glossa ordin.* (VI, 52A).   [6] *Solil.*, I, 6 (PL 32, 875).   [7] *De Trin.*, XIV, 7 (PL 42, 1043).   [8] *Retract.*, I, 4 (PL 32, 589).   [9] *De An.*, III, 4 (429b 25); 7 (431a 4).

the motion of the body of the heavens. But it is clear that, just as all corporeal movements are reduced to the motion of the body of the heavens as to the first corporeal mover, so all movements, both corporeal and spiritual, are reduced to the absolutely First Mover, Who is God. And hence no matter how perfect a corporeal or spiritual nature is supposed to be, it cannot proceed to its act unless it be moved by God. Now this motion is according to the plan of His providence, and not by a necessity of nature, as the motion of the body of the heavens. But not only is every motion from God as from the First Mover, but all formal perfection is from Him as from the First Act. Hence the action of the intellect, or of any created being whatsoever, depends upon God in two ways: first, inasmuch as it is from Him that it has the form whereby it acts; secondly, inasmuch as it is moved by Him to act.

Now every form bestowed on created things by God has power for a determined act, which it can effect in proportion to its own proper endowment; and beyond this act it is powerless, except by a superadded form, as water can heat only when heated by the fire. And thus, the human under-standing has a form, viz., intelligible light itself, which of it-self is sufficient for knowing certain intelligible truths, viz., those we can come to know through sensible things. Higher intelligible truths the human intellect cannot know, unless it be perfected by a stronger light, viz., the light of faith or of prophecy, which is called the *light of grace*, inasmuch as it is added to nature.

Hence we must say that for the knowledge of any truth whatsoever man needs divine help in order that the intellect may be moved by God to its act. But he does not need a new illumination added to his natural light in order to know the truth in all things, but only in those that surpass his natural knowledge. And yet at times God miraculously instructs some by His grace in things that can be known by natural reason, even as He sometimes brings about miraculously what nature can do.

Reply Obj. 1. Every truth, by whomsoever spoken, is from the Holy Ghost as bestowing the natural light, and moving us to understand and to speak the truth; but not as dwelling in us by sanctifying grace, or as bestowing any habitual gift superadded to nature. For this takes place only with regard to knowing and speaking certain truths, and especially in regard to such as pertain to faith, of which the Apostle was speaking.

Reply Obj. 2. The material sun sheds its light outside us, but the intelligible Sun, Who is God, shines within us. Hence the natural light bestowed upon the soul is God's illumination, whereby we are illumined to see what pertains to natural knowledge; and for this there is required no further illumination, but only for such things as surpass natural knowledge.

Reply Obj. 3. We always need God's help for every thought, inasmuch as He moves the intellect to act; for to understand anything actually is to think, as is clear from Augustine.[10]

Second Article

WHETHER MAN CAN WILL OR DO ANY GOOD WITHOUT GRACE?

We proceed thus to the Second Article:—

Objection 1. It would seem that man can will and do good without grace. For that is in man's power of which he is master. Now man is master of his acts, and especially of his willing, as was stated above.[11] Hence man, of himself, can will and do good without the help of grace.

Obj. 2. Further, any being has more power over what is according to its nature than over what is beyond its nature. Now sin is against nature, as Damascene says;[12] whereas the work of virtue is according to the nature of men, as was stated above.[13] Therefore, since man can sin of himself, much more would it seem that of himself he can will and do good.

Obj. 3. Further, the good of the intellect is truth, as the Philosopher says.[14] Now the intellect can of itself know truth, even as every other thing can perform its natural operation of itself. Therefore, much more can man, of himself, do and will good.

On the contrary, The Apostle says (*Rom.* ix. 16): *It is not of him that willeth,* namely, to will, *nor of him that runneth,*

---

[10] *De Trin.,* XIV, 7 (PL 42, 1043).   [11] Q. 1, a. 1; q. 13, a. 6.
[12] *De Fide Orth.,* II, 4; 30 (PG 94, 876; 976); cf. *op. cit.,* IV, 20 (PG 94, 1196).   [13] Q. 71, a. 1.   [14] *Eth.,* VI, 2 (1139a 27).

namely, to run, *but of God that showeth mercy*. And Augustine says that *without grace men do nothing good when they either think or will or love or act*.[15]

I answer that, Man's nature may be looked at in two ways: first, in its integrity, as it was in our first parent before sin; secondly, as it is corrupted in us after the sin of our first parent. Now in both states human nature needs the help of God, as First Mover, to do or will any good whatsoever, as was stated above. But in the state of integrity of nature, as regards the sufficiency of operative power, man by his natural endowments could will and do the good proportioned to his nature, which is the good of acquired virtue; but he could not do the good that exceeded his nature, which is the good of infused virtue. But in the state of corrupted nature, man falls short even of what he can do by his nature, so that he is unable to fulfill all of it by his own natural powers. Yet because human nature is not altogether corrupted by sin, namely, so as to be shorn of every good of nature, even in the state of corrupted nature it can, by virtue of its natural endowments, perform some particular good, such as to build dwellings, plant vineyards, and the like; yet it cannot do all the good natural to it, so as to fall short in nothing. In the same way, a sick man can of himself make some movements, yet he cannot be perfectly moved with the movement of one in health, unless by the help of medicine he be cured.

Hence in the state of the integrity of nature, man needs a gratuitous strength superadded to natural strength for one reason, viz., in order to do and will supernatural good; but in the state of corrupted nature he needs it for two reasons, viz., in order to be healed and, furthermore, in order to carry out works of supernatural virtue, which are meritorious. Beyond this, in both states man needs the divine help that he may be moved to act well.

Reply Obj. 1. Man is master of his acts, both of his willing and not willing, because of the deliberation of reason, which can be bent to one side or another. And although he is master of his deliberating or not deliberating, yet this can only be by a previous deliberation; and since this cannot go on to infinity, we must come at length to this, that man's free choice is moved by an extrinsic principle, which is above the human mind, namely, by God, as the Philosopher proves in the chap-

[15] *De Corrept. et Grat.*, II (PL 44, 917).

ter on *Good Fortune.*[16] Hence the mind even of an uncorrupted man is not so master of its act that it does not need to be moved by God; and much more needy is the free choice of man weakened by sin, whereby it is hindered from good by the corruption of its nature.

Reply Obj. 2. To sin is nothing else than to fail in the good which belongs to any being according to its nature. Now, as every created thing has its being from another, and, considered in itself, is nothing, so does it need to be conserved by another in the good which pertains to its nature. For it can of itself fail in good, even as of itself it can fall into nonexistence, unless it is conserved by God.

Reply Obj. 3. Man cannot even know truth without divine help, as was stated above. And yet human nature is more corrupted by sin in regard to the desire for good, than in regard to the knowledge of truth.

Third Article

WHETHER BY HIS OWN NATURAL POWERS AND WITHOUT GRACE MAN CAN LOVE GOD ABOVE ALL THINGS?

We proceed thus to the Third Article:—

Objection 1. It would seem that without grace man cannot love God above all things by his own natural powers. For to love God above all things is the proper and principal act of charity. Now of himself man cannot possess charity, since the *charity of God is poured forth in our hearts by the Holy Ghost Who is given to us,* as it is said *Rom.* v. 5. Therefore man by his natural powers alone cannot love God above all things.

Obj. 2. Further, no nature can rise above itself. But to love anything more than itself is to tend to something above itself. Therefore without the help of grace no created nature can love God above itself.

Obj. 3. Further, to God, Who is the Highest Good, is due the highest love, which is that He be loved above all things. Now without grace man is not capable of giving God the highest love, which is His due; otherwise it would be useless to add grace. Hence man, without grace, cannot love God above all things through his natural powers alone.

[16] Cf. *Eth. Eudem.,* VII, 14 (1248a 14).

On the contrary, As some maintain, man was first made with only natural endowments.[17] In that state it is manifest that he loved God to some extent. But he did not love God equally with himself, or less than himself, or otherwise he would have sinned. Therefore he loved God above himself. Therefore man, by his natural powers alone, can love God more than himself and above all things.

I answer that, As was said above in the First Part, where the various opinions concerning the natural love of the angels were set forth, in the state of integral nature man could, by his natural power, do his connatural good without the addition of any gratuitous gift, though not without the help of God moving him.[18] Now to love God above all things is natural to man and to every nature, not only rational but irrational, and even inanimate, according to the matter of love which can belong to each creature. The reason for this is that it is natural to all to seek and love things according as they are naturally fit [to be sought and loved] since *all things act according as they are naturally fit,* as is stated in *Physics* ii.[19] Now it is manifest that the good of the part is for the good of the whole. Hence everything, by its natural appetite and love, loves its own proper good because of the common good of the whole universe, which is God. Hence Dionysius says that *God leads everything to the love of Himself.*[20] Hence in the state of integral nature man referred the love of himself and of all other things to the love of God as to its end; and thus he loved God more than himself and above all things. But in the state of corrupted nature man falls short of this in the appetite of his rational will, which, unless it be cured by God's grace, follows its private good, because of the corruption of nature. And so we must say that in the state of integral nature man did not need the gift of grace added to his natural endowments in order to love God above all things naturally, although he needed God's help moving him to it; but in the state of corrupted nature, man needs, even for this, the help of grace healing his nature.

Reply Obj. 1. Charity loves God above all things in a higher way than nature does. For nature loves God above all things inasmuch as He is the beginning and the end of natural good; whereas charity loves Him according as He is the

[17] Cf. above, *S. T.,* I, q. 95, a. 1.   [18] *S. T.,* I, q. 60, a. 5.   [19] Aristotle, *Phys.,* II, 8 (199a 10).   [20] *De Div. Nom.,* IV, 10 (PG 3, 708).

object of beatitude, and inasmuch as man has a spiritual fellowship with God. Moreover, charity adds to the natural love of God a certain quickness and joy, in the same way that every habit of virtue adds to the good act which is done merely by the natural reason of a man who has not the habit of virtue.

Reply Obj. 2. When it is said that no nature can rise above itself, we must not understand this as if it could not be directed to any object above itself; for it is clear that our intellect by its natural knowledge can know things above itself, as is shown in our natural knowledge of God. But we are to understand that nature cannot rise to an act exceeding the proportion of its strength. Now to love God above all things is not such an act, for it is natural to every creature, as was said above.

Reply Obj. 3. Love is said to be highest not only with regard to the degree of love, but also with regard to the motive of loving, and the mode of love. And thus the highest degree of love is that whereby charity loves God as the giver of beatitude, as was said above.

Fourth Article

WHETHER MAN, WITHOUT GRACE AND BY HIS OWN NATURAL POWERS, CAN FULFILL THE COMMANDMENTS OF THE LAW?

We proceed thus to the Fourth Article:—

Objection 1. It would seem that man without grace, and by his own natural powers, can fulfill the commandments of the Law. For the Apostle says (*Rom.* ii. 14) *that the Gentiles, who have not the law, do by nature those things that are of the Law.* Now what a man does naturally he can do of himself without grace. Hence a man can fulfill the commandments of the Law without grace.

Obj. 2. Further, Jerome says that *they are anathema who say God has laid impossibilities upon man.*[21] Now what a man cannot fulfill by himself is impossible to him. Therefore a man can fulfill all the commandments of himself.

Obj. 3. Further, of all the commandments of the Law, the greatest is this, *Thou shalt love the Lord thy God with thy whole heart* (*Matt.* xxii. 37). Now man can fulfill this command by his natural powers, by loving God above all things,

---

[21] Cf. Pelagius, *Epist.*, I, 16 (PL 30, 32).

as was stated above. Therefore man can fulfill all the commandments of the Law without grace.

On the contrary, Augustine says that it is part of the heresy of the Pelagians that *they believe that without grace man can fulfill all the divine commandments.*[22]

I answer that, There are two ways of fulfilling the commandments of the Law.—The first regards the substance of works, as when a man does works of justice, fortitude, and of other virtues. And in this way man in the state of integral nature could fulfill all the commandments of the Law; or otherwise he would have been unable not to sin in that state, since to sin is nothing else than to transgress the divine commandments. But in the state of corrupted nature man cannot fulfill all the divine commandments without healing grace. Secondly, the commandments of the Law can be fulfilled not merely as regards the substance of the act, but also as regards the mode of acting, *i.e.*, their being done out of charity. And in this way, neither in the state of integral nature, nor in the state of corrupted nature can man fulfill the commandments of the Law without grace. Hence, Augustine, having stated that *without grace men can do no good whatever*, adds: *Not only do they know by its light what to do, but by its help they do lovingly what they know.*[23] Beyond this, in both states they need the help of God's motion in order to fulfill the commandments, as was stated above.

Reply Obj. 1. As Augustine says, *do not be disturbed at his saying that they do by nature those things that are of the Law; for the Spirit of grace works this, in order to restore in us the image of God, after which we were naturally made.*[24]

Reply Obj. 2. What we can do with the divine assistance is not altogether impossible to us; for according to the Philosopher: *What we can do through our friends, we can do, in some sense, by ourselves.*[25] Hence Jerome concedes that *our will is in such a way free that we must confess we still always require God's help.*[26]

Reply Obj. 3. Man cannot, with his purely natural endowments, fulfill the precept of the love of God according as it is fulfilled through charity, as was stated above.

[22] *De Haeres.*, 88 (PL 42, 47).   [23] *De Corrept. et Grat.*, II (PL 44, 917).   [24] *De Spir. et Litt.*, XXVII (PL 44, 229).   [25] *Eth.*, III, 3 (1112b 27).   [26] Cf. Pelagius, *Libellus Fidei ad Innocentium* (PL 45, 1718).

Fifth Article

WHETHER MAN CAN MERIT ETERNAL LIFE WITHOUT GRACE?

We proceed thus to the Fifth Article:—

Objection 1. It would seem that man can merit eternal life without grace. For our Lord says (*Matt.* xix. 17): *If thou wilt enter into life, keep the commandments;* from which it would seem that to enter into eternal life rests with man's will. But what rests with our will, we can do of ourselves. Hence it seems that man can merit eternal life of himself.

Obj. 2. Further, eternal life is the wage or reward bestowed by God on men, according to *Matt.* v. 12: *Your reward is very great in heaven.* But wage or reward is meted by God to everyone according to his works, according to *Ps.* lxi. 13: *Thou wilt render to every man according to his works.* Hence, since man is master of his works, it seems that it is within his power to reach eternal life.

Obj. 3. Further, eternal life is the last end of human life. Now every natural thing by its natural endowments can attain its end. Much more, therefore, can man attain to eternal life by his natural endowments, without grace.

On the contrary, The Apostle says (*Rom.* vi. 23): *The grace of God is life everlasting.* And, as the *Gloss* says, this is said *that we may understand that God, of His own mercy, leads us to everlasting life.*[27]

I answer that, Acts leading to an end must be proportioned to the end. But no act exceeds the proportion of its active principle; and hence we see in natural things that nothing can by its operation bring about an effect which exceeds its active power, but only such as is proportioned to its power. Now eternal life is an end exceeding the proportion of human nature, as is clear from what we have said above.[28] Hence man, by his natural powers, cannot produce meritorious works proportioned to eternal life; but for this a higher power is needed, viz., the power of grace. And thus, without grace, man cannot merit eternal life; yet he can perform works leading to a good which is connatural to man, as *to*

---

[27] *Glossa ordin.* (VI, 15F); Peter Lombard, *In Rom.*, super VI, 23 (PL 191, 1412).—Cf. St. Augustine, *Enchir.*, CVII (PL 40, 282).
[28] Q. 5, a. 5.

toil in the fields, to drink, to eat, or to have friends, and the like, as Augustine says in his third *Reply to the Pelagians.*[29]

Reply Obj. 1. Man, by his will, does works meritorious of eternal life; but, as Augustine says in the same book, for this it is necessary that the will of man should be prepared with grace by God.[30]

Reply Obj. 2. As the *Gloss* says upon *Rom.* vi. 23 (*The grace of God is life everlasting*): *It is certain that everlasting life is meted to good works; but the works to which it is meted belong to God's grace.*[31] What is more, it has been said that to fulfill the commandments of the Law, in their due way, whereby their fulfillment may be meritorious, requires grace.

Reply Obj. 3. This objection has to do with the natural end of man. Now human nature, since it is nobler, can be raised by the help of grace to a higher end, which lower natures can in no way reach; even as a man who can recover his health by the help of medicines is better disposed to health than one who can in no way recover it, as the Philosopher observes.[32]

Sixth Article

WHETHER A MAN, BY HIMSELF AND WITHOUT THE EXTERNAL AID OF GRACE, CAN PREPARE HIMSELF FOR GRACE?

We proceed thus to the Sixth Article:—

Objection 1. It would seem that man, by himself and without the external help of grace, can prepare himself for grace. For nothing impossible is laid upon man, as was stated above. But it is written (*Zach.* i. 3): *Turn ye to Me . . . and I will turn to you.* Now to prepare for grace is nothing more than to turn to God. Therefore it seems that man of himself, and without the external help of grace, can prepare himself for grace.

Obj. 2. Further, man prepares himself for grace by doing what is in him to do, since, if man does what is in him to do, God will not deny him grace; for it is written (*Matt.* vii. 11) that God gives His good Spirit *to them that ask Him.* But

---

[29] Pseudo-Augustine, *Hypognost.*, III, 4 (PL 45, 1624).   [30] *Ibid.*
[31] Peter Lombard, *In Rom.*, super VI, 23 (PL 191, 1412)   [32] *De Caelo*, II, 12 (292b 13).

what is in our power, is in us to do. Therefore it seems to be
in our power to prepare ourselves for grace.

Obj. 3. Further, if a man needs grace in order to prepare
for grace, with equal reason will he need grace to prepare
himself for the first grace; and thus to infinity, which is impossible. Hence it seems that we must not go beyond what
was said first, viz., that man, of himself and without grace,
can prepare himself for grace.

Obj. 4. Further, it is written (*Prov.* xvi. 1) that *it is the
part of man to prepare the soul.* Now an action is said to be
the part of a man when he can do it by himself. Hence it
seems that man by himself can prepare himself for grace.

On the contrary, It is written (*Jo.* vi. 44): *No man can
come to Me except the Father, Who hath sent Me, draw him.*
But if man could prepare himself, he would not need to be
drawn by another. Hence man cannot prepare himself without the help of grace.

I answer that, The preparation of the human will for good
is twofold:—the first, whereby it is prepared to operate
rightly and to enjoy God; and this preparation of the will
cannot take place without the habitual gift of grace, which
is the principle of meritorious works, as was stated above.
There is a second way in which the human will may be
taken to be prepared for the gift of habitual grace itself. Now
in order that man prepare himself to receive this gift, it is
not necessary to presuppose any further habitual gift in the
soul, otherwise we should go on to infinity. But we must presuppose a gratuitous gift of God, Who moves the soul inwardly or inspires the good wish. For it is in these two ways
that we need the divine assistance, as was stated above. Now
that we need the help of God to move us, is manifest. For
since every agent acts for an end, every cause must direct
its effect to its end; and hence since the order of ends is according to the order of agents or movers, man must be
directed to the last end by the motion of the first mover, and
to the proximate end by the motion of any of the subordinate
movers. So, too, the spirit of the soldier is bent towards seeking the victory by the motion of the leader of the army—and
towards following the standard of a regiment by the motion
of the standard-bearer. And thus, since God is absolutely the
First Mover, it is by His motion that everything seeks Him
under the common notion of good, whereby everything seeks

to be likened to God in its own way. Hence Dionysius says that *God turns all to Himself*.[33] But He directs just men to Himself as to a special end, which they seek and to which they wish to cling, according to *Ps.* lxxii. 28, *it is good for Me to adhere to my God*. And that they are *turned* to God can only spring from God's having *turned* them. Now to prepare oneself for grace is, as it were, to be turned to God; just as whoever has his eyes turned away from the light of the sun prepares himself to receive the sun's light, by turning his eyes towards the sun. Hence it is clear that man cannot prepare himself to receive the light of grace except by the gratuitous help of God moving him inwardly.

Reply Obj. 1. Man's turning to God is by free choice; and thus man is bidden to turn himself to God. But free choice can be turned to God only when God turns it, according to *Jer.* xxxi. 18: *Convert me and I shall be converted, for Thou art the Lord, my God;* and *Lament.* v. 21: *Convert us, O Lord, to Thee, and we shall be converted*.

Reply Obj. 2. Man can do nothing unless moved by God, according to *John* xv. 5: *Without Me, you can do nothing*. Hence when a man is said to do what is in him to do, this is said to be in his power according as he is moved by God.

Reply Obj. 3. This objection regards habitual grace, for which some preparation is required, since every form requires a disposition in that which is to be its subject. But in order that man should be moved by God, no further motion is presupposed, since God is the First Mover. Hence we need not go to infinity.

Reply Obj. 4. It is the part of man to prepare his soul, since he does this by his free choice. And yet he does not do this without the help of God moving him, and drawing him to Himself, as was said above.

Seventh Article

WHETHER MAN CAN RISE FROM SIN WITHOUT THE HELP OF GRACE?

We proceed thus to the Seventh Article:—

Objection 1. It would seem that man can rise from sin without the help of grace. For what is presupposed to grace

[33] *De Div. Nom.,* IV, 10 (PG 3, 708).

takes place without grace. But to rise from sin is presupposed to the illumination of grace, since it is written (*Ephes.* v. 14): *Arise from the dead and Christ shall enlighten thee.* Therefore man can rise from sin without grace.

Obj. 2. Further, sin is opposed to virtue as illness to health, as was stated above.[34] Now man, by force of his nature, can rise from illness to health, without the external help of medicine, since there still remains in him the principle of life, from which natural operation proceeds. Hence it seems that, with equal reason, man may be restored by himself, and return from the state of sin to the state of justice without the help of external grace.

Obj. 3. Further, every natural thing can return by itself to the act befitting its nature, as hot water returns by itself to its natural coldness, and a stone cast upwards returns by itself to its natural movement. Now sin is an act against nature, as is clear from Damascene.[35] Hence it seems that man by himself can return from sin to the state of justice.

On the contrary, The Apostle says (*Gal.* ii. 21 [cf. iii. 21]): *For if there had been a law given which could give life, then Christ died in vain, i.e.,* to no purpose. Hence with equal reason, if man has a nature whereby he can be justified, *Christ died in vain, i.e.,* to no purpose. But this cannot fittingly be said. Therefore he cannot be justified by himself, *i.e.,* he cannot return from a state of sin to a state of justice.

I answer that, Man by himself can in no way rise from sin without the help of grace. For since sin is transient as to the act and abiding in its guilt, as was stated above,[36] to rise from sin is not the same as to cease from the act of sin; but to rise from sin means that man has restored to him what he lost by sinning. Now man incurs a triple loss by sinning, as was shown above,[37] viz., stain, corruption of natural good, and debt of punishment. He incurs a stain, inasmuch as he forfeits the adornment of grace through the deformity of sin. Natural good is corrupted, inasmuch as man's nature is disordered because man's will is not subject to God's; and when this order is overthrown, the consequence is that the whole nature of sinful man remains disordered. Lastly, there is the

---

[34] Q. 71, a. 1, ad 3.   [35] *De Fide Orth.,* II, 4; 30 (PG 94, 876; 976); cf. *op. cit.,* IV, 20 (PG 94, 1196).   [36] Q. 87, a. 6.   [37] Q. 85, a. 1; q. 86, a. 1; q. 87, a. 1.

debt of punishment, inasmuch as by sinning man deserves eternal damnation.

Now it is manifest that none of these three can be restored except by God. For since the adornment of grace comes from the illumination of the divine light, this adornment cannot be brought back, except God give His light anew. Hence a habitual gift is necessary; and this is the light of grace. Likewise, the order of nature can be restored, *i.e.*, man's will can be subject to God, only when God draws man's will to Himself, as was stated above. So, too, the guilt of eternal punishment can be remitted by God alone, against Whom the offense was committed and Who is man's Judge. And thus, in order that man rise from sin there is required the help of grace, both as regards a habitual gift and as regards the internal motion of God.

Reply Obj. 1. To man is bidden that which pertains to the act of free choice, as this act is required in order that man should rise from sin. Hence when it is said, *Arise, and Christ shall enlighten thee,* we are not to think that the complete rising from sin precedes the illumination of grace; but that when man by his free choice, moved by God, strives to rise from sin, he receives the light of justifying grace.

Reply Obj. 2. The natural reason is not the sufficient principle of the health that is in man by justifying grace. The principle of this health is grace, which is taken away by sin. Hence man cannot be restored by himself, but requires the light of grace to be poured upon him anew, as if the soul were infused into a dead body for its resurrection.

Reply Obj. 3. When nature is integral, it can be restored by itself to what is befitting and proportioned to it; but without exterior help it cannot be restored to what surpasses its limits. And thus human nature, undone by reason of the act of sin, remains no longer integral, but corrupted, as was stated above; nor can it be restored, by itself, even to its connatural good, and much less to the good of supernatural justice.

Eighth Article

WHETHER MAN WITHOUT GRACE CAN AVOID SIN?

We proceed thus to the Eighth Article:—
Objection 1. It would seem that without grace man can

avoid sin. For *no one sins in what he cannot avoid,* as Augustine says.[38] Hence, if a man in mortal sin cannot avoid sin, it would seem that in sinning he does not sin, which is impossible.

Obj. 2. Further, men are corrected that they may not sin. If, therefore, a man in mortal sin cannot avoid sin, correction would seem to be given to no purpose; which is absurd.

Obj. 3. Further, it is written (*Ecclus.* xv. 18): *Before man is life and death, good and evil; that which he shall choose shall be given him.* But by sinning no one ceases to be a man. Hence it is still in his power to choose good or evil; and thus man can avoid sin without grace.

On the contrary, Augustine says: *Whoever denies that we ought to say the prayer 'Lead us not into temptation' (and they deny it who maintain that the help of God's grace is not necessary to man for salvation, but that the gift of the law is enough for the human will) ought without doubt to be removed beyond all hearing, and to be anathematized by the tongues of all.*[39]

I answer that, We may speak of man in two ways: first, in the state of integral nature; secondly, in the state of corrupted nature. Now in the state of integral nature, man, even without habitual grace, could avoid sinning either mortally or venially, since to sin is nothing else than to stray from what is according to our nature—and in the state of integral nature man could avoid this. Nevertheless, he could not have done it without God's help upholding him in good, since if this had been withdrawn, even his nature would have fallen back into nothingness.

But in the state of corrupted nature man needs grace to heal his nature in order that he may entirely abstain from sin. And in the present life this healing is wrought first in the mind, since the carnal appetite is not yet entirely healed. Hence the Apostle (*Rom.* vii. 25) says in the person of one who is healed: *I myself, with the mind, serve the law of God, but with the flesh, the law of sin.* And in this state man can abstain from all mortal sin, whose source is in the reason, as was stated above;[40] but man cannot abstain from all venial sin because of the corruption of his lower appetite of sensual-

[38] *De Duab. Anim.,* X; XI (PL 42, 103; 105); *De Lib. Arb.,* III, 18 (PL 32, 1295).   [39] *De Perfect. Iust.,* XXI (PL 44, 317).   [40] Q. 74, a. 4.

ity. For man can, indeed, repress each of its movements (and hence they are sinful and voluntary), but not all, because, while he is resisting one, another may arise, and also because the reason is not always alert to avoid these movements, as was said above.[41]

So, too, before man's reason, wherein is mortal sin, is restored by justifying grace, he can avoid each mortal sin, and for a time, since it is not necessary that he should always be actually sinning. But it cannot be that he remains for a long time without mortal sin. Hence Gregory says that *a sin not at once taken away by repentance, by its weight drags us down to other sins,*[42] and this because, as the lower appetite ought to be subject to the reason, so should the reason be subject to God, and should place in Him the end of its will. Now it is by the end that all human acts ought to be regulated, even as it is by the judgment of the reason that the movements of the lower appetite should be regulated. And thus, even as inordinate movements of the sensitive appetite cannot help occurring since the lower appetite is not subject to reason, so likewise, since man's reason is not entirely subject to God, the consequence is that many disorders occur in the acts itself of the reason. For when man's heart is not so fixed on God as to be unwilling to be parted from Him for the sake of finding any good or avoiding any evil, many things happen for the achieving or avoiding of which a man strays from God and breaks His commandments, and thus sins mortally; especially since, when surprised, a man acts according to his preconceived end and his pre-existing habits, as the Philosopher says,[43] although with the premeditation of his reason a man may do something outside the order of his preconceived end and the inclination of his habit. But because a man cannot always have this premeditation, it cannot help occurring that he acts in accordance with his will turned aside from God, unless, by grace, he is quickly brought back to the due order.

Reply Obj. 1. Man can avoid each but not every act of sin, except by grace, as was stated above. Nevertheless, since it is by his own shortcoming that he does not prepare himself to have grace, the fact that he cannot avoid sin without grace does not excuse him from sin.

Reply Obj. 2. Correction is useful *in order that out of the*

[41] Q. 74, a. 3, ad 2.   [42] *In Ezech.*, I, hom. 2 (PL 76, 915).
[43] *Eth.*, III, 8 (1117a 18).

*sorrow of correction may spring the wish to be regenerate;
if indeed he who is corrected is a son of promise, in such sort
that while the noise of correction is outwardly resounding
and punishing, God by hidden inspirations is inwardly also
causing him to will,* as Augustine says.[44] Correction is therefore necessary, from the fact that man's will is required in
order to abstain from sin; and yet it is not sufficient without
God's help. Hence it is written (*Eccles.* vii. 14): *Consider the
works of God that no man can correct whom He hath de-
spised.*

Reply Obj. 3. As Augustine says, this saying is to be understood of man in the state of integral nature, when as yet he
was not a slave of sin.[45] Hence he was able to sin and not to
sin. Now, too, whatever a man wills, is given to him; but his
willing good, he has by God's assistance.

Ninth Article

WHETHER ONE WHO HAS ALREADY OBTAINED GRACE CAN,
OF HIMSELF AND WITHOUT FURTHER HELP OF GRACE,
DO GOOD AND AVOID SIN?

We proceed thus to the Ninth Article:—

Objection 1. It would seem that whoever has already obtained grace can, by himself and without further help of
grace, do good and avoid sin. For a thing is useless or imperfect, if it does not fulfill what it was given for. Now grace is
given to us that we may do good and keep from sin. Hence
if with grace man cannot do this, it seems that grace is either
useless or imperfect.

Obj. 2. Further, by grace the Holy Spirit dwells in us, according to *1 Cor.* iii. 16: *Know you not that you are the
temple of God, and that the Spirit of God dwelleth in you?*
Now since the Spirit of God is omnipotent, He is sufficient to
ensure our doing good and to keep us from sin. Hence a man
who has obtained grace can do the above two things without
any further assistance of grace.

Obj. 3. Further, if a man who has obtained grace needs
further aid of grace in order to live righteously and to keep
free from sin, with equal reason he will need yet another

---

[44] *De Corrept. et Grat.,* I (PL 44, 921).   [45] Pseudo-Augustine,
Hypognost., III, 2 (PL 45, 1621).

grace, even though he has obtained this first help of grace. Therefore we must go on to infinity; which is impossible. Hence, whoever is in grace needs no further help of grace in order to work righteously and to keep free from sin.

On the contrary, Augustine says that *as the eye of the body, though most healthy, cannot see unless it is helped by the brightness of light, so neither can a man, even if he is most perfectly justified, live righteously unless he be helped by the eternal light of justice.*[46] But justification is by grace, according to *Rom.* iii. 24: *Being justified freely by His grace.* Hence, even a man who already possesses grace needs a further assistance of grace in order to live righteously.

I answer that, As was stated above, in order to live righteously a man needs a twofold help of God—first, a habitual gift whereby corrupted human nature is healed, and after being healed is lifted up so as to work deeds meritorious of eternal life, which exceed the capability of nature. Secondly, man needs the help of grace in order to be moved by God to act.

Now with regard to the first kind of help, man does not need a further help of grace, that is, a further infused habit. Yet he needs the help of grace in another way, *i.e.,* in order to be moved by God to act righteously; and this for two reasons: first, for the general reason that no created thing can put forth any act, unless by virtue of the divine motion; secondly, for this special reason—the condition of the state of human nature. For, although healed by grace as to the mind, yet it remains corrupted and poisoned in the flesh, whereby it serves *the law of sin* (*Rom.* vii. 25). In the intellect, too, there remains the darkness of ignorance, whereby, as is written (*Rom.* viii. 26): *We know not what we should pray for as we ought;* since, because of the various turns of circumstances, and because we do not know ourselves perfectly, we cannot fully know what is for our good, according to *Wis.* ix. 14: *For the thoughts of mortal men are fearful and our counsels uncertain.* Hence we must be guided and guarded by God, Who knows and can do all things. For this reason also it is becoming in those who have been born again as sons of God to say: *Lead us not into temptation,* and *Thy Will be done on earth as it is in heaven,* and whatever else is contained in the Lord's Prayer pertaining to this.

[46] *De Nat. et Grat.,* XXVI (PL 44, 261).

Reply Obj. 1. The gift of habitual grace is not therefore given to us that we may no longer need the divine help; for every creature needs to be preserved in the good received from Him. Hence, if after having received grace man still needs the divine help, it cannot be concluded that grace is given to no purpose, or that it is imperfect, since man will need the divine help even in the state of glory, when grace shall be fully perfected. But here grace is to some extent imperfect, inasmuch as it does not completely heal man, as was stated above.

Reply Obj. 2. The operation of the Holy Ghost, which moves and protects, is not circumscribed by the effect of habitual grace which it causes in us; but beyond this effect He, together with the Father and the Son, moves and protects us.

Tenth Article

WHETHER MAN POSSESSED OF GRACE NEEDS THE HELP OF GRACE IN ORDER TO PERSEVERE?

We proceed thus to the Tenth Article:—

Objection 1. It would seem that man possessed of grace needs no help of grace to persevere. For perseverance is something less than virtue, even as continence is, as is clear from the Philosopher.[47] Now since man is justified by grace, he needs no further help of grace in order to have the virtues. Much less, therefore, does he need the help of grace to have perseverance.

Obj. 2. Further, all the virtues are infused together. But perseverance is put down as a virtue. Hence it seems that, together with grace, perseverance is given when the other virtues are infused.

Obj. 3. Further, as the Apostle says (*Rom.* v. 20), more was restored to man by Christ's gift than he had lost by Adam's sin. But Adam received what enabled him to persevere. Therefore, all the more is there restored in us by the grace of Christ the ability to persevere. And thus man does not need grace in order to persevere.

On the contrary, Augustine says: *Why is perseverance besought of God, if it is not bestowed by God? For is it not a mocking request to seek what we know He does not give, and*

[47] *Eth.,* VII, 1 (1145b 1); 9 (1151b 32).

what is in our power without His giving it? [48] Now perseverance is besought even by those who are sanctified by grace; and this is seen when we say *Hallowed be Thy name,* which Augustine confirms by the words of Cyprian.[49] Hence man, even when possessed of grace, needs perseverance to be given to him by God.

I answer that, Perseverance is taken in three ways. First, to signify a habit of the mind whereby a man stands steadfastly, lest he be moved by the assault of sadness from what is virtuous. And thus perseverance is to sadness as continence is to concupiscence and pleasure, as the Philosopher says.[50] Secondly, perseverance may be called a habit whereby a man has the purpose of persevering in good until the end. And in both these ways perseverance is infused together with grace, even as are continence and the other virtues. Thirdly, perseverance is called the abiding in good to the end of life. And in order to have this perseverance man does not, indeed, need another habitual grace, but he needs the divine assistance guiding and guarding him against the attacks of the passions, as appears from the preceding article. And hence after anyone has been justified by grace, he still needs to beseech God for the aforesaid gift of perseverance, that he may be kept from evil till the end of his life. For grace is given to many to whom perseverance in grace is not given.

Reply Obj. 1. This objection regards the first mode of perseverance, as the second objection regards the second.

Hence the solution of the second objection is clear.

Reply Obj. 3. As Augustine says, *in the original state man received a gift whereby he could persevere, but to persevere was not given him. But now, by the grace of Christ, many receive both the gift of grace whereby they may persevere, and the further gift of persevering.*[51] And thus, Christ's gift is greater than Adam's fault. Nevertheless, it was easier for man to persevere through the gift of grace in the state of innocence, in which the flesh was not rebellious against the spirit, than it is now. For the restoration by Christ's grace, although it is already begun in the mind, is not yet completed in the flesh, as it will be in heaven, where man will not merely be able to persevere, but will be unable to sin.

[48] *De Dono Persev.,* II (PL 45, 996).   [49] *Ibid.*—Cf. also *De Corrept. et Grat.,* VI, 10 (PL 44, 922).   [50] *Eth.,* VII, 7 (1150a, 13).
[51] Cf. *De Corrept. et Grat.,* XII, 34 (PL 44, 937).

Question CXII

ON THE CAUSE OF GRACE

(*In Five Articles*)

WE MUST now consider the cause of grace, and under this head there are five points of inquiry: (1) Whether God alone is the efficient cause of grace? (2) Whether any disposition towards grace is needed on the part of the recipient, by an act of free choice? (3) Whether such a disposition can make grace follow of necessity? (4) Whether grace is equal in all? (5) Whether anyone can know that he has grace?

First Article

WHETHER GOD ALONE IS THE CAUSE OF GRACE?

We proceed thus to the First Article:—

Objection 1. It would seem that God alone is not the cause of grace. For it is written (*Jo.* i. 17): *Grace and truth came by Jesus Christ.* Now, by the name Jesus Christ is understood not merely the divine nature assuming, but the created nature assumed. Therefore a creature may be the cause of grace.

Obj. 2. Further, there is this difference between the sacraments of the New Law and those of the Old, that the sacraments of the New Law cause grace, whereas the sacraments of the Old Law merely signify it. Now the sacraments of the New Law are certain visible elements. Therefore God is not the only cause of grace.

Obj. 3. Further, according to Dionysius, *Angels cleanse, enlighten and perfect both lesser angels and men.*[1] Now the rational creature is cleansed, enlightened and perfected by grace. Therefore God is not the only cause of grace.

On the contrary, It is written (*Ps.* lxxxiii. 12): *The Lord will give grace and glory.*

I answer that, Nothing can act beyond its species, since the cause must always be more powerful than its effect. Now the gift of grace surpasses every capability of created nature, since it is nothing short of a partaking of the divine nature, which exceeds every other nature. And thus it is impossible

[1] *De Cael. Hier.*, III, 2; IV, 2; VII, 3; VIII, 2 (PG 3, 165; 180; 209; 240).

that any creature should cause grace. For it is as necessary that God alone should deify, by bestowing a partaking of the divine nature through a participated likeness, as it is impossible that anything save fire should enkindle.

Reply Obj. 1. Christ's humanity is an *organ of His divinity,* as Damascene says.[2] Now an instrument does not bring forth the action of the principal agent by its own power, but in virtue of the principal agent. Hence Christ's humanity does not cause grace by its own power, but by the power of the divine nature joined to it, whereby the actions of Christ's humanity are saving actions.

Reply Obj. 2. Just as in the person of Christ the humanity causes our salvation by grace, under the principal agency of the divine power, so likewise in the sacraments of the New Law, which are derived from Christ, grace is instrumentally caused by the sacraments, and principally by the power of the Holy Ghost working in the sacraments, according to *John* iii. 5: *Unless a man be born again of water and the Holy Ghost he cannot enter into the kingdom of God.*

Reply Obj. 3. Angels cleanse, enlighten and perfect angels or men, by instruction, and not by justifying them through grace. Hence Dionysius says that *this cleansing and enlightenment and perfecting is nothing else than the assumption of divine science.*[3]

Second Article

WHETHER ANY PREPARATION AND DISPOSITION FOR GRACE
IS REQUIRED ON MAN'S PART?

We proceed thus to the Second Article:—

Objection 1. It would seem that no preparation or disposition for grace is required on man's part, since, as the Apostle says (*Rom.* iv. 4), *To him that worketh, the reward is not reckoned according to grace, but according to debt.* Now a man's preparation by free choice can be only through some operation. Hence it would do away with the notion of grace.

Obj. 2. Further, whoever continues sinning is not preparing himself to have grace. But to some who continue sinning grace is given, as is clear in the case of Paul, who received

[2] *De Fide Orth.,* III, 19 (PG 94, 1080).   [3] Cf. *De Cael. Hier.,* VII,
3 (PG 3, 209).

grace while he was *breathing out threatenings and slaughter against the disciples of the Lord* (*Acts* ix. 1). Hence no preparation for grace is required on man's part.

Obj. 3. Further, an agent of infinite power needs no disposition in matter, since it does not even require matter, as appears in creation, to which grace is compared, for it is called *a new creature* (*Gal.* vi. 15). But only God, Who has infinite power, causes grace, as was stated above. Hence no preparation is required on man's part to obtain grace.

On the contrary, It is written (*Amos* iv. 12): *Be prepared to meet thy God, O Israel;* and (*1 Kings* vii. 3): *Prepare your hearts unto the Lord.*

I answer that, As was stated above, grace is taken in two ways.[4] First, as a habitual gift of God. Secondly, as a help from God, Who moves the soul to good. Now taking grace in the first sense, a certain preparation of grace is required for it, since a form can be only in disposed matter. But if we speak of grace as it signifies a help from God moving us to good, no preparation is required on man's part, anticipating, as it were, the divine help, but rather, every preparation in man must be by the help of God moving the soul to good. And thus even the good movement of free choice, whereby anyone is prepared for receiving the gift of grace, is an act of free choice moved by God. And it is thus that man is said to prepare himself, according to *Prov.* xvi. 1: *It is the part of man to prepare the soul;* yet it is principally from God, Who moves the free choice. Hence it is said that man's will is prepared by God (*Prov.* viii. 35), and that man's steps are guided by God (*Prov.* xxxvi. 23).

Reply Obj. 1. A certain preparation of man for grace is simultaneous with the infusion of grace; and this operation is meritorious, not indeed of grace, which is already possessed, but of glory, which is not yet possessed. But there is another imperfect preparation, which sometimes precedes the gift of sanctifying grace, which yet is from God's motion. But it does not suffice for merit, since man is not yet justified by grace, and merit can only arise from grace, as will be seen farther on.[5]

Reply Obj. 2. Since a man cannot prepare himself for grace unless God prevent and move him to good, it is of no account

whether anyone arrive at perfect preparation instantaneously, or step by step. For it is written (*Ecclus*. xi. 23): *It is
easy in the eyes of God on a sudden to make the poor man
rich*. Now it sometimes happens that God moves a man to
good, but not perfect good, and this preparation precedes
grace. But He sometimes moves him suddenly and perfectly
to good, and man receives grace suddenly, according to
John vi. 45: *Every one that hath heard of the Father, and
hath learned, cometh to Me*. And thus it happened to Paul,
since, suddenly when he was in the midst of sin, his heart was
perfectly moved by God to hear, to learn, to come; and hence
he received grace suddenly.

Reply Obj. 3. An agent of infinite power needs no matter
or disposition of matter, brought about by the action of some
other cause; and yet, looking to the condition of the thing
caused, it must cause, in the thing caused, both the matter
and the due disposition for the form. So, likewise, when God
infuses grace into a soul, no preparation is required which
He Himself does not bring about.

Third Article

WHETHER GRACE IS NECESSARILY GIVEN TO WHOEVER PRE-
PARES HIMSELF FOR IT, OR TO WHOEVER DOES WHAT
HE CAN?

We proceed thus to the Third Article:—

Objection 1. It would seem that grace is necessarily given
to whoever prepares himself for grace, or to whoever does
what he can, because, on *Rom.* v. 1 (*Being justified . . . by
faith, let us have peace*, etc.) the *Gloss* says: *God welcomes
whoever flies to Him, otherwise there would be injustice with
Him.*[6] But it is impossible for injustice to be with God.
Therefore it is impossible for God not to welcome whoever
flies to Him. Hence he receives grace of necessity.

Obj. 2. Further, Anselm says that the reason why God does
not bestow grace on the devil is that he did not wish, nor
was he prepared, to receive it.[7] But if the cause be removed,
the effect must needs be removed also. Therefore, if anyone
is willing to receive grace it is bestowed on him of necessity.

[6] Peter Lombard, *In Rom.*, super III, 21 (PL 191, 1360).   [7] *De
Casu Diab.*, III (PL 158, 328).

Obj. 3. Further, good is diffusive of itself, as appears from Dionysius.[8] But the good of grace is better than the good of nature. Hence, since natural forms necessarily come to disposed matter, much more does it seem that grace is necessarily bestowed on whoever prepares himself for grace.

On the contrary, Man is compared to God as clay to the potter, according to *Jer.* xviii. 6: *As clay is in the hand of the potter, so are you in My hand.* But however much the clay is prepared, it does not necessarily receive its shape from the potter. Hence, however much a man prepares himself, he does not necessarily receive grace from God.

I answer that, As was stated above, man's preparation for grace is from God, as mover, and from free choice, as moved. Hence the preparation may be looked at in two ways. First, as it is from free choice, and thus there is no necessity that it should obtain grace, since the gift of grace exceeds every preparation of human power. But it may be considered, secondly, as it is from God the mover, and thus it has a necessity—not indeed of coercion, but of infallibility—as regards what it is ordained to by God, since God's intention cannot fail, according to the saying of Augustine, in his book *On the Predestination of the Saints,* that *by God's good gifts whoever is liberated, is most certainly liberated.*[9] Hence if God intends, while moving, that the one whose heart He moves should attain to grace, he will infallibly attain to it, according to *John* vi. 45: *Every one that hath heard of the Father, and hath learned, cometh to Me.*

Reply Obj. 1. This *Gloss* is speaking of such as fly to God by a meritorious act of their free choice, already *informed* with grace; for if they did not receive grace, it would be against the justice which He Himself established.—Or if it refers to the movement of free choice before grace, it is speaking in the sense that man's flight to God is by a divine motion, which ought not, in justice, to fail.

Reply Obj. 2. The first cause of the defect of grace is on our part; but the first cause of the bestowal of grace is on God's, according to *Osee* xiii. 9: *Destruction is thy own, O Israel; thy help is only in Me.*

Reply Obj. 3. Even in natural things, the form does not

---

[8] *De Div. Nom.,* IV, 20 (PG 3, 719).   [9] Cf. *De Dono Persev.,* XIV (PL 45, 1014).

necessarily follow the disposition of the matter, except by the power of the agent that causes the disposition.

Fourth Article

WHETHER GRACE IS GREATER IN ONE THAN IN ANOTHER?

We proceed thus to the Fourth Article:—

Objection 1. It would seem that grace is not greater in one than in another. For grace is caused in us by the divine love, as was stated above.[10] Now it is written (*Wis.* vi. 8): *He made the little and the great and He hath equally care of all.* Therefore all obtain grace from Him equally.

Obj. 2. Further, whatever is a maximum cannot be more or less. But grace is a maximum since it joins us with our last end. Therefore there is no greater or less in it. Hence it is not greater in one than in another.

Obj. 3. Further, grace is the soul's life, as was stated above.[11] But there is no greater or less in life. Hence, neither is there in grace.

On the contrary, It is written (*Ephes.* iv. 7): *But to every one of us is given grace according to the measure of the giving of Christ.* Now what is given in measure is not given to all equally. Hence all have not an equal grace.

I answer that, As was stated above, habits can have a double magnitude.[12] One concerns the end or object, as when a virtue is said to be more noble through being ordained to a greater good; the other is on the part of the subject, which participates more or less in the habit inhering to it.

Now as regards the first magnitude, sanctifying grace cannot be greater or less, since, of its nature, grace joins man to the highest good, which is God. But as regards the subject, grace can receive more or less, inasmuch as one may be more perfectly illumined by the light of grace than another. And a certain reason for this is on the part of him who prepares himself for grace; since he who is better prepared for grace receives more grace. Yet it is not here that we must seek the first cause of this diversity, since man prepares himself only inasmuch as his free choice is prepared by God. Hence the first cause of this diversity is to be sought on the part of God,

[10] Q. 110, a. 1.   [11] Q. 110, a. 1, ad 2.   [12] Q. 52, a. 1 and 2; q. 66, a. 1 and 2.

Who dispenses His gifts of grace variously, in order that the beauty and perfection of the Church may result from these various degrees; even as He instituted the various conditions of things, that the universe might be perfect. Hence, after the Apostle had said (*Ephes*. iv. 7): *To every one of us is given grace according to the measure of the giving of Christ*, having enumerated the various graces, he adds (*verse* 12): *For the perfecting of the saints . . . for the edifying of the body of Christ*.

Reply Obj. 1. The divine care may be looked at in two ways. First, as regards the divine act, which is simple and uniform; and thus His care looks equally to all, since by one simple act He administers great things and little. But, secondly, it may be considered in those things which come to creatures by the divine care; and thus, inequality is found, inasmuch as God by His care provides greater gifts for some, and lesser gifts for others.

Reply Obj. 2. This objection is based on the first kind of magnitude in grace; since grace cannot be greater by ordaining to a greater good, but inasmuch as it ordains more or less to a greater or lesser participation of the same good. For there may be diversity of intensity and remission both in grace and in final glory as regards the subjects' participation.

Reply Obj. 3. Natural life pertains to man's substance, and hence cannot be more or less; but man partakes of the life of grace accidentally, and hence man may possess it more or less.

Fifth Article

WHETHER MAN CAN KNOW THAT HE HAS GRACE?

We proceed thus to the Fifth Article:—

Objection 1. It would seem that man can know that he has grace. For grace is in the soul by its essence. Now the soul has most certain knowledge of those things that are in it by their essence, as appears from Augustine.[13] Hence grace may be known most certainly by one who has grace.

Obj. 2. Further, as science is a gift of God, so is grace. But whoever receives science from God, knows that he has science, according to *Wis*. vii. 17: The Lord *hath given me*

---

[13] *De Genesi ad Litt*., XII, 25; 31 (PL 34, 475; 479).

the true knowledge of the things that are. Hence, with equal reason, whoever receives grace from God, knows that he has grace.

Obj. 3. Further, light is more knowable than darkness, since, according to the Apostle (*Ephes.* v. 13), *all that is made manifest is light.* Now sin, which is spiritual darkness, may be known with certainty by one that is in sin. Much more, therefore, may grace, which is spiritual light, be known.

Obj. 4. Further, the Apostle says (*1 Cor.* ii. 12): *Now we have received not the Spirit of this world, but the Spirit that is of God; that we may know the things that are given us from God.* Now grace is God's first gift. Hence, the man who receives grace by the Holy Spirit, by the same Holy Spirit knows the grace given to him.

Obj. 5. Further, it was said by the Lord to Abraham (*Gen.* xxii. 12): *Now I know that thou fearest God, i.e.,* I have made thee know. But He is speaking there of chaste fear, which is not apart from grace. Hence a man may know that he has grace.

On the contrary, It is written (*Eccles.* ix. 1): *Man knoweth not whether he be worthy of love or hatred.* Now sanctifying grace maketh a man worthy of God's love. Therefore no one can know whether he has sanctifying grace.

I answer that, There are three ways of knowing a thing. First, by revelation, and thus anyone may know that he has grace, for God by a special privilege reveals this at times to some, in order that the joy of safety may begin in them even in this life, and that they may carry on toilsome works with greater trust and greater energy, and may bear the evils of this present life, as when it was said to Paul (*2 Cor.* xii. 9): *My grace is sufficient for thee.*

Secondly, a man may, of himself, know something, and with certainty; and in this way no one can know that he has grace. For certitude about a thing can be had only when we may judge of it by its proper principle. Thus it is by indemonstrable universal principles that certitude is obtained concerning demonstrative conclusions. Now no one can know he has the science of a conclusion if he does not know its principle. But the principle of grace and its object is God, Who by reason of His very excellence is unknown to us, according to *Job* xxxvi. 26: *Behold God is great, exceeding our knowl-*

edge. And hence His presence in us and His absence cannot be known with certainty, according to *Job* ix. 11: *If He come to me, I shall not see Him; if He depart, I shall not understand.* And hence man cannot judge with certainty that he has grace, according to *I Cor.* iv. 3, 4: *But neither do I judge my own self . . . but He that judgeth me is the Lord.*

Thirdly, things are known conjecturally by signs; and thus anyone may know he has grace, when he is conscious of delighting in God and of despising worldly things, and inasmuch as a man is not conscious of any mortal sin. In this sense it is written (*Apoc.* ii. 17): *To him that overcometh I will give the hidden manna . . . which no man knoweth, but he that receiveth it,* because whoever receives it knows, by experiencing a certain sweetness, which he who does not receive does not experience. Yet this knowledge is imperfect, and hence the Apostle says (*I Cor.* iv. 4): *I am not conscious to myself of anything, yet am I not hereby justified,* since, according to *Ps.* xviii. 13: *Who can understand sins? From my secret ones cleanse me, O Lord, and from those of others spare Thy servant.*

Reply Obj. 1. Those things which are in the soul by their essence are known through experimental knowledge, in so far as through his acts man has experience of his inward principles. For example, we perceive our will by willing, and by exercising the functions of life, we observe that there is life in us.

Reply Obj. 2. It belongs to the nature of science that a man should have certitude of the objects of science; so, too, it belongs to the nature of faith that a man should be certain of the things of faith, and this, because certitude belongs to the perfection of the intellect, wherein these gifts exist. Hence, whoever has science or faith is certain that he has them. But it is otherwise with grace and charity and the like, which perfect the appetitive power.

Reply Obj. 3. Sin has for its principal and object a mutable good, which is known to us. But the object or end of grace is unknown to us because of the greatness of its light, according to *I Tim.* vi. 16: *Who . . . inhabiteth light inaccessible.*

Reply Obj. 4. The Apostle is here speaking of the gifts of glory (*I Cor.* ii. 10), which have been given to us in hope, and these we know most certainly by faith, although we do not know for certain that we have grace to enable us to merit them.—Or it may be said that he is speaking of the privileged knowledge, which comes of revelation. Hence he adds (*verse 10*): *But to us God hath revealed them by His Spirit.*

Reply Obj. 5. What was said to Abraham may refer to the experimental knowledge which we have through our deeds. For in the deed that Abraham had just wrought, he could know experimentally that he had the fear of God.—Or it may refer to a revelation.

BIBLIOGRAPHY[1]

The following list of books does not pretend to be a bibliography either of St. Thomas himself or of all the literature on which the *Summa Theologica* depends. Such a bibliography is scarcely necessary, since there are in existence excellent and exhaustive Thomistic bibliographical monographs. For the years down to 1920, one may consult the *Bibliographie Thomiste* of P. Mandonnet and J. Destrez (*Bibliothèque Thomiste*, vol. I, Kain: Le Saulchoir, 1921). The years 1920 to 1940 are covered by the recent work of V. Bourke (*Thomistic Bibliography*, St. Louis: St. Louis University Press, 1945). On the writings of St. Thomas Aquinas himself, their authenticity, chronology, etc., there are the well known works of Mandonnet and Grabmann (cf. P. Mandonnet, *Des écrits authentiques de s. Thomas d'Aquin*, 2nd ed. [Fribourg: Imprimérie de l'Oeuvre de Saint-Paul, 1910]; M. Grabmann, *Die Werke des Hl. Thomas von Aquin*, 2nd ed. [*Beiträge zur Geschichte der Philosophie und Theologie des Mittelalters*, Band XX, 1-2, Münster: Aschendorff, 1931]).

These ample works of reference dispense with the need of reproducing here any general bibliography on St. Thomas Aquinas. I have therefore restricted myself to including in the following list only such primary sources, collections of documents and secondary works which have been used in the annotations to the text of St. Thomas Aquinas.

I

Abelard, Peter:
   Introductio ad Theologiam, PL 178, coll. 987-1114.
Alain of Lille:
   Theologicae Regulae, PL 210, coll. 621-684.
Albert the Great, St.:
   Opera Omnia, 38 vols., ed. A. Borgnet (Paris: Vivès, 1890-1899).
   De Quindecim Problematibus (in P. Mandonnet, *Siger de Brabant et l'Averroisme Latin au XIIIme Siècle*, Louvain: Institut Supérieur de Philosophie de l'Université, Pt. II, 1908, pp. 29-52).

---

[1] The only abbreviations which may require explanation are two: PL stands for *Patrologia Latina* (*i.e.*, J. P. Migne, *Patrologiae Cursus Completus*, Series II, 221 vols., Paris, 1844-1864, with later reprints); PG stands for *Patrologia Graeca* (*i.e.*, J. P. Migne, *Patrologiae Cursus Completus*, Series I, 162 vols., Paris, 1857-1866, with later reprints).

De Animalibus Libri XXVI, nach der Cölner Urschrift, ed. H. Stadler (in *Beiträge zur Geschichte der Philosophie und Theologie des Mittelalters*, Bände XV-XVI, Münster, Aschendorff, 1916-1921). *Summa de Bono* (cf., below, O. Lottin, *Le droit naturel*).

Alcher of Clairvaux (Pseudo-Augustine):
De Spiritu et Anima Liber Unus, PL 40, coll. 779-832.

Alexander of Aphrodisias:
De Intellectu et Intellecto (in G. Théry, *Alexandre d'Aphrodise* [*Autour du décret de 1210*, II] *Bibliothèque Thomiste*, vol. VII, Kain: Le Saulchoir, 1926, pp. 74-82).

Alexander of Hales:
Summa Theologica, 3 vols. (Quaracchi: Ex Typographia Collegii S. Bonaventurae, 1924-1930).

Alfred of Sareshel (Alfredus Anglicus):
De Motu Cordis, ed. Cl. Baeumker (in *Beiträge zur Geschichte der Philosophie und Theologie des Mittelalters*, Band XXIII, 1-2, Münster, Aschendorff, 1923).

Ambrose, St.:
Opera Omnia, PL 14-17.

Ambrosiaster:
Commentaria in XII Epistolas Beati Pauli, PL 17, coll. 47-536. (Pseudo-Ambrose)
Quaestiones Veteris et Novi Testamenti, PL 35, coll. 2215-2422. (Pseudo-Augustine)

Anonymous (Pseudo-Hugh of St. Victor):
Summa Sententiarum septem Tractatibus Distincta, PL 176, coll. 41-174.

Anselm of Canterbury, St.:
Opera Omnia, PL 158-159.
S. Anselmi Opera Omnia, I-II (continens opera quae Prior et Abbas Beccensis composuit), ed. F. S. Schmitt (Secovii: Ex officina Abbatiae Secoviensis in Styria, 1938-1946).

Aristotle:
Aristotelis Opera, 5 vols., edidit Academia Regia Borussica, ex recognitione I. Bekker (Berlin: G. Reimer, 1831).
The Works of Aristotle, 11 vols., ed. W. D. Ross (Oxford: Clarendon Press, 1928-1931).
The Basic Works of Aristotle, ed. and with an introduction by R. McKeon (New York: Random House, 1941).

Augustine, St.:
Opera Omnia, PL 32-47.

Averroes:
Aristotelis Stagiritae Libri Omnes . . . cum Averrois Cordubensis variis in eosdem Commentariis, 11 vols., Venetiis apud Juntas, 1550-1552.

Avicebron:
Avencebrolis (Ibn Gebirol) Fons Vitae. Ex Arabico in latinum

translatus ab Johanne Hispano et Dominic Gundissalino, ed. Cl. Baeumker (in *Beiträge zur Geschichte der Philosophie und Theologie des Mittelalters,* Band I, 2-4, Münster, Aschendorff, 1892-1895).

Avicenna:

Opera in lucem redacta ac nuper quantum ars niti potuit per canonicos emendata, Venetiis, 1508.

Basil the Great, St.:

Opera Omnia, PG 29-32.

Bede the Venerable, St.:

Opera Omnia, PL 90-95.

Bernard of Clairvaux, St.:

Opera Omnia, PL 182-184.

Boethius:

Opera Omnia, PL 63-64.

Bonaventure, St.:

Opera Omnia, 10 vols. (Quaracchi: Ex Typographia Collegii S. Bonaventurae, 1882-1902).

Cassiodorus:

Opera Omnia, PL 69-70.

Chalcidius:

Timaeus . . . translatus et in eundem Commentarius (in *Fragmenta Philosophorum Graecorum,* ed. G. A. Mullach, Paris: Firmin-Didot, 1867, vol. II, pp. 147-258).

Cicero, Marcus Tullius:

Scripta Quae Manserunt Omnia:

Fasc. 1: (Anonymous) *Rhetorica ad Herennium,* ed. F. Marx (Leipsig: B. G. Teubner, 1923).

Fasc. 2: Rhetorici Libri Duo (De Inventione), ed. E. Stroebel (Leipsig: B. G. Teubner, 1915).

Fasc. 39: De Re Publica, ed. K. Ziegler (Leipsig: B. G. Teubner, 1929).

Fasc. 42: Academicorum Reliquiae cum Lucullo, ed. O. Plasberg (Leipsig: B. G. Teubner, 1922).

Fasc. 43: De Finibus Bonorum et Malorum, ed. Th. Schiche (Leipsig: B. G. Teubner, 1915).

Fasc. 44: Tusculanae Disputationes, ed. M. Pohlenz (Leipsig: B. G. Teubner, 1918).

Fasc. 45: De Natura Deorum, ed. W. Ax (Leipsig: B. G. Teubner, 1933).

Fasc. 46: De Divinatione, De Fato, Timaeus, ed. O. Plasberg—W. Ax (B. G. Teubner, 1938).

Fasc. 48: De Officiis, ed. C. Atzert (Leipsig: B. G. Teubner, 1932).

Topica (in *M. Tullii Ciceronis Opera Rhetorica,* vol. II, Leipsig: B. G. Teubner, 1893).

Costa-Ben-Luca:
  Liber de Differentia Animae et Spiritus, trans. by John of Spain, ed.
  C. S. Barach (in *Excerpta e Libro Alfredi Anglici De Motu Cordis
  item Costa-Ben-Lucae De Differentia Animae et Spiritus Liber,*
  Bibliotheca Philosophorum Mediae Aetatis, vol. II, Innsbruck, 1878,
  pp. 115-139).

Dionysius the Pseudo-Areopagite:
  Opera Omnia, PG 3-4.

Fulgentius:
  De Fide ad Petrum, sive De Regula Verae Fidei Liber unus, PL 40,
  coll. 753-780. (Pseudo-Augustine)
  *Liber de duplici Praedestinatione Dei, Una Bonorum ad Gloriam,
  Altera Malorum ad Poenam,* PL 65, coll. 153-178.

Gennadius:
  Liber de Ecclesiasticis Dogmatibus, PL 42, coll. 1213-1222; PL 58,
  coll. 979-1000.
Gilbert de la Porrée:
  Commentaria in Boethium, PL 64.
  (?) *Liber de sex Principiis Gilberto Porretano Ascriptus,* ed. A.
  Heysse (in *Opuscula et Textus,* Series Scholastica, fasc. VII, Mün-
  ster: Aschendorff, 1929).

Giles of Rome:
  *De Erroribus Philosophorum Aristotelis, Averrois, Avicennae, Al-
  gazelis, Alkindi et Rabbi Moysis* (in P. Mandonnet, *Siger de Brabant
  et l'Averroisme Latin au XIIIme Siècle,* Louvain: Institut Supérieur
  de Philosophie de l'Université, Pt. II, 1908, pp. 3-25).
  De Erroribus Philosophorum. . ., ed. J. Koch and trans. J. O.
  Riedl (Milwaukee: Marquette University Press, 1944).

Glossa Ordinaria. . ., 6 vols. (Basileae, 1506-1508).
Gratian:
  Decretum. Cf. *Corpus Iuris Canonici.*
Gregory of Nyssa, St.:
  De Hominis Opificio, PG 44, coll. 123-256.
Gregory the Great, St.:
  Opera Omnia, PL 75-79.
Grosseteste, Robert:
  *Die philosophischen Werke des Robert Grosseteste Bischofs von
  Lincoln,* ed. L. Baur (in *Beiträge zur Geschichte der Philosophie
  und Theologie des Mittelalters,* Band IX, Münster: Aschendorff,
  1912).
  "An unedited text of Robert Grosseteste on the Subject-matter of
  Theology," ed. G. B. Phelan (*Revue néo-scolastique de philosophie,*
  vol. XXXVI, *Mélangés de Wulf,* Feb. 1934, pp. 172-179).

Gundissalinus, Dominicus:
   De Anima, ed. J. T. Muckle (*Mediaeval Studies*, II, 1940, pp. 23-103, with an introduction by E. Gilson).

Hermes Trismegistus, Pseudo-:
   Liber XXIV Philosophorum, ed. Cl. Baeumker (in *Abhandlungen aus den Gebiete der Philosophie und ihrer Geschichte*, Festgabe Hertling, Freiburg, 1913, pp. 17-40).
Hilary, St.:
   Opera Omnia, PL 9-10.
Hugh of St. Victor:
   Opera Omnia, PL 175-177.

Isaac Israeli:
   Liber de Definicionibus, ed. J. T. Muckle (*Archives d'histoire doctrinale et littéraire du moyen-âge*, vol. XII-XIII, 1937-1938, pp. 299-340).
Isidore of Seville, St.:
   Opera Omnia, PL 81-84.

Jerome, St.:
   Opera Omnia, PL 22-30.
John Chrysostom, St.:
   Opera Omnia, PG 47-64.
John Damascene, St.:
   Expositio Accurata Fidei Orthodoxae, PG 94, coll. 789-1228.
Josephus:
   Josephus, ed. and trans. H. Thackeray and R. Marcus (Cambridge, Mass.: Harvard University Press, 1926-).
Justinian:
   Institutiones; Digesta; Codex. Cf. *Corpus Iuris Civilis*.

Kilwardby, Robert:
   De Natura Theologiae, ed. F. Stegmüller (in *Opuscula et Textus,* Series Scholastica, fasc. XVII, Münster: Aschendorff, 1935).
   Liber de Causis, ed. R. Steele (in *Opera hactenus inedita Rogeri Baconi*, fasc. XII, Oxford: Clarendon Press, 1935).

Macrobius:
   Macrobius, ed. F. Eyssenhardt (Leipsig: B. G. Teubner, 1893).
Moses Maimonides:
   The Guide for the Perplexed, trans. from the original Arabic text by M. Friedländer, 2nd ed. (London: G. Routledge, 1936).

Nemesius (Pseudo-Gregory of Nyssa):
   De Natura Hominis, PG 40, coll. 503-818.

Origen:
   Opera Omnia, PG 11-17.

Peter Lombard:
   Libri IV Sententiarum, 2 vols. (Quaracchi: Ex Typographia Col-
   legii S. Bonaventurae, 1916).
   Collectanea in omnes Divi Pauli Epistolas, Rom., I Cor., PL 191,
   coll. 1297-1696; others, PL 192, coll. 9-520.
Peter of Poitiers:
   Sententiarum Libri quinque, PL 211, coll. 783-1280.
Peter of Spain:
   Summulae Logicales (Cologne, 1489).
Plato:
   Platonis Opera, 5 vols. in 6, ed. J. Burnet (Oxford: Clarendon Press,
   1905-1913).
   The Dialogues of Plato, 5 vols., trans. B. Jowett (Oxford: Claren-
   don Press, 1871).
   The Dialogues of Plato, 2 vols., trans. B. Jowett with an introduc-
   tion by R. Demos (New York: Random House, 1937).
Plotinus:
   Enneads, 6 vols., ed. and trans. into French by E. Bréhier (Paris:
   Société d'Edition "Les Belles Lettres," 1924-1938).
   Enneads, 5 vols., trans. by S. McKenna (London and Boston: The
   Medici Society, 1917-1930).
Porphyry:
   Isagoge, trans. into Latin by Boethius, PL 64, coll. 77-158.
   The Introduction of Porphyry (in *The Organon or Logical Treatises
   of Aristotle,* trans. by O. F. Owen, vol. II, London: G. Bell, 1887,
   pp. 609-633).
Proclus:
   The Elements of Theology, ed. E. R. Dodds (Oxford: Clarendon
   Press, 1933).
Prosper of Aquitaine:
   Opera Omnia, PL 51.
Ptolemy:
   *Liber Ptholemei quattuor tractatuum (Quadripartitum) cum Cen-
   tiloquio . . .* (Venetiis, 1484).
   Syntaxis Mathematica, 2 vols., ed. J. L. Heiberg (Leipsig: B G.
   Teubner, 1898-1903).

Rhabanus Maurus:
   Opera Omnia, PL 107-112.
Richard of St. Victor:
   Opera Omnia, PL 196.

Simplicius:
In Aristotelis Categorias Commentarium, ed. C. Kalbfleisch (in *Commentaria in Aristotelem Graeca*, edita consilio et auctoritate Academiae Litterarum Regiae Borussicae, vol. VIII, Berlin: G. Reimer, 1907).

Themistius:
Paraphrases Aristotelis, 2 vols., ed. L. Spengel (Leipsig: B. G. Teubner, 1866).

Thomas Aquinas, St.:
Opera Omnia, ed. E. Fretté and P. Maré, 34 vols. (Paris: Vivès, 1872-1880).
S. Thomae de Aquino Ordinis Praedicatorum Summa Theologiae, cura et studio Instituti Studiorum Medievalium Ottaviensis ad textum S. Pii Pp. V iussu confectum recognita. Vols. 1-4, 1941-1944 (Ottawa: Impensis Studii Generalis O. Pr.).
S. Thomae de Aquino Doctoris Angelici Summa Contra Gentiles. Editio Leonina Manualis (Romae: Apud Sedem Commissionis Leoninae, 1934).
Le "De Ente et Essentia" de s. Thomas d'Aquin, ed. M.-D. Roland-Gosselin (*Bibliothèque Thomiste*, vol. VIII, Kain: Le Saulchoir, 1926).
S. Thomae Aquinatis Opuscula Omnia, 5 vols., ed. P. Mandonnet (Paris: P. Lethielleux, 1927).
Basic Writings of St. Thomas Aquinas, ed. Anton C. Pegis (2 vols., New York: Random House, 1945).

William of Auvergne:
Opera Omnia, 2 vols. (Paris, 1674).
William of Auxerre:
Summa Aurea in quattuor Libros Sententiarum (Paris, 1500).
William of Sherwood:
Introductiones in Logicam, ed. M. Grabmann (Sitzungsberichte der Bayerischen Akademie der Wissenschaften, Philosophisch-historische Abteilung, München, 1937, Heft 10).

II

Arnou, R.:
"Platonisme des pères" (*Dictionnaire de théologie catholique*, vol. XII, 2, 1935, coll. 2258-2392).

Baeumker, Cl.:
Witelo, ein Philosoph und Naturforscher des XIII Jahrhunderts (in *Beiträge zur Geschichte der Philosophie und Theologie des Mittelalters*, Band III, 2, Münster: Aschendorff, 1908).

Bareille, G.:
"Anges, II" (*Dictionnaire de théologie catholique,* vol. I, 1909, coll. 1192-1222).

Bergeron, M.:
"La structure du concept latin de personne" (*Études d'histoire littéraire et doctrinale du XIIIe siècle,* deuxième série, 1932, Ottawa: Institut d'Études Médiévales, pp. 121-162).

Capelle, G. C.:
Amaury de Bène. Étude sur son panthéisme formel (*Autour du décret de 1210,* III [*Bibliothèque Thomiste,* vol. XVI], Paris: J. Vrin, 1932).

Chenu, M.-D.:
"Contribution à l'histoire du traité de la foi. Commentaire historique de II-II, q. 1, a.2" (*Mélanges Thomistes* [*Bibliothèque Thomiste,* vol. III], Kain: Le Saulchoir, 1923, pp. 123-140).

"Grammaire et théologie aux XIIe et XIIIe siècles" (*Archives d'histoire doctrinale et littéraire du moyen age,* vol. X, 1935-1936, pp. 5-28).

Corpus Iuris Canonici, 2 vols., ed. E. L. Richter- E. Friedberg (Leipsig: B. Tauchnitz, 1922).
Vol. I. *Decretum Gratiani.*
Vol. II. *Decretalium Collectiones.*

Corpus Iuris Civilis, 2 vols. (Berlin: Weidmann. Vol I, 15th ed., 1928; Vol. II, 9th ed., 1915).
Vol. I. *Institutiones,* ed. Paul Krueger; *Digesta,* ed. Theodore Mommsen, revised by Paul Krueger.
Vol. II. *Codex Justinianus,* ed. and revised by Paul Krueger.

Denifle, H., and Chatelain, E.:
Chartularium Universitatis Parisiensis, 4 vols. (Paris: Delalain, 1889-1897).

Denzinger, H., and Bannwart, C.:
Enchiridion Symbolorum Definitionum et Declarationum de Rebus Fidei et Morum, 16th-17th ed. by J. P. Umberg (Freiburg: Herder and Co., 1928).

De Vaux, R.:
Notes et textes sur l'avicennisme latin aux confins des XIIe-XIIIe siècles (*Bibliothèque Thomiste,* vol. XX, Paris: J. Vrin, 1934).

Duhem, P.:
Le Système du Monde, 5 vols. (Paris: Hermann, 1913-1917).

Gaudel, A.:
"Péché originel (*Dictionnaire de théologie catholique,* vol. XII, 1930, coll. 275-606).

Gilson, E.:
"Pourquoi saint Thomas a critiqué saint Augustin" (*Archives*

d'histoire doctrinale et littéraire du moyen-âge, vol. I, 1926, pp. 1-127).

"Les sources gréco-arabes de l'augustinisme avicennisant" (*Archives d'histoire doctrinale et littéraire du moyen-âge,* vol. IV, 1929, pp. 5-149).

Kleineidam, E.:
Das Problem der hylomorphen Zusammensetzung der geistigen Substanzen im 13. Jahrhundert, behandelt bis Thomas von Aquin (Breslau, 1930).

Kors, J. B.:
La justice primitive et le péché originel d'après s. Thomas (*Bibliothèque Thomiste,* vol. II, Kain: Le Saulchoir, 1922).

Landgraf, A.:
"Studien zur Theologie des Zwölften Jahrhunderts" (*Traditio,* vol. I, 1943, New York: Cosmopolitan Science and Art Service Co., pp. 183-222).

Lottin, O.:
"Les dons du Saint-Esprit chez les théologiens depuis P. Lombard jusqu'à S. Thomas d'Aquin" (*Recherches de théologie ancienne et médiévale,* vol. I, 1929, pp. 41-97).
Le Droit Naturel chez Saint Thomas d'Aquin et ses prédécesseurs, 2nd ed. (Bruges: Ch. Beyaert, 1931).
"La composition hylémorphique des substances spirituelles. Les débuts de la controverse" (*Revue néo-scolastique de philosophie,* vol. XXXIV, 1932, pp. 21-41).

Mansi, J. D.:
Sacrorum Conciliorum Nova et Amplissima Collectio, 54 vols. (Paris and Leipsig: H. Welter, 1901-1927).

Muckle, J. T.:
"The *De Officiis Ministrorum* of Saint Ambrose" (*Mediaeval Studies,* vol. I, 1939, pp. 63-80).
"Isaac Israeli's Definition of Truth" (*Archives d'histoire doctrinale et littéraire du moyen âge,* 1933; vol. VIII, pp. 5-8).

Parent, J.-M.:
"La notion de dogme au XIIIe siècle" (*Études d'histoire littéraire et doctrinale du XIIIe siècle,* première série, 1932, Ottawa: Institut d'Études Médiévales, pp. 141-163).

Von Arnim, H.:
Stoicorum Veterum Fragmenta, 4 vols. (Leipsig: B. G. Teubner, 1921-1924).

MODERN LIBRARY COLLEGE EDITIONS

T74 AQUINAS, ST. THOMAS –
Introduction

T73 ARISTOTLE –
Introduction

T72 AUGUSTINE, ST. –
Confessions

T1 AUSTEN – Pride and
Prejudice *and* Sense
and Sensibility

T2 BALZAC – Père Goriot
and Eugénie Grandet

T42 BELLAMY –
Looking Backward

T86 BLAKE – The Selected
Poetry and Prose

T62 BOSWELL – The Life
of Samuel Johnson

T3 BRONTE – Jane Eyre

T4 BRONTE –
Wuthering Heights

T43 BROWNING –
Selected Poetry

T5 BUTLER –
The Way of All Flesh

T44 BYRON –
Selected Poetry

T57 CAESAR – The Gallic
War and Other
Writings

T69 CAMUS – The Plague

T6 CERVANTES –
Don Quixote

T84 CHEKHOV – Best Plays

T55 CICERO – Basic Works

T52 COLERIDGE – Selected
Poetry and Prose

T63 CONRAD – Nostromo

T45 CRANE – The Red
Badge of Courage

T7 DANTE – The Divine
Comedy

T8 DEFOE – Moll Flanders

T9 DICKENS – A Tale of
Two Cities

T10 DICKENS –
David Copperfield

T11 DOSTOYEVSKY – Crime
and Punishment

T12 DOSTOYEVSKY – The
Brothers Karamazov

T66 DOSTOYEVSKY – The
Best Short Stories

T13 EIGHT FAMOUS ELIZA-
BETHAN PLAYS

T80 EIGHTEENTH-
CENTURY PLAYS

T14 EMERSON –
Selected Writings

T68 FAULKNER –
Light in August

T78 FAULKNER –
Absalom, Absalom!

T61 THE FEDERALIST

T15 FIELDING – Tom Jones

T16 FIELDING –
Joseph Andrews

T17 FLAUBERT –
Madame Bovary

T18 FRANKLIN –
Autobiography and
Selected Writings

T19 GOETHE – Faust

T82 GOGOL – Dead Souls

T20 HARDY – The Mayor
of Casterbridge

T46 HARDY – Tess of the d'Urbervilles

T21 HAWTHORNE – The Scarlet Letter

T76 HEGEL – Philosophy

T54 HERODOTUS – The Persian Wars

T22 HOMER – The Iliad

T23 HOMER – The Odyssey

T56 HOWELLS – The Rise of Silas Lapham

T24 IBSEN – Six Plays

T83 IBSEN – The Wild Duck and Other Plays

T47 JAMES – The Portrait of a Lady

T59 JAMES – The Bostonians

T48 KEATS – Complete Poetry and Selected Prose

T25 MACHIAVELLI – The Prince *and* The Discourses

T75 MALRAUX – Man's Fate

T70 MEDIEVAL ROMANCES

T26 MELVILLE – Moby Dick

T27 MEREDITH – The Ordeal of Richard Feverel

T28 MILTON – Complete Poetry and Selected Prose

T29 MOLIERE – Eight Plays

T65 MONTAIGNE – Selected Essays

T71 PLATO – Works

T58 POE – Selected Poetry and Prose

T49 POPE – Selected Works

T67 PROUST – Swann's Way

T79 RESTORATION PLAYS

T30 SEVEN FAMOUS GREEK PLAYS

T50 SHELLEY – Selected Poetry and Prose

T85 SIX MODERN AMERICAN PLAYS

T31 STERNE – Tristram Shandy

T32 SWIFT – Gulliver's Travels and Other Writings

T53 TACITUS – Complete Works

T60 TENNYSON – Selected Poetry

T33 THACKERAY – Vanity Fair

T34 THACKERAY – Henry Esmond

T35 THOREAU – Walden and Other Writings

T51 THUCYDIDES – Complete Writings

T36 TOLSTOY – Anna Karenina

T37 TROLLOPE – Barchester Towers *and* The Warden

T38 TURGENEV – Fathers and Sons

T39 VIRGIL – Works

T64 VOLTAIRE – Candide and Other Writings

T40 WHITMAN – Leaves of Grass and Selected Prose

T41 WORDSWORTH – Selected Poetry

The Best of the World's Best Books
COMPLETE LIST OF TITLES IN
THE MODERN LIBRARY

*A series of handsome, cloth-bound books, formerly
available only in expensive editions.*

76 ADAMS, HENRY: *The Education of Henry Adams*
310 AESCHYLUS: *The Complete Greek Tragedies*, Vol. I
311 AESCHYLUS: *The Complete Greek Tragedies*, Vol. II
101 AIKEN, CONRAD (Editor): *A Comprehensive Anthology of American Poetry*
127 AIKEN, CONRAD (Editor): *20th-Century American Poetry*
145 ALEICHEM, SHOLOM: *Selected Stories*
104 ANDERSON, SHERWOOD: *Winesburg, Ohio*
259 AQUINAS, ST. THOMAS: *Introduction to St. Thomas Aquinas*
248 ARISTOTLE: *Introduction to Aristotle*
228 ARISTOTLE: *Politics*
246 ARISTOTLE: *Rhetoric and Poetics*
160 AUDEN, W. H.: *Selected Poetry*
263 AUGUSTINE, ST.: *Confessions*
264 AUSTEN, JANE: *Pride and Prejudice* and *Sense and Sensibility*

256 BACON, FRANCIS: *Selected Writings*
299 BALZAC: *Cousin Bette*
193 BALZAC: *Droll Stories*
245 BALZAC: *Père Goriot* and *Eugénie Grandet*
116 BEERBOHM, MAX: *Zuleika Dobson*
22 BELLAMY, EDWARD: *Looking Backward*
184 BENNETT, ARNOLD: *The Old Wives' Tale*
231 BERGSON, HENRI: *Creative Evolution*
285 BLAKE, WILLIAM: *Selected Poetry and Prose*
71 BOCCACCIO: *The Decameron*
282 BOSWELL, JAMES: *The Life of Samuel Johnson*
64 BRONTË, CHARLOTTE: *Jane Eyre*
106 BRONTË, EMILY: *Wuthering Heights*
198 BROWNING, ROBERT: *Selected Poetry*
15 BUCK, PEARL: *The Good Earth*
32 BURCKHARDT, JACOB: *The Civilization of the Renaissance in* [Italy
241 BURK, JOHN N.: *The Life and Works of Beethoven*
289 BURKE, EDMUND: *Selected Writings*
136 BUTLER, SAMUEL: *Erewhon* and *Erewhon Revisited*
13 BUTLER, SAMUEL: *The Way of All Flesh*
195 BYRON, LORD: *Selected Poetry*
24 BYRON, LORD: *Don Juan*

295 CAESAR, JULIUS: *The Gallic War and Other Writings*
51 CALDWELL, ERSKINE· *God's Little Acre*

249   CALDWELL, ERSKINE: *Tobacco Road*

352   CAMUS, ALBERT: *The Fall & Exile and the Kingdom*

109   CAMUS, ALBERT: *The Plague*

349   CAMUS, ALBERT: *Notebooks 1935–1942*

339   CAMUS, ALBERT: *Resistance, Rebellion and Death*

353   CAPOTE, TRUMAN: *Selected Writings*

79   CARROLL, LEWIS: *Alice in Wonderland*, etc.

165   CASANOVA, JACQUES: *Memoirs of Casanova*

150   CELLINI, BENVENUTO: *Autobiography of Cellini*

174   CERVANTES: *Don Quixote*

161   CHAUCER: *The Canterbury Tales*

171   CHEKHOV, ANTON: *Best Plays*

50   CHEKHOV, ANTON: *Short Stories*

272   CICERO: *Basic Works*

279   COLERIDGE: *Selected Poetry and Prose*

251   COLETTE: *Six Novels*

235   COMMAGER, HENRY STEELE & NEVINS, ALLAN: *A Short History of the United States*

306   CONFUCIUS: *The Wisdom of Confucius*

186   CONRAD, JOSEPH: *Lord Jim*

275   CONRAD, JOSEPH: *Nostromo*

34   CONRAD, JOSEPH: *Victory*

105   COOPER, JAMES FENIMORE: *The Pathfinder*

194   CORNEILLE & RACINE: *Six Plays by Corneille and Racine*

130   CRANE, STEPHEN: *The Red Badge of Courage*

214   CUMMINGS, E. E.: *The Enormous Room*

236   DANA, RICHARD HENRY: *Two Years Before the Mast*

208   DANTE: *The Divine Comedy*

122   DEFOE, DANIEL: *Moll Flanders*

92   DEFOE, DANIEL: *Robinson Crusoe* and *A Journal of the Plague Year*

43   DESCARTES, RENÉ: *Philosophical Writings*

173   DEWEY, JOHN: *Human Nature and Conduct*

348   DEWEY, JOHN: *John Dewey on Education*

110   DICKENS, CHARLES: *David Copperfield*

204   DICKENS, CHARLES: *Pickwick Papers*

308   DICKENS, CHARLES: *Our Mutual Friend*

189   DICKENS, CHARLES: *A Tale of Two Cities*

25   DICKINSON, EMILY: *Selected Poems*

23   DINESEN, ISAK: *Out of Africa*

54   DINESEN, ISAK: *Seven Gothic Tales*

12   DONNE, JOHN: *Complete Poetry and Selected Prose*

205   DOS PASSOS, JOHN: *Three Soldiers*

293   DOSTOYEVSKY, FYODOR: *Best Short Stories*

151   DOSTOYEVSKY, FYODOR: *The Brothers Karamazov*

199   DOSTOYEVSKY, FYODOR: *Crime and Punishment*

55   DOSTOYEVSKY, FYODOR: *The Possessed*

5   DOUGLAS, NORMAN: *South Wind*

206   DOYLE, SIR ARTHUR CONAN: *The Adventure and Memoirs of Sherlock Holmes*

8   DREISER, THEODORE: *Sister Carrie*

69   DUMAS, ALEXANDRE: *Camille*

143   DUMAS, ALEXANDRE: *The Three Musketeers*

227   DU MAURIER, DAPHNE: *Rebecca*

338 ELLISON, RALPH: *Invisible Man*
192 EMERSON, RALPH WALDO: *The Journals*
91 EMERSON, RALPH WALDO: *Essays and Other Writings*
331 ERASMUS, DESIDERIUS: *The Praise of Folly*
314 EURIPIDES: *The Complete Greek Tragedies, Vol. V*
315 EURIPIDES: *The Complete Greek Tragedies, Vol. VI*
316 EURIPIDES: *The Complete Greek Tragedies, Vol. VII*

271 FAULKNER, WILLIAM: *Absalom, Absalom!*
175 FAULKNER, WILLIAM: *Go Down, Moses*
351 FAULKNER, WILLIAM: *Intruder in the Dust*
88 FAULKNER, WILLIAM: *Light in August*
61 FAULKNER, WILLIAM: *Sanctuary*
187 FAULKNER, WILLIAM: *The Sound and the Fury* and *As I Lay* [*Dying*
324 FAULKNER, WILLIAM: *Selected Short Stories*
117 FIELDING, HENRY: *Joseph Andrews*
185 FIELDING, HENRY: *Tom Jones*
28 FLAUBERT, GUSTAVE: *Madame Bovary*
102 FORESTER, C. S.: *The African Queen*
210 FRANCE, ANATOLE: *Penguin Island*
298 FRANK, ANNE: *Diary of a Young Girl*
39 FRANKLIN, BENJAMIN: *Autobiography*, etc.
96 FREUD, SIGMUND: *The Interpretation of Dreams*

36 GEORGE, HENRY: *Progress and Poverty*
327 GIDE, ANDRÉ: *The Counterfeiters*
177 GOETHE: *Faust*
40 GOGOL, NICHOLAI: *Dead Souls*
291 GOLDSMITH, OLIVER: *The Vicar of Wakefield and Other* [*Writings*
20 GRAVES, ROBERT: *I, Claudius*
286 GUNTHER, JOHN: *Death Be Not Proud*

265 HACKETT, FRANCIS: *The Personal History of Henry the Eighth*
163 HAGGARD. H. RIDER: *She and King Solomon's Mines*
320 HAMILTON, EDITH: *The Greek Way*
135 HARDY, THOMAS: *Jude the Obscure*
17 HARDY, THOMAS: *The Mayor of Casterbridge*
121 HARDY, THOMAS: *The Return of the Native*
72 HARDY, THOMAS: *Tess of the D'Urbervilles*
233 HART & KAUFMAN: *Six Plays*
329 HART, MOSS: *Act One*
250 HARTE, BRET: *Best Stories*
93 HAWTHORNE. NATHANIEL: *The Scarlet Letter*
239 HEGEL: *The Philosophy of Hegel*
223 HELLMAN, LILLIAN: *Six Plays*
26 HENRY, O.: *Best Short Stories*
255 HERODOTUS: *The Persian Wars*
328 HERSEY, JOHN: *Hiroshima*
334 HESSE, HERMAN: *Steppenwolf*
166 HOMER: *The Iliad*
167 HOMER: *The Odyssey*
141 HORACE: *Complete Works*
302 HOWARD, JOHN TASKER: *World's Great Operas*
277 HOWELLS, WILLIAM DEAN: *The Rise of Silas Lapham*
89 HUDSON, W. H.: *Green Mansions*
35 HUGO, VICTOR: *The Hunchback of Notre Dame*

340 HUME, DAVID: *Philosophy*
209 HUXLEY, ALDOUS: *Antic Hay*
 48 HUXLEY, ALDOUS: *Brave New World*
180 HUXLEY, ALDOUS: *Point Counter Point*

305 IBSEN, HENRIK: *Six Plays*
307 IBSEN, HENRIK: *The Wild Duck and Other Plays*
240 IRVING, WASHINGTON: *Selected Writings*

 16 JAMES, HENRY: *The Bostonians*
107 JAMES, HENRY: *The Portrait of a Lady*
169 JAMES, HENRY: *The Turn of the Screw*
269 JAMES, HENRY: *Washington Square*
244 JAMES, HENRY: *The Wings of the Dove*
114 JAMES, WILLIAM: *The Philosophy of William James*
 70 JAMES, WILLIAM: *The Varieties of Religious Experience*
234 JEFFERSON, THOMAS: *The Life and Selected Writings*
355 JOHNSON, SAMUEL: *Johnson's Dictionary: A Modern Selection*
124 JOYCE, JAMES: *Dubliners*
300 JUNG, C. G.: *Basic Writings*

318 KAFKA, FRANZ: *The Trial*
283 KAFKA, FRANZ: *Selected Stories*
297 KANT: *Critique of Pure Reason*
266 KANT: *The Philosophy of Kant*
233 KAUFMAN & HART: *Six Plays*
273 KEATS: *Complete Poetry and Selected Prose*
303 KIERKEGAARD, SØREN: *A Kierkegaard Anthology*
 99 KIPLING, RUDYARD: *Kim*
 74 KOESTLER, ARTHUR: *Darkness at Noon*

262 LAOTSE: *The Wisdom of Laotse*
148 LAWRENCE, D. H.: *Lady Chatterley's Lover*
128 LAWRENCE, D. H.: *The Rainbow*
333 LAWRENCE, D. H.: *Sons and Lovers*
 68 LAWRENCE, D. H.: *Women in Love*
252 LEWIS, SINCLAIR: *Dodsworth*
221 LEWIS, SINCLAIR: *Cass Timberlane*
325 LIVY: *A History of Rome*
 56 LONGFELLOW, HENRY W.: *Poems*
 77 LOUYS, PIERRE: *Aphrodite*
 95 LUDWIG, EMIL: *Napoleon*

 65 MACHIAVELLI: *The Prince* and *The Discourses*
321 MAILER, NORMAN: *The Naked and the Dead*
317 MALAMUD, BERNARD: *Two Novels*
 33 MALRAUX, ANDRÉ: *Man's Fate*
309 MALTHUS, THOMAS ROBERT: *On Population*
182 MARQUAND, JOHN P.: *The Late George Apley*
202 MARX, KARL: *Capital and Other Writings*
 14 MAUGHAM, W. SOMERSET: *Best Short Stories*
270 MAUGHAM, W. SOMERSET: *Cakes and Ale*
 27 MAUGHAM, W. SOMERSET: *The Moon and Sixpence*
176 MAUGHAM, W. SOMERSET: *Of Human Bondage*
 98 MAUPASSANT, GUY DE: *Best Short Stories*
 46 MAUROIS, ANDRÉ: *Disraeli*
119 MELVILLE, HERMAN: *Moby Dick*
253 MEREDITH, GEORGE: *The Egoist*

134 MEREDITH, GEORGE: *The Ordeal of Richard Feverel*
138 MEREJKOWSKI, DMITRI: *The Romance of Leonardo da Vinci*
296 MICHENER, JAMES A.: *Selected Writings*
322 MILL, JOHN STUART: *Selections*
132 MILTON, JOHN: *Complete Poetry and Selected Prose*
78 MOLIÈRE: *Eight Plays*
218 MONTAIGNE: *Selected Essays*

343 NASH, OGDEN: *Verses From 1929 On*   [tory of the United States
235 NEVINS, ALLAN & COMMAGER, HENRY STEELE: *A Short His-*
113 NEWMAN, CARDINAL JOHN H.: *Apologia Pro Vita Sua*
9 NIETZSCHE, FRIEDRICH: *Thus Spake Zarathustra*
81 NOSTRADAMUS: *Oracles*

67 ODETS, CLIFFORD: *Six Plays*
42 O'HARA, JOHN: *Appointment in Samarra*
211 O'HARA, JOHN: *Selected Short Stories*
323 O'HARA, JOHN: *Butterfield 8*
342 O'NEILL, EUGENE: *Ah, Wilderness! and Two Other Plays*
146 O'NEILL, EUGENE: *The Emperor Jones, Anna Christie and The Hairy Ape*   [the Sea
111 O'NEILL, EUGENE: *The Long Voyage Home: Seven Plays of*

232 PALGRAVE, FRANCIS (Editor): *The Golden Treasury*
123 PARKER, DOROTHY: *Collected Short Stories*
237 PARKER, DOROTHY: *Collected Poetry*
267 PARKMAN, FRANCIS: *The Oregon Trail*
164 PASCAL, BLAISE: *Penseés and The Provincial Letters*
86 PATER, WALTER: *The Renaissance*
103 PEPYS, SAMUEL: *Passages from the Diary*
247 PERELMAN, S. J.: *The Best of S. J. Perelman*
153 PLATO: *The Republic*
181 PLATO: *The Works of Plato*
82 POE, EDGAR ALLAN: *Selected Poetry and Prose*
196 POLO, MARCO: *The Travels of Marco Polo*
257 POPE, ALEXANDER: *Selected Works*
284 PORTER, KATHERINE ANNE: *Flowering Judas*
45 PORTER, KATHERINE ANNE: *Pale Horse, Pale Rider*
120 PROUST, MARCEL: *The Captive*
220 PROUST, MARCEL: *Cities of the Plain*
213 PROUST, MARCEL: *The Guermantes Way*
278 PROUST, MARCEL: *The Past Recaptured*
59 PROUST, MARCEL: *Swann's Way*
260 PROUST, MARCEL: *The Sweet Cheat Gone*
172 PROUST, MARCEL: *Within a Budding Grove*

194 RACINE & CORNEILLE: *Six Plays by Corneille and Racine*
62 READE, CHARLES: *The Cloister and the Hearth*
215 REED, JOHN: *Ten Days That Shook the World*
140 RENAN, ERNEST: *The Life of Jesus*
336 RENAULT, MARY: *The Last of the Wine*
10 RICHARDSON, SAMUEL: *Clarissa*
200 RODGERS & HAMMERSTEIN: *Six Plays*
154 ROSTAND, EDMOND: *Cyrano de Bergerac*
243 ROUSSEAU, JEAN JACQUES: *The Confessions*
53 RUNYON, DAMON: *Famous Stories*
137 RUSSELL, BERTRAND: *Selected Papers of Bertrand Russell*

280 SAKI: *Short Stories*
301 SALINGER, J. D.: *Nine Stories*
90 SALINGER, J. D.: *The Catcher in the Rye*
292 SANTAYANA, GEORGE: *The Sense of Beauty*
335 SARTRE, JEAN-PAUL: *The Age of Reason*
52 SCHOPENHAUER: *The Philosophy of Schopenhauer*
281 SCHULBERG, BUDD: *What Makes Sammy Run?*
2,3 SHAKESPEARE, WILLIAM: *Tragedies*—complete, 2 vols.
4,5 SHAKESPEARE, WILLIAM: *Comedies*—complete, 2 vols.
6 SHAKESPEARE, WILLIAM: *Histories*
7 SHAKESPEARE, WILLIAM: *Histories, Poems* } complete, 2 vols.
19 SHAW, BERNARD: *Four Plays* [*and the Lion*
294 SHAW, BERNARD: *Saint Joan, Major Barbara,* and *Androcles*
112 SHAW, IRWIN: *The Young Lions*
319 SHAW, IRWIN: *Selected Short Stories*
274 SHELLEY: *Selected Poetry and Prose*
159 SMOLLETT, TOBIAS: *Humphry Clinker*
312 SOPHOCLES I: *Complete Greek Tragedies,* Vol. III
313 SOPHOCLES II: *Complete Greek Tragedies,* Vol. IV
60 SPINOZA: *The Philosophy of Spinoza*
332 STEIN, GERTRUDE: *Selected Writings*
115 STEINBECK, JOHN: *In Dubious Battle*
29 STEINBECK, JOHN: *Of Mice and Men*
216 STEINBECK, JOHN: *Tortilla Flat*
157 STENDHAL: *The Red and the Black*
147 STERNE, LAURENCE: *Tristram Shandy*
254 STEWART, GEORGE R.: *Storm*
31 STOKER, BRAM: *Dracula*
11 STONE, IRVING: *Lust for Life*
261 STOWE, HARRIET BEECHER: *Uncle Tom's Cabin*
212 STRACHEY, LYTTON: *Eminent Victorians*
351 STYRON, WILLIAM: *Lie Down in Darkness*
188 SUETONIUS: *Lives of the Twelve Caesars*
100 SWIFT, JONATHAN: *Gulliver's Travels and Other Writings*
49 SYMONDS, JOHN A.: *The Life of Michelangelo*

222 TACITUS: *Complete Works*
230 TENNYSON: *Selected Poetry*
80 THACKERAY, WILLIAM: *Henry Esmond*
131 THACKERAY, WILLIAM: *Vanity Fair*
38 THOMPSON, FRANCIS: *Complete Poems*
155 THOREAU, HENRY DAVID: *Walden and Other Writings*
58 THUCYDIDES: *Complete Writings*
85 THURBER, JAMES: *The Thurber Carnival*
37 TOLSTOY, LEO: *Anna Karenina*
347 TOLSTOY, LEO: *Selected Essays*
354 TOLSTOY, LEO: *Short Novels*
346 TOLSTOY, LEO: *Short Stories*
41 TROLLOPE, ANTHONY: *Barchester Towers and The Warden*
21 TURGENEV, IVAN: *Fathers and Sons*
162 TWAIN, MARK: *A Connecticut Yankee in King Arthur's Court*

357 UPDIKE, JOHN: *The Poorhouse Fair and Rabbit, Run*

190 VASARI, GIORGIO: *Lives of the Most Eminent Painters, Sculptors and Architects*
63 VEBLEN, THORSTEIN: *The Theory of the Leisure Class*

MODERN LIBRARY

156 VINCI, LEONARDO DA: *The Notebooks*
 75 VIRGIL: *The Aeneid, Eclogues* and *Georgics*
 47 VOLTAIRE: *Candide and Other Writings*

178 WALPOLE, HUGH: *Fortitude*
170 WARREN, ROBERT PENN: *All The King's Men*
219 WEBB, MARY: *Precious Bane*
225 WEIDMAN, JEROME: *I Can Get It for You Wholesale*
197 WELLS, H. G.: *Tono Bungay*
290 WELTY, EUDORA: *Selected Stories*
299 WHARTON, EDITH: *The Age of Innocence*
 97 WHITMAN, WALT: *Leaves of Grass*
125 WILDE, OSCAR: *Dorian Gray* and *De Profundis*
 83 WILDE, OSCAR: *The Plays of Oscar Wilde*
 84 WILDE, OSCAR: *Poems* and *Fairy Tales*
126 WODEHOUSE, P. J.: *Selected Stories*
268 WORDSWORTH: *Selected Poetry*

 44 YEATS, W. B. (Editor): *Irish Fairy and Folk Tales*
179 YOUNG, G. F.: *The Medici*

207 ZIMMERN, ALFRED: *The Greek Commonwealth*
142 ZOLA, ÉMILE: *Nana*

MISCELLANEOUS

288   *An Anthology of Irish Literature*
330   *Anthology of Medieval Lyrics*
326   *The Apocrypha*
201   *The Arabian Nights' Entertainments*
 87   *Best American Humorous Short Stories*
 18   *Best Russian Short Stories*
129   *Great Spanish Stories*
     Complete Greek Tragedies
310 Vol. I (Aeschylus I); 311 Vol. II (Aeschylus II); 312 Vol. III
(Sophocles I); 313 Vol. IV (Sophocles II); 314 Vol. V (Euripides
I); 315 Vol. VI (Euripides II)
101   *A Comprehensive Anthology of American Poetry*
226   *The Consolation of Philosophy*
 94   *Eight Famous Elizabethan Plays*
345   *Eight Spanish Plays of the Golden Age*
224   *Eighteenth-Century Plays*
 73   *Famous Ghost Stories*
139   *The Federalist*
 30   *Five Great Modern Irish Plays*
144   *Fourteen Great Detective Stories*
108   *Great German Short Novels and Stories*
168   *Great Modern Short Stories*
238   *Great Tales of the American West*
203   *The Greek Poets*
356   *Hellenistic Philosophy*
217   *The Latin Poets*
149   *The Making of Man: An Outline of Anthropology*
183   *Making of Society*
344   *Medieval Philosophy*
133   *Medieval Romances*
  1   *The Modern Library Dictionary*
258   *New Voices in the American Theatre*
152   *Outline of Abnormal Psychology*
 66   *Outline of Psychoanalysis*
287   *Restoration Plays*
337   *Roman Comedies*
158   *Seven Famous Greek Plays*
 57   *The Short Bible*
276   *Six Modern American Plays*
 38   *Six American Plays for Today*
118   *Stories of Modern Italy*
127   *Twentieth-Century American Poetry—revised*
341   *Twenty German Poets*

MODERN LIBRARY GIANTS

A series of sturdily bound and handsomely printed, full-sized library editions of books formerly available only in expensive sets. These volumes contain from 600 to 1,400 pages each.

THE MODERN LIBRARY GIANTS REPRESENT A
SELECTION OF THE WORLD'S GREATEST BOOKS

G76 ANDERSEN & GRIMM: *Tales*
G74 AUGUSTINE, ST.: *The City of God*
G58 AUSTEN, JANE: *Complete Novels*
G70 BLAKE, WILLIAM & DONNE, JOHN: *Complete Poetry*
G2   BOSWELL, JAMES: *Life of Samuel Johnson*
G17 BROWNING, ROBERT: *Poems and Plays*
G14 BULFINCH: *Mythology* (Illustrated)
G35 BURY, J. B.: *A History of Greece*
G13 CARLYLE, THOMAS: *The French Revolution*
G28 CARROLL, LEWIS: *Complete Works*
G15 CERVANTES: *Don Quixote*
G33 COLLINS, WILKIE: *The Moonstone* and *The Woman in White*
G27 DARWIN, CHARLES: *Origin of Species* and *The Descent of Man*
G43 DEWEY, JOHN: *Intelligence in the Modern World: John Dewey's Philosophy*
G70 DONNE, JOHN & BLAKE, WILLIAM: *Complete Poetry*
G36 DOSTOYEVSKY, FYODOR: *The Brothers Karamazov*
G60 DOSTOYEVSKY, FYODOR: *The Idiot*
G51 ELIOT, GEORGE: *Best-Known Novels*
G41 FARRELL, JAMES T.: *Studs Lonigan*
G82 FAULKNER, WILLIAM: *The Faulkner Reader*
G39 FREUD, SIGMUND: *The Basic Writings*
G6 ⎫
G7 ⎬ GIBBON, EDWARD: *The Decline and Fall of the Roman Empire*
G8 ⎭   (Complete in three volumes)
G25 GILBERT & SULLIVAN: *Complete Plays*
G76 GRIMM & ANDERSEN: *Tales*
G37 HAWTHORNE, NATHANIEL: *Compl. Novels & Selected Tales*
G78 HOLMES, OLIVER WENDELL: *The Mind and Faith of Justice Holmes*
G19 HOMER: *Complete Works*
G3   HUGO, VICTOR: *Les Miserables*
G18 IBSEN, HENRIK: *Eleven Plays*
G11 JAMES, HENRY: *Short Stories*
G52 JOYCE, JAMES: *Ulysses*
G4   KEATS & SHELLEY: *Complete Poems*
G24 LAMB, CHARLES: *The Complete Works and Letters*
G20 LINCOLN, ABRAHAM: *The Life and Writings of Abraham Lincoln*
G84 MANN, THOMAS: *Stories of Three Decades*
G26 MARX, KARL: *Capital*
G57 MELVILLE, HERMAN: *Selected Writings*
G38 MURASAKA, LADY: *The Tale of Genji*
G30 MYERS, GUSTAVUS: *History of the Great American Fortunes*
G34 NIETZSCHE, FRIEDRICH: *The Philosophy of Nietzsche*

MODERN LIBRARY GIANTS

G88 O'HARA, JOHN: *49 Stories*
G55 O'NEILL, EUGENE: *Nine Plays*
G68 PAINE, TOM: *Selected Work*
G86 PASTERNAK, BORIS: *Doctor Zhivago*
G5   PLUTARCH: *Lives* (The Dryden Translation)
G40 POE, EDGAR ALLAN: *Complete Tales and Poems*
G29 PRESCOTT, WILLIAM H.: *The Conquest of Mexico and The Conquest of Peru*
G62 PUSHKIN: *Poems, Prose and Plays*
G65 RABELAIS: *Complete Works*
G12 SCOTT, SIR WALTER: *The Most Popular Novels* (Quentin Durward, Ivanhoe & Kenilworth)
G4   SHELLEY & KEATS: *Complete Poems*
G32 SMITH, ADAM: *The Wealth of Nations*
G61 SPAETH, SIGMUND: *A Guide to Great Orchestral Music*
G92 SPENGLER, OSWALD: *The Decline of the West* (one volume)
G91 SPENSER, EDMUND: *Selected Poetry*
G75 STEVENSON, ROBERT LOUIS: *Selected Writings*
G53 SUE, EUGENE: *The Wandering Jew*
G42 TENNYSON: *The Poems and Plays*
G23 TOLSTOY, LEO: *Anna Karenina*
G1   TOLSTOY, LEO: *War and Peace*
G49 TWAIN, MARK: *Tom Sawyer and Huckleberry Finn*
G50 WHITMAN, WALT: *Leaves of Grass*
G83 WILSON, EDMUND: *The Shock of Recognition*

MISCELLANEOUS

G77 *An Anthology of Famous American Stories*
G54 *An Anthology of Famous British Stories*
G67 *Anthology of Famous English and American Poetry*
G81 *An Encyclopedia of Modern American Humor*
G47 *The English Philosophers from Bacon to Mill*
G16 *The European Philosophers from Descartes to Nietzsche*
G31 *Famous Science-Fiction Stories*
G85 *Great Ages and Ideas of the Jewish People*
G89 *Great Classical Myths*
G72 *Great Tales of Terror and the Supernatural*
G9   *Great Voices of the Reformation*
G87 *Medieval Epics*
G48 *The Metropolitan Opera Guide*
G46 *A New Anthology of Modern Poetry*
G69 *One Hundred and One Years' Entertainment*
G90 *Philosophies of Art and Beauty: Readings in Aesthetics from Plato to Heidegger*
G21 *Sixteen Famous American Plays*
G63 *Sixteen Famous British Plays*
G71 *Sixteen Famous European Plays*
G45 *Stoic and Epicurean Philosophers*
G22 *Thirty Famous One-Act Plays*
G66 *Three Famous Murder Novels, Before the Fact,* Francis Iles, *Trent's Last Case,* E. C. Bentley, *The House of the Arrow,* A. E. W. Mason
G10 *Twelve Famous Plays of the Restoration and Eighteenth Century* (1660–1820) Dryden, Congreve, Wycherley, Gay, etc.
G56 *The Wisdom of Catholicism*
G59 *The Wisdom of China and India*
G79 *The Wisdom of Israel*